INDIA'S
FORGOTTEN
COUNTRY

'This collection of insightful and keenly political writings is the result of an extraordinary life that has been lived on the front lines, years before they were recognized as the front lines of the most important battles facing us today. This book is a gift to readers'—Arundhati Roy, writer

'Bela Bhatia's book, far from being a self-glorifying account of her efforts, is the story of a life lived with no acclaim but with total conviction. Everyone who reads it will have to introspect on the worth of one's own contribution. This book is indispensable documentation for future generations'—Naseeruddin Shah, actor

'Bela Bhatia's writing is driven by a fierce commitment to the poor and oppressed of India. In this collection of her articles, she reveals the paths this has led her to in the last thirty-plus years. She uncovers the inequalities, exploitation and brutality that underpin a deeply entrenched rural hierarchy, while never underestimating the great difficulties that stand in the way of forging a more equitable society. In this, she refuses to valorize violent solutions, showing how in armed conflict the powerless are often the worst sufferers'—David Hardiman, emeritus professor of history at the University of Warwick

'In achingly beautiful prose, Bela Bhatia, an activist of immense credibility, constructs a harrowing and necessary record of India's forgotten people. Combining impeccable scholarship with a profound allegiance to justice, Bhatia bears first-hand witness to India's catastrophic upheavals of caste and communal massacres, untouchability, ferocious caste discrimination, bonded labour, land hunger, widowhood, armed uprisings and forced displacement. Her searing log also draws within its sweep a wide gamut of resistances to injustice—individual and collective, peaceful and violent. Her book is a lodestar for the public conscience, a stirring reminder of the people the nation has brutalized in so many ways'—Harsh Mander, author and peace worker

'Bela Bhatia is as committed to scholarship as to activism. She brings an exactitude and commitment to both that is unparalleled. This collection of essays spans the length and breadth of the country and of her vision. She has always stood by the marginalized and brought to our notice lives and realities India's shameless governments and elites do not want to see. Without Bela Bhatia, our understanding of India would be immeasurably poorer'—Ashley Tellis, independent researcher and LGBTQIA+ activist

'The twenty-five accounts contained in this important chronicle by one of our committed activist scholars, Bela Bhatia, sensitively expose the gangrenous heart of the Indian system on the one hand and the predicament of the struggling masses on the other. I had read some [accounts] earlier in various journals but still found them as refreshing as the first read for their vividness. India is well-known as the land of paradoxes but every time you confront her reality, she shatters you. The last paradox: when India is gasping for breath from the continual attacks from her rulers she is being projected by them with all kinds of embellishments, à la vishwaguru! This book is a must-read to understand the real India'—Anand Teltumbde, author, political commentator and civil rights activist

'Bela Bhatia's book is breathtaking. Written with a deep sense of empathy for the marginalized, its twenty-five essays unravel the underbelly of India's republic and the amoral political economy of the Indian state. They throw scorching light on the cosmetic character of democracy in India, where struggles for better conditions of living by vulnerable segments of society are met with repression and violence. Bela's writings are at once deeply personal and deeply political, a reminder of the unredeemed promises of social, economic and political justice. This is a book that will or should stir the conscience of its readers'—Uma Chakravarti, feminist historian and democratic rights activist, and Anand Chakravarti, retired professor of sociology, University of Delhi

'We have known Bela Bhatia as a human rights lawyer and activist of great commitment and courage, volunteering to work in the most difficult circumstances and places. In this book, we discover the same qualities, increasingly rare in today's world, in her role as an insightful author and thoughtful researcher. Her reports from a dozen states on the lives of people from marginalized sections, or those trapped in dire circumstances, are marked with deep sincerity and a resolve to report the truth as she sees it'—Bharat Dogra, independent journalist

'Bela Bhatia, a very sensitive researcher and committed activist, has presented an in-depth analysis of the oppression faced by classes, castes and communities—Dalits, Adivasis, women and others—who bear exclusion and deprivation over generations. When she worked with us at Shramjivi Samaj and the Narmada movement in Gujarat, her commitment was extraordinary. This book depicts not only her heartfelt experience but also her research into the societal and statutory contempt of the toiling masses. Her life and work will certainly inspire the youth to follow the path we all look forward to traversing, towards equity and justice'—Medha Patkar, social activist and co-convenor of the National Alliance of People's Movements

'India became independent with the hope that it would move from formal principles of the freedom movement towards substantive values. However, feudal values often persisted, sparking diverse social movements over the years. Bela Bhatia has not only been part of many of these movements but also been an empathetic chronicler of the struggles of Dalits, Adivasis, women and other marginalized groups. Her essays, covering a wide canvas across eleven states, are lucid and insightful. This absorbing book shows the mirror to a large part of Indian society. And in her own words, she is part of what she observes and what she observes becomes part of her writings'—Ram Puniyani, author and communal harmony worker

'Drawing on thirty-five years of research, fieldwork and activism, this important book explores the darker side of India's experiment with nationhood and democracy. The focus throughout is on the most vulnerable and victimized sections of our society including Dalits, Adivasis, women, and religious and ethnic minorities. Their stories and testimonies are a sharp indictment of the oppressive aspects of the Indian state as well as of the legal system. Bela Bhatia's analysis is rich, insightful and empathetic but never polemical. This rigorously researched book is a valuable corrective to the boosterism of the Indian government and of the corporate elite. The fault lines that Bhatia identifies and the conflicts she writes about remain unresolved. Every Indian who cares for the present and the future of our country should read this book'—Ramachandra Guha, historian and writer

INDIA'S FORGOTTEN COUNTRY

A View from the Margins

BELA BHATIA

PENGUIN
VIKING
An imprint of Penguin Random House

VIKING

Viking is an imprint of the Penguin Random House group of companies
whose addresses can be found at global.penguinrandomhouse.com

Published by Penguin Random House India Pvt. Ltd
4th Floor, Capital Tower 1, MG Road,
Gurugram 122 002, Haryana, India

First published in Viking by Penguin Random House India 2024

10 9 8 7 6 5 4 3 2 1

The views and opinions expressed in this book are the author's own and the
facts are as reported by her which have been verified to the extent possible,
and the publishers are not in any way liable for the same.

ISBN 9780670093342

Typeset in Adobe Garamond Pro by Manipal Technologies Limited, Manipal
Printed at Thomson Press India Ltd, New Delhi

www.penguin.co.in

For my parents,
Santosh and Raj Pal Bhatia

Why I write

These words
I write
try to tell
the story of your life
your suffering
muted, unmeasurable
your struggle
quiet and determined
the path you attempt to pave
against all odds
the questions that you ask
the answers that you explore
even as you attempt
with all your strength
to fight
the dark clouds
that tend to descend.

Certainly, this time
it is not darkness but light
not only your plight but
your might
which will be the mark,
the imprint,
a firm footprint.

To those who have suffered
intolerably
as long as they can remember
as their tired, questioning eyes
seem to say
as the deep furrows on their faces
betray
as do the gnarled, coarseness of
work-worn hands
the cracks on the feet
on broken sand
blow inflicted
upon old blow
humanity,
how could you
fall so low?
To those who dare
to look up at the open sky
nay, be the sky
to feel the earth below
their earth
to be the very air
pure and clear
to stand straight
and tall and high
to look straight in the eye
to dream
of justice, equality, freedom
for they know
it is better to dare
than to give in to despair
the flame must be kept alive
it may flicker
but must never die.

I am invisible, understand, simply because people refuse to see me . . .
When they approach me, they see only my surroundings, themselves,
or figments of their imagination, indeed, everything and anything
except me . . .

That invisibility to which I refer occurs because of a peculiar
disposition of the eyes of those with whom I come in contact.
A matter of construction of their inner eyes, those eyes with which
they look through their physical eyes upon reality.

—Ralph Ellison, *Invisible Man* (1952), p. 7

Contents

PART III: THE FLAMING FIELDS OF BIHAR

PART IV: BASTAR IN THE CIRCLE OF UNREASON

PART V: KASHMIR AND THE NORTH-EAST

Introduction

Sojourning for Truth

Beginning to Know

There is a time while growing up when we merely grow. And another, when we start understanding how things around us function. Some things make sense and some don't—and we begin to ask why. We begin to think. Suddenly, life takes on a meaning and we search for more meanings.

From the beginning of our existence, consciously or unconsciously, we all have tried to make sense of the world around us. Indeed, we do this most of the time. It is like a never-ending conversation we have with ourselves. This conversation about what is outside of us is invariably also about what is inside us. The observer and what they observe are a continuum—I am a part of what I observe, what I observe is a part of me.

Growing up as I did in Bihar in the 1960s, an early brush with poverty was inevitable. And as first impressions go, this left a deep mark on me. Here is a vignette of personal reminiscence in this respect.

It must have been 1967. A famine raged in Bihar's countryside, claiming lives and impoverishing many. While my family lived a sheltered life in a modern township, I, a four-year-old then, can recall the large number of bedraggled persons who came to our neighbourhood every day. I would watch them closely. One day, when a person came to our door, begging, I asked my mother:

'Who is he, mother?'

'He is a poor man,' she replied.

That was the first time I heard about poverty. When I think about it today, I realize the extent to which a person marked by poverty is bereft of an identity. His poverty becomes his identity.

My memories of Bihar until 1975—when my family moved from there to Gujarat—include many such impressions of poverty as well as violence. Stories of the political turmoil of those times often wafted into our sheltered world, including some about dismembered corpses found in sacks in a place mysteriously called 'zero-mile', dead bodies on the railway tracks, protests by thousands of labourers on the roads of Begusarai escalating further as the Emergency unfolded and more.

The Bihar of my childhood was not one of moderation. It was too cold in winter, too hot in summer and often flooded during the monsoon, when embankments gave way. An impression I carried of the personality of Biharis was also tinged with this brush of extremity: if they loved you, they would do anything for you, and if they hated you, you had it. These feelings were to return much later, in the mid-1990s, when I went back to Bihar with a new purpose.

First Steps

It was in 1985, when I started working as an activist in the Sabarkantha district of north Gujarat, that I took my first tentative steps to 'bring about change'. There was a kind of hope then. This was not just how I felt but also the mood of my colleagues and the movements we were part of at that time. The mid-1980s were a time when autonomous movements burgeoned in various parts of the country and diverse attempts were being made to organize different sections of the population.

I was young then.

When one confronted deep-rooted problems such as poverty, inequality, oppression and injustice of various kinds, there was a feeling that India's democracy could and would ultimately deliver; that it was indeed possible to bring about radical change. We felt the experiment that had begun in 1947 was still at a fledgling stage, with a majority of people still mired in the darkness of illiteracy and oppressive social practices born out of a caste system that perpetuated social and economic inequalities. The challenge was to retain the good in our culture and history and discard without any feeling of loss the traditions that came in the way of India achieving the promises it had made to itself. We believed that this could be achieved through non-violent struggles for rights and justice. This is how we saw the democratic framework and our engagement with it.

As I turn sixty, I find that the heart of India has hardened.

It was naïve perhaps to think that there was one idea of India, while the reality is and has always been throughout India's tumultuous history, that several varying ideas of India have jostled with each other for dominance. In recent times, an attempt has been made by some powerful sections of society to redefine India and take it back to the old conflicts. Instead of living by the liberating human values that we thought had prevailed and made India and us Indians part of the universal quest for the betterment of humankind, we find ourselves mired in sectarian thought and divisive, backward-looking politics again.

The recent disquieting trends in our country, reflected also in some other parts of the world, show that true appreciation of democratic values needs greater work and time. We must remind ourselves that we are just in a moment of history and that there is no need to give up hope.

New Horizons

In Sabarkantha, I was working with Shramjivi Samaj, a *sangathan* (collective) of agricultural labourers and marginal farmers. Shramjivi Samaj was born of a struggle for land led by Dalit, Adivasi and other marginalized communities with little or no land (see Chapter 5—Ekaki). They had fought for possession of government land in the catchment area of a local dam, assigned to them by a government resolution (GR) in 1962. They faced fierce opposition in the process, from the propertied classes as well as from various arms of the state, including mounted police on one occasion. But they won in the end and formed eight agricultural cooperatives to cultivate the land they had claimed—nearly 1400 acres. These collectives are a rare example of relatively successful cooperative farming in rural India. They became the foundation of Shramjivi Samaj, a registered trade union.

After working with Shramjivi Samaj for five years, I felt the need to understand ideology-led movements. I guess I did so because of the burden I felt as the only middle-class activist among eight full-time activists of Shramjivi Samaj. At that time, we were primarily engaged in 'consciousness raising'—helping people to understand their rights and organize to demand their realization. In practical terms, this often translated into struggles for better implementation of government laws, policies and schemes. At the end of five years, we had made a women's wing of the union, Shramjivi Mahila Sangathan, and expanded our work to some forty villages of Bhiloda taluka as well as to neighbouring talukas of Sabarkantha district. However, this horizontal expansion, despite being a result of meaningful struggles for land, Dalit rights, gender equality and so on, did not make clear how to proceed. The 'burden' mentioned earlier emerged because I found that, understandably, there are certain expectations from the more educated activists to provide some guidance and mark the next step. We were engaged in fighting for our rights 'within the system' and hoping to change it in the process. While I had learnt a lot during my years in Bhiloda—indeed, they were my most valuable lessons in Indian sociology and politics—I felt ill-equipped to guide our sangathan further. I acutely felt the need to educate myself about other possible ways of bringing about lasting and radical change.

Wondering how to go about it, I toyed with the idea of pursuing a PhD. There are various means of acquiring knowledge, and while a PhD may not be the best, at the time I felt I wanted to 'study' more and believed that it would provide me with the necessary tools to find answers to the questions that troubled me. The site of the PhD work was clear in my mind—it had to be Bihar. The Bihar of my childhood had never left me. The stark poverty I had witnessed there had remained, making me want to return and rediscover Bihar with adult eyes. I knew that in order to understand what I should do next, I had to study other social and political movements, especially those driven by specific pro-people ideologies.

My initial idea was to study the pre- and post-1947 movements in the undivided district of Gaya in Bihar. Gaya had seen progressive caste-based mobilization, socialist and Sarvodaya movements, and different strands of the Naxalite movement. Diverse and even opposing ideologies flourished there and coexisted at times. I was intrigued to find that people in the same area had supported each of these movements passionately. How did people relate to ideologies? I wondered. On the ground, however, I found that the only active contemporary movement was the Naxalite movement, which was itself factionalized. Thus began my tryst with the Naxalite movement.

Studying the movement for my doctorate led me to spend time with the poorest households in around fifty villages of five districts of then-central Bihar. The mass base of the Naxalite parties, then as now, was amongst the landless Dalits and other marginalized sections of the rural population, earning for it the name 'garibon ki party' (party of the poor).

Two years of 'fieldwork' gave me a close understanding of the abysmal existence of agricultural labourers and their families in rural Bihar. It also gave me an insight into the meaning of feudalism and a taste of the oppressive attitudes that had persisted—and continue to do so—amongst the dominant landlords who depended on the hard labour of the landless multitudes to cultivate their large properties. These dominant sections belonged to the Bhumihar and Rajput upper castes, or in some areas, to middle castes, such as Kurmi and Yadav.

Bihar exposed me not only to the harshness of acute deprivation but also to the ruthless social oppression and political marginalization that created a sea of people who lived in darkness and daily humiliation. Their mud homes were only marginally better than the shelters they built for their pigs; their dishevelled and worried faces brought back some of the memories of the 1967 famine survivors from my childhood days in Begusarai. The reality I witnessed in the mid-1990s did not seem very different from my memories of the late 1960s.

The study of the Naxalite movement in Bihar plunged me into a more complex reality and afforded me a better understanding of the various shades of left and revolutionary politics as well as of the socialist politics of Bihar's past.

I had come home in more ways than one.

In the mid-1990s, besides the structural violence that afflicted the poor and Dalits at the lowest rungs daily in Bihar, there were more dramatic eruptions of physical violence, such as massacres of Dalit labourers by upper-caste 'senas' (literally armies, but actually gangs), as well as internecine conflicts between the three major Naxalite parties that were active in central Bihar at that time. The violence of those times, and the violence I witnessed or heard of later in other parts of the country—from Nagaland and Kashmir to Bastar, whether it was inflicted on those exercising their right to self-determination, or on Dalits, Adivasis, women or minorities—

kept reminding me that some sections of the Indian society are as ruthless, violent and unfeeling as any other power-lusting human beings anywhere. The mutual civility of upper-caste men does not stop them from being extremely exploitative and violent towards the labourers they employ or the women of their own households.

This book, I hope, gives a sense of the life experiences and struggles of ordinary people in the vast stretches of rural India. I would like to emphasize that to a large extent, people live their own lives and manage themselves. They are part of the 'system', and they are not. Those of us who attempt to understand them and their circumstances are able to do so only to some extent, for their reality is layered, and their real life and feelings are only partially visible—not unlike a hill that presents a neat outline when seen from afar, but from closer proximity, reveals many different sides and shades that defy a single reading.

India's Forgotten Country

The essays in this book draw on my experiences and journeys in the last thirty-five years or so, when like many others, I grappled with the fundamental questions of our times. They are stories of life and death, of despair, but also of resistance and struggle.

These essays were not planned. They emerged one by one, as and when different issues took me to various parts of the country. Some go back to my early years in Gujarat. Others are an offshoot of my research on the Naxalite movement, not just in Bihar, but also in other states such as Telangana and Chhattisgarh. Some were written as and when I was led to investigate, individually or as part of a team, human rights violations in different areas. The more recent ones deal with the ongoing conflict in Bastar, where I live and work today. Taken together, the essays build on first-hand investigations in eleven states—Bihar, Chhattisgarh, Delhi, Gujarat, Jharkhand, Maharashtra, Manipur, Meghalaya, Nagaland, Rajasthan and Telangana. To this I should add Kashmir, now reduced to a union territory, but it has a special place in this book and my heart.

The book, however, is not just a collection of writings and studies from different states. The idea is also to bring to the fore some general issues that are pertinent to India as a whole.

Hard Lives

One obvious theme of the book is the harsh nature of people's lives in India's 'forgotten country'—the hamlets, villages and slums that remain out of sight of the privileged classes. All of us know, of course, that many people in India don't have much money. Still, it is easy to forget that so many people live on so little—the simplest food, tattered clothes, a bare house and very little to spare for children's education or healthcare. Further, lack of money is only one aspect of their pervasive hardships and restricted freedoms—daily worries, diverse insecurities, indebtedness, illness, powerlessness, humiliation and violence also follow them around like shadows. As an elderly widow in Bhiloda once explained to me: a life of poverty sometimes feels like '*dukh no dungar* [a mountain of sorrow]'.

This is not to deny that people's living conditions often improve over time. The Bhiloda of today is more prosperous than 'my' Bhiloda. Even the Bihari *mazdooras* (labourers) described in Chapter 12 (The Mazdooras of Bihar) are likely to have better food, clothes and shelter today than they used to have in the mid-1990s— when I spent time with them—and their children are now more likely to go to school than to work as wage labourers. Yet, their living conditions remain abysmal, and the fact that some crumbs fell their way as India's economy grew by leaps and bounds does not justify the government's neoliberal economic policies. Besides, it is not as if people's living conditions always improve. Some have lost much of the little they had as they were displaced by dams or other projects— forced displacement in the Narmada Valley, discussed in Chapter 10

(Forced Evictions in the Narmada Valley), is a dramatic example. And even amongst those who have experienced some improvement in material terms, there are many who look back with nostalgia to the lives they used to lead a few decades ago. In Bastar, for instance, people reminisce about the time when they could roam about the jungles without fear before the entire region turned into a war zone, causing so many of them to be displaced, jailed, tortured or killed.

And what to say of Kashmir? Unbeknown to the Indian public, living standards in Kashmir are higher than in most Indian states. Most people there have spacious houses, warm clothes and plenty to eat. Wage rates are higher than almost anywhere in India—no wonder migrant workers from Bihar, Jharkhand and other states brave the distance and cold weather to seek work in Kashmir. At first sight, life in Kashmir would look good not only to Bihari workers but perhaps even to many Gujarati tourists. But in fact, it has become hell for the Kashmiris, living as they do under the boot of India's security forces and constantly exposed to harassment, searches, beatings, arrests and torture. The incidents and atrocities mentioned in Chapter 22 (A Stone in My Hand), based on the events that occurred in mid-2010, have become routine for the people of Kashmir.

Social Oppression

Another theme touched upon in this book is the way oppressive social practices ruin people's lives, especially those of Dalits, bonded labourers, women and other downtrodden groups. Dalits, of course, are amongst the worst victims of oppressive social practices in India. Bihar is well-known for its history of atrocities against Dalits, including abominable feudal customs such as *dola pratha* (which compelled every new bride to spend her first night after marriage with the local zamindar), practised not so long ago. More recently, Bihar has become infamous for barbaric massacres of Dalits by upper-caste militias, such as the Ranbeer Sena (also known as

Ranveer Sena)—see Chapters 2 (Massacre on the Banks of the Sone) and 13 (The Naxalite Movement in Central Bihar). Caste-based oppression and exploitation, however, are not confined to Bihar—they persist to varying degrees across the country. As mentioned in Chapter 4 (Dalit Rebellion against Untouchability in Chakwada), Dalit resistance against untouchability in Chakwada goes back to the 1930s and was prominently mentioned by Dr Ambedkar in *The Annihilation of Caste*, but close to 100 years later, their struggle for equality continues.

Other victims of extreme social oppression include widows, condemned as they are to a life of hardship and loneliness. Chapter 5 (Ekaki) focuses not only on their sorrows but also on their struggles to resist oppression, individually or collectively. Bonded labourers are also amongst the worst victims of social oppression, compounding their economic oppression. Bonded labour is thought to have disappeared, but as the stories in Chapter 3 (Of Human Bondage in Baran) illustrate, it is, in fact, still rampant in some parts of the country. Its victims are exploited to the limit of physical endurance throughout their short lives, and the condition of bondage often ends up being transmitted from generation to generation.

Dalits, widows and bonded labourers are just some of the victims of India's oppressive social practices. Patriarchy has invaded every home and the caste system, every public space—and these are just two of the insidious systems of oppression that envelop us, ultimately degrading the oppressors as well as the oppressed. No wonder some consider that nothing short of a revolution is likely to sweep them away.

State Repression

Another concern covered in this book is state repression and how social inequality and state repression feed on each other. The privileged sections of the society will perhaps find this a little difficult to understand and relate to because they tend to see the kinder face of the state. The government provides them with electricity and water, helps them in times of disaster, defends the country's borders and keeps the poor in their place—that seems like a good deal, in exchange for surrendering a small portion of their income in the form of taxes. Unless they choose to indulge in criminal activities, there is little danger of the police barging into their homes at midnight, of a forest guard burning their homes or of them spending years in jail as undertrials. That sort of 'special' treatment is reserved for the poor and powerless.

Poor people have a very different experience and view of the Indian state. Most chapters in this book deal with state repression in one form or another, almost invariably directed at powerless people. From police firings in the Garo Hills (Chapter 23—Student Protests in the Garo Hills) and fake encounters in Bastar (Chapter 17—Salwa Judum and After) to forced evictions in the Narmada Valley (Chapter 10—Forced Evictions in the Narmada Valley) and rampant human rights violations in Kashmir (Chapter 22—A Stone in My Hand), the tales of brutality against ordinary citizens are endless. In addition to these highly visible acts of state repression, there is also a long record of what might be called 'passive repression' of a deliberate sort, where the state plays an oppressive role by failing to act on people's complaints or to protect their rights. In the case of massacres by caste senas in Bihar, for instance, the killings were carried out by private militias, but the state turned complicit by failing to take action on the killers and to ensure justice for the victims (Chapter 15—Justice, Not Vengeance). The story is the same in Chakwada, where the state failed to protect the rights of Dalits who were prevented from using the village pond (Chapter 4—Dalit Rebellion against Untouchability in Chakwada), and in Sabarkantha, where the government allowed right-wing Hindu militias to torment local Muslims without any fear of retribution (Chapter 1—A Step Back in Sabarkantha). There is not a single instance, in this book, of the state firmly taking the side of oppressed people and upholding their rights.

Struggle and Resistance

The essays in this book are not just stories of suffering and repression. They are also about people's courageous efforts to resist oppression and stand up for their rights, individually or collectively. These efforts take many different forms, some more visible than others. Some people resist individually, often at great personal risk. Such is the case of Ratanben, a widow branded as a witch, who fought with exemplary courage for her right to land and ended up being murdered by her own in-laws (Chapter 5—Ekaki).

Others resist collectively, in one way or another, without necessarily forming a structured organization. As Dr Ambedkar hinted in his famous slogan 'Educate, agitate, organize', agitation often comes before and without organization. It is a natural tendency for oppressed people to rattle their chains and shed their shackles whenever possible. All over the country, there are inspiring examples of their efforts to stand up for their rights. Some examples are explored in this book, including Dalit resistance against untouchability in Rajasthan (Chapter 4—Dalit Rebellion against Untouchability in Chakwada), Adivasi resistance against displacement in Jharkhand (Chapter 9—Resistance and Repression in Koel-Karo), collective action by single women in Gujarat (Chapter 5—Ekaki) and Adivasi protests against paramilitary camps in Bastar (Chapter 17—Salwa Judum and After). In recent times, we have seen many more examples of similar struggles, from the campus agitations of 2016 and the nationwide protests against the Citizenship Amendment Act of 2019 to the powerful farmers' protests of 2020–21. In most cases, these collective struggles involved peaceful means, yet they have been met with brutal repression.

Organized non-violent struggle is another approach. That is what much of my early work in Gujarat was about. As mentioned earlier, Shramjivi Samaj began with a relatively successful attempt by rural labourers to establish possession of contested agricultural land

and then to form cooperative societies to cultivate it. Later, we fought for a range of social and economic rights, from minimum wages and drought relief to food rations under the public distribution system. The union members were mostly Dalits, Adivasis and those at the lower rungs of the Other Backward Classes, such as Banjaras and Thakardas, struggling not only for a better life but also for dignity and equality. When I returned there in 2019, I found that Shramjivi Samaj had become relatively inactive, yet the political consciousness it had created had a lasting impact. Many Dalit members of the organization had found new inspiration in Dr Ambedkar, and some of them had even converted to Buddhism.

And then, of course, there is armed resistance by revolutionary organizations or parties. The Naxalites and their organizations are not to be forgotten easily. There are many endearing aspects of the Naxalite—one who devotes her life to people, lives like them, with them, remains invisible, and even forsakes her name and identity (real names get known only after their often-violent deaths). The selflessness of the Naxalite—who works towards ushering the 'next light' as some labourers used to perceive it in Bihar—cannot be denied. And yet, despite the many sacrifices of so many over the last fifty-six years of Naxalite insurgency, I am not convinced that this is the best path to radical change in India. The oppressed have every right to fight their oppressors, but as discussed in Chapter 16 (On 'Revolutionary Violence'), there is a downside to organized violence that cannot be ignored. Inevitably, real issues get eclipsed when a spiral of violence gets unleashed from both sides, and everything gets sucked into the vortex of violence. Something like that happened in parts of Bihar in the mid-1990s, as the 'Diary of Violence' at the end of Chapter 15 (Justice, Not Vengeance) illustrates. Paradoxically, it is always the weakest in the society who get caught in the crossfire and suffer the most even as the revolutionary movement aims or claims to work for their liberation. In Bihar and elsewhere, I have found more meaning in the powerful movements of the open and democratic fronts of the Naxalites or similar autonomous movements. They seem to me to hold more promise than the delusional struggle to seize power through 'revolutionary violence'.

The future of the Naxalite movement is uncertain. On the one hand, policies and circumstances that pushed people to join or support the movement continue. Counter-insurgency operations themselves, freely overstepping the rule of law, have contributed to the survival and spread of the movement. On the other hand, reliance on violence and fear can have corrupting influences, and that applies to the Naxalites as well. Perhaps the time has come for the Naxalite movement to reinvent itself.

Symbolic Democracy

Finally, the essays in this book bring out, I hope, the cosmetic nature of Indian democracy. There is not a single case, in the book, where democratic institutions made it possible for people to secure a timely and effective response to their grievances. Nor did democratic institutions restrain state repression. On the contrary, democratic institutions connived to maintain a status quo that continued to benefit a small elite at the cost of large sections of Indian society.

The Dalit struggle against untouchability in Chakwada (Chapter 4) is an enlightening example. At every step, the tendency of the state was to side with the powerful. When the local Bairwas (Dalits) complained to the police that they were prevented from using the village pond, a whole string of government officers—station house officer, tehsildar, deputy superintendent of police and even assistant collector—told them that they should respect the village tradition and avoid escalating the conflict. Even after the Bairwas filed a first information report (FIR) under the Scheduled Castes and the Scheduled Tribes (Prevention of Atrocities) Act, 1989, the police failed to take action, as it routinely happens in that area. Further, no political party took a firm stand on the side of the Bairwas; even the local MLA, a Dalit himself, took the side of the oppressors. In this respect, he vindicated Dr Ambedkar's prediction that seat reservation without separate electorates would produce pliable Dalit representatives who avoid antagonizing the upper castes for fear of losing their votes.

Democratic institutions in India have been equally ineffective in curbing state repression. It is extremely rare for security personnel or other government officers to be punished for human rights violations, or for complicity with atrocities committed by others. From police firing in the Garo Hills and the Bathani Tola massacre in Bihar to fake encounters in Bastar and even gang rapes of Adivasi women by the security forces there, state authorities have acted with impunity again and again.

None of this is to say that democratic institutions have no value. The way forward is to be more democratic, not less. But the first step is to recognize how little has been achieved so far.

Moving Forward

This book only provides a glimpse of the lives of marginalized people in rural India—where the bulk of the population lives. At the end of the day, an overwhelming impression one has after having lived and worked with poor communities is that, to a large extent, they manage their lives on their own. They suffer on their own, they survive on their own. Governance is an important concept, and much is made of it. But if you think about it, the lives of the poor are largely 'self' governed. The entity called 'government' interjects with their lives in particular ways—sometimes helpful, sometimes not, and sometimes positively harmful.

The essays in this book are intended as a small contribution to the social history of rural India. They were written at different times over a long period. I have not tried to update them, except by adding a few endnotes here and there, but some recent developments are briefly discussed in the Epilogue. In each chapter, an opening footnote mentions the date and context of writing. The date matters to follow the events, but the issues discussed in these essays are much the same as they used to be.

In some chapters (as indicated), people's names have been changed to protect anonymity, but in most cases, the original names have been retained. All place names are authentic.

I consider it my good fortune to have had the occasion to spend so much time over so many years in rural areas—in some beautiful landscapes, in the company of some very fine people. These places and people have certainly made my life meaningful.

Chuditekda, Dantewada
12 June 2023

1

A Step Back in Sabarkantha*

Riots, I was told, had broken out in Sabarkantha too. The thought of Sabarkantha brought back many memories, for it was from here that I began my working life many years ago. The quiet low hills of the Aravalli range all around, camels meandering at their own pace, the nomadic Bharvads squatting in the fields with their herds of sheep, mud huts, scorching heat during drought relief works, local struggles against caste oppression, for minimum wages and over land—those were my early years of getting to know rural life amidst the tears and laughter of the local communities: Adivasis, Vanjaras, Bhambis, Vankars and Thakardas. Many years had since passed and I decided to go back to Sabarkantha—only to find that the Sabarkantha I used to know had changed drastically.

Sabarkantha now had scars on its heart that would take a long time to heal and forget. A district that had no significant history of communal strife was engulfed in the wave of violence that swept

---

* This essay, originally published in *Seminar* in April 2002, was written after spending a month in Sabarkantha in March–April 2002. I had lived and worked there for five years in the second half of the 1980s. Sabarkantha district was later bifurcated into two districts: Sabarkantha and Aravalli. This version is in the past tense and includes added notes.

1

through Gujarat in March 2002. Asking anyone on the streets, you would learn that the *toofaan* (storm, as this wave of violence was called) had stuck almost every village of the district where Muslims resided. Probing a little further, you would hear numerous stories of what had happened everywhere—how Muslim women, men and children had to flee leaving their dinner half-eaten, some without even wearing their slippers or locking their doors, how they sought refuge in fields, trudged through the hills, walked for days to reach the safety of the relief camps, hungry, tired and frightened, with thorns in their feet and tears in their eyes. This is what it must have been like during Partition. Perhaps the Partition story is not over—it remains half-written and continues to tear at the soul of India.

Sabarkantha[1]

Sabarkantha, named after the Sabarmati River that flows along its western border, came into existence in 1949 following the merger of twenty-nine princely states and estates with a portion of the former Ahmedabad district in the then Bombay State. While the Sabarmati separates the district from Banaskantha and Mehsana districts on the west, the Aravalli hills form a natural boundary with Rajasthan on the northern and eastern sides, and Ahmedabad, Kheda and Panchmahal districts touch its southern boundaries.

The administrative history of the district is divided into the early period (up to 1412 CE), the Muslim period (1412–1700), the Maratha period (1750–1811), the British period (1820–1947) and the post-Independence period (1947 onwards). The earliest settlers, both the rulers and the ruled, were Bhils and Kolis. The entry of the Rajputs into the district can be noted from the eighth century onwards. Many of the Rajputs married the local Kolis, thereby losing the Rajput caste but retaining the clan names such as Makvana, Dabi and Bariya.

About 90 per cent of the population of the district lives in rural areas.[2] The economy of Sabarkantha is dominated by agriculture, both irrigated and (mainly) unirrigated. Only a small part of the population is engaged in industrial activities or the tertiary sector.

According to the 1981 census, 8.6 per cent of the population in Sabarkantha consists of Scheduled Castes (SCs) and 16.7 per cent of Scheduled Tribes (STs). Amongst the SCs, the more prominent ones are the Vankars, Bhambis, Bhangis and Chenvas. The main Adivasi groups are the Bhils, Bhil Garasias and Dungri Garasias. They are concentrated in four of the thirteen talukas of the district, including Bhiloda where I used to live and work.

A large part of the land is owned by influential cultivating castes such as Patels, Kolis and Rajputs. Political power is also heavily concentrated among these communities. In fact, Sabarkantha is a stronghold of the farmers' lobby in Gujarat.

Those with large landholdings are sometimes called *kampawala*s. Most of them originally came from Kheda, Surat and Kutch districts. They came in the days of the Idar princely state when forests covered much of the land. They used to live in camps while clearing the forests, hence the term 'kampawala'. The kampawalas started growing cash crops such as cotton and groundnut in Sabarkantha and soon ginning factories and spinning mills also came up. 'Patelvaad' (the domination of Patels) has existed in Sabarkantha in diverse ways.

The proportion of Muslims in Sabarkantha's population is small—about 6 per cent according to census data. Muslims work largely as traders, artisans, labourers and, to a lesser extent, cultivators. They are scattered across the district, with some pockets of higher concentration such as Himmatnagar (the district headquarters) and Modasa. Muslim communities such as the Mansuris, Ghanchis and Memons have resided in the villages of Sabarkantha for generations.

The temples and other religious structures of Sabarkantha point to a diversity of beliefs and faiths. The excavations at Devni Mori (Bhiloda) have revealed that a Buddhist Vihar was built there in the third century CE. Jain influence is evident from Jain marble temples at Lakhena (Vijaynagar). There are ancient Sun temples at Roda, and Khedbrahma gets its name from a standing image of Brahma—no other place in India, except Pushkar in Rajasthan, has a Brahma shrine of this sort.

Amongst the Hindu gods, Shiva (known here as Mahadev) and Krishna (known as Shamaliya Bavji by the Adivasis) are the popular ones. The Shamlaji temple in Bhiloda taluka was built in the eleventh century. Ram and Hanuman had no special status until recently.

From recent events, however, it appeared that attempts were made to obliterate this diversity by organizing and uniting the majority community against the minority community.

The Storm[3]

After the Godhra incident on 27 February 2002 (when dozens of Hindus returning from Ayodhya died in a suspicious train fire), the reaction in Bhiloda town was almost immediate. On 28 February, a *bandh* (blockade) was called—shops were shut down and vehicles stopped plying. Looting and burning started the next day, on 1 March. Jahoorbhai's *lathi* (a yard of wood, cement and other building materials) was one of the first to be looted. Jahoorbhai died long ago but his lathi, now run by his son, has been part of the Bhiloda landscape for many decades. Numerous shops, houses and hotels were looted in Bhiloda that day including prosperous shops of electronic items, ready-made clothes, household utensils, etc. People were seen carrying the loot to their homes. Many of these shops were burnt.

There were rumours of similar incidents across Sabarkantha district—not just in urban areas, the usual site of communal violence in Gujarat, but also in rural and Adivasi areas. As some observers put it, 'The question is not where it has happened but where it has not happened'. In the days after the Godhra incident, there was a wave of anger against the Muslims. This, combined with concerted mobilization by right-wing Hindu nationalist organizations over the last decade or so, led to a spate of violence that was intense and frightening. According to some, without the Godhra incident, none of this would have happened. According to others, things had been planned for 6 March and Godhra only hastened matters.

It is interesting how the dates, timing and method of communal violence coincided in village after village. While violence broke out in the town areas of Khedbrahma and Bhiloda talukas the very next morning after the Godhra incident, action in the villages happened on 1 and 2 March, mostly around 7.30 or 8.30 in the night. The houses and shops of most Muslims in each village were looted first, and then they were torched. Houses and shops were spared mainly when they were close to the houses of the Hindus, or where Hindus were owners or tenants. In some villages, houses of single Muslim women, widowed or old, were spared at the request of neighbours. The patterns that emerge confirm that this was not a 'riot', as the term is normally understood. It was neither spontaneous nor sporadic, but premeditated and systematic.

Aggressors were reported to be *baharnas* (outsiders) or *aaju-baju na gamdanas* (from nearby villages). Even though the participation of people of the same village was deemed to be negligible, some support is a certainty, for how else would it be possible for outsiders to know the exact targets? The attackers came in large mobs—the strength of which varied from a hundred to hundreds—in tractors, jeeps or on foot. In some villages, they were armed with *trishuls*, swords and local agricultural implements such as spades and lathis. In some villages they were also reported to be wearing saffron headbands and sashes, holding Hindutva flags and shouting slogans that clearly identified them with right-wing Hindu-nationalist groups.

Whatever was done, was done by *tola*s (groups). It seems that there was a clear division of tasks. There were the *todwawalas* (those who were destroying), *lootwawalas* (those who were looting) and *baadwawalas* (those who were burning). One influential local community was routinely mentioned as playing a leading role in these attacks, but poorer communities also participated in the looting. In many villages, it was emphasized that it was the *sukhi* (rich) people who were carrying off the loot and not the *dukhi* (poor) people.

Within a few hours, Muslims who had been residing in these villages for decades or even longer were rendered destitute and homeless. Forced to flee with only what they were wearing, they had to trudge for days through fields and *dungar*s (hills) with their infants and children, leaving most of the old people behind. Some of them initially headed to the houses of their relatives in nearby talukas of Sabarkantha or in adjoining areas of Banaskantha (the neighbouring district), only to find that their relatives too were experiencing a similar fate. After days of hunger, hardship and anxiety for lost family members, they finally reached the safety of relief camps. When I met them in the camps, they had already been living there for nearly two months as refugees in their own land, wondering about their future, too scared to go back.

The objective seems to have been to target the Muslims economically, boycott them socially and spread fear and terror. By forcing them to leave their places of residence en masse and without warning, an attempt was made to change the demography of the villages. That is why the most popular slogan was '*Muslai ne gaam ma thi kado* [Force the Muslims—pejoratively called 'muslai'—out of the village].' Altogether, 2161 houses, 1461 shops, 304 smaller enterprises (including small shops called *galla*s, handcarts, *fairia*s or mobile salesmen), 71 factories, 38 hotels, 45 religious places and 240 vehicles were completely or partially destroyed in the Sabarkantha district. The total loss in monetary terms was estimated at Rs 30.7 crore as of 4 April 2002.[4] Needless to say, the actual figures were likely to be much higher.

Muslims on the run fled to areas where they felt safe— mainly areas where their relatives lived or where members of their own community resided in greater numbers. Muslim religious organizations in these places started collective service. These areas later became relief camps recognized by the government. In March 2002, there were twelve such camps in the district. Eleven of these were being run by Muslim organizations, where the camp members were all Muslims. The twelfth camp was for Hindus and was run by a Hindu welfare organization in Modasa. It is sad to note that even the relief camps were divided by community and there were no multi-faith camps.

As of 9 April 2002, there were as many as 10,569 persons in these camps, of whom 10,041 were Muslims. A week-wise comparison of total numbers in the camps revealed that the peak occupation was in mid-March at 10,718. These figures suggest that the situation on the ground was yet to improve in early April. With their homes empty and charred, no source of livelihood and uncertainty about the reception of others in the village, what indeed did the victims have to go back to?

'They did not leave even a *chamchi* [spoon] with which I could take my medicine,' said elderly Nuresabibi from Derol village in Khedbrahma—later in Vadali camp. '*Humara vatan yahin hai, hum kahan jayen* [This is our land, where should we go]?' asked Hirabhai Ghanchi of Mudeti village in Idar taluka. '*Hum Hindustan ke vatni hain. Jab marenge to do gaz zameen to milegi? Unka kehna hai ki inko jala denge, to yeh do gaz zameen bhi nahi mangenge* [We are people of Hindustan. When we die, will we get enough land for our burial? They think that if they burn us, then we will not ask for even that],' said Zafarbhai Mansuri of Bhiloda taluka. These broken people had been pushed to the wall. In the midst of their pain, they remembered the help and support given to them by many of their neighbours and friends, knowing how difficult it was for them to do so. In numerous instances, those who protected them were also threatened. But despite the prevailing climate of hate and violence, many of their Hindu friends came to leave them at the camps, and many others were still going to the camps to get them back. While there were a few stray examples of Muslims who were able to return to their villages and resume their earlier lives, in most cases, their attempt to return home proved short-lived. Continued threats of further violence forced them to go back to the camps.

It was widely acknowledged, however, that some communities—in particular, Darbars and Dalits (especially Bhambis)—had supported the Muslims. Darbars—the erstwhile Rajwads (members of the former royal family) of the Idar state and *jagirdars* (landlords) of smaller *jagirs* (land)—were said to have openly challenged the onslaught, sometimes with their guns. One of them, I was told, had sheltered Muslim families on the terrace of his house for fifteen days. Being of relatively higher social status and economic standing, the Darbars proved a powerful ally for the Muslims. They could not be threatened easily, as happened to some of the Dalits who gave refuge to Muslim families or kept their possessions safe for them. In villages such as Leelcha in Bhiloda taluka, some Bhambi shops were looted along with those of the Muslims.

Despite these acts of solidarity, the general atmosphere was of suspicion and animosity between communities. The common perception of Muslims was that 'they live in Hindustan, but their heart is in Pakistan' or that 'when Pakistan wins in cricket matches, they burst crackers'. Comparing them with other minorities, someone said, 'If they want to live in India, let them learn to live like the Parsis—there will be little problem.'

Police Complicity[5]

The complicity of the police with the perpetrators was not in doubt; everyone seemed to be clear about it. 'The violence happened in front of their very eyes', 'It happened in front of the police station', 'When we phoned them for help, they did not come' and 'Policemen themselves were inciting bystanders to help themselves to the loot' were some of the observations I heard from numerous witnesses. In towns such as Himmatnagar, Bhiloda and Khedbrahma, it was *after* a curfew had been imposed on 28 February that shops and business establishments were looted and destroyed. One found few instances of action taken by the police—be it the use of tear gas or lathi charge. Notably, in the aftermath of violence too, urgent action that was necessary and possible was missing. For instance, there were no signs of search operations to retrieve looted goods. Instead, in some locations a truck was simply kept in a public place and people were ordered to return what they had taken, suggesting that no action would be taken against them personally.

I heard many complaints of police stations refusing to admit FIRs. As we know, a delay in lodging an FIR is detrimental to the attainment of justice. Where FIRs were being admitted, people were actively discouraged from mentioning the names of individuals and asked to mention only a tola. In some police stations, only one FIR per village was being accepted. Aggrieved Muslims got around this by faxing their complaints directly to the Deputy Superintendent of Police (DSP). Besides, 137 Muslim businessmen of Himmatnagar lodged a petition in the Gujarat High Court against the police inspector, Himmatnagar town, as well as the DSP, stating that they were not recording FIRs, nor were they carrying out investigations (*Times of India*, 26 March 2002). The petition was subsequently withdrawn when assurances were given by the respondents that due process would be followed. As of 9 April 2002, 393 FIRs had been lodged in the entire district (these are single FIRs with multiple complaints), but not a single person had been charged with any crime. In one way or another, the criminals were clearly being protected.

The functioning of the police clearly suggests that the violence was politically motivated. Saffronization of a large part of the police force itself cannot be ruled out. Out of fifty-two policemen in Himmatnagar town police station, for example, only two were

જય શ્રી રામ

વહાલા હિંદુ ભાઈઓ –ભગિનીઓ તેમજ માતાઓ….. સૌને જય શ્રી રામ

આપ સૌને ખબર છે કે હિન્દુસ્તાનમાં છેલ્લા બારસો વર્ષથી મુસલમાનોએ હિંદુઓ ઉપર ભયંકર જુલ્મો ગુજાર્યો છે. આપણા હજારો મંદિરો તોડી મસ્જિદો બનાવી દીધી છે. બહેન દિકરીઓની ઇજ્જત લૂંટી છે. ચિતોડ રાજસ્થાનની દશ હજાર થી વધારે પદ્મીનીઓનું અગ્નિ સ્નાન જગ જાહેર છે. વર્તમાનમાં ગોધરા રેલ્વે કાંડ ની ઘટનાથી સૌ વાકેફ છીએ. ૫૮ જેટલા નિર્દોષ ભાઈઓ બહેનો – બાળકોને અકારણ જીવતાં બૂંજ નાખ્યાં છે.

હિંદુ સમાજના આધારે જીવતાં આ નાપાક દેશદ્રોહી તત્વોની શાન ઠેકાણે લાવવા -તેમને મરણતોલ ફટકો મારવા હવે સમય પાકી ગયો છે. આપણે હિંદુ સમાજના તમામ ઘટકો કોઈપણ પ્રકારના ભેદભાવ ભૂલીને હવે સંગઠિત એવં લડાયક બનવું પડશે. આપણી આવનાર પેઢીઓની સુખાકારી - સમૃધ્ધિ - સલામતિ તેમજ ઠાયમી શાંતિ માટે સમગ્ર હિંદુ સમાજની ભલાઈ માટે - હિંદુ સનાતન ધર્મ તથા સંસ્કૃતિના રક્ષણ માટે ટૂંકમાં આપણા રાષ્ટ્ર માટે…. ઔરંગઝેબ અને બાબરની ગદ્દાર - દેશ દ્રોહી ઓલાદના ખાત્મા માટે આપણે છત્રપતિ શિવાજી મહારાજ તથા મહારાણા પ્રતાપ બનવું જ પડશે.

હે હિંદુઓ આ નઝૂત અને ગદ્દાર પ્રજા કદી પોતાના સગા બાપ-ભાઈ કે બહેનની થઈ નથી વિશ્વાસઘાત પ્રપંચ અને ધોખા બાજીથી ભરેલો તેમનો ઇતિહાસ છે. આવી બાબર-બિલાલોની પ્રજા હિંદુઓ માટે વિશ્વાસપાત્ર બની શકે જ નહિ. માટે તેમનો કદી પણ ભરોશો કરવો નહિ નહિ તો પાછળથી પસ્તાવાનો પાર નહિ રહે.

દુશ્મનોને - નાલાયક દેશદ્રોહી ગદ્દારોને ઠાયમી ખતમ કરવા તેમનો **આર્થિક અને સામાજિક બહિષ્કાર** કરવાનો ભગવાન રામની સાક્ષી એ દ્રઢ સંકલ્પ / નિશ્ચય કરો આજથી જ હું તેમજ મારા પરિવારના સભ્યો-પાડોશી, મિત્ર મંડળ, સગાસંબંધી સહુને જાણ કરીશ કે હવેથી જીવન પર્યંત ………. નીચેના મુદ્દાઓનો અમલ કરી રાષ્ટ્રના સજાગ પ્રહરી બનીશ હવે અમે પૃથ્વીરાજ ચૌહાણ જેવી ભુલો થવા દઈશું નહીં.

- મુસલમાનોની લારી કે દુકાનમાંથી શાકભાજી, મિઠાઈ, દારૂખાનું, પતંગ, જેલીને ઉપયોગી વસ્તુઓ, ઘર વપરાશની વસ્તુઓ કોઈ પણ ચીજ ખરીદીશ નહિ (ભલે ગમે તેટલી સસ્તી કેમ ન આપતો હોય)
- ગદ્દારોના ગેરેજમાં મારુ સ્કૂટર, જીપ, ટ્રક, ટ્રેક્ટર કદી રીપેર કરાવીશ નહિ. અને પંક્ચર પણ કરાવીશ નહિ.
- મુસલમાન છોકરા - છોકરીની દોસ્તી કરવી તે જીવનું જોખમ છે. માટે સર્વથા રાખવો નહી
- મુસલમાનોના ટ્રક , ટ્રેક્ટર, જીપ, કદી પણ ભાડે કરીશ નહિ તેમના સાધનોમાં પણ બેસીશ નહિ.
- મારા ઘરમા મુખ્ય દ્વારા પર ૐ ચીતરાવીશ, કપાળ ઉપર તિલક કરીશ ૐ ચીતરેલ વાહન જીપમાં માં જ બેસીશ.
- મુસલમાનો સાથે કોઈપણ ધંધા વેપાર ભાગીદારી કરીશ નહિ. તેમને પ્રોત્સાહિત કોઈપણ રીતે કરીશ નહિ.
- મારા ઘરમાં કોઈપણ પ્રકારના સંરક્ષક હથિયાર રાખીશ અને જરૂર પડ્યે હિંદુ સમાજના સંરક્ષણ માટે તેને ધારણ કરતાં ખચકાઈશ નહિ. અને ડરીશ નહિ.
- મુસલમાન ફકીરોને ચુપિયાંની ચુમાડી માટે એકપણ પૈસો આપીશ નહિ.
- આપણી બહેન દીકરીઓ સ્કૂલો, કોલેજોમાં, નોકરી કે અન્ય રીતે મુસલમાન છોકરાઓની સંગત કે માયાજાળમાં ફસાય નહિ તે માટે સજાગ રહીશ.
- મુસલમાન શિક્ષક, પ્રોફેસર પાસે ટ્યુશન કે કાંઈ શિખવા ખાનગી રીતે જઈશ નહિ.
- દેશદ્રોહીઓની હોટલો તેમના અભિનય વાણી સિનેમાનો દિલથી બહિષ્કાર કરો.
- મુસલમાનોની લાટીઓ માંથી સિમેન્ટ, પતરાં કે કોઈ પણ વસ્તુ ખરીદવી નહિ. લાકડાં વહેરવાનું કામ પણ ત્યાં ન કરાવવું.

યાદરાખો :–

મુસલમાનો હિંદુ ગ્રાહકોને આકર્ષવા માટે શરૂઆતમાં અન્ય વેપારીઓ કરતા પોતાની વસ્તુ સસ્તા ભાવે વેચવાનું ષડયંત્ર શરૂ કરો. માટે કોઈએ ક્ષણિક લોભથી લલચાવું નહિ. તેમની મોહજાળમાં ફસાવું નહિ.

ઉપરોક્ત બાબતો સાથે આપણા ધ્યાનમાં આવે તે તમામ ઉપાયોનો કડક અમલ કરી... એવીજડ બેસલાક આર્થિક નાકાબંધી નાપાક તત્વોના શ્વાસ રુંધી નાખો. એમની કરોડરજ્જુ ભાંગીને ભૂક્કો થઈ જશે. પાકિસ્તાન ઝીંદાબાદ ના નારા બંધ થશે. આર્થિક નાકા બંધીના અમલથી કોઈપણ મુસલમાનની તાકાત નથી કે તે આપણા સમાજ સામે માથુ ઉંચકી જીવી શકે. આ પત્રિકાનો ગામે ગામ, ઘેર ઘેર પ્રચાર કરો બહેનો ભાઈઓને સમજાવો અને અમલ કરે તેમ આગ્રહ કરો.

આ પત્રિકાનો અમલ ન કરે તેને ભગવાન શ્રી રામચંદ્રજી - હનુમાનજીની આણ છે.

જય શ્રીરામ… જય શ્રીરામ… જય શ્રીરામ…

તા.ક. આ પત્રિકાની જરૂર પડ્યે ઝેરોક્ષ નકલો વહેંચી શકાય. આ પત્રિકા વાંચો… વંચાવો અને અમલ કરો.

[Translation]

Jai Shri Ram
Dear Hindu Brothers, Sisters and Mothers . . . To All Jai Shri Ram

All of you know that for the last 1200 years Muslims have committed atrocities on the Hindus in Hindustan. They have destroyed thousands of our temples and built mosques. They have raped our sisters and daughters. The whole world knows that more than 10,000 Padminis had to immolate themselves by fire in Rajasthan's Chittaur. All are aware of the recent Godhra incident. 58 innocent brothers, sisters and children were roasted alive without reason.

The time is ripe to give a death blow to the power of these nefarious anti-national elements who have been living on the goodwill of the Hindu society. All sections of our Hindu society will have to forget whatever differences there may be between us and get organized and become fighters. For the happiness, progress, security and permanent peace of the coming generations and well-being of the entire Hindu society, Hindu *sanatan dharma* (eternal religion) and the protection of culture, in short for our *rashtra* . . . for the decimation of traitors and anti-national children of Aurangzeb and Babar, we will have to become Chhatrapati Shivaji Maharaj and Rana Pratap.

O Hindus! These deceitful people could not be loyal to their own father, brother or sister. Their history is full of cheating and treachery. These descendants of Babar-Bilal can never become trustworthy for Hindus. Therefore, they should never be trusted otherwise you will keep regretting it later.

Let us take an oath, with God Ram as witness, to finish off our enemies forever—these useless, anti-national traitors—by starting an **Economic and Social Boycott** against them. From today, I as well as my family members, will persuade our neighbours, friends and relatives to implement the following as long as we live and thereby become alert guardians of our nation. Now, we shall not allow mistakes like those made by Prithviraj Chauhan to happen again.

- I shall not buy anything from the hand-cart or shop of a Muslim whether it is vegetables, sweets, liquor, kites, household items or anything else (however cheaper the price may be).
- I shall never give my scooter, jeep, truck or tractor for repair in the garage of these traitors, or even go there to fix a puncture.
- To befriend a Muslim boy or girl is a risk to life. Therefore, I shall have no relation with them.
- I shall never rent a truck, tractor or jeep owned by a Muslim nor sit in their vehicles.
- I shall keep the Om sign on the entrance of my house, shall wear a tilak on my forehead and shall sit only in a jeep or vehicle that has Om written on it.
- I shall not employ a Muslim as a driver for my private or business vehicle.
- I shall not have Muslims as partners in any kind of trade or business. I shall not do anything to encourage them in any way.
- I shall keep some type of weapon for my self-protection and, if need be, for the protection of the Hindu society, I will not hesitate or be afraid to use it.
- I shall not give a single paisa to Muslim mendicants who habitually go around with incense smoke and expect small change.
- I shall be alert that my sisters and daughters do not befriend or fall into the love trap of a Muslim at school, college, office or any other place.
- I shall not go to any Muslim teacher or professor for private tuitions or to learn any art.
- Wholeheartedly boycott the hotels of the traitors as well as their acting, songs and films.
- I shall not buy any cement, stone or other material from the yards of the Muslims, nor will I go to them for any carpentry work.

Remember:

In order to attract Hindu customers, in the beginning Muslims may conspire to lower the price of whatever they are selling compared with other businessmen. Therefore, no one should fall into the temptation of momentary gain. Don't get entangled in their sweet trap.

In addition to what is listed above, use whatever means comes to your mind for this purpose. It is this kind of economic boycott that will suffocate these evil elements. It will break their backs and make them destitute. The slogan of 'Pakistan zindabad' will end. With the implementation of economic boycott, no Muslim will be able to live in front of our society with his head high. Publicize this leaflet from village to village and house to house. Make sisters and brothers understand and insist that they implement this.

Anyone who fails to follow this leaflet will have to face Shri Ramchandraji and Hanumanji.

Jai Shri Ram . . . Jai Shri Ram . . . Jai Shri Ram . . .
**Note: If needed, copies of this leaflet can be distributed. Read this leaflet . . .
get others to read it and follow it.**

Muslims. Sincere lower-level officials were often helpless in the face of their superiors. As a lower-level official at Bhiloda police station admitted: '*Amari halat chai jaivi churi vachai supari* [Our situation is like that of a betelnut in the middle of knives].'

Spread of Hindutva

How was such a large-scale operation carried out? As mentioned earlier, Sabarkantha at the time was a largely rural district and a stronghold of the farmers' lobby in Gujarat. A large part of this lobby was represented by the Bharatiya Kisan Sangh (BKS), a farmers' organization founded by Dattopant Thengadi, a leading ideologue of the Rashtriya Swayamsevak Sangh (RSS).[6] The BKS had an extensive network in the villages and was with the Bharatiya Janata Party (BJP). This village network, combined with the economic resources of the Patels (Rajputs played a protective role this time), political patronage of the BJP (the party in power in the state and the district—six of the district's eight MLAs were from the BJP) and concerted spread of the Hindutva ideology over the last decade were some of the key factors that helped organize the violence. Technical progress in the means of communication also played a vital role. A decade earlier, it was difficult to find a single telephone in most villages; by 2002, telephones and STD booths had mushroomed all over and could be found in interior villages too. Written propaganda material was also used. The preceding leaflet ('Jai Shri Ram')—widely circulated in Sabarkantha at that time—was a striking illustration of the poisonous and inflammatory nature of Hindutva propaganda.

There was a widely held view that Adivasis played a central role in what happened in Sabarkantha. However, stories from various villages across the district as well as the viewpoints of Muslim leaders and camp dwellers suggested that, by and large, Adivasis were used by upper-caste and upper-class Hindus in their pogrom against the Muslims. As one Muslim leader put it: 'Adivasis are not our *dushman* (enemies). After four years of continuous drought and hardship, they may loot our shops but they are not against us. Given the opportunity, they may loot the shops of Hindus too.' In many villages, Adivasis were mobilized to loot with the promise that there would be no police action afterwards; in some cases, they were also paid a small amount to do the work. Adivasis of Gambhirpura village in Bhiloda taluka admitted as much when their names appeared in the FIR. In villages where there are only Thakardas (another poor community, from the OBC category), they too were mobilized in similar ways.

In north Sabarkantha, Adivasi-dominated Khedbrahma taluka remained comparatively undisturbed despite right-wing Hindu-nationalist organizations having made it a base of sorts to further their saffron agenda and break the Congress base in the area. Major incidents in the current wave of communal violence were reported only from town areas where Kutchi Patels lived. In interior villages like Lambadiya and Poshina that had some history of communal tension, nothing happened. The Khedbrahma assembly constituency was then the only reserved ST constituency in the district; one of the two Congress MLAs of the district was from Khedbrahma.

In Vijaynagar taluka, on 3 March, the violence was initiated by members of right-wing Hindu-nationalist groups who came in large numbers in jeeps, tractors and tempos, sporting Hindutva flags and shouting that no Muslim should be allowed to remain in the taluka. Around 5000 Adivasis assembled in the town that day, beating their drums and blocking the roads. Some of them participated in the looting. The police opened fire that day, killing three Adivasis.

The pattern in affected villages of Vijaynagar, Bhiloda and Meghraj talukas was similar: activists from right-wing Hindu-nationalist groups came in vehicles and took the lead in destroying and burning Muslim properties, while Adivasis were mobilized for looting. In Kalyanpur village of Bhiloda, only one section of the Adivasis was under the sway of these organizations and turned aggressive while others remained supportive of Muslims. The sole Muslim resident of this village—a widow—was dressed in a sari, with a bindi on her forehead, and was helped to escape.

The Hinduization of the Adivasis in Sabarkantha was not a new phenomenon. The Adivasis in Sabarkantha defined themselves as Hindus even though they acknowledged that Hindus did not consider them as equals. Pictures of Hindu gods and goddesses were common in Adivasi households. Historic places in Adivasi areas, such as Shamlaji in Bhiloda taluka, had been named after the famous temple of Shamaliya Bavji, or Krishna. Like the Hindus, the Adivasis of Sabarkantha too had been practising untouchability towards the Dalits. When, how and why the Adivasis of Sabarkantha started thinking of themselves as Hindus is a question that requires closer scrutiny. An increase in education and income levels may have led to rising Adivasi aspirations to join the Hindu mainstream. It is possible that the official policy of identifying Adivasis as 'Hindu Bhil Garasia' or 'Hindu Dungri Garasia' in school leaving certificates also contributed to the making of their Hindu identity.

Saffronization amongst the Adivasis, however, had intensified in the recent past. In the late 1980s, when bricks were being collected for the construction of the Ram temple in Ayodhya, there was some response in villages in Sabarkantha too, but this remained confined to the upper and dominant castes. Dalits and Adivasis at large had not heard about the VHP or Bajrang Dal. By 2002, however, most of them were familiar with the Bajrang Dal. The Bajrang Dal had tried to widen its base in villages by building local organizations with young persons as office bearers, often on its payroll, and organizing popular events such as sports meets. Wall writing based on Bajrang Dal propaganda could be found in public places—for example, 'Talwar niklegi mayan se, Hindu rashtra banega shaan se [The talwar (sword) will be drawn from its sheath and the Hindu rashtra will be proudly built]' at Khedbrahma bus stand, or 'Is desh mein rahna ho to *Jai Shri Ram kehna hoga* [Those who want to live in this country will have to say Jai Shri Ram]' in Himmatnagar. Besides the Bajrang Dal, some efforts were also made by women members of the VHP to organize meetings with Adivasi women in some interior villages of Bhiloda taluka. The plan to include the Adivasis in the Hindu fold was evident from this slogan on a Gujarat Vanvasi Kalyan Parishad poster: *Nagar, gram aur vanvasi, hum sab Hindu Adivasi* (Whether in cities, villages or forests, we are all Hindu Adivasis).

In step with the spread of Hindutva, temples sprung up everywhere. In 1995 alone, 1400 Hanuman temples were built in different parts of the district. Many small ones were built overnight and were therefore called *Chamatkari* Hanuman (Hanuman the magician). Hanuman in Sabarkantha had many different names. The most famous was *Hulladiya* Hanuman ('hullad' roughly translates as hullabaloo and also means riots).

Outlook

The story of the rise of Hindutva in Sabarkantha is far from over. The tremors seemed to have just begun in 2002. Shortly before I left, a leading RSS leader of Bhiloda taluka, Narendrasingh Rajput openly told me, '*Hum itna hi keh sakte hain ki hum apni lakeer aage kheechte hi jaenge* [We can only say this much that we will continue to stretch our line forward].' What did the future hold? Where would this politics of hate lead? Would humanism prevail? One could only draw some hope from the many moving stories of support that people offered to their Muslim neighbours and friends.

As I left Sabarkantha in April 2002, it was a relief of sorts to travel from Ambaji to Abu Road and cross over to Rajasthan, leaving the madness behind as I thought then. But soon I realized that the relief was illusory. A middle-aged person sitting next to me in the passenger jeep—a shopkeeper in Idar—turned out to be from Bhilwara in Rajasthan. Initially, we were jointly celebrating the fact that sanity prevailed in Rajasthan. But soon he was arguing against secularism and for a Hindu rashtra. He said, in one breath, that—unlike the Hindus—the Muslims had no *daya* (compassion) and that they deserved what they got. The soft-spoken Lal Bahadur Shastri himself, he claimed, had said, '*Eent ka jawab patthar se dena hoga* [Bricks will have to be fought with stones].'

Evidently, the ground had already been prepared for communal violence well beyond Gujarat.

2

Massacre on the Banks of the Sone[*]

The Sone River flowed placidly as far as the eyes could see. A lone boat, the wide expanse of sand, the tar trees swaying sedately in the breeze—all served to dispel the fact that this site was witness to the worst massacre in the history of Bihar just a few days earlier, on 1 December 1997. The assailants came and escaped through the Sone. It was on its banks that the sixty-one victims of the attack were cremated on one single *chita* (funeral pyre), the rising flames of which were watched by villagers on both sides of the river—amongst whom, no doubt, were sympathizers of the victims as well as some of their killers.

When I reached Laxmanpur-Bathe (also called Bathe), the village in the Arwal block of Jehanabad district where the massacre occurred, a long black line was still visible on the sand very close to the bank.[1] 'That is where the chita was,' said Vakil Chaudhary, the youngest son of Gariban Chaudhary who had come from Delhi—where he worked—upon learning the news. He had lost nine members of his family, including his parents, brothers, their wives and children. He said that he did not feel like seeing the remains of the chita. His

---

[*] This essay originally appeared in *Economic and Political Weekly* in December 1997. This version is in the past tense and includes added notes.

17

last images of them, when he had come for Dussehra, were more comforting.

He was waiting for me on the edge of the village. I walked towards the river on the soft sand. It was a long stretch, for the river in that season had receded. Those hundred-odd men must have also taken these many steps towards their target and back. What remained of the chita was forty steps long. The ground was strewn with *khatias* (string cots) and bamboo stretchers on which the bodies must have been brought, some cast-off clothing, quilts and hair from the heads of the mourners. But what was difficult to look straight at were the fourteen skulls scattered amongst odd-sized bones and grey-black ashes. Deep, empty sockets—which must have held the eyes and noses—of the undifferentiated skeleton reveal little of what the structure of the human face must have been. Just five days earlier, some of them were either the beautiful Manmatiya in the prime of her youth, militant Sohar, sixty-year-old Erbati or ten-year-old Rohan, who his father said was very good in studies.

Hundreds of people came to watch their funeral. Many more watch them die every day—the oppressed and marginalized people of the other India who struggle to live even when alive. The sudden death of the massacre victims and their ashes now mixed in the sand of the Sone posed a single question: Why?

Eye-witness Accounts[2]

It had been drizzling that evening. By 9 p.m., Batanbigha *tola* (hamlet)—also known as Subhash Nagar after Subhash Chandra Bose—of Bathe, was quiet;[3] the inhabitants were inside their homes, most of them already in bed. A few were engaged in the usual end-of-the-day chores or talking to each other in the dim light of the *dhibri* (makeshift kerosene lamp)—its small, flickering flame casting shadows on the brown mud walls. Children, like one-year-old Chotelal and slightly older Sumanti, were fast asleep, snuggled inside the warmth of their *puvaal* (hay) beds with cotton *gamcha*s (used by their fathers as sweat cloths when at work) tied around their heads to ward off the cold.

Near the Sone, there was more activity. According to one version of the events of that evening, a group of more than a hundred members of the Ranbeer Sena—a private militia of upper-caste Bhumihar landlords—alighted from two boats which came from the Bhojpur side. They took three Mallahs who were fishing by surprise. The next morning, these three were found with their throats slit. Two other Mallahs, one of whom had been sleeping on the sand, were found a little further up, also with their throats slit. Another Mallah was able to save his life when he observed the scene from a distance and fled. It was only in the case of these five that the assailants did not use their guns as they did not want to alert the unsuspecting members of the tola they were about to attack.

Without electricity, the tola was pitch dark. Any outsider unfamiliar with the layout would have failed to find his way. Not only did the assailants find their way, but they were successful in breaking into fourteen specific houses and shooting the occupants at close range. This made local involvement a certainty. Amongst the sixty-one massacred were members of four families who were completely wiped out. Nineteen men, twenty-seven women and fifteen children who were less than ten years old were killed; the youngest was a year old. Eight of the women were pregnant, five were found in positions suggesting rape and the breasts of three had been cut off. In caste terms, thirty-three victims were Dalits (Rajwad, 20; Paswan, 7; Pasi, 5; Nai, 1) and twenty-eight belonged to backward castes (Mallah, 23; Koeri, 5). Three children and one woman had to be hospitalized in Patna for bullet injuries.[4]

Eighteen-year-old Vinod Paswan, who had a narrow escape, was the main witness; it is based on his complaint that an FIR was filed. He haltingly described to me the sequence of events:

My whole family was sleeping in two rooms. I had been sleeping with my brother Rohan in one and the rest were in the other. *Jab goli chalne lagi, Rohan ma ke paas bhaga* (when we heard the sound of gunfire, Rohan ran to our mother). My sister, Rita, married just last year—the bamboo *mandap* is still intact—told me to crouch in the corner near the *kothi*s (mud containers used to store grain). She quickly covered me with a *soop* (winnowing basket). She then ran back into the other room; that room had a door while the one I was in did not. They bolted the door from inside.

His father, Ramchela Paswan, added: 'First, they tried to break open the western door leading to our courtyard, but then they changed their minds. When I heard them tearing at the eastern door, I knew that there was little chance. By then my family was inside the room *aur hum apni jaan le kar bhage* [and I ran for my life]. There was nobody in the lane outside the western door. I ran and hid in the *badhar* [open fields].'

Meanwhile, the attackers had managed to break the door. Vinod continued:

I heard them shouting, '*Is samuchay tola ko maro. Ghar mein eko ko nahi chhodna hai.* (Wipe out this whole tola. Don't leave a single person in any house).' I then heard them breaking the door of the other room. I heard the screams, then *dhai . . . dhai*, and then silence. Later, around twenty men entered the room I was in. Some of them had rifles in their hands, a few had torches. I recognized some who had their faces uncovered. Thinking there was nobody there, they left.

Vinod Paswan's elderly *bua* (father's sister), who had come after hearing the news, showed me the interior of that room, with the door the family had thought was safe. One has to stoop in order to enter. At first, the eye can see little in the darkness. It is a small room. Two huge kothis divide the sleeping area from the kitchen, where there is a *chulha* (stove), some *matkas* (pots), some rice. From a hole in the thatch above, a streak of light reveals a patch of darker earth near the kothi, where Rohan in desperation had tried to hide. But he was not able to escape the bullets; neither were his mother, his sisters—sixteen-year-old Rita and twelve-year-old Kabutri, or his brothers—nine-year-old Amar, seven-year-old Kuwar and five-year-old Anuj, who were killed in that room. '*Bahut khoon tha. Kudal se maati ko kaat kar phir se lep kiya hai, phir bhi yah dhabai, jo aap dekh rahi hain, rah gai hain* [There was a lot of blood. With a spade, we tried to remove the blood-soaked mud plaster and re-plaster the floor, but the blood that you see remains].' Ashutosh Pratap, their three-year-old neighbour, was still looking for his playmates.

To the south of Vinod's house was the house of Sohar. The door of Sohar's house was taken out of its hinges. This seems to have been the general pattern. Where this was not possible, the door was broken down. Another common feature was that they moved into each house in groups of twenty to twenty-five. The villagers rightly pointed out that they would not have been able to do what they did if they were one or two. Sohar, his two sons and his daughters-in-law were all killed. The lone survivor of the family, ten-year-old Bimlesh, escaped the bullet which grazed his cheek. Bimlesh and two other children, eight-year-old Manoj and ten-year-old Mahesh, who were hit by bullets in their legs, had been admitted to the government hospital in Patna. They reminded me of five-year-old Saddam, who had survived the massacre at Bathani tola (also by the Ranbeer Sena) on 11 July 1996 for a few days and later succumbed to his injuries in the same Patna hospital.[5]

The villagers claimed that they heard the miscreants shouting slogans hailing Ranbeer Sena and Bajrangbali.[6] A group of women reported:

Channi ka, Saroja ka balatkar kiya, Manmatiya ka bhi. Meena ka chhaati kata, Sita aur Phulvanti ka bhi chhaati kata. Hum gareeb ka kya raha? Jab chhaati kaat lete hain to aur kya bacha? Hum kaise jiyen? (Channi, Saroja were raped; so was Manmatiya. Meena's, Sita's and Phulvanti's breasts were cut off. What is left of us poor people? When they don't even spare our breasts, what remains? How do we live?)

They said they had covered their dead bodies with blankets so that others would not see them.

It was reported that the firing continued from 9 to 10.30 p.m., with 100–200 rounds of ammunition being fired. The police later recovered forty-three empty cartridges from various houses. The sound of gunfire had also reached the neighbouring tolas, but in the darkness, nobody dared to come to investigate or help.

Some managed to survive. One-year-old Ramesh sat quietly in his grandmother's lap. Wearing a red sweater and a monkey cap, he stared on. When she asked him, 'Babu, where is your *maiya* [mother]?', '*Unnai* [there],' he replied, pointing towards the main door. Ramesh had a narrow escape. When his mother, Basanti Devi was shot, he fell from her hands and was saved when she pushed him under the bed. Etbari Devi's son, daughter-in-law and two grandchildren also escaped from the back door to the fields. Etbari Devi and her daughter were found dead in their beds.

Those who survived continued to feel insecure, for they had heard their attackers had pledged to kill a hundred. They feared that the worst was not yet over and that they were going to come back. Fear was the dominant emotion in the area. '*Hum logo ko bariyari maar diya. Hum logo ka khota hai, jab yahan bhi aa kar mar diya, to kahan jaen?* [They have killed us by force. When they killed us in our own nests, then where do we go?],' said a relative of one of the victims.

Possible Motives

Why did they choose Bathe? One speculation was that the Ranbeer Sena targeted Bathe because CPI (ML) Liberation and CPI (ML)

Party Unity were active in the village.[7] There was indeed some history of political activism in the village, which used to be a local base of the CPI and Forward Bloc (hence the name Subhash Nagar for Batanbigha);* followed by the Indian People's Front in the early 1980s and Party Unity around 1990, though both Liberation and Party Unity maintained that their base in the village was not particularly strong.

About eight years prior to the massacre, a strike was called by the labourers, leading to a rise in wages. There were also various land-related conflicts in the village and the area, of which the details are less clear. According to the district magistrate (DM), Arun Kumar Singh, some *parcha*s (title deeds) related to land that became available under the Land Ceiling Act were given to a few individuals in the village in 1973. The villagers, however, said that no effort was made to demarcate the land or ensure possession. Also, the very same parchas were given to families in neighbouring Parshurampur. The problem remained unresolved, though, after the massacre, the DM was quoted in the local media as saying that he would resolve all outstanding land issues in Jehanabad district within a week!

There is a similar story about *bhoodan* (land donation) land, for which some parchas had been distributed in the early 1980s, but no further step was taken by the local government to ensure possession. Four individuals had also got some parchas related to *gairmajurwa* land (common land), but again official action remained limited to paperwork. More recently, Liberation and Party Unity tried to take direct action in the case of around thirty-two bighas of land belonging to Upadhyay Nath Pandey. This landowner, who had no heir, had already sold around forty bighas of his land to local Bhumihar farmers, ignoring the claims of his tenants. These outstanding land issues—claims and counterclaims—had caused

---

* Subhash Chandra Bose founded the Forward Bloc as a faction of the Indian National Congress in 1939. It later became an independent political party.

tensions in Bathe that continued to simmer for many years. Having said this, the level of political activity and conflict in Bathe was far from unusual for this area. Conflicts, past and present, had not led to significant violence; even the labour strike was resolved peacefully ('*mithe mithe*', as one woman put it).

A more plausible explanation for Bathe being targeted by the Ranbeer Sena, invoked by some villagers, is simply that Bathe was a soft target, both geographically and socially. Indeed, Liberation and Party Unity also maintained that the Ranbeer Sena had until then never targeted any of their strongholds. The fact that both Bathe and Batanbigha were located right above the banks of the Sone made it easy for the assailants to reach the Dalit households as well as to escape. Also, they did not have to fear much resistance in this village. As one survivor put it: '*Yeh tola ka kisi se takrahat nahi tha. Sab nirdosh mara gaya. Unko laga ki gareeb hai, maar do toh kya karega? Yehi un logon ko hota, to humara khal ukhad lete* [The people of this tola had no conflict with anybody. All those who were killed were innocent. They thought—they are poor, kill them, what can they do? Had this happened to them, they would have skinned us].'

Several theories were advanced regarding the motivation behind the massacre. A general view was that Ranbeer Sena had done this to reassert its supremacy and '*atank phelane ke liye* [to spread terror]'. It was widely acknowledged that the class struggle being waged by the Naxalites in the last three decades had seriously undermined the economic, social and political hegemony of the upper castes and classes. Massacres of the poor and the struggling peasantry were part of the effort of the upper class to reinforce their feudal domination.

The Ranbeer Sena and the BJP enjoyed a close relationship in the area.[8] The rising influence of the BJP in state politics and the strengthening of the Ranbeer Sena went hand in hand. It was no secret that the BJP was providing political patronage to the Ranbeer Sena; in return for this, the party received political support during the then parliamentary elections (e.g., in Ara constituency, Ranbeer

Sena members supported the BJP-Samata candidate). According to Liberation, the massacre was part of a general pre-election strategy of creating tension and fear in the area so as to discourage Dalits from active political participation.

The Bathe massacre was also seen by some as an effort on the part of the Ranbeer Sena to realign its forces and consolidate its base beyond Bhojpur. It had tried for some time to be active in the border areas of Bhojpur as well as in Patna and Gaya districts and had several skirmishes with Party Unity in these regions. A notable development in 1997 was that the Ranbeer Sena had also targeted Party Unity supporters in Haibaspur village of Patna district, killing ten Dalits—in retaliation against an encounter with Party Unity in Jalpura village (also in Patna district) in which four activists of the Ranbeer Sena were killed.[9] These incidents, as well as the Bathe massacre, point at the intention of the Ranbeer Sena to not only root out Naxalism from the plains of central Bihar, as it had promised to do in one public meeting earlier that year, but also to nip all efforts at organizing the rural poor in the bud.

The labouring poor of the region understood this well. As a Bathe labourer said, '*Yeh sab pait ke karan hi ho raha hai. Hum log aadha pait kha kar ke aapka kaam karte hain. Jab poora pait khane ke liye mangte hain to maare jaate hain* [All this is a matter of hunger. With half-filled bellies, we work for you. When we ask for a full stomach, we get killed].' Indeed, what alternative did agricultural labourers have but to raise their voices? As a woman labourer said, '*Hum log sahi majdoori ke liye nahi mange toh kya karein? Un logo ka kheti bhi hai aur naukri bhi. Majdoor ka keval majdoori hai. Vah mangega nahi* [If we do not ask for fair wages, what do we do? They have land as well as secure jobs. A labourer has only her wage. How can she not ask for more]?'

After the Massacre

In the post-massacre phase, the response of the government included the usual relief and development package which follows most massacres. In this case, due to the large number of victims, the response was more generous—cash payments of up to Rs 2,30,000 per victim, houses under the Indira Awas Yojana, 50 kg of wheat rations and a handpump amongst other relief measures. Besides, agencies such as the Red Cross provided daily-use items such as blankets, dhotis and biscuits. In the case of families where there were no survivors, there was the question of who would receive the compensation. As an old woman put it, '*Jiske vahan diya barne ke liye bhi koi nahi bacha, vahan kisko denge* [Where there is nobody left even to light the lamp, to whom will they give]?' Widowed daughters such as Rukmini Devi, who was dependent on her father Gariban Chaudhary and brother Mahendra Chaudhary, hoped to receive part of the compensation. There were other cases where sons-in-law staked their claim. Besides, the government finally approved long-pending proposals for development projects in the area, including a power substation at the Arwal and Agnur hydel project.

On the night of 6 December, I was witness to the first day of a *kudki-japti* (confiscation of property) operation by the police in Bathe. The huge walls on each side of the narrow lanes made it clear that we were in the upper-caste part of the village. Five days had elapsed since the killings—enough time to allow miscreants to escape to safer locations. No villager was visible in the now almost empty tola. In the wake of the massacre, all the able-bodied had fled. In this somewhat half-hearted raid led by the police with the help of thirty chowkidars of nearby villages, what was missing was the tension that comes with a sense of purpose and urgency. Household items like chairs, quilts, tin trunks, etc., had been confiscated from three houses according to the chowkidars, five houses according to the DM who visited the village that night and ten houses according to the DSP.

As of 6 December 1997, the police had arrested five suspects, four of whom belonged to the Rajput caste, of whom three were named accused: Ashok Singh (Rajput), Baleshwar Singh (Bhumihar) and Surendra Singh (Rajput). Police sources claimed that as many as thirty-five upper-caste men would soon be arrested from various villages in Sahar block. Meanwhile, top Ranbeer Sena leaders like Brahmeshwar Singh, the *mukhiya* (headman) of Khopira village (Udwantnagar block, Bhojpur district) remained free.[10]

Incidentally, when the Ranbeer Sena was formed in late 1994 in Belaur village (also in Udwantnagar block, Bhojpur district), its composition was exclusively of Bhumihar landlords and farmers of the area. The Sena was named after the legendary Bhumihar of Belaur, Ranbeer Chaudhary, who in the early part of the twentieth century is said to have driven out the Rajputs from the village. Due to local Bhumihar-Rajput animosity, Rajput involvement in the Ranbeer Sena was doubted until the Bathani Tola massacre on 11 July 1996—discussed in Chapter 15 (Justice, Not Vengeance).

The general population seemed to have lost all faith in the police. According to media reports, the police had prior information of the impending violence, but no precautions were taken. In fact, in recent months many police pickets were withdrawn from central Bihar districts on the dubious grounds that they were ill-equipped. As it is, the police camps and pickets had proved to be both ineffective and biased.[11] Rarely did one find examples of preventive action. Instead, there were many cases where the police force openly colluded with the upper caste-class senas against the Naxalites. Three recent examples from Patna district made this clear: On 1 February 1997, in the Jalpura village of Patna, district police and the Ranbeer Sena fought shoulder-to-shoulder against a Party Unity squad in an eighteen-hour encounter. Likewise, in the wake of the Haibaspur massacre of ten Musahars by the Ranbeer Sena on 23 March 1997, the police were informed within two hours of the killing but arrived twelve hours later, even though the police station was only 5 km away. In contrast, on 21 April 1997, after a retaliatory action by Party Unity in Raghopur, a Bhumihar village, the police arrived within half an hour of the killing and pursued the Party Unity squad.[12]

State Abdication

Did the government do enough? As has been the case with many other massacres in the post-Independence history of rural Bihar, there was a heady central and state government response in fast-forward mode immediately after the Bathe massacre. But soon there was total silence. In response to massacres which are due to social and economic inequities, feudal agrarian relations and violation of basic democratic rights, the central and the state governments do everything other than what really needs to be done. No attempt is made to address the roots of class and caste conflicts. No attempt is made to answer the question that stares at anybody who cares to look into those mud hovels where almost every item is made of mud—be it the chulha, the kothis or the matkas, where a sturdy door is a luxury. Despite being ill-fed, ill-clad, their children shivering in the winter cold, these people—even in the wake of a personal tragedy—had enough humanity left in them to inquire: 'Have you eaten? Do you have a place to sleep tonight? Are you warm enough?' How can a government face these people and not address the root causes that are behind the violence?

A responsible government could implement existing laws and ensure that the labourers get their basic entitlements: fair wages, implementation of tenancy laws, distribution of ceiling surplus and gairmajurwa, bhoodan and *math* lands to the landless. Further, it could ensure that they have basic amenities—roads, electricity, schooling and health facilities of the same standard as the government provides for privileged families in Patna or Delhi. Why should labourers be expected to settle for less? On what basis can a policymaker justify a different standard for them?

Unfortunately, not much can be expected from the state government in the current landscape of electoral politics. That year, Laloo Prasad Yadav was moving towards a tie-up with the Congress, winning over the Rajputs to his camp and thus adding 'R' to his

'MY' (Muslim and Yadav) base, making it 'MRY' in one humorous update of his well-known acronym. His party, Rashtriya Janata Dal (RJD), was not interested in antagonizing the leftover upper-caste, upper-class Congress supporters who had not as yet moved to the BJP. Even though the then RJD MLA of Arwal constituency, Rajinder Singh, was a former Liberation cadre, it was widely believed that the ruling party would do little to address the real needs of the people. Instead, it would follow the old strategy while dealing with the victims of massacres in central Bihar: the more unsatisfied they were, the greater the chance that they would lose confidence in the Naxalite leadership and seek protection with the ruling party.

During the state assembly election campaign in Bhojpur in 1995, Laloo Prasad Yadav was quoted in the local media as saying, *'Maale ko Bhojpur se ukharne ke liye main narak ki takato se bhi samjhauta karne ke liye taiyar hoon* [In order to uproot CPI(ML) from Bhojpur, I am ready to compromise with the forces of hell].'[13] Here the reference was to the BJP, the known patron of the Ranbeer Sena. During the Lok Sabha election campaign in 1996, another prominent Janata Dal leader even demanded a lifting of the official ban on the Ranbeer Sena.

BJP's Sushil Kumar Modi, then leader of the opposition in the Bihar Assembly, while condemning the massacre and asking for the resignation of the chief minister, maintained silence over the question of the Ranbeer Sena. Even though BJP leaders repeatedly denied any links with the Sena, they did not press for the arrest or disarmament of Ranbeer Sena members. Each political party was using the massacre to score points over its opponent and take advantage of the situation. Even a large number of brutal killings of Dalits was not able to touch whatever was human in these individual politicians, nor persuade them to do their duties as elected representatives.

A helipad had been installed on the banks of the Sone. The children of Bathe had never seen a helicopter, or so many cars. Even the serious occasion could not disguise the absurdity of the scene. Imagine a pantomime and the main character announcing, '*Logon* [people], didn't you always ask: Who is the *sarkar* [government]? Where is the sarkar? Let's open the car doors and find out. Meet the *mukhya-mantri* [chief minister], the *raksha-mantri* [defence minister], the DM sahib, the DGP sahib and so many more in this long cavalcade. The word "*sarkar*" means "Sir" plus "Kar", does it not?'

Basanti, a young *bahu* (daughter-in-law) who was not allowed to venture out of her home, watched everything from the threshold of her house. She observed: '*Bahri aadmi lashon ko tamashe ki tarah dekhe hain. Par hum logon ka toh parivaar tha, hadas ke chalte nahi dekh sake* [Visitors were looking at the dead bodies as though it was a ring show. But they were our family, we could not bear to see their lifeless bodies in our grief].'

3

Of Human Bondage in Baran[*]

Even imagination, audacious as it may be at times, has limits. While India's dazzling rates of economic growth have won it wide acclaim, there exist within its boundaries citizens not just mired in poverty, but bondage—at the mercy of oppressive jagirdars, some for decades. Bonded labour may be dismissed as an aberration by those who believe that even remnants of feudalism no longer exist in India, but it is a sombre ground reality in no less than sixteen states of the country.[1]

Baran district of south-east Rajasthan is one region where this pernicious and immoral labour arrangement is still alive, mainly in two of its eight tehsils—Kishanganj and Shahbad. Locals point out that the practice is not new and has persisted for a long time in the form of the *hali* system. In such an arrangement, a labourer—called *hali*—typically enters an annual labour contract with the landlord,

---

[*] This essay originally appeared in *Economic and Political Weekly* in June 2012. It draws on my contribution to a joint enquiry report submitted to the National Commission for the Protection of Child Rights (NCPCR) in January 2012. The other members of the enquiry committee were Asha Mishra and G. Sampath A few notes and references have been added.

often in exchange for a prior loan. In scholarly literature, this is known as debt bondage.

Baran and the Sahariyas

Baran became a district in 1991 when it was carved out of Kota district. It is a largely rural district, with poor social indicators even by Rajasthan's low standards. For instance, it has lower literacy rates and higher child mortality rates than the state average. There have been recurrent stories of starvation deaths in Baran, notably in 2002–03, when a wave of starvation deaths was reported amongst the Sahariyas and the survivors were subsisting on wild grass.[2] Deaths of three Sahariya children below the age of five in October 2011 were also attributed to malnutrition.[3]

In Baran, the Sahariyas are concentrated in Kishanganj and Shahbad. In these two tehsils—demarcated as Shahbad subdivision—there were about 21,000 Sahariya families (approximately 1,00,000 people) in 2011.[4] Sahariyas are one of seventy-five indigenous groups of India officially known earlier as 'primitive tribal groups' (PTGs) and now as 'particularly vulnerable tribal groups' (PVTGs).[5] This category, aptly renamed, draws our attention to the deprived living conditions of the Sahariyas. This is due, in part, to the degradation of their natural environment: the traditional occupations of the Sahariyas (e.g., selling *mahua* and *tendu*, or making baskets) have been heavily dependent on forest resources, which have disappeared rapidly in eastern Rajasthan in recent times. Even the forest resources that were not degraded have often been appropriated by vested interests.

The land of the Sahariyas has been alienated or usurped over the decades by local dominant castes and communities as well as enterprising outsiders who migrated into these regions—mainly Sikh farmers from Punjab (locally known as 'sardars'), who became owners of large tracts of land and acquired not only economic but also political power. As a result, whenever Sahariyas tried to reclaim possession of their illegally occupied small holdings, their efforts were mostly frustrated by local government functionaries, such as the *patwaris* (revenue officers at the gram panchayat level) or forest guards or police officers, who sided with the occupiers. Reservation norms help the Sahariyas have some space amongst elected representatives, but Sahariya leaders are not always able to stand up for the interests of their community. Loyalty to the party (typically Congress or Bharatiya Janata Party, in this region) tends to be far more important for their political career.

Bonded Labour in Baran

Any visitor to the area is likely to come across the *sahrana*—as a Sahariya settlement is called—usually located outside the main village. There are local histories about how the Sahariyas had to move to the fringes, sometimes due to cultural or natural causes (such as floods in the Banganga river, in the case of Sunda-Chenpur village), but also due to the oppressive circumstances they endured when they lived in the main village. Amongst the dominant castes and communities in the area are the Sikh farmers mentioned earlier, who migrated to the area a few decades ago. The influx may well be related to the political turmoil of those days in Punjab, not unlike the previous in-migration at the time of Partition. Sikh settlements already existed in regions such as Kota, and spilling over to Baran (then part of Kota) must have happened gradually, just as these farmers had begun expanding to Shahbad district in 2012. Though most of the lands in the tribal tracts were under intermittent cultivation (since the Sahariyas practised shifting or slash-and-burn agriculture), this was often invisible on paper in the absence of up-to-date land surveys and 'records of rights'. While a more detailed study of the history of land tenure in these parts is required, there is no doubt that Sahariyas are indigenous people of this region—the etymology of 'Sahariya' also relates them to the *sahara* (jungle) as well as to animal life within the forest.

Sahariyas are the poorest people of Baran, have few resources and constantly struggle to survive. Even as the corridors of power are abuzz with perfunctory concern about the 'primitive', 'backward' or 'poor', and as huge funds continue to be earmarked for Sahariya 'development' schemes, the most crucial issues related to their well-being remain unaddressed. These have to do with assured access to their basic resources: land, forests and labour arrangements that respect the law. Sahariyas have had to contend with uncertainty and insecurity in each of these areas; the same governments that show enthusiasm about 'schemes' turn lukewarm and lethargic when it comes to recovering the lost lands of the Sahariyas. The Sahariyas have been able to survive only on the strength of their labour, which has been ruthlessly exploited by the upper castes and landed gentry. While the situation of those who work as halis has been abysmal, those who are engaged in *khuli majdoori* (unattached labour) have done only marginally better.

The following account is based on a visit to three villages of Kishanganj tehsil. In two of them (Ganeshpura and Sunda-Chenpur), we were able to speak to the labourers as well as the landowners, but in the third (Iklera), we spoke only to the labourers.

Ganeshpura

In 2012, Ganeshpura was a medium-sized village of 140 households in Kankhra gram panchayat. Besides Ganeshpura, there were ten other villages in this gram panchayat, all located within a radius of two kilometres. Sahariyas represented 95 per cent of the total population of the gram panchayat; the remainder was made up of other castes such as Gujar, Chamar, Ahir, Aud and Sikhs.

The hundred-odd Sahariya families of Ganeshpura were distributed over three mohallas. A little over half of them (sixty families) lived in the Sahariya sahrana in Ganeshpura proper. The rest were spread over two mohallas: Danda (twelve families) and Joi (about twenty-five families). The thirty-five Sikh families lived in the main Ganeshpura mohalla. The differences of land ownership (agricultural and homestead) and living conditions between the Sikhs and Sahariyas were sharp and glaring.

The existence of the Sahariyas was dominated by everyday insecurity. They did not even have legal titles for homestead lands. While families of the Danda mohalla had received some land from one Chaudhari as bhoodan many years ago, they did not have any papers. Enquiries at the Bhoodan Board office proved futile. 'No titles are given for bhoodan land,' they were told. The Joi mohalla families said that their houses were constructed on *junglat* (forest land), so they had no papers either. The Ganeshpura Sahariyas, who also said that their houses were built on forest land, were in a similar situation. They recalled that more than a decade ago they used to get tax notices, and had paid taxes for around five years, but after that, they stopped receiving the notices. All the Sikh families, except five whose homes were also on bhoodan land, had titles for homestead land.

The Sahariyas of Ganeshpura were either completely landless (like the inhabitants of Danda and Joi mohallas) or marginal farmers with small landholdings (roughly two to three bighas each). In contrast, all the Sikh families except two had *khate-vali jameen* (arable land with legal titles). Some of them had large holdings. For instance, *up-sarpanch* (vice-sarpanch) Keshvant Singh told us that his father owned seventy bighas—the largest holding in the village, though it was divided between his brother and himself. Similarly, Jasvinder Singh alias Sabi said that his father and uncle together cultivated 250 bighas, out of which seventy bighas was their own land in Ganeshpura, and the rest was land taken on lease in different villages.

Keshvant informed us that aside from five Sikh families who owned more than thirty bighas, eight had fifteen to twenty bighas, while a larger group of twenty or so owned five to ten bighas. The Sikh farmers of Ganeshpura grew a rich variety of crops—wheat, rice, mustard, soyabean, bengal gram (chana) and red lentils (masoor). 'However, it is not as though the sardars are uniformly well off— many even had to do labour work under MGNREGA last year to survive—you can check the muster rolls,' he maintained. Rain-fed agriculture was not always possible and not all could afford to dig bore wells.

While the Sikh families had to reckon with a lean year every now and then, for the Sahariya families, most years were bleak—their small landholdings yielded little even in a normal year. Most of the land they owned was of poor quality and all of it was rain-fed. In the absence of land, education or other resources (we did not come across any Sahariya who owned a cow or a buffalo), they survived mainly on wage labour. This put them at the mercy of the Sikh landowners. It was only recently that MGNREGA works had emerged as an alternative, besides the odd chance to work, say, as a *hamal* (load carrier) in the town or for a contractor in brick kilns.

It is worth noting how the Sikh families came to own and occupy land in this area—similar stories can be heard in other villages (like Sunda-Chenpur below) too. Keshvant, then in his mid-forties, was born in Ganeshpura. He said that the settlement in Ganeshpura owed its existence to five Sikhs who had come there around fifty years earlier, including his maternal grandfather who had migrated from Bikaner. These five farmers initially gained control over 200 bighas. Keshvant's father moved to this village after his marriage. Later, his uncle also followed. They took good care of his grandfather's land and received seventeen bighas from him as a reward. Slowly, they expanded, and by the time of his death some years ago, his father owned seventy bighas.[6]

Anandi, a Sahariya elder, explained how the Sahariyas became condemned to a life of servitude. '*Sahariya ne mar-mar kar zameen banai. Bana-bana kar di. Us samay se hali ban gai. Unka khet badhta*

raha. Hum mazdoori kar ke khate rahe. Hali mein zindagi nikal gai
[Sahariyas nearly died making the land cultivable. They prepared the
land and gave it (to them). We have become halis since then. Their
land kept expanding. We continued to labour—and survive. Our
lives were spent as halis].'

Hali thus became a source of minimalist survival and the bane of
their existence. Until some years ago, one or two members from each
Sahariya family were working as halis. A closer look at the experience
of even one hali sheds light on this labour arrangement and how it
determined the contours of the limited lives that the Sahariyas were
forced to lead.

'I started work as a hali when I was seven'

Ashok of Joi mohalla in Ganeshpura knew the hali system well. Then
in his mid-twenties, he had already worked as a hali for seventeen years.
He started early, with his elder brother Anarsingh, then twelve. Their
first job was as goatherds for a Banjara farmer who lived in Hoshiarpur
village, about 20 km away. Their employer agreed to pay them Rs 3000
for the year, and by doing so, earned rights over them as he had over
the fifteen goats they were supposed to look after. Every morning they
headed with their charges to the forest, guiding the goats three or four
kilometres inside the sometimes treacherous terrain. At that time, their
father was working as a hamal in the local bazaar and their mother, as
a khuli. A younger brother and sister stayed at home; no member of
Ashok's family was literate. At the end of the year, they were told that
they owed Rs 6000 for a goat that had died in their care—even though
she had died due to illness. So, a thousand rupees were deducted (from
Rs 3000) and the rest was stated as *karja* (debt).

After that, the two brothers returned home and worked as halis
for two years. They were paid Rs 1500 per year each. It took two
years of their combined earnings to clear the debt they had incurred
for the dead goat!

Ashok's next nine years were spent working as a hali for Gyaniji. His work would begin before 6 a.m. and end at around 7 or 8 in the evening. In the course of the day, he was required for different chores—getting fodder for the cattle, diesel for the engine, operating the mill, etc. He was paid Rs 1500 the first year, with a raise every year. In his ninth year, he was earning Rs 14,000 annually, paid to him in advance. However, this was far from sufficient to meet his own expenses, let alone contribute to his family's. Moreover, his father disapproved of his late hours and they had regular arguments about this. Ashok decided to quit. But he was not a free man yet since he learnt that he owed Gyaniji Rs 7000 for expenses (food, medicine, etc.) that he had incurred on him. They agreed that Ashok would repay this within a year.

Mandip Singh then hired him at Rs 20,000 per year. At the end of the first year, Ashok was able to clear his debt to Gyaniji. He stayed for another year with Mandip and then left to work for Janak Singh (of the Thakar Rajput caste) in Sunda-Chenpur village, where he worked for three years.

The first year with Janak started at Rs 12,000 as an advance. His boarding, lodging and other miscellaneous expenses were borne by Janak, who also maintained the accounts, as did all landlords. At the end of the year of full-time work, Janak told him that he owed him Rs 20,000 (for food and other charges). Ashok explained:

I did not have money, so I continued to work for him and cleared the debt (Rs 20,000) the following year. So, that year I was left with no money. I continued to work for him for the third year. At the end of that year, he said I owed him Rs 30,000. I was now quite desperate.

That is when we heard about the developments in Iklera. We heard that a girl had been raped there. We also heard about the efforts of the *sanstha* (organization) that took up her case and fought on her behalf. A few of us decided to meet the sanstha people. We went there and met Vijay and *master-saab* (teacher; the reference here is to Motilal) and told them our story.[7]

In 2010, I became active in their campaign and started participating in the *dharnas* (sit-ins). We went to Jaipur twice. One was the *do sau din wala* dharna (where the demand for 200 days [of MGNREGA work] was raised). The second dharna was about the *bandhaks* (bonded). I liked being in the dharna. We spoke about our situation to the government officials in Jaipur and the Collector. *Phir hum chhoote* (then we were released [from bondage]). In our village, thirty-two halis were released. *Ab hamein mukti mil gai hai. Ab bandhak mein nahi jaenge. Badi mushkil se chhoote hai.* (Now we are free. Now we will not go for bonded work. We have been able to secure our release with great difficulty.)

However, more than a year after these thirty-two halis were released or declared themselves free, only five had received the *mukti praman patra* ('released from bonded labour' certificate). When we spoke to him, Ashok himself had not received it. And none of them had received the full rehabilitation package. The certificate is very important since it is the first step of the rehabilitation process. As we have seen in Ashok's case, being in bondage means being caught in a cycle of indebtedness. These labourers and their families don't have any backup—be it property, savings or well-off relatives and friends. Any delay in their rehabilitation pushes them towards accepting an exploitative labour arrangement. At the time of our enquiry, these released bonded labourers were surviving on daily-wage work (at Rs 100 per day) in the locality, or travelling to Baran or Kelwada to work as casual labourers. None of them had gone back to their former employers.

During the year, government officials came once and took the testimonies of the thirty-two bonded labourers and their employers. After that, however, there was silence from the government and the former bonded labourers had to fend for themselves.

Sunda-Chenpur

Sunda-Chenpur village, in Khandela gram panchayat, was widely acknowledged at that time—even by the sardars of neighbouring villages—as the bastion of Sikh landlordism. In 2012, it was a small village of fifty-three households: forty-five Sahariyas, seven Sikhs and one Rajput family. The Sahariyas lived in one sahrana—known as Chenpur—though some of their houses were dispersed. The Rajput household was adjacent to the Sahariya sahrana, facing the road beyond which flows the Banganga river. Beyond the river were the lands of Sikh families. The Sikhs had made individual houses on their farms and the size of each farm was so large that as you drove through, you saw only large expanses of green fields with hardly a house or a rooftop. The houses were large, built in the typical farmhouse style one sees outside Delhi or in prosperous parts of Punjab.

If a visitor were to meet Pravin Singh alias Bitta, grandson of one of the seven Sikhs who first settled in Sunda, and then Matralal, a Sahariya elder, as we did, the local history and politics of this area would not be difficult to surmise. Even their appearance and the circumstances of their daily life spoke volumes of the reality of their existence—as the oppressor and the oppressed.

'This land was our own'

Matralal did not look it, but he was said to be ninety years old when we met him. A thin reed of a man, he came doggedly holding his bamboo staff. Devilal, an articulate ex-bonded labourer, had insisted that if we wanted to hear their story from olden times, then Matralal was the man to meet. But Matralal had other things on his mind. His indignation almost palpable, pointing at a half-built stone structure nearby, he said:

> The *junglat* people (forest department) came yesterday and forcibly stopped the construction, claiming that this was forest

land. We wanted to build a grain bank, so that in times of need, grain can be provided to the needy and we do not have to go to the landlords for help. Why did the *junglat* fellows stop us, when this land belonged to our forefathers—when it was our own?

Since many Sahariyas of Sunda-Chenpur had become free one year earlier, this grain bank was a critical attempt to ensure their self-reliance. All the people in the sahrana had contributed towards the cost of the building. Devilal explained why the Sahariyas were so upset: their grain bank, occupying less than a bigha of land, had been stopped, while ten bighas of land occupied by three Sikh farmers as *chakks* (threshing floor) had never been questioned, let alone hindered. 'This is the kind of official discrimination we face here regularly,' said Pappu and Kishore, both ex-bonded labourers.

'We have brought the stay and can continue to cultivate'

We were able to appreciate Pappu's remark better when we went to Bitta's house and saw for ourselves the results of 'official discrimination'. His house was less than a couple of kilometres from the Sahariya sahrana, but what a world of difference it was. While the Sahariyas lived in small kaccha or semi-pucca houses and owned only a few valuable household items like a cot, steel utensils and the odd goat, landlord Bitta's house was like a palace in comparison—a two-storeyed building with a high compound wall, a few vehicles parked outside (jeeps, tractors, motorcycles), dogs, and then Bitta himself, perhaps in his forties, lording over the house with his rounded pink cheeks. While one wished Bitta good health, one could not help being shocked by the contrast.

Bitta's family was said to own thousands of acres of land (4000 according to one estimate) in many different villages. According to the ex-bonded labourers who had worked on his land, his grandfather owned 1300 bighas of land in this village alone, which were now under the joint ownership of Bitta and his brother Rampi, who lived and worked in Kota.

Bitta's family also controlled a large parcel of Chenpur land (450 acres according to Bitta) that belonged to the Bigoda Cooperative Society, registered in 1969–70 by a group of Sikh farmers and a few token Sahariyas. According to local labourers, Bitta's father (or perhaps grandfather) Umraon Singh sold society land as if it were his private land. The society was also an advantageous arrangement in other ways, since, as Bitta explained, government loans for agricultural purposes are more easily available to a society. This scam was terminated by ex-collector R.S. Ghatala and the land was distributed to the Sahariyas. We could not gather the full story but learnt that a legal suit was subsequently filed by Bitta, who managed to obtain a stay, enabling him to retain control of the land until the final judgement.

The injustice of this interim arrangement was in full view as we sat talking to him in an open space in front of his house—next to a large shed with at least fifty robust buffaloes. After our interview was over, he took some of us to see how jaggery was being prepared from the sugarcane that grew in his fields, going past huge stacks of hay, stores of grain, large jaggery cakes, tractors, other expensive implements and quite a few retainers and more humble-looking hired hands who were busy with their chores—we were clearly amidst affluence.

This was not the only land that Bitta or others like him were alleged to have usurped. As mentioned earlier, Sahariyas owned little land, if any. In Chenpur, only seven or eight out of forty-five Sahariya families were said to be landowners; the largest landholding, Matralal's, was barely fifteen bighas (see below). Further, due to the complicity of government revenue officials with landlords, the land of the Sahariyas was generally of poor quality. Further, any plot of land adjoining the landlord's ran the risk of illegal occupation by him. Four allegations reported to me by local Sahariyas illustrate these problems:

Matralal owned just over fifteen bighas of land. Out of this, twelve bighas were in his possession (he cultivated about half of that as the other half was stony). The rest, according to Matralal, was occupied by Bitta and another Sikh farmer.

Babulal, Shyamlal and Pappu (sons of Jagna) jointly owned eight bighas of land. They were cultivating four bighas and alleged that two bighas—adjacent to Bitta's house—had been occupied by Bitta's family for the last two decades. The occupied land was good, they said, as a government canal passed nearby. According to Babu, 'The patwari did not measure the land properly. The patwaris are under the influence of the landlords. Whenever they come to the village, they first go to the landlord's house and he accompanies them to the land; therefore, they work under his guidance and influence. Sahariyas inevitably have *pathar, nalla, khada* (land unfit for cultivation) as their share, while the landlords get the more fertile land. I used to cultivate that land, but now it has been lying fallow for two decades.'

Devilal owned ten bighas adjacent to Babulal's land. He said that one bigha of his land was under Bitta's occupation.

Mukesh, Ramsingh, Mohan and Pappu (sons of Gopal) owned about twelve bighas of land. They cultivated eight bighas. The rest was under the occupation of Sikh farmers.

Bitta, of course, denied having occupied any parcel of land that belonged to the Sahariyas. As one might expect, his family members had an influential role in local politics. Some Sikhs felt that one reason why the bonded-labour story had gained prominence recently was the intra-Sikh community tension that emerged after Bitta's mother switched to the BJP from the Congress—the party favoured by the Sikhs so far—in order to be made chairperson of the *mandi* (local market). The Bitta family came under some criticism for this transgression of loyalty.

There were not many places the Sahariyas could go to for justice. In each of the two gram panchayats we visited, the sarpanch was a Sahariya and the up-sarpanch a Sikh, but it was understood that the Sikhs had a dominant influence over the gram panchayat. As one Sahariya labourer put it: *'Zamindar gram panchayat par haavi hain* [Landlords dominate the gram panchayats].' If most institutions of local governance are dominated by powerful landlords, what hope of justice would vulnerable groups like the Sahariyas have?

Iklera

Iklera village made history of sorts in late 2010. It is from here that the rebellion started. Sixteen halis of the Sahariya sahrana of the village decided to break free and paved the way for many other halis, far and near.

Iklera was off the main road on the way back to Baran. As the jeep sped on the tarred road, we saw very few signs of life in the arched light of its headlights—the roads become quiet soon after dark in these parts. Suddenly, the jeep lurched leftward into the dark fields. A few more bumpy minutes and we had reached—it seemed to us—nowhere. It took us a little while to discern the faint outline of huts, immersed in darkness. Sand and other building materials were piled here and there. A single solar street lamp stood downcast at a distance. We headed towards it, and soon people started assembling.

And there, sitting on a hurriedly brought string cot, with the help of a torchlight, we wrote our notes while the labourers sat and stood around. It was cold and one could see how ill-clad they were—their appearances, like their stories, were heart-wrenching.

This settlement, still in the making, was made up of rebels—those who had already quit, some recognized by the government and others still waiting to be recognized as 'bonded labourers'. This would make them eligible for the rehabilitation package—much sought after, yet only a little more than crumbs, as we were soon to discover.

In Iklera, the eleven landlords who had employed sixteen halis were not Sikhs, as in Ganeshpura and Sunda, but they belonged to local dominant castes and communities, including Dhakad (Chandravanshi Rajputs, known by their surname Nagar) and Muslims. In Rajasthan, Dhakads are officially recognized as 'backward' and included in the OBC list, as are many Sikhs (e.g., Jat Sikhs).[8]

The stories of Kanhaiya and Prakash, narrated below, are representative of the general pattern of servitude in the area. While the story of Ashok from Ganeshpura revealed the relationship between indebtedness and bondage, and how entire families get trapped for years, these stories reveal the reasons that may compel someone to 'choose' this labour arrangement. They also bring forth the similarities between the hali system and slavery.

'I needed twelve thousand for my son's marriage'

Kanhaiya (son of Hiralal), in his mid-thirties, was landless and his family had eight members. He said that he became a hali because he needed Rs 12,000 for his son's marriage. After three years of continuous work on landlord Roopnarayan Nagar's fields, he was told that his debt had increased to Rs 20,000 even though, according to Kanhaiya, no expenses had been incurred on him except for medical expenses of Rs 100. 'My lunch would come from home, and on days when food could not be sent, I had to work without food,' he recalled.

The customary terms of employment applied. For instance, there were no work timings—he often had to work during early mornings or late evenings, at the convenience of the landlord. On days when he was absent (naga), double the 'wage' due to him was deducted from the landlord's ledger.

He was also a hali for Jagdish Chotulal (of the Meena tribe) in Aalampora village for one year, after borrowing money for his little daughter's tonsure ceremony. One day, when he was irrigating the fields, the engine stopped. The landlord came and beat him up for being careless. 'That night after work, I ran away and came here. Aalampora is many kilometres away and it took me one day and one night to reach.'

'He sold me for twenty thousand to Chotman'

Prakash (son of Prahlad, thirty years old) was also seated with Kanhaiya and the others. He said:

> We were landless and were bandhak with Chotman (Chothmal Nagar) and Hansraj Dhakad. I worked for Hansraj for five years. At the end of five years, Hansraj told me that my *karja* had become Rs 15,000. *Bees hazar mein usne mujhe Chotman ko bech diya* [Hansraj sold me for Rs 20,000 to Chotman].
>
> I worked for Chotman for five years. My daughter fell ill and was hospitalized. I donated blood to get blood for her. After that, I felt weak and stayed home for four or five days. Then, Hansraj came and said that Chotman was calling me. Hansraj took me with him to Chotman's grain store and both of them beat me ruthlessly. I started bleeding from my nose and mouth. They also pulled my hair and beat my head against the wall. They continued until Chotman's wife intervened and said, '*Itna mat maro nahi toh mar jayega* [Don't beat him so much, otherwise he will die].' I was then told to stop crying and to clean the cattle shed. For the next two hours, I was made to fill around forty *tagari* (baskets) of cow dung and pile them up in one place. After this, they instructed me to go and irrigate the fields. Having given this instruction, they left for Kishanganj. As soon as they left, I ran home and told my wife (Gitabai) all that had happened. We decided to file an FIR. But

at the police station at Kishanganj, the *thanedar* (police officer) refused to register one.

Finally, his testimony was taken but not his signature. He was told that the miscreants would be arrested by the evening. When no action was taken for the next five days, his wife and he decided to join the Jagrut Mahila Sangathan, whose members were going to attend the dharna at Jaipur. There, they related their story as well as the circumstances of the other halis.

This issue was then taken up in a major way by the dharna participants with higher government officials, including the Chief Minister, who then summoned the Collector. On their instructions, the Sub-Divisional Magistrate (SDM) and the tehsildar went to Iklera and conducted an enquiry. The following day, the Collector also visited Iklera and talked to the halis. It was after that, we were told, that Sahariya households in Iklera (forty-five of them) received ration cards and MGNREGA job cards for the first time. Also, fourteen labourers received the mukti praman patra.

On the day of our visit, there was much consternation amongst the labourers because Kalulal and Rukbeer had been refused recognition as bonded labourers and denied the mukti praman patra. Their assertion that they had worked as halis for two and four years respectively—after which their employers claimed that their initial debt had nearly doubled—was ignored by the authorities. Instead, erroneous conclusions were drawn on grounds that didn't hold water. In Kaluram's case, in the meeting where the certificates were distributed, he was asked by the SDM if he knew the name of his employer's grandfather. He did not. And this seems to have been used against him. 'Why was he asked this question and how did his response matter?' asked Kaluram's friends, who suspected foul play.

In Rukbeer's case, the SDM informed him that he had been excluded from the list because of lack of 'proof'. The labourers considered this unjust because they were now aware of the fact that under the law, the onus of proof was on the employer.

Rehabilitation Package

Fourteen others in Iklera who did get certificates received the rehabilitation package two months later (on 16 January 2011; see Chronology below). This rehabilitation package from the central government was worth Rs 20,000. Of this, Rs 1000 was to be paid in cash when the certificate was delivered. The remainder was to be paid in kind. The 'beneficiaries' mentioned that each of them had received ten goats. They had also received two small quilts, two tin sheets and measly food items—10 kg rice, 10 kg sugar, 5 kg jaggery, 2 kg oil, 2 kg lentils and 100 gm tea leaves—that included nothing for infants. Most of them sold off their goats after two died due to some illness in the first week. Aside from this package, they also received job cards and ration cards.

We took a small sample from one of the quilts. It did not seem like wool, but we thought we would check with someone more knowledgeable. When we met the Principal Secretary (Labour) in Jaipur, he promptly confirmed that it was 'kachra' (waste).

The rehabilitation package was far from adequate. It was first designed in 1978 when the assistance of up to Rs 4000 per bonded labourer was approved. This was raised to Rs 6250 in 1986, Rs 10,000 in 1995 and Rs 20,000 in 2000. At the time of our enquiry in 2012, it was still at that low level.

Struggle for *Mukti*

The struggle of the Iklera labourers made waves in the area. Many labourers started coming to Iklera. The chronology of events below attempts to capture the main developments of the first few months of the struggle—from October 2010 onwards. According to a list prepared by Jagrut Mahila Sangathan and Sankalp, as of late January 2012, 151 labourers had applied for release and forty-four had received their certificates. Only fourteen, however, had received the full rehabilitation package.

What we saw in Iklera convinced us that despite sporadic relief from the district administration, no systematic arrangements had been made for the safety and 'just and proper resettlement and rehabilitation' of the released bonded labourers. Breaking free from the old patterns of servitude and leaving their employers without any preparedness had been very difficult for them. However, as one of them said, it was bad enough not to know where their next meal would come from, but worse to live in constant fear of retaliatory persecution from their former employers. There had already been a few instances of a former employer coming to the Sahariya settlement, raining abuses at his one-time hali and dragging him back. Such belligerence, the labourers felt, could be checked only if the police and administration took firm action.

Despite their tribulations, the residents of Iklera had hope. They had borne their earlier distress with fortitude and now too, it was their own reserves of strength and solidarity that sustained them.

Chronology of Events

(October 2010—February 2011)[9]

2010

27 October: Sixteen Sahariyas from Iklera village, who had been working as halis for eleven landlords of the same village, broke their silence by speaking out at the Mazdoor Haq Satyagraha in Jaipur. Pressure from civil society groups resulted in the district administration ordering an investigation, declaring fourteen of them bonded and officially releasing them on 13 November. On 16 January 2011, they were given the rehabilitation package from the centre, along with job cards and ration cards.

29 November: A second group of **six** labourers from Rajpura, Karvarikala, Pinjana and Jaitpura (Kishanganj tehsil) came forward to break free from their bondage and lodged a complaint with the administration. Their testimonies were taken by the Sub Divisional Officer (SDO), Kishanganj, on 13 and 17 December. Investigations in all these cases were completed, but they were declared to be ineligible for rehabilitation. Re-investigation in four cases was requested.

24 December: A group of **ten** labourers from Kelwada (Shahbad tehsil), Karjuna (Ataru tehsil) and Mayda ran away from their employers and came to Iklera. They had been working as halis for periods varying between one and seven years. Their cases were presented to the administration.

2011

10 January: Malkhan and Roopchand (from Rampuriya-Lakhakhedi village) and Tejkaran (from Bhawadgadh-Premnagar) demanded to be freed from bonded labour. Ghasi, Malkhan and Roopchand's father, had also been working as halis for a Meena landlord for years. The SDO Kishanganj asked them to come on 18 January to present their testimony. On the same day, the landlord came to the SDO's office and took them away. Malkhan ran away to Kota, but Roopchand resumed working for the landlord again. A frustrated Ghasi said: 'We are being asked for proof, what proof can we give?'

12 January: A group of **nine** labourers from Sunda demanded freedom from bondage. They were all working as halis for Pravin Singh, Pratap Singh and Balvir Singh for six to fifteen years. Their testimonies were taken on 21 January. Three of them did not have a ration card and one did not have a job card.

24 January: Twenty-one labourers from four villages of Kishanganj tehsil—Sunda (sixteen), Khankhra (two), Khedla (two) and Acharpura (one)—came forward for their release. They had also been working as halis for sardar farmers. Seven of them did not have ration cards and four did not have job cards.

3 February: Twenty labourers from Ganeshpura, Khankra, Jawaipura and Gordhanpura (Kishanganj tehsil) applied for release. In this group, some had been halis for nine to twenty years. Four of them did not have ration cards and two did not have job cards.

4 February: Four labourers from two villages of Kishanganj tehsil—Sunda (three) and Jawaipura (one)—submitted their demand for release.

7 February: Five dalits from Muhal village (Shahbad tehsil), who had been working as halis for farmers of the Kirad caste, demanded their release. After giving their testimonies, they stayed at home. These were the first cases of non-Sahariyas in bondage who came forward for their release.

8 February: In the first half of January, a group of **fourteen** halis from Alampura (Chabra tehsil) escaped from their oppressive landlords and came to Iklera after hearing about the released bonded labourers through a milkman. Amongst them were women who had been sexually harassed. On 29 January, their employers came to Iklera and threatened to tie them up with ropes and drag them back. Finally, on 8 February, the SDO of Chabra tehsil recorded their testimonies. None of them had ration cards or job cards.

4

Dalit Rebellion against
Untouchability in Chakwada*

21 September 2002: The morning air on this otherwise ordinary
September day seems to hold an indefinable expectancy. In a small
wayside tea stall in Dudu—as I wait for my friends to arrive for the
sadbhavna rally (peace and harmony march)—I talk to the only other
person who is also sipping tea. A fine-featured villager in Rajasthani
attire with earrings and *pagadi* (turban), he is not too forthcoming at
first. But the mention of Chakwada provokes an immediate reaction:
'The Bairwas [Dalits] have their own ghat which is *nyare* (separate),
so where is the injustice? Now they are thinking of entering the Shiv
temple. How can they when this is forbidden?' A farmer of the Jat
caste from a nearby village added that Jats from the surrounding area
were going to assemble in Phagi to counter the rally. The tea-shop
owner, quite poor, didn't say much, but the nods and shakes of his
head made it clear that he agreed.

Later in the morning, en route to Madhorajpura, where we were
planning to join the rally, we stopped at a village called Devriya. The

---

* This essay appeared in *Contributions to Indian Sociology* in 2006. A few notes and
references have been added.

Chakwada incident was known there too. Some women and older persons who had stayed back told us that many from their hamlet had gone for the rally. This was clearly a Dalit hamlet. In their village, they said, they lived discriminated lives at the hands of those the women kept referring to as '*aado*' and '*dhando*' (the obstructive and stubborn ones).

The rally could not continue from Madhorajpura. The rallyists decided to avoid a confrontation with the Jats, who were assembled in thousands in Phagi—the next big junction on the scheduled route.[1] Since they were armed with lathis and in a belligerent mood, violence seemed inevitable. Policemen trying to disperse the assembly became targets of Jat anger and according to local media reports, forty-four of them sustained minor injuries in the clash that followed.

The Issue

Chakwada, a little-known village around 50 km from Jaipur, in Phagi tehsil, was in the midst of a social upheaval. The issue was the ever-persisting one of 'untouchability'. The most basic of all human rights—to be regarded as a human at par with others—is still out of reach for many citizens of our country. For them, this basic freedom continues to be like stars in the sky—sparklingly attractive, but very distant.

The story began in December 2001. After several years of continuous drought, the water in the village pond had receded. The pond was large and impressive even in its depleted state. It was said to be more than five hundred years old. Herdsmen liked to stop by this pond, as did *yatris* (travellers) from far away. It was a popular halt due to the shade of many different trees nearby as well as the Shiv temple located at one end of the pond. However, according to the *parampara* (tradition) of the village, not all yatris or inhabitants of the village had equal access to the pond.[2] The parampara allowed bathing rights to all except those who were *avarna*, i.e., outcaste (also identified with castes presently listed as Scheduled Castes, i.e., Dalits). This rule, made by the elders of *savarna* Hindus (also known as 'caste Hindus'), allowed access even to the Muslim and Adivasi residents of the village, but not to Dalits.[3]

Since olden times, the Chakwada pond had four ghats where the *gaon wale* (or the 'general castes', as all castes and communities other than the Dalits, including Muslims, were referred to by the Dalits) were allowed to bathe. These ghats were in a semi-circle, at the end of which stood the Shiv temple. Beyond the Shiv temple, there were a few slabs of stone where the Dalits would bathe. The Dalits had to struggle to get a ghat built for them at this location about fifty years ago. But the Dalit ghat remained nameless, even as all the other four ghats had dignified Hindu names (Jorawar, Narsingh, Mahadev and Ganesh). 'That is the ghat of the poor. It has no name. They call it *bairwaon ka ghat* (the ghat of the Bairwas),' said Phoolchand, a young Bairwa.

Even after the Dalits had a ghat of their own, their problems were not resolved. Their ghat, located on a higher ground, always had less water than the other ghats. In drought years, it dried up completely. This unfavourable location, combined with the continuing prohibition of access to the other ghats, led to the rebellion that took place in 2001 and 2002.[4] Following a collective decision to break this unjust tradition, Babulal Bairwa and Radheshyam Bairwa took a dip at Ganesh ghat (close to the Shiv temple) on 14 December 2001, acutely aware of the mayhem that might follow. As expected, this sparked an unprecedented social outrage.

The trajectory of this resistance highlights many crucial aspects of the predicament of Dalits in rural Rajasthan: the continuation of untouchability in brazen violation of the law; the absence of government initiative in this matter; the difficulties Dalits face in claiming their basic democratic rights; the nexus between government officials and dominant castes; the complexity of caste divisions and alliances (even amongst Dalits), amongst other issues. A close look at the Chakwada rebellion can help us to understand these issues, especially the persistence of untouchability and the state's passivity towards it, even in the face of rebellion.

The Setting

I visited Chakwada for the first time on 25 September 2002. Alighting from a local passenger jeep, my very first sight was the large pond—the stage of this confrontation. Even though four days had lapsed since the Phagi skirmish, I expected the atmosphere to be tense. Feeling like an unwanted cactus in this somewhat desolate and even hostile landscape, I made my way to a nearby shop. Besides the young shopkeeper, another man (who turned out to be a Jat) was present. After answering the usual questions posed to an outsider, I asked what the conflict in Chakwada was about.

'*Yahan nahane-dhone ki ladai hai* [The conflict here is about bathing and washing].'

'*Yahan moochh ki ladai hai* [The conflict here is about keeping the moustache (manly honour) intact].'

'*Kiski moochh* [Whose moustache]?'

'*Jaaton ki, Bairwaon ki. Bairwa kahte hain ki veh Brahmin ho gaye* [Of the Jats, of the Bairwas. The Bairwas are claiming that they have become Brahmins].'

'*Bairwaon ne to hamein aise rakha hua hai jaise jeebh hoti hai danton ke beech. Thoda sa bahar nikle to kat jaye. Thoda sa kahe to chhua-chhoot ka case ho jata hai* [Bairwas have kept us like a tongue between the teeth. If it comes out just a little, it gets cut. Even if just a little is said, an atrocity case is slammed on us].'[5]

The other man was worried about the repercussions in his village Pachala (three kilometres away), which also had Bairwas, a strong Jat community and a pond with separate ghats. Bidding them farewell, I proceeded towards the Bairwa hamlet, encouraged by the tacit acknowledgement that the Bairwas had a moustache and felt entitled to keep it!

In Chakwada, the 'general castes' consist predominantly of Jats—roughly half of the village's 525 households (261 households to be precise) in 2002. Jat domination has been a common feature of many villages in this region. Amongst the upper castes, there were nearly 100 Brahmin households. Rajputs, traditionally the dominant upper caste in Rajasthan, were a small minority in Chakwada (three households). Meenas, a well-off community listed as a Scheduled Tribe in Rajasthan (thirty-two households), along with thirty-five Muslim households, made up the remainder of the 'general castes' as the Dalits viewed them.

There were 102 Dalit households. The Bairwas (known as Chamars elsewhere) were numerically the strongest (seventy households), followed by the Balais (thirty households) and Bhangis (two households). The Member of the Legislative Assembly (MLA) of Phagi reserved constituency—under which Chakwada falls—was then a Balai. As we shall see, he sided with the Jats in this conflict. At first sight, judging from the mostly fair-sized and at least semi-*pucca* houses of the Bairwas, the Dalits in Chakwada seemed to be economically better placed than their counterparts in other states such as Bihar. This illustrates the fact that social equality does not necessarily follow economic mobility.

Much as in other parts of India, public positions in Chakwada were dominated by the upper castes. This was evident, for example, from the caste background of the gram panchayat functionaries. The then sarpanch, Pushpadevi Sharma, was a Brahmin, as was the previous sarpanch, Bhagwansai Sharma. Chakwada gram panchayat is a reserved seat for women, but it was common knowledge that Pushpadevi's husband, Nandkishore Sharma, was the de facto sarpanch.

Jats have been the most powerful caste in Chakwada. The Jat community has not only been numerically strong but also owned most of the land. Formally in the Other Backward Classes (OBC) category, most of them have been Congress supporters, though a significant number were believed to have shifted to the BJP in the Assembly elections of 2003 and the Parliamentary elections of 2004. An important reason for this shift was the Vajpayee government's granting of their long-standing demand for caste reservations soon after it came to power in 2002.

Untouchability: Past and Present

The contemporary face of untouchability in Chakwada and surrounding areas is nuanced in some respects, and blatant in others, but remains a major social evil that causes pain, humiliation and rage amongst the victims. While many humiliating practices of the past have changed, caste discrimination continues and the present remains troubled due to the unresolved caste question.

The recorded history of caste conflict in Chakwada goes back at least to the mid-1930s when Dr Ambedkar referred to it in his famous work *Annihilation of Caste*:

A most recent event is reported from the village Chakwara in Jaipur State. It seems from the reports that have appeared in the newspapers that an untouchable of Chakwara who had returned from a pilgrimage had arranged to give a dinner to his fellow untouchables of the village as an act of religious piety. The host desired to treat the guests to a sumptuous meal and the items served included ghee (butter). But while the assembly of untouchables was engaged in partaking of the food, the Hindus in their hundreds, armed with lathis, rushed to the scene, despoiled the food and belaboured the untouchables who left the food they were served with and ran away for their lives. And why was this murderous assault committed on defenceless untouchables? The reason given is that the untouchable host was impudent enough to serve ghee and his untouchable guests were foolish enough to taste it. Ghee is undoubtedly a luxury for the rich. But no one would think that the consumption of ghee was a mark of high social status. The Hindus of Chakwara thought otherwise and in righteous indignation avenged them for the wrong done to them by the untouchables, who insulted them by treating ghee as an item of their food which they ought to have known could not be theirs, consistently with the dignity of the Hindus. This means that an untouchable must not use ghee even if he can afford to buy it since it is an act of arrogance towards the Hindus. This happened on or about the 1st of April 1936![6]

This story told and retold, is part of the oral history of the Bairwas of Chakwada. When I met them, they recalled how the meal was being served to the rows of seated people when the attack occurred. Armed with lathis and hurling abuses, the attackers threw mud in the food. Their pressure tactics, however, could not contain a revolt against the unjust ban on ghee consumption—Dalits of Chakwada continued to consume ghee on special occasions as and when they could afford it. Today, this rule stands broken and the Bairwas take pride in their ancestors' fight for dignity.[7]

There are other examples of unjust rules that have died out over time. One is the practice of giving water to Dalits through an iron or wooden pipe called a *pandala*. Even in a *piau* (public drinking-water point) and public places such as hotels, Dalits would be thus humiliated.[8] Caste discrimination at school was also the norm. Ramlal Bairwa, for instance, recalled that twenty-five years earlier, when he was in primary school, '*Ham pyase khade rahte the jab tak savarna jati ka koi baccha hamein matke se pani pilata* (We had to remain thirsty until a high-caste child would give us water from the pitcher).' There were also other forms of caste discrimination at school, such as separate seating arrangements. Ramlal Bairwa added that as children, he and his friends couldn't understand why they were considered 'dirty', even when they were actually cleaner than some of the high-caste children.

While some discriminatory practices had ceased, discrimination in other guises persisted. Untouchability at school was no longer as common as it used to be, but some parents complained that Dalit children were often made to sit in the back rows. There was a separate cremation ground for the Dalits. Further, water sources such as wells remained separate. And while all could draw water from the government handpumps, Dalit women often had to fight to get others to respect the queue. Also, the public handpumps were sometimes deliberately so placed that access to them became difficult for the Dalits. Describing a recent instance of this, Jamku Devi said, 'There is an old Hanuman temple in our village. Four months ago, as part of the drought relief works, a raised platform was built near the temple and a handpump was installed in the centre. Then a boundary wire was fixed and a gate constructed, and soon a sadhu made himself at home there. The handle of the handpump was installed only after the gate was in place in order to control the use of the handpump. Now, Jagdish Jat prohibits us from entering the gate and filling water from that handpump. He says, "*Puja karna hai to dur se karo, tilak lagana hai to dur se lagao, matha tekna hai to dur se teko*" (If you want to worship, do it from afar). Except SCs, all are allowed to fill water from that handpump.' As we can see in this instance, *pani* (water) and puja were strategically so mixed that Dalits were effectively barred from both.

Similarly, Dalits in Chakwada were yet to gain the right of temple entry. None of the five big *sarvajanik* (public) temples in the village were accessible to them.[9] In fact, they were not even allowed in the vicinity of the temples. Kanhaiyalal Bairwa related one such incident:

This happened eight years ago. I was making a rope near the Mahadev ghat. As the length of the rope increased, I had to move backwards and soon I was quite close to the temple. I was fined Rs 500 for this. They said I had no right to come near the temple.

The fact is that we have no right to bathe in the ghats or even sit under the shady trees near the temple, nor can our children play in that area. After that incident, they constructed a wall around the temple.' Kanhaiyalal continued, 'Ironically, it is the labourers (usually Dalits) who lay the foundation of the temple and create its splendid form, but as soon as the structure is complete and the *murti* (idol) installed, it belongs exclusively to the savarnas and Dalits become outcastes.

Parampara or *buzurgon ke niyam* (rules made by the ancestors) are invoked as reasons in defence of these discriminatory practices. The fact that these rules were made by and for the dominant castes is conveniently overlooked.

The Conflict

As mentioned, the conflict of 2002 began when Babulal Bairwa and Radheshyam Bairwa took a dip in the Ganesh ghat of the pond on 14 December 2001, around 9 a.m. This was not a spontaneous action; it followed a collective decision of the Bairwa community to rebel against the existing norm that prevented them from accessing all ghats.

Late in the evening on the same day, the upper castes held a meeting near the pond and shouted slogans against the Bairwas. Babulal and Radheshyam stayed indoors. They made a phone call to the police station at Phagi and informed the Station House Officer (SHO) of the situation. They were told that nothing could be done that night and that they should file a complaint at the police station the following morning.[10]

The next day, the SHO and tehsildar—one a Brahmin, the other a Jat—came to the village. On reaching the village, they sent word to the Bairwas that they should come to meet them near the pond. When the Bairwas came, they were roundly scolded for breaking the village tradition. They were told not to do anything that would escalate the conflict. On the same day, the Deputy Superintendent of Police and the Assistant Collector cum Magistrate also came to the village. They held a meeting of the Bairwas and the upper castes in the village community hall. The same message was repeated: the Bairwas should, in accordance with the village parampara, desist from bathing in the ghats 'reserved' for the upper castes. None of the government officials who visited the village that day or in the following days visited the Bairwa hamlet or talked with the Bairwas separately. This censorious and unsupportive attitude of the government officials only increased the isolation and fear of the Bairwas.

On 16 December, the general castes of the village organized a meeting to which the Bairwas were summoned. Babulal Bairwa was asked why he had bathed at the prohibited ghats. To this he replied, *'Main bhi insaan hoon, kya mujhe nahane ka adhikar nahi hai* [I am also a human being; don't I have the right to bathe]?' The Bairwas were asked to sign a statement admitting that they had broken the village parampara and called the police. They were told to sign the statement or face the consequences. When the Bairwas refused to sign, another meeting was held. In this meeting—allegedly attended by a local Vishwa Hindu Parishad (VHP) leader—a fine of Rs 51,000 was imposed on Babulal and the Bairwa community. The meeting held that by bathing in the ghat meant for the upper castes and involving the police and administration in the internal affairs of the village, the Bairwas had broken the village parampara and lowered the dignity of the village.

The Bairwas refused to pay the fine. Explaining this, one of the Bairwas argued, *'Hamne gai thodi maari hai, ya khoon thodi jo kiya hai* [It's not as though we have killed a cow or committed a murder].' Following their defiance, a social and economic boycott of the Bairwa community was announced on 21 December. The boycott meant that no landowner would employ them or lend farm implements to them, no one would sell them vegetables or a cup of tea, the local doctor would not treat them, the fair-price shop manager would not serve them, the local mechanic would not repair their bicycles and so on. Further, if anyone broke the boycott, a fine of Rs 5000 would be imposed on that person.

The next day, the Bairwas filed a police complaint on the basis of which an FIR was lodged against seventeen persons under the Scheduled Castes and Scheduled Tribes (Prevention of Atrocities) Act, 1989. They had been planning to do this for some time, but they were waiting for the return of Harishanker Bairwa, a relatively knowledgeable member of their community who had gone to Gujarat. The police, however, remained indifferent and did not take any action on the FIR. In the village, the Bairwas continued to face verbal abuse and threats of physical abuse if they did not fall in line. In the absence of any action by the police and the local administration, the Bairwas finally approached the Rajasthan State Human Rights Commission (SHRC) for protection and justice. The SHRC, however, did not initiate an independent inquiry. Instead, it ordered the Superintendent of Police to investigate the case.

On 3 January 2002, some police officials were sent to the village and the Bairwas were able to bathe in the ghat under police protection. However, when they tried to bathe again the next day—without police protection—they were chased away by a mob of dominant-caste men. The Bairwas were now convinced that they would not get any sustained help from the government and decided to approach other groups like the People's Union for Civil Liberties (PUCL) and the Centre for Dalit Human Rights (CDHR) in Jaipur. These groups started putting pressure on the administration.

Under this pressure, the District Collector (a Brahmin again) visited the village with the Superintendent of Police (Rural). Even though the Collector affirmed that the law had primacy over any village tradition and that everyone would have to abide by the law, no punitive action against those accused in the FIR was taken. Instead, on 6 January 2002, the local administration forced the Bairwas to enter a compromise with the upper castes. This included the Bairwas having to sign a statement saying that there was no prohibition on the Bairwas and that they were free to bathe in the pond. Under pressure, some of the Bairwas signed the statement, even though in practice this was not the case. On hearing about this compromise later, the SHRC closed the Chakwada file—three months after the initial application—on grounds that during this period none of the Bairwas had approached them with any further complaint; also because the matter had by then been taken up by the National SC/ST Commission. Thus, the grievance of the complainants and the Bairwa community was not addressed adequately, either by the state machinery or by the SHRC.

In the absence of any government action, the CDHR along with PUCL and several other organizations initiated the 60 km long sadbhavna rally to Chakwada on 20–21 September 2002. The objective of this rally was to sensitize the public as well as the administration to the problems faced by Dalits. The rally started from Chaksu on 20 September and covered an initial distance of 45 km. Meanwhile, a rumour spread that the Dalits were planning not only to bathe in the pond, but also to enter the Shiv temple. In reaction to this, the upper castes of Chakwada began a *Ram dhuni* programme near the pond, thereby blocking access to it as well as to the temple. This Ram dhuni is said to have had the support of various local leaders, including an MLA and some VHP members. The next day, on 21 September, a large mob assembled in Chakwada itself, while another mob of around 15,000 assembled in Phagi—the next big junction on the scheduled route of the rally. The mob consisted mainly of Jats, armed with lathis. Since violence seemed imminent, the rally was called off before it could reach Phagi. Following the rally, the administration managed to enable the Bairwas to bathe in the ghats late at night on 24 September, under police protection. Even though the sustained struggle of the Bairwas secured them bathing rights, their confidence that this would continue remained tenuous.

Subsequent Developments

After the Chakwada rebellion and the subsequent Phagi confrontation, the situation in the surrounding area was tense. Dalits, particularly Bairwas, were frightened of repercussions. Their apprehension that they would be made targets of Jat anger proved right. Several cases of caste-based harassment and excesses on Bairwas were reported in the Phagi-Chaksu area. The actual number of cases is likely to be larger as many of the victims may not have reported these incidents to the police or higher authorities for fear of reprisal. The following is a sample of some of these cases—they illustrate how diverse forms of discrimination were used to humiliate the Bairwas.[11]

1. On 21 September 2002, Jats of Kansel village participated in the Phagi action in large numbers. That night, after dining in Chakwada, they returned to Kansel on their tractors. They stopped in the Bairwa hamlet, where they abused the Bairwas in casteist terminology, challenging them to come out of their homes and face them. The Bairwas remained indoors.

2. On 22 September 2002, Dhanpal Bairwa of Khera village and Laduram Bairwa of Jharana village were travelling from Madhorajpur to Phagi in a private bus, as they had done countless times before. But unlike previous times, that day they were abused and humiliated by upper-caste co-travellers. These passengers claimed that '*ham savarn jati ke logon ko in achhoot, neech Bairwa logon ki badboo aa rahi hai* [we upper caste people are having to suffer the stink of these untouchable, low-birth Bairwas].' They waved the objections of the driver and the conductor aside, promising them full payment of the tickets owed to them, and compelled them to stop the bus midway and evict the Bairwas. Severely outnumbered, Dhanpal and Laduram stepped down, but their trial was not yet over. They were spat at from the windows of the bus, abused and threatened with dire

consequences—that their family members would be lynched—if they dared to inform the police. Frightened for their families, they did not make a police complaint.

3. On 25 September 2002, the dominant castes of Kansel deposited a large quantity of faeces in the drinking water well of the Bairwas in their village. This action was severely criticized by elders in the village, and the well was cleaned up. However, the following day the act was repeated. An FIR was then lodged in the Phagi police station, with no immediate effect. Subsequently, the police along with the local administration contacted the Bairwas, only to persuade them to accept a compromise. Besides getting the police to act on their behalf, the dominant castes tried to confuse the situation by getting some of the Bhangis of the village to complain against the Bairwas.

4. In Chapri village, a more direct and drastic method was used to deprive the Bairwas of drinking water. Here, the drinking water well in the Bairwa hamlet was filled with stones and mud and then sealed with wooden planks.

5. During this period, individual Bairwas were also victimized in diverse ways. For example, on 12 October 2002, a Jat trader who ran a dairy in Gokulpura village refused to accept milk from Gopal Bairwa. 'I do not accept the milk of Chamars in my dairy,' he shouted as he ran after Gopal brandishing his shoe, mouthing casteist abuses and threatening to kill him. Gopal, who had been delivering milk to the same dairy throughout the previous year, lodged an FIR in the Phagi police station on the same day. But no action was taken. A discouraged Gopal wrote to CDHR requesting them to intervene. 'I am a poor Scheduled Caste person, that is why the police have not taken any action against the culprits based on my report,' he wrote. The CDHR immediately wrote to the SHRC, but nothing happened afterwards.

6. Attempts were also made to revive old untouchability-related practices. For example, in a tea shop in Ladana village, a few

dominant-caste customers forced a Bairwa to wash his glass after drinking tea, against the wishes of the shop owner.[12] The matter escalated and reached the sarpanch. The sarpanch took a clear stand against this act of discrimination, but his views were disregarded and his authority ignored. The miscreants announced that all teashops that catered to the Bairwas would be closed. A similar incident occurred in another tea shop in Mohanpur Prithvi Singh village, where the Bairwas were prohibited from using the water jug and glass as well as from sitting on chairs and benches. They were insulted and physically threatened if they dared to disobey.[13]

All these cases came under the jurisdiction of the Phagi police station. The response was the same each time; the police failed to take responsible action as per provisions of the law. The Dalits had to cope on their own and wait for the situation to return to normal. As the Phagi events shows, the 'rule of law' comes into effect only after much prodding, especially by civil society organizations. Pleas of the people, often made in a tone of respectful expectation rather than an assertion of rights—*aap hum par meharbani karein, doshi par karyavahi karein* (please oblige us by taking legal action)—are ignored. The bottom line is that the police station personnel feel no sense of responsibility or obligation to act, nor any fear of punishment if they don't.

The anti-Bairwa sentiment also pervaded the pre-poll calculations during the Assembly elections of 2003. There was an unspoken understanding amongst the dominant castes in the Chakwada area that '*kisi bhi halat mai Bairwa ko jeetne nahi dena hai* [on no account should a Bairwa be allowed to win]'. The Bairwas were equally determined that only a Bairwa should win. With this in mind, the Bairwas voted for the BJP candidate, Laxmi Narayan Bairwa, who also happened to be the President of the all-India Bairwa Mahasabha, even though he did not speak out against the upper castes forcefully enough, they admitted. 'We have habitually voted for the Congress, but this time it became a caste fight,' said Babulal Bairwa.[14]

The caste fight that Babulal was referring to was a fight to ensure the victory of a Bairwa candidate, not a fight between Dalits and the upper castes. The Bairwas themselves acknowledged that the Congress candidate, Mukesh Valmiki, was an able person and sympathetic to the cause of the Dalits, unlike Laxmi Narayan. Yet they voted for Laxmi Narayan because he was a Bairwa. Another reason was that they did not feel that Mukesh Valmiki would be able to defeat Ashok Tanwar, the previous MLA who was contesting as an independent candidate. A Balai, Ashok Tanwar had opposed the Bairwa rebellion and the Bairwas were keen to trounce him, come what may.

In the Lok Sabha elections (2004), the Bairwas voted for the BJP candidate again. The BJP candidate, a Brahmin, had their favour this time because Ashok Tanwar was backing the Congress candidate, a Rajput. A Congress victory would have added to Ashok Tanwar's clout. Thus, ironically, in both elections, the Bairwas ended up voting for the very party (the BJP) that wanted to retain the traditional social order that had hurt them and led to their rebellion.

This illustrates the complexity of caste identities in rural areas. Caste equations manifest themselves more sharply and clearly than ever at election time. The politics of reserved constituencies further undermines Dalit solidarity as different Dalit castes (e.g., Bairwas and Balais) are pitted against each other and compete for their respective candidates or parties. This was evident in the case of Ashok Tanwar, who was known to enjoy the patronage of the Jats. He openly told us that it was quite understandable that the Jats were not allowing the Bairwas to bathe in their ghats considering how dirty the Bairwas usually were.[15] In fact, his attitude struck us not just as anti-Bairwa, but as anti-Dalit. It reminded us of Dr Ambedkar's apprehension that Dalit parliamentarians would not truly represent the interests of the Dalits unless they were elected by separate Dalit constituencies. Dalit parliamentarians elected by general constituencies, he had argued, would not be accountable to Dalits but to a larger constituency, which were effectively dominated by the privileged castes. Phagi constituency has a 'reserved' seat, but a Scheduled Caste candidate was unlikely to win there without the support of the Jats, and despite being Dalit, Ashok Tanwar gave the impression of being a virtual spokesperson of the Jats. To some extent, this also applied to Laxmi Narayan Bairwa, the BJP candidate.

On returning to Chakwada in May 2004, a year and a half after my earlier visits, I learnt that the Bairwas were now bathing in the pond regularly. However, this did not mean that equality had been achieved. In fact, the upper castes had stopped bathing there altogether—from the very day when the Bairwas started bathing—as they now considered the pond to be 'impure'. They were now themselves flouting the much-protected buzurgon ke niyam by walking with their slippers on the ghat, polluting it in many ways, not watering the plants and trees on the banks and even cutting some. Untouchability thus continued in another garb. The argument against this social practice in modern times, the efforts (however half-hearted) of the government officials and the attempts at sadhbhavna by civil society organizations did not seem to have made a dent in caste prejudices.

Even amongst Dalits, the right to bathe in the pond had not been extended equally. While all the Bairwa men bathed there regularly, the younger generation of the Balais only did so occasionally; despite the rebellion, they did not dare to challenge the parampara. The two Bhangi families rarely used the pond, that too only for washing clothes. Women of all castes, for their part, were still barred from using the pond.

Further, there was a deterioration in the relationship between the Bairwas and the Bhangis after the rebellion. The Bhangis had stopped working for the Bairwas. The Bairwas felt that the Bhangis enjoyed greater patronage from the upper castes and had done this under their influence.

Caste Power and Rights

Caste continues to be a major force in the villages of Rajasthan. Caste-based hierarchy and power are at the heart of the traditional social order and determine, to a large extent, the kind of lives that people live. It comes into play, for example, in village conflicts.

Conflicts, known as *vivaad*, abound locally, and lead to acrimonious exchanges of words and sometimes, more than words. Some conflicts can be seen as those that inevitably emerge in community life, even within a caste or class. Others, however, are imbued with caste or class aspects. For example, a fairly common incident is for an errant goat or cow to cross into someone else's field. Whether the response is one of mild irritation or wild anger may depend less upon the damage than upon who owns the animals. The waywardness of the cattle may be seen as the willfulness of the owner. A motive-less incident may be attributed motive and read as a form of everyday domination or resistance. Caste offers little escape and 'small matters become big issues' (*chhoti-chhoti baatein badi ho jati hain*) as age-old distrust and disdain come to the fore.

Caste hierarchy is also reflected in village institutions such as gram panchayats and even in traditional water management systems, as shown in this study. Such traditional systems have been widely admired for their effectiveness and ecological sustainability. However, by and large, the propertied sections of society have designed them for their own purposes. The interests of Dalits, women, the landless and other marginalized groups have been overlooked.

Extreme gender inequality is another oppressive aspect of the traditional social order. Like the caste hierarchy, it is reflected in traditional water-related institutions: women in Chakwada, like the Dalits, were not allowed to bathe in the pond. Until recently, a wooden board near the Shiv temple made it clear that women of *all* castes were excluded from bathing in the pond. Interestingly, this did not become an issue during the 2002 struggle.

The Chakwada story highlights the difficulties Dalits face while resisting traditional forms of oppression. Any attempt to challenge the traditional social order makes them vulnerable to repression and violence as well as to isolation. One might have expected that in this struggle, the intermediate castes would side with them against the upper castes. On the contrary, the intermediate castes—in this case, the Jats—sided with the upper castes and even led the backlash against Dalits. Further, other groups such as the Muslims and the Meenas also endorsed the practice of untouchability.

Special mention should be made of the collaboration of the Jats with the Meenas (a Scheduled Tribe). According to some Bairwas: 'The Meenas in this village are our real problem; the Jats are not fighting directly but getting Meenas to fight on their behalf.' They explained that the Meenas, being STs, could not be prosecuted under the Atrocities Act, making it convenient for the Jats to use them. The Meenas, in any case, are closer to the Jats than to the Bairwas, as they have a relatively high status in this area.[16]

Even amongst the Dalits themselves, significant divisions have weakened the struggle in Chakwada—for instance, the lack of solidarity between the Bairwas and the Balais. It is not clear when and how their antagonism developed, despite notable instances of cooperation among them in the past. The most important, about fifty years ago, concerned the same pond. Both communities had struggled together for a ghat for the Dalits, instead of mere stone slabs. The pond managing committee finally agreed to contribute Rs 1500 towards material costs, and the Dalits—Bairwas and Balais—provided the rest, including labour.

The unease between the two communities does not seem to be restricted to Chakwada. A brief look at the history of these communities may help explain the matter. The Bairwas and the Balais, also the Jatavs, Meghvals and Chamars have the same root occupation, i.e., working with leather.[17] In the late 1930s and early 1940s, the Bairwas—then called Chamar—fought against the compulsion to engage in this occupation. '*Is kaam ko nafrat kar ke bahishkar kiya. Yah log jabardasti yah kaam karvate the. Tab sangharsh kiya. In sab logon ne hamse bair kiya. Ham dabe nahi. Dare nahi. In sab se bair kar ke hamari jeet hasil hui. Is liye hamne apna naam Bairwa rakha* [Hating this occupation, we boycotted it. These people would force us to do this work. We launched an agitation. All these people became our enemies. But we did not give in to fear or intimidation. Out of this enmity (*bair*) and our struggle was born the name 'Bairwa'].[18]

In Rajasthan, as in many other parts of India, Chamars have led many resistance struggles. According to P.L. Mimroth of the Centre for Dalit Human Rights (CDHR), this is for several reasons: in numerical terms, it is a large community, perhaps larger than any other Dalit community; many of them have given up their traditional occupation as a mark of protest and adopted other means of livelihood; and as a result, many of them have also improved their economic situation. This also means that they are less dependent on the upper castes than many other Dalit castes. Educationally, they have done relatively well and this is also reflected in their political participation. All these factors have led to their emergence as leaders amongst Dalits. In many regions, this has exposed them to major atrocities. It has also alienated them to some extent from the other Dalits. In Rajasthan, for example, the Regars, Kolis, Khatiks, Valmikis and other Dalit castes that are considered 'weaker' than the Chamars do not cooperate with them. According to Mimroth, this is because in their perception the Chamars pick fights with the upper castes without adequate cause. He feels that some others who are still working with leather, like Balais, do not cooperate with them because of the somewhat superior attitude the Chamars acquired after giving up leather work.

Some of these reasons apply in Chakwada: Bairwas are numerically stronger and economically better off. Unlike the Balais, most of the Bairwas own land on account of an earlier struggle waged by them against upper-caste encroachment. This local history of successful resistance has increased the confidence of the Bairwas and improved their status amongst the Dalits in Chakwada.

Caste hierarchy and related problems have also crept within the Dalit fold. While there is greater social equality between the Bairwas and the Balais, untouchability towards the Bhangis is the norm. In a long interview on this issue, Babulal Bairwa, as well as an elderly Bairwa from Akoda village (Dudu block), admitted that they practised untouchability with the Bhangis, i.e., they did not drink the same water or share their food. In fact, the Bairwas refer to the Bhangis as 'Harijans', arguing that while they (the Bairwas) had 'always had their own caste', Gandhiji had renamed the Bhangis as Harijans. The Chakwada rebellion was mainly a Bairwa rebellion, with other disadvantaged communities including the Balais, Bhangis, Muslims and Meenas standing by or even siding with the upper castes.

The Chakwada rebellion also brings out other issues related to Dalit existence in the area, such as the question of religious identity. To resolve this issue, some of them joined the VHP. However, their bitter experience with the Sangh Parivar only intensified their frustration and anger. Recalling this experience, Harishanker Bairwa said:

> There was an RSS *shakha* (cell) in this village. About twenty to twenty-five of us Bairwas used to attend it. It continued for about two years. But when we felt that we were not being treated equally, we all left. After that, the shakha was disbanded. Before participating in this shakha, some of us also participated in similar activities in other villages. In appreciation of the participation from Chakwada, our village had also received a *reshmi jhanda* (silk flag) from the RSS, but now they have taken it back. Three of us had also gone to Ayodhya for *kar sewa* at the time of the demolition of the Babri Masjid. *Main kar sewa mein raha, maine Hinduon ki sewa ki, phir bhi mere se bhedbhav ho raha hai, toh ismein rahne se*

kya faida (I went for kar sewa. I served the Hindus, even then I am being discriminated against, so what is the point of remaining within Hinduism)?

After the ghat incident, we sent a petition to the VHP office in Jaipur and VHP workers came to investigate. There are some RSS workers in our village too. But all of them have kept silent on this issue. If the VHP, Sangh and BJP were really close to the Dalits, from their *atma*, then the continuation of untouchability would not be possible and the country could be saved. If they openly stand by us, then the general castes can't do anything. *Par VHP aur Sangh ki niti Daliton ke prati saaf nahin hai. Jab dharm parivartan ki baat hoti hai to aa jaate hai. Apne swaarth ke liye lete hain aur phir baad mein dhakka maar dete hain* (The policy of the VHP and the Sangh towards the Dalits is murky. They come when there is talk of conversion. They use us for their own selfish purposes and later push us out).

It is because of this character of the Sangh Parivar that Harishanker Bairwa left the BJP after supporting it for eight years. The Congress, he felt, did not help them either: '*Wahan bhi andar kuchh, bahar kuchh* [There, too, there are double standards].' The Congress leadership was in the hands of a few who did not allow others space to grow. The Dalit MLA himself repressed the rights of the Dalits.

Harishanker subsequently joined the Bahujan Samaj Party (BSP). He said that most of the Scheduled Castes would eventually join the BSP because they would see some hope in it. At the time of our interview, he was also toying with the idea of conversion to Islam. He commented in passing that this would be more effective than conversion to Buddhism because Muslims have greater numerical strength than Buddhists, and if the numerical strength of Dalits is added to it, 'Hindus will be hurt the most.'[19]

Even though Harishanker was the most articulate Bairwa leader in Chakwada, his stand was not always clear. He was not immune to the influence of the upper castes and at one point, he even supported their petition to be allowed the exclusive use of one ghat in the pond.[20] Babulal turned this request down by saying, 'If this request had been made at the time of negotiations, we might have conceded, but now that we have got this right after being crushed under their *jootis* [shoes], we will not give up our rights so easily.'

The Nature of Official Response

The Chakwada events throw some useful light on the relationship between state power and social power in rural India today. Constitutional provisions and related laws are meant to protect Dalits from social discrimination and exploitation. In practice, however, a large majority of Dalits are unable to access these laws or get them implemented in their favour. In the eyes of the law-enforcing agencies, they remain unequal citizens. The police and the state machinery fail to protect their constitutional rights and often end up aligning with forces that suppress them. There are several reasons for this: state officials often belong to privileged sections of the society, in terms of class and caste; even if they do not, they may imbibe the same attitudes in their own self-interest. And even if they have a different worldview, they are often constrained to cave in under pressure from the powerful, either within the government system or from outside. Rare is the officer who has the motivation and courage to stick his neck out in favour of the rights of the Dalits. In fact, such officers are so rare that they often become part of local folklore. Thus, the socially powerful are often able to wield state power to their advantage and thereby maintain the status quo.

It is not that the state is unable to intervene, or never intervenes. In fact, even in the Chakwada case, whenever the officials responded, it made a difference. For example, after the conflict, the presence of the police force in the village made the Dalits feel more secure. As Kanhaiyalal Bairwa said, 'When the administration is around, we feel more secure, otherwise, we are scared.' In the absence of the *prashasan* (administration), the *shashan* (rule) of the dominant castes prevails.

However, as we saw, the administration fails in its duty on many occasions and even takes the side of the upper castes from time to time. In fact, the first reaction of senior officials was to urge the Bairwas in Chakwada to abide by the parampara, allegedly for the sake of avoiding an escalation of the conflict and maintaining 'law and order'—a rather ironical argument since the Bairwas were trying to enforce the law.

The local administration also violates its duty to take proactive measures to protect the rights of Dalits. Unequal access to ponds and other forms of caste discrimination are known to be rampant in the area, yet the administration acts only in response to 'incidents', that too with much reluctance.

On a revisit to the Phagi thana in May 2004, I attempted to find out what the record of the thana was in addressing cases registered under the Atrocity Act. Accessing these old records was difficult. But the information that I could gather was revealing enough. I discovered that out of 268 FIRs filed under this Act during 1991–2004, a majority (143) were judged as '*adam baku*' or '*jhoot*' (a lie), and therefore dismissed at the thana level itself. As for the 121 cases where a chargesheet was filed, they were first heard in the Dudu court and then transferred to the Special SC & ST Court in Jaipur. What happened afterwards nobody knew. According to the SHO, the fate of these cases was reported back to the thana annually, but registers were not up to date and therefore, no entries had been made. Records available for the year 2000 indicated that out of twenty-two FIRs lodged that year, fifteen had been declared as *jhoot* (lie), and out of the seven for which chargesheets had been filed, two were pending, one had led to a *rajinama* (compromise) and in the remaining four cases, the accused had been acquitted. When I drew his attention to this, the SHO said, '*In case-on mein saja kahan hoti hai* [When is punishment ever given in these cases]?'

Time spent at the thana also gave me an inkling of how the indifferent and even hostile environment at the thana must have stifled many a cry for justice. To start with, the SHO and almost all his predecessors belonged to privileged castes. Going by the attitude of the last two SHOs, whom I had a chance to meet, and what one heard from the villagers, the thana police personnel tended to be on the side of the upper castes. They routinely dismissed complaints from Dalits as jhoot, refused to register their FIRs (or dictated FIRs on their own terms) and openly made disparaging comments about them. These attitudes were in sharp contrast to the official notifications prominently posted on the walls of the thana, informing the Dalits of their rights and of the assistance they could expect from the police.

The Atrocity Act has been deliberately derailed in Rajasthan. Section 4 of the Act explicitly states that a public servant who wilfully neglects his duties under the Act is liable to be severely punished. Instances of deliberate neglect are plentiful in Rajasthan, but at that time, not a single officer had been prosecuted under this section of the Act in the state.

Dalit atrocities in Rajasthan continue unchecked. According to some Dalit human rights activists, more than 50 per cent of the cases go unreported. Even in much-publicized cases—like the Kumher carnage, in which seventeen Jatavs were lynched and burnt alive by a mob in 1992—the wheels of justice move slowly and it takes decades to secure a verdict, if it happens at all. The SHRC, for its part, does not have teeth. As Mimroth puts it: 'The SHRC is just like a post office. We have sent as many as 300 cases to them from all over Rajasthan. All they do is forward the petitions to the concerned collectors or police officials and resend their replies to us. No independent enquiry is held, no relief or protection [offered] to the victims.'

Having said this, the potential power of the Atrocity Act cannot be denied. The Act empowers the Dalits and 'dominates' the dominant castes, both in terms of the intellectual argument against untouchability and in terms of the power it gives to the state and society to curb untouchability in practice. No doubt this power is resented by the dominant castes; in fact, some of them go so far as to accuse the Dalits of misusing the Act, as we saw in the conversation cited earlier in this essay. Even though stray cases of misuse cannot be ruled out, this general allegation against Dalits reflects indignation and anger at their newfound power. The power of the Act could be even greater if it was taken seriously by the authorities.

Traditional caste norms are increasingly coming into conflict with modern legal rights. Amongst Dalits, the more conscious are aware of their rights under the Constitution and this enhances their confidence. As one of them put it, '*Ab hamein samaanta ka adhikar mil gaya hai* [Now we have the right to equality].' However, legal rights require assertion on an everyday basis because others may view modern rights as a transgression from the normal. And what has been traditionally normal, they argue, is also the 'right' practice (*sahi reet hai*). In short, the legal rights of the marginalized are in contest with what is understood as right in the moral and social universe of the dominant. A legal right, however, can positively affect the understanding of what is right (*sahi*) in the moral and social universe of the villagers, as the following example illustrates.

'When we go to fill water the Bairwa women tell us to stand in the queue,' complained an affronted Jat woman. The logic of the queue, its intrinsic fairness, is outside the pale of legality. However, it can be seen as an extension of the general legal and constitutional right to equality. Insistence on maintaining the queue by the Dalits stems from the notion of it as a 'right', over and above its intrinsic fairness. Even if the latter may not impress the Jat woman who prefers the traditional norm, she may nevertheless have to respect the Dalits' insistence on the queue.

Social and political consciousness amongst Dalits has increased with the spread of education, better jobs, reservation policies, development, migration, pro-Dalit laws and political mobilization. This awareness, however, has little impact on the concerns of political parties and the state machinery. In the Lok Sabha elections that followed the Chakwada rebellion, in 2004, the two main parties in Rajasthan (BJP and Congress) fielded candidates in all the twenty-five parliamentary constituencies, but Dalit and Adivasi candidates were fielded only in reserved constituencies (four and three respectively). There was not a single exception to this.[21] Issues of social discrimination and exclusion were also absent from the agenda of these political parties.

The gram panchayat in Chakwada has also failed to uphold the legal rights of Dalits. The panchayat is governed by modern law, and the abolition of untouchability is one of its twenty-nine main duties, yet it did nothing positive to support the Dalits in the present case. On the contrary, the sarpanch and other prominent members of the panchayat are said to have been supportive of the upper castes during the entire period when the Bairwas were in crisis. It is only after the bathing right was affirmed by the administration that the husband of the sarpanch visited the Bairwas.

In the absence of timely government intervention, when incidents go unquestioned again and again even after the Dalits have drawn the attention of the administration towards them, Dalits are increasingly losing confidence in the promise of equal citizenship, especially equality before the law. The relationship of the Dalits with the state in Rajasthan has so far not taken an aggressive turn; in fact, Dalits have been respectful towards the law and no incident of violence has occurred. However, continual foot-dragging by the state functionaries and their pro-upper-caste bias may well result in Dalits being pushed towards violent forms of struggle, as has already happened in other parts of the country.[22]

A struggle for bathing rights in a public pond may seem insignificant, but in rural Rajasthan it made history. The Chakwada story carries important lessons about the predicament of Dalits at the village level and the challenges of Dalit liberation. Not least among these challenges is to link struggles for specific rights with a larger vision of social equality. In this respect, the Chakwada rebellion was somewhat restrictive as it focused specifically on the rights of the Bairwas, without really involving broad-based Dalit solidarity or a vision for wider social change. Further, women's rights did not feature at all in the entire struggle, or even in the consciousness of the resisters. It remains to be seen whether, in the future, the Dalit liberation movement will be able to overcome these limitations and pose a principled challenge to the traditional social order in Rajasthan.

Conclusion

The Chakwada story sheds some interesting light on ongoing questions that have arisen in recent sociological literature on caste, in particular the question of persistence or erosion of caste hierarchy. An influential school of thought holds that the caste system is becoming more and more a matter of 'difference' than one of 'hierarchy'. For instance, contesting the view that the caste system is made up of a single, clearly ranked hierarchy, Dipankar Gupta has argued that most castes 'proclaim exalted origins'—that they have their own perception of the caste hierarchy, often at variance with the Brahminical view—and that 'such hierarchies are idiosyncratic and *equally* valid'.[23] In other words: 'No matter which way one looks at caste, the system, such as it was supposed to have been, has clearly collapsed. Where there was once a seeming tranquillity of caste relations, ordered by a status hierarchy, howsoever localized in character, we now have a plethora of assertive caste identities, each privileging an angular hierarchy of its own.'[24]

This argument does not do justice to the complexity of the situation as it emerges in Chakwada. The existence of several 'assertive caste identities' in Chakwada does not alter the fact that there is also a well-defined hierarchy, imposed and ruthlessly enforced by the privileged castes. The Chakwada story as well as similar stories from other states in the country point out that the dominant castes in rural India are fighting tooth and nail to maintain the traditional caste hierarchy, their power and control over the rest of the village members. The inter-relationships may seem 'tranquil' up to the point when the poor attempt to give voice to the turmoil within by organizing themselves for a better deal—often to begin with economically, but also socially and politically. As 'power' begins to change houses, the contest for this power begins—to retain it or to share it—as the case may be. For the Jats of Chakwada, for instance, suppressing the Dalit rebellion was part of the assertion of their own caste identity and supremacy. It was in the name of protecting their *jati* (caste) and dharm that they came out in large numbers—as they had not done in recent times for any other reason—and also armed themselves with lathis. Their mobilization was clearly an attempt to impose their view of the caste hierarchy on others, as they had done in the past due to their economic privilege, numerical strength and political power. A similar belligerence can be observed in other parts of India; in states like Bihar where the gun culture prevails, dominant castes are coming out with guns. The indignation and anger are the same. Their motivation is also the same in at least one crucial respect—to keep those who were 'below' them in their place. Assertion of caste identities is therefore of many types and carried out with diverse motivations. When viewed from the upper or upper-middle end of the ladder, it is to break even the possibility of a transition from hierarchy to difference.

From the point of view of the disadvantaged castes, the phenomenon of 'assertive caste identities' has to be seen in the context of a rigid social system, where these castes have no choice but to cope with an identity that is given to them. For instance, proclaiming 'exalted origins' may be seen as a contestation of the prevailing caste hierarchy; but it can also be seen as a way of rationalizing and coping with one's place in the caste hierarchy—a place one can alter only in the realm of imagination. The exalted origin is something that may have existed in the past and can thus be invoked to justify aspiration for it in the future but is of little relevance to the often-dismal present.

Indeed, the issue is not just how different castes 'perceive' themselves, but also the objective power that some castes have over others. The disadvantaged castes may have their own perceptions of 'exalted origins', but they also know that they are way down in the caste hierarchy and are expected to stay there. This applies even to those amongst them who have achieved some economic mobility by getting high-placed jobs in the city and who have improved their material conditions in the village and may now look and speak like the upper classes. In the eyes of the upper castes and other castes as well, one's rank at birth based on the traditional caste hierarchy continues to be the most fundamental fact. In this sense, a Brahmin is a Brahmin and a Bairwa, ultimately a Bairwa.

Castes at the receiving end of the hierarchy are fighting the discrimination that emanates from this hierarchy and to this extent, it can be argued that they are struggling for 'difference'—a difference which may allow their castes to transcend into communities at par with others.[25] However, one finds that while on the one hand, there exists a struggle for a 'difference' in the structure, there co-exists a struggle with one's own social identity. Do those who 'assert' from within the confines of a caste identity—an identity which was given—really identify with that identity? The fact remains that they have no choice in the matter. If they had a choice, they would cast off their old identities and take on new ones—not just as myths of origin but as realities of existence.[26]

In fact, those who can, do attempt to 'cast off', to distance themselves from their pasts—from the domain of memories. Painful and humiliating, memories continue to define, defile, draw down and come in the way of stepping out as a new being in the present. The social histories of individuals and groups who have been victims of the caste system are made up of these memories. These memories can be firmly put in the past where they belong only if the current realities bear no similarities to past existence and experience. It is only when these individuals are free from all social tyrannies and are treated as humans at par with other humans, when as individuals their human worth and well-being are valued and as a group, they can stand up, that hierarchies will really be obliterated. The 'hierarchy' aspect of social identity derives from the 'differences' in opportunities that are available to different groups from the time of birth: differences in home environment, quality of education, health facilities and so on. Dalit liberation is therefore not just a matter of 'assertion', but also of changing their life circumstances.

In urban areas, where such 'differences' of actual opportunities have been reduced, some change can be discerned. But even over there, the erosion of the caste hierarchy is slow and uncertain. In fact, even here, it is mostly the cover of 'anonymity' rather than the comfortable co-existence of caste identities that enables some Dalits to avoid the oppression of a hierarchical caste system. Otherwise amicable social relations may suddenly turn sour when caste identities are revealed. This is well conveyed in *Joothan*, Omprakash Valmiki's moving autobiography, described by the author as a 'narrative of pain'. For instance, Valmiki describes an incident where a friendly conversation in a train compartment turned into abrupt silence after his fellow travellers discovered his caste. In another incident, an intimate friendship between Valmiki and a Brahmin girl came to an end after the girl discovered that he was a Dalit. 'How can you be an SC?' she asked—the girl and her family had mistaken him for a Brahmin as Valmiki is a Brahmin surname in Maharashtra.

Further, the assertion of caste identities often reflects a failure to challenge the caste system itself, either because of a lack of vision or because of the powerlessness of the disadvantaged castes. This failure was quite apparent in Chakwada. For the Bairwas, assertion (specifically, the struggle for bathing rights over the pond) was couched in the language of opposition to untouchability and discrimination and argued under the rubric of *insaniyat* (humanism), suggesting a need to distance from and go beyond the caste system. This concern for insaniyat, however, was essentially self-centred and did not stem from a general commitment to social equality: even as the Bairwas fought against untouchability insofar as it affected them, many of them continued to practice untouchability against the Bhangis. Therefore, their struggle against untouchability can be viewed as a fight for their own self-interest, but not against the principle on which it is based or the system that it is part of.

Social mobility in the Indian context results in the weakening of some features of the caste system but does not do away with the system itself. What it does is to increase understanding and thereby change the way in which a disadvantaged individual perceives her own self and her history. These revised perceptions about self and society, however, do not change the position of the person in the social hierarchy acquired at birth. The child that she gives birth to also takes on that identity even if it has lost all meaning in the changed circumstances. This identity certainly does not have the old meaning; whether it can acquire a new meaning de-linked from the old is a question which at present can only have an uncertain answer. At present the old system is being retained in a new garb. The question is: can redefinition happen within the confines of the old system, or can new definitions be born only when the old system and the premises on which it was based are discarded?

5

Ekaki

The Pain of Lonesome Marginality*

The notion of marginality essentially means that you do not count. You are on the margins. On the edges, you are of marginal interest, unlike the main characters around whom the story revolves. Those on the margins are often alone with their pain, seen yet unseen, part of the whole, yet excluded. Even though the jagged rough edges of these marginal lives are not expected to speak, sometimes they do. Sometimes they not only speak but tear, pierce and break the silence, and in doing so, strike out a path for themselves and others in similar pain. The story of the widows of rural India is something like that.

This essay presents an account of social action with rural widows in Bhiloda taluka (north Gujarat), led by Shramjivi Mahila Sangathan, the women's wing of Shramjivi Samaj, a union of agricultural labourers and marginal farmers. This effort took place in the late 1980s when years of drought drew our attention to the

---

* This chapter is adapted from two essays published in the late 1990s (Bhatia, 1998c, 1998d). It draws on my experience of work with Shramjivi Samaj in rural Gujarat in the second half of the 1980s.

extreme vulnerability of rural widows. The essay also includes a brief discussion of widows and land rights in the Narmada Valley. Before turning to collective action, two individual stories may help to convey the social isolation that many widows experience in rural India.

A Child Widow and an Alleged Witch

Called *ekaki* (a woman alone) in north Gujarat, the lonesome nature of a widow's life at once becomes clear. Most widows have to face a personal tragedy with multiple dimensions—emotional, economic and social—compounded by social and governmental neglect. The stories below (one from Bihar and one from Gujarat) illustrate their vulnerable lives and lonely struggles.

Rampuneet Devi: A Bhumihar Child Widow

I met Rampuneet Devi in 1992 in a village where she had sought refuge after fleeing from Mujamallika village (Saraiya block, Muzaffarpur district, Bihar), where she came as a bride at the age of sixteen, thirty-four years earlier. Of the Bhumihar caste, Rampuneet Devi was widowed after eight days of marriage. She continued to live in the same house because her father-in-law was a kind man who ensured that she had a respectful position in the house. Her brother-in-law was then unmarried. Even after his marriage, they continued to live peacefully for twenty-five years while her father-in-law was alive.

After his death, the quarrels began. With time, these became more frequent and intense. Verbal abuse would often be followed by physical beatings, mainly from her sister-in-law, who would shout and say, 'Get out. You have no rights here.' Her brother-in-law started threatening her and telling her to transfer her share of the land—six bighas—to his name. She refused. For the next six years, these exchanges became a daily routine. Around midnight, one day, she was woken up and summoned to their room. As she told me:

Suddenly they jumped on me—all three of them, my sister-in-law, her daughter and her daughter-in-law. They pulled my hair and threw me on the floor. One of them sat on my chest and the other held my feet. Hot scalding water, which had been boiled with chilli-powder, was then thrown on me. I was almost unconscious. Meanwhile, my brother-in-law and the daughter-in-law's father also came in, but they did not intervene.

Our neighbours, fortunately, heard my cries for help and came to my rescue. They put me in a hired jeep and rushed me to the police station. An FIR was filed. I had to be hospitalized for many weeks and had to borrow Rs 35,000 from some of our caste leaders to meet the hospital expenses.

My brother-in-law was sent to jail, but he quickly managed to bribe his way out. I heard that he gave Rs 10,000 to the district superintendent of police, Rs 10,000 to the doctor, Rs 14,000 to the *daroga* (police officer) and distributed Rs 20,000 amongst a few distinguished members of the village. Five kathas of land were also given to two other persons as a reward for their help. Out of fear, I could not go back to Mujamallika.

When I met her, Rampuneet Devi was living in a seed store made available to her as a shelter by an influential member of the village where she had taken refuge. By then, other incidents had occurred: her rice crop had been forcibly harvested by her brother-in-law, saplings were uprooted from a field she had painstakingly sown, she was prevented from using the wood of a tree she had got felled to make a bed in her new dwelling, and so on. Her brother-in-law had also induced local officials to ignore her application for her due share of her husband's land, even after she paid the prescribed fees with some difficulty. He was able to misuse his unjust power over her because there was nobody to question him or support her. The caste leaders did not help her (some even supported her brother-in-law), nor did the police take any action on her complaints.

Despite her circumstances, Rampuneet Devi continued to fight back doggedly. She had filed two cases in the local court against her in-laws. Summing up her experience, she said: 'Nobody is bothered about the destitute and the helpless. I do not have a husband or a son, and so I do not have any *pratishtha* [respect]. For fear of loss of the pratishtha of the whole village, the people of the village tried to prevent my aggressors from being jailed. My running away from the village and living here has also incensed them since they feel that their pratishtha has been ruined. But the assault, humiliation and ordeals I have suffered in that village did not affect their pratishtha. Now I do not want to go back and face the possibility of further assault. All I want is my *haq* [rights].'

Rampuneet Devi's resolve was inspiring. The support she received from her brother's family was crucial to sustain her through adversity, but so was her fighting spirit. The fact that she had received some school education also contributed to her confidence. This was apparent in the words she often used while describing herself, the words I remember every time I think of her: '*Main bhi satmi pass hun. Padhi-likhi, hoshiar, kabil* [I have also passed the seventh standard. I am educated, intelligent and capable].' At the same time, the odds against her were heavy and perhaps it was only because she left the village that her life was saved—unlike that of Ratanben, thousands of miles away in Gujarat.

Ratanben: An Adivasi Widow Branded as a Witch

An Adivasi widow from north Gujarat, Ratanben tried every possible step to defy the oppression she faced. A grim struggle ensued, ending in her murder in July 1990. What follows is an edited extract from the *panchnama* (document prepared by an official called the panch) recorded on the night of her murder.

On the night of 20 July 1990, widow Ratanben Jeevabhai Asari was murdered in village Vejpur (Bhiloda taluka, Sabarkantha district) in Gujarat. Her murder was '*iradapurvak*' (with premeditation). Before attempting to kill her, the murderers ensured that all electricity connections were disrupted. The bulb outside her house had been removed and thrown away. A bamboo stick was used to disconnect the wires in the nearby electric pole.

A leather belt, used to tie bullocks, was used to exert pressure on her neck in order to kill her. Her ribs and chest showed evidence of severe beating, perhaps with wooden poles. There were injuries on her chest and stomach. Blood was oozing out of her mouth. The nails of her hands had turned black.

It was clear that more than one person was involved in her murder. After she died, her body was brought to the room at the rear of her house and laid on the bed, with a *chadar* (sheet) draped over it, as though she were sleeping, so as not to attract any suspicion. It would seem that the murder was committed by those who were close to Ratanben.

All the above-mentioned injuries were seen by present residents of Vejpur, Ratanben's son and all the relatives who had come from her natal village, Andharia.

Ratanben, a stockily built woman in her mid-forties, used to live in her *sasural* (in-laws' house) at Vejpur village. Her husband, Jeevabhai Babrabhai, died in 1983. Her son, a government employee, used to live outside Sabarkantha district; her daughter was married and lived in her own sasural. As a result, Ratanben used to live by herself in Vejpur. She used to survive by leasing her land to a sharecropper. (Living alone in these villages is not an easy proposition. Houses tend to be far apart because local Adivasis generally build their homes in the midst of their respective fields.)

The police report alludes to a land dispute within the family as a possible motive for the murder. The dispute was about the distribution of land belonging to Ratanben's father-in-law, Babrabhai Asari. The land had been distributed earlier between his three sons, but the land records had not been updated. The land apportioned to Ratanben's husband was thirty-seven *gunthas* (a local area unit) and had been cultivated by Ratanben and her husband for many years.

After her husband died, Ratanben's father-in-law agreed to enter the names of her son and daughter in the land records as the rightful heirs of their deceased father's land. But when the formal process was initiated by Ratanben, her *diyar* (younger brother-in-law) Dharmabhai induced the *talati* (revenue officer of the village panchayat) to enter his name instead. When Ratanben learnt about this, she wrote complaints objecting to her diyar's claims over her land. It is possible that this act of rebellion led some of her in-laws to plan or instigate Ratanben's murder.

The animosity Ratanben's brothers-in-law felt against her soon after she was widowed is evident from various incidents. One such incident occurred on 18 May 1984, when Punjabhai (son of Hirabhai, Ratanben's elder brother-in-law) physically assaulted Ratanben's son, Nanjibhai and threatened to kill him. Nanjibhai reported this to the *mukhi* (traditional police) of the village.

The following day, the village elders and caste leaders met to bring about an amicable solution to the conflict, as is customary in the community. But Punjabhai refused to sign the *samadhan patra* (a statement recording the terms of reconciliation), scuttling the whole effort. In the years that followed, the harassment continued.

In early 1990, Hirabhai died. This led to new tensions. Her diyar accused Ratanben of being a *dakan* (witch) and threatened to kill her, saying '*Jamin mara namai karvani chai. Tema koi dakhal giri karish to goli mari nakhis* [My name should be entered in the land records. If anyone interferes, I will shoot them].'

Ratanben's brothers had tried to persuade her to move to her natal village and live with them, but she was determined to remain in her sasural and claim her legitimate right over land. Unfortunately, both the community and the government failed to respond to her brave assertion of rights.

Single Women Fight Back

Shramjivi Samaj

Shramjivi Samaj, as the name suggests, is a union of agricultural labourers and marginal farmers who survive from their *shram* (labour). Active in Bhiloda and Idar talukas of Sabarkantha district in north Gujarat, this union consists of people belonging to the disadvantaged castes and communities of the rural society in Sabarkantha.[1]

This organization was formed after a subaltern movement of twenty-seven landless Bhambi (Chamar) families of Mau village in Bhiloda taluka, who successfully claimed forty-six acres of *gochar* (pasture) land in their village in 1974. This movement gave a big boost to land-related struggles in the area. The Dalit leaders of this movement subsequently played a crucial role in many land struggles, especially a historic land struggle initiated in the late 1970s for the implementation of a progressive GR of 1962.[2] This GR stipulated that land submerged by a medium-sized local dam on the Hathmati River, which became available for cultivation every year during the dry season, should be distributed among the landless and small farmers of the area for cultivation on a yearly contractual basis. This struggle faced strong opposition from the upper castes, who had occupied that land earlier.

This land struggle involved the mobilization of Dalits, Adivasis and other disadvantaged groups in the surrounding villages, and had to face severe repression. They were ultimately successful in taking possession of nearly 1400 acres of land. This struggle culminated in the formation of eight agricultural cooperative societies in 1981 and of Shramjivi Samaj in 1983.[3]

Women (including single women) of all the concerned castes, tribes and communities had participated in these struggles wholeheartedly. The cooperative society that was formed after the Mau struggle consisted of members of all the twenty-seven Bhambi families including four widows. The first *karobari* (working committee) had seven members, two of whom were women; one was a widow named Rajiben. Currently, eight of the twenty-seven members of the Mau Cooperative Society are widows.

In all the eight agricultural cooperative societies of the Shramjivi Samaj, widowed women are members and have a share in the land like any other member. In fact, in the joint cooperative of Kalidungri and Janali Tanda villages, where members are mostly Adivasis and Vanjaras, widows were given an extra share because their economic condition was particularly poor and a large amount of land was available. These women lease out their land to sharecroppers. The sharecropper is usually a member of the widow's *kutumb* (extended family) and also of the cooperative. The widow and her children also work as labourers on the cooperative land, for which they get wages like everyone else.

Notwithstanding some sensitivity to the plight of widows, the male leadership of the land movement failed to recognize women as equal members of the movement. Women were not treated at par with men, whether in the membership, decision-making or leadership roles. This omission was not deliberate but more a reflection of inadequate consciousness of women's capabilities and the value of gender equality.

In late 1984, however, the seeds of a women's wing of the union were sown. This was facilitated when Setu, a small non-governmental organization based in Ahmedabad, started giving non-financial support to Shramjivi Samaj. In practice, this took the form of women activists of Setu working as an integral part of the Shramjivi Samaj team. This eventually led to the formation of Shramjivi Mahila Sangathan (union of working-class women), the women's wing of Shramjivi Samaj.[4]

Shramjivi Mahila Sangathan started in eight villages and soon spread to around twenty villages of Bhiloda taluka. The first few years of the Sangathan were indelibly marked by a severe drought in 1986–88. This had a direct bearing on the issues that were taken up by the Sangathan in its initial phase, such as mobilization for the implementation of drought-relief worksites, just and timely wages, removal of corruption at relief worksites, effective functioning of the public distribution system, adequate drinking water facilities, etc.

These years of mass impoverishment in rural Gujarat highlighted the plight of those who suffered the most. As women activists, we had intimate insights into the lives of women in the Sangathan. In village after village, we could not help but notice that households of single women were the worst affected. Towards the end of the drought, one of the Sangathan villages was part of a larger study on widows in rural India, which further contributed to our awareness of their condition.[5]

This awareness had to be translated into action. But first, it was necessary to understand the problem in greater depth and confer with women in the Sangathan, especially those who were single. To start with, the issue was brought up at the Sangathan's village-level meetings. There it was felt that the best thing would be to bring single women from as many villages as possible on to one platform—a *sammelan* (mass gathering) at the taluka headquarters in Bhiloda. This open forum, it was hoped, would give women an opportunity to explain their situation and discuss it with government representatives from the taluka, district and state levels.

The Sammelan

The sammelan took place on 18 November 1988. Prior to that, a village-to-village campaign was launched in the forty-odd villages where Shramjivi Samaj worked. Also, in order to cover the entire taluka, a small group of single women and other members of Shramjivi Mahila Sangathan prepared a *patrika* (leaflet) explaining the problem, calling for change and proposing specific demands. This patrika was distributed far and wide.

The response was tremendous. Women came to the sammelan in large numbers and some even came with small children. Rajput women, who are not allowed to go out of their houses, also had the courage to come for the meeting. Brahmin and Dalit women sat side by side and shared their problems. The participants also included *niradhar* (destitute) men and women, the physically or mentally disadvantaged and even tuberculosis patients. About 500–700 women attended the meeting.

In Their Own Words

The sammelan was inaugurated by Kamliben, an old widow of the Vanjara caste and one of the leading members of the Shramjivi Mahila Sangathan. Kamliben and the Sangathan activists encouraged women participants to speak. The sammelan was to be 'their' gathering.

Asking the women to describe their own situation was no small request. For many of them, this was the first public event of their lives.[6] Some had also come to the taluka headquarters for the first time. It was an act of courage for them to speak knowing that a speaker would have to get up in front of the whole crowd and speak into the microphone, that her voice would carry as far as the local market, and that the audience included not only fellow women but men from various villages, invited officials from the taluka and district headquarters, and countless spectators and bystanders who had stopped to watch and listen to this unusual gathering.[7]

Under these difficult circumstances, it was heartening to see women from different castes and communities get up to speak. Their halting words gave us a small glimpse of their lives. Here are some excerpts:

> *Hun ugadi padi. Sasu-sasra koi nathi. Balka chai. Koina sahara nathi* [I was thrown in the open. I have no mother or father-in-

law, nobody is there. I have children. I do not have the support of anybody].

—Laxmiben

Balka nathi ane vidhwa chun. Mari saame jo jo [I have no children and I am a widow. Take care of me].

—Muliben

I have been a widow for the last five years. We do not have enough food to eat. If some government help comes our way, our situation may improve. I do not have land or any other property. I do not have a son either. Please do something.

—Khemiben

After I became a widow, my mother- and father-in-law, as well as my elder brother-in-law harassed me, severely beat me and forcibly took possession of the plot of land that had previously been given to me by the government. As a result, I lost some of my teeth. I live by myself in my house. I do not have any support from anyone.

—Kamlaben

I was widowed fifteen years ago. Another sister of mine has separated from her husband. What help can we expect from our brothers? We hope we will get some assistance from the government.

—Shardaben

We are Rajputs, so we cannot do any labour work. I have a house but no land.

—Kamlaben

How many women are suffering in this world? Rajput women are prevented from going out of the house due to the

restrictions of our community. The government has ignored so
many women.

—A woman from a Rajput caste

We have come here with the hope that the government will be able
to provide us with some support. One man had come and filled
out a form. He asked me to get a certificate from the doctor, so I
got him that; he later asked me to get a photograph and I got that
also. In spite of all these efforts, in the end nothing happened. The
money spent on transport was also wasted.

—Ramilaben

Women who had received pensions under a government scheme
were not too happy either:

I got a pension for six months, then no more. Why was it
discontinued, is what I would like to know. What do we eat now?

—Gangaben

The government gave me monetary support only for six months,
that too only Rs 60 per month. What can we do with so little
money? We should get more than that.

—Meenaben

Drawing attention to the plight of separated and divorced women,
Maniben, who lived in her parental village with her daughter, said:
'Women who are divorced or separated from their husbands often
have no support from their families. They should be provided
employment by the government.'

Many women were anxious because they were unable to pay for
their children's schooling. Though elementary education was free,
it still entailed some expenses for school uniforms, notebooks and
even transport. Their attempt to get scholarships for their children

often failed, as several testimonies revealed. Maniben, who is from a tribal village, said that she had spent over Rs 50 on her son's scholarship form, yet he did not qualify because—she was told—he had low marks.[8]

Some women stressed that they had spent a lot on transport to come for this meeting and that they would not like to go away without any of their hopes being met. Other speakers pointed out that rallies held by men were not unusual, but similar occasions for women were indeed extraordinary.

The first-hand testimonies of single women drew attention to many painful aspects of their daily lives, including poverty and hunger, harsh treatment from in-laws, alienation from land and other property, lack of support from their parental home, anxiety about children's upbringing, caste-based social restrictions, worries about debts, sexual harassment and above all a lonely existence. Some of them used the revealing expression 'ugadi padi' to describe their situation. Literally, this means 'out in the open'. This expresses the lack of security and support a woman often feels after becoming a widow—a feeling that she has to fend for herself against all odds.

These women survived by dint of incredible strength. Unfortunately, they had little else to help them change their situation. Still, the sammelan lit a small spark of hope.

What followed

After the sammelan, our first aim was to support widows in their collective demand for pensions.[9] As a starter, the Sangathan focused on a simple yet challenging step: helping as many widows as possible to send their pension application forms, duly completed, to the social security office. This line of action had some chance of success, and was less likely to lead to family or community tensions than, say, claiming land rights. We were clear, however, that this was only the starting point. Other areas of intervention we had in mind included improvements in the pension scheme, inclusion of single women in the BPL list, and greater control of single women over land.[10] Plans were also made to build a sustained campaign on these issues with other women's groups in Gujarat.

In the following months, the Sangathan was able to get pensions for over three hundred widows as well as over a hundred destitute elderly women. Prior to 1988, only five to eight pensions had been sanctioned in the whole district each year, on average. This experience helped us to understand all the frustrations involved in applying for a pension.

Initially, it was difficult to get copies of the prescribed application form from the Samaj Suraksha (Social Security) office at Himmatnagar, the district headquarters. The staff followed a 'one person, one form' policy. After the sammelan, they agreed to provide multiple copies and also allowed the Sangathan to photocopy the form.

While helping women to fill these forms (most of them were illiterate), we became aware of the difficulties they experienced in this simple task. To mention a few: the process requires the applicant to get various *dakhlas* (certificates) from the talati and the sarpanch. This constrains them to make numerous trips in search of these officials, which they describe as '*dhakka khava pade chai*' (futile comings and goings).[11] Often they are expected to pay bribes. These corrupt practices declined significantly after women started resisting them with the backing of the Sangathan.

After the form is submitted with all the required annexures, the *chakasni* (verification) process leads to further ordeals, delays and frustrations. Concerned officials lack concern, forms languish in drawers, and applicants are sent from pillar to post. On one occasion, a few forms were declared 'lost' because the responsible officer had been transferred. Even after the application is verified and forwarded to the district headquarters, it often takes over a year before the *sahay* (help) is granted, or 'passed' as local people call it. The Sangathan had to be vigilant and keep urging officers to expedite the process.

Every pensioner is expected to join some training programme and submit an attendance certificate. Only then does the pension continue for three years. Even during that limited period, pension payments are often irregular.

The Sangathan also fought for better access of widows to the public distribution system (PDS). Two thousand women participated in a rally on this in Himmatnagar, demanding a regular supply of the stipulated quota. Eleven women also went on indefinite fast outside the district collectorate. The demand was met, but only by diverting PDS supplies from neighbouring talukas. This drew our attention to the need for policy-level intervention and a larger campaign for a just PDS. We also learnt that many widows found it hard to secure their fair share of the monthly PDS quota from other family members who shared the same ration card. This led the Sangathan to demand official recognition of single women as household heads with their own ration cards. Similarly, single women demanded their own BPL cards and employment under the Jawahar Rojgar Yojana, with varying success. Some of them even contested gram panchayat elections.

A few months after the sammelan, we conducted a quick survey to assess the impact of the pension campaign and other actions. Many single women felt that earning a pension improved their economic security, self-confidence and status in the family. The campaign was also remembered by many widows as an empowering experience. These actions increased their awareness of the possibilities of change, and perhaps more importantly, they gave widows a sense of togetherness and collective power.[12] This increased awareness also brought to light more difficult challenges (for example, related to caste restrictions and land rights), which the Sangathan was not always able to take up effectively.

Some Unresolved Issues

The Shramjivi Mahila Sangathan was able to address some of the problems which destitute single women perceived to be the most important. However, in the course of our campaign and survey, we became acutely conscious of several unresolved issues. Some of them are as follows.

Land Rights

In Bhiloda, women's awareness of their land rights is low. Most women 'renounce' their inheritance rights to a share of their father's land (in favour of their brothers) as a matter of course.[13] As a general rule, there is no practice of including the names of women, whether single or married, in the land records.

It is only after becoming a widow that a woman is recognized to have some right to her husband's land and even that usually takes the form of usufructuary rights only, to be shared with the sons. It is extremely rare for a widow to have her name entered in the land records after her husband's death. Even the realization of these usufructuary rights often depends on the 'goodwill' of her brothers-in-law, especially if her sons are young, even though their help is not given for free—she usually enters a sharecropping contract with them. These usufructuary rights are almost non-existent in the case of a childless widow, especially if she is young—childless widows are encouraged and sometimes forced to return to their natal village. Similarly, the chances of fair treatment are considerably reduced in the case of a widow who has only daughters. Upon widowhood, therefore, the woman is seen to have access to the land only through her sons. She is not seen to have a right of her own but is more of a caretaker of the rights of her sons.

Deprivation of land rights is an even more serious problem for separated, deserted and divorced women. Unlike widows, these women are not even recognized to have any usufructuary or other rights on their former husband's land. The plight of such women— barred from access to land, both in the natal village as well as in the husband's village—is truly miserable.

Aside from having very restricted customary rights to land, a widow is often a victim of harassment and collective violence by her in-laws (including women), who are usually keen to grab as much of her land as possible. An extreme form of such harassment is the practice of witch-hunting in the Adivasi community.[14] In Bhiloda, we woke up to this when Ratanben (mentioned earlier) was brutally killed.

While the Sangathan was successful in building up public opinion against the culprits and their heinous acts, it failed to achieve justice through legal or other means. The nexus between government officials and the police on one hand and the culprits and their accomplices (including caste panchayat leaders) on the other, and the fear of the villagers to stand witness, combined with the absence of effective laws and policies against witch-hunting, all contributed to our failure to bring the culprits to book.[15] Ratanben's own relatives, who were initially interested in taking up the issue, were not able to see it through. Aside from the specific problem of witch-hunting, the general issue of women's land rights has not been effectively addressed by the Sangathan so far. All the attempts that were made to work on this issue brought home to us its complex, challenging and potentially conflictual nature.

Children's Needs

Many destitute single women are very anxious about the needs of their children, especially the need for education.[16] A widow often has to withdraw her children from school soon after being widowed due to economic hardship. Many children of widows and other destitute single women end up working (e.g., grazing cattle, collecting wood or doing wage labour in nearby towns) in order to supplement the family income. The need to work at an early age affects the well-being and future of these children, especially in the case of occupations where children are overworked, exploited or exposed to health hazards.

Child Marriage

Child marriage remains common in Gujarat, despite legislation against it. In 1983–84 alone, 1231 complaints of child marriage were received by the department of social security in Sabarkantha district. And this is only the tip of the iceberg since most cases of child marriage go unrecorded.[17]

It is worth mentioning that the reason for the persistence of child marriages is not so much that the families involved consider child marriage to be a good thing. In many cases, the main reason is simply convenience: marrying a child at a young age, usually at the same time as his or her elder sibling(s), makes it possible to avoid an expensive marriage.

The persistence of child marriages creates a special problem of widowhood in the younger age groups. The plight of young widows is particularly harsh among the higher castes, where remarriage is prohibited even if the widow is childless.

Social Attitudes and Norms

Most widows have to suffer being treated as inferior members of society. Some symptoms of low social status that are frequently mentioned by widows are: not being able to participate on an equal basis in social occasions, being expected to wear austere clothing, generally being treated as an inauspicious person, having to constantly project the image of a suffering woman and restricting social interaction (even with children, in the case of some childless widows).

These oppressive norms and attitudes are very difficult to challenge. They are particularly difficult to challenge for individual widows on their own, given the enormous pressure to conform. The only hope for change is some form of collective action. The chances of success will be greater if married women are as involved as the widows themselves. Even better would be to involve men as well as women.

The Role of Caste Panchayats

In some parts of rural India, caste panchayats (*jati panchayat*) still play an active role in governing the social life of their members. These panchayats are guided either by a set of written rules called a *bandharan* (constitution) or by unwritten rules which have been passed on to the current generation by oral tradition. The customary law laid down by these caste panchayats is as important as modern law in terms of practical impact on social life. This applies in particular to the social practices that affect widows.

I was able to study look at caste panchayats of four castes and communities: Bhambis, Adivasis, Rajputs and Vankars.

Bhambis

The Bhambi caste has a bandharan (its latest version is dated 1991), which along with the unwritten rules of this caste, governs a wide range of social practices, including marriage and remarriage.[18] The normal procedure of widow remarriage is as follows.

Six months after the death of the husband, remarriage proceedings can be initiated; while the first marriage is called *lagan*, the second one is called *natru*. As a first step, the widow is taken to her *pihar* (mother's house or village), where her parents or brothers—whoever may be there—ask her if she wishes to remarry. If she does, the permission of the in-laws is sought. Normally they agree and then both families search for a suitable husband.

Usually, widows who are still young and childless are ready to remarry. There is no pressure on the widow either way (note also that there is no practice of leviratic remarriage—marriage with the dead husband's brother—amongst the Bhambis). If the widow wishes to remarry, her brothers (*pihar paksh*) and her brothers-in-law (*sasri paksh*) are involved; the pihar paksh are never alone in this. In the final stage, the decision is taken by the caste leaders of her present *sasri* (marital) village and the village into which she is being married. The objective of the meeting of the caste leaders of the two villages is to take an assurance from the family and the community in which the widow remarries that they are responsible for her happiness and that she will be treated respectfully.

If a widow is taken as a second wife because the first wife cannot bear children, then a written *dastavej* (agreement) is taken from the man and the family in which she is being married. As witnesses, signatures are taken from leaders of the village, representatives of her pihar and the family elders in the old sasri. If the agreement is broken, then initially an attempt is made to sort things out at the village level, and if this fails, the matter is taken up at the *samaj* level because the samaj is considered to have the ultimate responsibility (samaj here refers to the whole jati panchayat).

The Bhambi panchayat is an example of a caste panchayat that has remained quite active and involved in social reform, perhaps because some of its members have also been members of Shramjivi Samaj. The caste panchayat has been meeting regularly, taking up cases of transgression of social norms and changing the written norms laid down in the constitution from time to time. The social condition of widows is intimately related to this process.

Adivasis

Unlike the Bhambi Samaj, the Adivasi Samaj does not have a very active panchayat. A bandharan was constituted around 1914,

applicable to 220 villages, but it has not been revised since. Some of
the rules laid down in the bandharan—e.g., having an annual general
body meeting—used to be observed in the past but are increasingly
ignored. This declining influence of the panchayat can be attributed
to the increasing non-Adivasi influence on the community (e.g.,
through modern education and Christian missionaries) and the
growing reliance on modern institutions such as the courts and the
police to solve local conflicts. Some Adivasi leaders feel that the
panchayat no longer exercises an important influence on the social
life of their community (*samaj ni koi pakkar nathi*).

The failure of the Adivasi panchayat in playing a progressive
role as far as widows are concerned became dramatically clear after
Ratanben's murder. The panchayat did not take any action, even
though it was strongly suspected that Ratanben's murder had been
instigated by some of her in-laws, who had accused her of being a
witch. Many of the community leaders believe in witches and some
of them are known to have taken part in harassment, including
murder, of female relatives accused of witchcraft. In Ratanben's case,
the leaders deliberately turned a blind eye despite being fully aware
of the facts. As one of them commented, '*Sasla nai badha pakde, pan
sihn nai kon pakadwa jai* [Everyone is ready to catch a rabbit, but
who will chase a lion]?'

Rajputs

The Rajputs of Bhiloda taluka have no written bandharan, no active
caste panchayat, and no recognized leaders. However, there is still a
strict code of behaviour which most members of the caste know and
abide by. This code of behaviour severely restricts what women can
do. For instance, married Rajput women are not allowed to go out of
the house (some of them told me that they did not even know where
the family fields were), remarry, divorce or take up wage employment.
They also play a subordinate role within the household. In sharp

contrast, married men are free from any restrictions of this kind and are even allowed to have several wives (one old Rajput in Bhiloda taluka is said to have had thirteen wives).

The case of the Rajputs illustrates the fact that social norms can be very strong even in the absence of a formal caste panchayat. Thus, social change among these communities will have to be brought about by other institutions.

Vankars

Like the Bhambis, the Vankars (weavers) have active caste panchayats. The Vankars in the area are divided into Ramanandis (who worship Ram) and Pranamis (who worship Krishna). The Ramanandis constituted a bandharan twenty-five years ago when about 5000 of them assembled together and conferred for ten days. This bandharan was revised in 1987 when separate bandharans were written for different groups of villages. The Pranamis have different bandharans, even though they intermarry with the Ramanandis.

The bandharans of the Vankars include sections dealing with widow remarriage, divorce and related matters. The existence of these written rules and their continued influence on social practices provide some scope for reform, in so far as future revisions of these bandharans may be used as an opportunity to foster progressive changes.

Widows and Land Rights in the Narmada Valley

The unjust treatment of widows within the family, caste and community finds reflection in public policy. As discussed in Chapter 10 (Forced Evictions in the Narmada Valley), even the relatively progressive resettlement policy of the Sardar Sarovar Project in the Narmada Valley has failed to recognize widows as household heads and omits them from the very definition of project-affected persons except as dependents. There again, I observed how the denial of land rights placed widows in a condition of extreme vulnerability.

Consider Kashiben Mansukhbhai of Surpan village in the Narmada area of Gujarat. She was one of the intrepid few who resisted displacement. Kashiben did not get any compensation land because she is a widow and is not considered the head of a household, in spite of the land being in her name. Her younger son, with whom she lives, was below eighteen in 1987, and therefore, not eligible for compensation either. 'Without land, I will not go,' she said firmly when I met her in 1993.

The resettlement policy of the Narmada Valley Project in Gujarat prescribes that a widow who lost her husband before 1980 cannot be counted as a household head and must be considered a dependent. Widows like Kashiben, even if they are *khatedar* (registered landowners), are not entitled to land compensation—the same rule applies to house ownership. If a widow is counted as a dependent but is not, in fact, being taken care of by her sons or other relatives, her situation is very precarious.

The resettlement policy also prescribes that major sons who were below the age of eighteen in 1987 are not entitled to compensation. According to local tribal customs, a widow is normally looked after by her youngest son. In a situation where the youngest son was below the age of eighteen in 1987, neither he nor his widowed mother are entitled to compensation. Many widows in the submerged villages and the resettlement sites suffer, in diverse ways, as a result of this anti-women policy. I have heard the question over and over again, 'If our men were alive, would they also be treated in this way?' Widows have been assumed to live with their sons and their families and to be well taken care of by them. In reality, the situation of many widows is quite different.

Sanchiben Dhorabhai presently resides in the Kamboya Kuwa resettlement site with her only son Naran Dhora. She is a *khatedar* and used to own sixteen acres of land in her own village before resettlement. However, she has not received either cash or land as compensation for being displaced. The main reason given to her is that she was widowed prior to 1980. Her son, Naran Dhora, has received only five acres of land—three acres of which is uncultivable. Neither the mother's rights nor the son's have been respected.

The situation of Januben Bacchubhai of Nishad *falia* (hamlet) in Gadher village is no better. Januben is fifty-five years old and a widow. She herself has a land title for sixteen acres. Januben showed me two different notices she had received from the government. The first notice, dated 21 February 1990, informed her that she had been declared as a 'project-affected person' (PAP) and that she could select five acres of land for resettlement. This notice gave her only ten days to accomplish the selection. The second notice, dated 25 January 1993, informed her that because she had major sons, her name had been omitted from the PAP list dated 20 July 1989.

Naniben Makanbhai is a blind sixty-year-old widow and a resident of Mandir falia of Surpan. Before she lost him, her husband was given seven acres of land at the Ambawadi resettlement site. But when he died, instead of Naniben's name being entered in the land records, the name of her eldest son, Chuna Makan, had been entered. Chuna Makan has now moved to the resettlement site with his family and does not take care of Naniben. Naniben, who is deprived of land rights, lives in Surpan as a dependent of her youngest son, Bacchu.

Similar is the story of Rukiben Jhinga, the mother of Varsan Jhinga, who has been a widow for twelve years. Her husband had received a sum of Rs 6776 as compensation for his 3.2 acres of land, and Rs 4742 for the house. The money was deposited in his bank account. After his death, the account was transferred to the name of his youngest son, Varsanbhai. Rukiben now lives as a dependent of Varsanbhai. Had the account been transferred to her name, she would have had a source of economic security and would have been less dependent on the goodwill of her son for her survival.

Even widows who have been allotted land are not completely secure. Lalliben, originally a resident of Gadher village, was allotted land in Kasata village. However, her son Ambalal was allotted land in Kamboya Kuwa, which is 30 km away, three years earlier. How can she go and live alone in Kasata? Lalliben has preferred to remain with Ambalal and to leave her Kasata land uncultivated.

It is not clear how these widows are expected to survive in the new sites. They have not been recognized as household heads and have been totally omitted from the definition of an oustee family, except as dependents. In many cases, their sons have been resettled at different sites.

Concluding Remarks

Most of the women mentioned in this chapter are fighting for their basic survival—their right to exist. They are all victims of patriarchy at its worst, whether it be within the family, caste, community or even in public policy. These women draw our attention to the predicament of a very large number of widows and single women—there were 43 million widows in India at the time of the 2011 Census, and their number is likely to be even larger today.[19]

These women have also, through their own example, shown us the power of individual and collective action. There is scope for action of different types—from small steps such as fighting for pensions to more radical demands such as equal land rights. The primary concerns and demands of single women also include dignity and respect. These psychological and social aspects of well-being are of great significance even for those who live extremely deprived lives in material terms. Be it Ratanben, Rampuneet Devi or Kashiben, each of them stood up for their right to dignity against all odds.

When we are talking of the marginality of women, we must bear in mind that a woman is up against 'intimate enemies', and this is particularly so in the case of widows. A widow's family, the most basic unit of succour and support, itself becomes her battlefield, for a battle that largely remains invisible. The caste, community or neighbourhood are also on the side of the dominant male members of her family. Other female members who could have been her allies are also vulnerable and often turn against her as well. The torture of Rampuneet Devi and the murder of Ratanben are extreme examples of the fate that often strikes those who dare to rebel against the established order.

6

In the Crevices of the City*

What does it feel to be a part, yet apart? To belong but with uncertainty? A philosopher would perhaps argue that such is the nature of belonging, and yet it is to such pegs that the human being hangs on to, or hangs herself on—for life!

However, there are many who live lives more uncertain than most. As India is becoming a land of opportunities, even to NRIs, there are those who never left her shores—nor their wretchedness—behind. Among them are the slum dwellers: a sea of people who live in a *kacchi basti*, *jhuggi-jhopadi*, or *jhopadpatti*, as slums are known in some parts of India, tucked away in the crevices of the city. Many of them live and die in the by-lanes of non-existence, grappling with life. They are seen—perhaps every day—but remain unseen, often forgotten by history and commentary.

Delhi city. A rickshaw puller dies while pedalling because he has no money to treat his diabetes. Childhood passes by as young girls labour on mundane jobs to keep their families alive. Mothers take on

---

* Initially written in 2007 and partly published at that time in an article co-authored with Jean Drèze ('Rang de Basti', *Hindustan Times*, 7 May 2007). Sanjay Basti is alive and well—demolition plans are still on hold. I lived there for seven years, from late 2000 onwards.

more acceptable Hindu names in order to get domestic work, looking after other homes and kids while their own are left unattended in capricious dwellings. Unemployed youth dream wistful dreams as they take another drag of a harmful drug. Puffs of smoke. Wasted lives. Happiness that does not last long enough. Human potential is lost to humanity.

Officially, there are about 675 slums in Delhi. These settlements throb with pulsating life close up but are invisible from the flyovers and official maps. They came into existence as waves of impoverished landless or near-landless rural folk made their way to the city, hoping for a better existence. Children laboured with their parents to build a life. Some were able to make sturdier homes. But lasting security remained elusive and displacement a constant threat.

Their lives—shaped by their ingenuity and labour—are brave attempts at remaining 'legal'. Legality requires proof at every turn, even as they ward off pressures that pull them into the vortex of 'illegality'. People know well how the system works. They have seen how the police and political representatives can be accomplices of drug dealers, real estate owners, and others who exploit them and keep them down. 'Law' often enters their lives like the lash of a cruel whip in the shape of a false case or crime they did not commit.

A *basti* is a mosaic of many stories that draw us into the worlds of working children and youth, single women, a range of degrading and unrewarding occupations, sex workers, untreated illness, disability, self-taught intellectuals, old and new cultures, amongst others. Their stories provide valuable insight into the webs that poverty weaves and the many meanings that social marginalization takes.

Sanjay Basti, Timarpur, Delhi 110054

It was a day like any other. Two women neighbours in the basti were arguing. The issue was the use of the common space in front of their homes. As happens in bastis, space is always short and its uses many. Soon a small group of women had gathered. Tempers were flying high, and voices were raised. The habitually high-pitched tones of one had led the other to follow suit lest the sheer force of volume of her opponent persuade the listeners. Moreover, this was perhaps the only way to get heard. Low tones in the basti are often not listened to, but mistaken as a sign of weakness.

The conversation soon strayed from the issue at hand. Incidents that had occurred in the past were invoked, as though the present could be explained only by patterns of the past. The tone, tenor and substance of what was being said had now taken on a theatrical quality. Gaining the sympathy of the onlookers had become as important as arguing with the other. The power of these onlookers was apparent. With a simple nod of the head, a comment or two, they could shift the balance this way or that, even though their expressions depended less upon the validity of the argument and more upon their prior relationship with the side they chose to favour.

Most quarrels have a time limit. After going through the necessary octaves, the high notes of this one too dropped and finally came to a close. The points had been made but nothing was resolved. Slowly the crowd dispersed. Tension, like a live wire, continued to make itself felt for some time between the two neighbours until this incident too, like others before, was relegated to history to be invoked no doubt at some future time. The ebbs and flows of life in the slum continued. The following days, however, were witness to correction in the usual practice in the use of the common space. The views of the other were being accommodated. However grudgingly, some change had been wrought in.

An everyday quarrel in a slum, but with all the components, twists and turns, that make up dialogues on war and peace at higher levels!

Sanjay Basti is a non-descript 'squatter' settlement located near Timarpur Police Station in north Delhi. Much of it lies on the grounds of Balak Ram Hospital, a children's health centre, though the settlement overflows on both sides of the main road that runs through Timarpur. Across the road from the Balak Ram grounds are modest middle-class flats—a 'colony' as this sort of enclave is aptly called. The two communities on each side of the road live their own lives, with little interaction except on Wednesday evening when they all mix together in the weekly vegetable market.

Most of the 'houses' in Sanjay Basti are small, single-room dwellings (perhaps a hundred square feet on average), with thin brick walls usually painted in bright colours, and asbestos roofs often padded with plastic sheets, rubber tyres and assorted items to protect them from wind and rain. Some of the residents 'own' their house, others have taken it on rent. Minimum facilities such as a few public water taps, illegal electricity connections, and open drainage are available, but little beyond that. There are two toilet blocks on the edge of Sanjay Basti, but they are sparingly used as the visitors are charged. 'One rupee per visit' may not seem unreasonable, but it quickly adds up, especially in large families. The Balak Ram grounds are more popular, never mind the pigs.

Most of the residents of Sanjay Basti came to Delhi from neighbouring states such as Uttar Pradesh, Rajasthan and Bihar. Some were born in Delhi and relocated to Sanjay Basti from other places. Many of them are vegetable vendors, others work as domestic helpers, rickshaw pullers, casual labourers, hawkers and skilled workers (electrician, mechanic, mason, painter, driver, embroidery worker, etc.) in some cases. Those with no special skills probably earn Rs 50 to 100 a day on average. This is enough to feed the family, buy clothes from time to time, send the children to the nearest government school, and furnish their one-room home with the basics, but little more. Those with better jobs have gradually acquired some consumer durables (mainly second-hand or from the local *kabadiwala*): television, cooler, and even the odd fridge or mobile phone, though that is relatively recent. In Sanjay Basti as in most settlements of this type, there are sharp inequalities within the community, even though it may look like an undifferentiated 'slum' from outside.

While hunger is rare in Sanjay Basti, exposure to disease is common and lack of health care facilities often ruins the quality of life. It is a cruel irony that, in spite of the slum being located on the grounds of a children's health centre, many children in Sanjay Basti are undernourished or suffer from diarrhoea, anaemia, scabies and other ailments. Adults too, especially women, struggle with health problems and wonder where to go when they are sick. There is little to choose between exploitative private doctors and ramshackle government hospitals.

Police harassment is a regular irritation—or worse—in Sanjay Basti. The police station is very close and the basti is a handy source of pocket money for the constables. They take hefty *haftas* (regular bribes) from most of the vendors and hawkers in Timarpur and rarely miss a chance to extract tips, often from both sides, when a dispute or incident occurs. If someone in Sanjay Basti dares to start building an extra room or a stone roof, the police somehow get a whiff of it in no time and rush there on their motorcycles to enquire, threaten, smash or turn a blind eye—at a price—if it suits them.

In common parlance, Sanjay Basti is a 'slum' or 'encroachment', but these pejorative terms fail to convey the real character of this settlement. Most of the residents have patiently transformed their humble dwellings into real 'homes'. Without much help or subsidies, they have made thoughtful use of every inch of space, often by recycling middle-class 'waste'. Their houses are tidy and functional, and what is more, they have their own special touch. In this respect, this 'slum' compares favourably with the dull middle-class quarters across the road, built at considerable public expense. As a form of low-cost urban housing, Sanjay Basti is not doing badly.

Four Women

Every house in Sanjay Basti hides a unique story of survival and struggle. By way of illustration, I include here a few lines about four of the seven women who filed a civil petition in the Delhi High Court when Sanjay Basti was threatened with demolition in 2007.*

Kanta Devi, forty years old, is a mother of five children. She came to Delhi from Bulandshahar with her husband Basant Lal after her marriage at the age of sixteen. Kanta came from a very poor weaver's family. Basant Lal's family was also poor: his father worked as a coolie, lifting sacks of grain for a daily wage. Basant Lal, like his other siblings, started to work with his uncle who was a tailor when he was only ten. For nine years, Kanta Devi and Basant Lal lived in a rented jhuggi in Sundernagari. Later they moved to Sanjay Basti, where they had a close relative, and bought their own jhuggi for Rs 6000. Right now, Basant Lal is employed in someone else's shop since he does not have his own sewing machine. He gets paid Rs 2000 a month, of which he has to spend Rs 300 on transport alone. To supplement the family income, Kanta and her daughter spend long hours doing embroidery work at home on ready-made shirts that a local contractor supplies to them. They get a paltry sum of three rupees for every shirt, after spending a similar number of hours on it. They are barely able to earn Rs 300 a month. They realize that their labour is being exploited, but they have no alternative. Kanta's eldest son is now twenty years old and has begun to work as an apprentice, but he earns just enough to meet his own expenses. Three of Kanta's children are studying in the local government school. One of them, her fourteen-year-old son studying in Class 7, has a physical disability.

Zireen Bano, thirty-five years old, is a high-school pass. She is originally from Lucknow and came to Sanjay Basti ten years ago. For

---

* This petition was an impleadment in case number W.P. (C) No. 4582 of 2003.

the first two years, Zireen and her husband Nasim Ahmad stayed in a rented jhuggi, paying Rs 500 per month. Later they bought one in instalments, for Rs 12,000. Zireen was married at the age of thirteen and has six children—five daughters and one son, aged between eight months and thirteen years. Four of them are going to the local government school. The family lives on the earnings of her husband who works as a mechanic in a scooter garage for Rs 100 a day. In the first year, he could not find any fixed premise for his work and used to offer his services here and there on the road, earning Rs 10–20 a day. Then he managed to find a regular spot, where he used to earn Rs 50 a day. This arrangement continued for four years or so. For the last five years, he has been working in the garage where he earns a better wage. The garage is in Inderlok, and Nasim cycles back and forth.

Kiran Devi, fifty-one years old, came to Sanjay Basti about fifteen years ago from Daudkhan Haipur village in Railka Tehsil, Aligarh. She has eight children. She recalls that her husband, Bhola Ram, started working ever since he was ten years old. His father died early and he used to stay with his father's only brother. Initially, he used to take the cattle out to graze. He would be out all day but all his *chachi* (aunt) gave him to eat was roti with chutney. Then his uncle sold the cattle and bought land. Bhola Ram then started working in a factory that used to make *chhalai* (iron rings). He would be paid only Rs 2 or 2.50 per day. Bhola Ram and Kiran Devi moved to Delhi after the birth of their first two children. They first lived in Kishanganj (in front of Filmistan), where they rented a single room for Rs 150 per month. They lived there for eighteen years. The rent kept increasing, and by the time they left in 1992, the monthly rent was Rs 2000. There, Bhola Ram used to sell tikki and golgappe and they were usually able to save a small amount of money every day. Kiran gave birth to five children in Kishanganj. After moving to Sanjay Basti, Bhola Ram joined other vegetable vendors there. He goes to the mandi every day before dawn to buy vegetables wholesale and then sells them on the road for the rest of the day. Sometimes he is able to save Rs 100, sometimes much less. There are days when he loses quite a bit of money too.

Charan Devi, forty-two years old, is the most articulate and enterprising woman in Sanjay Basti. She and her husband Inderjeet have been in Sanjay Basti since 1989. Inderjeet had first come to Delhi from Bulandshahar when he was just eight years old as life was very hard in the village where he had lived in a large, landless family with few assets. His parents used to work as agricultural labourers, earning just five rupees a day at that time. Their house was too small for the growing family. So, they migrated to Delhi in search of a livelihood. Charan Devi spent her own childhood in Paharganj (Delhi) and experienced her own share of hardships. Her father died young and her widowed mother brought up her children by selling flower garlands. 'It is only now that we have started wearing clothes that we have bought ourselves,' said Charan Devi. 'Those days we could never afford to. My mother used to get some food from one or the other family she supplied garlands to. That is how we seven children grew up.' Her husband has tried his hand at many different occupations, from selling vegetables and driving to running a tea shop. They have six children of whom three are going to school.

There are some interesting parallels between these stories. In each case, a young woman and her husband fled from the village to escape a life of destitution or humiliation. They came to the city in search of livelihood, without any specific opening. Initially, they struggled to survive, but eventually, they found some sort of place in the urban economy. Their children are going to school and they have a vague chance of leading a better life than their parents.

Ready for Demolition

The residents of Sanjay Basti live in permanent insecurity, since the settlement may be razed to the ground at any time. In fact, similar settlements nearby have already been demolished. About three years ago, Durga Basti, a large slum in Khyber Pass near Mall Road was flattened in a single day, to make space for a depot of the Delhi Metro. The residents were given a few hours to pack their most precious belongings, then the bulldozers came under heavy police guard and pulverized the houses one by one. The families had a chance to relocate to a resettlement colony, but with a catch or two: the colony is more than 25 km away and an advance payment of Rs 7000 was expected for each tiny plot, aside from regular instalments later on. This brutal operation deprived many of their source of livelihood since they could not afford long and expensive bus journeys from the resettlement colony to their ordinary places of work near Khyber Pass. Children were also torn away from decent government schools, without any immediate alternative in the resettlement colony.

From time to time, rumours were rife that the same was about to happen in Sanjay Basti. And indeed, on 1 March 2007, a terse notice appeared here and there in the neighbourhood. Posted by the Central Public Works Department (CPWD), it directed the residents to vacate by 27 April or face removal soon after that. The notice did not explain the purpose of this forcible removal, specify the area to which the order applied or mention any relocation plan. Nor did it provide a contact number or address where further details might be sought—so much for the right to information. As far as the authorities were concerned, Sanjay Basti was ready for demolition.

Ever since the eviction notice came up, the people of Sanjay Basti have been worried, fearful and confused even if their everyday lives continue much as before. The notice did not come as a surprise—they have always felt that it was only a matter of time. More than once, the basti had already come close to demolition. Yet it survived each time, and even seemed to take root: election cards were made, some ration cards were distributed, children were admitted to local schools and some lanes were cemented. But now, part of Sanjay

Basti is already rubble; as a starter towards full demolition, a row of shops and houses on the edge of the road was razed to the ground on 6 March 2007. This swift and ruthless operation made it clear that the eviction notice had to be taken seriously.

All these little shops served a purpose and added to the colour. Some were tiny, like a tea shop run by a widow on the corner of the lane that led to Balak Ram—just a wooden bench in a hut with a mud floor. Then there was Inderjeet's shop. He was the 'capitalist' of his lane. His shop was perched on a raised platform, one had to climb a step or two, and he had two benches as well as a small second-hand TV. He always looked quite content making tea from a height. In his shop, one could also get various snacks to eat: matthi, phen, biscuits, toffees, and even eggs and buns. One year earlier, he had acquired some sort of cooler box, so he was also selling '*thanda*' (cold drinks). Little by little, he had improved his shop over the years. His wife Channi (Charan Devi), now an enterprising woman herself and not to be left behind, had opened another shop outside their home. This was a *kirana* (grocery) shop, where she also sold vegetables, rakhis, churis and other items. One day she also started selling chowmein for a few hours every evening. There were other, smaller shops around—a sweetmeat shop, a paan stall, and a smaller kirana shop run by ten-year-old Gopal with admirable acumen. The old Dunlop sofa outside one of the tea shops that had a TV was a popular spot where children, as well as grown-ups, often hung around to watch a Bollywood film.

All this was reduced to rubble in no time. Bricks that held together to make up a whole—a grocery shop, a garbage dump, a taxi stand, a tailor's cubicle, a barber's room, a vegetable vendor's platform, a corner where a dhobi ironed clothes—were torn apart. Those who made a living from these shops and those who used their services are readjusting to the new circumstances. And soon, we hear, the homes will go too— 'Perhaps after the *chote* elections (municipal elections) on 23 April,' said one. 'The roads are going to be broadened,' said another. 'The municipality is reclaiming the land, they will make a big mall here,' claimed a third.

And so, the landscape changes, and with it change lives.

Double Standards

In principle, Sanjay Basti is well protected from arbitrary demolition under existing policies and laws. The Delhi Laws (Special Provisions) Act 2006 prohibits any slum demolition for the time being unless the land is required for a 'specific public project', which is conspicuous by its absence in this case. Indeed, persistent enquiries from countless offices failed to uncover any specific reason for the demolition of Sanjay Basti.

Further, the Delhi Master Plan 2021, which has statutory force, declares and mandates a policy of in situ upgradation or relocation as per strict specifications (provided for in the Plan itself) of all slums and 'jhuggi-jhopadi' clusters, and a continuance of these settlements in the interim. The impending demolition of Sanjay Basti violates this Master Plan as well as the 2006 Act. For good measure, it is also contrary to the slum policy of the Municipal Corporation of Delhi.

These laws and policies, unfortunately, are being overridden by reckless High Court orders aimed at 'cleansing' the city from settlements of this kind. Indeed, Sanjay Basti is only the latest target in a long series of slum demolitions carried out under pressure from the Delhi High Court and its offshoots—notably the Commissioners and Monitoring Committees appointed to oversee the progress of demolition orders.

These orders are based on the notion that slums are parasitical settlements that tarnish the urban environment if not dens of crime and filth. They overlook the fact that slums serve an essential economic purpose: they provide low-cost housing to masses of workers who service the city, and for whom no provision has been made in urban development planning. For many of them, it would be impractical or expensive to commute long distances from the outskirts of the city. For instance, street vendors and roadside workers (barbers, tea stall owners, cycle mechanics, and so on) need equipment that would be difficult to carry back and forth. Similarly, it is the short distance between work and home that enables many women to work as part-time domestic helpers in the neighbourhood, even as they continue to handle child care and other household tasks.

Slum demolition drives also overlook another important fact about squatter settlements in Delhi: they occupy very little space. Indeed, squatter settlements in Delhi cover barely *one per cent* of the total land area in the city. This point can also be appreciated by examining Google Earth's high-resolution maps of Delhi. It is a striking fact that slums are virtually invisible on these maps. The reason is that squatter settlements are tucked away in the nooks and crannies of the city, too small to be easily visible on aerial maps.

On this one per cent of the total Delhi area, live some three million people who keep the informal economy going and for whom no shelter provisions have been made. When the situation is seen in that light, the case for removal looks much weaker than when slums are regarded as an eyesore and a nuisance. Would it really be unwise to allocate one per cent of the land for in situ improvement of existing slums, and spare the trauma of forced eviction to millions of people, except possibly when essential public purposes are at stake?

It is interesting to contrast the harsh treatment meted out to 'slums' with current policies towards another category of squatters—motorized vehicles. Delhi's private cars alone (there are more than 12 lakh) occupy a larger area, for parking purposes, than all the city's slums.* In many neighbourhoods, it has become difficult to move around as public spaces are jammed with private cars. Cars also cause endless noise, pollution, accidents, disputes and traffic jams, among

---

* More recent figures place the number of 'registered motorized vehicles' in Delhi at a startling 134 lakh, as on 31 January 2022 (*Hindustan Times*, 1 February 2022).

other nuisances—rapidly turning the whole city into a living hell. Yet, little is done to stem the runaway growth of vehicular traffic.

This contrast is one symptom, among others, of the class character of urban development in Delhi. The housing needs of the poor are ignored, while the city is redesigned to suit the aspirations of the privileged classes. As the Master Plan puts it, the top priority is to convert Delhi into a 'world-class city'—whatever that means.

7

Lush Fields and Parched Throats

Groundwater Politics in Gujarat*

Introduction

The years 1985–88 will be remembered for a long time in rural Gujarat as 'dry years' or 'thirsty years'. These will be harsh memories: unending stretches of parched land, ceaseless search for water, back-breaking labour on relief worksites, the scorching heat, exhaustion, anaemia and even death in the shape of hundreds of decaying skeletons of cattle lying on the wayside.

And yet, breaking this sepulchral landscape like a mirage, there were lush fields with healthy stalks and shiny leaves, swinging in a casual breeze while freshwater flowed beneath, tickling their roots.

---

* This is a highly condensed version of the original article (Bhatia, 1992), published in *Economic and Political Weekly*, which includes detailed evidence of groundwater exploitation in Gujarat as well as a fuller discussion of possible interventions. This study was motivated and informed by my experience of social action in rural areas of Sabarkantha district (north Gujarat) during the period 1985–90, which included a severe drought and acute water shortages. It reflects the situation that prevailed by the end of the 1980s, but the basic issues discussed in this chapter are still relevant today.

Clear water through which one could see fertile soil, unaffected by the surrounding desolation, rich with the promise of bountiful yields. But the dream turned sour when one observed not only that the neighbouring field was barren, but also that its owner and her family hardly had enough water to drink. Their own well was drying up, even as their richer neighbours were reaching deeper and deeper to extract groundwater. And as the water table went down, their dependence on their neighbours for water kept increasing.

These were also years of fierce debates about the use of groundwater resources in India. The discussion drew attention to India's vast groundwater resources and some argued that these resources were mostly unharnessed and untapped. Some experts and planners saw in them a latent potential for irrigation, development, increased food production and mitigation of the drinking water crisis. Others voiced warnings that in certain areas, especially in states like Gujarat, the groundwater table had reached a dangerously low level. The discussion also raised questions about social and economic equity in the distribution of water resources as well as about the role played by water markets, state intervention and other regulatory mechanisms. At the same time, deeper questions received insufficient attention: Who owns groundwater resources? Who benefits from their use? Who causes and who suffers from their overexploitation? How can we make sure that these resources are utilized to meet real needs rather than to enrich a privileged minority?

This ongoing debate as well as the personal experience of rural life under drought conditions in Sabarkantha district (north Gujarat) motivated the present study. The study focuses on two alarming aspects of water utilization patterns in Gujarat: *overexploitation* and *inequity*. While the overexploitation aspect is discussed from macro data, the inequity aspect, in the absence of adequate secondary data, is examined at the village level.

The Groundwater Crisis

The Changing Nature of Droughts

Drought is not a new phenomenon in Gujarat; it has an important place in the written as well as oral history of this region. However, the nature of droughts and their impact on rural life are quite different now from what they used to be.

History of Droughts and Famines in Gujarat

The earliest authentic records of scarcity and famine available for the state relate to the seventeenth and eighteenth centuries. Scant information is available for earlier periods. In most cases, famine seems to have followed a massive crop failure resulting from drought, or, in some years, from pests or invasions of locusts, rats and caterpillars.[1]

Alexander Loveday, writing on famines in India, observes that between the years 297 and 1907 CE, the less severe famines tended to recur in cycles of about five years and the more severe ones in cycles of fifty years or so.[2] He advanced the hypothesis that after an exceptional period of drought, a time of comparative prosperity generally followed, varying in length from forty to fifty years.

For Gujarat specifically, the years known for 'severe famines' are 1631, 1696, 1718, 1731, 1747, 1791, 1812, 1899 and 1901. Of these, famines that are still remembered today with dread because of high mortality are Satyasyo (1631), 1718, Sudtalo (1791) and Chappaniyo (1899–1900).[3]

Large-scale starvation and mortality were commonly reported during the Mughal and Maratha periods and to a lesser extent during the British period. No such events have occurred in the post-Independence period. As a result of public intervention, the main damage caused by drought is no longer a sharp increase in mortality. On the other hand, as discussed below, the hardships caused by shortage of water and fodder in drought years have become increasingly serious.

It may help to recall why drought often led to famine in the pre-Independence period and how famines have been prevented since Independence. On the former question, Baird Smith, in his famous report on the famine of 1860–61, aptly described Indian famines as 'rather famines of work than of food'.[4] In other words, the reason why droughts often precipitated famine in the pre-Independence period was not so much that they reduced the availability of food, rather they disrupted economic activity and employment, especially in rural areas. The Famine Commission of 1880 described this process thus:

> [As] a general rule, there is an abundance of food procurable, even in the worst districts in the worst times; but when men who, at the best, merely live from hand to mouth, are deprived of their means of earning wages, they starve, not from the impossibility of getting food, but for want of the necessary money to buy it.[5]

Following this diagnosis, the relief policy outlined in the Famine Codes—introduced towards the end of the nineteenth century—put great emphasis on the creation of wage employment through relief works. To this day, public works remains the main plank of famine prevention in India. Since Independence, strong political incentives to respond to crises have ensured that this strategy usually works well enough to avert a disaster.[6]

While pre-Independence accounts of droughts and famines extensively mention hunger and starvation deaths, fodder scarcity is only occasionally discussed, while water scarcity is hardly ever mentioned.[7] All sorts of descriptions can be found of how people coped with hunger (e.g., by eating roots and seeds), but there is no corresponding account of the survival strategies they adopted to cope with water scarcity.

This observation applies, for instance, to Bhailalbhai Patel's brilliant account of the Chhapaniyo drought (1899–1900).[8] In his autobiography, Bhailalbhai Patel, a leading politician in Gujarat and able engineer gives a vivid picture of the impact of drought on people's lives in his own village in Baroda district. The failure of crops was followed by distressed sales of milch animals and household assets. Land alienation, indebtedness and begging increased sharply. The author also describes heart-rending scenes of countless bodies being dumped in a local well, while human skeletons could be found on the waysides and fields long after the end of the drought.

There is, in Bhailalbhai's narrative, no corresponding account of hardship caused by groundwater scarcity. In fact, Bhailalbhai uses the revealing expression *panine mule* (literally, at the cost of water) to convey that land was being sold for a pittance. The use of this metaphor fits with the idea that groundwater continued to be available during pre-Independence droughts in Gujarat, in sharp contrast with the present situation.[9]

Water Scarcity and Relief Policy

Interestingly, the continued availability of groundwater during droughts in pre-Independence India went hand in hand with enthusiasm for the construction of water extraction mechanisms in times of drought. The building of water extraction structures is mentioned as early as 1343 when Muhammad Tughlak took out advances from the treasury for the digging of wells during a famine. Akbar also had canals made for the rich and the poor alike. Historical records give credit to the Muslim rulers for the construction of canals and to the Hindus for the construction of tanks and the digging of wells. Similarly, after the heads of state in Kutch, Palanpur (Banaskantha) and Kathiawar adopted a policy of 'food for work' in 1812, the relief works consisted mainly of the construction of tanks, wells and roads. The post-Revolt period (after 1857) was marked by further developments in this direction, including the large-scale development of irrigation. In 1883, the British government enacted the Land Improvement Loans Act with the objective of encouraging land improvement and relieving the distress of poor cultivators in times of famine. This was done by providing aid to the *ryots* for financing permanent improvements, particularly the digging of wells and the construction and repair of tanks and water channels. In the Chhapaniyo drought of 1899–1900, one of the important relief measures was the digging of wells. This was also the case in Kheda district during the drought of 1918–19, when the government liberally provided loans for the deepening of wells.

Thus, traditional relief policies have included an effort to build water extraction mechanisms, both to generate large-scale employment and to reduce vulnerability to future droughts. In both cases, the main preoccupation was to avert starvation and mortality, rather than water scarcity as such. From 1960 onwards, however, water scarcity emerged as one of the most alarming aspects of drought in Gujarat.

Emergence of Water Scarcity

Acute water scarcity was noted during the drought of 1960–61 in Gujarat and the subsequent droughts of 1961–62 to 1968–69—when drought occurred year after year in one part of Gujarat or another—1972–73, 1974, 1979 and 1985–88. The number of villages without adequate access to water or 'no source' villages rose from 3,844 in 1979 to 12,188 in 1986.[10] In 1987, as many as 16,351 villages out of a total of 18,114 were classified as 'no source' villages.[11]

Drought relief measures since then have been increasingly geared to this growing problem of water scarcity. The public supply of water through tankers first occurred during the drought of 1960–61 in parts of Ahmedabad and Bharuch districts. In subsequent drought years, water was supplied by tankers and bullock carts, wells were dug or deepened, bores sunk, village tanks deepened or repaired, tagavi loans were given for diesel engines and water was arranged for cattle by hiring *koshias*.[12] During the drought of 1972–73, drilling rigs were imported to drill tube wells, and during the drought of 1985–88, the state went so far as to transport water to Rajkot by train across a distance of more than 250 km!

The growing seriousness of the water crisis in Gujarat can also be gauged from the sharp rise in the allocation of funds to drinking water supply in the relief budget of each consecutive drought year. The provision of drinking water has now become one of the principal planks of the government's relief policy.

In 1985–86, the government spent Rs 87 crore on supplying drinking water to villages and towns by various means. But this left the problem as acute as ever, for a repeat performance happened in 1986–87 and again in 1987–88. During the first seven months of 1987–88, the government spent Rs 115 crore on drinking water supply schemes, including both 'short-term' measures like deepening of wells and supply of tankers and 'long-term' measures such as installing deep tube wells and water pipes to transport water over long distances. In the three years from 1985–88, as many as 36,901 deep tube wells were constructed, and a mammoth sum of Rs 248 crore was spent on these relief operations. The number of bores drilled increased year after year, from 6,612 in 1985–86 to 8,125 in 1986–87 and 11,247 in 1987–88.

One can therefore argue that while starvation deaths are now rare in Gujarat, drought still plagues this state in different—and no less serious—manifestations. In addition to the traditional threat of a 'famine of work', there is now an acute need to deal with the threat of a 'famine of water'.

The significance of the water crisis does not end there. As will be seen further on, the water crisis is no longer confined to drought years. The depletion of groundwater resources affects the livelihood of the rural population on a permanent basis.

Indications of Groundwater Scarcity[13]

The most perceptible and widespread manifestation of groundwater scarcity in Gujarat is the decline of water tables.[14] Officials dealing with the subject are particularly concerned about the tapping of resources which are beyond the reach of seasonal recharge and are therefore most vulnerable to depletion. Shocking reports have appeared in the newspapers—like the water table in parts of Mehsana district reaching a depth of 1200 feet.[15] Less spectacular, but still alarming, is the rapid decline of groundwater levels reported in many districts of north Gujarat, Saurashtra and Kutch.

In 1988–89, the regional office of the Central Ground Water Board (CGWB) in Ahmedabad initiated district-wise reappraisal surveys in districts which had been systematically covered by earlier surveys. These district-wise reports pointed to large-scale groundwater overexploitation during the previous two decades.

Phadtare (1988) reports official analysis of historical groundwater level data from the National Network of Hydrograph Stations (established by CGWB). Based on hydrographs and the long-term trend of groundwater levels, the decline and rise in water levels were calculated for 1979 to 1987. The results pointed to an overall decline of water levels in almost all regions. In most of the state, water levels had fallen by more than two metres over this short period. In many areas, they had fallen by more than four metres.

The decline of water tables over that period is partly attributable to the drought conditions that prevailed in 1987. Indeed, Phadtare's own report clearly shows how water tables tend to decline quite drastically in drought years. Having said this, the decline of water tables was not just a short-term, drought-induced phenomenon. There was, in fact, much evidence of a long-term decline in water tables in most areas of Gujarat; while the downward trend had a tendency to accelerate during droughts, it was not confined to drought years alone. For instance, declining trends in water level for the period 1981–90 were observed in eighty-six out of ninety-five observation wells monitored by the CGWB (Bhatia, 1992, Table 7). The total decline over this ten-year period, calculated for each well based on the observed time trend, was larger than four metres for nearly half of these wells.

Causes of the Current Crisis

By the end of the 1980s, there was abundant evidence of an acute and growing problem of water scarcity in Gujarat—not only in drought years but also in other years, especially during the summer months. The water table had receded, water extraction through dug wells and handpumps had become increasingly difficult and groundwater had become inaccessible for those who could not afford modern extraction devices.

Broadly speaking, this crisis has two interrelated causes. First, the depletion of groundwater is one aspect of a broader ecological crisis, involving particularly the disruption of the hydrological cycle. Second, there are important economic forces at work, especially the indiscriminate use of modern water extraction devices and the expansion of water-intensive crops in areas of groundwater scarcity.[16] Both factors are discussed below.

Groundwater Depletion and the Environmental Crisis

The term 'hydrological cycle' refers to the continuous circulation of the earth's moisture through evaporation and precipitation. The excessive pumping of groundwater, beyond the recharge rate, can disrupt this cycle and lead to the depletion of this otherwise renewable resource. The recharge rate depends on the extent of rainfall and on the rates of percolation and run-off.

The rate of percolation depends chiefly on the characteristics of soil. For instance, percolation is fast in coarse sandy soils, but very slow in fine clayey soils. The extent of run-off depends on the depth, porosity and compactness of the soil and the underlying material, the steepness and configuration of the surface, and the character and density of the vegetation. In the absence of plant cover, the run-off rate is higher. In Gujarat, denudation has played an important role in accelerating run-off and reducing groundwater recharge. Conversely, the disruption of the hydrological cycle itself contributes to the disappearance of forests. The latter is a matter of deep concern in its own right.

Since plant cover helps to increase rainwater percolation, the soil water reservoir under a forest cover tends to be preserved for a longer period compared with barren land. Moreover, forests play an extremely important role in controlling floods by reducing or regulating water run-off, thus also reducing soil erosion and landslides. As two leading environmentalists observe:

> From an uncut, unburned and ungrazed forest, rarely will any water emerge as surface flow even during heavy rainfall. Almost all water is transmitted downwards . . . According to one calculation, if the soils of India's forest area had good forests on them, they would have the capacity to store more than all the rainwater that falls in an average year on a temporary basis and more than half of it on a prolonged basis . . . Once forest lands are denuded, soil loss can increase by as much as 400 times.[17]

The National Forest Policy (1952) prescribes that, of the total land area, 33 per cent should be covered by forests. Official statistics of the Government of Gujarat show that the land area under forests more than *doubled* between 1960–61 and 1980–81—from 5.1 per cent of the total land area to 10.4 per cent.[18] However, independent studies lend little support to this extraordinary claim. Satellite-based data released in mid-1984 by the National Remote Sensing Agency (NRSA) show, on the contrary, that Gujarat's forest cover shrunk by almost 50 per cent between 1972–75 and 1980–82—from 5.3 per cent of the total land area to 2.8 per cent.[19]

The experience of desertification has found deep expression in oral histories and local folklore. Celebrated poet Umashankar Joshi talks about his native village in Bhiloda taluka of Sabarkantha district as the 'most beautiful spot on earth' with its dense forests, rich foliage and freshwater streams and rivers. But today, the hills at the edge of the Aravalli range around Bhiloda are completely bare of vegetation.

The real brunt of this forest loss is borne by the poor villagers, especially tribals who often depend on forest resources for their livelihood. Women not only have to walk longer distances for water but also have to spend several hours every two or three days on fuelwood collection. The growing scarcity of fuelwood, which is as precious as food or water, is one of the most alarming aspects of the environmental crisis in Gujarat.

The unscrupulous exploitation of forest resources for commercial and industrial purposes is a major cause of growing wood scarcity. It is a bitter irony that the poor are themselves being driven to participate in the destruction of the environment on which their own survival depends. For lack of gainful employment, many poor villagers in north and south Gujarat are forced to trade a head-load of wood for a small amount of cash, or in exchange for a pitcher-full of buttermilk. This practice enables the higher-caste rich farmers to maintain stacks of fuelwood for their own needs in spite of the general scarcity. Meanwhile, the poor become losing participants of this vicious circle of destitution and environmental destruction.

Government policies have failed to prevent this process. To a large extent, these policies have taken the negative form of attempting to 'bar' people from the forests, instead of taking positive steps to promote alternative sources of energy and livelihood. The alleged success of official 'afforestation' programmes is little more than a myth, based as they are on the large-scale promotion of ecologically suspect species such as the water-guzzling eucalyptus. Further, in some cases government policies have directly contributed to the destruction of the environment, for instance, through the submergence of rich forests following the construction of large dams.

Groundwater Overexploitation

The Emergence of Modern Irrigation in Gujarat

The large-scale development of irrigation in Gujarat, as in the rest of the country, began after 1951—the year when planned development in India was initiated. Prior to 1951, the use of groundwater for irrigated agriculture accounted for around 25 per cent of the total groundwater resources harnessed at that time in the country. At the beginning of the planning era, the full potential of underground aquifers was not known. The availability of pumping equipment and the energy needed to operate them were also restricted.

However, once the realization came that groundwater was a very cheap and 'efficient' alternative to major and medium irrigation works, the exploitation of groundwater began at an accelerated pace. The comparative advantage of groundwater over other sources of irrigation is well described by B.B. Vohra:

> [G]roundwater requires no expenditure for storage and transport
> and can be harnessed by the farmer with his own efforts—except
> possibly for a short-term loan—within a matter of weeks if not
> actually days and can therefore be developed through the efforts of
> millions of private individuals on an infinitely wider decentralized
> front and practically in all parts of the country within a far shorter
> period of time than surface water. It also involves no environmental
> problems such as the submergence of good lands under storage
> and canals, and no evaporation and seepage losses which take
> away more than 50 per cent of the water released from reservoirs

before they reach the farmers' fields. It also creates no problem of waterlogging. Above all, it is a resource entirely under the farmer's control and requires no huge and corrupt bureaucracies before it can be put to work. It can thus be applied exactly when and to the extent required by the crop or land . . .[20]

Irrigation facilities expanded at a frantic pace in Gujarat in later decades of the twentieth century. Between 1960–61 and 1984–85, the percentage of gross area irrigated to gross area sown nearly quadrupled. And while the area irrigated by wells slightly declined over time in proportionate terms—mainly due to the expansion of canal irrigation, wells remained the main source of irrigation throughout this period.[21]

At the same time, a dramatic change took place *within* the 'wells' category. In earlier times, irrigation through wells meant the use of kos and similar water-lifting devices, manually operated with the aid of bullocks. Later, however, well irrigation began to involve energized water extraction mechanisms such as electric tube wells and diesel pumpsets. Thus, the dug wells or open wells of the 1960s increasingly gave way to the tube wells of the 1970s and 1980s. The dramatic increase in area irrigated from the 1950s was largely due to the rapid expansion of these modern water extraction mechanisms. The number of these modern wells in Gujarat grew at a phenomenal rate, while that of dug wells comparatively stagnated. The overexploitation of groundwater in Gujarat has been closely related to these trends.

The Role of Electrification

The massive expansion of modern water extraction devices was partly due to the official promotion of groundwater exploitation, beginning with the Grow More Food campaign launched in 1953 at an all-India level. Another important factor was the electrification of villages, which led to the rapid energization of pumpsets and tube wells. Electrification was particularly rapid in Gujarat. While in 1960–61, only 823 villages were electrified, by 1985–86 this figure had shot up to 17,053 (out of a total of 18,114 villages). A large increase was also observed in the number of pumpsets and tube wells that were electrified: from 5,401 in 1960–61 to 3,17,403 in 1985–86. In other words, within this twenty-five-year period, there was almost a *sixty-fold* increase in the number of electrified pump sets and tube wells in Gujarat.

For diesel pump sets, steady growth can be observed until 1976. After that, the rate of growth seems to have slowed down. At the field level, one observed that many of these pump sets were not in use. Sometimes, this was because the dug well on which a pump set was installed had little or no water and the owner did not have the capacity to deepen his dug well or to get an in-well bore drilled. But, in some areas, it was also the result of a switch from diesel to electricity, the latter being a cheaper source of energy.

Interestingly, the largest proportionate increase (340 per cent) in the number of electrified pump sets and tube wells over a period of five years occurred in 1966–71. The late 1960s was the period when the Green Revolution was gaining a foothold in Gujarat. It was also a period of frequent drought conditions—drought was declared in all the districts of Gujarat in 1965–66, and in sixteen out of nineteen districts in 1968–69. The expansion of electrified pump sets and tube wells was also rapid during the drought of 1985–88. Describing the uneven impact of these structures on subsistence farmers and prosperous farmers in times of drought, Bandyopadhyay (1987) rightly states:

> While drought is getting mitigated for the farmers growing cash crops, energized pump sets are creating new drought for marginal and poor peasants by drawing down the water table to below their reach.

Private Profits and Government Subsidies

What were the reasons for the proliferation of pump sets in general and of electric pump sets in particular? An obvious factor was that within the prevailing structure of incentives and property rights, energized water extraction mechanisms represented a far more lucrative technology than dug wells in most environments.

The profitability of investment in tube wells was greatly enhanced by various government policies. These included highly subsidized electricity pricing and liberal financial assistance. Liberal provision of subsidized credit in agriculture began with the Five-Year Plans. After the formation of the state of Gujarat in 1960, agricultural credit was mainly provided through the agency of the Gujarat State Cooperative Land Development Bank. By the late 1980s, most of the credit extended by the Land Development Bank was allocated to investment in modern water extraction devices. A large share of the credit channelled through later institutions and schemes such as NABARD and the Integrated Rural Development Programme also supported such investments, especially during and after the drought years. In the absence of government support in these and other forms, the profitability of modern water extraction devices would have been greatly reduced.

Overexploitation and Inequity

The depletion of groundwater resources in Gujarat must be seen in the context of a larger environmental crisis. It not only means that traditional wells dry up and that drinking water must be fetched over longer and longer distances. It also means a dangerous and possibly irreversible disruption of the 'hydrological cycle'.

As we saw, a major cause of this disastrous trend is the overexploitation of groundwater. The expansion of modern water extraction devices is one aspect of the gradual transformation of

Indian agriculture—beginning with the 'Green Revolution'—towards more intensive cropping patterns and practices. The adverse consequences of this transformation on the environment must be seriously considered, along with any possible gains that could be realized through increases in productivity or employment.

Aside from this problem of overexploitation, growing inequity in groundwater use is both a critical consequence and a major cause of overexploitation. This growing inequity compounds earlier economic inequalities based on land ownership, with the result that the agricultural community in Gujarat is increasingly sharply divided between a minority of prosperous farmers who monopolize most of the land *and* water and a majority of small farmers and agricultural labourers who are increasingly alienated from both of these means of production.

Inequity and overexploitation are, thus, twin aspects of the groundwater crisis in Gujarat, ultimately inseparable insofar as their common cause lies in the anti-social appropriation of groundwater by a minority of large farmers. They can be seen as two sides of the same coin.

A Case Study

This section presents the main findings of a case study undertaken in eight villages of Bhiloda and Idar talukas of Sabarkantha district in the summer months of 1988 (the broad features of Sabarkantha district were introduced in Chapter 1—A Step Back in Sabarkantha). The aim of the study was to understand the distribution of and access to groundwater in these villages. Two types of questionnaires were used, for interviews with big and small farmers respectively. A few case studies of each category were attempted. Besides this, general socio-economic information on the villages was collected. The emphasis of the fieldwork was less on the collection of quantitative data than on a qualitative assessment of the situation prevailing in the villages that were studied as well as on informal discussions with the people concerned.

Inequity and Groundwater Use

Economic inequality is a persistent feature of rural India, but its manifestations and intensity do change over time. This observation applies to the ownership of water extraction mechanisms. As we shall see, traditional inequalities in the ownership of dug wells have sharply increased with the acquisition of modern accessories such as pump sets and bores.

In order to examine the 'distribution' of water extraction mechanisms, we need some indicators of the economic status of different households or groups. Household income (or per-capita income) is frequently used for this purpose. However, household income is extremely hard to measure in rural India and it varies widely from year to year, so the *current* income of a household may be a misleading indicator of its long-term economic prosperity, especially in a drought year. An alternative is to use land ownership as an indicator of economic status. This, perhaps, would have been the best approach in this context. However, given the difficulty of obtaining and interpreting land records, another route was adopted.

In this case study, we begin by looking at the distribution of irrigation assets between different castes. This indicator is obviously not very reliable if we are interested in the economic status of individual households. However, to divide households into broad *groups* of different levels of affluence, caste is a very useful indicator in the study area. For instance, it can be said with confidence that, say, Patels represent a 'rich' and influential caste in the study villages, while Vankars—a Scheduled Caste—are extremely poor in comparison.

More precisely, the different castes encountered in the eight villages can be divided into three broad groups according to their level of economic prosperity.[22] First come the well-off, land-owning, well-educated, advantageously employed and politically influential caste groups, including particularly Patels, Rajputs, Barrots, Banias, Desais and Sonis. At the other extreme are the Scheduled Castes like Bhambis and Vankars. Households from these castes are mostly poor, landless and illiterate. Many of them have also suffered severely from the loss of their traditional occupation—for example, manual weaving in the case of Vankars. An intermediate position is occupied by households from Other Backward Classes (OBCs) in some cases. These households tend to own small pieces of land, which has enabled them to rise somewhat above Scheduled Castes in economic terms. However, their condition remains quite depressed. Over time, their holdings have become very small due to land fragmentation, and in the some cases, due to large-scale alienation of land resulting from indebtedness. The labouring classes consist almost exclusively of households belonging to the last two of these three broad groups.

The distribution of irrigation assets between different caste groups is shown in Tables 1 and 2, with a specific focus on bores in Table 1. It is useful to concentrate first on the village of Bhadresar. For this village, information is available for all water extraction structures, and detailed information on the caste composition of the population can also be accessed. As Table 2 indicates, the ownership of modern water extraction devices in Bhadresar is overwhelmingly concentrated amongst the privileged castes, especially the Patidar caste, including Patels and Desais. For instance, in Bhadresar, *all* the bores are owned by Patels and Desais, even though they represent only 23 per cent of all the households in the village.

As one might expect, the inequity of ownership is more pronounced for modern irrigation devices like bores and pump sets than for dug wells. In contrast to their total monopoly of bores, Patels and Desais own 'only' a little above half of the dug wells in Bhadresar.

The ownership of dug wells amongst other castes—even the poorer ones—is widespread. Yet, the distribution of dug wells is itself far from equitable. For instance, while the number of households per well is only 1.4 amongst Patels and Desais, it is as high as thirty amongst Vankars—with ninety households in Bhadresar.

In other villages too, the privileged castes have a virtual monopoly of modern water extraction devices, as Table 1 illustrates. While precise information on the caste composition of these villages is not available, in terms of the broad groups defined earlier, the composition of these villages is similar to that of Bhadresar. The pattern of sharp and increasing inequalities observed in Bhadresar thus applies in those villages as well.

TABLE 1
Number of Bores Owned by Different Caste
Groups in Eight Survey Villages

	Patel	Other privileged castes[a]	Thakarda	'Harijan'	Other deprived castes[b]	Total
Bhadresar	1	28	0	0	0	29
Choriwad	27	1	0	1	0	29
Mau	8	11	0	0	1	20
Messan	30	0	0	0	0	30
Munai	33	1	1	0	0	35
Naranpura	7	10	2	0	0	19
Takatuka	24	6	0	0	0	30
Umedpura	25	2	1	0	0	28
Total	155	59	4	1	1	220

[a] These include castes such as Barrot, Chauhan, Bhatt and Kolis. Individuals with the Desai surname (used by some Patels as well as by Rabaris) have been included in this group for want of further information. In these villages, the Desais are mostly found in Bhadresar.
[b] These include Turi, Ghanchi, Nayak, Kumhar, Pandaya, Talal, amongst others. A small number of Muslims have also been included in this group.
Source: Field survey and survey conducted by the talatis of these villages in June–July 1988.

TABLE 2
Caste-Wise Ownership of Modern Water Extraction Devices in Bhadresar

	Patel	Other privileged castes	Thakarda	'Harijan'	Other deprived castes	Total
Bores	1	28	0	0	0	29
Pump sets	7	20	0	6	1	34
Electric motors	21	99	0	2	6	128
Number of households	160		100	130	150	540

Source: Field survey and survey conducted by the local talati. For details of the different caste groups, see Table 1.

Land and Water

Inequalities in the ownership of water extraction mechanisms are closely related to inequalities in land ownership. Two of the survey villages, namely Munai and Mau, illustrate this starkly.

In Munai, marginalized communities, including disadvantaged castes, tribals and Muslims, represent almost two-thirds of the total population. Yet only a minute proportion of the total cultivable land in the village is in their possession. There has been a continuous process of land alienation, especially amongst the Thakardas, many of whom have lost their land after mortgaging it to the higher castes.[23] Those who do own land, like the Bhambis and Vankars, own at most two to 2.5 acres. Moreover, this land tends to be of very poor quality, most of it being of the type locally known as *khada-tekra*, i.e., uneven land, good only for the cattle to graze on.

The same picture can be observed in Mau, as far as the Thakardas and the Harijans (as they are known in the area) are concerned. Amongst the Scheduled Castes, the Bhambis, who have been traditionally landless, had to struggle for seven long years for forty-six acres of pasture land to be allocated to them for cultivation on a collective basis (see Chapter 5–Ekaki).

As was observed in the preceding section, the distribution of water in these villages is also very unequal and follows a similar caste pattern. Thus, inequalities of land and water ownership are seen to reinforce each other.

We can further illustrate this point by comparing the situation of Mohanbhai Shamalbhai Patel, a rich farmer of Choriwad village, with that of Dhanabhai Madhabhai Vankar, a poor farmer in the same village. The former owned sixteen acres of land and two bores with depths of 140 feet and 130 feet respectively. He shared one of the bores with a relative. The other bore was drilled a few months prior to the survey. He had incurred an expenditure of Rs 50,000 from his own savings to install these two bores. He was able to afford the investment on the second bore thanks to the large income generated from the use of the first bore. He would grow three crops each year on his well-irrigated land. For 1987–88, the *third* consecutive year of severe drought in Sabarkantha, he reported an annual income much above Rs 100,000 from cultivation alone, not including other sources of income such as the sale of milk from his four buffaloes. Interestingly, the substantial income he earned from fodder crops that year came from sales to relief organizations running cattle camps for drought-affected farmers.

The fate of Dhanabhai during the same year is in direct contrast to this story of opulence amidst general hardship. During the drought, Dhanabhai's family was totally dependent on relief works for its survival. Dhanabhai and his wife both participated in relief works and earned approximately Rs 50–60 per week. There were five members in this family at the time of the survey.

Dhanabhai owned 3.4 acres of land and a well which was 38 feet deep. In 1986–87, when there was still a little water in his well, Dhanabhai had managed to grow a small seed plot, from which he earned Rs 900. However, he was not able to deepen his well since, unlike Mohanbhai, he did not have the necessary resources. As a result, his well dried up the next year and he was not able to grow any crops. Further, his family had to depend on the neighbouring wells and bores for drinking water and other domestic needs.

One might expect that during a drought, big landowners who derive their income mostly from agriculture might be amongst the worst affected (in relative terms). This would be the case but for the inequitable ownership of irrigation sources. The possession of these irrigation sources gives large landowners a virtual monopoly over water and fodder resources during drought years. For many large farmers, a drought year can turn out to be a boon year.[24]

Drinking Water

One of the worst groundwater-related inequalities concerns drinking water. This applies in both drought and non-drought years. Even in non-drought years, access to drinking water is highly unequal. This arises partly from the uneven ownership of private water extraction mechanisms and partly from the fact that the more powerful sections of the population also gain privileged access to public sources of drinking water such as wells and handpumps.

During a drought, when the ordinary sources of drinking water of many poor people dry up, the situation becomes particularly critical. Although government relief policies officially include schemes for drinking water supply, in practice, these schemes often end up helping the rich more than the poor. The more influential groups and individuals, like the sarpanch, usually succeed in getting the public handpumps installed near their own houses. When poor people, especially from oppressed castes, try to get access to these handpumps, they often face hostility or even violence. When they get water at all, it is usually after a long time of queuing, while richer or higher-caste people jump the queue and fill their numerous matkas and buckets.

In one of the eight villages, a newly constructed public handpump had found its way into the higher-caste hamlet, despite it being much smaller than the other hamlets. When some of the women from the other hamlets braved the hostility of their neighbours and tried to get water from it, they were greeted with abuses, threats and stones. Some of them had their matkas broken. They obtained their rightful share of water only after a long struggle against the rural elite and the bureaucracy.

In another village, Munai, the poor had to depend on private drinking water sources during the drought, because the public sources had all dried up. While the propertied classes were able to draw water from their own private sources, women from poor households had to walk a long distance to the fields of a rich Patel farmer to draw water from his well. The latter did not miss this opportunity to make them feel their dependence on him; in fact, he regularly threatened to discontinue the water supply. In this case, too, people had to organize and take their grievances to the *mamlatdar* (taluka officer). They held a rally and dharna outside his office, after which the mamlatdar granted their demand for the installation of public handpumps in the poor hamlets of Munai. His promises, however, only partly materialized.

These two stories are by no means isolated cases. Every Thursday, during the drought, when the mamlatdar was available to hear public grievances, his office would resound with a cacophony of complaints, while a crowd of anxious villagers waited expectantly in the compound. Many complaints related to lack of drinking water and unequal access to public water sources.

What People Said

To conclude this case study, this section reports a few observations from the respondents about what can be done to remedy the present situation.

Many small and marginal farmers were of the view that the government should install bores for public use and should not allow private bores. This would enable people from all castes and classes to share the benefits of modern irrigation. A small farmer from Naranpura, for instance, said that he and other small farmers had asked the Bhiloda mamlatdar for a public bore so that they could have a share in the underground water, instead of it being appropriated by the rich.

Aside from the equity angle, public bores would enable a better spreading of risk over large groups of people:

> I have not attempted to dig a bore, because the bores which have been tried in the vicinity of my field have failed. Hence, I do not want to take the risk. I feel that the government should install bores for irrigation purposes. This way, those who do not own bores could also get water. If the government is ready to do that, I do not mind giving my land for free. I have written to government offices in Ahmedabad and Baroda, but I am still waiting for a reply.
>
> (Vithalbhai Barrot, a small farmer from Naranpura)

> If the government makes a bore for us and if we strike water, then we can, within a set period, return the money invested by the government, with interest. If we do not strike water, then naturally we will not be able to return the money.
>
> (Mohanbhai Jeevabhai Patel, a small farmer from Messan)

With public ownership of bores, better planning of their location—aimed at sustainability as well as equity—would also be possible:

> We do feel that bores which could be used by a collective and owned by the government should be encouraged instead of private bores. From such a government-owned bore, water could be bought by individual farmers. The principle of equal distribution

could be kept in mind. The place of the installation of the bores could be such that it falls in the centre of a group of farmers. Initially, the expenditure of the bore could be borne by the government. After the drought, in a few good years, the group of farmers could together return the amount to the government and the bore could then be of collective ownership.

(A small farmer from Naranpura)

One reason why many small and marginal farmers aspired to some kind of government intervention was that they had little hope of being able to discipline the large farmers on their own. For instance, Lallubhai Shankarbhai Ghant of village Naranpura felt that the bores of large farmers were definitely responsible for the drying up of wells, but also that one could not question them since they were digging the bores on their own land and with their own money. He felt that only external control exerted by the government would help and that a regulation should be introduced for this purpose.

In contrast to these constructive and imaginative responses from small and marginal farmers, many rich farmers were reluctant to discuss the problem of groundwater overexploitation. Those who spoke mostly showed a lack of concern for the problem, a reluctance to acknowledge their own responsibility for it and a negative attitude towards all forms of government intervention.

These views are well illustrated by the case of Ramjibhai Dhanabhai Thakarda, who owns one bore of about 190 feet depth from which he irrigates six acres of land. Initially, Ramjibhai was very suspicious and refused to talk. When his reaction was sought regarding the new depth limit of 160 feet, he replied: 'What is the sense of a limit of only 160 feet? We have been able to strike water at 190 feet. We had initially constructed a well which was 50 feet deep, but since we did not strike water, we had to dig a bore.' When asked whether he had taken a permission from the government authorities, he argued: 'There was no existing rule of this kind, so why should I take permission?' He further added: 'How can I be said to have committed an offence? If there was a government regulation and I had broken it, then it could be said that I have committed an offence.'

He was asked whether he realized that a bore as deep as his could affect the water table of the nearby wells. His reaction was: 'I can install as many bores as I feel like on my own land. Am I digging on someone else's land? Are we preventing the others from digging if they want to?' When asked if he felt that the government would take concrete steps, he confidently said that it would not.

Generally, the big landowners felt that they were not *guneghars* (at fault) since they were not breaking any government rules or laws.

If the government had attempted to introduce a rule or law earlier, we would not have been able to dig this bore. But since the government has not made this law, we are not at fault because we have not broken an existing law.

(Sevarbhai Raghjibhai Bamania, a farmer from Naranpura who owns seven acres of land and a bore 190 feet deep.)

The attitudes of large farmers towards government intervention were resoundingly negative.

The government's limit is only 160 feet. If I attempt to dig a bore and it fails, the government can make as many rules and regulations as it wants to, but I am ready to go as deep as 500 feet and nothing will stop me. After that, if the government wants to punish me, let it do so.

(Jethabhai Patel of Takatuka)

The government should not attempt to introduce any kind of regulation detrimental to the interests of the farmers. The more the farmers are able to produce, the more is the gain for the government and society—is it not?

(Madhabhai Gajibhai of Bhadresar)

If any control is exerted now, then whatever little greenery is left will also dry up. What will the cattle feed on then?

(A farmer from Naranpura)

An interesting aspect of the responses of large as well as small farmers, which emerges in several of these statements, is that they attach some importance to the *legality* of the situation. Some went so far as to envision the prospect of actual legal action on groundwater issues.

Only the government knows the depth to which a bore should be installed in particular areas and how it needs to be regulated. We do not understand this. If the well of a small farmer dries up due to the installation of a bore nearby, then he can file a case and stop the functioning of the bore.

(Rambhai Dhirubhai Patel, a middle farmer of Munai)

Some farmers, however, had difficulty in conceiving of a change in currently accepted property rights. For instance, Jethabhai Lakhabhai Vankar, a small farmer from Choriwad, exclaimed: '*Bijana kua ke bore par haq lage? Na lage*! [Can one have a right over somebody else's bore or well? No!]'

The Political Economy of Groundwater

The groundwater crisis in Gujarat is unlikely to go away in a hurry. It is not that means of intervention are lacking, but most of them are likely to encounter some resistance.

Means of Intervention

Broadly speaking, it is possible to identify four types of intervention to prevent the overexploitation of groundwater resources: (1) state regulation of the private sector, (2) public management of water resources, (3) community management and (4) changes in property rights.

Regulation can be direct or indirect. Direct regulation seeks to impose direct controls on the use of groundwater. Indirect regulation operates through other variables such as electricity pricing, minimum support prices and credit policies. As discussed earlier, some direct regulations were supposed to be in place in Gujarat at the time of my fieldwork. For instance, a licence was required to build a new borewell beyond a certain depth. Direct regulation, however, has been staunchly resisted by privileged landowners. On at least three occasions (1977, 1988 and 1989), their influence prevented the state legislature from introducing regulatory measures that would have helped slow down the overexploitation of groundwater resources in Gujarat.

As far as indirect regulation is concerned, one powerful means of action is electricity pricing. The two main alternative pricing systems are *flat-rate* pricing, involving a fixed annual charge per electric motor, and *pro-rata* pricing, where the user pays for each unit of electricity consumed. Pro-rata pricing is clearly preferable from the point of view of groundwater conservation since it imposes a cost on every extra unit of water extracted. Despite this, Gujarat switched in June 1987—in the middle of a drought—from pro-rata to flat-rate electricity pricing! This, too, happened under the influence of privileged interests—specifically, a three-year agitation led by the politically powerful farmers' lobby.

It is possible to combine flat-rate and pro-rata charges in a way that ensures some equity and rationality in electricity pricing. One example would be a pricing policy where (1) the pro-rata charge is area-specific, with higher charges in areas of more severe water scarcity, and (2) the flat-rate charge varies between users based on equity principles (e.g., by linking it to landholding size). There is every reason to demand this sort of departure from the irrational and inequitable system that has emerged as a result of political pressures from influential farmers.

Turning to public management of water resources, one important possibility is more active development of small-scale surface-water conservation structures. As B.D. Dhawan puts it, 'Wisdom lies in paying more attention to the development of surface water irrigation works so that a sizeable fraction of surface waters ends up in the groundwater table.'[25] Labour-intensive schemes of surface water development have the merit of simultaneously protecting groundwater and promoting employment.

Community management, in principle, is an important alternative to state intervention in this field. The village community has a collective stake in preventing the depletion of groundwater. There is, thus, some scope for mutual agreement on rational groundwater use. The main difficulty is to enforce the agreement, especially on those who are doing well from unrestrained groundwater exploitation. Successful community management may require a drastic change in perceptions of ownership over water resources. As things stand, landowners have a legal right to unrestrained use of the water that lies beneath their land.

This brings us to the issue of property rights. The existing structure of property rights is quite astonishing as far as groundwater is concerned. The Indian Easements Act of 1882 makes a crucial distinction between underground running streams and underground percolating water. Rights over the former are governed by the doctrine of 'riparian rights', which essentially states that 'each co-riparian has the right to have the water flow pass his lands undiminished in quantity and unimpaired in quality'.[26] For underground percolating water, however, the opposite principle applies: 'A landowner has the right to appropriate water percolating in no defined channel through the strata beneath his land; and no action will lie against him for so doing, even if he thereby intercepts, abstracts or diverts water, which would otherwise pass to or remain under the land of another.'[27] This provision removes all barriers to the private extraction of percolating groundwater.

The resulting status of (percolating) groundwater has been described as a 'fugitive resource', 'for which private property rights exist, but these rights are indefinite among the overlying landowners'. This creates a situation where 'each user protects his rights by capturing the groundwater in the fastest possible way, as the user knows that the deferred use is subject to great uncertainty since other users would capture the resource in the meantime'.[28]

This aberration is the result of the indiscriminate adoption of British legislation. In England, percolation is abundant, irrigated agriculture is practically non-existent and landholdings tend to be quite large so that the problem of 'interference' between groundwater users is less serious. In this context, these legal provisions are perhaps justified. But the situation is completely different in India, where the depletion of groundwater is a real danger and where small, contiguous holdings share common aquifers. The Indian Easements Act 1882 is a relic of the colonial period.

The need for legislative change is clear enough. What is less clear is how alternative property rights should be defined. One option would be to limit the right of private water extraction to sustainable levels. A more radical departure would be to treat groundwater as a collective resource of some kind. Of course, legal rights of this sort would not be easy to define and enforce. Quite likely, they would often be violated, as is the case with riparian rights today. But this does not mean that legislative changes of this kind would be useless. Indeed, social perceptions of what are 'legitimate' uses of groundwater *are* influenced by the legality of the matter and changes in these perceptions, in turn, can influence groundwater extraction practices in various ways—for instance, through bargaining between conflicting parties, community decisions, 'lok adalats', social sanctions, popular protests and so on. Had easy enforceability been regarded as a condition of legislation, laws such as those prohibiting child marriage or bonded labour would not have seen the light of day.

Public Ownership of Bores

As mentioned earlier, a recurring demand of small and marginal farmers in Sabarkantha was that the ownership of bores should be 'socialized', even if motors continue to be privately owned. To understand this idea, we must remember that a bore (the metal pipe running vertically from the ground to the underlying aquifer) and a motor (the engine that draws the water through the pipe) are two separate objects, which need not be owned by the same person. Indeed, it is a common practice in north Gujarat (as in many other parts of India) to put a motor on a mobile cart and to attach it to different bores (including, possibly, bores belonging to other persons) according to the circumstances. In most villages, the services of a motor or a bore can be easily hired at standard rates.

These arrangements make it possible to envisage a situation where the bores are publicly owned, while motors remain privately owned with their services being hired by the users. The socialization of bores would have some major advantages (many of which were clearly mentioned by the small farmers quoted earlier). First, it would help to prevent overexploitation, since public control could be exercised on the number and depth of bores in a particular area. Second, it would facilitate a rational location of bores through coordinated planning. In particular, the problem of 'well interference' could be greatly reduced. Third, public ownership of bores would permit a more equitable distribution of groundwater, since large farmers would no longer have the virtual monopoly of access to this resource.

Fourth, this arrangement would ensure better spreading of the risks involved in drilling bores, by transferring these risks from private individuals to the community or the government.

Last but not least, the social ownership of bores could facilitate the emergence of various forms of community management. Indeed, if bores are owned by the community rather than by private individuals, their *use* could also be more easily regulated. For instance, if a simple technology for monitoring the amount of water extracted by different individuals becomes available, it may be possible to introduce and enforce collective rules for the allocation of groundwater.

The socialization of bores would be a creative *combination* of the different forms of intervention discussed earlier. It is interesting that, this practical and effective approach should be so alive in the minds of the farmers we interviewed (particularly the smaller ones), even as it has been largely overlooked—so far—in the literature on groundwater management in India.

Concluding Remarks

The protection of groundwater resources in Gujarat ought to be a lively social issue. There is sustained pressure from influential farmers to adopt or perpetuate policies that allow the unrestrained use of these resources for short-term private gain, but no countervailing pressure for the protection of groundwater. The plunder goes on with little resistance.

Ultimately, this is perhaps the most important cause of the groundwater crisis. But this situation can be changed. In India as in many other parts of the world, environmental issues are receiving increasing attention in democratic politics. Within this emerging political movement, the groundwater question deserves an important place.

8

Fighting the Invisible Enemy in Jadugoda*

Jadugoda, literally meaning 'magic land', intrigues an outsider. The promise of magic enthrals, the mystery of the unknown attracts. Closer proximity, however, reveals not innocence but an intention—dangerous and deliberate. In the early 1960s, the Uranium Corporation of India Limited (UCIL) pitched its tents in Jaragoda, a land surrounded by forests and hills. The indigenous Santhal and Ho inhabitants called their land after the plant Jarabindi, which grows in abundance in this region and is considered very beneficial as the oil extracted from its seeds is used for healing purposes. By the mid-1960s, however, the UCIL was firmly in place and mining operations in uranium-rich Jaragoda had begun in earnest. The healing touch of Jarabindi had given way to sinister nuclear sorcery.

Jaragoda had now become Jadugoda.

Contaminated Environment

Jadugoda is located in the Potka and Mosabani blocks of east Singhbhum district in Jharkhand, about 25 km from Jamshedpur.

---

* Originally written in July 2001 and published in the annual *Survey of the Environment* published by *The Hindu*.

Uranium for the country's nuclear programme is being mined from three underground mines, 1600 to 2000 feet below the earth's surface, in Jadugoda (since 1964), Bhatin (since 1983–84) and Narwapahar (since 1989–90). A fourth mine has been inaugurated recently in Turamdih in Jamshedpur block. Besides these mines there are three 'tailing' ponds; a fourth one is in the offing. The official term 'ponds' is a misnomer, for in reality, these are small dams constructed for the purpose of storing nuclear waste.

This waste, known as 'tailings', comes from the mines and mills at Jadugoda as well as from Hyderabad. After the uranium ore has been mined, it is sent for purification to a mill. In this process, uranium concentrate is separated out. Popularly called yellow cake, this uranium concentrate is sent to the nuclear fuel complex in Hyderabad for making fuel rods. The waste from this process is packed into drums and sent back to Jadugoda to be dumped into the tailing dams. The contents of the tailing dams are highly radioactive, for even though uranium has been extracted, the remaining materials called 'uranium tailings' or 'uranium decay products' (thorium-230, radium-226, radon-222, polonium-210 among others) remain radioactive—some of them for thousands of years. This poisonous nuclear waste has the potential to cause unimaginable damage.

It is frightening to see that these radioactive dams are located very close to inhabited villages. Scientists the world over have acknowledged that there is no safe way of storing nuclear tailings. According to local sources, the dams have not been constructed in accordance with prescribed safety norms. When the first tailing dam was constructed, the waste was just dumped in the acquired area. Children used to play football on it and cattle grazed there freely. Tailings and waste ore have also been used for the construction of roads, schools, playgrounds and tailing dams themselves.[1]

Under public pressure, UCIL has classified areas close to the tailing dams as 'prohibited'. These areas have been cordoned off with barbed wire. In most places, these wires were found broken or there were no wires at all. Goats, sheep, cows and buffaloes continue to graze within the prohibited areas. Those going to the forests to collect firewood are also using this route. 'There is no other place, where will we go?' asked one villager, 'government land which we used for grazing purposes also got acquired for the tailing dams.' The route through the prohibited areas is the one they used to take before. It remains more convenient than the alternative route, which requires a long and arduous detour.

Contamination of groundwater and surface-water sources was another common complaint. Residents of Chatikocha, next to Tailing Dam 3, observed: 'Water in wells and nalas has become black . . . sometimes the water tastes salty . . . soap does not produce enough foam, our clothes remain unclean.' UCIL has cordoned off such ponds and wells and provided taps and handpumps instead. On an average, one tap has been provided for every thirty-five households. This is inadequate for basic human needs, let alone for domestic animals. Streams and nalas continue to be used (especially by animals) for bathing, washing and drinking. In addition, during the dry season, radioactive dust from the tailing dams gets carried away by winds. Likewise, during the monsoon, there have been overflows from the tailing dams and the connecting drains; residue water from the tailing dams is sent for purification through these drains after the solid tailings have settled down. These overflows fall into the Gudra River, a tributary of the Subarnarekha.

Radiation is an invisible enemy. Its slow and insidious effects are perceived by the Adivasis from the quiet changes happening to nature. Indeed, nature for local Adivasis often works like a signpost of what to expect in life. For instance, upon finding a nest of the Lippi bird in the field, one Adivasi tells another that there is still time before it rains, for a Lippi would not be so foolish as to let her eggs drown in the rain. Similarly, the direction which the entrance of the nest points to indicates that a storm will not come from that side.

These sharp observers of nature pointed out the following changes in plant and animal life. Some trees, like the mahua and room have decreased to the extent that leaves of the mahua tree now have to be bought during festivals (the leaves are an essential part of Ho religious rituals). The fruits of some others, such as *kendu* (elsewhere called *tendu*), are either seedless or have deformed seeds. Fruits and leaves of other trees which are consumed (e.g., drumstick) do not taste as sweet as before. The fate of rice is similar: produce has decreased and the taste has diminished.

Fertility amongst the hens has also been affected. In Mechua, villagers said that the yolk from the eggs was missing. In some cases, it was also reported that only one egg out of sixteen was fertile. In some places, tails of cows and buffaloes were said to be shorter and with less hair and calves were born with deformities. Fishes in a pond located within the premises of the Narwapahar mines died in large numbers due to the periodic release of a poisonous gas. In some other ponds, fishes were without tails and had boils on their skin.

One widespread response of the birds and animals to the contaminated environment has been migration. 'Now all the Lippis have gone, only Lippiguttu remains,' lamented a villager. So abundant were the Lippis in this region that villages were named after them; in fact, not only villages but also beautiful girls, for both Lippi and Peo (which has also become scarce) are known for their captivating beauty and sweet voice. Mynahs, hariyals (a pigeon-like bird) and owls have also decreased, as have monkeys and honeybees. With the honeybees gone, Khadiya and Birhor Adivasis have also been forced to migrate, since their livelihood depended on them. Their absence has affected other communities in diverse ways. For example, *tokris* (bamboo baskets) used during religious rituals of the Hos have always been woven by the Birhors. Now they have to be brought from other villages.

Health Hazards

The people in the Jadugoda area are affected not only by radiation from tailing dams but also by the lack of safety at the mines. UCIL has been accused of practising unsafe mining for the last thirty years, the effects of which have now begun to show. Fatigue, lack of appetite and respiratory ailments are widespread. Increases in the incidence of miscarriages, impotency, infant deaths, congenital deformities such as Down's syndrome, skeletal deformities like fused fingers, skin diseases, cancer, leukaemia and thalassemia have also been reported. Amongst the miners, tuberculosis (TB) and lung cancer are rampant. Besides physical ailments, mental illness is also common.[2]

Sumitra Soren has lived in Jadugoda all her life, first near Jadugoda mines and now in the Harijan basti near Tailing Dam 1, and has therefore been exposed to low-level radiation from birth. Her husband has also worked in the mines for two years. Sumitra's first three children died almost immediately after birth. Her fourth child survived and is now eighteen months old, but she is very sickly. Her fontanelles remained too soft for too long and so Sumitra fears brain-related problems in the future. The plight of Balika Rani, also eighteen months old, is no better. Dali Kendu, her mother, complains that Balika has little strength in her limbs and cannot stand up unassisted. Six-year-old Babulal Bhumij (in Tuwar Dumridih) is blind in his left eye and has been mentally impaired since birth. Many other children in the Jadugoda area have similar problems. Unfortunately, parents who are working in the mines were reluctant to speak out for fear of victimization.

The incidence of tuberculosis among the miners is very high, although there is a possibility that many of the cases diagnosed as TB are actually lung cancer. Bhatin village is a case in point. This village is located close to the Bhatin mines and is 2 km from Tailing Dams 2 and 3. In Rassi tola of Bhatin village, men were found lying on a cot in many houses, too tired to do anything. All of them were said to have been diagnosed with TB.

In some cases, TB has become a family illness. Mahi Murmu's father-in-law, Dasma Murmu, was working in the UCIL for many years. He developed TB and opted for voluntary retirement. His son, Risa Murmu, who got his father's job (as is the rule with the voluntary retirement scheme), has had TB since last year. At present he is at home on a half-salary basis. His brother, Logen, died in October 1999 after nine years of illness. He was not working in the mines, yet he died of TB.

Chotrai Soren has been suffering from TB for the last two years. He is also living at home on a half-salary. He has worked in the underground section of the Jadugoda mines for the last thirty-one years. He is unable to understand why he is not getting better. He said that in his department there were many who presently had TB and that many others had died of it. TB-afflicted poor as well as better-off miners alike, as the dust which pervaded the underground mines affected their lungs sooner or later. TB, in the life of a uranium miner, is almost inevitable. Besides, since TB is a contagious disease, it does not remain confined to the miner. But UCIL does not bear any responsibility for non-UCIL individuals. Chotrai Soren is now worried that the company might ask him to resign if he remains unfit. In effect, the uranium miners have a job until they contract TB.

Even though the retirement age is sixty years, rarely does one meet a uranium miner who has retired after serving his full term. If they have sons, miners usually opt for early retirement after being afflicted by some disease. Others who do not have this option try to stick to the job on a half-salary basis during the period of their treatment and then go back to work. However, most of them do not feel completely well even after prolonged treatment and some even die.

Besides miners, labourers who have worked on the tailing dams have also been afflicted by many illnesses, like Bhonjo Tudo who worked on one of the tailing dams as a contract labourer. He contracted TB after a year's work and died six months later.

Displacement and Resistance

According to the UCIL policy, all villages within 5 km of the mines and tailing dams should be evacuated. Yet little has been done to evacuate even those houses that are barely 100–200 metres away. Resettlement of the fifteen-odd villages within the 5-km radius has been far from satisfactory. The resettlement policy of the UCIL has not been uniform over the years, nor does it follow any national guidelines. Those whose lands were acquired in the last decade have been more demanding and have done better by way of compensation than those in the previous two decades. The residents of Tuwar-Dumridih (literally meaning orphaned-Dumridih), for example, were displaced from Dumridih village thirty-six years ago. These twenty-five families lost their homes and land to Tailing Dam 1. But no compensation was paid (except in the form of employment for some), nor was any help given to them to transfer their belongings or to build their new homes. Instead of being resettled in a safe location, oddly, they have been resettled close to a tailing dam. 'They did not tell us that this was a hazardous location. Finding the place free we decided to settle here,' explained one villager.

The residents of this hamlet are deeply unhappy. Ram Patro, a retired miner who worked in the UCIL mines for twenty-five years said:

> We live here like birds in a cage. The company says there is no radiation, but then why has it filled the local canal with earth? Our cows and buffaloes used to drink water there, we used to wash our clothes there, during birth and death ceremonies we used to bathe there. Now they have closed all this and not given much instead. There is no provision for grazing either. Except for a gate, there is

a fence all around our hamlet. Where should our children go to urinate? Would the big people have tolerated a situation where their women have to defecate in full view of the security guards? All this is a ploy to treat us badly so that we get fed up and leave without adequate resettlement. On 5 January, we were given a notice by the forest department saying that the land on which our houses are built is the forest department's land and that we should vacate it or face the bulldozers. The government does not take people like us seriously.

In the nearby Chatikocha hamlet, eighteen houses were bulldozed with minimal warning in 1996, to make way for Tailing Dam 3.

Several local organizations have come up to resist the UCIL, such as Manjhi Pargana Mahal, Jharkhandi Organization Against Radiation (JOAR) and Adivasi Samanvay Samiti. Of these, JOAR is the most prominent. Its major task has been to spread awareness on radiation and its ill-effects among the local population. Diverse means have been used to achieve this: village-level and public meetings as well as the use of popular media such as a film on the issue. The organization has also helped organize scientific surveys of the health and environmental consequences of uranium mining. Programmes have been organized on Children's Day as well as on Hiroshima Day when children with mental and physical disabilities were brought together. There have also been anti-nuclear rallies in Jamshedpur and other actions to put pressure on the authorities, sometimes involving national and international organizations. JOAR is also supporting a public interest litigation in the Supreme Court. A slogan in a recent JOAR rally asserted: 'Our land, our water, our forests, our rights!'

Resistance has not been without problems. Radiation is an elusive enemy and inadequate understanding of this issue has been the greatest hurdle. Ever since the UCIL has been operating in the area, people have been kept in the dark. Little effort has been made to enlighten them about radiation and its ill-effects. There are no scientific studies of the impact of radiation in India, though some studies are available for other parts of the world. In the absence of scientific know-how, even medical and environmental experts who have noted anomalies have not always been able to say with certainty whether these are due to radiation. However, in the case of Jadugoda the adverse effects are so serious that they have been clearly acknowledged by the Environment Committee of the Bihar Assembly in a report submitted in 1998, following a detailed survey.

Before the mines opened, the local people were entirely dependent on agriculture and forest produce for survival. As in the rest of Jharkhand, Adivasis in this region too own some land, though landholdings have shrunk over generations due to repeated sub-division. In the absence of irrigation, only one crop can be grown. Working in the mines or mills is therefore very common in these villages. For example, out of approximately 410 households in Tilaitand village, all but twenty-five had at least one member engaged in mines. Thus, over the years, economic dependence on the UCIL has become acute and at the same time, these very mines have also come to represent unknown danger, destruction and death. This paradoxical situation stands in the way of effective resistance. Many local as well as non-local employees of the UCIL, despite being personally affected, are not ready to speak out for fear of unemployment or victimization.

According to locals, the actions of the UCIL authorities have ranged from timid efforts to threats, harassment and denial. UCIL's official stand continues to be that radiation levels are low, that there is no adverse impact whatsoever and that they have been following international atomic energy guidelines. But these claims inspire little confidence in light of the ground reality. On important matters such as the possibility of radiation and its ill effects, there has been a shroud of secrecy legitimized by the Official Secrets Act. People's right to information has been suppressed on many important issues. For instance, the results of periodic health check-ups of the miners conducted by the UCIL hospital are not available to them. Miners as well as the local population are therefore unable to take control of their own circumstances.

The Jadugoda question has become an international issue, drawing attention to the ominous aspects of India's nuclear programme. What is happening in Jadugoda amounts to nothing less than a criminal act of human and environmental destruction. The government does not tire of reiterating that India's nuclear option is for self-defence. But at whose cost have such decisions been taken and whose 'self-defence' are we talking about? As the people of Jadugoda see it, the devastating consequences of uranium mining are ruining their lives and those of the future generations.

9

Resistance and Repression in Koel-Karo[*]

A faded green flag flies atop the Shaheed Smarak (Martyrs' Column) in Tapkara village of Ranchi district. The flag is changed every year on 2 March, I was informed, in memory of five *shaheeds* (martyrs) killed that day in a police firing at this very site in 1946. Their crime? They were demonstrating along with many thousand Munda Adivasis of the region for the formation of a separate Jharkhand state. Ironically, history repeated itself on 2 February 2001, in the newly formed Jharkhand. The police opened fire on an unarmed assembly of around 5000 Mundas including children, women and men.[1]

According to eyewitness accounts collected a few days after the event, the police fired more than 150 rounds, killing five on the spot. Five others succumbed to their injuries in the following hours, bringing the toll to ten. As many as twelve, who had sustained bullet injuries, were being treated in the Rajendra Medical College and Hospital (RMCH) in Ranchi, besides many other wounded who were being treated locally. Eight persons from six villages were still reported missing. The dead have been declared as shaheeds of the Koel-Karo

---

[*] Originally published in *Frontline*, 3 March 2001. Ranchi district was bifurcated later on and Tapkara is now in Khunti district. The Koel-Karo project was scrapped in 2003, soon after the firing incident reported here.

165

Jan Sangathan and have been buried next to the old Shaheed Smarak. In Tapkara Chowk, 1946 and 2001 have become one.

Testimonies of the Incident

Amrit Gudia, a retired army man, was returning from the jungle with a load of firewood on the afternoon of 1 February 2001 when he saw a police jeep break the barricade outside Derang village, drag it for a short distance, and then lift it on to the jeep. This barricade, which looks like the bamboo checkpost on a highway, was first erected in 1984 by the Koel-Karo Jan Sangathan to prevent National Hydroelectric Power Corporation (NHPC) and government officials from going to Lohajimi, a village beyond Derang, where a dam on the Karo river is expected to be built. In 1995, the government announced its decision to restart the project. In protest, a 'janata curfew' was imposed by the Sangathan and more such barricades were installed on the road leading to the dam site. A round-the-clock vigil was maintained at the barricades to prevent officials and police from entering the area without permission. These barricades, therefore, were no ordinary checkposts, but a powerful symbol of people's resistance to the project.

A furious Amrit Gudia now dropped his load, ran onto the mud road and obstructed their progress. 'Why had they broken the barricade?' he asked. 'They should have at least consulted with the people.' His protests met with abuse. The police officers in the jeep are reported to have shouted '*Maro, Maro* . . . [Beat him, beat him . . .]'. He was then beaten with lathis and the butts of guns by four or five policemen. The police later claimed that he was drunk. This action of the police was viewed by the people as purposive and provocative.

Pointing to a path by the side of the barricade, Soma Munda, president of the Sangathan pointed out, 'While going, the police jeep used this path, why then did they not return the same way but instead, chose to break the barricade? Neither the road nor the land on which the barricade had been constructed is government land; it is *raiyati* land belonging to two individuals, late Marcel Barjo and late Nathniyal Topno.'

No action was taken by the Sangathan that night. It was decided to assemble the following day. People started coming by around 8.30 a.m. from surrounding villages, and by 3.30 p.m., when the firing started, there were around 5000 or so people sitting outside the Tapkara police outpost and in adjoining areas. It should be emphasized that the movement has relied entirely on non-violent means during its nearly three-decade struggle; this tradition was respected during this *dharna* too. Nobody had come armed with any weapons—neither the traditional bows and arrows nor lathis. 'We would not have let our children come with us if we wanted to use violence,' said Biswasi Gudia of Derang village.

The assembled people waited for the DSP of the Khunti sub-division, F.K.N. Kujur, to arrive. The DSP and an official of magistrate rank (who has the power to order a firing) arrived at 11 a.m. R.N. Singh, the daroga of Tapkara outpost (under Torpa police station), as well as Akshay Kumar Ram, the daroga of the adjacent Rania police station, were already present. Altogether there were around forty policemen in the Tapkara outpost that day. While the assembled people waited, their leaders presented the demands of the Sangathan. First and foremost, the people demanded an explanation from the police authorities for breaking the barricade. Linked with this were three principal demands: that the officials who had ordered the beating of Amrit Gudia be suspended; that he be given monetary compensation of Rs 50,000; and that the police respectfully reinstall the barricade to the earlier state.

The DSP stated that he could not meet their demands since he had no power to suspend. Not satisfied with this outcome, the assembled people refused to move. In order to resolve the stalemate, the intervention of the local member of legislative assembly (MLA) was sought. He was brought on a motorcycle from Torpa. The MLA confirmed the Sangathan's demands to be just. He affirmed that R.N. Singh was arrogant and had in the past treated the public at large as well as the MLA himself with contempt. He was also corrupt. On many occasions, he had allegedly forced the Adivasis to get good quality wood from the forests and the non-Adivasi carpenters to make sofas and beds which he would then sell for profit.[2] The MLA's support of the Sangathan's demands did not satisfy the officials who decided to contact the Superintendent of Police (Rural). Soma Munda, Paulus Gudia and other activists of the Sangathan then came out of the outpost, as did the MLA.

By this time, it was around 3.30 p.m. The people had been sitting peacefully for six or seven hours, waiting for a response to their demands. According to eyewitness accounts, the Sangathan leaders had just started explaining the situation to the assembly when the two darogas came running out of the police station shouting 'Aadesh mila . . . aadesh mila [got the order . . . got the order]' and began the lathi charge.[3] Women and children who were sitting right in front were the first to be hit. People say that everything happened quickly afterwards. Almost at the same time as the lathi charge, the police began firing in the air. This was not done in full view of the public but from inside the outpost. Countless holes in the roof of the outpost bear testimony to this fact. Firing at the assembly followed immediately afterwards. Some who ran towards the back of the outpost also reported tear gas. Utter chaos prevailed. People started throwing stones at the firing policemen even as they ran to protect themselves. Some, like Lucas Gudia of Gondra village, forgot that theirs was an unequal combat and stones were hardly a match for bullets. Lucas is reported to have gone right up to the window of the police station in order to aim better. He was shot at and died on the spot. As young Adivasi activist–writer Sunil Minj points out, the history of Adivasi struggles in Jharkhand shows that whenever Adivasis get killed in similar incidents, they rarely die of shots fired from behind. An Adivasi faces and fights authority, even if he is unarmed. This fact was reiterated by other Sangathan members: 'If we wanted to use violence, no policeman would have gone back alive. Their firearms would not have stopped us. We were in thousands.'

In the stampede that followed, Kumulen Gudia (of Koynara village), who was five months pregnant, fell and was trampled on by running feet. She was carried later by other women till Dumkel village, two and a half kilometres away. She was then put on a cycle and wheeled on for another three kilometres of uneven terrain to her own village. She remained unconscious for two days.

Samuel Topno of Gondra village was tortured by the police in his injured state. Admitted in the neuro-surgery ward of RMCH in Ranchi, he said, 'As soon as the firing began, I started running towards the back of the police station. Four policemen chased me and fired. A bullet hit me on my left foot and I fell. Three boys tried to help me but fled when the policemen came after us. They put me on a sack and carried me to the police camp. Initially, they thought I was dead and left me. But when they realized I was alive, they started debating on how to kill me. "If we use our bare hands or fire from close range we could be in trouble," I heard one of them say. They brought a log of wood and placed it on my neck. Two policemen then stood on either end of the log. When I still did not die, they just kicked me on the head with their boots.'

Another person who had a similar experience is Francis Gudia, also of Gondra village. After being shot in the top-right part of his chest, he tried to drag himself and escape from the site of firing. 'Some of my companions were helping me when the police came. They threatened us by using abusive language. They took me to the police camp where they dumped me next to the dead, kicked me with their boots and then left me.' Samuel Topno, Francis Gudia and two others were sent by the police to the RMCH a few hours after the firing. No attempt was made, however, to dress their wounds, which continued to bleed. One of the injured died on the way to the hospital. Most of the others who had sustained serious bullet injuries were treated locally that night. Vijay Gudia, the general secretary of the Sangathan, pointed out the difficulties they had in trying to transport the injured to Ranchi that night itself. In the general atmosphere of terror that prevailed, nobody with private transport was willing to go. Nine of the seriously injured were taken by the Sangathan members in the early morning bus to Ranchi.

School-going children had also joined the dharna on their way back from school. Of the five who died on the spot, three were in secondary school. Some other children were wounded, like a Class IV student from Derang village whose legs were injured. According to some sources, a woman was also hit, though she could not be located. In the days immediately after the firing, the Sangathan activists were going from village to village in order to ascertain the situation: how many were killed, how many were injured and how many were missing. The exact numbers were hard to ascertain.

On the evening of 2 February, after the firing, the police broke into a house where Silai Gudia, a youth from Lohajimi village, had taken refuge. Sticking the butt of a gun on his chest, the policemen accused him of throwing bricks; after beating him, they took him to the Tapkara outpost. The police also broke into the houses of four non-Adivasis who were living close to the police outpost and arrested them. These four had been residing in Tapkara for many years and were engaged in masonry, carpentry and brick-making locally. They were taken to the outpost and locked in a room. Later that evening they were released and made to load all the stuff from the outpost into standing vehicles. The police vacated the outpost at around 1 a.m. with all their belongings as well as the dead bodies. The arrested were taken to Torpa police station and locked inside the inspector's room for the night. The following morning, they were made to unload the stuff from the vehicles. Naresh Gupta, one of those arrested, said: 'We were made to work like labourers. We were not given any bedding or blankets even though the night was cold, nor did we get anything to eat or drink until our release the following day at 4 p.m.'

A burnt police jeep stands outside the Tapkara outpost. A motorcycle in a similar state stands close by. The outpost itself is almost completely destroyed. Its three rooms have a scarred look: the perforated asbestos sheets of the roof, the torn doors and window frames, debris and ash everywhere and brick pieces lying scattered on the ground outside. Among what remains of the outpost, one can just about make out the words 'Satyamev Jayate [truth alone triumphs]' inscribed on the front wall.

People claim that the police had burnt the vehicles and wrought the destruction themselves. This was part of a strategy to enable them to allege that the public had turned violent and that the police firing was justified. Pointing to the missing tyres of the charred jeep, traders who live opposite the outpost said that the police had first taken the tyres off before setting the vehicle on fire. The motorcycle—a private vehicle seized by the police a few days earlier—was then cast into the flames.

Not far from the outpost is a huge banyan tree. Its leaves are dry and burnt, like the charred remains of three upturned jeeps lying below. According to local sources, these three jeeps were set on fire by the civilians of Tapkara after the firing began. Some newspapers also carried photographs of the burnt body of a policeman found at some distance from the outpost. R.N. Singh as well as two dozen policemen were reported to have sustained some injuries as bricks were thrown at them.

Several explanations have been offered for the incident. The official version is that the police had received information about the presence of Maoist Communist Centre (MCC) activists in the area and that the patrolling was part of ongoing anti-Naxalite operations. However, there is wide speculation that this is a pretext and that the truth lies elsewhere. It is interesting to note that even though police patrols in the area had ceased since the imposition of the 'janata curfew' in 1995, the DSP had gone to patrol the area as recently as 22 December 2000. Some people are wondering whether this patrolling had anything to do with the incident on 2 February.

Who ordered the firing? Was it ordered by the Superintendent of Police (Rural), whom the police officers in the outpost were trying to contact, or by the magistrate who was already present? Or was the decision to fire taken on the spot without official sanction? Whoever ordered the firing and whether or not it had official sanction, *post facto* the police are claiming that the situation had so developed as to justify the firing. Official action following the firing seems to be based on this assumption. The Deputy Commissioner (DC) and the Deputy Inspector General (DIG) are reported to have visited the Tapkara outpost that night, but no attempt was made by them to contact the people. No other government official has visited the site since. The police officials involved in the firing have not been suspended. When asked why this was so, the Senior Superintendent of Police (SSP), Neeraj Sinha, said that *prima facie* there was no justification for immediate suspensions. Official action would follow only after a high-level enquiry.

Members of the Sangathan feel that the MCC was used as a pretext to justify police repression. The real reason was to weaken the people's resistance against the Koel-Karo project and to pave the way for NHPC again. 'When in the height of the struggle no incident occurred, why now? *Lashon ko gira kar Koel-Karo naheen bandhega. Jab gaonwale raji honge tabhee* [Koel-Karo dams will not get built by laying down dead bodies, but only with people's agreement],' said Santosh Horo.

The Sangathan has put forward the following demands to the government: (1) a judicial inquiry should be set up to probe the incident, (2) the police officers and personnel responsible for the killings should be identified and punished, (3) compensation of Rs 5 lakh to the families of those killed and Rs 2 lakh to those seriously injured should be awarded, (4) only Adivasi police officers and personnel should be appointed to police stations in Adivasi-majority areas of Jharkhand, and (5) the Koel-Karo project should be cancelled. Accordingly, when a cheque of Rs 2 lakh was offered to the relatives of each deceased, it was refused. On 8 February, a *Sankalp Diwas* (pledge day) was organized. Thousands of people vowed that they would not allow the construction of the Koel-Karo dams to take place. They also resolved to keep the movement non-violent, as it had been in the preceding decades.

The police firing is a clear violation of the democratic rights of the people of Koel-Karo. That people should expect the police to be accountable for their actions is an important part of democracy in practice. Breaking the barricade was not an insignificant act. '*Hamare gaon mein hamara raj* [Our rule in our land]' may be just a slogan, yet to be realized in other parts of the country, but in the heart of the Munda 'country'—as S.C. Roy described the Mundas and their land in the early years of the twentieth century—it has been the practice for a long time. The social and political system of the Mundas is far more advanced than that of mainstream Indian society. Decision-making, for example, is based on consensus. There may be heads like Mundas and Parha Rajas but they do not expect others to be subservient to them, nor would the others allow that. Each Munda Adivasi, like members of other Adivasi communities in Jharkhand, expects to be part of the decision-making process. The fact that people belonging to such a society and culture should assemble in large numbers to defend their rights and demand an explanation for objectionable behaviour should not be surprising. Citizens are told time and again that they should not take the law into their own hands, but what happens when the police do the same?

This is not the first time that the state government has used gunpowder to silence people's power in Jharkhand. Indeed, police firing has become part of the 'dialogue' that the state has with the people when they have tried to practice democracy.[4] More often than not, Adivasis have been the main victims and in quite a few cases, police firing occurred in the context of people's resistance to forced displacement. This applies, for instance, to the police firings in Chandil in 1978 and in Icha in 1982, where people were protesting against the construction of big dams elsewhere (part of the Subarnarekha multi-purpose project) without proper resettlement of displaced people.[5] In both Chandil and Icha, the firings had an adverse impact on the incipient movements, which took some time to reorganize. The people of Koel-Karo are aware of the history of such incidents and are determined to ensure that what happened elsewhere should not happen to them.

The Koel-Karo Project and the Koel-Karo Jan Sangathan

The Koel-Karo Hydroelectric Power project was initiated in 1973 by the Bihar Electricity Board. In 1980–81, this project was handed over to the National Hydroelectric Power Corporation (NHPC). The project aims to generate 710 MW of electricity by building two dams on the rivers Koel and Karo. The submergence zone of the project is spread over Gumla, Ranchi and Singhbhum districts. Official estimates of the extent of displacement have tended to vary. In 1973, the government stated that forty-two villages would be submerged. In 1986, when the resettlement plan was prepared, this figure was revised to 112 villages. According to non-official sources, however, even the revised figure is an underestimate and in fact, 256 villages will face submergence, of which 135 will be submerged completely, affecting approximately 1.5 lakh people, most of them being Adivasis. Besides submerging villages, the project will also submerge 66,000 acres of prime land, of which roughly half is presently under cultivation and half is forest land. Importantly, at least 152 *sarnas* (groves of trees which were part of the original forests before they were cleared for settlement and are considered sacred) and 300 *sasan-diris* (stone slabs which form the ancestral graveyard of each family of *khuntkattidars*; these family *sasan-diris* make up a village *sasan*) will also get submerged.

As with other 'development' projects initiated in other states, in the case of Koel-Karo too, the state government did not deem it necessary to consult the people while planning the project or even to inform them about it in advance. The people got to know about the project only when government officials started coming to their villages and the first moves towards land acquisition were made. It was then that the people of the Koel region in Gumla district formed the Jan Sangharsh Samiti and those in the Karo region in Ranchi district formed the Jan Sanyojan Samiti. During 1975–76, both these organizations united to form the Koel-Karo Jan Sangathan. In the last twenty-six years, the Sangathan has shifted from a cooperative stance towards the government and the project to uncompromising opposition.

In its first communication with the government after its formation, the Sangathan had actually stated that it was willing to welcome the project if the government was willing to consider it as a people's project and accordingly make its policies and plans transparent to the public. However, the government's indifferent attitude on these questions made the Sangathan initiate a *Kaam Roko* (stop work) campaign in 1977–78. The campaign was a great success. All work came to a grinding halt; even cement sacks were not allowed to be unloaded from trucks. Ultimately, the government authorities agreed to have a tripartite meeting including the Sangathan, the project authorities and government representatives. A decision was made to conduct a joint socio-economic survey of the affected villages. A detailed questionnaire was prepared and the survey was conducted in two or three villages. But this process got interrupted when filled-in schedules vanished from the project office!

The Sangathan then prepared a document which defined *sampoorn punarvas* (total resettlement) as the people saw it. It observed that total resettlement was possible only if besides economic resettlement, social, cultural and religious resettlement were also taken into consideration. The Sangathan now proposed that the government should first resettle two villages as an example. If the people were satisfied, the government could go ahead with the resettlement programme. Even though this was agreed upon, nothing was done. Instead, in July 1984, the government announced that force would be used to advance work on the project.

Armed police arrived in the area but soon had to pack their bags and withdraw. The nature of people's resistance was such that their day-to-day survival had become impossible. They were stopped from cutting trees for their camps; nobody sold them any wood for fuel; a rumour was spread that the water in the well had been poisoned; and they were not allowed to defecate in the forests. The police had to go all the way from Lohajimi to Torpa, 12 km away, to get fuelwood and water for their everyday needs. An end was put to this too when women decided to sow on the mud road on which their jeeps plied, claiming that it was private land and not a public thoroughfare; if they still drove their jeeps over it, they would have to face their bows and arrows!

That same year, a writ petition was filed in the Supreme Court. The Supreme Court ordered that the project be stopped until the state complied with certain conditions regarding resettlement. This led to the government's announcement of a resettlement policy in 1991. In 1995, the Bihar government decided to restart the project and announced that the foundation stone would be laid on 5 July by the then Prime Minister, Narasimha Rao. This move of the government led to renewed and vigorous mobilization in the area. Thousands of people participated in rallies and *satyagrahas* organized in many villages, culminating in the imposition of 'janata curfew' from midnight of 1 July in the project area. Three barricades were erected on the road leading up to the dam site and have been in place since then. The Prime Minister decided to cancel his visit. The foundation stone of the Koel-Karo project is yet to be laid. The Sangathan's stand is now firm—no compensation, no resettlement and no project!

10

Forced Evictions in the Narmada Valley[*]

Introduction

The Sardar Sarovar Project (SSP), one of the largest irrigation and power projects in the world, is likely to displace a larger number of people than any other development project in India. The extent and possibility of 'just and proper' resettlement of displaced persons have occupied a central place in official discourse and public debate on the project.

In this case study of five submerging villages of Gujarat and eleven corresponding resettlement sites, an attempt has been made to examine whether there is any evidence of 'forced evictions' of the affected families. This term covers the United Nations' notion of forced eviction as 'involuntarily removing people from their homes against their will'. In this study, the scope of this definition has been further expanded to include any eviction which had already taken place or was taking place at the time of research, without the full

---

[*] This essay is an abridged version of the original article (Bhatia, 1997), itself based on a larger report submitted to the Gujarat High Court in July 1993. The report was a contribution to a public interest litigation (PIL) initiated by Lok Adhikar Sangh, a human rights organization based in Ahmedabad. Senior Advocate Girish Patel was arguing the case on behalf of the Sangh.

satisfaction of stipulated requirements, or under circumstances in which the displaced persons were unable to exercise their own free will and judgement.

While the SSP resettlement package is often regarded as exemplary, serious doubts about the practical feasibility of this package have been expressed by independent commissions such as the Morse Commission which undertook an independent review of the resettlement and rehabilitation (R&R) aspects of the project for the World Bank in June 1992, and the report of the World Bank Review Mission in July of the same year. Based on these two reports, the World Bank decided to set resettlement and rehabilitation targets, often called 'benchmarks', in October 1992. The fulfilment of these benchmarks before 31 March 1993 became a crucial condition for further disbursement of the World Bank loan to the Sardar Sarovar Project.[1]

However, contradictory claims continued to be made about the extent to which the Gujarat government was able to fulfil the official R&R norms while displacing families from the affected villages of Gujarat. This study seeks to survey the extent to which Gujarat 'oustees' have been resettled according to the stipulated norms and regulations of official policy, as spelt out in government resolutions, in loan agreements with the World Bank and in the award of the Narmada Water Disputes Tribunal (NWDT).[2]

The study chooses to focus on the resettlement situation of Gujarat oustees for one significant reason: with few exceptions, the affected people in the nineteen submerging villages of Gujarat have not resisted the dam or the resettlement process. In fact, they have patiently cooperated with the government for the last fourteen years. In this sense, resettlement in Gujarat has taken place in comparatively favourable conditions and the case studies presented below may provide a useful basis for assessing the credibility of the resettlement programmes associated with the Sardar Sarovar project.

The Study Villages

The five villages included in this study are Gadher, Katkhadi, Mokhadi, Surpan and Vadgam. These five villages, situated in Nandod taluka of Bharuch district in south-west Gujarat, were among the six first-phase villages to be affected by submergence. The Gujarat High Court passed a stay order on 24 February 1993, restraining the government of Gujarat from forcibly removing people from these six villages and from displacing them without due compliance with the R&R provisions. It was, therefore, considered necessary to review the extent to which this order had been respected by the implementing authorities. There was also an urgent need to examine the plight of the people still remaining in the submerging villages as well as of those who had moved to the resettlement sites (particularly after the stay order had been granted) and to complete this exercise before the lands in their original villages got submerged. All these were important concerns in the PIL that was being fought in the Gujarat High Court at that time.

The eleven resettlement sites in which the survey was conducted are Baroli, Chametha, Kamboya Kuwa, Chhatiambli, Chichadia, Kalitalavdi, Kantheswar, Khokhra, Kodi Kuwa, Malu and Sankwa. These sites are located in Naswadi and Tilakwada talukas of Bharuch district and Sankheda and Dabhoi talukas of Baroda district. Displaced persons from four of the five study villages were resettled at these sites.[3]

The Survey Period

This report is based on fieldwork carried out in two phases from March to May 1993. It is important to mention some significant features of this period:

1. The fieldwork immediately followed the Gujarat High Court order of 24 February 1993, restraining the government of

Gujarat from forcibly removing people from these five first-phase villages.

2. During the first phase of the fieldwork, the government was frantically trying to meet the R&R benchmarks before the 31 March deadline set by the World Bank.

3. The second phase of the research included two significant events: the Government of India's decision (on 30 March 1993) to renounce the balance of the World Bank project loan, and the central government's decision (on 22 April 1993) to step in and provide the necessary funds for the completion of the project.

4. On 30 April 1993, the High Court passed a further order elaborating its earlier interim stay of 24 February 1993. This order reiterated a Supreme Court directive (dated 9 August 1991) that the people must be fully resettled at least six months prior to actual submergence. The High Court made it clear that the earlier stay also applied to the forcible removal of people on account of submergence caused by the project and ruled out any displacement, even temporary, during the monsoon of 1993. In spite of these orders, many families were displaced during the month of May. I was able to assess the process involved in displacing and relocating them, aside from observing the plight of those who had been resettled earlier.

5. The last phase of this study (late May 1993) witnessed a heavy police presence in a number of villages of Gujarat and Maharashtra, especially in Manibeli, the first village on the Maharashtra side to face submergence. The nearest town from the five study villages, Kevadia, was turned overnight into a police town. Human rights observers who witnessed this situation described it as a 'police siege'.[4]

In short, this was a period of considerable political turmoil. The facts presented in this report should be read in this light.

The Survey Method

This study is based on in-depth interviews with residents of the study villages and resettlement sites. In the study villages, the first phase of fieldwork focused on households which were scheduled to be submerged during the monsoon of 1993.[5] They were at various stages of relocation, e.g., some were dismantling their houses and leaving for the resettlement sites, others were waiting for land to be allotted to them and others still had come back after the stressful experience of living in a resettlement site for a few years. During the second phase, particular attention was given to households which had resisted displacement during April and May.

At the resettlement sites, the primary focus during the first phase of fieldwork was on households which had moved their houses after the 24 February stay order. During the second phase, the focus was on those who had moved their houses after the 30 April order of the Gujarat High Court.

Affected Families in the Study Villages

Also called 'dam site' villages on account of their proximity to the dam, the five study villages are predominantly tribal. Most of the inhabitants belong to two tribal groups: Tadvis and Vasavas (originally Bhils), with a large majority of Tadvis in each village. Village-wise profiles of the project-affected persons (PAPs), and some basic demographic features of the study villages, are presented in Table 1.

In this section, I shall present some findings relating to one village, Katkhadi, based on the first phase of fieldwork. While particular resettlement issues are more pertinent in some villages than in others, the general resettlement situation did not differ greatly between different villages. Katkhadi is not representative of the study villages in every respect, but it does provide a good illustration of the general situation.

Table 1

Demographic Profile of Project Affected Persons in the Study Villages

	Number of Households	Population	Literate Population		Landed	PAPs[a]			
			Female	Male		Landless	Major Sons	Total	
Gadher	370	2399	59	360	260	56	418	807
Katkhadi	52	331	16	71	24	9	77	110
Mokhadi	225	1337	4	182	207	15	200	422
Surpan	76	417	16	65	72	12	51	135
Vadgam	315	1730	65	360	235	27	292	554
Total	1038	6214	160	1038	798	119	1038	2028

Source: Columns 2, 3, 4 and 5 are based on Census of India 1981; Columns 6-9 are based on 'Submerging Village Profile' prepared by the Sardar Sarovar Narmada Nigam, Baroda, Gujarat.

[a] The numbers of PAPs in different categories are based on government records. For Gadher, the figure in the 'total' column is a little higher than the relevant row total; this is a case of internal inconsistency in the official figures. Also in Gadher, landless households include 21 'encroachers'.

Case Study: Katkhadi

At the time of the 1981 census, Katkhadi had a population of fifty-two households and 331 individuals, divided in three hamlets or *falias* (Nishad, Gaman and Bhagor falias). The population had increased to 375 by 1989.[6] Over 90 per cent of the people in the village belong to the Tadvi tribe.

In 1993, the official number of PAPs in Katkhadi was 110 (see Table 2). Of these, seventy-seven PAPs belonged to households classified as those of 'major sons'. At the time of the first phase of the survey in March 1993, thirty-four PAPs were still in the village. At least fifteen eligible major sons had not yet been included in the PAP list.

Table 2
Village-Wise Resettlement of PAPs

	Number of Hamlets	Number of Declared PAPs	Number of Resettlement Sites[a]
Gadher	12	807	32+
Katkhadi	3	110	6
Mokhadi	3	422	8+
Surpan	4	135	6+
Vadgam	14	554	27+

Source: Field survey conducted during March–May, 1993.
[a] The figures in the last column are approximate minimum numbers of resettlement sites, based on the information available from the displaced persons.

Among the Katkhadi PAPs who could be included in the survey, thirty-five had returned from Timbi resettlement site in 1992, after having lived there for three years. These thirty-five were later allotted land in four sites, namely Kalitalavdi (15), Chichadia (4), Sankwa (3) and Nada-Dabhoi (13). In spite of having been allotted land, seventeen of the thirty-five Timbi returnees were still in Katkhadi at the time of the survey.

The resettlement process was underway when I first visited the village. Households which were to move in the near future were getting their fodder and cattle transported in trucks to their respective resettlement sites. These would be kept on the house plot allotted to them. Some members of the family were seen accompanying these trucks. The house material was always the last to be taken away.

Most of the villagers were busy chopping as much wood as they could when I visited them. They told me that they were trying to take enough to last them for at least a year. They were aware that at the new sites they would face a serious shortage of fuelwood.

Heaps of cow dung were also being moved away. I learnt that this was *chan khatar* (organic fertilizer), and that these truckloads were not heading towards the resettlement sites, as I had thought, but had been sold to contractors for a mere Rs 80–100 per truckload. The contractors were making a quick buck by reselling this fertilizer for profit in nearby villages. The villagers could not take this to the new site for use as fuel since it was mixed with mud. Their intention had been to move to the new site the following year, so they had prepared this fertilizer for their fields for the coming agricultural season. Now that they were being forced to move immediately, they had decided to sell the stock they had at whatever price it would fetch.

The main R&R problems confronting the villagers, as expressed by them during group discussions, were the following: some of the PAPs had still not been allotted any land; others had been given less than the official minimum of five acres; some eligible residents had not yet been declared PAPs; many major sons had been excluded from the PAP list; in many cases, the *kutumb* (extended family) had been split up; the government was removing people and emptying the village in the absence of an adequate resettlement process; and difficult conditions were expected at the resettlement sites. Some evidence and examples of these different problems follow.

Inadequate Land Allotments

Ramabhai Ukkadbhai was given a house plot at Kantheswar, but only a part of the land that he had been offered was located in Kantheswar; the rest was three kilometres away. One part of the land was also taken up by a small stream passing through it.

Kila Shiva had been offered less than five acres of land, at Chichadia resettlement site. He was determined not to move until he and his major son were given land and house plots in the same place.

Most of the other PAPs who had been allotted land mentioned the numerous difficulties they had in selecting land that found approval with the government officers. Often, the price of the land they had selected was more than the amount the government was willing to pay. They contended that no uniform policy was followed by the government on this issue. While they were told to select land in the range of Rs 6000 to 7000 per acre, there were other PAPs who had been allotted land priced at Rs 23,000–27,000 per acre.

The Situation of the Non-PAPs

Lalji Hura had been working as a cattle-grazer for the Katkhadi residents for over two decades. Now that there were so few people left, how could he survive in the same job? Since people of the village had been dispersed to so many sites, he could not even resume the same occupation in some other site. He had been compensated for his house but was not allotted any land because he was not declared a PAP, even though he clearly fell under the definition of an oustee as spelt out in the Tribunal award.[7] Similarly, two *gharjamais* (sons-in-law who live in the fathers-in-law's houses), married to sisters of

Chiman Shiva, had also not received benefits as PAPs since they had not been recognized as 'oustees'.

The Problems Faced by Major Sons

Major sons, i.e., those who had attained the age of eighteen on 1 January 1987, was another group of persons who often ended up being unfairly excluded from the PAP list. The Tribunal award states that every major son should be treated as a separate family. The problems faced by major sons can be summed up in the words of one of the residents: 'They were promised a *naukari* (service, in this context government service)—they did not get it. They were promised land—they did not get that either.' There were as many as fifteen to twenty major sons amongst the remaining households in Katkhadi, many of whom were married and had children but had not been declared PAPs. All of them had been asked to produce certificates proving that they had attained the age of eighteen in 1987. Acquiring a certificate was possible only for those who had attended school. Others were required to get these certificates from the talati, who inevitably expected a bribe. Many of them had submitted these certificates to the government office in Kevadia without keeping a copy for themselves. They were now unable to prove their age to any other officer when asked for the same evidence.

Community Resettlement

Community resettlement has been laid out as an important principle of the resettlement process. However, except for twenty oustees from Gaman falia, others in Katkhadi have not been resettled on a community basis as required by the Tribunal award. The fifty-six PAPs of Nishad falia found themselves scattered in six different sites. People pointed out that no resettlement site had been found for them where contiguous, good quality agricultural land was available, enabling community resettlement. High land prices also proved to be a major obstacle. As a result, people had to be scattered in various sites. 'We did not want to be dispersed. We wanted to go together so that *samp rahe* [we remain united].[8] We tried to complain but nobody listened. They are not bothered about us tribal people.' Such was the general feeling expressed by most of the affected people.

The problem of failure of community resettlement is by no means unique to Katkhadi. As Table 2 indicates, PAPs from the study villages have been relocated in dozens of different sites (at least thirty-two for Gadher alone).

Inadequate Resettlement Process

The people felt that the government had moved them without a proper resettlement process and that their village leaders had been bribed and pampered by the authorities so that they would raise no objections nor make any demands for the welfare of the village community as a whole. Many fraudulent practices which had occurred during the resettlement process were mentioned. One striking instance was that of Mansingbhai Chunilal and five other PAPs, who were shown land in the thick of the night with a torch and also made to sign the *dastavej* (written agreement) in the night— more about this in the following section (The 'Resettled' Oustees).

Problems Envisaged at the Resettlement Site

Some of the expected problems at the new sites that worried the villagers were related to the availability of fuel, fodder and work opportunities. Already, many of them had experienced some of these difficulties at the Timbi resettlement site. As one of the oustees put it: 'Here we have free access to fuel and fodder. At the new site, how will we be able to keep our cattle alive? How many of our needs can we fulfil with five acres of land? Here, if we do not have kerosene, we can use wood—what will we do there?'

Regarding labour opportunities at the new sites, people said: 'In this area there are many different types of labour opportunities we can benefit from. There is work at the dam site. There is environment-related labour work. We can also collect timru leaves [a local shrub] and be paid for that. Leaving our own land and going to work for wages on someone else's land is something that we normally don't do.'

Difficulties related to housing added to these anxieties. The houses of tribal families in these areas need major repair and maintenance every few years, since they are made of bamboo, mud and wood. How would they be able to do this at new sites with almost no tree cover?

Drinking water facilities at the resettlement sites were also inadequate. Many families had been asked to move to the new sites even though satisfactory arrangements had not been made there for drinking water and other civic amenities. One example was that of Chiman Mohan and his family, who had been asked to move to Sankwa barely two weeks after being allotted land.

Oustees resettled at Kalitalavdi, like Kashiram Chunilal and his brothers, were worried on account of the fragmentation of the land allotted to them. This not only caused difficulties in cultivation but also made collective irrigation impossible, unless tubewells were constructed with government help.

General Observations

In the second phase of fieldwork, the five study villages were revisited after the 30 April stay order granted by the Gujarat High Court against forced evictions. Despite the stay order, more than 200 families of PAPs had been moved from these five villages during the preceding two months.

The critical question is whether people were forced to move. Considerable evidence suggests that direct and indirect means were used to pressurize people. In Mokhadi, government officers had come in April and May and informed the people that if they did not move, the authorities would bring bulldozers to remove them. People of Vadgam village, most of whom had been resettled at Malu resettlement site the previous year but had returned to their original village after an unhappy experience there, were also issued two additional notices urging them to move back to Malu. In this village, indirect measures were also used to cause considerable distress to the people still residing there. The intentions of the government became perfectly clear when the main road leading to the village was dug out at various places and the local school was closed, a few months before my visit. In most villages, trees such as mahuda, a major source of income for tribal communities, were being cut and loaded onto standing trucks by the government.[9]

Besides these direct and indirect coercive methods, the ever-increasing height of the dam was a source of escalating fear. The prospect of certain submergence as the monsoon approached and the risk of possible destruction of their houses, belongings and cattle created a climate of panic which led many oustees to feel they had no option but to take what they could get from the government and shift to the new site.

As we shall see, most of these families were moved under false pretences and through misleading promises. They were told, for instance, that all the required amenities were available at the resettlement sites. Those who had not been allotted any land were told that they would be given land at the earliest.

Talking to the people, I came to the distressing conclusion that the High Court stay order had been ineffective in avoiding forcible evictions during the month of May. People were not only kept in the dark about the order, but also removed in a hurry according to previously set targets. Among those who were being displaced were

PAPs whose land was scheduled to be submerged in the monsoon of 1993 as well as 1994 and 1995 (as in the case of Gadher). This was a blatant violation not only of the stay order, but also of the Tribunal award and of other official agreements. It made a farce of the government's loud and incessant claims of commitment to the 'just and proper resettlement' of the affected people.

The 'Resettled' Oustees

This section focuses on two of the eleven resettlement sites I surveyed: Khokhra and Chichadia. These two case studies illustrate the nature of the difficulties involved in the resettlement process and also highlight some qualitative aspects of people's lives at the resettlement sites. Some observations from the other sites are presented in summary form in Tables 3 and 4.

Khokhra

In early April 1993, fourteen families from two hamlets in Gadher and one family from Katkhadi were resettled at this site which is located in an area with a large Vasava population. This case study highlights one problematic aspect of land compensation—failed land allotments. It also draws attention to the government's determination to move people even when crucial R&R norms remain unfulfilled.

The land allotted to the resettled families belonged to a farmer called Atul Premji. On 11 February 1992, when the land agreement was executed, people were given a simple receipt—the land was not entered under their names in the official records of the talati, nor were any formal papers (e.g., a copy of the signed agreement) given to them. This later became a source of endless problems. In practical terms, it meant that in spite of having notional land allotments, the displaced PAPs were unable to gain effective *kabja haq* (right of possession) over their land. The landlord prevented them from

Table 3
Condition of Nine Resettlement Sites, May 1993

Resettlement site	Original village	Number of resettled PAPs	Time when shifted in 1993	Drinking Water	Facilities available				Fuel Shortage
					Electricity	Cremation Ground	Gochar Land		
Baroli	Gadher	70	20 in late March	1 well (incomplete)	No (few poles)	No	No		Yes
Chametha	Gadher	52	17+ in late April	1 well (non-potable water)	No (few poles)	No	No		Yes
Chhatiambli	Gadher	5	Mid-May	1 handpump	No	No	No		Yes
Chichadia	Katkhadi Gadher Vadgam	50+	Early April (from Katkhadi)	1 handpump; natural stream close by	No	No	No		Yes
Kalitalavdi	Katkhadi Gadher	19	Early April	tanker (saline water)	No	No	No		Yes
Kantheswar	Surpan	44	Late April	tanker	No	No	No		Yes
Khokhra	Gadher Katkhadi	15	Early April	1 handpump	No (few poles)	No	No		Yes
Kodikuwa	Gadher	2	Early May	private well	No	No	No		Yes
Sankwa	Katkhadi Gadher	5	Mid-April	no source; dependent on host village	No	No	No		Yes

Table 4
Main Problems Reported by the PAPs
Living at the Resettlement Sites

Resettlement Site	Main Problems[a]
Baroli	• Threat of this site being submerged in the monsoon as a result of the blocking of drains of the SSP canal constructed nearby. • Severe drinking water shortage.
Chametha	• Almost 70 per cent of the affected people have been allotted land which is of inferior quality or uncultivable. • Many of them have been allotted less than five acres of land. • Serious problem of non-potable drinking water.
Chhatiambli	• Land allotted to some of the oustees is of inferior quality. • Eligible major sons have not been included in the PAP list. • There has been no follow up from the government officers after their relocation.
Chichadia	• Five PAPs and two major sons relocated forcibly without being allotted any land, house plots or tin sheds. Subsequently, twenty-seven days after moving there, two of them were allotted land which was less than 5 acres. • House plots were not cleared before the oustees were brought to the site. PAPs had to remove the stumps of Eucalyptus trees themselves. There are, approximately, 40 such stumps in each house plot. • Eight oustees have been allotted low-lying land which gets submerged during the monsoon, making cultivation impossible. Cultivation is possible only during the winter.
Kalitalavdi	• PAPs have not been given possession of the land because the landowner has not been paid. • Land has not been cleared or demarcated, nor have land records been completed. • Five PAPs have been allotted land which is less than 5 acres; land allotted to four PAPs is of inferior quality and 8 major sons have not been allotted any land. • Water in the area is saline. • Many oustees have not yet received compensation for their houses in their original village. • Tin sheds are not ready for all the oustees.

Kantheswar	• Land allotted to most of the oustees is less than 5 acres. • Some of the land that has been allotted is uncultivable. • In most cases, allotted land is not yet demarcated. • Dastavej of the land has been completed but kabja haq has not been given. The original owner continues to cultivate. • Tin sheds are not ready for all the oustees.
Khokhra	• The PAPs have been allotted land but have not got the kabja haq. The original owner threatens them from entering the land and continues to benefit from the land. • Some oustees have either been given less than the stipulated 5 acres or the cultivable area of the land received is less than 5 acres. • A few oustees have still not been included as PAPs.
Kodi Kuwa	• No tin sheds were constructed for the people before they moved to the site as is the government norm. • A few PAPs have been allotted less than 5 acres of land.
Sankwa	• The resettled oustees have not been allotted house plots. • They have no source of drinking water at the site. They are facing extreme difficulties in getting potable drinking water from the host village.

Source: Field survey, March–May 1993.
ᵃ At *all* sites, resettled persons, especially women, complained about a serious shortage of fuel and fodder.

cultivating the land during the monsoon as well as the winter season in 1992.

The same story was repeated in the monsoon of 1993. At the beginning of the season, Shevanti Utran, on the advice of a senior government official (Mr Gandhi, the Deputy Collector), decided to sow his land. But he found that Atul Premji had already sown it. The response of the official to this fraudulent act was: 'Don't worry, he will give you your share.' But the PAPs did not get anything. The same happened during the winter season.

This seemingly insoluble problem, which developed while they were still in their original villages, discouraged the PAPs from moving their houses to the resettlement site. They knew that any move to the resettlement site would be irreversible and that after such a move their resettlement would be deemed complete. Their plight also restrained other families from moving without full R&R provisions.

However, they were unable to stand their ground for very long. In late March 1993, and again in early April, the government sahibs came in several jeeps and said to them: 'All of you have to move immediately. We are responsible for emptying this village. You will have to go—there is no other way.' The people explained the land situation to the officers. They were told that their problem would be solved at the earliest. Atul Premji, by way of a compromise, suggested: 'All of you can start cultivating and give me part of the produce.' Even though this was hardly a just solution, the PAPs decided to accept the deal as a temporary compromise. They were under intense pressure and felt they had little choice. But after they went to Khokhra, the promises did not materialize; neither did the government officers pay them a visit, nor did the landlord allow them to enter the land. Instead, he threatened them in the following words: 'Don't you dare step on my land. If you do, then just a clap of my hands would fetch all the heavy-weights from Videshia, Nakhalpur and other nearby villages—you will then know who you are up against.'

Kantibhai Mansukbhai was an exception—his land was demarcated and there were even irrigation facilities on his land. During the winter season, he sowed wheat. But Atul Premji did not allow him to reap the harvest, on the grounds that as long as the land allocated to the oustees was not recorded in the books of the talati, he would not allow them to cultivate it.

On 16 April, the landlord threatened them again. The PAPs felt insecure. Against someone so powerful, who had clearly stated that he had already 'pleased the Deputy Collector', resistance seemed futile. They did not know any way out of their predicament and felt completely helpless. When I visited them, they were using up their stocks of makai (maize) and jowar (millet). Many of them had to buy grain from the market. Their overwhelming worry was the imminent

monsoon, only two weeks away. It was time for them to prepare
their fields. If they were unable to cultivate the monsoon crop, what
would they eat? Where else could they go? They had heard that part
of the land they had been cultivating for generations in Gadher (the
government wasteland) had been used by the forest department to
plant saplings. The land for which they had land titles still remained.
They felt that if the government did not solve their problem soon,
they would have no option but to return to their village, where they
could at least subsist on forest produce and hope to be able to sow
their fields.

Apart from the basic problem of access to land, the people
who were being resettled at Khokhra had to cope with many other
problems, including the following: five families had a road passing
through their agricultural plots, reducing the effective land area to
less than five acres; two families of *gharjamais* (sons-in-law who stay
at their wives' home), who had been living in Gadher for the last
thirty years and had come under the official definition of 'project-
affected persons', had not been recognized as such; many other
project-affected people had also not been declared as PAPs. Further,
prescribed facilities such as electricity, *gochar* (pasture) land, schools
and cremation grounds were mostly absent or inadequate.

The fact that people moved to this site despite knowing that they
would face these acute problems clearly points to the coercive nature
of their displacement and resettlement.

Chichadia

In Chichadia, I learnt about the plight of a number of families who
had been resettled from Katkhadi. These families were among the
thirty-five families who had returned from the Timbi resettlement
site, after living there for three years (see 'Case Study: Katkhadi'
earlier). Lack of integration with the host community as well as
inferior quality of allotted land were their main grievances. On

return, they were shown alternative land at various sites. Attempts to resettle them in haste involved various instances of fraud. One such incident is described below.

Mansing Chunilal and five others were taken to select land in the Dabhoi area at night and shown land with a torch. They were not interested in seeing that land but had been compelled to go there. They were brought back at 4 a.m. The same day, they were taken to Kevadia and from there back to Dabhoi in the evening. The land agreement was signed at 2.30 a.m. in the presence of many government officers. The absence of the landowner (who, they learnt, was also a tribal) made them suspect that he too was unaware of the deal. They refused to sign the documents but were forced to do so. However, all this was of little use since they refused to go to the site.

In April 1993, more than thirty families from Katkhadi were moved. Only around five to eight houses remained. One day the project officers came to remove these houses too. When the people appealed to a senior R&R officer, he agreed that they should be given another chance to select land of their choice and provided a vehicle for this purpose. Thereafter they selected land at Chichadia and were asked to move immediately. They were reluctant to go because, even though they had selected the land, the documents had not yet been executed, nor had they been provided with house compensation and house plots at the new site. It was, however, made clear to them that unless they moved immediately their houses would get submerged. 'The officers used to come in vehicles every day and threaten to come with the police if we did not move. Ultimately, we had to depart to the new site.'

On reaching Chichadia, they found that the tin sheds (temporary shelters to be provided by the authorities during the transition phase) were not ready. All the families had to live in the open, in the middle of the summer, for nearly a month. When I visited them, I found women cooking in a makeshift kitchen, little children and older women sitting under shades made of dried leaves and twigs, men trying to clear their homestead plots of tree stumps. Those who had cleared their plots had started building their sheds with material brought from their previous houses and with tin sheets they found at the site. Since there was no electricity at the site, and all their household belongings were out in the open, they had to stand guard in the night. Even then, some of their material got stolen a few days after their arrival.

'Not a single government officer came to enquire about our condition since we arrived a month ago. When we were in our villages, two or three officers used to come every day, but now we are left to fend for ourselves. We had to go to Kevadia a number of times at our own cost. We have told the officers that unless the documents are executed and the land allotted to us in the near future, we would prefer to go back to Katkhadi.' After many such applications, Mansing Chunilal and Raising Chunilal were able to get the documents executed for nine acres of land, but many others are still without land titles.

This is another clear case of forcible eviction. Commenting on the way the government had treated them, Raisingbhai said: 'They removed us as they would remove a dead body.' When I left them, the foremost question on their minds was—what will happen if we are not allotted land before the monsoon? Already, having exhausted their food stocks and cash resources, they were surviving by borrowing food from relatives.

Some Resettlement Issues

Among the major concerns of displaced people are, first and foremost, those immediately related to their survival. While economic issues are central, changes in their social life are no less important. This section discusses four specific concerns, based on their experiences so far: land compensation; water, fodder and fuel; house compensation; and intra-family conflicts.

Land Compensation

Land compensation is the most important and challenging aspect of resettlement and rehabilitation. To start with, traditional landholding patterns in the study villages are quite complex. Briefly, cultivable land falls into four categories: (1) revenue land (*khata valli jameen*); (2) waste land (*kharaba*); (3) forest land (*jungle jameen*); and (4) river-bank land (*narmada kath vallo kacho kharabo*). Of these, only the first category is registered. Most of the remaining land is said to be 'encroached'. While the law in Gujarat prescribes that forest land cultivated prior to 1968 should be regularized, this has not been done in these areas.

In all the villages I visited, plots of revenue land tended to be very small due to repeated partition within the kutumb. Further, most of them were unregistered, as the land records had not been updated. The R&R rules and regulations recognize only registered revenue land as 'land owned' by the family. The affected people have, therefore, lost out on land compensation. Other problems related to land compensation are illustrated below.

Inadequate Compensation

Though the land acquired in the early 1980s was taken over under the Land Acquisition Act of 1894, many affected people have not received any compensation for it. Many PAPs (landed, landless and 'encroachers') have still not been allotted any land or have been given less than five acres. Landed oustees who owned more than five acres of land, but less than the land ceiling in the state, have simply been given five acres like other displaced families. I did not come across a single case where they were compensated according to R&R provisions.

Widowed women have not been compensated for their land even if they are *khatedars* (registered landowners). Many major sons who were eighteen in 1987 have not received their allotment of land, if they have been listed as PAPs at all. Further, major sons who were in the age group of 18–24 years at the time of the survey rightly argued that age at the time of displacement is a more appropriate basis of eligibility than age in 1987.

Unfulfilled Promises

One recurring complaint was of rosy promises made by government officials before the signing of the dastavej, which were then evaded after the land was allotted. Displaced persons were being given less than five acres, often fragmented into several small plots. In many cases the land was of poor quality or even uncultivable (e.g., waterlogged, sandy or saline).

Sometimes government officials roundly cheat the PAPs, e.g., by showing them a particular piece of land and making them sign for another or by allotting them land which does not correspond to the survey number they signed for. A copy of the dastavej, or a receipt acknowledging the agreement, is rarely given to the people. Without such evidence, people have been unable to assert their claims.

The oustees' problems do not end with the signing of the dastavej and land allotment. Some farmers have lost part of the land allotted to them after it was re-acquired for canal construction. Some oustees have not been able to take possession of their land as the original owner continues to exercise control over it. To compound these problems, government officials are lax in updating land records and ensuring that these are in line with land allotments.

Disregard for Official R&R Criteria

During the process of resettlement, R&R norms have been openly flouted. For example, R&R provisions specify that the acquired land should be compensated with irrigable land and that the authorities should make the land ready for cultivation prior to resettlement.

None of the oustees I met had been provided with any irrigation facilities, and except for a few stray cases, they had to use their own labour and resources to make their land cultivable. Those who were unhappy with the land allotted to them and tried to get it transferred to a new site faced official hostility or outright refusal.

Widows and Land Rights

One of the main flaws of the R&R package is that it has followed a patriarchal notion of property rights. The package does not give equal rights to men and women; land entitlements are given to major sons but not major daughters. And widows—one of the most vulnerable groups—have been further marginalized and dispossessed as a result of the resettlement process.

The resettlement policy in Gujarat prescribes that a widow who has lost her husband before 1980 cannot be counted as a household head and must be considered a dependent. This implies that such widows, even if they are khatedars, cannot receive land compensation; nor are they eligible for house compensation. Some of the widows I met had held land titles of as much as sixteen acres but had not been compensated either in cash or in kind.

Even when widows have been provided with land, many of them have had to forgo their entitlement because the land allotted to them was far away from their sons, or because it was of very poor quality. For instance, Lallliben, originally a resident of Gadher village, was allotted land thirty kilometres away from the site where her son Ambalal had been resettled (see Chapter 5—Ekaki). Unable to live alone, she decided to stay with Ambalal.

Protection of Land Rights: A Basic Minimum

Land compensation, which is at the core of a satisfactory R&R process, is clearly inadequate and rarely meets official standards. The tribal oustees of SSP were promised a basic minimum in exchange for their whole life system. As it is, they have been uprooted from their natural environment and social milieu; they have forgone their customary rights and their relationship with the forest and river. Displacement has undermined the basis of their economic and social support systems. Against this background, protection of their land rights is the basic minimum necessary for their survival. In the absence of adequate land compensation, their survival is threatened.

Water, Fodder and Fuel

As indicated in Table 4, problems related to water, fodder and fuel were endemic at the resettlement sites. To illustrate, consider Kamboya Kuwa and Chametha. Due to the lack of common pastureland, the villagers in both sites had to meet all their fodder and fuel needs out of the five acres that had been allotted to them. This severely restricted their freedom to grow other crops.

Drinking water concerns were acute at both sites, in different forms. In Kamboya Kuwa, very little care had been taken to maintain the facilities provided by the implementing agencies. None of the four handpumps were in working condition. Efforts to dig a well had begun, but could not be completed before the monsoon, rendering all the work useless. People had to rely on the goodwill of the owners of private wells for their own water needs.

The situation in Chametha is no better. Only one of the handpumps is working and the water (yellowish in colour) has a bad taste. Neither the villagers nor their cattle can drink from the handpump and people are forced to bring water from a private well. Due to the poor quality of drinking water, a number of people had fallen sick, as had some cattle. Naranbhai Dhorabhai, a resident of Kamboya Kuwa, described how the cattle had been falling ill after drinking water from a pond near Kalediya. One of the bullocks he was given as part of the rehabilitation package had died a few days earlier.

House Compensation

Housing entitlements are crucial for the well-being of the PAPs. The resettlement policy only considers houses constructed prior to 1980 for compensation, which is unfair. In tribal communities, people marry young, and sons usually set up a separate household after marriage. A young man who married at the age of eighteen in 1980 and built a house for himself at that time would have been thirty-one in 1993 (when the research was conducted) and would have been paying the *ghar vero* (tax) for thirteen years. He would be eligible for land compensation as a major son, but not for house compensation.

According to a Gujarat government resolution dated 1 January 1987, residential plots should be given free of charge to all PAPs including major sons. A significant number of major sons would, therefore, be given a plot if not house compensation. Many oustees, however, complained that they had not been allotted house plots. Some of them were being offered house plots more than 3 km away from their sites. Some were offered cash instead, at the rate of Rs 2000 for five gunthas of land (the standard area for a house plot). All of them had refused this because they preferred land; moreover, they felt that the amount being offered was only about a fourth of the real value of a residential plot.

Temporary shelters, usually called 'tin sheds', are provided by the authorities for displaced people at the resettlement sites, until they rebuild their own houses. However, this arrangement is far from satisfactory. At roughly 9 feet by 12 feet, the sheds are too small for the families to accommodate children, household items, stocks of fuel and fodder and sometimes even cattle. They are forced to tie some of their possessions on the roofs or walls of the shed, or even to keep them outside, taking the risk of theft and weather-inflicted damage. The sheds are unbearably hot in the summer; they are not waterproof and so tend to get flooded or damaged during the monsoon; and most of them are not electrified. This is in stark contrast with the better built houses of some community leaders, not to speak of the pacca houses built for the government officers in charge of these resettlement sites.

Intra-family Conflicts

The resettlement process often leads to the emergence or intensification of intra-family discord. In some instances, the recipients of compensation money refused to share it, even with close family members, as happened with Narsima Roopa of Chametha. After his father's death, the compensation amount of Rs 55,000 was transferred to the account of his uncle, Mansukh Roopa. Now Mansukh Roopa refuses to share the compensation money with his brothers and their heirs. In other cases, family members who have been reasonably fortunate with their land allotments are not willing to help relatives who were not so lucky. This is what happened with Bhimabhai, also a resident of Chametha, whose father had been given less than five acres. Bhimabhai's brother Kanu refused to share his land with his father on the grounds that the land had been given to him as an individual. Bhimabhai himself was not eligible for compensation as a major son, as he was younger than eighteen in 1987, the cut-off year.

The Resettlement Process

On my return to Baroda from fieldwork in late March, I travelled with two R&R officers, who were kind enough to give me a lift in their jeep. One of them was thirsty and ordered the driver to get him some water to drink. The jeep soon stopped in front of a little house made of rough stone. At the driver's request, the occupant of the house respectfully brought the officer a jugful of water and a glass. As the officer drank the water, his relief was apparent. He asked the owner, 'How cool the water is—do you have a cooler?' (He was not joking). Hesitatingly, the person replied, 'No, Sahib, this is water from a *matla* [an earthen pitcher].' 'Oh, matla!' said the officer, suddenly losing interest as comprehension dawned on him.

As the jeep sped on, I reflected on the absurdity of the situation. What did government policy-makers and functionaries know about the lives of the Adivasis? Yet they had the power to take decisions that determined their fate.

The defective implementation of the R&R package in Gujarat reflects the dependence of the resettlement process on an alienated and inefficient government machinery. The limitations of the government bureaucracy have been amply demonstrated in other contexts—how can we expect it to perform differently when it comes to resettlement and rehabilitation? The implementation machinery is the same, with all its flaws, further compounded by deep prejudices and biases against Adivasis and a profound lack of understanding of their way of life.

Aside from this general problem, specific flaws in the resettlement process include the following:

No consultation with PAPs: No consultation with PAPs has taken place either at the inception of the project or at any later stage.

Failure of information and communication: The implementing agencies have failed to ensure timely communication with the PAPS. More often than not, the affected people are uninformed, inadequately informed or even misinformed about the R&R provisions, the submergence schedule, their rights and responsibilities vis-à-vis the implementing agencies and official plans for their future. This creates immense confusion and generates widespread feelings of insecurity and fear.

Disregard of cultural differences: The literacy rate in the submergence villages is very low and some of the Adivasis (especially those living in the interior villages) have had little or no contact with outsiders. With complete disregard for this issue, the implementing authorities send them notices set in small font and couched in legalistic language, which even a well-educated person would find difficult to understand. Similarly, people have been suddenly introduced to institutions, procedures and systems which are beyond their world view. In village after village, PAPs often brought their records, passbooks and documents to me, hoping that I would explain the meaning of these mysterious papers to them.

Irregular land compensation procedures: As we saw earlier (section entitled 'Land Compensation'), the actual process of land compensation, which is the most basic of all R&R provisions, violates many of the official norms and principles.

Fraud and corruption: Fraud and corruption are an integral part of the resettlement process. Selective appeasement of village leaders, for example, is a common tactic. Many of these leaders also take bribes from their own people.[10] The villagers are known to have paid bribes not only to their own village leaders but also to the talatis, surveyors, forest-department officers and even officers from Kevadia. The talati demanded a bribe for issuing age certificates to major sons (see 'Case study: Katkhadi'). Forest department officers also expect payment in return for releasing the 'passes' which allow wood-laden trucks to go through the checkpoints. Officials at higher levels often extract payments in kind rather than in cash. The irresistible attraction of government officers for *marga* (chicken) and *daru* (country liquor) was much in evidence in the study villages and resettlement sites.

False promises: The resettlement process is replete with false promises. 'I will look into this' must be the most widely used phrase in the vocabulary of the government officers. The villagers, in their innocence, usually believe what they are told (at least in the initial stages). These false promises are usually given prior to displacement. Once the PAPs have shifted to the new sites, the government officers settle into a pattern of avoidance behaviour towards the oustees, who do not get any response to their grievances. '*Thasai, thasai* [will be done, will be done]' then becomes the refrain.

Absence of grievance redressal procedures: The resettled oustees showed me many applications and petitions they had sent to government officers at various levels—Kevadia, Baroda and Gandhinagar. Often, they would send these applications by registered post at great personal cost. The oustees also expressed much frustration at being incessantly pushed from one office to another without genuine attention being given to their problems. Indeed, there is virtually no official follow-up after the PAPs are resettled. Displacement, relocation, resettlement and rehabilitation are the four stages of R&R. Without the full satisfaction of each of these four stages, R&R cannot be said to be complete. In practice, however, the resettlement process often stops at relocation.

Coercion and Human Rights Violations

Another sinister aspect of the resettlement process is the frequent use of coercion and the flagrant violation of human rights. Examples include forced eviction, forced stay and physical harassment.

Forced Eviction

In submerging villages as well as resettlement sites, I asked the people whether they would have moved if the R&R provisions were offered to them as a 'development' package, without the existence of the dam. Their answer was always unequivocally in the negative. The same sentiment is also expressed in the reply of the oustees when asked if they would like to go back to their original villages in the event where the dam is not built. The answer is always, unhesitatingly, in the affirmative. In addition, the fact that (1) there have been violations of crucial directives, (2) R&R provisions have not been fully met, and (3) pressure tactics and other coercive methods have been used, all point toward the practice of forced evictions by the government of Gujarat to remove these Adivasi oustees.

The fact that from amongst the more than 260 oustee families who were moved in the month following the High Court Stay order of 30 April, at least twenty-four were not allotted any land, twenty-six were allotted land of inferior quality, forty-one did not have kabja haq over the land allotted to them and at least fifty-seven were allotted less than five acres of land, is clear evidence that people were moved under duress. A number of specific examples have been given earlier.

Some oustee families were evicted in flagrant violation of judicial orders expressly prohibiting this course of action. The High Court order dated 30 April 1993 explicitly stated that removal as a consequence of submergence would also be regarded as forcible removal and refused permission to the authorities to shift people temporarily. It reiterated that PAPs should be resettled at least six months prior to the proposed submergence of their lands. Yet gross violations of this order could be observed in April and May. One example is the notice put up near Surpan, Vadgam and Mokhadi villages, which reads as follows:

> *Warning:* The houses of these *falias* are likely to be affected by floods from the Narmada during the current monsoon season. They are, therefore, asked to move themselves to a safer place along with their belongings so that the people and their property may not suffer damage.
>
> —BY ORDER

The text of this notice makes it amply clear that the impending monsoon floods were not altogether unexpected as the government later maintained. The official submergence schedule notwithstanding, people were not resettled in good time and were instead asked to move 'temporarily', at the cost of permanent destruction of their homes and other property. Issuing such a notice itself was a violation of the Court's order.

Forced Stay

The forced stay of resettled people at the new sites is another violation of their human rights. In order to avoid situations where displaced persons are forced to stay at resettlement sites against their wishes, land in the original villages should not be submerged until the resettlement has been satisfactorily completed. As the following example illustrates, a long period of adjustment may be required before the final stage of rehabilitation is achieved. Instead, the tendency is to give oustees very little time before they are deprived of their freedom to return, forcing them to accept a diminished standard of living at the resettlement site.

As an illustration of this issue, consider the experience of the PAPs of Vadgam. One of the resettlement sites they had moved to is Malu, in Dabhoi taluka of Baroda district. Various problems at the site induced twenty-four PAPs to return to their original village in 1992. Others chose to stay back at the resettlement site. When I visited Malu in April 1993, they told me repeatedly that they did not want to live there any longer. They had sent several petitions to the authorities, asking for alternative land, but these applications were rejected on the grounds that they had already stayed at the site for more than two years.

While the quality of land in Malu was reasonably good, the soil type only allowed cultivation during the winter season and that too of particular crops such as cotton, tuar and jowar. This was a major problem since agricultural produce was people's only source of income. They felt that their standard of living had declined at the new site. Nanniben Bachubhai described the situation in the following words: 'We do not have enough cash to buy even the basic things we need like salt, chillies, cooking oil, tobacco and clothes. We cannot get wage employment worth even five paise. Even if there are ten adult members in the house, what use are they when they have to lie around without any work? We were better off in Vadgam.'

Lack of social adjustment in the resettlement area was another major concern. The site had been plagued by frequent robberies, increasing their insecurity and discomfort. 'We have to work in the fields during the day-time and during the night, we have to keep awake—this cannot continue forever. Here, they may even kill us. We have written many applications to the government, asking for transfer to another site. We have not heard from them until now. We have decided to wait until the monsoon and then return to Vadgam. It is a drastic measure, but what can we do?'

The people emphasized that they were taking that decision only after trying to adjust at Malu for nearly three years. They had tried but failed—was their request for relocation unjustified?

Repression as a Means of Eviction

Repression is often used as an instrument of control of the powerless by the powerful. In the Narmada valley too, intimidation, threats and repression have frequently been used to evict people from their villages. Diverse means have been used, even rape.

On 13 April 1993, we went to Antras village to investigate the rape of a local Adivasi woman—let us call her Khemiben Vasava.[11] Khemiben was raped by two policemen and the *patel* (headman) of her village on 4 April 1993. Khemiben and her husband, Indiyabhai, were one of the earliest members of the Narmada Bachao Andolan from Antras. Khemiben, known to be a militant woman, had actively resisted several attempts at eviction (in one instance, by lying in front of an official truck).

Antras is a village of approximately sixty houses, known as an 'interior village' because of its inaccessibility in comparison to other dam-site villages. All the villagers belong to the Vasava tribe. In Kundabari falia of this village, thirty households still remained when we visited them. These households are part of the anti-dam agitation spearheaded by the Narmada Bachao Andolan.

Most of the thirty oustee families decided not to move after they were given inferior-quality land at the resettlement sites of Sanoli and Pata. There were six other project-affected families in Kundabari falia, who wanted to be resettled but were only willing to move the following year. In early April, they were under pressure to move. A police contingent, approximately seventy persons according to locals, was stationed in the village. Sent there to evict people, they were determined to evict these six families as well as those who were resisting displacement. Amongst the resisters determined not to move were Khemiben and her family, who lived in a neighbouring falia, where their house was the only one left.

In this tense atmosphere, a conflict arose between those who wanted to go and those who wanted to stay, around the issue of wood. Those who agreed to go wanted to cut the trees for fuel at the new sites. Those who wanted to stay objected that the trees were crucial to their survival. This quarrel led to a physical fight. A few days later Khemiben, seen as the leader, was arrested, taken in a jeep to an isolated spot and then raped by two policemen and the local patel.

Khemiben's rape personifies the coercive nature of the current resettlement process. The government's apathy extended to this act of major repression too. None of the rapists whom Khemiben had painstakingly identified in an identification parade were arrested. The fact that the police department, alleged to be responsible for the rape, was also in charge of the investigation highlights the profound lack of official committment to social justice and tribal welfare. This rape effectively served as a pressure tactic to quell any further resistance.

What People Said

This section presents a selection of further personal testimonies from the oustees, in their own words.

> *Ame shu kareai* (What can we do)? Every day four or five vehicles come here. Gandhisaheb—the Deputy Collector—comes and says: 'You don't move . . . you trouble us so much that the blood in our bodies has turned into water . . . the tyres of our vehicles have given way. If you do not want to go, then give it in writing with your signature.' Every day, all these vehicles. We feel truly sick and tired, sister!
>
> [Kesubhai, on being asked why he was leaving, despite being allotted land of inferior quality and receiving no compensation for his house]

> Here we have to get everything from the shop. At this moment in our village, there are many different kinds of fruits like mango, *mor*, mahuda, *tar*, *bor*, etc. Here, if we want to eat ripe mangoes, we have to spend Rs 9 a kilo. One raw mango costs one rupee. Only if we have this much money can we eat mangoes. And only if we have money in our pocket, can we even eat. There, we would have everything for free. We would fish, go to the forest and collect leaves of the *saragva* tree. The government really causes us a lot of pain.
>
> [Resettled oustees in Chametha]

> When the fodder in our fields gets depleted, we have to buy it. I have four cattle heads. One head of cattle requires a minimum of 6 *pudas* of fodder per day. One puda costs Rs 3. Now you can count how much it will come to. Having spent so much on our cattle while raising them, you can imagine how unhappy we must be to see them die!
>
> [Naranbhai, resettled at Kamboya Kuwa.]

Only after we pull water ten to fifteen times from the well, is it enough for our cattle to drink. There is no water for them to bathe in. We are waiting for the rains when small puddles will form and our cattle will be able to drink and feel the coolness of water like they used to enjoy in the Narmada River.

[Women at Chametha resettlement site]

Jaldi nahi karvu joie—jaldi no kaam shetan no kevai (Things should not be done in a hurry. Work done in a hurry is the work of the devil).

[Shankarbhai, an oustee from Gadher, commenting on the hasty and ad hoc nature of resettlement operations]

Manso rarta-rarta jata raya (The people went away in tears). Can one call this a government? Is the government for killing the people or giving them life?

[A resident of Surpan, commenting on the plight of those who had to move to Kanteshwar]

Pani lavta-lavta radu aavi jai (When I have to go to get water, I feel like crying). Where should I go to get water? We are not allowed to take water from the private wells.

[Malkiben Mohanbhai, resettled in Sankwa from Katkhadi, commenting on the water situation at the resettlement sites. The tin sheds are at some distance from the host village, Sankwa, and no drinking water facilities are available near the tin sheds.]

The government showed one plot and gave another. The agreement was signed, without seeing the land. Then they told us that we would have to accept the land. The government has cheated us very badly . . . We never get any response to any of the complaints we submit to the office. We do not know whether they tear up our applications.

> [Raijibhai Kadwa, resettled in Chametha from Gadher]

It is very hot inside the tin sheds. There, we did not feel the heat. Here we have to face water shortages; living here is anguish. They call us every day to Kevadia; then no work gets done and we have to go again. Strong winds come often and blow during the night; so strong that our tin roofs can fly off. Our relatives live close by, that is why I chose to come here. *Mara juna ghar ni yaad to bau aave, pan shu kari shakiye* (I miss my old house very much, but what can we do)?

> [Mohanbhai, resettled in Sankwa from Katkhadi;
> he fell terribly sick after coming to the new site]

'Thasai, thasai' (Will be done, will be done'), saying this they moved our houses. But nobody pays attention to us anymore. Jeep after jeep would come to our village; no jeeps come here.

> [Ranchodbhai Magan, a major son who has been relocated to
> Chhatiambli from Gadher, without being allotted any land]

I came, and that is why the others did. After coming here, I have been very unhappy. If others had not come, then I would have gone to them and warned them, 'Beware! Do not move your houses.' I have borne pain, but I would not allow pain to fall on others.

> [Shankarbhai Girdarbhai, at Chametha resettlement site]

Colony wala to bhagya kevay, bhagidari ma paisa khai (The colony people are like sharecroppers—they make money through partnerships).

> [Shankarbhai Girdarbhai, commenting on the
> behaviour of government officers in Kevadia]

Our desire is only one. We do not wish to stay here. We would like to send an application to the government stating that we do not want any facilities.

> [Bachubhai Lallubhai, at the Malu resettlement site,
> which people want to leave. Bachubhai and the others
> felt that if the government were to spend money on
> amenities at Malu, it would later say that having spent so
> much, it could not afford to resettle people elsewhere.]

In our old village, many government vehicles would come. Government officers would say, 'All of you will drown like rats if you do not move', 'We will bring the police' or 'We will break the roof-tiles of your houses.' But now nobody comes.

> [An old woman, resettled in Baroli from Gadher]

We will not move our houses until all facilities are provided at the new sites and all our demands are met. *Ame abhan chai pan ganda nathi—hoshiyar chai ekdam.* (We may be illiterate, but we are not foolish—we are very intelligent.)

> [Umedbhai from Mokhadi]

Conclusion

The facts and testimonies presented earlier speak for themselves. Before concluding, I would like to reiterate that the residents of the study villages and resettlement sites have never resisted the dam. They have, in fact, been willing partners of the government's stated R&R policy. The achievements of the government should be examined in this light. The state has had the full cooperation of the affected people as well as of the NGOs which represented them (notably ARCH-Vahini). And yet, the resettlement situation is a disaster. This leads to the crucial question: If this is the quality of R&R achieved after fourteen years of effort to resettle approximately 4500 families in relatively favourable conditions, how can the government of Gujarat possibly assume responsibility for the resettlement of 40,000 families to be displaced by the Sardar Sarovar Project?

11

Forest Rights

Competing Concerns[*]

The night was falling when my companion and I reached the Chintaguda hamlet of Allampalli panchayat of Adilabad district in Andhra Pradesh. On the way, we passed through 12 km of thick jungle and met very few people. When we saw a couple with loads on their heads on the path, we stopped to talk. They turned out to be Kolam Adivasis, traditionally bamboo workers, who are among the poorest Adivasi communities of Andhra Pradesh. They said that they used to live on forest land in Dharmajipet from where they, along with about sixty other Kolam families, were evicted by the

---

[*] Originally published in *Economic and Political Weekly*, 19 November 2005. The final version of the Forest Rights Act, formally called The Scheduled Tribes and Other Traditional Forest Dwellers (Recognition of Forest Rights) Act, 2006, addresses some of the concerns expressed here, reflecting the consultative process that led to revisions of the Bill. The Act did succeed in halting mass evictions of Adivasis from forest land across the country. Beyond that, however, the implementation of the Act has been very poor and many Adivasis (and other traditional forest dwellers) who were not successful in claiming land rights are still at risk of eviction today. Also, the provisions of the Act are frequently undermined by other policies, laws or rules aimed at facilitating corporate entry in forest areas. On recent developments, see forestrightsact.com, maintained by the Campaign for Survival and Dignity.

forest department and the police two years ago. Their homes were burnt and razed to the ground without warning. Those who were present in the hamlet could save their few possessions; the belongings of the rest were all burnt. Rendered homeless overnight, they headed for Utnoor (the nearest tehsil headquarters) and camped outside the tehsildar's office for a few weeks. There they contacted a local Naxalite leader who helped them resettle in the forests not far from the original site. This is where seven of the households were now; the others were working as casual labourers in a neighbouring town.

Landless, these families had come to Dharmajipet forests around a decade ago from another part of Adilabad district in search of land. With some difficulty, they had cleared a small patch of land, built their homes and started cultivation. When I met these families at the new site, I could see how hard-pressed they were to make ends meet in this cut-off area. The nearest road was 12 km away. A casual job was possible only in Utnoor, at a distance of 25 km. Gathering minor forest produce (such as honey) and making bamboo baskets helped but it was not always enough to ward off hunger. Interestingly, these Kolams did not hunt (even birds or small animals) because they did not know how to—their parents being bamboo workers had not taught them—nor did they own bows and arrows considered customary for most Adivasi communities.

A Historical Injustice

The land question came up again and again during my travels in Adilabad over the following days. The stories were nearly always the same whether one talked to a Gond, Pardhan, Naikpod, Thoti or Andh Adivasi—stories about land, forests and insecurity of tenure, about the problem of non-tribals in tribal land. Their present condition was reminiscent of the descriptions of their problems by Haimendorf, who lived and worked among them in the 1940s: '. . . dozens of Gonds from other villages came to see us and tell us tales of woe . . . Thus, I learnt from numerous individual stories that in the 1940s the Gonds of the district had already been ousted from many villages and large tracts of land once held by their forefathers.'[1]

Adivasis have lived since before the age of written records on lands where their cultures and civilizations were born and have thrived. According to Verrier Elwin, the Baigas of Madhya Pradesh claimed 'to have been born from the womb of Mother Earth before the foundation of the world and to be the Bhumia Raja, veritable lords of the earth'. But already in 1936, Elwin reports that '[t]heir most tormenting and readily-remembered dreams are the nightmares of anxiety and hunger'.[2]

The land was theirs, but forests were declared and reserved without settling their traditional rights. Oral tradition in these districts describes how their lands and forests were taken away from them. According to historian Ajay Skaria, for instance, the Bhils of the Dang district of Gujarat narrate, in their *vadilcha goth* (stories of the elders), how their ancestors were shown three sacks by the British and asked to pick one. 'We felt the sacks. We could make out that the first contained earth—why would we need earth, we thought, when we had plenty of land? We felt the second sack, and could feel the bark of trees—why would we need trees when we had plenty of forests? We felt the third sack. This seemed to contain coins—we were always short of money so we chose the third sack.'[3]

It is stories such as these that make up the 'historical injustice' mentioned in the prelude of the Forest Rights Bill, 2005, which it seeks to correct. Many layers of such injustices have befallen the Adivasis, like blows of an axe on a tree. Adivasis have attempted to fight this in their own ways in their everyday life.[4] They have attempted to cope even by migrating to far-off places, not to speak about the many who were shot or hung by the colonial rulers for fighting for their rights. Every tribal district of the country has its 'heroes' who have become a part of their folklore. Adivasis often begin to describe their present by relating stories of these past rebels, as though like stories of all agonies this one too needs to be told from the beginning.

Rather than improving, the situation of Adivasis has worsened in recent times. During the last three years, systematic 'eviction drives' have been conducted all over the country by the forest department to remove so-called 'encroachers' from forest land. These eviction drives were triggered by an order dated 3 May 2002, whereby the inspector general of forests instructed state governments 'to evict the ineligible encroachers and all post-1980 encroachers from forest lands in a time-bound manner'.[5] Diverse coercive means were used for this purpose, from setting fire to houses or destroying standing crops to molesting women, trampling people's dwellings with elephants, and even firing. These atrocities are a grim reminder of similar agonies that have been the lot of Adivasis in India for the last 200 years. History—ruthless and unrepentant—seems to be only repeating itself.

Forest Rights Bill, 2005

It is against this background that a promise was made in the Common Minimum Programme of the United Progressive Alliance (UPA) government: 'Eviction of tribal communities and other forest-dwelling communities from forest areas will be discontinued'. In pursuance of this commitment, the Ministry of Tribal Affairs (MoTA) prepared legislation to protect the Adivasis from forced evictions.

The aim of the bill is to give legal entitlements to forest land that the Adivasis may have been cultivating for a long time, as well as other forest rights such as grazing rights and access to minor forest produce. For instance, the bill will give Adivasis titles to forest land they have been cultivating since before 1980, up to 2.5 hectares per nuclear family. Similarly, the bill will give Adivasis secure entitlements to minor forest produce such as fuelwood, bamboo, honey, gum, mahua, tendu patta, roots and tubers. Other forest rights covered by the bill include the right to *nistar* (collection of forest products for subsistence needs), the right to conversion of 'forest villages' into revenue villages, the right of settlement of old habitations, community rights to intellectual property related to forest biodiversity and cultural diversity, and 'any other traditional right customarily enjoyed by the forest-dwelling scheduled tribes . . . excluding the right to hunting'.

A unique feature of the bill is that the rights of Adivasis go with responsibilities of conserving the forests and protection of wildlife. The bill also seeks to end the exploitative hold of the forest department over the Adivasis by recognising the gram sabha as the authority to recognize and verify claims.

Common Misconceptions

A lively debate began when the bill entered the public domain. This debate, however, has been clouded by several misconceptions.

Land distribution: Some opponents of the bill claim that it intends to distribute 2.5 hectares of land to each Adivasi nuclear family in the country.[6] This creates a fear that entire forests will get wiped out. In reality, the bill only seeks to recognize what is already there, i.e., to give land rights to people who have been cultivating forest land for generations (before 1980), often in circumstances where the forest was 'reserved' without due settlement of traditional land rights. Even this recognition is subject to a maximum of 2.5 hectares per nuclear family.

According to the ministry of environment and forests, the total area of forest land under 'encroachment' (whether by Adivasis or other communities) is 13 lakh hectares. This is less than 2 per cent of the recorded forest area in the country.[7] Seen in this light, the potential adverse impact of the bill on the forest cover is quite limited.

Old rights vs new rights: A related misconception is that the proposed bill confers new rights on the forest-dwelling scheduled tribes. In fact, the entitlements to be created under the bill are consistent with the existing policy framework, in particular the '1990 guidelines' formulated (and partially implemented) by the ministry of environment and forests. These guidelines put in place a procedure for the regularization of so-called 'encroachments' that occurred prior to the cut-off date of 1980. The basic purpose of the bill is similar and the same cut-off date is being used.

Tigers vs Adivasis? Another misconception is that the bill takes the side of Adivasis at the expense of India's dwindling tiger population. This is quite misleading. For one thing, this issue arises only in certain 'protected areas' (national parks and sanctuaries) that account for about 22 per cent of the total forest land.[8] For another, even in those sanctuaries, an accommodation is often possible between the interests (and rights) of Adivasis and the protection of tigers, as the recent report of the Tiger Task Force recognizes.[9] This is not to deny that special provisions may be required to protect the interests of wildlife in these sanctuaries.

The spectre of vanishing tigers has been actively used to create opposition to the bill. The tiger issue is a serious one, but it has been somewhat exaggerated in this context. Contrary to the notion that tigers are rapidly vanishing in India, figures from the tiger censuses indicate that India's tiger population remained fairly stable during the ten years preceding the last census, in 2001–02. Perhaps there was some decline after 2002. But if that is the case, the post-2002 decline cannot be attributed to 'encroachments', since very few new encroachments must have happened during this period of active eviction drives. As the case of the Sariska tiger reserve in Rajasthan illustrates, other factors (such as commercial poaching, often with the complicity of the reserve staff) are often more important.[10]

Critical Appraisal

These misconceptions have overshadowed other important aspects of the bill that require critical discussion. For instance, a serious criticism is that the 1980 cut-off date is too conservative. There is a strong case for a more recent cut-off date such as 2001. This section briefly highlights other shortcomings of the bill.

Non-tribal forest-dwellers: One major flaw of the bill is that it is restricted to Adivasis (more precisely, Scheduled Tribes) and does not apply to other forest-dwellers. Life in the forests is harsh for Adivasis and non-Adivasis alike and there is no reason to discriminate between the two. The real distinction that needs to be made is between those who are in the forests for survival and livelihood reasons, and those who are there for commercial purposes and to make profits. It is the latter category that needs to be prevented from gaining access to forests. This is the real fight.

Non-scheduled Adivasi communities: There is also an issue of fairness amongst Adivasi communities. Some Adivasi communities do not figure in the list of Scheduled Tribes in a particular state. For example, Lambadas are considered a Scheduled Tribe in Andhra Pradesh but not in Maharashtra. There is no reason why the forest rights bill should give a different treatment to the same Adivasi community in two different states simply because it is listed as a Scheduled Tribe in one state and not the other.

Adivasis in the 'diaspora': In order to cope with their distress, Adivasis have often migrated to, and even settled in, far-off places. Oraons of Jharkhand, for example, can be found today labouring in the tea gardens of Assam where they have lived for many decades.[11] These 'dispersed' Adivasis ought to be eligible for rights to the land which they had traditionally inhabited and cultivated. However, there is no provision for this in the bill.

Treatment of non-eligible persons: The bill gives little protection to Adivasis and other forest-dwellers who started cultivating after the 1980 cut-off date. All it says is: 'Save as otherwise provided, no member of a forest-dwelling scheduled tribe shall be evicted or removed from forest land under his occupation till the recognition and verification procedure is complete in such manner as may be prescribed'. Aside from failing to clarify the conditions under which people may be displaced, this provides no guarantee that displaced persons will get an adequate resettlement package, and be treated in a fair and humane manner.

The land question: The bill prescribes 2.5 hectares as the upper limit of forest land that an Adivasi nuclear family may be given. This ceiling is much below the existing land ceiling in most states.[12] It is not clear why Adivasis should be subject to a lower ceiling. It would make better sense to lift the present ceiling of 2.5 hectares and instead stipulate that an Adivasi nuclear family can own land (forest and revenue) up to the prescribed ceiling in the concerned state.

There are other land-related gaps in the bill. For instance, there is no provision for the restoration of tribal land acquired through illegal or unfair means. This type of land alienation has occurred on a large scale in many parts of the country, including scheduled areas, in spite of various laws and policies aimed at protecting the Adivasis from exploitation. In order for such provisions to be effective, the bill needs to stipulate that all land records in the scheduled areas should be up-to-date and transparent. This will help to monitor future misappropriations as well as to restore tribal land that has already been alienated. Similarly, there are no special provisions for tribal communities with a tradition of collective ownership of land (e.g., in parts of Arunachal Pradesh).

Women's land rights: The bill also needs improvement from the point of view of gender equity in land rights. The bill does not define the term 'nuclear family'. It seems to endorse the standard definition of a nuclear family as husband, wife and their children. Accordingly, the bill states that land titles 'shall be registered jointly in the name of the male member and his spouse'. Thus, at present, the land rights of single-headed households have gone unacknowledged. Since the bill explicitly mentions the male member, it can be assumed that even if he does not have a spouse, his land rights may still be protected. But the converse may not be true: the rights of households headed by single women (e.g. widows) are unclear. Further, it is not clear how a widow living (say) with her married son and his nuclear family would be treated under the bill—whether the household would count as two nuclear families, or just one.

Role of the gram sabha: The bill states (Section 6) that 'the gram sabha shall be the authority to initiate any action for determining the extent of forest rights that may be given to the forest-dwelling scheduled tribes within the local limits of its jurisdiction'. However, it is not clear from the bill where the actual decision for 'determining the extent of forest rights' actually resides. Section 6 essentially states that a subdivisional-level committee 'shall examine the decision by the gram sabha', and that a district-level committee shall give 'final approval' to the record of forest rights prepared by the subdivisional-level committee. Further, the composition of these committees is left to be prescribed by the government in the rules. In short, the actual powers of the gram sabha, and the relation of the gram sabha to other authorities, are far from clear.

Concluding Remarks

The forest rights bill is a useful attempt to correct the relationship of the Adivasis and other forest-dwelling communities with the state. However, it has to be viewed in the light of the larger political economy. In this respect, the bill and the debate around it are quite limited. They are silent, for instance, on the commercial interests and powerful lobbies (the timber lobby, the land mafia, the tusk business) that exploit the forests for profit.

Besides, the bill and the subsequent act shall be born in a climate of economic liberalisation, globalisation and the growing power of the corporate sector. Adivasis know more than others the havoc that new economic policies have caused to them and the environment. These policies allow not only the government but also multinationals and private companies to operate in tribal areas, even Fifth Schedule areas, and give them access to natural resources such as land, water or minerals. In the name of 'public purpose' (as with uranium mining) or 'development' (as with dams and mines), sanctions have been given to such projects without the prior knowledge, let alone consent, of the local people. In many cases, approval of these projects is in open violation of existing laws and constitutional safeguards. These projects have also been sites of serious transgressions of human rights: when people have protested, the state has often responded in the language of coercion and violence.

It is ironic that even as negotiations on the forest rights bill are underway, destructive projects continue to be sanctioned. According to the ministry of environment and forests, close to 10 lakh hectares of forest land have already been released for various projects such as mining and industrial development. This area is almost as large as the same ministry's estimate of the total forest land area under 'encroachment' (13.4 lakh hectares).[13]

This inconsistency is a reflection of the character of the Indian state. When the choice is between furthering the interests of the propertied sections and protecting the property or even the life of the poor, the state often chooses the former. Likewise, in Fifth Schedule areas the interests of propertied classes are protected even at the expense of Adivasis and other forest-dwelling communities.

12

The Mazdooras of Bihar[*]

Few places match Bihar's reputation for poverty, oppression, violence, corruption and crime. All were on full display in central Bihar in the mid-1990s, at the time of my initial years of fieldwork on the Naxalite movement (discussed in Chapter 13—The Naxalite Movement in Central Bihar). However, Bihar also had a rich political life and vibrant social movements. This essay introduces the economy and society of rural Bihar as they stood at that time. It also discusses living conditions in the study villages—a group of fifty-odd villages in Patna, Jehanabad, Gaya, Aurangabad and Bhojpur districts where I conducted detailed inquiries.

The Land of Bihar

Agrarian Relations

Land is central to the understanding of Bihari society, economy and politics for several reasons. First, Bihar is an overwhelmingly rural

---

* This essay is based on my doctoral thesis (Bhatia, 2000) submitted to the University of Cambridge. It reflects the living conditions of rural labourers at the time of my fieldwork in the mid-1990s, with occasional updates in the notes. The term 'central Bihar' should be understood here with reference to the geography of undivided Bihar (including the districts that are now part of Jharkhand, earlier 'south Bihar'). This region is now in south Bihar, in terms of the geography of post-2000 Bihar.

state. Second, most people in rural areas depend on agriculture for their livelihood. The proportion of the rural workforce depending on agriculture was as high as 87 per cent in 1981 (the second-highest figure amongst all Indian states) and marginally *higher* at 88 per cent in 1991.[1] Third, land deprivation is a major cause of mass poverty, especially in view of the low level of economic diversification in rural areas. Amongst all major states, Bihar has the second-highest proportion (55 per cent) of landless or quasi-landless households in the rural population.[2]

At the dawn of India's independence, there was much popular hope of radical change, including land reform. The Congress was under pressure to respond to these hopes, but at the same time, it had to contend with opposition from landed interests within itself. The policy of the Congress on agrarian issues was contentious even prior to Independence and had contributed to a split between its left and right sections. This vacillation remained the attitude of the government in states where the Congress became the ruling party.

The main outcome of these contradictory pressures was the enactment of the zamindari abolition laws.[3] Bihar was the first state to introduce a zamindari abolition bill in 1947. The central aim of the bill was to abolish all intermediary interests in land—in particular, the zamindari system—and vest them in the state. As a result, the tillers of the soil were meant to become either owners of the land or tenants of the state.

However, this legislation was very limited in some respects.[4] First, the abolition of zamindari interests did not include any redistribution of land but was restricted to granting secure ownership rights to the existing *raiyat*s (tenants). It was irrelevant to the landless. Second, the government retained a favourable attitude to the interests of the zamindars to the very end. This was apparent in its decision to pay compensation for the surplus land taken from them.

Zamindari interests in Bihar used every means at their disposal to stall basic land reform legislation—the Bihar Abolition of Zamindari

Bill of 1947, which was passed into an Act in 1948. Zamindari obstruction included challenging this Act in the court and getting an injunction against its implementation, subsequently leading to its repeal with the stated intention of replacing it with a more comprehensive legislation called Bihar Land Reforms Bill 1949, which became an Act in 1950. This new Act was again challenged by zamindari interests in the Patna High Court and subsequently in the Supreme Court of India, which finally upheld the validity of the Bihar Land Reforms Act in 1952. All this was enough warning of the resistance to land reform that would continue for decades.

One consequence of these delays was the large-scale eviction of tenants. Eviction of tenants was a means used by many zamindars to avoid losing their land since the zamindari abolition law did not include the government taking over self-cultivated land. As Joshi describes it: 'Almost all evaluation studies on land reforms have reported that land reform legislation led in its wake to evictions of tenants by the landlords on a scale which was without precedent and parallel in recent Indian history. In fact, land reform, which was introduced with a view to promote security of tenure for the poor tenants, was itself instrumental in creating insecurity on a scale unheard of before.'[5] Evicted tenants were constrained to survive on smaller holdings when they were not landless.

Thus, the agrarian structure in Bihar remained highly unequal after the zamindari's abolition. This inequality, combined with sub-human living conditions and social oppression of the landless agricultural labourers, gave rise to many militant movements. These movements brought the middle peasants and the labourers in direct conflict with the erstwhile zamindars or *barahils* (managers for absentee landowners), or with the raiyats of the pre-abolition phase who were able to avoid eviction and emerged as the big landowners after abolition.

'Land reforms' initiated since the abolition of zamindari have been minimal, in terms of both policy and—more so—implementation. The main steps that have been taken are the following:

1. *Land ceilings*: Land ceilings have been introduced with the stated intention of redistributing 'surplus land' to the landless. In practice, this measure has been largely ineffective, both because of large-scale evasion—e.g., through *benami* (owned by proxy) transfers and gifts to relatives—and because the ceilings were high in the first place.[6]

2. *Tenancy legislation*: Some attempts have been made to introduce legislation to regulate tenancy arrangements and protect the rights of tenants. In practice, however, this legislation has rarely been enforced.

3. *Gairmajurwa land*: This refers to 'common' land, meant for purposes such as common pastures, access roads, cremation grounds and panchayat buildings.[7] In central Bihar, landlords have staunchly resisted the surrender of gairmajurwa land and much of this land remains intensely contested.

4. *Math land*: In various parts of Bihar, Hindu religious institutions (*maths*) own large amounts of land attached to particular temples. Legislation was introduced to limit the amount of land owned by maths and redistribute some of the excess land.

In each case, left-wing organizations—including not only Naxalite organizations but also the CPI, CPI(M) and socialist movements such as Chhatra Yuva Sangharsh Vahini (Students and Youth Struggle Force) in Bodh Gaya as well as other movements like the Bhoodan movement—have tried to ensure the enforcement of whatever legislation had been introduced. Despite local successes, however, the overall impact of these struggles has been quite limited. Land ownership, therefore, continues to be highly unequal in Bihar, and landlessness is widespread.

Caste Structure

Caste is an essential feature of Bihar's social structure. Caste considerations pervade every aspect of social life including marriage, employment, education, politics and government. Caste is also of paramount importance in political alignments and voting patterns.

The caste composition of Bihar in 1931 is known from census data.[8] At that time, 13.6 per cent of the population belonged to the upper castes. In central Bihar, the most influential upper castes are Bhumihars and Rajputs. Both castes have a history of control over land, political supremacy at the local level and violent oppression of the lower castes. Next in the caste hierarchy are the Yadavs, Koeris and Kurmis (sometimes called 'upper backward castes'). These are cultivating castes which largely come in the category of 'middle peasants', though their members include some landless households as well as some large landowners. The demographic and social importance of these three castes is a special feature of Bihar. Yadavs, in particular, are the largest single caste in numerical terms and have gained considerable social and political influence in the post-Independence period.

The above castes, which are the main landowning castes in most regions with varying degrees of influence, accounted for one-third of the population of Bihar in 1931. The 'lower Shudras', i.e., Nai, Teli, Dhimar and other service castes, accounted for another third. The rest were divided between Muslims, Scheduled Castes and Scheduled Tribes.[9] By and large, members of these groups own little or no land, with some exceptions—e.g., Muslims are the major landowners in some areas. Except for Muslim landowners, they represent the most disadvantaged and oppressed sections of the population.

The remainder of this section gives further details of specific castes in central Bihar.

Brahmin: In Bihar, as elsewhere, Brahmins occupy the top position in the caste hierarchy. In central Bihar, Brahmins tend to be seen as less oppressive than some of the other privileged castes, even though they are a landowning caste, like the Bhumihars. They are also less dependent on land since the traditional *jajmani* system continues to bring them some income from priestly functions (they also have a high share of white-collar jobs). Their relationship with other castes involves multi-faceted interdependence and is not always antagonistic.

Bhumihar: Bhumihars (from *bhumi*, land) are one of the distinctive castes of Bihar and eastern Uttar Pradesh. In central Bihar, Bhumihars are the largest landowning caste. Their ethos is deeply authoritarian and patriarchal; they are viewed as prone to arrogance and abuses of power.[10] Bhumihars, who consider themselves as Brahmarishi Brahmins, do not have priestly prerogatives. In their own perception, they are Brahmins of a different kind—those who produce *dhaan* (rice) and give *daan* (alms) instead of begging for it.[11] The Bhumihars of central Bihar have been politically active for a long time.

Rajput: Rajputs, often regarded as a martial caste, are another dominant caste in the area, also owning a lot of land. Like Bhumihars, Rajputs have a strong reputation for tyranny. In central Bihar, there has always been a struggle for supremacy between the Rajputs and the Bhumihars.[12] One symptom of this antagonism is the fact that today, both castes are rarely found in the same village.

Yadav: Amongst the 'backward' castes, the Yadavs—an influential cultivating caste—deserve special mention. The upward economic mobility of the Yadavs in the past few decades in Bihar is noteworthy. This has been on account of their numerical strength, which gave them importance as a vote bank. Also, as cultivating landowners, they benefitted both from the abolition of zamindari and from rising agricultural productivity. The Yadavs have been the most important power base of the Janata Dal and later the Rashtriya Janata Dal, which have ruled the state off and on. Yadavs are generally considered hard-working and enterprising, but not always highly educated.

Koeri and *Kurmi*: These are also enterprising intermediary castes of Bihar, which seem to be doing well economically. Like the Yadavs, Koeris and Kurmis are enthusiastic cultivators. A popular saying states that 'the Kunbi [Kurmi] is always planting, whether his crop lives or dies'. Women from these cultivating castes, too, work in the fields and are known as hard-working—'A basket on her head and a child on each hip, by this you may know the Kunbin [Kurmi woman]'.[13]

Scheduled Castes: In central Bihar, the main Scheduled Castes are the Bhuiyas, Musahars, Chamars, Dusads, Doms, amongst others.[14] Generally, members of the Scheduled Castes do not own any land, except possibly homestead land, though there are some exceptions (e.g., Chamars sometimes do own small amounts of land). Their main occupations are casual labour and sharecropping. They have low literacy levels and little employment in the formal sector. Most of them live in extreme poverty.[15]

Bhuiyas and *Musahars*: Within the Scheduled Castes, Bhuiyas and Musahars are amongst the most deprived communities.[16] They usually live in hamlets outside the main village, called Bhutoli or Mustoli (*toli* means hamlet), and survive from agricultural labour, rearing pigs, rickshaw pulling, gleaning and similar activities. Almost without exception, they are landless. In areas that are under Naxalite influence, many of them are strong supporters of the movement.

Poverty and Oppression[17]

Bihar, to a layperson in India, is a symbol of deprivation, destitution, degeneration and decay. If, in the international perception, India is associated with poverty, within India, *garibi* (poverty) often brings Bihar to mind. In the mid-1990s, Bihar was the only Indian state where a *majority* of the population lived below the poverty line.[18]

The intensity of poverty is best understood by looking at the most deprived groups, especially agricultural labourers. Bihar has the second-highest proportion (37 per cent) of agricultural labourers in the workforce amongst all major states. In central Bihar districts, agricultural labourers and their families account for 30 to 40 per cent of the rural population.[19] Most of them belong to the Scheduled Castes, Scheduled Tribes and Other Backward Classes (OBCs).

Agricultural labourers and tenants, historically, have been a highly exploited category. They have been subjected to *begar* (forced labour) and arbitrary *abwab*s (cesses) besides the exaction of due revenue and rent. The nomenclature of labour contracts in historical records like G.A. Grierson's *Bihar Peasant Life* (1885) brings out the complex and exploitative nature of these contracts. According to some historians, until quite recently, the real wages of agricultural labourers in Bihar were no higher than those paid to casual labourers by the East India Company in the early eighteenth century, or to the drudge labourers employed on state works in the Magadh state two-and-a-half millennia ago.[20]

In the post-Independence period, agricultural wages have been a contentious issue and a prominent focus of mass organizations. Real agricultural wages in Bihar stagnated and even declined in many areas until the late 1970s; it was only from the 1980s onwards that a slow upward trend emerged.[21] Even today, real agricultural wages in Bihar are extremely low.

This is a gross violation of the Minimum Wages Act 1948 and its subsequent revisions, even though the official norms themselves are highly inadequate. As of 1995, the minimum wage in Bihar was Rs 30.50 per day. At the district level, the minimum wage is often translated in kind. In Jehanabad district, for instance, the prescribed minimum in the early 1990s was four kilograms of paddy and 500 grams of sattu (flour of parched gram, barley or millet) or *chura* (flattened rice) as *nashta* (snack). Instead, in most areas where the labourers were unorganized, they received just 2 to 2.5 kilograms of coarse grain per day.

Agricultural labourers have also been victims of social oppression, for instance, in the form of widespread sexual exploitation of poor labouring women. In the early twentieth century, in some places like Shahabad (the present Bhojpur and Rohtas districts), this had been ritualized in practices like the *dola pratha*, which compelled every new bride to spend her first night after marriage with the local zamindar. The *dola* tradition prevailed in the Rajput and Bhumihar-dominated regions of Shahabad, and many legends in the region are associated with it.[22] The rape of labouring women by Rajputs and Bhumihars was almost a tradition, 'an accepted social evil, a fate which many bore unquestioningly', as recently as the 1970s in parts of central Bihar, like Bhojpur.[23] There are other instances of villages, like the Masurha zamindari (Patna district), where similar exploitation of tenant womenfolk was so rampant that tenants outside Masurha were unwilling to get their daughters married there.[24]

The condition of agricultural labourers in these areas in the late 1970s has been described well by Mukherjee and Yadav (1980):

> The landless *Chamars* and *Musahars* [who often work as *banihar*s or *halwaha*s] lived like animals in hovels less than a man's length, subsisting on three to five rupees per day and the master's *kesari*— an animal feed made of husk which produced painful skin disorders and arthritis . . . Though begar was a thing of the past, the banihar worked often for nothing. Wearing a clean dhoti, remaining seated in the presence of the master even on a cot outside his own hut, walking erect, were taboo. When the evenings fell or in lonely stretches of field, the rape of his womenfolk by landlords' *latheiths* (musclemen) and scions completed a picture of unbridled Rajput-Bhumihar overlordship.[25]

Interestingly, it was from Masurha that the Kisan Sabha—which grew into a formidable peasant force in Bihar—made its beginning in 1928. Similarly, Mahtin Dai's memory (see note 22) and the continued exploitation of lower-caste women, in addition to economic oppression, were instrumental in the political organization of agricultural labourers in central Bihar for what they called *izzat ki ladai* (fight for dignity). The virtual state of war that has since existed between these political mass organizations of the rural poor and the dominant classes has earned for the central plains the reputation of being the 'flaming fields of Bihar'.

The Study Villages

My fieldwork in central Bihar included personal visits to fifty-one villages of Patna, Jehanabad, Gaya, Aurangabad and Bhojpur districts. My primary interest was in villages that were situated in or near areas of influence of the Naxalite movement (the subject of my doctoral thesis). In each village, I had detailed discussions with residents, especially men and women from the working classes and marginalized sections. The discussions were guided by a simple questionnaire, but these conversations also led me to listen to what people themselves wanted to share.

Who Lives Where and Why

A gaon in Bihar usually consists of a main settlement and a cluster of tolas located around it. While the tolas tend to be smaller than the main village, they are often large enough to be considered a separate village. For somebody new to central Bihar, it is at first difficult to distinguish the village from the tolas, for a tola may have a distinct name of its own.

On closer look, however, the difference between the main village and the tolas is apparent. The main village tends to have a more prosperous appearance. The houses are larger and pucca, the lanes are paved, the drains cemented and public facilities like schools, medical dispensary, post office (or post box), market, etc., insofar as they exist, are also located in the main village. In contrast, the tolas have few facilities and the houses are semi-pucca or kaccha and often located in a disorderly fashion.

Some tolas are also called tolis. Some authors have suggested that the difference between the two is one of size, a toli being smaller.[26] However, one finds that only the tola of the oppressed castes, irrespective of its size, is referred to in this way. For instance, a tola of the Musahars or the Bhuiyas is called Mustoli or Bhutoli, but a Bhumihar tola, which could also have been abbreviated as Bhutoli, never is. Instead, the tola where the upper castes reside is considered the main village. This can be understood as an extension of the way in which the upper castes regard and refer to members of the oppressed castes and classes.

The origin of the tolas often arises from repression of the disadvantaged castes by the upper castes. For instance, members of a particular caste or community may have been forced to flee the main village and seek refuge in another tola or create a new one (as happened in Bathani tola—see Chapter 15—Justice, Not Vengeance). Tolas may also have sprung up for other reasons such as the settlement of labourers who were brought from outside; population pressure and the need for space; or state policy such as that of settlement of the landless on gairmajurwa land. The main village is therefore almost always older than the tolas.

The main village usually houses the *dabang* (dominant) castes and classes of the village. These may be upper castes, locally known as *aagda* or 'forward' jatis, or dominant castes in the upper layer of the 'backward' jatis. The upper-caste households tend to be located at the centre of the village in caste-specific quarters. It is common to find upper castes such as Brahmins and Kayasths along with either the Bhumihars or Rajputs in a village. However, their presence is largely inconspicuous. Seldom is a village in central Bihar known after Brahmins or Kayasths; mostly, it is either *Bhumiharon ka* or *Rajputon ka* (i.e., of Bhumihars or Rajputs).

In the study villages, as in much of central Bihar, land is concentrated in the hands of the upper or dominant castes. Further, there is a close tie between the physical location of castes in a village and their occupations. Generally, landowners live in the main village, those whom they need on an everyday basis live close to them and those whom they may need on a casual or seasonal basis live at some distance. Amongst the castes required on an everyday basis are those whose occupations relate to the 'domestic' realm, such as Kahar (who work as domestic labourers), Dhobi (washermen), Nai (barber), Mali (gardener) and even some from the Scheduled-Caste category, like Chamar (leather tanners). Besides them, there may also be shopkeepers (Banias) and OBCs often owning some land of their own such as Yadavs, Koeris and Kurmis. The main village therefore tends to be multi-caste, with the dominant castes residing at the centre and other castes in the peripheries, while tolas are of a single caste or a group of castes of similar status.

Those living in the tolas are largely landless households or marginal farmers (many of them, sharecroppers). However, there are exceptions. Yadavs, for example, who often have significant land holdings, often live in a tola by themselves. Interestingly, the Yadavs are sometimes split in two tolas, or between the main village and a tola—a pattern rare amongst the upper castes. Families of an upper caste always tend to reside together. The Scheduled Castes also usually live in a tola by themselves. Their tolas are often situated to the south of the main village—a direction considered inauspicious.

Land and Class

As mentioned earlier, land reforms in Bihar have remained no more than a paper exercise. In stray cases where some action has been taken, for example with respect to gairmajurwa or bhoodan land, it has been left incomplete. In the absence of land reforms, class conflict continues to pervade agrarian relations.

The Maliks

The exact pattern of land ownership in central Bihar is difficult to ascertain for want of reliable data. Land records are in a dismal state. Cobwebbed and dirty, the offices that house these records illustrate the state of affairs. The last land survey conducted for the region was the cadastral survey of 1912–13. In the absence of reliable land records, conflicting claims and land disputes abound.

In the study villages, I tried to ascertain land ownership patterns from the landlords as well as the labourers. Not surprisingly, the land that the landlords claimed to own was always below the stipulated ceiling and often ridiculously small in comparison to what the labourers alleged they had. Some exaggeration is possible on the part of individual labourers, but their collective knowledge of these matters seemed fairly reliable.

The study villages illustrate an important aspect of land ownership in central Bihar: the absence of large land estates and zamindars. The largest landholding in a village is often smaller than 100 bighas, and sometimes as small as 40 bighas; the largest landholding in all the study villages is in the range of 300 bighas.[27] This contrasts with the land situation in north Bihar—where large estates and powerful landlords are common—as well as with the historical situation in central Bihar itself.

Land, however, continues to be highly concentrated among the upper castes.[28] The higher one is placed in the caste hierarchy, the higher are the chances of being propertied. Thus, caste and class go hand in hand in central Bihar. Further, in the absence of large individual holdings, the power of the upper castes is of necessity a shared power held on the basis of intra-caste and inter-upper-caste cooperation. One example of this is the caste 'sena' phenomenon (see Chapter 15—Justice, Not Vengeance).

Even though landowners are seldom big landlords, labourers refer to them as zamindar or *malik* (master) and their class as *baraka log* or *babu log* (big people); so do the poorer members of upper castes. Why does the use of these terms persist? Several explanations are possible. First, the memory of the zamindari system has a lasting influence even though agrarian relations are less oppressive today. Second, in the near absence of economic diversification, labourers continue to live in a state of insecurity and dependence on the landowners. In that sense, the old malik remain the malik and the baraka in the village remains the baraka. Third, the *vyavhar* (behaviour) of many maliks continues to be *saamanti* (feudal)—another reminder that a complete break with the past has not yet been achieved.[29] Feudal behaviour reflects the self-perception of the upper castes as the legitimate holders of power and this self-perception adds to the other reasons to continue seeing them as maliks.

Yet there is a difference. A labourer may call someone zamindar or malik, but not with the same submissiveness as before. A sense of dignity marked with defiance has slowly crept in. The term may be the same, but the tone has changed. Not only the form of address but the way of address, not only what is said but how it is said is important. In the minds of many labourers today, the word malik may even mean enemy more than a master. As discussed in Chapter 13 (The Naxalite Movement in Central Bihar), this sense of dignity is one of the positive achievements of the Naxalite movement.

The Mazdooras

Agricultural labourers as a class are known as mazdooras or *majuras*.[30] There are different categories of labourers. A *mazdoor* (labourer) may be *chuta* (free) or *bandhua* (attached). A chuta labourer is one who is employed on a daily basis, while a bandhua labourer is employed on a seasonal or yearly basis and is not free to work for anybody else during the period of the contract.

Bandhua Mazdoora and Begari

The nature of bondage in central Bihar has changed over time. The current nature of bondage is different from the sense in which the term 'bonded labour' is understood in the rest of the country, or may have been understood in central Bihar in the past. Traditionally, a bonded labourer has been understood to be an attached labourer who has lost his freedom due to indebtedness (see also Chapter 3—Of Human Bondage in Baran). Even though the initial *karj* (debt) may have been a paltry sum, the landowner cum moneylender charged an exorbitant rate of interest and often manipulated the accounts to keep the labourer in debt. The labourer ended up enslaving himself and his family, often for generations.[31] While bonded labour of the traditional type does exist in some parts of Bihar, there was little evidence of it in the study villages. According to local CPI(ML) Liberation (or Liberation for short) activists, this type of *pusht dar pusht* (generation upon generation) servitude no longer exists in central Bihar.

In Bihar, certain forms of illegal cesses (*abwab*s) and forced labour (*begari*) had taken an institutional form during the colonial period. In the study villages, little mention was made of abwabs, but the mention of begari was frequent. Its incidence is negligible today, but the fact that the memory of begari lives on suggests that it did exist until recently.

Not only bandhua but casual labourers were also expected to comply with begari. The tasks that labourers could be asked to perform were numerous and diverse. Examples include taking the cattle of the zamindar out to graze, making fuel cakes from cowdung, filling water and making muri (puffed rice). Some tasks could be long and painstaking, yet no wages were paid. For example, labourers were sometimes told to take some freshly-harvested grain to the landlord's relatives in town, walking all the way with sacks on their backs—sometimes for two or three days. All the labourers got at both ends was food and water.

The significance of begari lay in the complete control—economic and social—that the landlord exercised over the labourer. Economic exploitation is often possible because the person exploited is not just poorer but also has a lower status in the social hierarchy. Begari represented not only economic but also social exploitation and was a crucial part of the overall social oppression of the rural poor. For the upper castes, the lower castes were nothing more than manual workers who, as a class, were there only to serve them.[32]

But now the situation has changed. In the study villages, mazdooras who are called bandhua are those who are employed as attached labourers on a contractual basis. Such a contract is usually for one agricultural year. The main task of such a bandhua mazdoor is ploughing; since timely ploughing is very important, the landlords prefer to avoid depending on the availability of casual labourers by engaging a labourer on a longer-term basis.[33] Such a mazdoor may also be called *halwaha* or *harwaha* (ploughman), or, depending on the terms of employment, *sthai* mazdoor (labourer in place or fixed)—somebody who has been 'guaranteed' for the year! The description of these attached labourers as bandhua can be understood as a continuation of the old usage, even though the terms of bondage have changed.

Chuta Mazdoora

Workers employed on a casual basis, male or female, are known as chuta mazdoora. During the agricultural season, it is common to see the *barahils* of the landlords come to the hamlets of the labourers in the evenings to strike a deal with them on the next day's work. Until recently, this did not include any discussion of work timings, when the wages would be paid or the quality of grain to be given as wages. Today, however, landlords can no longer take these matters for granted.

The wages paid to the chuta labourers are known as *roj* or *rojina* and those paid to the halwahas are known as *harwahi*. In many respects, the system of wage payments today is much the same as that described by Grierson in the second half of the nineteenth century.[34] However, there are also important changes.

Wages of casual labourers vary for different agricultural tasks. Broadly, the wages differ in the two agricultural seasons: *ropni* (transplanting) and *katni* (harvesting). The wages have always been paid in kind. Earlier, a system existed where an advance was paid and the wages due to the labourer at the end of a week or two-week period were adjusted against the advance. The wages received by casual labourers used to be coarse grain of poor quality, usually *khesaari*. The latter is known to cause paralysis, and was already considered unhealthy in Grierson's days: 'It is unwholesome for human beings, but bullocks eat it greedily, e.g., in the saying: *Turuk taari, bail khesaari, Baaman aam, Kaayath kaam* [Toddy is necessary for a Musalman's happiness, *khesaari* for a bullock's, mangos for a Brahman's, and employment for a Kayasth's].'[35] The terms and conditions of payment of the halwahas were similar to those of chuta labourers, though in addition, a small piece of land was given to the halwaha for self-cultivation during the contractual period to ensure that he remained sthai.

Previously, there used to be no specific work timings. Labourers tended to get up at daybreak and to depart for the malik's fields after the essential morning tasks. The workday ended when the sun set. There were no scheduled breaks. When nashta or khana (a meal) was given, these periods would serve as break times. Payments were not regular either. Even though chuta labourers were employed on a daily basis, they were often not paid daily. A similar plight applied to the halwaha. He would be paid after two weeks, a month, or even two months. In need, he would go to the malik's house and often be told day after day that the *malikini* (malik's wife) was not there, or to come the next day for some other reason.[36]

Now the situation has improved. In many villages, this happened only after a wage struggle. Labourers continue to be paid in kind, but the quality of grain has improved. Instead of khesaari, labourers are usually given rice or wheat flour. The wages vary a lot not only from district to district, but also between villages. In the study villages, wages range from 2 to 3.5 kgs of rice per day, with or without nashta and khana. Nashta normally includes a sherbet made of jaggery (usually unlimited), sometimes accompanied with a fixed number of rotis. Khana, if given, includes a set number of rotis (not more than four) or *sattu* with green chilli, a few slices of onion and sometimes a pickle. Where khana is given, it is only to male labourers.

Aside from a rise in wages, the employment conditions of labourers, including halwahas, have also improved in other respects. Timings are now fixed, with a break at mid-day. Wage payments are regular. In most villages, women receive the same wages as men. Supervision is less stringent, and there are fewer instances of sexual harassment or assault in the field. The begari system, as mentioned earlier, has largely disappeared.[37]

In spite of these improvements, wage rates are well below the prescribed minimum (Rs 30.50 per day at the time of fieldwork). In Jehanabad, for instance, the district administration itself acknowledged that minimum wages were not paid in 785 out of 934 villages; of the 785, 157 villages were further identified where even the accepted local rate was not being paid.[38]

Even though the wage rates are below the prescribed minimum, most labourers feel that their situation has improved. In many villages, labourers, especially older ones, mentioned that no longer did they see days of hunger and that they were now '*khush-haal*' (in a contented state). Of course, this is in comparison with the extreme deprivation they faced in the past. What is important is that because of their organized strength, they now have greater control over their situation.

The Bataidar

Besides employing labourers on a casual or contractual basis, the landlords also enter into *bataidari* (sharecropping) arrangements with them. Since few of the upper-caste landlords are self-cultivators, a large proportion of their land is sharecropped.

Who does mazdoori (wage labour) and who, bataidari? By and large, the landless do mazdoori and halwahi and the marginal farmers do bataidari. The Scheduled Castes such as Dusadh, Paswan, Chamar and Manjhi are almost always landless and depend primarily on mazdoori for their livelihood. Castes in the middle category such as Yadavs, who have some land, rarely do mazdoori. Instead, they prefer to take land on lease. The reason why the lower castes are unable to do so is that they cannot afford the cost-sharing arrangements.

Tenancy contracts are of different types. The terms vary between different areas. Briefly, there are four main arrangements: *batai, manni batai, nagdi* and *ijara*. Batai is an ordinary sharecropping contract. In manni batai, the tenant gives the landowner an agreed-upon quantity of grain per bigha (measured in *man*, a local measure of weight approximating 20 kgs) after the harvest, irrespective of the produce of the field. The nagdi system is similar except that the rent is paid in cash and in advance. In the ijara (mortgage) system, the landowner mortgages his land to the tenant for a fixed amount and retrieves the land if and when he is able to return this amount to the tenant.

In sharecropping arrangements, the shares depend on the quality of the land, the crops being grown, the cost-sharing capacity of the tenant and the respective bargaining powers of the tenant and landlord, among other factors. The *ek-chauthai* (one-fourth) system was widespread until recently. In this system, all the expenditure for seeds, fertilizer and irrigation was borne by the landowner, who kept three-fourths of the final produce. Another variant is *ek-tihai* (one-third), where the tenant receives one-third of the final produce. In the study villages, an increasingly common arrangement is that the final produce is shared equally, along with the cost of fertilizer and irrigation, while seeds and labour are provided by the sharecropper. This is known as *batai*.

These arrangements are similar to the systems described by Grierson for the second half of the nineteenth century.[39] According to Grierson, the norm then was a system known as *nausatta* (nine-sixteenths) whereby the landlord received nine-sixteenths of the crop. *Adhiya*, the system where the landlord got half of the total produce, has also been described by him, although this seems to have been an exception: 'The division into equal shares is rare and is confined to the cases of high caste tenants, or where a tenant has obtained a decree of the Civil Court restricting the landlord's share to one-half.'[40]

As mentioned above, the norm until recently seems to have been ek-chauthai. This would suggest that since Grierson's days, there has been a deterioration from the point of view of the tenants. This may have been on account of an increase in population while there was no corresponding increase in land productivity. In recent years, however, a shift towards a more egalitarian crop-sharing arrangement can be seen. Batai is becoming the norm with an increased awareness regarding existing legislation in favour of the tenants. However, this has been achieved only after considerable struggle and the shift to batai is far from complete.

Living Conditions

Labourers in Bihar are not difficult to recognize. You have only to look at them—their faces, hands, feet, posture, expression. When you visit their mud houses, you often find that they have no doors; a sturdy wooden door is a luxury. Inside the house, there are few possessions and whatever they have is largely made of mud—be it the *chulha* on which they cook, the *kothi* in which they store grain or the matka in which they store water. Just to seat you, they may have to borrow a *khatia* (string cot), or sometimes even a gunny bag. Few houses can afford a khatia, the size of which gives away the class of its owner: in comparison to the small-sized khatia of the Dalits, those of the upper castes are always longer and wider.

Similar scenes are found in hamlet after hamlet. When women are not labouring, one may find them sitting in small groups, the old and young talking, making ropes from hay or picking lice out of each other's hair. Children may be playing close by. Often, the surroundings are filthy with plenty of scattered garbage. In the absence of a drainage system, pools of stagnant water add to the dismal and unhealthy surroundings. Pigs and other animals roam around freely, mixing with the children.

The food of the poor in Bihar is very basic: mainly cereals— rice after the winter harvest and wheat in the summer, with simple seasonal supplements such as saag (green leaves) of various standing crops, potato, chilies, mango pickle, etc. Few can afford dal (lentils). *Sattu* is a common supplement eaten in various forms. During the rainy season, small fish are sometimes caught in the irrigation channels. Items such as milk and meat are consumed only during festivals. Among the Musahars, field rats are often caught by the children and eaten roasted.

The poverty of the people also shows in their clothing, or the lack of it. The worn-out look—of clothes that have been washed far too often and repeatedly repaired or patched over—speaks much about their lives. Most poor women do not have more than two sarees; some have just one. The sarees are meant to be bright-coloured but often look dull, having seen many a season. Likewise, men may have to wear the same clothes day after day after simply rinsing them in plain water for want of soap.[41] A *ganji* (vest) may not be discarded until it has quite a few holes. Small children go around with minimal garments except the privileged few who have school uniforms. In the winter, rarely does one find sweaters or shawls. Many people avoid wearing their slippers except on special occasions, e.g., if they go out of the village. Some have no slippers at all.

There are few material luxuries in the life of a Bihari labourer. Glass bangles and *sindhur* worn by women add some colour. Country liquor and tobacco, consumed by men and women, provide

occasional relief. Fairs, *natch* (dances of women and young men—
londas—masquerading as women), *natak* (plays) or open-air films
organized in the village, the local *haat* (market), marriage feasts,
festivals like Durga Puja, Holi, etc., are some of the few diversions in
their hard lives. Political rallies too have some entertainment value,
especially for the uninitiated.

The hardest part of people's lives is poor health. A simple illness
like diarrhoea may lead to death, as happened to fifty infants in
Jehanabad district in the monsoon of 1995. Without immunization,
children remain vulnerable to infectious diseases like polio, tetanus,
diphtheria, etc.[42] Undernourishment and anaemia are endemic.
A relatively simple problem like poor eyesight becomes a cause
for daily pain since few can afford glasses or an eye check-up. For
women, the lack of private space to bathe and defecate is a constant
hardship. Any kind of complication during pregnancy or childbirth
may prove fatal.

Health services are practically non-existent in the study villages.
Much the same applies to other public services. The villages in the
region are literally immersed in darkness. In only one of the study
villages did I come across electricity, that too a single bulb in an
entire house. The only paved roads are the link roads between major
towns and even those are in a state of serious disrepair. There are
no public transport facilities. To go to town, most villagers have to
walk to the nearest road and then wait for one of the private buses
(operated by local landlords and businessmen) that ply the main
roads. The public distribution system, though functional in some
villages, delivers much less than it is supposed to do.

Among all local public services, only schools achieve a semblance
of continuity and effectiveness.[43] Most villages have a government
primary school, some also have a secondary school. The functioning
of the government schools, however, varies a great deal in terms of
attendance rates, teacher regularity, quality of teaching, etc. Among
schools that are not functioning effectively are those located in

Musahar tolas, where lack of motivation on the part of the parents is part of the problem. In upper-caste tolas, the situation is somewhat better: facilities are minimal and the quality of teaching leaves much to be desired, yet there is some order and activity. Private schools have proliferated in the region, but they charge fees and tend to be used mainly by better-off households. Lack of schooling facilities not only contributes to harsh living conditions for the poor but also affects the future of their children.

Social Oppression

Stories of *daman* (oppression) and *soshan* (exploitation) abound. I shall describe here three examples of oppressive practices that are most resented in the study villages. Though these practices are much less common today than in the past, people have had to fight hard against them.

One of the first complaints mentioned by Dalits is the way in which they used to be (and sometimes still are) addressed by the upper castes, even by children. The common form of address was a nameless '*arrey*' (hey) as if they had no identity and were invisible as distinct individuals. When the name of the person was mentioned, a derogatory suffix of '*wa*' would be added—for example, Deepa would become Deepwa. Often a rain of abuses accompanied whatever was being said. This is one of the deepest hurts of the people. Their minimum demand from the upper castes and classes is that they be addressed by name and not in an abusive language.

While 'Arrey' symbolizes their invisibility, it is also a symbol of all that they were not supposed to do. A Dalit person was not supposed to attract attention to himself or herself, whether by speech, action or demeanour. For example, he or she could not dare to wear clean clothes, to wear slippers in the presence of the landlord or to look straight into his eyes while speaking. Only by stooping would they be showing appropriate respect for the *huzoors* or maliks.

Second, the Dalits had to abide by some rules not only in the presence of the upper castes and classes but also in their own homes. Sitting in front of their own houses on a khatia was forbidden as a daring affront to the maliks—khatia for some reason is considered to be 'pure' and thus unfit for the 'impure'. Even though the Dalits today do sit on khatias in their own homes or outside, even in a relatively progressive upper-caste household, only a *chowki* (a bed made of plain wooden planks, considered more appropriate for Dalits) will be offered to them.

Third, sexual exploitation of women otherwise considered 'untouchable' by the upper castes was the norm. Women were routinely abused while working in the fields or elsewhere.

These and other oppressive practices are seen by the labourers as an attack on their *izzat* (dignity). In the depths of anguish and humiliation is born a rage, a cry for restoration of their izzat. In the notion of izzat, we see not only a culmination of anguish and anger, but a basic assertion of their selves as persons, as human beings. That is why the labourers continuously return to the question of izzat while discussing their plight.

13

The Naxalite Movement in Central Bihar[*]

Khet par adhikar ke liye lado, desh mein jaanwad ke liye badho
(Fight for land rights, march towards democracy
in the country—CPI (ML) Liberation slogan)

*Saamantshahi ke kille ko dwasth karen, janwad ke durg ko nirman
karen*
(Let us smash the castle of feudalism and build
the fort of democracy—CPI (ML) Party Unity slogan)

Apni satta, apna kanoon
(Our power, our law—Maoist Communist Centre slogan)

Introduction

The Naxalite movement is a revolutionary communist movement,
which traces its origins to the Naxalbari uprising of 1967 in West

---

[*] This is an abridged version of an earlier essay (Bhatia, 2005) based on my
PhD thesis (Bhatia, 2000). The term 'central Bihar' refers to the geography of
undivided Bihar—see Chapter 12 (The Mazdooras of Bihar), where the study
villages were also introduced.

Bengal. Widely considered one of the most significant among the radical agrarian movements that emerged in the post-Independence period, the movement sharply captures the turbulence of the Indian countryside. It also represents one possible means of overcoming the failures that have led to that turbulence.

In the layperson's mind, the word 'Naxalite' evokes various images. Either it is an image of unreasonable gun-toting extremists (an image painted by the state and most of the media), or it is a heroic picture reminiscent of Che Guevara's idealism and self-sacrifice. While much of the latter image applies to some Naxalites, there is a need to go beyond these stereotypes and pay attention to the ground realities.

The aim of my research on the Naxalite movement in central Bihar was to develop an understanding of the movement from the perspective of the people who make up its mass base including members, supporters and activists at the village level. Valuable as they are, most scholarly accounts of the Naxalite movement in Bihar have neglected this important dimension, i.e., the point of view of the participants.[1] These accounts tend to be based either on the experiences and writings of the leaders or on secondary literature such as media and government reports. A view of the Naxalite movement as politics of the people needs to be developed.[2] In this view, people are seen not just as supporters but also as actors and thinkers who—with others—shape the movement. This approach involves asking who these people are, what they think, how they act and why they think or act the way they do. Answering these and related questions is indispensable to developing an understanding of the movement's inner life.

This essay draws on two years of fieldwork in rural areas of central Bihar in 1995 and 1996. During this period, I visited (and often revisited) more than fifty villages under the Naxalite influence and talked with the participants of the movement, their opponents and the representatives of the state. More recent developments are briefly discussed in the postscript of this essay.

The Naxalite Movement in Central Bihar

The Naxalite movement in Bihar can be divided into two phases: the formative phase, from 1967 to 1977, and the current phase, from 1977 onwards.[3] Prior to the imposition of the Emergency in 1975, the movement had been able to spread in parts of two or three districts, but during the Emergency, it faced heavy state persecution and had to lie low. However, by the late 1970s, it had been able to reorganize itself and was once again on an upswing. The phase after 1977 therefore saw the revival of the movement, significant reformulations of its political line and the emergence of new Naxalite groups.

During the formative phase, local struggles initially sprung up in the Mushahari region of Muzaffarpur district in north Bihar, in parts of Bhojpur and Patna districts in central Bihar and in Hazaribagh, Ranchi, Singhbhum and Dhanbad districts of south Bihar (now Jharkhand). These struggles were modelled after the Naxalbari uprising of 1967 and were initiated by various members of the All-India Coordination Committee of Communist Revolutionaries (AICCCR) or its successor, the CPI (ML), as well as by Naxalite groups outside the AICCCR fold (mainly the Maoist Communist Centre [MCC]).[4]

Many of these actions were sporadic and were not part of a sustained movement. In Bhojpur, however, the Naxalite movement took root starting from village Ekwari, where Jagdish Mahato, a local teacher who had forged links with Naxalite leaders from West Bengal, led a protracted struggle against exploitative landlords. The Naxalites who came to Bhojpur belonged to the 'pro-Lin Piao group', which later developed into the present CPI (ML) Liberation, also known as 'Liberation'.

The Naxalite movement in Bihar, as in other Indian states, is heavily factionalized (see Chart below for a summary of party history from 1967 to 1982, as viewed by Liberation). At the time of my fieldwork, in 1995–96, at least seventeen Naxalite groups functioned in different parts of Bihar. Except for the MCC, all others were CPI (ML) groups. The most important groups were Liberation, Party Unity and MCC. These factions, discussed below, broadly represented the three main trends within the movement in Bihar and in the country as a whole: on the Naxalite spectrum in Bihar, MCC was considered to be on the extreme left, Liberation was drifting towards the 'parliamentary path' and Party Unity was somewhere in between. The other Naxalite groups in Bihar are outside the scope of this essay.

Liberation[5]

Central Bihar is the stronghold of Liberation. It was here that Liberation first found a firm footing, in Bhojpur, in the late 1960s and early 1970s. From Bhojpur, Liberation spread to adjoining areas of central Bihar as well as to parts of south Bihar (now Jharkhand) and north Bihar. At the time of my fieldwork (1995–96), the Liberation group functioned in approximately thirty districts of undivided Bihar, including eleven districts of central Bihar.

Even though the Liberation group considers itself the true inheritor of the CPI (ML) legacy, its political line has changed dramatically from that of the original CPI (ML). In 1978, a 'rectification campaign' was launched by the party to bring about changes in its style of work. The campaign went well beyond this initial objective, as the need for fundamental changes in the party line and practice began to be voiced. These changes were formalized in a special party conference held in July 1979. The most important outcome of this conference was the decision to begin open mass activities through the formation of appropriate mass organizations.

This ushered in a phase of mass politics. The Indian People's Front (IPF) and the Bihar Pradesh Kisan Sabha (BPKS) were formed in the early 1980s. The aim of BPKS was to lead the peasant

Party History at a Glance 1967–82

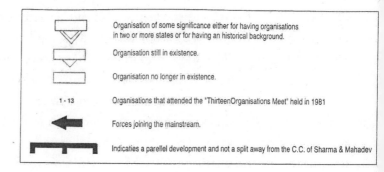

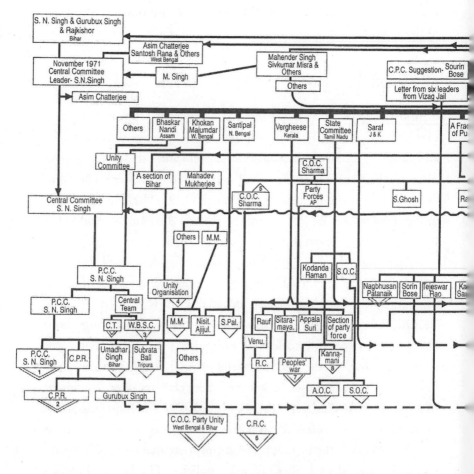

Source: CPI(ML) Liberation. 1983. Documents of the Third All-India Co...

Note: Forces owing allegiance to the C.P.I. (ML) have been shown on the
and from non-party to party by wavy line. During the period after ...

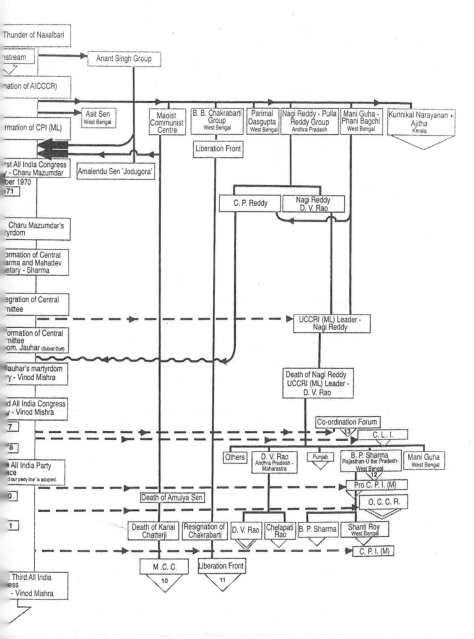

Thunder of Naxalbari

nstream

Anant Singh Group

nation of AICCCR)

| Asit Sen
West Bengal | Maoist
Communist
Centre | B. B. Chakrabarti
Group
West Bengal | Parimal
Dasgupta
West Bengal | Nagi Reddy - Pulla
Reddy Group
Andhra Pradesh | Mani Guha -
Phani Bagchi
West Bengal | Kurnikal Narayanan +
Ajitha
Kerala |

rmation of CPI (ML)

Liberation Front

rst All India Congress
/ - Charu Mazumdar
ber 1970
71

Amalendu Sen 'Jodugora'

| C. P. Reddy | Nagi Reddy
D. V. Rao |

Charu Mazumdar's
yrdom

rmation of Central
arma and Mahadev
etary - Sharma

egration of Central
nittee

UCCRI (ML) Leader -
Nagi Reddy

ormation of Central
nittee
om. Jauhar (Subrat Dutt)

Jauhar's martyrdom
y - Vinod Mishra

Death of Nagi Reddy
UCCRI (ML) Leader -
D. V. Rao

d All India Congress
/ - Vinod Mishra

Co-ordination Forum

7   13   C. L. I.

'8

| Others | D. V. Rao
Andhra Pradesh -
Maharastra | Punjab | B. P. Sharma
Rajasthan-U ttar Pradesh-
West Bengal | Mani Guha
West Bengal |

All India Party
nce
d our party line' is adopted.

12

Pro C. P. I. (M)

0   Death of Amulya Sen

O. C. C. R.

1 | Death of Kanai
Chatterji | Resignation of
Chakrabarti | D. V. Rao | Chelapati
Rao | B. P. Sharma | Shanti Roy
West Bengal |

C. P. I. (M)

| M .C. C.
10 | Liberation Front
11 |

Third All India
ess
- Vinod Mishra

arty of India (Marxist-Leninist), 26-30 December, 1982. Unpublished party document.

ces are shown on the right side. Change of party forces to non-party forces shown by broken line
d the groups have been joining the mainstream of the party. This process has not been shown here.

movement in Bihar, while IPF was to intervene in the national political scene. Both organizations flourished. The BPKS led vibrant peasant struggles in central Bihar in the 1980s and remained a significant force for many years. The IPF also developed into a powerful people's movement. Its initial vision was to become a broad forum of communist revolutionary organizations and other democratic forces in the country. This vision, however, could not be sustained because the party (Liberation) held on to a leadership role and failed to develop IPF as an autonomous confederation. IPF therefore did not develop beyond a mass organization of the Liberation group, though a powerful one.

Quick on the heels of the decision to initiate open mass activities was the decision taken by the party at its third congress in December 1982 to contest elections on tactical grounds (initially under the banner of IPF).[6] In a special conference convened in July 1990, the party decided to resume open functioning. This decision was formalized at its fifth congress in December 1992. In 1994, the Indian People's Front was disbanded. The party was recognized by the Election Commission in 1995 and was able to contest the 1995 assembly elections and 1996 parliamentary elections as CPI (ML).

Party Unity[7]

As the name indicates, Party Unity's original aim was unification. It came into existence on 1 January 1982 with a merger between two CPI (ML) groups: CPI (ML) Unity Organization (henceforth UO) and Central Organizing Committee CPI (ML) (henceforth COC). In the following years, three other CPI (ML) groups joined.[8] Party Unity itself merged with the CPI (ML) People's War Group (PWG) in August 1998; the united group was called CPI (ML) People's War (PW). Since the merger took place after the end of my fieldwork in 1996, this Naxalite faction is referred to as Party Unity (PU) in this essay.

As PU leaders see it, all the parties that merged to form the present PU were part of the 'third trend' in the CPI (ML) camp in the early 1980s. Parties of the third trend upheld the Naxalbari uprising, the historical role of the original CPI (ML) and its founding leader Charu Mazumdar, and the basic line of the original CPI (ML). However, these parties conceded that deviations and mistakes had occurred and were keen to make appropriate corrections to theory and practice.[9] PU's example illustrates the fact that while the history of the CPI (ML) party and movement is replete with splits and factionalism, there is also a history of mergers.

Jehanabad is a stronghold of Party Unity. Besides, PU-led peasant movements are also strong in parts of the adjoining Gaya and Patna regions and in Palamau. The most popular open front of Party Unity is Mazdoor Kisan Sangram Samiti (MKSS), banned in 1986 and renamed Mazdoor Kisan Sangram Parishad (MKSP) in 1994.[10]

Maoist Communist Centre

In its self-identity and political image, MCC represents the 'hardline wing' of the Naxalite movement. Completely banned, MCC leads an entirely underground existence.[11] As a result, reliable information on MCC is difficult to obtain. The following account is based on a series of interviews with the MCC spokesperson in Bihar in July–October 1996, and some primary literature supplied by him.

MCC was formed on 20 October 1969. The initial differences between the MCC and the CPI (ML) are spelt out in a document circulated by MCC in June 1971.[12] MCC considered the CPI (ML)'s political line and practice until 1971 to suffer from 'left deviationism' and asserted that this trend would have to be opposed, just like its right counterpart (represented by the CPI[M]).

Even though MCC's central critique of the CPI (ML) line was its then extreme position, paradoxically, it is MCC that later faced accusations of being *kattarpanthi* (extremist) in the Naxalite camp. Even before the ban of its open fronts in 1994, MCC's emphasis was on underground party action and its mass fronts were relatively confined. In its inner-party functioning, particularly in the implementation of the principle of democratic centralism, MCC is known to be more centralized than democratic.

As it turns out, MCC has achieved little success in building a mass People's Army for guerrilla warfare. Instead, it has become known for actions that have invited condemnation not only from bourgeois circles but also from the Naxalite movement itself. For example, on several occasions, MCC has retaliated against massacres by upper-caste landlords by carrying out counter-massacres of upper-caste men (it is after such a counter-massacre that MCC was banned in 1987). Other examples of actions that have attracted wide criticism include brutal punishments in people's courts (justified as 'the will of the people') and severe threats against those who participate in elections.

MCC is most active in districts that are now part of Jharkhand. In central Bihar, it is considered to be the strongest in Gaya, followed by parts of other districts such as Jehanabad, Aurangabad and Patna.

Who are the Naxalites?

Some broad features of the Naxalite movement are relatively easy to identify. The social base of the movement in central Bihar consists overwhelmingly of the landless, small peasants with marginal landholdings and to a lesser extent, middle peasants. In caste terms, the base of the movement consists of lower and intermediate castes.[13] This applies to the Hindu as well as Muslim communities. The movement, however, also has some supporters among the higher castes and classes. Their presence is particularly strong in the leadership of the movement. Beyond these features, also observed by other scholars, little is known about the identity, motives and worldview of the Naxalites. In this section, I attempt to shed some light on this based on my fieldwork in Liberation and especially PU areas in 1995–96.[14] The discussion relies primarily on people's testimonies: perceptions of members and supporters of the movement and wherever possible, of their opponents.

People's Perceptions

The Term 'Naxalite'

Even though the term Naxalite is part of people's vocabulary in central Bihar, it is understood in different ways. 'Everybody calls you Naxalites. What is your understanding of who a Naxalite is and what does the term mean?' The responses to this question reflected diverse perceptions of the term and of the Naxalite movement itself. Below is a sample of the responses to this question obtained from members, supporters and local cadres of the Naxalite movement in different villages:

Do we know how to read and write that we can tell you?
                              (A common answer)

We may be called Naxalites or by another name . . . but we do not go anywhere nor come from anywhere . . . we just do our work.

Before the sangathan came to our village, we had heard that the sangathan is Naxalite. It cuts *mundis* (heads). It is dangerous. We did not have a lot of knowledge or information then. When we came closer and got a chance to talk, our knowledge grew.

Dushman varg (enemy class) spoke about them with fear. Others considered them *acche log jo hamare haq mein hai* (good people who are in our favour).

In English 'lite' means *prakash* (light), right? So, we say *naksha-lite*—making a new map (*naksha*) for Bharat (India) with our light. We wish that the *aam janata* (ordinary people), those whose houses are in darkness, be influenced by our light. We wish to bring light to the darkness . . . to take those who are in the dark out of it.

Aanewala prakash (the next light) is Naxalite.

Naxalite means [pointing at the back of the neck] *nas kaat kar prakash lana* (cutting the nerve and bringing light).

The zamindars say Naxalite. We say Naxalbari. We support the Naxalbari movement and its objectives. We are following the *vichardhara* (ideology) of Naxalbari. We are walking on the same path. But our zamindars say, 'This is a Naxalite who cuts *nas* (nerves) of the upper castes and carries out their *safaya* (annihilation).' They say that the Naxalites want to keep you under their control with the butt of their rifles. They say this so that others may hate the Naxalites and fear them.

No, we are not Naxalites! We fight for our children, for our *haq* (rights). We ask for three kilos of grain as *mazdoori* (wages). We do not consider Naxalite as Naxalite. It is a party . . . Who is Naxalite? Those who have been oppressing us and sucking our blood, or we, who are trying to change the situation?

We are *Naxalvadi* (Naxalite). *Sarkar* calls us *ugravadi* (extremists), but we are not ugravadis. Those persons are ugravadis who are exploiting and oppressing. Then there is one more word which the sarkar uses—*aatankvadi* (terrorist). When in our country, a neighbouring country enters, terrorizes and then leaves, that is called aatankvadi. The *shashak varg* (ruling class) says that these are the Naxalites, but that is not the case. They do not say anything to the real aatankvadis. But Naxalvadi we are.

If somebody who demands his rights is a Naxalite, then we are also Naxalites. We ask for our rights—you may call us Naxalite or what you will.

People who decided to join or not join the Naxalites had in most cases heard about the Naxalites before they actually met them. A large majority of the people in Jehanabad, some of whom subsequently joined the movement, had initially understood the Naxalites to be people who indulge in *maar-kaat* (beating and hacking), *jo che-inch chhota karte hain* (those who shorten [the body] by six inches). These initial perceptions changed after they came in contact with some leaders or members of Naxalite factions at the village level. This made them realize that the maar-kaat of the Naxalites was with a difference and that they were *acche log* (good people) with good intentions. Many of them joined the movement based on this perception; others joined in the hope that the Naxalites would deal with their oppressors.

After joining the sangathan, their understanding of its objectives grew. Some cadres were now able to relate it to Naxalbari and the movement which spread subsequently. These cadres clearly affirm: 'Yes, we are Naxalites!' However, a large majority continue to express their understanding in popular terms. As the testimonies above indicate, some of these popular perceptions of the term are: *naksha-lite* (a new map and light), *aanewala prakash* (the next light), *nas kaat kar prakash lana* (cutting the nerve and bringing light). Historically less conversant but politically no less astute, those who offer these explanations identify themselves as Naxalites less through the label than through the actions of the movement. The initial association with maar-kaat faded away with the shift in emphasis from 'annihilation' to open mass movements and people's own participation in these movements. The Naxalite movement began to be understood by them as a struggle for basic rights.

The testimonies convey an anti-system sentiment. There is awareness of the existence of classes in society, that the interests of one class may clash with those of another and that in order to draw the 'map' (naksha) anew, those in darkness would need to be taken towards 'light'—the future vision being metaphorically conveyed as light. The testimonies suggest that the Naxalites have a fair idea of the important components of their struggle for basic rights as well as a knowledge of their opponents—the zamindars, the sarkar, the punjipati and the shashak varg. In their self-identity, therefore, the Naxalites clearly see themselves as individuals who have chosen a path which clashes with the existing order.

However, their struggle for basic rights has met with fierce opposition and condemnation. Their attempt to assert the 'right' has turned them into 'wrong' in the eyes of a large part of the world. The Naxalites and their movement have been abused for so long by the state, the establishment and the upper classes, that the negative connotation of the term Naxalite has been internalized by some of the Naxalites themselves, as we can see from the testimony of the person who began by exclaiming, 'No, we are not Naxalites!' Like him, some Naxalites deny all the wrongs that are commonly attributed to the movement and may even distance themselves from the term itself. They define who they are by who they are not, and in doing so, affirm the positive values of the Naxalite movement.

In the perception of the Naxalites, therefore, the term 'Naxalite' defies a single interpretation. The various participants understand it in their own terms. However, behind these differences, there lies a common theme of basic values such as justice, freedom from oppression and standing up for one's rights.

On Revolution and the Party

Feudalism will have to be rooted out steadily, otherwise it will uproot you. *Saamantvaad har aadmi par chaya hua hai* (feudalism lies like a shadow on every person). Until feudalism is rooted out, *kranti* (revolution) cannot be achieved.[15]

Before the sangathan came, we did not have a lot of *gyan* (knowledge). The sangathan gave us *shiksha* (education) regarding the present system and the need to overthrow it (*palatna*). India is a *ardh-saamanti* (semi-feudal) and *ardh-upnivaishik* (semi-colonial) country. There is also foreign capital in our country. We must stop using this foreign capital and utilize the capital of our own country. The downtrodden people must rise above the system. Each individual should get education. Each individual should get food.

We got books to read about Marx, Lenin and Mao. From these we learnt that Marx was a revolutionary, and so were Lenin and Mao. We have not read a lot, but we understand what Marx and Lenin wanted to say—this *sadi-gali vyavastha* (rotten system) should be destroyed, the exploitation of one human being by another should end, humankind should be liberated from this. This is what Marx and Lenin wanted to say.

The Naxalite movement has a long-term agenda of achieving a revolution. How do the people who join the movement conceptualize 'revolution'? People do not have a textbook understanding of revolution, but they do have some notion of radical change. They use the word *badlav* (change) more often than kranti. One can safely say that badlav represents their own understanding while kranti or *nayi janwadi kranti* (new democratic revolution) are additions to their political vocabulary. They understand badlav as a change in their existing situation; their newly learnt notion of kranti adds a vision of building a new society which is more equitable and just. They also understand revolution to be a *ladai* (struggle) between them (i.e., their party) and their opponents (i.e., landlords, police and government).

Do the members and supporters of a revolutionary movement such as the Naxalite movement perceive themselves as 'revolutionaries'? Within the Naxalite movement, *krantikaris* (revolutionaries) are understood to be those who are ready to give up everything, even their lives, for the cause. They recognize it to be a long process for which they have seen many of their comrades die. The self-perception of the people as krantikari can be felt more at the cadre level than at the level of people in the villages. Similarly, it can be felt more in the underground party organization than in the open fronts. Outside the former, people rarely call themselves krantikaris.

Why do People Join the Movement?

Diverse reasons motivate people to join a revolutionary movement. A broad distinction can be made between ideological and non-ideological motives.

Ideological Motives

In this category, a distinction needs to be made between 'formal' ideology and the 'informal' understanding or popular perception of such an ideology. Individuals who choose to join the movement with full knowledge of its ideology and revolutionary agenda can be understood to be motivated by the formal ideology. Leaders of the movement at the block level and upwards tend to fall into this category. We can also call these individuals 'informed revolutionaries'.

Aside from them, there are 'instinctual revolutionaries'. These are individuals who have an instinctive urge to fight against injustice and who get attracted to the revolutionary message of the movement. These revolutionaries may have witnessed the oppression perpetrated on or by their own families and caste and instinctively rebel against this injustice. Their coming across Marxist-Leninist ideology and joining the movement is more like finding partners with the same concern. There are many committed and inspiring Naxalites in this category of instinctual revolutionaries. A large majority of the cadres, especially those at the village level, and of the people who comprise the backbone of the movement are in this category.

People in both categories can be seen to have revolutionary intentions. However, these categories are not clear-cut. I am not suggesting that informed revolutionaries are not instinctual or vice-versa. Instinctual revolutionaries also, in their own ways, make 'informed' choices, though the basis is different.

Ideological motives of some kind apply to both groups, even though only the first has a clear understanding of the formal Marxist-Leninist ideology. At the village level, with a few exceptions, there is little understanding of the formal ideology of Marxism-Leninism amongst the people who constitute the mass base of the movement. In fact, very few have heard of Russia or China, leave alone Marx, Lenin and Mao. Thus, at the village level, few people have joined the Naxalite movement on the basis of its formal ideology. This, however, does not mean that people have no ideological motivations. It is just that their ideological motivations are based on their own interpretation and understanding of the revolutionary ideology.

When we try to determine the salient aspects of the ideology which resonate with the deprived sections, we find that people who support the Naxalite movement do so mainly because they feel that the Naxalites share their sense of injustice, are ready to live and suffer like them and fight on their behalf. The Naxalite ideology also strikes a chord with the people because it finds expression in concrete struggles on immediate issues that concern them, like land distribution, minimum wages, and so on.

Need and Survival

Many people join the movement, especially its open fronts, for non-ideological reasons and with non-revolutionary intentions. They recognize the injustice of their circumstances and realize that only a collective struggle is likely to redress it. It is in this respect that the 'class struggle' appeals to them.

Among the needs that the people hope the party will address are better wages, land redistribution and freedom from harassment. Many individuals also approach one or the other Naxalite faction with specific personal requests such as retribution for rape, protection in the face of threats and arbitration of property disputes.[16] Interestingly, the form and language of such requests (e.g., petitions to the local party committee) are often similar to those of petitions made to the government. In fact, the Naxalite parties are also known in some areas as *lal sarkar* (red government).

Sometimes, joining the Naxalite movement is a matter of survival. The nature of local politics in central Bihar is such that it is often impossible for people to remain neutral. People belonging to the oppressed castes and classes, more often than others, join the movement for this reason. In central Bihar, the CPI (ML) is the only party which gives priority to their interests and has a strong presence at the local level. The fact that the Naxalites are armed adds to their attraction in this respect.

Opportunism

Members of different classes sometimes choose to align themselves with whatever Naxalite faction happens to be locally powerful and is likely to be beneficial to them, irrespective of its ideology.

There are many specific forms of opportunism. For instance, some individuals may join the Naxalite movement to settle scores with their enemies or to gain advantage in a private conflict over issues such as division of family property. Another type of opportunism is based on fear—some high-caste landlords and rich peasants join the movement out of fear of becoming the next 'target'. Similarly, in situations where the upper castes (e.g., Rajputs and Bhumihars) are in conflict with each other, one of the sides may align with a Naxalite group for the sake of self-protection. Sometimes individuals simply join the Naxalite movement as a shortcut to achieving local power.

Other Motives

Aside from the motives discussed so far, other factors of a seemingly more superficial nature can also influence people's decision to join the Naxalite movement or a particular Naxalite faction. For instance, the popularity of different factions often depends simply on 'who came first'. Whichever faction is the first to set foot in a particular area is likely to win broad support—if it talks about justice and rights and has the power to take cudgels on behalf of the underprivileged. Another example is the occasional transmission of political preferences from generation to generation. I have come across families in Bhojpur where one can meet second-generation or even third-generation Liberation cadres. Last but not least, the personality factor (personal appeal of cadres) has a strong influence on the popularity of different Naxalite groups in particular areas—a leader of high integrity and reliability, who is able to guide the people and be with them through thick and thin, often attracts many followers. A sound ideology may have little following if its proponents are not individuals of high calibre.

Collective identities like caste, class and gender also play a crucial role in determining who joins the movement and why. By and large, an individual follows the family, the family follows the caste and the caste is influenced by other social groups of similar status. A caste may be factionalized and have more than one leader; political allegiance may be divided accordingly.

Case Study: Challenge to *Saamanti Dabdaba* in Ekwari

Bhojpur today is sitting on a volcanic edge. During the last three decades, ever since the struggle described by the labourers as izzat ki ladai began, many battles have been fought. The struggle of the Dalits against the *saamanti dabdaba* (feudal power) of the upper castes and classes continues unabated. This struggle has plunged the villages of five blocks of Bhojpur district (where the Liberation group is active) into an extended period of turmoil, the end of which is nowhere in sight. The story of Ekwari village illustrates the situation.

Ekwari is a village at war. The mood is tense, the class divide sharp and clear. People of both sides, participants and witnesses to the class war, can often be found discussing the latest events in low voices in small groups. These events are often dramatic. For instance, on 25 November 1995, when I was returning from the Dalit tola of Ekwari to the main village with a local woman, we met another woman. In whispers, the latter related to my companion that the police had unearthed a dead body from the nearby mango grove.

The deceased, a Brahmin, was from a neighbouring village. He had been reported missing for around ten days. According to one version of the events, he had been kidnapped by members of the Ranbeer Sena before being killed. This version, one among others, came from a Bhumihar, who claimed to be among the kidnappers and maintained that he had tried to dissuade the others from killing the victim as he was a Brahmin. The story and the sight of the unearthed body aroused some curiosity from adults and children alike. By the evening, however, the same villagers were engrossed in an open-air film. Clearly, there is nothing unusual about death in Ekwari. Since the Naxalite movement began, as many as eighty-five individuals have been killed on the side of the landowners, and perhaps an equal or larger number on the side of the poor.

Ekwari is one of the largest villages in Sahar block, with a population of approximately 9000 in 1995. Roughly, one-third are *kisans* (farmers) and the remaining two-thirds are mazdoors, who are either completely landless or have marginal landholdings. Bhumihars (about 250 households) are the major landowners in Ekwari. As

Sankh Singh—a prominent Bhumihar leader who was on the 'hit list' of the Naxalites—tried to emphasize, the landed in Ekwari were not zamindars but kisans who used to be ryots of the zamindars of Banaras before independence.[17] The largest landholdings in the village today are below 100 bighas. However, landowners in Ekwari are called zamindars by the labourers since they not only own a major share of the land, but also retain overwhelming political control over village institutions such as the gram panchayat.

It was this insistence on maintaining political control that got the Bhumihars in trouble in 1967. During the fourth state assembly elections that year, Jagdish Mahato, an educated youth of the Koeri caste, was severely beaten by the henchmen of the landlords for attempting to prevent them from rigging votes.[18] Meanwhile, news of the Naxalbari uprising (which took place the same year) had spread far and wide. Naxalite slogans calling for armed revolution had also started appearing on the walls of towns like Ara of Bhojpur. The Naxalite message caught the imagination of Jagdish Mahato, who started looking for like-minded friends. In this endeavour, he was joined by Rameshwar Ahir, a Yadav dacoit-turned-rebel who had returned to Ekwari after serving a twelve-year sentence for murdering a constable.[19]

The izzat ki ladai had begun.

At this stage, Jagdish Mahato is reported to have travelled to West Bengal to forge links with Naxalite leaders there. The Naxalites who subsequently came to Bhojpur developed into the present CPI (ML) Liberation.

Initially, the focus was on annihilation of oppressive landlords and their henchmen, and on fighting against the state. The struggle against the landlords was not only over land but also against their saamanti (feudal) attitudes and behaviour. Jagdish Mahato is said to have described this hangover from the past in the following words: 'The landlord's moustache has got burnt but the twirl still remains.' Jagdish Mahato and Rameshwar Ahir were killed in 1972 and

1975, respectively. Sometimes fondly called Marx and Engels, these two founders of the Naxalite movement in Bhojpur had no prior communist background.

After the formation of the mass fronts of the Liberation group in the early 1980s, the movement started focusing on other issues, such as land and wages. Diverse means of struggle were used, including strikes, dharnas, roadblocks and *gheraos*. These struggles on different issues were often against the same landlord. One example is the struggle of the Naxalites against Sankh Singh and his family.

Sankh Singh was considered as the leader of the anti-Naxalite group in Ekwari in 1995. He and his relatives, including his sons and nephews, were said to be leading members of the Ranbeer Sena, a Bhumihar-based militia formed in 1994 (see Chapter 15—Justice, Not Vengeance). When I interviewed Sankh Singh in November 1995, he mentioned that his land had been lying *parti* (fallow) for five years due to the *aarthik nakebandi* (economic blockade) imposed on his family by the Naxalites. Before 1990, he said, he had employed around 150 labourers on an average in his fields. The blockade extended to all economic activities. One truck and two buses plied by one of his close relatives were destroyed; his tractor was burnt. Any attempts to overcome the blockade were thwarted and sometimes had serious repercussions, including many instances of firing from both sides. Five members of his family had been killed, beginning with his father, Nathuni Singh, in 1972.[20]

A casual observer in Ekwari may be confused as to what really is the issue at the centre of the class war that has torn the village apart year after year. Ceiling-surplus land does not exist in Ekwari. Wages remain below the legal minimum and low in comparison to the levels that prevail in struggle areas of Jehanabad. Sankh Singh and the *mukhiya*, Baijnath Singh, contended that, '*kuch baat ki ladai naikhe, gundai ki ladai ba* [there is no issue involved in this fight, it is only hooliganism]'.[21] On asking who the hooligans were, they pointed to the Naxalite leaders, whom they said had incited the mazdoors against them.

And yet, all this ladai has not been without results. The power of the landed upper castes and their saamanti dabdaba have been decisively challenged. The dignity and rights of landless agricultural labourers have been asserted. This local 'freedom struggle' has also created unprecedented political consciousness among the labourers.

The Ekwari story is exceptionally grim, but similar stories apply to many other villages of Bhojpur. In Dhanwar Bihta and Belaur, for instance, bitter struggles have been fought against local tyrants. Notable struggles against saamanti dabdaba have also taken place in other villages such as Gorpa, Gulzarpur, Baruhi, Nannor and Nadhi. The outcome of these battles is much the same everywhere: feudal power has been undermined and the dignity of the labourers has been restored, but protracted violence has also left a long trail of blood and tears.

The Struggle on the Ground

The Naxalite movement is best understood through its actions on the ground. Its ideology is understood by the people from these actions. In the remainder of this essay, I shall focus on 'the struggle on the ground'—the specific issues that the movement has taken up and the strategies and tactics it has followed.[22]

Basic Economic Rights

As the preceding section illustrates, the struggle issues actively taken up by the Naxalite movement reflect the practical needs and expectations of its mass base. These relate primarily to what may be seen as basic economic, social and political rights. Among the economic issues that have been taken up by the movement are land rights, minimum wages, common property resources and housing.

Land Rights

In Naxalite areas, one occasionally comes across a red flag resolutely planted in the middle of a field. This means that the land is contested and that the Naxalites have staked their claim over it. This land is usually 'surplus land' (above the legal ceiling) or misappropriated gairmajurwa land. In some cases, the land belongs to an absentee landlord.

If the claims of the Naxalites are uncontested by the landowner, the transfer of land is fairly smooth. However, this is rarely the case. Usually, the landowner contests the claim and a prolonged battle begins. If the issue cannot be resolved through peaceful means, it often results in violent clashes. If the Naxalites win, the land is subsequently distributed to the poor for agriculture or housing purposes. There have also been instances of land remaining in the hands of the party (instead of being distributed) and being leased to sangathan members on sharecropping basis. I have not come across any instances of land being distributed to women.

The movement has also attempted to change tenancy relations, for example, by demanding the implementation of tenancy regulations and better sharecropping terms. In some areas, the movement has attempted to enforce *batai* (equal shares for landlord and tenant), though this struggle has not been without problems. For instance, when the terms of sharecropping improve, landlords sometimes react by reducing the amount of land they lease out.

Minimum Wages

In many villages, prior to a wage struggle, the labourers were given approximately half *paseri kacchi* (1 kg and 750 gm) of coarse rice with some lunch, and sometimes also breakfast, as daily wages. There was no knowledge of an officially stipulated minimum wage. Today, in struggle areas, even though the wages are not uniform, they tend to be in the range of 3 to 3.5 kg of grain per day. This increase has had a positive impact in the non-Naxalite villages too.

There has also been an increase in the wages paid to the labourers at harvest time. Prior to the wage strikes, the harvesters used to receive one *bojha* (headload) for every twenty-one bojhas of harvested crop; this has risen to one bojha for every ten bojhas. The increased rate benefits not only the casual labourers, but also the halwahas or bandhuas (who are employed for one agricultural year). In addition, some other positive changes have been achieved, including a set number of work hours, an increase in the quality of grain paid and, in some areas, an equal wage for women.

A unique aspect of these wage strikes is the degree of unity, not only among the labourers of a particular village but also among the labourers of the surrounding area, making it impossible for a landlord to hire labourers from nearby villages. Often, these wage strikes are part of a general economic strike against a landlord, called aarthik nakebandi—as happened to Sankh Singh in Ekwari. Such a blockade includes a boycott of the landlord and his family by the labouring poor of different castes who refuse their services to him. As a consequence of these blockades, land may be left fallow for years. The situation can often take a volatile turn and lead to violence.

Struggle for just wages is one of the most important issues taken up by the Naxalite movement in central Bihar, with considerable success. The advantages of this issue were recognized early on: it could be taken up by the mass fronts of the CPI (ML) without much dependence on the underground squads; it could draw and unite a large number of labourers across castes on a class basis; and it had a good chance of success since an increase in wages was long overdue. For all these reasons, the wage issue was a useful starting point for the Naxalite groups.[23] But as stories from village after village in central Bihar reveal, even to achieve this basic minimum, long struggles had to be waged, which often became bloody battles or even took on the colour of war.

Other Economic Issues

The Naxalite movement has also fought for the rights of the poor to
common property resources. In doing so, the movement has asserted
the identity of the poor as equal members of a village. These struggles
are over gairmajurwa land as well as for full access to village ponds.
Used for washing clothes, bathing buffaloes, etc., these ponds are also
an important source of fish. The question of who has rights over the
fish has never been settled to the satisfaction of all the villagers. The
general government policy has been to auction the fish to the highest
bidder. Often, the local landlord gets the fish for a low price since
his bid goes unchallenged. This system is considered unfair by the
poorer sections of the village, for whom fish is a much-needed food
supplement. The Naxalite movement has challenged the landlords'
monopoly, established control over ponds on behalf of the poor and
devised a fairer system of distribution.

Another economic issue often taken up by the Naxalite movement
relates to housing. Owning a residential plot is very important for
the poor since it means some security. Living on homestead land
belonging to the landlord (the standard arrangement in earlier days)
increases the dependence of labourers on their employers. With the
help of Naxalite groups, labourers are sometimes able to resettle on
reclaimed gairmajurwa land.

Basic Social Rights

The Naxalite movement in central Bihar has fought against exploitative
agrarian relations, not only in economic but also in social terms.
Izzat (dignity or honour) is one of the crucial social freedoms it has
attempted to restore. Even though the Dalits of the region continue
to face many deprivations, there is now a greater sense of confidence
and autonomy. Most importantly, the Naxalite movement has been
effective in its assertion of Dalits as human beings and individuals

entitled to equal rights. Instances of rape of Dalit women have decreased dramatically. Arbitrary beatings are no longer tolerated. Labourers are free to sell their labour to whoever they please. Many Dalit children are going to school. Labourers are now allowed to wear clean clothes, sit in front of their homes on *khatias* (string cots) and welcome their guests without interference from the landlords, amongst other gains. All this has come about because the landed are no longer in a position to exercise illegitimate power with impunity.

Another important social right is protection from violence and harassment. Insecurity and fear have always been part of the daily lives of the poor in central Bihar. To some extent this continues today; the Naxalite movement itself, and the repression it has unleashed, have contributed to the general atmosphere of fear, mistrust and suspicion. However, progress has been made in eliminating some earlier forms of violence, such as the violence of organized gangs.

Giroh (organized criminal gangs) proliferated in many districts of Bihar since the 1960s. These *saamanti rangdaar* (feudal hooligans) did not belong to any particular caste, though a large number of them were Bhumihars, Rajputs or from middle castes such as Yadav and Kurmi. In 1978, when Party Unity first tried to build its base in Jehanabad district, it had to tackle the dominance of criminal gangs in the area. The most notorious gangs in Jehanabad then were those led by individuals known as Raja and Deepa, Ramanand, Hare Ram and Bindu Singh. As one of the activists said:

> Ever since I became old enough to understand, I have seen the people of my village and the surrounding area being in their vicious grip. The villagers were totally frustrated. One giroh specialized in stealing cattle (*maveshi chor*). They would come in the night and take bullocks, buffaloes, cows and even goats and pigs from the Dalits. Another giroh used to be called *motor chor*. After 1967, when electricity came to our villages for the first time, these gangs dismantled the new fittings and stole the cables and any other items

of value. Besides, there were numerous other instances of theft, molestation, rape, threats and intimidation. Except the landlords, who could organize their own protection and were recognized as *takatwar* (powerful) by the marauders, all others—the landless, middle peasants and even rich peasants—were affected.[24]

The Naxalite squads were effective in targeting the most notorious gang leaders and reducing the strength of these groups.[25] Elimination of criminal gangs has been a concern not only of Party Unity but also of other Naxalite groups. In this respect, they have brought some relief to the people of that region.

Basic Political Rights

Struggles for the economic and social rights mentioned earlier, by their very nature, involve an assertion of basic political rights. For example, when the poor struggle for minimum wages or land reform, they are asserting their constitutional right to justice. Similarly, when women who used to be constantly exposed to sexual harassment and even rape struggle to resist and punish their aggressors, they are also defending their constitutional right to personal liberty and dignity.

Here again, the Naxalite movement has achieved some success. The poor and oppressed of rural Bihar, who used to be invisible as far as upper classes and the state were concerned, are now a visible— even powerful—political force. Agricultural labourers are learning to think of themselves as citizens with the same political rights as the landlords and even to assert this equality in practice. Also, their perception of poverty as a matter of '*naseeb*' (fate) has changed; now they often see it as a matter of injustice. In other respects too, the poor of Bihar strike the observer for their political consciousness. In both rural and urban areas, people take strong interest in political matters and are well informed about political issues.

Another important political right, which has been denied to many in central Bihar, is the right to vote. People were often kept away from the polling booths by henchmen of the upper castes and classes who would cast the votes on their behalf in favour of their own candidate. Since Liberation considers participation in election as part of its political line, people in Liberation areas have been able to exercise their right to vote. In these areas, the party's candidates are contesting elections, with cadres oppose booth-capturing, and the party ensures that its supporters are able to caste their vote.[26]

Means of Struggle

Open and Non-Violent Forms of Struggle

The open and non-violent actions of the Naxalite movement have received little attention from the media or the state. However, in practice, many of the Naxalite movement's activities are 'non-violent'. This has been so in the second phase of the Naxalite movement—from 1977 onwards—when different groups began to organize open activities with varying degrees of emphasis. Over the years, non-violent protest has taken many forms and served varying objectives. Common forms of non-violent action include sabha (meeting), bandh (closure), aarthik nakebandi (economic boycott), samajik bahishkar (social boycott), jan adalat (people's court), dharnas (e.g., the fourteen-day dharna organized by Liberation in Ara in 1995 against Ranbeer Sena), gheraos (e.g., the famous gherao of the state assembly after the Arwal massacre in 1986), rallies (including silent marches and torch processions), chakka-jaam (road blocks), putla dahan (effigy burning) and, of course, work strikes. Even hunger strikes have figured in this rainbow of agitations—for instance, when Liberation MLAs and cadres launched an indefinite fast after the Bathani tola massacre in 1996, demanding an inquiry.

Cultural media (*sanskritik madhyam*) such as songs and plays have an important role in mobilization, especially since a large majority of the people in central Bihar are illiterate. Often, the songs are made by people themselves and convey their existing reality with great poignancy. The cultural fronts of the Naxalite movement, such as PU's Abhivayakti, are very popular. Some of their songs, printed in small booklets, are so popular that everyone seems to know them.

Underground and Armed Forms of Struggle

Underground and armed action has been an important part of the Naxalite movement from its inception. In the first phase of the movement, when mass mobilization was considered unnecessary, the movement relied almost exclusively on armed tactics. This changed with the formation of open fronts.

In the case of Liberation and MCC, people became familiar with the underground party before the mass organizations since the latter were formed only in the 1980s. Liberation's open fronts, in particular the Indian People's Front, were able to flourish because the party made a conscious decision to promote mass organizations. MCC, in contrast, continued to emphasize armed action and its open fronts never gained much popular support.

By the time PU was formed in the late 1970s, the importance of building mass movements was already felt. Accordingly, PU decided to begin with mass movements and then slowly build its armed wing. But in the very first meetings with labourers in Sikaria village (Jehanabad district), they realized the importance of building armed strength. According to a senior member of Party Unity, who was present in these meetings:

This was in 1979. There was an atmosphere of terror in the whole region due to the feudal forces and criminal gangs. Even though the labourers had heard about us and wanted to speak to us, they were too scared to invite us to their village. However, we were able to establish contact with a few active members of the JP movement and had asked them to arrange a meeting with some labourers, introducing us as individuals who belonged to a garibon ki party. On the agreed day, around midnight, we met in the *badhar* (open fields) outside the village. We expected a small group but were surprised to find around forty to fifty men waiting for us. They had come with lathis, *bhalas* and *gadasas*.

The terrorized villagers explained that they would have taken us to the village but could not because it was too risky. The maliks had warned them that if they brought the 'Naxalites' to the village, they would be severely punished. If an informer reported the meeting to the maliks, in all likelihood their hamlet would be burnt. 'Then who will protect us?' they asked. The labourers did not even have the right to meet. The attitude of the maliks was, '*Raad-raiyan* meeting *kare, aur hum log bardash karenge* [If the rabble dare to have a meeting, are we supposed to tolerate it]?'

In this initial meeting, we stressed that issues such as izzat, wages, land and basic democratic rights could be taken up. But we emphasized that the fight would have to be fought on our own strength. We would have to be prepared to face the feudal forces directly and not depend on the government. When we explained this, the labourers immediately said: 'We have understood. You are Naxalvadis [Naxalites] and you talk about *takat* [strength].'

People started coming in large numbers. After a few meetings, we began to feel that there was something they were hesitating to ask. Finally, one of them spoke out. He said that they had been coming to meeting after meeting expecting each time to get *hathiyar* (arms), but that even though we talked about the need for *samna* (confrontation) and *hathiyarband kranti* (armed revolution), we were not providing arms; when did we plan to do so? We understood then that they were actually demanding arms.[27]

In practical terms, underground armed action is undertaken by the *dasta* (squad). A dasta tends to have approximately six to ten members. Most dasta members are local residents from the labouring classes. Some squads also have middle-class members, possibly from other states such as West Bengal. These dastas are organized on militaristic lines, involving hierarchy, discipline and a uniform.

The squad functions under the directives of the party and undertakes a variety of actions such as safaya (annihilation) of a landlord, attack on a police picket (e.g., to snatch rifles and ammunition), or even a strike on another Naxalite faction. In the case of annihilation of landlords, advance warnings (including written warnings) are usually given and alternative measures such as boycotts are often tried before resorting to safaya. Landlords who agree to mend their ways have the option to 'surrender' in front of a *jan adalat*.

The most important role of the squad is to protect the open fronts, which are often attacked or repressed. The relationship between the open and underground movement, however, is not without tension.

Not all squad members are members of the party. In this respect, a squad member is like any other member of the open movement and has to pass the same criteria before he is accepted as a party member. The fact that squad members are armed gives them questionable power, considering that not all of them have been found suitable for party membership. On the other hand, being a squad member involves little private gain and considerable risks. Moreover, once a person chooses to be a member of a squad, he has few options. It is difficult, if not impossible, for him to revert to the life of an ordinary villager.

Mention should be made of the daily lives of squad members. These are individuals who have forsaken the sunlight and personal freedom. Their life begins in darkness when the village is asleep. A squad, for the sake of safety, has to be on the move all the time. It leaves its base late at night and has to reach a new shelter before dawn. Danger is always present. Squad members face the threat not only of 'class enemies', but also of possible informers within their own fold. They can never relax and have to be alert at all times.

The daily life of squad members also has its share of deprivations. They are almost totally dependent on the people for their survival. And since most of their supporters are poor, their food and shelter tend to be very basic. In their own self-perception, however, their living conditions have considerably improved. Pointing to his canvas shoes, one squad member mentioned that in the initial years, they could not even afford shoes, let alone a uniform. Wearing a *lungi*, they used to move barefoot in pitch darkness, unmindful of thorns or sharp stones.

Connections Between Open and Underground Actions

As we saw, each Naxalite group has its open fronts, even though the link between these fronts and the underground party is not always public knowledge. Each of these fronts has its own manifesto and organizational structure. Some of these open fronts, such as MKSS and IPF, have become very popular, not unlike some autonomous movements in other parts of the country, such as Chhattisgarh Mukti Morcha in Chhattisgarh and Kashtakari Sangathana in Maharashtra. However, there is a crucial difference between these movements and those led by the Naxalite fronts. The difference lies in the extent to which these movements are autonomous. In the case of the Naxalite fronts, the link with the 'party' is vital. However discreetly, the party provides leadership and protection to the open fronts. This link is both a strength and a weakness of these open organizations.

The party consists of selected people who subscribe to its ideology and revolutionary aims. Some party members may also belong to open fronts and work as a link between the two. The party, of necessity, must remain underground. It is the ultimate authority and is not answerable for its decisions or actions to the open fronts, though the latter need to hold the party in high esteem if the relationship has to work. While the party provides these organizations with protection, it also counts on their support in many diverse ways. For example, it depends on them for logistical support and relies on their cooperation to avoid being targeted by the police.[28]

The open and the underground are therefore intimately linked. Together they make a whole, each complementing the other. The relationship between the two is, however, far from simple and at times, even problematic. For example, in the mid-1980s a tension between Party Unity and its open front, MKSS, resulted in a split in the latter. In the case of Liberation too, IPF had to be disbanded in 1994 because it had become so popular that the identity of the party itself was at stake.

On Revolutionary Violence

People in the Naxalite villages do not comment openly on the question of arms. The following testimonies of leading members of MKSS in Jehanabad—some of whom may also have been members of the party—illustrate their perceptions in this regard:

> Without hathiyar, we feel that we shall not be able to fight. With arms we feel confident; we feel we have *shakti* (power). We feel that *final kar sakenge* (we shall be able to settle the fight).

> If we do not have hathiyarband shakti, then how will we counter the zamindar's anger? Can his anger be countered by just wagging our fingers at him? Without hathiyarband shakti, it is not possible to ensure *janata ki raksha* (people's protection).

> If we do not have arms, then nobody will take our committee [the MKSS village committee] seriously. Each will do according to his

will. They will think—'what can they do to us?'. When this shakti is there, they feel *dar* (fear). They know that if they do not obey us, then we have the power to destroy them.

To what extent are people prepared for the consequences of this kind of politics? By and large, people (especially cadres) are aware that incarceration, and even death, may be the price to pay. As one cadre said:

> There will be a lot of problems. We may even be killed. During this period, many have been martyred. *Kheti mein beej dala jata hai asha par ki ugega. Usi dhang se samajvaad ka ek sapna dekh kar hamlog chal rahe hai* (Seeds are sown in the field in the hope that they will grow. Similarly, with a dream of socialism we are going on).

Time and again, while talking about some 'martyred comrade', party workers remind the people that their tears need to become bullets. The fact that their politics hides in its fold possibilities of destruction as well as creation, death as well as life—is clear to all Naxalites. Even in the midst of grief and suffering, a Naxalite may unflinchingly affirm that armed struggle is essential. So did Suraj, a young PU squad member, as he sat leaning on the wall below the framed photographs of Pankaj, Manju and Aditya—his three *saathis* who had been martyred the previous year. The lower part of his body was covered with a blanket, and it took me some time to realize that one of his legs had just been amputated after an encounter with the police. I could discern no regret in his eyes, only some anxiety for his landless family which depended on him—the only son—for survival, as his father (also a squad member) had also been killed in action.

The perceived need for armed struggle is easy to understand. In central Bihar, killing of men who are guilty of extreme offences such as rape is to some extent culturally sanctioned—more so than in other parts of India. Safaya of oppressive landlords is accepted with similar relief. For labourers who have been at the receiving end of upper-caste violence for centuries, it is natural to seize the opportunity to protect themselves, and maybe even to retaliate. This is all the more so because the state has miserably failed to give them protection; instead, it has protected the privileged and their property.[29] For those who see the capture of state power as the ultimate aim of the movement, violence seems all the more necessary. Even the successful functioning of the open fronts, according to the party, depends heavily on the protection they receive from underground squads (called *suraksha dasta* or protection squads by the party).

The use of arms has been effective in some respects. For instance, zamindars and dacoits are no longer able to terrorize people with impunity:

> Because we have arms, the zamindars have shrunk with fear. Also, gangs of dacoits, who used to loot people's houses, have been vanquished. Because of these atrocities, the people used to feel very insecure. This has come to an end.

The possession of arms has also helped to resolve some conflicts without actual resort to violence. For example, in Nyona village (Jehanabad), the activists pointed out that the wage issue was resolved peacefully only because of the armed power of the sangathan. The same issue had been raised earlier by the labourers, using the same methods (e.g., negotiation and peaceful strike), but the zamindars had ignored their demands as they had no bargaining power.

> *Magar ham logon ke paas koi shakti to tha naheen ki us se ham un logon ko dabaen, to voh log mana naheen* (We had no power to put any pressure on them then, so they ignored our demands).

The practice of revolutionary violence, however, raises several problems. First, the use of violence has created a tension between safaya and sangathan, or between hathiyarband shakti (armed power) and lok shakti. Sangathan builds on lok shakti and the Naxalite movement owes much of its popularity to the open fronts. In contrast, armed actions such as safaya have to be highly secretive and rely on a hierarchical structure of power. It is difficult for the sangathan to be truly democratic and to fully realize the power of lok shakti as long as it is controlled by a secretive and hierarchical party. Moreover, even if the party owns up to its actions as it almost always does, the state can only target the visible actors, i.e., members of the open fronts. In that sense, the 'vanguard' party lets the people bear the brunt of its actions—which are undertaken on behalf of the people, but without their knowledge and consent.

Another problem is the danger of escalation, as violence breeds violence. While the need for *suraksha* (protection) is invoked to justify violence, it is not clear whether people are safer today than they used to be. They are better armed, but this has also led to a backlash on the part of upper classes and castes. While people are less vulnerable to unilateral violence from the landlords, they are more exposed to the spiral of retaliatory violence. The spiral of violence also runs the risk of reducing the revolutionary class struggle to a 'politics of revenge', well captured by what one hears at the local level on both sides—'*khoon ka badla khoon se lenge* [blood will be avenged with blood]'. Often, at the peak of a conflict between caste militias and one of the Naxalite factions, revolutionary activity gets reduced to a mere tit-for-tat strategy. In the process, other activities are neglected as most of the energy of the cadres is focused on defence and retaliation. The revolutionary value of this retaliatory violence is far from clear.

A third issue is the corrupting influence of armed power. Unprincipled individuals may join the movement out of attraction for armed power or for the sake of private gain. Also, there is always a risk that arms may not be used responsibly within the movement. Animosity or factionalism among Naxalite groups, for instance, has often taken a lethal turn.[30] Another corrupting influence of armed power, even if it is not misused, is that the mere possession of arms by some discourages criticism and dissent within the sangathan.

Finally, it should be borne in mind that the price of this retaliatory violence is paid first and foremost by ordinary people. Many parts of central Bihar have reached a war-like situation, where people live in a constant state of terror and suspicion and are exposed to the worst forms of violence on a daily basis. People have been living under these circumstances for many years and countless lives have been lost. Even if the spiral of violence has revolutionary value, the question remains whether it is justified.[31]

The Naxalite leaders argue that there was no alternative. However, the possibility of alternatives should not be dismissed lightly. The most prominent achievements of the Naxalite movement (increase in wages, assertion of izzat, resistance against social oppression, claiming illegally occupied land) could perhaps have been attained without large-scale violence if the Naxalites had greater faith in the power of popular mobilization. No doubt some lives would have been lost due to repression, but the spiral of retaliatory and wasteful violence might have been averted.

Concluding Remarks[32]

The declared goal of the Naxalite movement—revolution—remains unaccomplished. As we reflect on this, it becomes clear that revolution is not a widely shared goal in the movement, but rather a dream of the leadership. People do aspire to see badlav (change) in their lives and the society at large. Badlav, however, does not mean an affirmation of kranti. When people join the movement, it is assumed that they stand for kranti, or that they will do so in due course—with a rise in their 'political consciousness'. In fact, they often join the movement for short-term goals, in response to their immediate situation. Interpreting the movement in this light helps to assess its achievements and failures.

The main achievement of the Naxalite movement in central Bihar is that it has empowered the labouring and oppressed classes. The confidence of agricultural labourers, the poorest of the poor in this region, has increased remarkably. They have been able to challenge many oppressive practices, and the equations of power at the local and regional levels have changed drastically. In their self-image as well as in the perception of their former masters, they are no longer vulnerable or inconsequential. Power and fear have changed houses, at least to some extent.

The struggle for izzat has not been in vain.

Having said this, we need to ask to what extent this empowerment has translated into a better life. Respect and self-respect themselves are of course part of a better life—something the labourers value dearly. However, this is not the end of their aspirations. Like everyone else, they also long for an improvement in their everyday existence: better food and housing, education for their children, adequate employment, freedom from fear and violence, leisure and laughter. In that respect, the outcome of the Naxalite movement is mixed. Empowerment has been achieved only at the cost of considerable suffering. There has been freedom from old fears but not *all* fears— old fears have been replaced with new ones. Similarly, while there has been an increase in wages, reclaiming of gairmajurwa land for housing purposes and some seizing of ceiling surplus land for agricultural purposes, development has been a casualty. In the climate of tension and fear that prevails in central Bihar, development activity (both private and public) is extremely difficult. Naxalite leaders have taken little interest in enhancing the quality of life in the villages, arguing that all reform would have to follow revolution. In fact, development efforts like building roads have often been hindered, for example by extracting taxes from the contractors. The bottom line is that the Naxalite leaders are not interested in the 'development' of the region.

Some even consider that the more underdeveloped the region, the better are the prospects of revolution. They regard development as antagonistic to revolutionary consciousness. Also, darkness and inaccessibility—in the absence of roads and electricity—mean physical safety and some protection from state repression.

However, the dire conditions under which the Naxalite movement operates are taxing for the people as well as for the activists. An observer can sense a kind of tiredness, if not exhaustion, among the people. In many places where the Naxalite movement was active in the past, this has led to a situation of stalemate. Former activists often slip into being politically inactive, or defect to other political parties that are less demanding. After so much hardship, and with no imminent end to the strife, it is understandable that some of them should give up. Neither has revolution turned out to be a short-term affair, nor is a protracted 'people's war' easy to sustain.

Does the Naxalite movement have a future? One could argue that it has not lost its relevance and may even have considerable potential. The need for a movement committed to the interests of the poor remains undiminished. Mainstream political parties have paid lip service to popular slogans such as *garibi hatao* (remove poverty) and may be able to get the vote of the poor, but the poor are under no illusion that these parties represent them.

However, the Naxalite movement will thrive only to the extent that its vision resonates with the people. The wider the gap between the two, the higher the chances that the movement will fizzle out. The present formula is a marriage of convenience between leaders who dream of a Maoist revolution and people who aspire for practical change. In order to bridge this gap, the Naxalite leaders have to be ready to let people's concerns influence the vision of the movement.

When the movement has done this, it has been extremely popular. This is the experience of the open fronts. In the case of both Liberation and Party Unity, it is really the mass fronts (e.g., IPF and MKSS) that have caught people's imagination. People identify with the mass fronts because it is in these fronts that they really participate. When villagers refer to *hamra* party (our party), they are often referring to the mass fronts. The mass fronts are accountable to the people since they depend on people's support and cannot afford to ignore their concerns. It is between the underground party and the people that the danger of a gap of vision arises.

The main problems of the Naxalite movement relate to the party rather than to the open fronts. For example, factionalism is mainly a problem of the Naxalite 'parties'. Caught in the mire of internecine conflicts, the various Naxalite factions end up working against the interests of the very people they claim to defend. The quarrels between party leaders inevitably lead to divisions among the people themselves, for example, agricultural labourers of one faction being pitted against those of another. If people's concerns were to guide the vision of these individual factions, the risk of factionalism would be reduced. Indeed, there would be more common ground and ideological differences would take the backseat. If the Naxalite movement unites and focuses on people's concerns, it could make a real difference in central Bihar and beyond.

Postscript (2005)

Nine years have passed since the fieldwork for this essay was completed. Meanwhile, the situation in Bihar—and the new state of Jharkhand formed in 2000—has not changed much. In the continued absence of credible governance, the lives of the rural poor are still mired in deprivation, insecurity, strife and struggle. Corruption, crime and violence have further pervaded the fabric of the society and politics in the state. Real democracy in Bihar remains an elusive dream.

The Naxalite brand of politics continues to dominate and determine the contours of alternative politics in Bihar. A sharper polarization, however, has emerged between the major Naxalite groups, specifically between Liberation on the one hand and a consolidation of likeminded 'underground' parties on the other. Party Unity merged with the People's War Group on 11 August 1998 and formed People's War (PW). Meanwhile, with the strengthening of the Communist Party of Nepal (Maoist) after 1996 and the formation of the Coordination Committee of Maoist Parties and Organizations of South Asia (CCOMPOSA) on 1 July 2001, there was a stronger emphasis on unification of Maoist forces in South Asia. Even as PW continued its negotiations with MCC, the latter merged with several smaller groups, including its own splinter group Revolutionary Communist Centre (Maoist), which had split from it in 1999, and a Punjab based group, Revolutionary Communist Centre (Marxist-Leninist-Maoist). The new organization formed in January 2003 was called Maoist Communist Centre of India (MCCI). On 14 October 2004, PW and MCCI merged and formed the Communist Party of India (Maoist).

Among other significant changes is the spread of the movement to new areas. While central Bihar remains a stronghold, the movement has grown stronger in other regions. In the intervening years, it has made impressive inroads in north Bihar districts, especially in Champaran and Siwan. This applies both to the Liberation group and to the underground parties.

In the years following the merger with PWG in 1998, there has been a marked decrease in open and democratic forms of struggle and a greater focus has been placed on militaristic interventions in erstwhile PU areas. As it is, mass movements suffered due to the activities of the Ranbeer Sena, which spread beyond Bhojpur (where it emerged in 1994) to adjoining districts of Jehanabad, Gaya and Patna. However, this period has significantly also witnessed a weakening of the Sena on account of internal conflicts, which worsened after the arrest of the Ranbeer Sena founder, Brahmeshwar Singh on 29 August 2002. As a result, massacres of the poor have also declined in recent years.

In 2001–02, internecine conflict between PW and MCC on the one hand and Liberation on the other was at its peak. Even though this has decreased recently, Liberation nevertheless continues to be targeted on account of being 'revisionist' (e.g., participating in electoral politics). Meanwhile, in Liberation areas, the panchayat elections in 2001, held in Bihar for the first time after 1978, saw impressive participation of people and local leaders (including many Dalits) who had emerged in the last two decades of concerted mobilization and action. A significant number of Dalit mukhiyas have now replaced their upper caste-class predecessors.

Underground Naxalite groups have also made their presence felt at the national level by building alliances with other left movements in the country in order to fight the forces of imperialism and globalization. A notable effort in this respect was Mumbai Resistance, organized as a parallel event to the World Social Forum in January 2004. Links with the Communist Party of Nepal as well as other Marxist-Leninist-Maoist parties elsewhere have also been forged.

The state, for its part, continues to use diverse tactics to deal with the Naxalite movement. In the intervening years, a few instances of death of Naxalites in police custody and encounter killings have occurred, besides arrests of important leaders like Arvind of Party Unity. The Supreme Court on 15 April 2002 confirmed death penalty to four poor farmers from Gaya district who were involved in the Bara massacre led by MCC in 1992 (a mercy petition is pending with the President of India). After the Prevention of Terrorism Act (POTA) came into force in June 2002, it was extensively used in Jharkhand; in fact, Jharkhand has the largest number of POTA detainees in the country. And even as the present government at the centre has announced its intention to repeal POTA, its predecessor Terrorist and Disruptive Activities (Prevention) Act, 1985 (TADA) is still in force. Indeed, nine years after its lapse, TADA is alive and kicking in the plains of Bihar. On

2 April 2004, the Supreme Court convicted fourteen persons to life imprisonment under the Act.

On different lines, in Andhra Pradesh, peace talks were initiated with People's War and Janashakti leaders in October 2004 following more than five years of effort by the Committee of Concerned Citizens. The talks were widely welcomed, but they broke down in January 2005.

A Musahar house in rural Bihar—mud all around (Chapter 12).

Deepa Musahar, who was locked up by his landlord when he
asked for pending wages, leading to a backlash that played a role
in the formation of the Ranbeer Sena (Chapter 13).

A clandestine meeting of Party Unity supporters in a village of Jehanabad in the mid-1990s (Chapter 13).

A public meeting convened by Liberation and the Indian People's front in Arwal in the late 1990s. The open fronts of the Naxalites were very popular in those days (Chapter 13).

Cooperative ploughing in Bastar. The Adivasi economy and society, based on mutual aid and local democracy, have been severely destroyed by long years of conflict (Chapter 17).

SPOs being trained in Injaram camp, 2006 (Chapter 17).

An Adivasi woman in the ruins of her house, set on fire by the security forces in 2013; even her meagre rice stock was burned (Chapter 17).

Many schools in Bastar were destroyed by the Maoists, or even by the people themselves, for fear that they might be used as an outpost by the security forces (Chapter 17).

Aayti, Jabbo and Nendo, mothers of three girls who were killed in a fake encounter in Abujmarh in 2019 (Chapter 20).

The simple graves of Adivasis killed in a fake encounter in Nulkatong in 2018 (Chapter 19).

Two elderly women in Bastar share their grief for Lakhmu Punem, killed in a fake encounter in Gundam, 2023.

Adivasis displaced by Salwa Judum were often forced to migrate to the *mirchi badis* (chilly fields) of Telangana, walking long distances with whatever belongings they were able to carry (Chapter 17).

A meeting of Moolvasi Bachao Manch in Bastar, 2023 (Chapter 17).

Parveena Ahangar, founder of the Association of Parents of Disappeared Persons in Jammu & Kashmir; her own son Javed, a Class-11 student then, was abducted by the Indian Army in 1990.

A Kashmiri woman with a photo of her eight-year old son Samir, who was killed by the security forces in 2010 (Chapter 22).

Slogans such as 'Go India, Go' were all over the streets of Kashmir when we visited the Valley in 2010 (Chapter 22).

A *sangbaaz* (stone pelter): Countless youth in Kashmir have risked their life to throw a stone at the security forces, as an expression of protest (Chapter 22).

Sademjila and Temjenmongla, two of the women, who related to me the horrors of life in the camps during the 'grouping' period in Nagaland (Chapter 25).

'When you write, do not forget our sovereignty!'—these were Soupongyanger, Nungsangtemjen and C. Aliba's parting words after I met them in Nagaland (Chapter 25).

14

Might Is Right in Champaran*

Anyone who travels through West Champaran, a district in north Bihar bordering the Terai region of Nepal, would be impressed with the vast expanses of fertile land stretching all around. They would soon learn, however, that this land of plenty hides much degrading poverty. For Dalits and other deprived groups in this region, unequal distribution of land is a burning issue. On one side are huge estates of thousands of acres: Shikarpur estate, Bilaspur estate, Ramnagar estate, Dumaria estate—the last allegedly spread over 24,000 acres. On the other side are masses of landless labourers who, in the months of August-September 2002 (when I travelled in this area), were surviving by collecting *ghoghi* (snails) from the village pond and eating them with some boiled rice. The tiny ghoghi was able to do what the mighty sarkar failed to do—relieve their hunger.

The land issue in West Champaran is not confined to skewed distribution. It also includes illegal occupation, whether of ceiling surplus or gairmajurwa (village common) land. Besides land, other prominent issues in the area are non-payment of statutory minimum wages, sexual exploitation of Dalit and Adivasi women,

---

* Unpublished essay written in October 2002.

bonded labour and the virtual absence of public services. West Champaran is also the most notorious of all Bihar districts for its criminal gangs. Kidnappings and murders are frequent events. It is common knowledge that the zamindars, the criminal gangs and the police form a nexus and help each other to pursue their own vested interests. There is no government worth the name and what exists is unable to protect the underprivileged from this nexus, which is used to suppress the rural poor, especially those who dare to raise a voice against the status quo. As far as the poor of Champaran are concerned, democracy does not exist.

CPI (ML) Liberation, or Liberation for short, has been active in organizing the rural poor in some blocks of West Champaran for the last eight years or so. Having disbanded its armed squads, the struggles being waged are mainly through open democratic means. Among other issues, they are concerned with the implementation of laws related to land reform and minimum wages. However, these collective struggles have faced severe repression. In spite of complaints, petitions, rallies and dharnas, the official response is half-hearted and often hostile. A series of incidents in July and August 2002 illustrate the repression unleashed on the rural poor and the attitude of state authorities.

The Price of Resistance

On 6 July, in Mahuava village (Narkatiyaganj block), an agricultural labourer named Mohan Paswan was shot dead by armed criminals, believed to be goons of a prominent local zamindar. Mohan Paswan's crime was that he was part of the local sangathan which was demanding a raise in wages. Even though labourers aspired to the minimum wage of Rs 51 per day, they were asking for less. Still, Mohan and his fellow labourers had to pay a price. He lost his life, the houses of twenty-seven Dalit labourers were destroyed or looted, and many were beaten or injured. All this intimidation was carried out to teach people a lesson and make them withdraw their petitions. Some labourers were forcibly taken to the courts and made to sign pre-drafted statements. Much of this coercion took place in the presence of the police and with their connivance.

Just eleven days later, on 17 July, in Pahkaul village of Gaunaha block, Sushila Devi, a thirty-two-year-old Tharu woman and mother of four children, was beaten, stripped naked and taken to the house of her abductor, Sheshnath Panjiyar, who led this attack on her hamlet with about thirty others. She was kept there with her hands tied behind her head for three hours. Taking pity on her plight, a female member of Panjiyar's household put a bed sheet on her. She was finally released when the local thanedar came with his police force. They set her free but not before telling her to leave the 'Lal Salaam party'—as Liberation is known in these parts. In the presence of the police, her thumb impression was taken on a blank sheet of paper. They also asked her sardonically: 'So, did you get your minimum wages?' Needless to say, the thanedar did not think it necessary to ask any questions from the other side or make any arrests.

Sushila's nightmare did not end there. A few days later, she was asked to appear before the local *darbar* (court). Such darbars are organized and presided over by the landlords. She was firmly told not to make an issue of what had happened. After this, she was confined to her house and kept under constant surveillance. It was only after twenty days that she managed to escape under the pretext of going out to cut some grass. Accompanying her was another Tharu woman, Ramni Devi, whose house and grocery shop had been looted the same day that Sushila was beaten. Since there is no public transport in the area, the two women ran through fields to reach another village which is a Liberation stronghold. From there they took a train to Chanpatiya (another block) where the district party office is located. With the help of party activists, they were finally able to reach Bettiah, the district headquarters, where they lodged a complaint in the Chief Judicial Magistrate's court. They learnt later that by the time they had reached Bettiah, their adversaries, who had followed their trail in two jeeps, had also reached the city. Fortunately, this did not prevent Sushila from lodging her complaint.

When I met Sushila in early September, she said that she had not been able to return to her village after the complaint, for fear of reprisal. Her husband and two youngest children had joined her, and for the past month, they had been taking shelter in different villages where Liberation has a strong presence. Back in her village, her mother and two children were being constantly harassed and threatened by Panjiyar's men, who demanded that Sushila should withdraw her complaint. Meanwhile, even though a month had passed, no action had been taken on her complaint. In this atmosphere of insecurity, with the thanedar on the side of her aggressors, the court failing to intervene and the government abstaining from any arrests or other punitive action, how could she possibly return to her village?

Sushila had been victimized because, aside from demanding minimum wages and an end to the occupation of ceiling surplus and gairmajurwa land, she, along with other Tharu women of her village, had also been resisting sexual exploitation. Possibly because of their Nepali origins, Tharus generally tend to be fair-complexioned and are considered quite beautiful. The poverty of Tharu women therefore has been used to exploit them sexually for a long time. That is why the Tharvat region of north Champaran, where most of the Tharu Adivasis are settled, has come to be known as the 'Paris of Champaran'. Landlords, politicians, bureaucrats, policemen, criminals—all are known to have been involved in the sexual abuse of Tharu women.

For the rural poor, organizing politically often invites repression. As Sushila's case illustrates, even those who adopt the legal path sometimes end up becoming fugitives on the run.

State Collusion and Abdication

The collusion of the police with the landlords was apparent in another incident which occurred on 5 August in Chiotaha village (Mainatand block). Around 200 police surrounded the village that day. In the police action that followed, twelve-year-old Laxman Manjhi was shot dead, seventy Musahar households were looted, twenty-one labourers (including thirteen women) were arrested and several others were injured.[1] Laxman's relatives were not even given the dead body, which was disposed of by the police.

The main reason for the police presence, according to the officer-in-charge of the concerned thana, was that they had received information of an impending confrontation between the labourers and the local landlord, Markande Pande. Besides, they also needed to take action on an FIR lodged by Markande Pande, who had complained that the dynamo of his tractor had been stolen in the course of an attack on his house by Musahar labourers on 26 June. The thana officer claimed that they were forced to open fire because, when the police arrived in Chiotaha, the Musahars attacked them with lathis, bhalas, stones and even firearms.

Markande Pande is originally from Uttar Pradesh. According to the District Magistrate (DM), he owns around 300 acres of land, but most of it is in the name of twenty others, who cannot be traced. In other words, the bulk of Markande Pande's land is benami. According to the labourers, Pande's goons had also participated in the police action that day. Pande himself was present and there is evidence that six rounds were fired from his gun. The thana officer acknowledged this, but he argued that Pande could not be arrested on that count since his gun was licensed. Pande was arrested later, but then released on bail after one day.

The police–landlord nexus in this incident is starkly clear. According to the labourers, on visits to the village, the police usually take shelter in Pande's house—the officer in the thana did not deny this. Instead, he explained that the land belonged to Markande Pande and that the labourers were preventing it from being cultivated and even trying to occupy it. So, what option did Pande have but to defend his property? He claimed that some 'criminal types' were inciting the labourers.

The labourers of Chiotaha—all Musahars—are very poor. When I visited the village, many households were on the brink of starvation. They said that they were paid 3 kg of rice per day as wages; at Rs 4 a kilo, this is Rs 12—a far cry from the minimum wage of Rs 51. In protest, they started a strike on 25 June which has continued ever since. On 28 July, they were attacked by armed goondas who came in jeeps, tractors and motorcycles. The attackers fired many rounds in the air. People ran southwards towards Dhobni village and sought refuge in the sugarcane fields. The landlord's henchmen also harassed the labourers in other ways, such as looting their belongings, poisoning their pigs, stealing their hens, and even preventing them from defecating on the common land.

In protest against the police repression of 5 August, a demonstration was held by Liberation in Bettiah on 9 August. The demonstration was completely peaceful—even government officials admitted this. However, the day ended with Ramji Patel, a leading activist, being shot dead by the police at point-blank range. This happened when a group of departing participants were waiting at the Bettiah railway station for their train to arrive. They were sitting on the platform, eating some *chura* (flattened rice), when a group of policemen arrived. An altercation followed and in the course of this argument, a policeman aimed his gun at Ramji's head and killed him on the spot. This case has become controversial because the Superintendent of Police (SP) claims that there was a provocation by Liberation activists, while the DM has denied this and clearly acknowledged that the firing was done without a magistrate's order, as is prescribed by law. This is an exceptional case where a DM has maintained his independent stand. However, no punitive action has been taken so far.

Missing Democracy

The struggle of Dalits for basic izzat as human beings deserving equal respect has many dimensions. Besides struggle on economic issues, Dalits who are part of political movements in Champaran have also fought in panchayat elections and even won in some cases. This has resulted in sharper caste-class polarization and led to a *varchasva ki ladai* (a conflict for social dominance). For daring to compete with them, the upper castes have terrorised the whole Dalit community by diverse means including night attacks, burning of houses and everyday harassment such as preventing Dalits from using common land to defecate. The Musahars of Belwan Bahuwari village (Gaunaha block) have suffered greatly along these lines after Jogendra Manjhi, a Musahar leader, was elected mukhiya in the panchayat elections of 2001, defeating eighteen other candidates. Before him, Raghunath Sharan—previously Rashtriya Janata Dal (RJD), now Bhartiya Janata Party (BJP)—was the mukhiya for twenty-seven years! Mukhiya Jogendra Manjhi's life is under constant threat today and he is forced to live an underground existence. When I met him, he related the difficulties he faced in carrying out his official duties. For example, he narrated the story of how he had written to the Circle Inspector (in-charge of land records) innumerable times for information regarding the gairmajurwa land close to his village, which had been illegally occupied by two upper-caste families for a long time. But he was not getting any response—there seemed to be an unspoken understanding in official circles that they would not cooperate with a Dalit mukhiya. The gravity of the situation was well expressed by Jogendra Manjhi when he said, '*Sab se badi baat hai ki yahan nyonatam vetan mangne par goli chalti hai* [The biggest issue here is that firing takes place if you ask for minimum wages].'

The rule of law in Bihar seems like a fiction when one hears stories of blatant violation of it by Cabinet ministers. One recent example involved the Food and Civil Supplies Minister, Purnamasi Ram. A PIL filed in the Supreme Court by political activist Dayanand Dwivedi of Bagaha district accused him of complicity with large-scale corruption in the public distribution system (PDS). The petitioner claimed that food grains meant for below poverty line (BPL) families had been siphoned off to the tune of Rs 61 crore. Sometime in April 2002, according to local reports, a greatly incensed Purnamasi Ram went in a Gypsy with his bodyguards to Dayanand Dwivedi's house and kidnapped him in broad daylight. Dwivedi, who was just dressed in a lungi and ganji and was not even wearing his slippers, was taken to the Inspection Bungalow on the campus of the main office of the district police and then beaten black and blue. Many people who had gathered there witnessed the beating as the room in which he was being beaten had wide windows. Dwivedi was later taken to a jail, and then finally released. The minister, of course, went scot-free.[2]

This is just a sample of the stories one hears on a brief visit to rural Champaran. One after another, they reinforce the feeling that democracy does not exist in this corner of India.

15

Justice, Not Vengeance

Bathani Tola and the Ranbeer Sena*

Does our vision of ourselves as a 'developed' society include a self-understanding of also being 'just'? One would think the answer to be fairly obvious. The Bihar High Court verdict (16 April 2012) in the Bathani Tola massacre case, however, belies this simple assumption, compelling us to pause and think.

This small hamlet in the Sahar block of Bhojpur district was witness to a gruesome massacre of twenty-one Dalit and Muslim women and children one July afternoon sixteen years ago (1996) at the hands of the Ranbeer Sena, a private army of upper-caste landed local gentry.[1] Family members, relatives and comrades of the victims have since awaited justice. While justice could not bring back their loved ones, nor return their lost years or selves, it might have set right the contours of a worldview that had gone terribly wrong that afternoon when evil triumphed over good, and the extreme violence

---

* This essay, originally published in *Economic and Political Weekly* in September 2013, was written soon after the Patna High Court verdict on the Bathani Tola massacre in April 2012. It draws on fieldwork in Bhojpur district in the mid-1990s (see preceding chapters). The Bathani Tola case is now in the Supreme Court, but no progress has been made since the appeal was admitted in July 2012.

deployed by neighbour upon neighbour left in its wake a bereaved, bitter bewilderment at the unfathomable darkness of the human personality.

Their wait was a long one. On 5 May 2010, nearly fourteen years after the incident, the Ara sessions court convicted twenty-three of the sixty-eight accused, sentencing three to death and twenty to life imprisonment.[2] The High Court, however, reversed gear on 16 April 2012, acquitting all of them. The judgment, predictably, met with public outrage and was called a 'judicial massacre'.[3] On 16 July 2012, an appeal was admitted in the Supreme Court on behalf of the victims as well as the state of Bihar. The case has moved no further.

Before returning to the High Court verdict, we should take a closer look at the events that unfolded on that fateful day, the class conflict that prevailed then, and the everyday incidents of violence that the people of the area had been experiencing in the preceding two years, the build-up of which led to the Bathani Tola massacre and subsequently, other massacres. By way of background, the 'Diary of Violence' at the end of this chapter presents a partial list of violent incidents that took place in Bhojpur district in these two years.

This period included five major massacres aside from a long list of murders: in Sarathua (July 1995), Noorpur (August 1995), Chandi (February 1996), Nannor (April 1996) and Nadhi (May 1996). In this volatile state of almost daily violence, most of those who lost their lives were ordinary villagers. During this period, the tension in the area was palpable and a general atmosphere of fear, suspicion, insecurity and uncertainty prevailed.

The Massacre

The massacre took place in Bhojpur district, in Bathani tola of Barki Kharaon village in Sahar block. At a distance of 43 km on the Ara-Sahar road is Khera. A 3 km walk from there on a kaccha road leads to Barki Kharaon and after another ten minutes, one reaches Bathani

Tola, the site of the massacre. On the afternoon of 11 July 1996, nineteen poor Dalit and Muslim women and children were killed, while five sustained severe injuries. Two of the injured succumbed to their injuries the following month, bringing the toll of the massacre to twenty-one. Out of eight children who were killed, two were less than a year old.

The sky had been overcast that morning. Fierce clouds and the interminable drizzle seemed to portend another onslaught of heavy rains. Under the weak sun, Bathani Tola—tucked away in the midst of stretching fields on all sides—was silent except for the sounds of everyday life. Naimuddin, a thirty-five-year-old Muslim of the Churi-Pharosh (bangle sellers) caste and a local leader of the Communist Party of India (Marxist-Leninist) Liberation (hereafter Liberation), who lost five members of his family that day, said: '*Hum bargad ke ped ke niche baith kar khaini bana rahe the. Aur bhi kuch bhai sath baithe hue the* [I was sitting under the banyan tree and preparing khaini; a few other men were also sitting with me].' Besides these men, women were either engaged in their daily chores or huddled inside their homes taking an afternoon nap, while children continued to play in the slush and mud, their cries and laughter making the day seem like any other.

But it was not a day like any other.

A little after 2 p.m., the inhabitants were jolted when they heard shots in the air and realized that what they had dreaded for some time had happened—a mob of 100–150 armed men had surrounded their tola and were firing indiscriminately. Panic spread like wildfire. Shouts, screams and the sound of running feet seemed to rent the air. Trying to save their children, the women and men rushed to gather them and ran in search of a safe shelter. As many as fifty Muslim and Dalit families had run away in late April from the main village, Barki Kharaon, and sought shelter in this tola, where their new dwellings did not even have doors. These families searched for houses with sturdy doors. Naimuddin narrates: 'Gathering my family together, I put them in Marwari Mallah's house and ran to find a safe hiding place. They would not touch women and children, I thought.' Marwari Mallah's house, with a large aangan enclosed within a concrete wall, became a refuge for many families as well as for children like Kusum, who had no time to run to their own home. Her mother Armanodevi later bemoaned, 'If she had not gone to play that day, she would have been safe.'

The assailants attacked from three sides, and from the sound of their shots, it was clear that they were approaching fast. Soon, rising flames from the northern and western ends of the tola signalled that two houses on that side had been torched. In the next half an hour, another six houses were burnt, most belonging to those who had resettled recently, or to those who had dared to support and shelter them, like Marwari Mallah. The houses had been on fire for around half an hour when it started pouring. And in the rain, slush and mud, the rampage of killings began.

'Men carrying guns broke the door and came inside. They started cutting the throat of Bhauji with a *phasuli* [sickle]. I was scared and ran and hid under a chowki,' said Salma, five-year-old daughter of Naimuddin, who was amongst those who had taken refuge in the walled house of Marwari Mallah.[4] Inside the courtyard, women and children sat cringing and clinging on to each other under the mahua tree when the door finally gave way. Dressed in ganjis, lungis or dhotis tied as lungis, some of the attackers had covered their faces with gamchas, but most were not even trying to hide their identity. They were armed not only with guns and rifles, but also with swords, phasulis, *katas*, *gadasis* and lathis. In the frenzy that followed, the women and children tried to escape through whatever routes were available. Holding her three-month-old sister, Naimuddin's twenty-year-old daughter Dhanvarti Khatun was trying to escape when she was caught. She was pulled by her hair and a knife thrust through her. The infant's wheatish-coloured body was found face down on the muddy earth; according to some witnesses, she had been flung in the air and a sharp instrument pierced into her body as she fell. Najma Khatun, Naimuddin's daughter-in-law, was running with six-year-old Saddam Hussein when a bullet hit her thigh and she fell. When she felt that the attention of the assailants was no longer on her, she tried to run with Saddam again. She had hardly taken a step or two when another bullet hit her, this time in the ribs; she fell and her clutch on Saddam loosened. Saddam was then attacked by three or four men, who tried to chop him with swords and katas. Naimuddin's forty-year-old widowed sister, Jaibun Nisha, was found dead in the position she must have been before the attack—leaning against the wall of the aangan with five-year-old Amir Subhani in her lap. Her throat had been slit and a bullet had hit her chest, while Amir had been hit in the head. Lukhi Devi, a sixty-year-old woman of Dhobi mohalla of Barki Kharaon, who had gone to Bathani to return some freshly laundered clothes, had tried to save herself by hiding under the chowki, but she died due to asphyxiation and burn injuries. Marwari Mallah's wife, daughter-in-law and grandson, besides six other victims, were found burnt and dead in the aangan. Among other victims were Phool Kumari and Ramratia Devi, who were found dead near their houses in the rajwad and dusadh end of the tola.

Some did manage to escape. Amongst them was ten-year-old Rajudeen, who ran and jumped into the *aahar* (part of a traditional irrigation system) and then hid among a few overhanging shrubs for the next few hours. Similarly, two children of Babban Chaudhary were found hiding in *kothis* (high mud containers used for storing grain), speechless with fright.

There were other survivors who escaped, but who will continue to be haunted by those searing images. Radhika, an eighteen-year-old pregnant woman who had come to her parents' house from Aurangabad for her first delivery, related to a reporter how in the melee that ensued, she found herself on a heap of human bodies where she lay pretending to be dead. When all seemed silent, thinking that the marauders had gone, she got up only to find to her horror that the killers were still lurking around. Panic-stricken, she tried jumping over a wall, but one of them, Bacha Singh, twenty-five-year-old, ordered her to stop and then a second later, fired at her. She was one of the five who were found alive by the Bathani Tola men who had been anxiously watching their tola from their hiding places and returned to it soon after the marauders left. Others, like Naimuddin's wife Hasina Begum, had also been watching Bathani from the outskirts of a neighbouring village, where she had gone that morning to sell bangles. She also returned. Little Salma had by then come out from under the chowki and woven her way through the scattered, lifeless bodies to the banyan tree which stood witness to this carnage.[5]

Wails and cries now rented the air, heavy with the acrid smell of burnt houses. In the evening light, bodies lay strewn on the wet earth. Even as the men tried to brace themselves for the next task ahead—taking the wounded to the nearest hospital, the policemen from the police camp located just across a field in the middle school of Barki Kharaon finally made an appearance. When they asked the men of the tola to carry the bodies of the dead to the roadside, they were met with stiff resistance. These protectors of law had turned a deaf ear and a blind eye to the happenings of that afternoon, now they could at least carry the dead, people thought. With the help of the chowkidar, the police carried the bodies, while the relatives carried the wounded.

The laxity of the Bhojpur administration, both before and after the massacre, was an extension of the general apathy of the government machinery in Bihar. In this case as in many before it, one finds that the machinery is not only ill-equipped and ineffective, but also extremely biased. Initially, the district administration wanted the post-mortem to be done in a makeshift camp near the road itself, which the Liberation activists resisted, fearing foul play. The bodies were then brought to the government hospital in Ara, where, according to eyewitness reports, they were literally dumped in a muddy open space. No attempt was made to cover the bodies, even of women, who lay maltreated in their death as they were in their life. As a relative of one of the victims said, '*Marne ke baad bhi garibon ki izzat-aabru ki kisi ko padi nahi hai* [Even after they die, nobody is concerned about the respect and honour of the poor].' The surgeon is reported to have taken many hours to come to the hospital from his home in Ara. Angry Liberation activists broke a few chairs and other furniture in the hospital, for which a case was lodged by the district administration against the two Liberation MLAs, Ram Naresh Ram from Sahar and Rameshwar Prasad from Sandesh constituencies.

Of the five wounded, little Baby (barely nine months old, with a fractured thigh) and Shailendra (sixteen months) were treated in the hospital at Ara, while Radhika, Kusum and Saddam were rushed to Patna. Even though the quality of health services at Patna Medical College Hospital (PMCH) was reported to be a little better than that of Ara hospital, it was far from ideal. If doctors were available, medicines were not, and so on. The general situation of the whole ward improved after the victims of the massacre moved there and Liberation drew the attention of the media to the pathetic state of the medical services: ceiling fans were installed, bed sheets were given to all patients and the quality of food improved.

When I visited them, Radhika wore a stony look and talked only haltingly; a bullet was still embedded in her left shoulder. Saddam (born around the 1991 Gulf War and named after the Iraqi leader) had a deep horizontal cut on his neck, which was almost severed, making the insides visible. A nerve in the neck had been partially damaged, leaving a high probability of paralysis of his limbs. Lying prostrate on the hospital bed, Saddam showed the usual recalcitrance expected of a child of his age. Rarely quiet, he asked to be moved to a more comfortable position, or for his *mai* (mother) or Deena *chacha* (uncle)—a medically-trained Liberation cadre who nursed him and was obviously dear to him, or for another round of '*haitem*' (his word for Horlicks). Running a high temperature and in a delirium, he mumbled the names of those who had attacked him—Deepwawale, Belwa, Suberwa . . .[6]

Another time, a barely audible '*Didi tera dewar diwana* . . . [a popular Bollywood song]' escaped his lips, a poignant reminder of the child that he was. Beside his bed, little Salma, in a bright yellow frock and a string of colourful beads around her neck, stood quietly looking at her brother.[7]

The Context

As the name suggests, *Barki* (big) Kharaon is a large village of more than 400 houses, as opposed to the 100 houses of *Chotki* (small) Kharaon a little distance away. The village has three small tolas, which are almost like separate villages. Tandi Tola on the north-west has thirty-five Dalit households, including Rajwads, Paswans and Kanu-savs. South-west of Tandi is Ujwallia Tola, with approximately 100 houses of which sixty are Brahmin houses and the rest of other castes including Kahars, Paswans and Kanu-savs. South of Tandi is Bathani, a tola of sixty to seventy houses, including those of Kanu-savs (about thirty), Yadavs (twenty), Mallahs (fifteen) and Chamars (five). South-west of Bathani is Chotki Kharaon, with fifty households of Bhumihars and the rest of Dalits including Chamars, Paswans and others.

If one goes deeper into the history of the formation of these tolas, one often finds it to be rooted in some painful experience of oppression, which forced some people to forsake the place of their forefathers and reside elsewhere in order to be able to live without fear. Bathani Tola is a clear example of this phenomenon. The original settlers of Bathani were the Kanu-savs. The Chamars came fifteen to twenty years ago from Aurangabad district, due to severe repression by the Rajputs there, and settled in Bathani where the villagers accommodated them on the common (gairmajurwa) land.

The other castes, namely the Yadavs and Mallahs, used to be part of the main village of Barki Kharaon, but continued to break away after some instance of oppression or another. As Naimuddin said, '*Yeh log shuruati daur se hi daman-atyachari rahe hai* [These people (upper castes of Barki Kharaon) have been exploiters and oppressors from the very beginning).' The latest addition is a group of eighteen Muslim and thirty-two Dalit households (Kahars, Savs, Rajwads, Dusadhs, Mallahs), who decided to quit Barki after one Sultan Miyan was killed in broad daylight on 25 April 1996 (more on this below) and seek refuge in Bathani Tola. There they built around ten to twelve mud houses, with two to three families sharing one house. Some of the residents of the tola were extremely helpful, like Marwari Mallah, who opened his house for others, for which he was to pay a heavy price.

Barki Kharaon is one of those few villages in Bhojpur that have both Bhumihar and Rajput presence (Chotki has only Bhumihars). Both castes are roughly equal numerically (about sixty houses each), as well as in terms of land ownership. As one enters the village, the Rajputs are found towards the east (as the locals say '*purwari patti*'); a little lane separates this from the '*pachiari patti*', where the Bhumihars live. The Rajput area is also known as Kharaon Bujurg and the Bhumihar area as Kharaon Chaturbhuj. Even though these two upper castes together constitute less than half the total number of households, they have enjoyed uncontested supremacy. The Bhumihars and Rajputs are all in one area, while the Dalits and others are scattered all over. Besides these two dominant castes, other numerically strong castes include Muslims (thirty-five houses), who used to live right next to the Rajputs before they shifted, Yadavs (twenty-five), Koeri (twenty), Savs (twenty-five), Paswan (forty), Chamar (twenty), Dhobi (twenty) and others. The Rajputs and Bhumihars own most of the land. Even the gairmajurwa land is reported to be under their control.

Notwithstanding a previous history of oppressive agrarian relations, there was relative peace in and around Barki Kharaon after the four-month wage strike of 1988. Mazdooras of the three Barki tolas as well as those of nearby villages had joined the strike. The strikers were demanding a daily wage of Rs 21 along with breakfast and lunch, instead of *half paseri kacchi* (about 1 kg and 750 gm) of coarse rice which they had been getting for as long as they could remember. Oddly, or perhaps not so oddly considering their feudal mentality, their employers agreed to pay Rs 20, but not the last rupee. Finally, the Liberation cadres had to resolve the stalemate by suggesting that the labourers settle for that and start work again. There was an increase in the wages they received at harvest time too. Prior to the strike, the harvesters used to receive one *bojha* (headload) for every twenty-one bojhas of harvested crop. After the strike, this changed to one bojha for every ten bojhas.

The victims of the massacre said that even a few months earlier they were on talking terms with the Bhumihars and Rajputs, but this stopped after a series of events that made them insecure. The first incident occurred in February 1996, on the occasion of a Karbala Mukti March led by Liberation, when two upper-caste men from Barki Kharaon were killed.[8] From then on, there was tension in the area. On 24 April 1996, Gyanchand Bhagat of Ganeri caste from the nearby Dhanchua village was found murdered in the fields. The two murderers were identified as Jitendra Oza, a Brahmin youth of Ujwallia Tola and Ajay Singh, a Rajput of Barki Kharaon, both in their early twenties. No arrests were made. On the night of 24 April, villagers say, a meeting of the Ranbeer Sena was held in Barki Kharaon. Early next morning, Sultan Miyan, a youth in his early twenties, was killed by Ajay Singh and five other Rajputs of the village as he was going to the local shop to buy some soap.

A tussle followed about his body. Naimuddin, who had always stood up for the underdog even at the risk of antagonizing the upper castes, went out of his way to retrieve the body of Sultan Miyan. This had earned him the ire of the upper castes. After Sultan Miyan's murder, the thirty-five Muslim households felt that they had no other option than to leave their present dwellings. Their houses were right next to those of the Rajputs and they feared an attack any time. They decided to seek refuge in Bathani Tola, which was also a Liberation stronghold. After seeking the cooperation of the Bathani residents and locking their houses, they moved on 29 April with minimal belongings.

On 30 April, the then Superintendent of Police, C.R. Kaswan (of 'Arwal massacre' fame), who had just been transferred to Bhojpur, visited Barki Kharaon.[9] He sent for Naimuddin. 'I had nothing to fear and so I went,' said Naimuddin. But he was in for a surprise— he was taken to Sahar and arrested on a murder charge. Forty days after his arrest, his bail petition was accepted and he was released. Upon his return to Bathani, he realized that the displaced families had undergone a lot of tribulations. They had been attacked several times, but due to the armed response from the tola, the attacks were unsuccessful. The locks of their houses in the main village had been broken and all their belongings had been taken. Some upper-caste families were forcibly occupying their houses; for example, Gopali Singh made a door through the wall which used to separate his house from Naimuddin's. Some of the affected pointed out that '*Sarkar ne hi hamko yah dukh diya hai* [The government has only caused us this pain]'. Complaints had been sent to the District Magistrate, Amir Subhani, and to the SP, C.R. Kaswan, but no action was taken.

In the two months that followed, the situation in Barki Kharaon and nearby villages remained tense. A series of incidents of violence and even murder took place (see 'Appendix'). One incident led to another, and this spiral of violence culminated in the Bathani Tola massacre on 11 July.

The Making of a Caste Sena

Bhojpur, no stranger to militant politics, had been the site of a caste war since August 1994. New ripples on political waters had been created by the formation of the Ranbeer Sena—initially called Kisan Suraksha Sangharsh Samiti—regarded as the 'private army' of upper-caste Bhumihar landlords of the district. The Sena had made its presence felt only too frequently since its formation in the four blocks of south Bhojpur, namely Udwantnagar, Sahar, Sandesh and Charpokhari.

Since most of the assailants of the Bathani Tola massacre made little effort to conceal their identities, the survivors of the carnage knew many of them. From this and other evidence, there is ample proof that those responsible for the massacre were members of the Ranbeer Sena. A new aspect of the Bathani Tola massacre, however, is the allegation of Rajput participation. Until then, the Ranbeer Sena had been known as a Bhumihar outfit even though, like any other organization of that nature, the Sena did hire goondas of other castes, including Rajputs and members of the backward castes. The possible involvement of Rajputs, along with other members of the Ranbeer Sena, in the Bathani Tola massacre is significant because there is a history of antagonism between Rajputs and Bhumihars in the area. The two castes had rarely joined forces in the same caste sena in the past.[10]

The origin of the Ranbeer Sena is inextricably linked with Belaur village in Udwantnagar block, the largest village in the district with a large Bhumihar presence of 500 houses. Bhumihars, who consider themselves as Brahmarishi Brahmins (see Chapter 12—The Mazdooras of Bihar), are the dominant upper caste in Belaur today. However, according to oral sources this was not always the case. A century ago, there was a significant presence of Rajputs too, but they were driven away by one Ranbeer Chaudhary, a retired military jawan who had organized the Bhumihars in the village for this purpose and led several fights against the Rajputs before the final outcome.[11] Ranbeer Chaudhary is popularly known as Ranbeer baba amongst the Bhumihars of this area, especially in Belaur. He is revered as an exceptional person who had fought to preserve Bhumihar honour and supremacy. And thus, even today, whenever Bhumihars have to fight in order to preserve their supremacy, they turn to him for inspiration.

In 1993, Deepa Musahar, a mild, helpless-looking *banihar* (labourer) gave them the occasion to gather forces, bring out their guns, as they would their swords and clubs in the old days, and turn to Ranbeer baba for inspiration. All this, because this mongrel of a human being had the audacity to ask his malik Deep Narayan Chaudhary for wages that were due to him for the previous year. 'Deepwa', as the maliks liked to call him, had to be cut to size, and thinking thus, the malik locked him in a room.[12]

This was not the first time that landless agricultural labourers had been exploited and maltreated by their employers in this village. In this respect, Belaur was no different from the countless villages in this region which are replete with similar stories of exploitation, oppression and humiliation that many Deepa Musahars had to bear silently for centuries. One oft-mentioned form of social oppression in the old days was to prohibit labourers from sitting on a khatiya, even in front of their own homes. Even their guests were subject to the same rules. In other villages, labourers were required by the zamindars to register the name of every relative or outsider who visited them. Dalit boys were beaten if they were caught wearing good clothes. Another outrageous practice for which Belaur is known required Dalit brides leaving for their sasural to walk barefoot till the outskirts of the village, instead of sitting in a customary *doli* (palanquin) from their home. The izzat of Dalit women has always counted for little and many prominent upper caste men have been involved in raping them. For example, in the present case, the son of Deep Narayan Chaudhary is suspected of having raped several women, including a Yadav woman of the Bhagwanpur tola of the village. Deep Narayan Chaudhary, quite unconcerned, allegedly commented, '*Maine saand pala hai* [I have raised a bull].'

In his dealings with Deepa Musahar, however, Deep Narayan Chaudhary had not reckoned with the fact that times had changed. No sooner had the news of this event reached the other labourers that a *rasta roko* (road blockade) was organized in protest by local members of Liberation; the Belaur road (the main thoroughfare linking Ara with Sahar) was jammed. After the local administration and police intervened, the combined pressure made Deep Narayan release Deepa Musahar, who had been detained for four hours by then. This incident, besides other acts of Liberation such as winning seats in the state assembly elections, made some Bhumihar leaders—including Deep Narayan Chaudhary, Dharichan Chaudhary, and mukhiya Shiv Narayan Chaudhary, who were to play a crucial role in the bloody events that followed—feel that the Liberation base in the region was growing and that they had to pluck this thorn before it destroyed their very existence.[13] This led to their mobilization in the shape of the Ranbeer Sena. The Ranbeer Sena was banned in November 1995 but continued to operate in the area, as the Bathani Tola massacre and subsequent massacres show.

The High Court Verdict[14]

The history of legal proceedings on the Bathani Tola massacre is a sad tale of justice delayed and denied. As mentioned earlier, in May 2010, three of the accused were sentenced to death by the sessions court in Ara district and another twenty were sentenced to life imprisonment. In a stunning reversal, however, they were all acquitted by the Patna High Court in April 2012 on grounds of defective evidence.

The High Court judgment (henceforth HC-J) on the Bathani Tola case was shocking but not necessarily surprising. It prepares the ground for acquittal of the twenty-three convicted by the lower court judgment (henceforth LC-J) using old tactics: overplaying weaknesses of the prosecution and discrepancies in witness accounts to discredit the investigation and evidence. Having effectively done away with the witnesses, it invokes case law to justify acquittal.

The judgment revealed a clear leaning in favour of the accused. The closing observations of the judgment illustrate its biased treatment of the case: '. . . the investigation was not fair *in respect of the persons who perpetuated this ghastly crime*. . . . [it] *was directed in a particular direction far from truth* and not above suspicion. *Truth was deliberately suppressed* . . . only to project an involvement of the accused persons . . .' (HC-J: 56, emphasis added). On closer examination of the two judgments, it became clear that the HC-J was guilty of the bias it attributed to the LC-J. Some indications of this bias are as follows.

Prosecution and Investigation

The independence of the investigating agency is crucial to the affirmation of truth in any crime. In the Indian judicial process, however, the state has monopoly over prosecution in criminal proceedings. In cases where the state itself is implicated in the crime, this arrangement is problematic because it makes the prosecution, in effect, a dummy of the state. In the Bathani Tola case, the state is implicated on two counts: first, because there were three police outposts within a distance of 1.5 km of the carnage site and none intervened even as the carnage continued for hours in broad daylight; second, because the Ranbeer Sena enjoyed the patronage of powerful persons who were part of or close to the state. Affirmation of truth by a compromised prosecution, under such circumstances, is a challenge.

The case against the accused was also undermined by long delays in the proceedings. The police took almost two years to complete its investigations and submit the charge sheet. Delays continued after the case was admitted in the sessions court. As the HC-J notes sarcastically, 'Prosecution . . . [took] virtually nine years to examine 13 witnesses.' (HC-J: 22)

Another lapse is that, despite directions from the court, the test identification parade (TIP) of those arrested was not organized. The Investigation Officer (IO) maintained that the people were not ready for the TIP, but the prosecution witnesses said that they were never called for it (HC-J: 9). They were finally asked to identify the accused in court, a decade after the massacre. Not surprisingly, many of the accused remained unidentified. Similarly, some discrepancies naturally emerged in the statements of witnesses when they were verified in court after a decade or so. Two witnesses and two accused died in the intervening years.

Despite these drawbacks, some important material was made available to the court. The prosecution had an FIR based on a statement made by Kishun Choudhury, who lost his wife and two daughters that day. It had thirteen witness statements, including two eyewitness accounts of Radhika and Paltan Ram respectively. Both Radhika and Paltan Ram had named the accused in their statements, identified them during the identification parade in court and held their ground during cross-examination.[15]

The defence case rested on claiming false implication on three counts. First, it maintained that while statements of eight persons were taken within hours of the massacre, these were not admitted as *fardbayan* (information received by an individual); the fardbayan that became the basis of the FIR was recorded early the following morning, after having 'thoughtfully planned the accusation'. The 'authenticity, correctness and reliability' of the FIR thus stood challenged. Second, the accused were arrested 'like sitting ducks' soon after from the village and another location. Third, they were produced for remand in the Chief Judicial Magistrate's court after a delay of two days, and despite directions of the court, TIP was not arranged. Based on these lapses, the defence claimed 'false implication'.

Doubts and Discrepancies

In criminal proceedings, advocates often try to misuse the basic principle that 'charges against the accused should be proved beyond all reasonable doubt'. A common tactic is to ask irrelevant questions during cross-examination. Discrepancies on trivial points are then used to question the veracity of pertinent details. It is up to the judge to avoid this trap, sieve the relevant from the irrelevant and weigh the relevant discrepancies according to the circumstances of the case. In the present case, the HC-J brought up doubts and discrepancies with respect to the following.

Fardbayan and FIR

The HC-J made too much of a delay—about twelve hours—in recording the fardbayan. No consideration was given to the circumstances of the case, which involved mob violence of a particularly macabre nature. Individuals were expected to make statements while their houses were still burning, family members lay dead, and others needed urgent care. To expect coherence and accuracy of detail in such circumstances is unfair.

It was suggested that Kishun Choudhury, the informant, had perhaps consulted other members of his organization, the CPI (ML), in the intervening hours. In the villages of Sahar block in the mid-1990s, without mobile phones, this would have required a face-to-face meeting. Without convenient transport, moving in the rain and pitch darkness after losing three members of his family, Kishun Choudhury would, at best, have been able to talk things over with comrades of his village and a few others in nearby villages. The suspicion that he took this opportunity to cook up the FIR is gratuitous.

The High Court judges also questioned why the initial written message by the picket personnel, Raghuraj Tiwary (Defence Witness 1), was not treated as a fardbayan. This message mentioned cross-firing and the insinuation here is that this is the reason why the message was not admitted as a fardbayan. But cross-firing was not mentioned by anyone else, nor was there any other evidence of it (e.g., fallen cartridges or injury of any of the attackers). And even supposing that there was cross-firing, would the brutal murder of so many innocent women and children be less of a crime?

Importantly, nowhere does the HC-J ask why Defence Witness 1 did not intervene in the conflict. His statement that he was outnumbered is taken at face value. Why? If thirty or so police personnel had intervened, would the assailants not have been discouraged? At the very least, they would have become eyewitnesses. Why should the HC-J give so much importance to the statement of someone who abdicated his duty and was suspended for it? Why was his statement deemed reliable—without any evidence—while the statements of the victims and their relatives were not?

The HC-J also worried about minor discrepancies such as the time of the fardbayan—4.30 a.m. according to the Investigating Officer but 6.30 a.m. according to Kishun Choudhury. Details of this sort have been used to cast doubt on the authenticity of the FIR.

Unreliable Witnesses

The most shocking aspect of the HC-J bias is its treatment of the witnesses and especially of the survivors. Consider some of the key witness-statements.

Radhika Devi, as an adult survivor of a bullet injury, was one of the most important witnesses. She described how she was shot at point-blank range by Bacha Singh and also identified him and five others, including Bela Singh and Dilip Singh—who were sentenced to death by the sessions court. As someone who had sought refuge in the house of Marwari Mallah, she was also an important witness of what happened there. The sessions court had upheld her testimony as 'truthful and reliable' (LC-J: 35). However, the High Court casually dismissed it as unreliable after pointing to superficial gaps in the evidence. For instance, according to HC-J, an 'important thing to be noted is that although she alleges that her fingers were crushed to see whether she was alive, none of the injury reports show any injury on the fingers' (HC-J: 26). I leave it to the reader to decide whether finger injuries being left unmentioned in the medical examination of a person who has been shot at point-blank range is such an important lapse that the victim's entire testimony should be dismissed. It would also be interesting to know why, according to the High Court judges, the victim would invent such details.

Similarly, the HC-J has little time for Paltan Ram. While Radhika was allegedly a disoriented woman, Paltan Ram's flaw was his age (about sixty) and weak eyesight. The most important part of his statement was that 'his daughter, Phul Kumari, ran out of his house when Ajay Singh shot her and Nagendra Singh cut her arms. Nagendra Singh also shot the mother of Satyendra Prasad [Ramratia Devi]' (HC-J: 30). This is given no credence because the Investigating Officer claims that Paltan Ram failed to mention this when he gave his statement, while Paltan Ram affirms that he did, then as well as at the time of cross-examination.

> We find that what he stated is a bundle of lies. Police state that they had reached the village in the evening itself. He states that they had come in the next morning. Police state that there was no one in the village. He states that he was all along in the village. He admits that because of age he had weak eyesight and he had seen the miscreants for the first time on that day but still, he was able to identify them and give graphic details from his hiding place of what was happening (HC-J: 31).

In other words, the police's statements were taken at face value, but Paltan Ram was held to be a liar as soon as his statement conflicted with theirs, ignoring the fact that Paltan Ram had no reason to lie, while the police had obvious reasons to hide its dereliction of duty in this incident. On closer scrutiny, the HC-J chose to believe the Investigating Officer whenever his assertions worked in favour of the accused—e.g., when he contradicted key witnesses, and disbelieved him when they do not—e.g., on the fardbayan and FIR. As for Paltan Ram's 'weak eyesight', it would not have prevented him to see what he saw, though it might have prevented him (say) to read. Further, the claim that Paltan Ram had said that he saw Ajay Singh and Nagendra Singh for 'the first time' on that day is plain mischief. Both are residents of Barki Kharaon and Paltan Ram would have known them well. So here again, the HC-J casually dismissed a key witness, after the LC-J had taken the view that Paltan Ram's statement '. . . so far it relates to accused Ajay Singh and Nagendra Singh and deceased Phool Kumari and Ram Ratiya, has emerged truthful, reliable, intact and well corroborated by medical evidence' (LC-J: 52).

There are other instances of biased treatment of key testimonies in the HC-J, such as that of Naimuddin, who lost five members of his family in the massacre. As with Radhika Devi and Paltan Ram, the High Court dismisses Naimuddin's testimony by playing up alleged inconsistencies. The LC-J had already acknowledged minor inconsistencies in his testimony but did not reject it:

> Naimuddin has made some inconsistent statement in respect of identification of accused persons, but for these reasons alone the statement of PW11 (Prosecution Witness 11) Naimuddin cannot be brushed aside as his statement otherwise appears free of any infirmity, improvement and embellishment and was corroborated by [others] . . . therefore, evidence of PW11 appears truthful and reliable and so his statement is accepted (LC-J: 69).

In short, the High Court judgement is shot through with biases and inconsistencies, all in favour of the accused. This judgment raises deep questions not only on how the victims of the Bathani Tola massacre are supposed to get justice, but also about the fairness of the judicial system.[16]

When Justice Falters

Justice for the Bathani Tola massacre victims took a long time, and it came on a false note; what is public knowledge could not be proved in a court of law.

The Bathani Tola residents exercised restraint for many years. It must have been hard for the survivors of the carnage, families of victims, petitioners and witnesses to live alongside those they knew to be the killers of their loved ones all along. The fact that 'the court' was looking into the case gave them some hope. But fighting for justice had also made the families of the victims more vulnerable. We must not forget that in these regions, until recently (and to a large extent even now), just looking into the eyes of the malik while talking to him was considered audacious. So, taking them to court must have been an unimaginable affront.

Had justice been dispensed judiciously, it would have given strength to the victims and worked as a deterrent. Many other lives could have been saved—lives that were lost in the interim period as the Ranbeer Sena's activities continued and many other 'successful' massacres of Dalits and other oppressed groups in this region were perpetrated, especially against those who dared to rebel.

The Bathani Tola residents were seeking justice, not revenge. In a region where private revenge is common, seeking justice through the custodians of the 'rule of law' becomes an important step. It is a chance for a court of justice to intervene and make pronouncements that become a warning to—in the words of Simon Wiesenthal—'the murderers of tomorrow'. When this does not happen, people, especially the poor and oppressed, begin to doubt the capacity of the court to uphold justice and may well feel constrained to take the law into their own hands. Where justice fails, vengeance prevails.

Appendix to Chapter 15

A Diary of Violence

Behind the massacres that made headlines is a long history of day-to-day incidents of antagonism and violence. The following chronology of events (based on Liberation records as well as local media reports and some first-hand inquiries) helps to understand the build-up of tensions between the Ranbeer Sena and Liberation in Bhojpur district from the time of the former's birth in 1994 to the Bathani Tola massacre in July 1996. This chronology aims to convey the nature of the ground situation at the time, but it is only a partial picture—the full picture is likely to be worse.

All the places mentioned below are in Bhojpur district. The place names in brackets (after dates) indicate the name of the village where a particular incident took place, followed by the name of the block. The affected blocks are Udwantnagar in central Bhojpur; Sahar, Tarari and Charpokhari in the south; and Sandesh and Agiaon in the southeast.

1994

10 August (Belaur village, Udwantnagar block): At 10 p.m., a squabble took place between Sunil Chaudhury, a Bhumihar youth in his early twenties known to be a lumpen, and Sidhnath Sav, a local shopkeeper and Liberation supporter, over a cigarette. Sidhnath paid a heavy price for it.

Earlier that evening, Sunil had tried to buy a cigarette from Sidhnath's shop, but since Sidhnath could not figure out where his son (who helped him) had kept the packets, Sunil had to return empty-handed. Meanwhile, Sidhnath's son returned, found the cigarettes and sold one to another customer. When Sunil saw this person smoking a cigarette and learnt that it had been bought from the same shop, he was so incensed that, with some of his friends, he immediately set out to find Sidhnath, who had closed for the day. Angrily beating at the door, Sunil demanded that it be opened. Sidhnath refused but explained the situation through the window and offered him a cigarette too. Sunil's anger, however, was not to be appeased and angry poundings on the door continued. Fearing that the door would break, Sidhnath opened it. The five Bhumihar youths then nabbed him and his son and beat them black and blue.

11 August (Belaur, Udwantnagar): At 10 a.m., Birbal Yadav, a local Liberation leader who had come to the village to inquire about the previous night's incident, was attacked by around eight to ten Bhumihar goondas led by Sunil Chaudhary. They beat him with lathis and *raama*,[17] shouting, '*Pichada ka yahi man badhaya hai, maro isko* (He is the one who has incited the backwards, beat him up).' Birbal suffered a serious head injury. Even though the police were later notified, no action was taken against the assailants. Instead, a false case was lodged claiming that Sidhnath Sav and Birbal Yadav had thrown a bomb which had led to the assault; bail was granted to Birbal only two years later. This is one instance, among many, of the complicity of the police.

Tension soon enveloped the entire village. It was especially high in Bajar Tola and Chakardah, about half a kilometre away from the main Belaur village, where the Dalits live. Soon a group of around 500 of them had gathered near the bus stand at Bajar Tola. Early in the afternoon, this group, a large majority of whom were Liberation supporters, finally gave expression to their anger when a private bus owned by Dharichan Chaudhary of Belaur (a leading member of the Ranbeer Sena) stopped at the stand. Badu Chaudhary, the conductor of the bus, was pulled down and killed. However, there is some confusion as to who was responsible for the action.[18]

28 September (Belaur, Udwantnagar): Bhumihar goondas attacked Gung Tola (near the Bhumihar Tola) and fired at an old Dalit couple, Ramruchi Ram and Rajkeshwari. They left Rajkeshwari's dead body behind and disappeared with Ramruchi Ram's.

1 October (Belaur, Udwantnagar): 150–200 armed goondas attacked five tolas of backward and Dalit castes—Gung Tola, Siyarahi Tola, Balwahi Tola, Bajar Tola and Chakardah Tola. While the attackers completely ravaged Gung and Siyarahi tolas, where most of people's belongings (including their cattle) were stolen and their houses destroyed, they were unsuccessful in Bajar and Chakardah tolas because the occupants fired back in self-defence. The occupants of the ravaged tolas took refuge in Chakardah and Bajar tolas.

When I visited the site in November 1995, Gung and Siyarahi tolas wore a desolate and crumbling look. It was difficult to imagine that people lived there once. Near Chakardah Tola, sixty to hundred small, thatched huts had sprung up, and women and children were huddled in the nearby primary school building to protect themselves from the cold. The government had not given them any aid until then, except plastic sheets to about forty-five households. The displaced families had protested many times against the apathy of the district administration, but with little effect.

3 October (Maniach, Sandesh): One Sambhu Sav was kidnapped while cutting some grass in the fields which fall east of Belaur. He was later murdered.

17 October (Chasi, Sahar): Sri Bhagwan Bari, a Liberation cadre, had gone early in the morning to the fields to relieve himself when he was shot by a Bhumihar of his own village.

20 October (Belaur, Udwantnagar): Rajeshwar Paswan was in the wood business and used to go to Ara regularly to sell wood. He was returning from Ara on a tractor when, upon reaching Belaur, he was shot. He was rushed to the Patna Medical College Hospital but died on 18 November.

13 November (Belaur, Udwantnagar): A group of around fifty to sixty armed individuals attacked Chakardah Tola. Firing from both sides went on for four hours, after which they had to retreat.

14 November (Belaur, Udwantnagar): Prayag Sah, resident of Chakardah Tola, was killed as he was returning from the field after his morning ablutions. After killing him, the miscreants fired 300 rounds to intimidate the residents and force them to flee Chakardah. They attempted to take the dead body of Prayag Sah but failed to do so. By this time, Liberation had increased the armed capacity in Chakardah and residents were ready to retaliate and defend themselves.

27 November (Bara, Sandesh): Ramjag Mahato of Bara village went to Belaur to get some medicine for his cattle. He was kidnapped, killed and his body disappeared. Though not a Liberation supporter, he was killed because he belonged to a backward caste, clearly on the assumption that all members of that caste must be supporting Liberation.

1995

2 January (Bartiyar, Sandesh): Liberation cadre Suresh Thakur of Aahpura village was kidnapped and murdered in Bartiyar. His body was never found.

3 January (Bartiyar, Sandesh): Early in the morning, some of the Ranbeer Sena members started firing indiscriminately while walking on a village street. Vinod Sah was washing his face on his terrace when a bullet hit him and he was killed. That very day, a Dalit youth, Ranvijay, was returning to Bartiyar in a bus when some assailants shot at him and ran away. He was admitted in PMCH and survived the wound, but it could have proved fatal.

17 February (Belaur, Udwantnagar): Ramji Sah and Indrajit Ram of Chakardah Tola, Belaur, make their living by selling cloth. Their cloth bundles were snatched and they were fired at. Luckily, they survived.

22 March (Chasi, Sahar): Soon after the state assembly elections were held in this village on 20–21 March, Subhash Yadav was shot dead. The allegation against him was that he had protested against booth capturing and that he was a Liberation supporter.

26 March (Chasi, Sahar): Liberation cadre Lalkeshwar Yadav was shot dead in the morning as he was going to the fields to ease himself.

3 April: Ayodhaya Rai, a local landlord and office bearer of the Ranbeer Sena, was killed by Liberation activists.

4 April (Khopira, Sandesh): At 9 p.m., Ramanuj Mahato, Avadh Mahato and Kunj Bihari were in their fields guarding the chana (gram) crop, when they were attacked and killed.

After this incident, Liberation leaders approached the administration, but government officials remained indifferent. Tension in the area was now building up.

13 April (Gulzarpur, Sahar): Antu Ram was killed at six in the morning when he stepped outside his house to help his daughter defecate.

In the face of an indifferent administration, which at times had even sided with the Ranbeer Sena, the party decided to arm the people. The intention was to enable them to retaliate against particular targets, without hurting innocents. All this time, their aggressors were being supported by the ruling state government as well as mainstream political parties. The police targeted the poor and conducted many raids (*chapamari*) in their houses; similar actions in the houses of the upper castes and suspected members of the Ranbeer Sena were not attempted until much later. Whenever there were instances of encounter between the two sides, the administration always troubled members of Liberation. All this was adequate proof that the district administration was siding with the landlords. None of them were arrested, nor was a single weapon confiscated. After every killing of Liberation members or supporters, the party organized protests and rallies. Each time, they were promised monetary compensation but received nothing other than a few hundred rupees for cremation. Likewise, the government promised that the murderers would be arrested, but nothing of the sort happened.

Meanwhile the villagers had to cope with this situation. From every village where an incident had occurred, people who had alternatives left the village, but those who had none continued living where they were, in a state of terror.

14 April (Ekwari, Sahar): Rajkeshwari Devi, who was sitting outside her front door, was hit by a bullet and killed. Another woman, Janurata Devi, was injured. They were targeted because they were Dalits and belonged to a family which supported Liberation.

19 April (Belaur, Udwantnagar): Jibrail Ansari was known for his kindness. Over sixty years old and barely able to make a living as a vendor, he had supported his Bhumihar neighbour's widow and her children as best as he could for many years. On 19 April, the Bhumihars of Belaur killed him. They had seen him in Gulzarpur village a few days earlier with Gaffarmiyan, a Liberation cadre who was also Jibrail's brother-in-law. It was the son of the Bhumihar widow who found the missing body in the village pond after he spotted a leg amongst the overgrown weeds. At great risk to himself, he lodged an FIR with the police and the body was finally fished out two days after the event. According to some villagers he (the Bhumihar widow's son) left the village soon after that.

20 April (Gulzarpur, Sahar): Nagendra Ram, Liberation cadre from the neighbouring village of Dullamchak, had gone to Gulzarpur when he was kidnapped and murdered.

29 April (Khopira, Sandesh): Hiralal Sah was murdered at ten in the night when he was going to the women's quarter from the *dalan* (outhouse where the men sleep).

5 May (Chasi, Sahar): Shivnandan Prasad, a Dalit youth of village Pande Dehri, Charpokhari block, was on his way to Chasi village when he was shot at and seriously injured. He was going to Chasi that day to pay for a buffalo he had bought earlier from a Chasi farmer. Around twenty to twenty-five goondas who had fired at him later surrounded Chasi and started firing indiscriminately. The Dalits returned fire. Soon the police arrived but started firing at the Dalits too. This put a stop to the firing by the Dalits and enabled the attackers to escape.

5 May (Khopira, Sandesh): A fifty-year-old Dalit woman was fired at and suffered serious injuries. She had to undergo treatment in Patna for three months.

6 May (Gulzarpur, Sahar): A twenty-five-year-old Liberation cadre, Surendra Sah, was having a meeting with members of the party in the village when they were attacked and he was killed.

8 May (Ekwari, Sahar): Maura Musahar used to earn his living by carrying dolis. On this day, members of the Ranbeer Sena of this village summoned him with the message that they needed his services. Along with another person, Maura went to their place to fetch the doli. He was, however, nabbed and murdered shortly afterwards; his friend had a narrow escape. A bullock belonging to Angrahit Ram was also shot dead.

Soon afterwards, 100 Musahar households who lived close to Bhumihar households were attacked, their houses raided and set ablaze. They had no option but to run for their lives. These families now live at a distance of one kilometre from the main village, close to Hanuman Chapra, a tola with a large Scheduled-Caste and backward-caste population.

11 May (Ekwari, Sahar): Goondas of the Ranbeer Sena torched another eleven houses, this time of people of the kahar caste. One of them, Mahendra Ram, had a heart attack due to the shock and died.

13 May (Ekwari, Sahar): The target of attack now shifted to the Doms. The Ranbeer Sena goondas set fire to Badri Dom's house.

14 May (Chanargadh, Sahar): In this village close to Ekwari, some of these goondas tried to take away four buffaloes by firing several shots in the air, but they had to run when the villagers fired back.

15 May (Ekwari, Sahar): Approximately 100–150 goondas of the Ranbeer Sena attacked five households in the tola of the backward castes.

17 May (Ekwari, Sahar): As if to complete what they had started two days earlier, goondas entered the house of Baliram Sah in the night, beat up his wife Tetra Devi and mother Butna Devi, and then raped his twelve-year-old daughter Asha. While the rape was contested by the administration, Asha maintained that Pramod Singh, son of Sankh Singh and a noted criminal himself, had raped her.

17 May (Ekwari, Sahar): Nathuna Ram, a Dalit youth and Liberation cadre, was shot at in broad daylight and seriously injured.

18 May (Ekwari, Sahar): Seventy-year-old Sri Kahar and fifty-year-old Dashrath Kahar, who were sitting outside their homes, were shot at and killed.

After this incident, the administration seemed to wake up. The then Chief Minister, Lalu Yadav, ordered the police to take action. On the ground, however, this order was carried out only to harass Liberation supporters. Mukeshwar Yadav, the thana in charge at Sahar and known to be close to Lalu Yadav, played a key role in these one-sided proceedings. In one instance, he is reported to have asked, '*Tum log Janta Dal mein kyon nahi, Male mein kyon ho* (Why are you people not in Janata Dal, why in Liberation)?' On the pretext of looking for weapons, policemen raided the houses of Liberation supporters and caused much damage. In Ekwari, while carrying out a raid, the police beat up many women, broke earthen pots and used obscene language. Liberation's demand for an inquiry into police repression and transfer of the thana in-charge fell on deaf ears.

5 July (Ara town): The Ranbeer Sena organized a demonstration in Ara where they announced that all their members and supporters would stop employing labourers in that agricultural season. This was in solidarity with Sankh Singh, the Ekwari landlord, against whom an economic blockade was in force. The fields remained barren in Khopira, Gulzarpur, Ekwari and parts of Belaur. Other farmers of Belaur, however, broke the ban and cultivated their fields, undermining the Ranbeer Sena's strategy and creating frictions within the organization.

25 July (Sarathua, Udwantnagar): At around 10 p.m., an armed group woke the sleeping Musahars and asked them to show the way to the neighbouring village. They took eight Dalits with them. One managed to escape. After they had walked a kilometre away from the tola, six were shot dead. One was shot just below his knee and survived by pretending to be dead.

24/25 July (Salempur, Sandesh): Ajay Kumar, eighteen years old, was shot at and seriously injured.

29 July (Lahthan, Piro): Mubarak Ali's old mother (name not known) used to run a small shop. That day, a Bhumihar of the same village asked her to sell him some stuff on credit. When she refused, her angry customer fired at her, killing her on the spot.

5 August (Noorpur, Barhara): Six Dalits—Ganesh Bind, Tribhuvan Paswan, Sampat Bind, Laxman Bind, Dashrath Bind and Srihari Bind—were fishing in the Ganga when a group of Rajputs belonging to the Ganga Sena attacked them with guns and knives. They were seen as Liberation supporters because they were Dalits, were poor and had voted for Liberation in the state assembly elections; this was enough reason to teach them a lesson. The details of this attack became known only because of the exemplary courage of Srihari Bind, who dived into the Ganga and continued to swim towards the shore in spite of the serious cuts in his neck and stomach. He died soon after being rushed to PMCH in Patna, but not without giving his statement. The dead bodies of the others floated down the river and were ultimately found in Chapra. This massacre was widely rumoured to be the joint work of the Ganga Sena and Ranbeer Sena.

12 September (Ekwari, Sahar): Early in the morning as fifty-year-old Rameshwar Sharma was leaving his house, he was fired at and seriously injured. After this, thousands of people assembled near the village high school and demanded that the weapons of the Ranbeer Sena be seized and that the police should be impartial.

28 September (Lachidih, Tarari; Lathan, Agiaon): Shital Mahato and Wahida Khatun were killed in these two villages respectively.

7 October (Chauri, Sahar): Goondas attempted a raid in Chauri but had to retreat after meeting with stiff resistance. Bharat Sharma of Chauri, who was part of the gang of goondas, was injured.

11 October (Intor, Charpokhari): Lallan and Babban Musahar sustained bullet injuries after an attack on them.

12 October: Murder in Bagar (details not available).

14 October (Banwari and Chauri, Sahar; Karanth, Tarari): Supporters of Liberation and Ranbeer Sena had an armed encounter on the issue of fishing rights over the village pond, which lasted the whole day. Encounters also took place in Banwari and Chauri villages. In Karath village, Liberation supporters set fire to a private bus owned by one of the Ranbeer Sena members.

16-21 October (Ara town): To protest against these atrocities, Liberation launched a six-day dharna. The dharna went on day and night and was attended by hundreds of Liberation supporters from different blocks in the district. Among other demands, the dharna called for the arrest of Ranbeer Sena leader Brahmeshwar Singh, the main accused in the Sarathua massacre, who was roaming around freely in Ara at that time.

18 October (Ara town): A hand grenade planted under the main podium of the dharna exploded, seriously injuring ten Liberation supporters. One of them, Paras Ram of Mulkua village in Piro block, died on the way to the hospital. The attack was clearly aimed at killing some of the Liberation leaders who were addressing the people or sitting on the podium. Anticipating an attack, the party had asked the District Magistrate for security but this had been denied. A police van was present at the time of the explosion, but the police blamed Liberation, saying that they had planted the grenade. This proved to be a turning point in Liberation's strategy to deal with the Ranbeer Sena. The dharna continued as per schedule, but in the following days, Ranbeer Sena men were also murdered.

19 October (Imadpur, Tarari): Two men of the Ranbeer Sena were killed. That very day in Sonbarsa and Bartiyar villages, two Bhumihars were shot.

24 October (Gulzarpur, Sahar; Belaur, Udwantnagar; Pavar, Sandesh): On this day, within six hours, four murders took place. It all started in Gulzarpur when a twenty-year-old youth, Kamlesh Paswan, went to fish in the aahar early in the morning and was found murdered there. As some of the local Bhumihars themselves admitted,

Kamlesh was an innocent youth and liked by everybody in the village. When news spread to nearby villages, Umesh Chaudhary, thought to be close to the Ranbeer Sena, was killed in Belaur. At ten that morning, Nirmal Paswan of Pavar village, who was going about his duty as a postman, was found murdered around five kilometres from Belaur. Half an hour later Satya Narayan Singh, one of the alleged murderers, was shot dead by Liberation supporters.

2 November (Bartiyar, Sandesh): A Liberation cadre of Aahpura village was going to Bartiyar village to investigate the armed encounters that had frequently taken place there between Liberation and the Ranbeer Sena. He was killed by the Ranbeer Sena even before he could reach Bartiyar.

12 November (Bichiaav, Sandesh): One Ramji Kahar, aged 12 years, was found murdered.

1996

24 January (Ekwari, Sahar): Ram Lal Ram, father of a Liberation cadre, was sleeping with a few others in his dalan when he was attacked by a group. He was killed immediately, while his eight-year-old grandson, who was cuddled in his lap, sustained serious injuries.

7 February (Chandi, Charpokhari): Gorakh Ram, Raghunath Ram, Prahlad Ram and Kashi Kahar worked as halwahas (ploughmen hired for a year). That night, they were guarding their malik's rice crop, which had just been harvested, when an armed group attacked and shot them dead.

22 February (Baruhi, Sahar): Butan Sav had made an advance payment to a Bhumihar farmer for some rice, as is customary in the villages. When he went to collect the rice, he was shot at by another Bhumihar and died immediately.

22 February (Kosdihra, Sandesh): Gudri Yadav was found murdered.

7 March (Kaup, Charpokhari): Munidra Sav and Chandradeep Sav were killed by three goondas known to be members of the Ranbeer Sena.

9 March (Patalpura, Sahar): Aside from one Bhumihar house, there are approximately sixty to seventy houses of Dalits and backward castes in this village. Some Ranbeer Sena men from other villages attacked the Dalit tola in the evening when the residents were listening to the radio. Three Dalits—Tapeshwar Ram, Budhan Ram and Kaushal Kumar—were killed. According to Liberation sources, this attack was meant to dissuade the people of Patalpura and surrounding areas from participating in the Adhikar rally in Delhi on 11 March. Members and supporters of Liberation were scheduled to leave the next day.

17 March (Ekwari, Sahar): Rampujan Mistri was found murdered.

22 April (Nannor, Sahar): There were two *barat*s (marriage processions) in the village that day. In the evening, a film was being screened for their entertainment. Suddenly, at 1 a.m., an armed group attacked, killing four (Khurshid Miyan, Munna Miyan, Kallu Miyan and Aissammudin Miyan) and injuring thirteen others. One of the injured persons died in the hospital.

24 April (Dhanchua, Sahar): Gyanchand Bhagat of Ganeri caste of this village was found murdered in the fields between the two villages of Chakk and Barki Kharaon, where he had taken some buffaloes out to graze at two in the afternoon. The two murderers were identified, but no arrests were made.

25 April (Barki Kharaon, Sahar): Sultan Miyan, a youth in his early twenties was shot at by some Rajput members of the Ranbeer Sena early in the morning when he was going to the local shop to buy some soap.

5 May (Nadhi, Sahar): Nithali Miyan and Ramjan Miyan were killed by the Ranbeer Sena members of this village. In reaction to this or otherwise, armed Liberation cadres attacked the Bhumihar tola in three different locations and killed eight Bhumihar members of the Ranbeer Sena who were suspected of involvement in the Nannor massacre of 22 April.

11 May (near Barki Kharaon): One Rajeshwar Lal of Bhakura village (Tarari block) used to go from village to village to sell cloth. He was found murdered near Barki Kharaon.

19 May (Nadhi, Sahar): Sitaram and Chintamanidevi, a Dalit couple, were attacked in their house by armed men who first ordered them to take a position of sexual intercourse and then shot the man in the anus and the woman in her vagina. Another woman, Chanodevi of the same tola was also killed.

20 May (Dhanchua, Sahar): Tapeshwar Rai, a Liberation supporter of Bhumihar caste, was killed by other Bhumihars of the same village in the morning, when he was returning after easing himself. He had been under constant pressure for some time to join the Ranbeer Sena or support it with donations, but he had refused to comply. Tapeshwar had also spoken out against the Ranbeer Sena on a few occasions.

20 May (Belaur, Udwantnagar): At ten in the night, twenty-five-year-old Sunil Sav was returning home from his shop when he was shot at and killed. He was not a Liberation supporter, but was presumed to be one because of his caste.

25 May (Morath, Udwantnagar): Three Musahars of the same family were gunned down by Ajay Singh and Bhim Singh of this village. Rajputs are the dominant upper caste in Morath. Two months earlier, some houses were being constructed under the Indira Awas scheme in this tola for which money had been given directly to the Musahars. Ajay Singh had forcibly taken one thousand rupees each from twenty-seven Musahars. The Musahars filed a police complaint against him. Ajay Singh pressured them to withdraw it, but they refused. Incensed, Ajay Singh shot and killed Lal Mohar Musahar, his two-year-old grandson Sudhir and his relative Mita Musahar.

8 June (near Barki Kharaon): Nandu Chaudhury of Lodipur village was shot dead.

11 July (Bathani Tola, Barki Kharaon, Sahar): Nineteen Dalit women and children were killed in broad daylight. Two of the injured succumbed to their injuries, bringing the toll of the massacre to twenty-one.

As we can see, this period from August 1994 to July 1996 included six major massacres aside from a long list of murders: in Sarathua (July 1995), Noorpur (August 1995), Chandi (February 1996), Nannor (April 1996), Nadhi (May 1996) and Bathani Tola (July 1996).

16

On 'Revolutionary Violence'*

'*Saathiyon ke khoon se rangi raah par karna hoga aana jana . . .* [On the path coloured with the blood of our comrades, we will have to come and go . . .].' These lines of a song sung by the Naxalites in Bihar are laced with a certain sadness, as well as resignation to the inevitability of violence and bloodshed on their chosen path of *viplav* or kranti—as revolution is known in some Indian languages.

The communist revolutionaries, who gave birth to the Naxalite movement following the Naxalbari uprising in 1967, have since traversed a long distance. Some of them had remained outside the fold of the original Communist Party of India (Marxist Leninist) when it was formed on 1 May 1969. Those who were inside the party then, later split for many reasons; more splits and mergers followed over the years. Today it is difficult to say how many CPI (ML) parties there are. These parties, along with those who had remained outside the original CPI (ML), together form the Naxalite movement (also see Chapter 13—The Naxalite Movement in Central Bihar). Revolution remains their common aim; however,

* Originally published in *Economic and Political Weekly*, July 2006. My experience of the Maoist movement in Bastar, which came later, has not altered the views presented in this chapter.

there are differences on questions of strategies and tactics. Thus, while all acknowledge the need for armed resistance at some stage, their present emphasis on it varies. While the CPI (Maoist) leads a largely underground existence, others like CPI (ML) New Democracy are only partly underground, and some others like CPI (ML) Liberation function openly.

The case for armed struggle has to be assessed not only on theoretical grounds (e.g., the necessity of violence for the purpose of capturing state power) but also in the light of practical experience. Since the Naxalite movement claims to be a people's movement, it has to be accountable to the people, thus, open to public scrutiny. It is with this motivation that I draw attention below to some of the troubling aspects of revolutionary violence, based on my experience while studying the Naxalite movement in Bihar in the mid-1990s, and to a lesser extent, in the Telangana region of then Andhra Pradesh in the mid-2000s.

Practical considerations

Foremost among the practical fallouts of resorting to violence as a means of struggle is the organizational impact. An organization resorting to armed means has to adopt a certain kind of organizational structure as well as processes. Such an organization naturally cannot be as democratic as it may want to be otherwise. Instead, it needs a hierarchical and authoritarian structure on military lines. Of necessity, it has to be a secret organization and must guard this secrecy at all costs, by developing 'intelligence' within the organization, punishing any breach of discipline, etc. The political culture of such an organization is also oddly schizoid: camaraderie of an exceptional type on the one hand and deep suspicion (sometimes leading to virulent action) on the other.

Underground existence also raises a range of problems. It means secret hideouts, hide-and-seek with the police and intelligence agencies, clandestine courier services and other covert methods. Those who are 'sheltering' in the cities, towns or villages can live at best uncertain lives. Life is all the more difficult for squad members (called *dalam* in Andhra Pradesh and *dasta* in Bihar). Whether in the plains of Bihar or the forests of Andhra Pradesh, in the face of ever-present danger, they have to be on the move all the time and are often forced to lead a nocturnal existence. Squad members face the threat not only of the police and 'class enemies', but also of possible informers in their own fold. Their daily life has its share of deprivations. They are almost totally dependent on the people for their survival. And since most of their supporters are poor, their food and shelter tend to be very basic.[1]

Further, a political organization which utilizes arms has to acquire the ability to procure, maintain and use these arms purposefully and without compromising its principles. Since the movement's inception, the Naxalites have believed in procuring their arms by raiding police pickets and armouries. A lot of energy and human lives have been lost in such actions, sometimes with little result. In Bihar, I have personally known some very fine young persons who lost their lives in such raids. As the Naxalite organizations have grown and state repression has intensified, aspiration for advanced types of armament has increased, even though they cannot keep pace with the arsenal of the Indian state. Advanced technology means more money, high-level training and dynamics of a different kind. For this again, compromises on principled politics are hard to avoid. Since open funding for this purpose is not possible, the party has to rely on other means such as 'levies' on private contractors and development funds. Often, 'extortion' of big money is also involved. A considerable proportion of the material and human resources of Naxalite organizations is used up in this process.[2]

Sometimes the use of violence helps to achieve a short-term gain but intensifies violence from the other side, triggering a spiral of violence. Once this escalation process is in motion, it can be very difficult to contain and often goes out of control. Retaliatory violence acquires dynamics of its own, often out of proportion with the issues at stake. In this respect, class war has similar characteristics to other armed conflicts. There are many historical examples of violence going massively out of control through gradual escalation. Even the First World War, which started with a single assassination (in Sarajevo), is sometimes interpreted in those terms. In the context of a revolutionary movement, the tit-for-tat process sometimes takes over and retaliatory violence becomes the main focus of the movement, displacing all other activities. In the worst cases, revolutionary politics gives way to petty revenge.

Ethical considerations

Aside from practical problems, the use of violence also raises serious ethical issues. Even if violence is considered justified in some circumstances, it is not possible to confine armed struggle to these particular circumstances. For instance, even if the killing of some 'class enemies' can be defended, the armed struggle cannot be confined to particular 'targets' and is bound to engulf innocent victims who are caught in the crossfire or just killed by mistake. Besides individual killings 'by mistake', there are instances where many innocent people have been killed in a Naxalite action (e.g., in attacks on public transport or places). Further, even if a revolutionary organization is determined to avoid killing innocents and make restrained use of violence, there is no guarantee that the other side will do the same. Massacres of the labouring poor, including women and children by caste senas in rural Bihar, discussed in Chapter 13 (The Naxalite Movement in Central Bihar), illustrate the problem.

A related problem is that there is little respect for due process. Even in the bourgeois social order, nobody is supposed to be deprived of his or her life without the facts of the case being considered in a court of law based on impartial norms. By contrast, revolutionary movements, which aim to uphold progressive values and rights, sometimes end up inflicting capital punishment after a process where the same persons (possibly low-level cadres) are the petitioners, witnesses, jury and executioners.

The killing of suspected police informers is a telling example of this problem. When someone is suspected of being an informer, the safety of the movement may demand that he or she be killed, even if the suspicion is unconfirmed. If it is considered appropriate to kill someone when the chance of his or her being an informer is, say, 50 per cent, this implies that when many suspected informers are killed, about half of them are actually innocent.

In some cases, the killing of innocents is extremely disturbing from an ethical point of view. Consider, for instance, the case of a mid-day-meal cook in Karimnagar who was beaten to death because she was suspected of being a police informer.[3] Suppose that she was actually innocent. What possible ethical justification can there be for beating a poor innocent mid-day-meal cook to death? In this instance, the family members were also beaten up when they offered resistance. If the local people knew her to be innocent, we can imagine the impact that this incident might have on them and on the local organization.

Actions such as these might be easier to justify if there was a reliable process, but the question is whether, in politics of this kind, which is largely underground, such a process is possible. If it is not, then we can only conclude that these 'mistakes' are an inevitable part of politics of this type. A lot of subjective judgement is undeniably involved. A young woman in an Adilabad village explained this to me further. She had sheltered me for two nights and I was grateful for that. Giving that as an example, she talked about how sometimes closeness develops between the *annas* (brothers, as the Naxalite cadres are known in Andhra Pradesh) and those who feed or shelter them. And soon the annas may take any information provided by such persons as facts and act upon it, when in reality some hidden self-interests, old enmities, etc. may well be involved.

It is disturbing that the Naxalite discourse seldom refers to the ethical aspects of the use of violence. The premise seems to be that 'the end justifies the means'. As the Secretary of People's War put it in a letter to the Committee of Concerned Citizens dated 20 June 1999: 'The objectives and aims of the struggle are much more important than the forms and methods of the struggle. People will always have the freedom to choose the form of struggle necessary for achieving the objective.'[4] The last statement can be read as a licence for unaccountable violence. Sometimes the Naxalite discourse goes further and glamorizes violence as if it were a value and a marker of revolutionary commitment.

Political considerations

Much is expected from a political movement that aims to be transformative. Most importantly, it should be able to put into practice its own social vision. An important value that the Naxalites have tried to uphold in this respect is equality. Thus, it is natural that the movement should be tested on this account. Unfortunately, the Naxalite movement (not unlike some other autonomous movements in India) in its intra-party dynamics has not always been able to ensure equality for its disadvantaged constituents: Dalits and women. These and other political issues call for further discussion, insofar as they relate to the use of violence in various ways.

The Dalit critique of the Naxalite movement has been more vocal in Andhra Pradesh than elsewhere. Due to the movement's actions against big landlords and other feudal elements, social oppression and untouchability have considerably declined (in both Bihar and Andhra Pradesh). However, in recent times, questions have been raised by Dalits from within the party as well as observers of Naxalite politics. For instance, it has been pointed out that the hard and dangerous work of handling guns is mainly done by Dalits or individuals from underprivileged castes and classes; therefore, those who get killed are also mostly from these sections of society. An additional charge is that while Dalits and other disadvantaged communities comprise the bulk of the Naxalite support base, they are not adequately represented in the upper echelons of the party leadership. Due to these and similar issues, the Janashakti party in Andhra Pradesh underwent a split in the second half of the 1990s.[5]

A similar criticism is also made regarding the position of women within the movement. Even though women in the Naxalite movement have broken their traditional boundaries and their participation has been significant (for example, the proportion of women in the dalams in Andhra Pradesh is impressively high), nevertheless, by and large, they have remained invisible. Like the Dalits, women are almost negligible in leadership positions. The Naxalite movement has not been able to vanquish patriarchy, which permeates the functioning and ethos of the movement. The violent nature of the movement has contributed to this since patriarchy and violence have much in common and tend to reinforce each other. The Naxalite movement has also shown that armed resistance in the context of a class war does not always question violence that emanates from patriarchal norms. For example, in Andhra Pradesh, the number of dowry deaths is very high, but this has not become an urgent issue for action in the Naxalite movement.

Similarly, armed struggle has affected the Naxalite movement's commitment to human rights. When we view the positive contributions of the Naxalite movement, we could well describe it as a movement for human rights. However, there are many instances where the Naxalite movement itself has abused human rights; almost all these instances are excesses related to violence. These excesses have also had a serious impact on the image of the movement, making it possible for the state and the media to ignore the socio-economic causes that have given rise to Naxalite politics, disregard the essential humanism that motivates the Naxalite endeavour and dismiss it summarily as an 'extremist' movement.

The spread of violence in Naxalite areas has also exacted a heavy price in terms of development. Naxalite groups often oppose various forms of development, such as the construction of roads, which hamper their activities. Also, the overemphasis on violent action and 'war' with the police detract from other important issues that the Naxalites could otherwise have taken up. Naxalite areas are among the poorest in the country and there is no dearth of essential demands to struggle for in these areas—schools, electricity, water, health centres, etc. However, these issues get eclipsed since most of the Naxalite groups do not wish to engage with the present government, except as an enemy. Continuous conflict has also drastically reduced the democratic space for other forms of struggle. For instance, in Telangana villages, where direct state repression is ruthless, anybody who dares to question the government (even on basic issues such as water shortages or a non-functional PDS) runs the risk of being labelled as a Naxalite and persecuted. In Bihar, too, democratic space for non-violent struggle has been considerably reduced with the spread of armed conflict.

Another downside of armed power is that it has led to corruption in the ranks. At the local level, having a gun can make the person immensely powerful in his own eyes as well as in the eyes of others. Often, the squad members are young and this 'power' can go to their heads. There have been instances where individuals have misused such power for private gain. Likewise, attraction to armed power may lead unprincipled individuals to join the movement. Such corruption is not easily prevented by the party leadership, as it is not always able to control what happens at the local level. Also, those who implement the party line at the local level are not always 'imbibed' in the Marxist-Leninist ideology. Some of them have formed gangs after running away with party arms and turned against the party itself (e.g., Jagnandan Yadav group in Bihar). Thus, the fact that someone becomes a 'Naxalite' is no guarantee of principled behaviour on his or her part. For the Naxalites to be truly Naxalite, it is very important that they be subject to critical public scrutiny, especially by human rights defenders.

Finally, the use of violence affects the political culture of the movement. For instance, intolerance amongst the Naxalites towards those who hold a different political view has made itself felt time and again. This can be observed not only vis-à-vis political opponents from mainstream political parties but also towards other Naxalite parties. There is no dearth of instances of killing of sarpanchs and MLAs in the former category, or of internecine conflicts within the Naxalite fold.[6] Intolerance, of course, is also found in non-violent movements, but it does not find expression in a violent response. In a violent movement, on the other hand, intolerance and violence feed on each other. The shortcut of violence fans intolerance and even contributes to the making of somewhat arrogant individual personalities, and over time, also colours the organization as a whole.[7] Intolerance in turn finds expression in violent actions (such as the liquidation of political rivals) that have nothing to do with revolutionary struggle.

Party and People

There are many problematic aspects in the relationship of the underground party with the people. Many instances make us feel that for the Naxalites, the party is more important than the people. Sometimes the focus on the party is so pronounced that 'party' seems to encapsulate 'people' in the minds of the Naxalite leaders. Whenever there is a conflict, the interests of the party tend to be placed over those of the people, even though this may entail neglecting what the people think and want. For instance, even as far as the use of arms is concerned, people often defend their decision to take up arms by saying that 'the government does not listen to us otherwise'. However, the very same people also get tired of endless strife. In fact, the leaders of the People's War (PW) in Andhra Pradesh clearly admitted that 'the people want peace' as a reason for engaging in peace talks with the government in 2004. However, after the peace talks broke down and the ceasefire came to an end in January 2005, the CPI (Maoist)—formed by then as a result of a merger between People's War and the Maoist Communist Centre—had soon forgotten this, as was evident in the spate of killings from both sides (roughly equal in number) in the following months.[8] In Andhra Pradesh, this constant strife (encounters and counter-killings) has led to a situation where the people feel that they are caught between the state and the Naxalites.

It is ironic that a movement which promises 'liberation' can actually end up making people less free in some ways. Joining the movement entails repercussions of diverse kinds: being a target of the state and the social forces the movement is struggling against; the danger of being implicated in legal cases through false charges which are not small by any means (e.g., for murder); not being able to lead even a semblance of normal family life, etc. Joining Naxalite politics is basically inviting danger, death and destruction to oneself and one's family, sometimes even the community. In spite of these difficulties, it is a fact that the Naxalites have been able to win the support of the poor in the areas they have operated in. The possibility remains that many more would have joined or supported the movement if it was less taxing.

Besides, the dynamics of the movement are such that it often becomes difficult to tell whether the people are in it voluntarily or involuntarily. At times, people find themselves trapped in circumstances that make it hard to leave the movement. Once one is labelled as a Naxalite, it is difficult to return to normal existence or even a life relatively free from suspicion, fear and death. Also, if they participate in a Naxalite action and get charged, the poor become more dependent on the party to rescue them, as they are unable to deal with the police and the courts on their own. Thus, they may remain in the party because they need the party's protection.

If they do leave the party, they are constantly harassed by the state and made to prove their loyalty in various ways. For example, the government may ask them to sign a register at the local police station every week, give them election duty at polling booths during election time, make them run errands like rounding up the villagers when a government official comes, etc. However, even if they cooperate with the local officials, they remain in the black book of the police and are never above suspicion. Often, such 'surrendered' Naxalites are forced to join some other political formation that is more acceptable to the state, such as a mainstream political party, so that they can discard their old identity and find protection in a new one. Some end up doing what the police ask them to do, involuntarily or even voluntarily: they become police informers, coverts, members of a vigilante group, or even join the police force. Some of them are also harassed by the party and this pushes them further into the clutches of the police.

The problematic relation between the party and the people also manifests itself in similar problems between Naxalite parties and their 'open fronts'. People who join these open fronts do so based on the manifestos of these fronts, which are committed to basic rights as enshrined in the Indian Constitution. However, these fronts are not as 'autonomous' as they perhaps think, to begin with, for the link with the party is vital. This link has proved positive at times, for example, when the party offers protection to mass fronts at open mass meetings—in Bihar, labourers did not even have the right to hold a meeting in the eyes of the landlords—or acts in other ways as a *suraksha dasta* (protection squad). However, the link between the party and open fronts also has many problematic dimensions. For instance, if a peasant front is engaged in a struggle for ceiling surplus land and the party decides to 'annihilate' the landlord, the state is likely to target the members of the open front since they are the only visible actors. Thus, members of the mass front pay the price for actions taken by the underground party, even if the party owns up to its actions (e.g., through leaflets) as it usually does. In that sense, the 'vanguard' party lets the people bear the brunt of its actions, which are undertaken on behalf of the people, but without their knowledge and consent.

The basis of struggle by a mass movement is the notion of 'rights'. When arms are used, even though the use of arms aims to affirm rights and may do so, it also generates other dynamics. For example, it generates fear. The opponent is forced to yield, not because he or she has acknowledged the right and gives in to the collective power of the people who are claiming it, but often out of fear. Likewise, arms give power. Yes, in some ways they do give power to the people. However, this is an 'external' power, which is there only as long as arms are there. Failing that, the individuals or the social group are in a weaker and more vulnerable position than before. Moreover, such a power is not democratic, e.g., it is not and cannot be decentralized. Control does not rest amongst the people but in more specialized agencies. Thus, arms make the people dependent on these external agencies and do not prepare them to fight on the basis of their own strength.

Concluding Remarks

Something that was once beautiful may not be beautiful now—'. . . time and bad conditions do not favour beauty,' reminds Ngugi.[9] The story of the Naxalite movement on the ground certainly has had beautiful aspects and inspiring moments. However, the use of violence has taken a heavy toll. The downside of violence has been so wide-ranging that it may well end up negating what the Naxalites stand for.

The Naxalite movement has been a significant political movement of our times. Individual Naxalites, including many exceptionally fine human beings who have lost their lives for the cause of revolution, have been an inspiring example of idealism, sacrifice and commitment. Politically, the movement has raised important questions regarding India's democracy and underlined the need to bring about 'a people's democracy'. There have also been significant practical achievements in specific areas: curbing of feudal practices and social oppression; confiscation and redistribution of ceiling surplus land; more equitable access to village commons; higher agricultural wages; elimination of the stranglehold of landlords, moneylenders and contractors; protection from harassment by forest department officials and the police; heightened political consciousness and empowerment of the poor, amongst others.

The question remains whether the same results could have been achieved through non-violent or at least less violent means.[10] In the Naxalite movement, the inevitability of violence tends to be taken for granted on the grounds that there is no other way of overthrowing the state. In practice, however, the movement has, for the most part, not been involved in overthrowing the state but in practical struggles for land, wages, dignity, democratic rights and related goals that can be pursued no less effectively through open mass movements. In fact, it is worth noting that the success and popularity of the Naxalite movement itself owes more to the achievements of its open mass movements than to armed action. The growing displacement of open mass movements by militaristic action in recent years has been a loss for the movement, not a gain.

The preceding argument should not be read as a condemnation of all violence. I agree with Noam Chomsky that 'No person of understanding or humanity will too quickly condemn the violence that often occurs when long subdued masses rise against their oppressors or take their first steps towards liberty and social reconstruction.'[11] However, it is one thing to acknowledge that the downtrodden may resort to violence in situations of acute crisis or oppression, and another to endorse organized violence. Perhaps the time has come to revive the more humane approach advocated by Bhagat Singh: 'Use of force justifiable when resorted to as a matter of terrible necessity: non-violence as a policy indispensable for all mass movements.'[12]

17

Salwa Judum and After

Internal War as Counter-Insurgency*

The Bastar region in Chhattisgarh has been the site of intense warfare between the CPI (Maoist) and the Indian state since 2005. For the first time, the state used 'strategic hamletting'—the displacement of entire villages, usually from interior regions to roadside areas that security forces can patrol without difficulty—as a counter-insurgency measure against the Naxalite movement. During the first phase of the counter-insurgency (June 2005 to September 2009), the government also created and supported a ruthless vigilante group, Salwa Judum (which means 'purification hunt' in Gondi), to help it in its aim 'to wipe out the Maoists'. The results have been devastating—thousands were displaced, hundreds died, entire hamlets were burnt, more than a hundred women were raped.

---

* This essay, mostly written in 2009-11, focuses on the situation in Bastar prior to the Supreme Court judgement of July 2011. It draws on a small portion of the material I have collected there, and covers a fraction of the tragic events of that period. The situation did not improve much after 2011, as discussed in the postscript to this chapter. Some names (surname first, as per local custom) have been changed to protect anonymity.

News about Salwa Judum in Dantewada (undivided) district, the southern-most district of Chhattisgarh at that time, first started coming out in June 2005.[1] We heard stories of thousands of Adivasis who had been rendered homeless due to the intimidation and violence of the Salwa Judum and who were now in relief camps. It took some time for the contours and substance of Salwa Judum to become clear and to realize that the marauders were also the ones who had organized the relief, and that this was not a spontaneous popular resistance against the Maoists but an organized, state-sponsored counter-insurgency strategy. Far from being a 'peace movement' as the state claimed, Salwa Judum involved large-scale violence, killings and serious human rights violations. It was, in reality, the first operation in the intensive counter-insurgency that began in 2005. As this essay shows, the civilian actors in Salwa Judum were merely junior accomplices of the police and paramilitary—what happened at the time under the name of Salwa Judum would be more appropriately called 'Operation' Salwa Judum.

Despite the evident failure of this strategy, the government has continued to militarize the area and carry on its operations, notably Operation Greenhunt from September 2009 and other operations after that. Today, Bastar is considered as the most militarized zone in the country after Jammu and Kashmir. This offensive in Bastar is being used as a model for emulation in other Adivasi (tribal) areas of the country, for instance in Maharashtra, Odisha and Jharkhand.

In this essay, I attempt to understand the workings of this internal war at the ground level, based on several months of fieldwork in Bijapur and Konta tehsils of then Dantewada district, carried out intermittently between 2006 and 2009. The focus is on how Salwa Judum was perceived and experienced by those who were supposed to have a stake in this 'movement'—the Adivasi people of Dantewada. The concluding sections discuss how justice and peace have become a far cry for the people of this region.

'Operation' Salwa Judum

Region and People

Chhattisgarh was carved out of Madhya Pradesh in 2000. It is a largely rural state; 80 per cent of the population lives in rural areas. While 32 per cent of Chhattisgarh's population is tribal, the share of Adivasis in the population is much higher in the Bastar region: for instance, 79 per cent and 67 per cent in Dantewada and Bastar districts (undivided) respectively. Of the sixteen districts that constituted Chhattisgarh at the time of its creation in 2000, seven fell under the Fifth Schedule and another six were partially under the Fifth Schedule. The Constitution includes special provisions for the administration of Fifth Schedule areas. Further, the Panchayat Extension to Scheduled Areas (PESA) Act 1996 gives special powers to the gram sabhas in these areas, especially to safeguard traditional rights over natural resources. Under PESA, the gram sabhas have the power to prevent alienation of land and to take action to restore any unlawfully alienated land of a scheduled tribe.

A notable feature of Chhattisgarh is that it is rich in natural resources and forests. It has the highest area under forests in the country after Assam—two-thirds of the area of the state (nearly 80 per cent in the northern and southern regions) is under forests. There are abundant mineral resources including large deposits of iron ore, coal, diamond, bauxite, limestone, tin ore, etc. The inroad of private capital intensified after the state's formation in 2000. Numerous Memorandums of Understanding (MoUs) have been signed between the government of Chhattisgarh and private corporations, often blatantly bypassing the provisions of PESA. By August 2006, forty-two MoUs had been signed for steel plants alone, of which most people had no knowledge.[2]

The two main political parties in the Chhattisgarh Assembly are the Bharatiya Janata Party (BJP) and the Congress. The BJP came to power in the state assembly elections in December 2003, after replacing Ajit Jogi's Congress government, and remained in power until late 2018. Interestingly, on the question of economic globalization as well as lack of respect for due legal processes, especially in the Fifth Schedule areas, both parties think alike. Likewise, with a few exceptions in the Congress party, Salwa Judum enjoyed the support of both parties. The story of economic globalization in Chhattisgarh and the story of Salwa Judum have many points in common, even as both these incursions have been vicious in their own ways.

Dantewada district (undivided), the main theatre of Salwa Judum, was carved out of the old Bastar district in 1998. It had four tehsils: Bhopalpatnam, Bijapur, Dantewada and Konta. Except for a few small towns, Dantewada is largely rural (93 per cent) and forested (80 per cent). Like the rest of the Bastar Division, it comes under the Fifth Schedule. As mentioned earlier, a large majority of its population is made up of Adivasis, mainly Gonds including the Madias, Murias and Dorlas. In Bastar, the Gonds call themselves Koitur or Koi. The name Gond was given by outsiders, but it has gained wide acceptance.[3]

The Naxalite Movement

Around 1980, when members of the CPI (ML) People's War Group first entered Bastar, it was with the idea of using the area as a shelter zone since it was adjacent to some Telangana districts that were the main centre of their activity. Their influence spread amongst the Dorlas, with whom they came in contact first, since the areas of Bastar that border Khammam district in Telangana have a high proportion of Dorlas. As they expanded to the interior forest region where the Hill Madias reside, their base amongst them became stronger. Over time, they spread to the Abujhmad region across the Indravati (also populated by the Hill Madias) and adjoining areas.

Not unlike other tribal areas of the country, Bastar too has seen steady in-migration of non-tribals with a wide variety of business interests during the last two centuries. Over the decades, these non-tribals have become quite powerful economically and politically, and the Adivasis have been marginalized. It was mainly to end the exploitation of Adivasis by the police and the forest department on the one hand and by non-tribal traders and moneylenders on the other that the Naxalite movement took root in the hills and forests of undivided Bastar district since the early 1980s. For the Naxalites, their work in this region was also an experiment of a kind since they tried to develop it as a model area where besides the politics of resistance, they also attempted to put into practice their ideas regarding development.

As mentioned in Chapter 13 (The Naxalite Movement in Central Bihar), the CPI (ML) People's War Group merged with Party Unity in 1998, and then with the Maoist Communist Centre of India in 2004 to form a new party, the CPI (Maoist). In this chapter, the terms Maoist and Naxalite are used interchangeably, as tends to be done in Bastar. Strictly speaking, Naxalite is a broader, generic term for communist revolutionaries, but in Bastar there is no significant Naxalite presence other than the CPI (Maoist).

What is Salwa Judum?

As it had also happened in other states like Bihar, the Naxalites' attempt to organize the people in Bastar met with fierce resistance from some quarters. The first organized resistance occurred in 1989–91. The Jan Jagran Abhiyan (people's awakening campaign), as it was called, started and spread in some villages of Bijapur tehsil, but fizzled out in less than two years due to conflicts within the organization. In 1998, according to some sources, another counter-movement was initiated, but it was brief and did not make a notable impression. In mid-2005, discontent emerged again in one village of Bijapur tehsil. This discontent turned into organized dissent when some notable tribal and non-tribal elites, with the help of the government, gave it the shape of a counter-insurgency movement that they named Salwa Judum. Among them was Mahendra Karma, a local Congress politician who later became the most prominent leader of this movement. Salwa Judum was initially projected as a non-violent popular movement of local tribals against the Maoists, and it is possible that it did have that element when discontent first emerged. However, it soon became clear that Salwa Judum was not a spontaneous movement of dissent but a state-supported operation backed by massive funds, armed forces and glaring impunity.

Salwa Judum's trajectory has involved forcibly evicting people from their villages and forcing them into government-run camps, ironically called *Salwa Judum rahat shivir* (Salwa Judum relief camps). This was done as an intense drive during the first six months, from June to December 2005, in Bijapur and Bhairamgarh, and in the first few months of 2006 in Konta. *Padyatras* (rallies) were organized to round up the villagers. Typically, a rally would include a group of around 300, about half of which consisted of 'the force' (as the paramilitary and police are called locally), including members of the Indian Reserve Battalions (IRB) from Nagaland, the Central Reserve Police Force (CRPF), the Chhattisgarh State Police and Special Police Officers (SPOs); the rest consisting of Salwa Judum leaders, activists and followers. While the force would be armed with modern weapons, the accompanying activists and villagers were usually armed with local weapons like axes, swords, sticks and bows and arrows.

The group would descend on an Adivasi village and 'persuade' people to join the Salwa Judum. Threats, beatings, destruction of household items, burning of houses, sexual harassment and even rapes and killings were used freely as intimidation tactics. The message was clear and was conveyed as such: 'If you come with us, you are with the government, otherwise it will be understood that you are with them [the Naxalites].' In many cases where information about village *sangam* (village committee) members was available, more severe measures were used. Their houses were burnt, and if the sangam member was caught, he or she would be treated as a prisoner and often tortured. The initial rallies took place for the formation of the 'base camps' (as rahat shivirs were called in official parlance), and after such camps were set up, to increase the strength of the people in the camps.

The Salwa Judum led to the massive displacement of Adivasis. According to one conservative estimate, as many as a 1,00,000 people were displaced in the first year (mid-2005 to mid-2006). Roughly half found themselves in camps and the other half became fugitives and refugees overnight. These included people who had run away to the forests and those who fled across the state borders to Khammam and Warangal districts in Telangana (part of Andhra Pradesh at that time).

The Camps

The camps were set up and run by the Salwa Judum with government support. At what can be assessed as the peak (late 2006), there were thirty-six camps in Konta and Bijapur tehsils of Dantewada district with more than 50,000 residents. However, the number of camps and their population have been fluctuating over time. The rationale given in defence of this aggressive grouping of people was to protect them from the Maoists. However, this façade barely concealed the true intention—evident on the ground—to control the people, to separate them from the Maoists and thereby, weaken the Maoist support base. As one Salwa Judum leader put it: 'How can the fish survive without water?'

Thus, what we saw in Dantewada was a result of this odd hypothesis of the government that if people from villages of Maoist influence could be evicted, moved into government-run and monitored camps and confined there for an extended period, the Maoists would be 'finished'. As we shall see, extreme measures were adopted to achieve this extreme objective.

Salwa Judum in Konta Tehsil

Konta tehsil has fifty-nine gram panchayats and 248 villages, administered through two revenue circles: Konta and Jagargonda. The Konta revenue circle covers thirty-two gram panchayats and sixty-four villages. In November 2006, there were 30,000 people from approximately ninety villages in four camps: Konta, Injaram, Errabore and Dornapal, all located close to the Hyderabad-Jagdalpur national highway on the 40 km stretch between Konta and Dornapal.

According to local residents, around four or five padyatras of Salwa Judum took place in Konta tehsil in early 2006. Typically, the routes these rallies took and the villages they covered corresponded to the villages that were found in the camps. From the descriptions I heard, there was a mass exodus of people from villages located within 10 km of the highway. Beyond this are thick forests for a further 50 km; the villages located in this stretch remained comparatively untouched by the 'Judum', as Salwa Judum is called locally.

In the second half of November 2006, I visited Konta and Injaram camps for the first time. I found that many people had joined the camps due to direct coercion by the security forces and Salwa Judum, others out of fear of them because they perceived it to be a government order. Some also joined the camps because they were being targeted by the Maoists and needed protection from them. The camps were thus a refuge for a few and a coercive settlement for most, as the following stories and observations from the Konta camp illustrate (further testimonies from the camps are presented in the next section).

Konta Camp

Prema Joga, a Dorla of Itkal village (Banda gram panchayat), said that twenty-five of the thirty households in his village came to the

Konta camp. The rest went to Telangana. He said, *'Pehle bahut maar-peet kar rahe the, is liye dar se aa gaye* [Earlier they were beating people a lot, that is why we came, out of fear].'

Kattam Channa, also a Dorla, is from Murligudem (also in Banda gram panchayat). He said that, except for five of the seventy-two households in his village, all were in the Konta camp. The five missing families had gone to Telangana. He added: '*Yah hamare sarkar hai, ma-baap hai, is liye aa gaye. Judum wale kahte the ki base camp mein naheen rahoge to chawal naheen denge. Samajhdaar wale yahaan aa gaye, anpadh wale unke saath chale gaye* [They are our government, our mother and father, that is why we came. Judum people told us that only those in the base camp would get rice. The intelligent ones came here, the illiterate went with them (the Maoists)].'

Some of the camp residents related that in the early days and months, there was a lot of pressure on all villagers. All cyclists going to the market or returning after some work in Konta would be stopped and ordered to join Salwa Judum. Those who tried to run away after seeing the Salwa Judum men would be caught and taken to the *thana* (police station) for questioning. '*Thana mein jo samajhdaari se jawab dete, unko chod dete* [At the thana, those who replied smartly would be released].'

People mentioned that even after the establishment of the camp, every morning a contingent of fifty armed men, including security forces and Judum activists, would head towards the villages. On some days they would return with five or six persons, on others, more. Over time, they got most of those who had not run away to the forests or across the borders. Camp inmates had few possessions. Most were unable to bring anything with them. Slowly, some went back and retrieved some household items like cots and utensils.

When I visited the Konta camp in November 2006, I found it alive with activity. People were busy constructing new houses. The government had allotted Rs 12,000 per family, part of which was given in kind, for construction work. Those who could had also brought poles, doors and window frames from their old houses as though they knew that in the near future, they would not be able to return. I had expected to find temporary shelters in these 'camps', but the frames of the new houses arranged in neat rows suggested otherwise. I could see that plans were afoot to turn these camps into permanent settlements.[4] However, no official at the tehsil or the district level knew what the plan was. None saw an end in sight. The Konta tehsildar, for instance, said that the people would remain in the camps for as long as the Maoists were there and that food rations would continue to be provided to them—as though that was all that the people needed of the lives left behind in their villages.

The food rations were provided fortnightly. Every household member was eligible for two kilos of rice, one medium-sized glass of lentils, one small glass of dried peas, two onions and two potatoes. Periodically, they were also supposed to receive cooking oil, salt and condiments, though people said that they had not been given any oil after the floods in August 2006. The Konta tehsildar said that they were authorized to give provisions worth Rs 20 per person per day. He admitted that they were actually distributing rations worth Rs 8 per day. He said that giving the rest in kind would add to the administrative burden and ruled out paying it in cash since the 'order' permitted only payment in kind. Any modification, he claimed, would have to be taken up in the state assembly. This is a good example of the corruption that was rampant in the camp administration. One local trader from Bihar said: '*Yahaan vyapar chal raha hai* [Business is flourishing here].'

As a result, the camp dwellers—who were habitually non-vegetarians and consumed a wide variety of roots, tubers, fruits and other forest produce—were having to survive on the same frugal diet day after day. And even this basic existence was not without fear. The camps were administered by Salwa Judum leaders whose signature was necessary to release a family's rations. The camp inmates, who had no other means of livelihood, were thus totally dependent on the goodwill of these leaders. Even though government sources claimed that NREGA works had started under the Rs 1 crore package sanctioned for the four camps in Konta tehsil, I found no evidence of any ongoing or completed works, or even of anyone having a job card.

Some camp residents compared their situation to being in a jail. They had no source of livelihood and they were not allowed to return to their villages and land. They were unable to return out of fear of reprisals by the security forces, the Salwa Judum or the Maoists (who regarded them as 'enemies' for living in the camps). They were thus at the mercy of the Salwa Judum and the police, who were always on the lookout for people who might be in touch with the Maoists. They knew that they were under round-the-clock scrutiny. Anyone caught moving away was severely punished.

Nevertheless, some managed to run away from the camps. In the process, they were doubly displaced and had to face destitution all over again, since the few possessions they had gathered after coming to the camps had to be left behind.

Selected Testimonies

The best way of understanding the situation in Bastar is to hear the stories of the affected people from them. In this section, I present a small selection of testimonies that represent different perspectives on the situation, among many others that I collected in 2006 and the following years.

In those days, there was an atmosphere of fear and danger in the conflict areas (e.g. Bijapur and Sukma), and few people remained in the villages that had been targeted by Salwa Judum. Therefore, I looked for witnesses mainly in the camps and also in the chilli fields across the Telangana border, where many Adivasis from Bastar worked as casual labourers after being displaced from their villages.[5]

In the Camps

Karam Jogamma

At Injaram camp, I met nineteen-year-old Karam Jogamma from Irpaguda village (Injaram gram panchayat). Her testimony reflects the sentiments of the relatively privileged, who have no sympathy for the Naxalites. She said:

> There are thirty-one houses in Irpaguda. It was midday when the people of the village started shouting '*Naga wale aa rahe hain* [The Nagas are coming]'. When they came close, we saw that there were the Naga force as well as the Judum and SPOs. People got scared and decided to come to Injaram. Later some escaped to Andhra Pradesh.
>
> There was a *sangam* in Irpaguda. *Sangam walon ko bhee maar maar kar laye* (They also brought the sangam members, beating them up); not only that first time, but also on two later occasions. They were enlisted as SPOs.
>
> I did my primary and middle school from Injaram. For my secondary school, I went to Konta. That is when I first heard about Naxalites. During the summer holidays in my ninth class, when I came home, sangam members were calling everybody for a meeting. I asked my parents about them. But they discouraged my questions and said that I should keep away from them. 'Stay inside the house. They should not even be able to see you,' they said. My family members did not go for their meetings. Even then, they came a few times to call us. During my holidays, a woman Naxalite once came to my house and called me for a meeting. I told her that I wanted to study and could not come with her. They would ask us why we were not going. They accused us of listening to the police and not to them. We heard of people being beaten up; they had beaten my father once.

About the work of the Naxalites, she said:

> *Accha karte the, par ulta-seedha bhi karte the* (They did some good
> things, but also some mischief). They fought those who exploit the
> poor, and even killed them if they went too far. Two such persons
> were killed in my village. In one case, a man had a relationship
> with a woman and made her pregnant, but he was refusing to
> marry her. Police also used to come to our village, but there was
> no encounter between the two.
>
> Now the Naxalites are angry with us because *hum sarkar se
> chaval-dal kha rahe hai* (we are being fed by the government) and
> some amongst us have also become SPOs. Even if they call us, we
> will not go. In their recent posters and messages they are saying
> that 'all of you can come back to us, and if you come, we will
> not do anything to you'. They want us to return because they are
> not getting rice from us anymore, but there is no guarantee that
> they will not kill. They are scared only of the Naga force, not the
> police or CRPF. After the force goes, violent incidents will keep
> happening. People will not be able to escape.
>
> Salwa Judum is good. We have enlisted as SPOs so that if
> there is an incident, we can respond. If there is a firing, how do we
> protect ourselves otherwise?

She said that they will stay in Injaram camp until peace returns.

Rani and Janaki

Still in Injaram camp, Rani and Janaki spoke about their occasional
contacts with the Naxalites when they lived in the village, and how
they ended up becoming SPOs. In Rani's words:

> *Hum donon Naxalite ke 'Sinem'* [her name for the cultural wing of
> the Maoists] *mein jaane wale the. Sinem mein hum se chote-chote*

bhi rahte the. Nachne ka bahut maza aata tha. Uske baad training hoti thi, phir banduk milta tha. (Both of us were going to join the cultural wing of the Naxalites. Some members are even younger than us. We loved the dancing. After that, there would be training, then we would be given guns.)

Here in the Injaram camp, there are ex-dalam (armed squad) members also, as well as those who used to be part of the sangam. They were there in every *para* (hamlet) of the village—Konel para, Patel para, Pujari para and others. Now they are all SPOs—only three did not come.

Angrily, the Naxalites would tell people, 'You were with us for so long, how could you go with them [Salwa Judum]?', and they would hurt people for doing so with sticks and even knives or guns. I was with them. I have seen all this.

Madia people become Naxalites. They go from village to village and hold meetings. During the meeting, if the police comes, they run away. They are scared of the police. They had a meeting and told all of us not to go to Salwa Judum. They said that if Salwa Judum comes to your village, you can throw chilli powder in their eyes, but if we were to do this, would they just keep looking at us? Would they not harm us?

Naxalites severely punish all those who make mistakes. Somebody who brought a second wife would be made to rub his nose on the ground. They would come in the night and catch an offender, put a rope around his neck, pull it and drag him. If a girl was being forced into marriage, they would beat up those who were forcing her. They favoured love marriages. They told us that it was not good to get married when you are of tender age. You will not be able to care for your child properly. Land would be taken from those who had more land and distributed. They roam about in the dalams like brother and sister. I don't like this aspect of them—that they beat up people so easily. We call them *Narkator* in Gondi.

'Do the villagers not love them [the Naxalites]?' I asked. She replied:

> Those who like their work love them. They spend their time targeting the police. Some of us did not join Sinem willingly. But we enjoyed the dancing; nobody can dance like them.
>
> Both of us have joined the SPOs willingly. First, we accepted to go and learn to parade. The SPOs are becoming SPOs to kill the Naxalites.
>
> The Nagas hunt the Naxalites and kill them. They have killed many and also taken many as prisoners. The Injaram SPOs were trained by the Nagas and are now able to hunt and kill the Naxalites like them. Konta and Errabore SPOs are not like that. They are scared, like the CRPF. As soon as there is firing, the CRPF run away.
>
> If the SPOs are fired at, they fire. If they have been seen and do not fire, then they will be hounded and shot [by the Maoists] in the future. Yes, SPOs have also killed unarmed persons who are with the Naxalites. *Bahut gussa hai* (There is a lot of anger in them)!

Mala Netam

Mala Netam is from Misma village, 12 km from Dornapal. Her family is in the Dornapal camp, but she lives and works as an anganwadi worker in Injaram camp. She is the half-sister of Bodduraja, a Salwa Judum leader and *adhyaksh* (president) of Injaram camp. She belongs to one of the better-off Adivasi families in the camp. Even though such families tend to be hostile to the Naxalites, she has a relatively nuanced understanding of what occurred.

> We came to Injaram on 24 January 2006. *Hum iccha se naheen aye. Iccha se kaise aayenge* (We did not come of our own will—how could that be)? Around 100 Judum activists, armed with bows and arrows,

knives and other local weapons, used to round up the Adivasis on market days. *Judum kya hai, kisi ne logon ko naheen samjhaya* (No one explained to people what the Judum is). For a whole week, they would land up wherever a market was being held and accost people. '*Tum Judum mein kyon naheen judte* [Why are you not joining the Judum]?' they would insist. They also beat up many people.

People in this entire region got scared. They thought that if they did not go, the Judum would burn their houses. The villagers of the Injaram area have little education. They were worried. '*Yahaan rahenge, to veh mar denge, vahaan rahenge to yeh maar denge* [If we stay here, they (the Judum) will kill us, and if we go with them, then they (the Naxalites) will not spare us],' they thought. They were in a panic. There was no way out. Since they were not with the Naxalites in any case, they decided to go to Konta. It is difficult for people to leave their homes and everything they own. *Log iccha se naheen aye. Dar se aye. Jabardasti se laya gaya. Mahila ho, purush ho, ya baccha, chahe koi bhee ho, usko pakad pakad kar, teer-dhanush dikhate hue, Konta laye* (People didn't come of their own free will. They came out of fear. They were forced. Women, men, children, anyone—[the Judum] caught them, scaring them with bows and arrows, and brought them to Konta).

People on our side (Misma side, near Dornapal) are educated. They thought that even though they were not with the Naxalites, it was better not to leave their village in a hurry. They preferred to wait and watch. *Soch kar dekhenge, samajh ke, phir jaenge* (We shall think, understand and then go). However, later they thought, '*Kahe ko maar khana?* [Why should we get beaten]?' After the Dornapal rally, when the decision was taken to set up camps in Injaram and Dornapal, they also decided to move.

In those days, the Judum and the forces used to beat up people because they knew that without the use of force, people would not submit. But later, people forgot the beatings. *Ab apne aap ko Judum wale bolte* (Now they refer to themselves as part of the Judum). Most men are part of it. They are fools who do not understand anything. *Padh-likh jae, to bahut dur tak ja sakte hain* (If people get educated, they can go a long way).

She felt that their future was bleak. '*Jayenge to bhi marenge, rahenge to bhi marenge. Aisa hi sab sochte hain* [Everyone thinks that if we go, we will die, and if we stay, we will still die].' Meanwhile they just continued to live in the camp. Her parting words conveyed the helplessness of the people, especially those with little education:

> *Log aisa soch rahe hain ki gai, bail, bakri, murgi, suar, ghar, ghar ka pura andar ka saamaan—dhan, lakdi, kapda, aadi—bahut nuksaan hua. Logon mein bahut chinta hai. Log soch rahe hain, hum kyon ghar chode? Aisa kyon hua, kaun kiya, kyon kiya? Public jo thoda padha-likha hai, usko samajh mein aa raha hai, aisa kyon hua. Jo kuch bhee hua, galat hua. Yah bahut galat tarika hai* (People think that they have lost everything—cattle, goats, hens, pigs, their house and all their household belongings—rice, fuelwood, clothes, etc. They are very worried. They are thinking—Why did we leave our homes? How did this happen? Who has done this and why? Those who are a little educated are able to understand why this happened. Whatever happened, it was wrong—terribly wrong).

Across the Borders

Across the state border, in Telangana, I heard many similar stories from those who had fled from Bastar, about the circumstances that made them flee from their homes and villages.

Sudru and Budhram

Sudru and Budhram are from Savnar village (Todka panchayat, Bijapur tehsil). They work as casual labourers in the *mirchi badi* (chilli fields) of Warangal, near the border, and camp on the banks of the Godavari. In the evening when I reached their camping site, I saw about ten blue tents made of simple poles and plastic sheets. Lots of potlis hung from the poles. There were piles of firewood, clothes lines, women and small children everywhere. There was a lot of activity and chatter as people had come home after a hard day's labour and were preparing for dinner.

Sudru said that they had walked for five days to reach there. Each year only the men came, but this year, 'chote-bade sab aye [young and old, everyone came]'. I asked him to explain why they had left their villages. He said, 'Our houses have been burnt, and even the school has been destroyed.' There are three paras in the village, and he estimated that sixty out of eighty houses had been burnt in Patel para, thirty out of sixty in Muka para and all hundred houses in Gunda para. Those who had not come to Telangana were living partly in the village and partly in the forest near their village.

> In September 2005, they burned approximately 100 houses. But we did not run away. We stayed and rebuilt our houses. This [the burning] was repeated the following year, when about 150 houses were burnt. That year, they did not burn the houses in one go. They used to come every ten to twenty days and burn one lot each time. We rebuilt again. In August 2007, they torched all the houses again. Some houses were half-burnt. Since then, some men have stayed in the village but they kept their rice store in the jungle. They were also able to save cows, but not pigs, goats and hens that the Salwa Judum took for their consumption.

Budhram said that his house in Patel para was burnt twice. They had rebuilt it, but it was burnt again. Salwa Judum goondas would come in a group of 100–150 with CRPF, Nagas and SPOs, carrying modern weapons. In the first year, they took around 400 people to the Cherpal camp. They beat up many of those who were taken away and even killed some. They burnt their houses—about 100 of them—two months later.

> People were shocked that their houses were burnt even though they had gone to the camp. We stayed in the camp for another two months and then surreptitiously, giving different reasons, we escaped to our village four km away.

According to Sudru and Budhram, the Salwa Judum and security forces combine killed four people from their village in 2006: Ayta (female, twenty-one years), who was raped and killed on 2 March when she ran away from the police; Punem Unga (male, thirty-five years) whose throat was slit in July when he had gone to another village and was caught there; Hemla Sannu (male, twenty years) who was shot dead in the village on 18 September during one of the Salwa Judum raids; and Kursam Setu (male, sixteen years) who was caught in the village in December, beaten with a stick and killed with a *tangia* (axe). Another four men were killed in 2007: Punem Mangu (fifty years), Hemla Suku (forty years) and Hemla Lachu (forty-five years) were caught and killed the same day in February, and Hemla Budru (thirty years) was stabbed to death in September.

Sudru and Budhram maintained that none of these eight were members of the sangam. While burning their houses, they would be told, '*Tum log Naxalite ko khana khilate ho, sangam mein rahte ho* [You feed the Naxalites and you are in the sangam].'

Uikilakshmi

On 18 November 2006, I met Uikilakshmi, a Dorla woman from Gorkha village (Konta tehsil), in a village close to Mallampeta in Chintur mandal, Khammam district. Uikilakshmi is a typical case among many bewildered Adivasis who were displaced from their village after their houses were burnt and herded into camps, but eventually escaped from the camps. She said that after a neighbouring village Chintagufa was burnt, Salwa Judum activists told them: 'If you do not come with us, your houses will also be burnt.' Later, Gorkha was burnt, along with her house, in broad daylight. Other villages in their neighbourhood like Banda and Murligudem met the same fate. 'They came in large numbers—armed men in uniforms as well as others who were our Adivasis. They burnt our houses because we did not join them,' she said.

Gorkha was a medium-sized mixed village with twenty-five Dorla and thirty Madia houses. People from this village went in three different directions—to the forests, to the camps and to the border. Since Uikilakshmi had relatives in Chintur, she came there with her husband, three children and some cattle, before the monsoon in 2006. 'They took my mother away. My brother managed to run away. My husband and I were made to lie down with our arms stretched out. Then, they stepped on our palms and beat our backs. We went to Injaram camp and stayed there for a month. One day, we told them that we would go to our village and return, and saying this, we ran away. Before Salwa Judum,' she said, '*gaon theek tha* [life in the village was alright]. *Salwa Judum hamare hi log hain* [Salwa Judum is made up of our people only]. Some have gone that side, others have remained as before.'

Later that day, I met another Dorla woman (wife of Madavi Ramu), also in a village close to Mallampeta. She said that she was from a village on the road from Konta to Golapalli, and that she had come to live with her parents around two months earlier because she was scared that the forces (Naga battalion and Salwa Judum) would forcibly take her. She was also sheltering someone else from her village. People from her village had all run away because all the neighbouring villages had been burnt—Gorkha, Banda, Chintagufa. People from some thirty to forty villages in that area had also run away. None of them wanted to go with the 'samiti' in Konta (reference here is to Salwa Judum). '*Kai log bhag gae, kai log junglon-pahadon mein ghoom rahe hain* [Many people ran away, many are roaming about in the forests and hills].' Her brother and mother stayed back to look after the cattle. They did their best to watch their cattle because they were afraid that the Naga force might butcher them for consumption as they had done in some other villages. Her family owned five acres of land. They used to grow paddy and til (sesame) and produced three bags of each annually. While living in the forests, she said, her brother had managed to sow the seeds in their fields that season (in 2006) without getting caught. But they were unable to go to the forests to collect minor produce due to perpetual fear.

Korsa Samta

Korsa Samta, fifth standard pass, belongs to a group of five Madia families from Sarkeguda (Korsaguda panchayat, Bijapur district) that came to Warangal together.

> Salwa Judum came in 2006 and burnt the entire village in one go. In 2007, they came again and caught hold of Chinna Korsa, and took him with them to Basaguda thana. They killed him with a *tangia* and threw his body in a river near Basaguda.

A woman who had seen all this gave the following account.

> After our village was burnt in 2006, people started living elsewhere but would return to the village from time to time to salvage some belongings that had not been burnt. Chinna had also gone back for a similar reason when he was caught. Now there is nobody in the village. After Chinna's death all of us came here. That was a month ago. We shall work for another month and go home.

Home for them, after their village got burnt, is in the jungle. That is where they have settled for now. They have built small shelters, cultivate a little land, and also collect mahua and other forest products for sale.

There was an ashram school in the village, up to the fifth standard. But after the Judum started, children stopped going to school. The *andarwale* (Naxalites) and *gaonwale* (villagers) destroyed the school to prevent the security forces and the Salwa Judum from using it as their base. This happened in many other villages too.

Killings in Camps

As we saw, violence attributed to Salwa Judum includes killings, rapes and torture of many hundreds of local Adivasi men and women besides loot, plunder and decimation of entire villages. The *modus operandi* of Salwa Judum involved coercion at every step—based on the use of direct force as well as indirect means such as intimidation, threats and rule by fear and gun power. The complicity of the civil administration and the impunity enjoyed by the security forces, Salwa Judum and the SPOs have been documented by many human rights organizations.[6]

While more than 500 persons were killed, over 100 women raped and thousands of houses burnt in the first two years (2005 and 2006), the spate of violence continued in the following years, not only in the forests, villages and marketplaces, but even in the camps. I include below two examples of killings by the security forces in two camps of Bijapur district in 2008.

Killings in the Matwada Camp

Three Adivasi inmates of Matwada camp, Bhairamgarh (Bijapur district), were brutally killed in the camp on 18 March 2008: Madkami Mudda, Madkami Deva and Mandavi Hidma. A police press release initially stated that the Maoists had killed them. However, the wives of the victims—who had witnessed the killings and were beaten when they protested—claimed that a police officer from Jangla police station and two SPOs stationed at the same camp were the killers.[7] They wrote to the Superintendent of Police (SP) in Bijapur, requesting that an FIR be lodged. The SP took their oral statement behind closed doors and took their thumb impressions on statements he had drafted himself. Later, when inquiries were made about the FIR, the SP is reported to have said that an FIR had already been lodged against unknown Maoists, so there was no need to lodge another FIR. Later, on 8 April 2008, the wives of the victims and a survivor of the violence filed a writ petition in the High Court at Bilaspur with the help of voluntary organizations.[8]

The Matwada camp was one of eight camps that were set up in Bhairamgarh during the first wave of the Salwa Judum (June–August 2005). In June 2008, the camp had 184 families, including 150 from nearby Kotrapal village. Since this village had cooperated with the Salwa Judum, one would not expect many Kotrapal residents to have lost their lives at the hands of the Salwa Judum. But this is not the case: as many as eleven of them were killed in 2005–06, when the security forces–Salwa Judum combine was trying to 'persuade' people to join them. For good measure, six women were raped and around sixty houses burnt.

If a village has been targeted by the Salwa Judum, one might assume it to be safe from Maoist violence. But that is not the case either. The Maoists have also spilled blood in Kotrapal, albeit of those they call 'people's enemies'. In fact, the killings in the camp on 18 March 2008 were a reaction to earlier killings by the Maoists, of two persons who were caught when they had gone to the village from the camp to plough their land. The incident of 18 March was described as follows by Kudami Somdu, the sole survivor:[9]

A week after Madkami Sukko and Podiyami Maso were killed in front of all the villagers in Kotrapal, the SPOs said that if they met anyone from Kotrapal village, they would kill them. All of us were in the Matwada camp and we decided not to go to the Tuesday bazar out of fear. Around 4 p.m., ten to fifteen SPOs and the thanedar came to [the] camp. Mudda was near the boring and the SPOs asked him to work the hand pump. When he himself bent to drink, they hit him from behind with a stick. Deva, Hidma and I were coming from the stream after having bathed. The SPOs said, 'Come, there is a meeting.' The SPOs took us some distance and hit us all with sticks and rifle butts; after we fell unconscious, water was put on us and we were hit again. Wives of the others came and tried to stop the beating, but the SPOs hit them also. All the SPOs were drunk.

The CRPF was observing all this from a distance and did nothing. Nobody from the camp was allowed to come near us. By this time, it was dark. The other three, Mudda, Deva and Hidma, were tied and taken to a stream nearby. They were first cut with knives and then hit with a big stone. The SPOs then fired in the air so that they could claim there was an encounter and left the bodies there. I somehow managed to escape and went and hid in a neighbouring village. I have been very badly beaten and tortured. After a week, we came to Vanvasi Chetna Ashram and told Himanshu Kumar what had happened. We are no longer safe in Matwada camp. Our families are being threatened for telling the truth. I am scared for my life.

Killings in the Cherpal Camp[10]

The camp inmates reported that the CRPF entered the Cherpal camp (Bijapur district) at 3.30 a.m. on 23 May 2008, started beating on the doors of houses and told people that they should assemble near the road. They were abusing people in filthy language and gave no reason for the sudden summons. Within half an hour, the people gathered. The women were asked to sit on the road and the men in the adjoining field.

The commandant of the CRPF battalion (no. 181) then came out of his barrack and shouted that if any villagers made any sound, they would be shot. The people were sitting quietly when one CRPF officer (Tirupati Rao) abruptly opened fire, killing a twenty-two-year-old woman (Shambai, from Sarkanti village) who was sitting in the front and a three-year old boy (Andrick Raju). Two children, aged three and seven, and a twenty-seven-year old woman were also injured. People started screaming. CRPF forces began a lathi charge, caught four youth and took them to their barracks where they started beating them. By now, angry people surrounded the CRPF barracks. Calm was restored only after the intervention of the SP, who took the four boys with him and promised that they would receive medical treatment. But the story released to the media from his office later states that the four boys were Naxalites who had been caught as they were trying to escape, and that the woman and child had been killed accidentally when the CRPF jawan opened fire at the boys. A case has since been lodged in the High Court of Chhattisgarh.

Impact of Salwa Judum on People's Lives

By 2008, Operation Salwa Judum was drawing to an end. But it had already had a devastating impact on people's lives. The Adivasis of this area, who used to be by and large self-sufficient, were reduced to a life of penury and destitution.

Their situation became such that basic citizenship rights were denied to them on both sides of the state border. Some government policies in this respect are quite astounding. In Konta tehsil, for example, the government had withdrawn development funds (e.g., for education and health) from all the 'inside' villages of the tehsil after Salwa Judum began. Instead, these funds were diverted for the use of people in the camps, as though the government was not responsible for the rest of the population.

Even though the camp dwellers were being provided basic food, education and healthcare, this was at the cost of their freedom and old way of life. They were being kept away from their land and forests. Thousands of hectares of patta land in the tehsil lay vacant until 2007–08 when the situation started normalizing somewhat, though not for long, besides the forest lands which the Adivasis had also been cultivating for generations and for which they still did not have pattas.

Purchasing power also decreased because the Adivasis were no longer able to go and collect non-timber forest produce such as tamarind, tendu, mahua, honey, etc. This was an important source of income and sustenance and enabled them to acquire simple items in exchange. Further, many local markets shut down and some traders also decided to wind up business and moved out after the Salwa Judum offensive began. This also had an adverse effect on the local economy.

Those who ran away to the forests or across the state borders have been living uncertain lives. Those living on the borders, for example in the forests of Khammam, are having to face the wrath of forest department officials in Telangana who have burnt their huts— in some hamlets not once but many times. The situation of these 'internally displaced people' is very serious. Their condition is not recognized by the government since India does not have a policy for the conflict-induced displaced, therefore, destitute though they may be, they are ineligible even for the meagre benefits available to other rural citizens: the public distribution system, employment under public works programmes, education and health facilities, and so on. In time, a couple of NGOs started working with them. They have found, in the course of their work, that hunger and malnutrition is widespread amongst them.

The social fabric of the Adivasi society has also been severely ruptured. Communities, villages and even families have been divided. The psychological impact on the population is anyone's guess since the violence that the people of this region have seen or endured since 2005 is unprecedented.

From 'Purification Hunt' to 'Green Hunt'

Despite its brutality, the Salwa Judum operation did not succeed in crushing the Maoist movement in Bastar—far from it. In fact, it drove many more Adivasis into the Maoist fold, and the movement expanded into new areas. State repression was seen as an unjustified assault on ordinary villagers. Salwa Judum activists and the security forces would tell people that 'you are either with us or with them', but the response was not always what they expected. Those who went with the forces voluntarily or involuntarily were blacklisted by the Maoists. In order to avoid the camps, people had no alternative but to flee across the state border, hide in the jungle, or align with the Maoists. It was often a collective response—in Adivasi society, people tend to stick together.

As the Salwa Judum started faltering, there was a realignment of security forces around 2008. Civilian actors were gradually replaced by or turned into SPOs, who had been recruited from late 2005 onwards. The role that had been played by the IRB from Nagaland and later Mizoram was increasingly taken over by the CRPF. Suddenly, we started hearing about Operation Green Hunt and a new wave of state repression in Adivasi areas under Maoist influence.

We also started hearing about Operation Green Hunt from Maoist areas of other states including Odisha, Jharkhand and Maharashtra. This term does not seem to be officially acknowledged, but its mission is to crush the Maoists by force quickly and decisively. The 'purification hunt' (Salwa Judum) in Bastar had given way to Green Hunt.

In practical terms, this meant killing Maoists or presumed Maoists in encounters real or fake, using devious means to make some of them 'surrender', turning surrendered Maoists against their former comrades, throwing suspected sympathizers in jail under fabricated charges, setting up numerous paramilitary camps across the region, and as far as possible, silencing all dissenting voices in Bastar.

Aside from routine encounters, there were shocking instances where many Adivasis were killed in the course of an attack. Just to illustrate, two massacres occurred in quick succession in a small area of Sukma (then part of Dantewada district) in late 2009—in Gachanpalli on 17 September and Gompad on 1 October.[11] Both villages are located in the Konta tehsil, an area considered a Maoist stronghold. In Gachanpalli, six villagers were brutally killed including elderly persons (see below). In Gompad, seven persons were killed including three women and a twelve-year old girl. The fingers of an infant were allegedly chopped after his mother who was carrying him was attacked and killed. According to eyewitnesses, this massacre was perpetrated by SPOs.

In both cases, the police made strenuous efforts to prevent witnesses from speaking freely. I experienced this myself when I tried to meet Sodi Sambo, one of the main witnesses of the Gompad massacre, in Maharani Hospital in Jagdalpur where she had been admitted due to a bullet wound in her leg. The women's ward and even the corridor leading to it were heavily guarded by police and it is only after much argument and insistence that I was allowed to go inside the ward, with the strict instruction that I could 'see' Sodi Sambo but not speak to her. Later, she disappeared, apparently whisked away by the police.[12]

These are just some of the more prominent incidents in the series of atrocities that happened in that period. They are not the worst—an even worse massacre reportedly happened in Singaram on 8 January 2009, involving the 'alleged killing of seventeen tribals including four women in an alleged encounter between a group of naxalites and a police party' according to the National Human Rights Commission.[13] As one might expect, the Maoists reacted to this new wave of terror strongly. Among other major acts of retaliation is the Tadmetla ambush of 6 April 2010, when seventy-six jawans lost their lives. Hundreds of them had gone on a searching and combing operation and were on their way back when the ambush happened. This was a period of successive operations and ambushes from both sides.

In March 2011, another major operation was launched against the Maoists. In Sukma area, reports and images appeared of hundreds of houses being burnt and women being assaulted in Tadmetla, Morpalli and Timmapuram. When Swami Agnivesh and others tried to reach the affected villages, they were stopped and roughed up.[14] Soon after, a team of human rights activists (including myself) and journalists were successful in taking three tractors full of rice, lentils and jaggery for the affected population of the three villages. It was a sad statement of the times that we could not take a straight route to deliver the food but had to take a longer back route with constant fear of being stopped by the security forces. We saw the burnt houses and the rice stores that had been reduced to ashes. The list of relief recipients was the first reliable estimate of the number of houses burnt. When a government thinks nothing of burning the rice stocks of poor Adivasi households, can it really hope to win people's support?

Operation Green Hunt was no more successful than Salwa Judum in weaning Adivasis away from the Maoists, but it did intensify the militarization of the Bastar region and unleash a new wave of oppression.

The Gachanpalli Massacre

It took a long journey by foot and bicycle to reach Gachanpalli, an interior village of Dantewada (now in Sukma district).[15] The nearest pacca road is 32 km away. This Adivasi village of about ninety houses of Dorla and Madia Gond spread over four paras was bereft of all basic facilities except a lone functional handpump. Most people in this village had no ration card or voter ID. Their children were not immunised. The village used to have a school, but it was demolished by the Maoists for fear that it might be used by the security forces.

When we reached the village in early November 2009, it looked deserted. Perhaps most people had fled after the massacre of 17 September. After some time, we found two men in the nearby forest, Mada and Raja. They told us what had happened that day. Mada, sixty-seven years old, was lucky to get away with a severe beating:

> It was not yet dawn and we were still in bed when they came. They were about a hundred of them, all in uniform. All of them were speaking in Hindi. I cannot say whether there were any Adivasis with them or not. They caught me and beat me badly with an *uspal* (a rod used to pound rice). They also caught six elderly women of this para, tied us all to each other with a rope and marched us to the jungle. We were near Koliguda when it started raining heavily. Everyone ran for cover, and in the confusion, we were able to escape. Hiding and running, we somehow came back.

Mada showed me an X-ray (dated 13 October 2009) of his broken ribs. The women had also been beaten. Others had a worse fate, as Raja explained.

> My father Joga and at least four others were killed that day. After the force arrived, my father expected them to burn the house, so he started throwing our belongings outside in order to save them. But they caught up with him, shot him in the side of the neck and also put a knife through his side.

Mada and Raja related some of the other killings as follows. Madkam Sula (sixty years old) was going to his field that morning to set the cows free to graze when he saw the Force. They called him. When he went to them, he was knifed and shot at from close range.

Madavi Adma (in his early thirties) was getting ready to plough his field when he was caught by the Force. They used the cow rope that he was carrying to tie his hands behind his back. He was then taken to the open space that is used as a dancing floor by the village youth and made to lie down. His clothes were taken off, his private parts cut, and then he was knifed and shot.

Kawasi Ganga (a half-blind seventy-year old man) was awake and sitting on his *khat* (string cot) when he was caught, knifed and shot.

Dudhi Muye (a seventy-five-year old woman who could barely walk) was also killed. Raja said that her breasts were cut, a knife was thrust through her, and then she was shot.

Aside from killing these five and beating many others that day, the Force also looted thirteen Madia houses and then set them on fire. They did not even spare the rice stores.

According to Mada and Raja, nobody from this village had ever been jailed. Nobody joined the Salwa Judum, nor did anyone become an SPO. Nobody joined the Naxalites either. They said that after the incident the Naxalites had come once, saw what had happened, and went.

I asked them why they thought they were targetted? They said, 'We don't know. While beating us, the Force was telling us that "you people feed the Naxalites".'

Later, we found some local residents in one of the paras of Gachanpalli and talked to them together. We heard further stories of brutality on 17 September. For instance, one woman related how her husband, who had sought refuge in a tamarind tree out of fear, was shot from below.

The gratuitous cruelty of these killings is shocking even by Bastar standards, and may seem unbelievable. But these accounts are consistent with independent testimonies collected later by *The*

Hindu,[16] and also with further testimonies submitted to the Supreme Court by residents of Gachanpalli.[17] It is possible that this rampage was a case of blind revenge for a Maoist ambush: early media reports suggest that six police personnel were killed the same day in that area in an encounter with the Maoists.[18] Whatever their reason, nothing can excuse this sort of atrocities.

Judging the Judgment on Salwa Judum[19]

On 5 July 2011, the Supreme Court pronounced what is widely seen as 'a landmark judgment' on Salwa Judum. This judgment was the culmination of a prolonged PIL aimed at restraining state atrocities in the area.[20] Written in an easy style, the judgment has many parts which warm one up, as one does in the company of the like-minded. A full reading makes one concur, even applaud, but on quieter consideration, some gaps register and call for a comment.

The judgment has two important aspects. First is the banning of Salwa Judum. Second is the disarming and discontinuation of SPOs (Special Police Officers) in combat operations. Thus, Salwa Judum and vigilante movements of a similar character that the state may create, support or use against insurgent movements are no longer tenable. Such movements would be deemed to be what they are—unconstitutional. A person like Mahendra Karma, for instance, will not be able to be the leader of the opposition in the Chhattisgarh state assembly—as he was in 2005—as well as a leader of Salwa Judum, nor will government officials or representatives be able to hobnob with the Salwa Judum brethren under the open sky. The prohibitory order on the functioning of SPOs in combat operations will help to ensure that local tribal youth are not pitted against other tribal people and guerrillas, thus reducing the risk of their becoming human shields for the paramilitary or soft targets for the Maoists. Besides, SPOs and SPO-like formations exist in other conflict areas of the country and this ruling is likely to have far-reaching consequences in undoing such aberrations as well as in underlining the limits of what can be construed as 'legitimate' counterinsurgency in a democracy.

Who is Culpable?

However, the question remains whether removing these two actors—Salwa Judum and SPOs—from the war scenario in Dantewada would rein in all the perpetrators of large-scale human rights violations? To my mind, the main culprits are the security forces, who escaped unscathed in the judgment. Except for some allusion to them in the philosophical-contextual preamble, the judgment makes no mention of the Indian Reserve Battalions (IRB) or the CRPF, not to speak of the other state and district level forces (including the police) that are deployed in Bastar and played the leading role in the excesses that occurred. Salwa Judum, even when it had full teeth, was only an assistant. The beatings, killings, rapes, arson and other atrocities that happened during that season of indiscriminate, ruthless and relentless violence were not the work of Salwa Judum alone.

In their accounts of these events, the survivors typically mention both the 'force' (sometimes more specifically Nagas, CRPF, and so on) and the Judum as part of the mob that descended on their village. Sometimes, the term 'Judum' is used as a composite term that includes both. The 'force' was always there.

The SPOs came on the scene in late 2005 and were pressed into combat operations actively the following year. They included some erstwhile members of the Judum, sons and daughters of camp dwellers who often joined for lack of another source of income (camp inmates were not free to seek work outside), others who also needed employment, and some ex-Maoists or victims of Maoist actions who had a personal axe to grind. In discussions of excesses that occurred in the post-SPO phase, people would still refer to the 'Judum', but on further probing it often turned out that they meant the *vardi wale* (those in uniform, the SPOs). This was also because of the close relationship that existed between the local Salwa Judum leaders and the SPOs; these leaders played a key role in the administration of the camps and were perhaps (at least some of them) in the inner circle of official planning. The SPOs and the Salwa Judum, thus, often became interchangeable in popular perception.

Deliberate Strategy

As we saw, what occurred in 2005–06 was part of the Indian state's deliberate counterinsurgency strategy of 'strategic hamletting', in which Salwa Judum became a partner. The success of such a strategy rests first and foremost on granting impunity to the forces; an impunity that, in this case, was also extended to the SPOs and the civilian partner, Salwa Judum. All these actors together—but principally the security forces and the masterminds behind and above—turned this area into a 'heart of darkness', as the judgment aptly describes it. The Armed Forces Special Powers Act (AFSPA) did not apply to these parts, but the ground reality was as though it did.

Consider, for instance, the following conversation I had with a relatively friendly member of the 'Naga force' in Injaram camp in November 2006 (he had been there for a month or so).

I began by asking him what his duty was.

'To protect the people in the camp and to provide them relief.'

'How were these camps formed?'

'People here used to live with the Naxalites. The government said we should gather them all together [*ek saath jama karna hai*]. When we went to the villages, people used to run away. We would catch them and check whether they are [with the Naxalites]—*sangam wala hai ya dalam wala hai.*'

'How did you identify them as such?'

'With the help of the sarpanch.'

'What else did you do when you went to the villages?'

'We asked people—do you want to live or die? We burnt many houses.'

'Why?' I asked.

'Because if we burn their house, they come here [to the camps]— *jalae toh yahaan aate.*'

'Did you also burn houses afterwards?'

'Yes. If we don't burn the houses, then they will run away. And in many villages, we burnt houses again, to prevent the Naxals from living there.'

'When you go to the jungle, what do you do?'

'If we meet someone who is in the sangam or dalam, we kill him.'

'If someone is in a uniform, with a gun, but he is not using his gun, will you kill him?'

'Yes, we kill him.'

'If he is in a uniform, but doesn't have a gun, will you kill?'

'Yes, we kill.'

'What if you meet a villager who is not in uniform?'

'We stop him and talk [*discuss karte*]. Then we kill.'

'Why?'

'Because if it was just a member of the public, he would be with the Judum.'

'Those who are in the sangam, why don't you just arrest them?'

(He could not relate to the notion of 'arrest' and was non-committal even when I used other words like *giraftar*.)

This was the 'rule of law' in Bastar then, as it is now, under the aegis of Operation Greenhunt, initiated by the Indian government in mid-2009 in the tribal areas (starting again from Bastar), despite the dismal failure of its strategy in the first phase of the war against the Maoists there. This failure undermined the operation's very raison d'être. For not only did violence in the region increase manifold in comparison to the pre-2005 phase, the strength of the Maoists and the areas under their influence also expanded.

The judgment, in its wisdom, accepts that people do not take up arms 'for no rhyme or reason'. Indeed, the systemic failure to uphold constitutional ideals and values in these regions, which was the main reason for people joining the Maoists, got compounded many times by the direct state violence in the post-2005 period. It changed people's lives to such an extent that they could no longer recognize their old life in its tattered remains. The 'people's war' found recruits at an unprecedented speed—recruits who are fighting for a revolutionary change to their circumstances in the here and now.

Surprisingly, Operation Greenhunt finds no mention in the judgment. The judgment banned the Salwa Judum, which by then was already in the past tense. Banning the 'idea' of Salwa Judum, or what it was, is not without value and has wider implications. But banning something which is causing harm now in the same way has a different value. Salwa Judum was deemed unconstitutional, but Operation Greenhunt—the present face and phase of the war—was not?

Foot Soldiers

SPOs are the foot soldiers in this war. Their number (a few thousands) is small in comparison to the total number of the central, state and district forces. Even though the State is squirming after the judgment regarding the SPOs, it is not clear how deep the discomfort really is. Its character is such that it may get round this hitch by regularizing them, for there is no restriction on recruitment of tribals in the police force or a bar on police expansion. The average of 200 'encounter' killings that Andhra Pradesh saw annually for more than a decade in its fight against the People's War Group did not need SPOs.

The judgment rightly points out that far more SPOs have been killed and injured than paramilitary or police personnel (in proportion to the strength of each force), and it is commendable that it should seek to protect young tribals from being killed as 'cannon fodder' in this war. But if the state continues to give people reasons to join an armed revolt against it, young tribals will still get killed like ants. Tribal combatants have been getting killed on both sides—as SPOs, tribal guerrillas and jan-militia—besides the many tribal non-combatants who are getting killed in this war. The army training school that is being set up in Abujhmad and the recent army announcement that it would strike back in 'defensive' actions suggest preparations for a long battle. Viewed thus, if the Supreme Court does not take—in its orders—a wide angle view but restricts itself only to the SPOs, then it is like saying: 'You can keep the AK-47s but you'll have to give up on the desi kattas [country-made pistols]!'

Indictment

The judgment is an indictment of some aspects of the modus operandi of the war—not the war itself.[21] This war between the state and the Maoists is a disproportionate and amoral war. It is disproportionate because there was little in the Maoist movement, until the early 2000s, that called for such warfare. It is amoral because it seeks to protect what the judges have called the 'amoral political economy' of the Indian state. The Planning Commission document *Development Challenges in Extremist Affected Areas*[22] quoted in the judgment had warned against such a war, based as it is on a 'security-centric' view concerned more with state security than with people's security, which rests in protecting their interests and rights. Such a strategy, the report maintained, 'delegitimizes politics, dehumanizes people, degenerates those engaged in their 'security', and above all, represents abdication of the state itself. It should be undone immediately . . .' But the government chose to ignore the report's recommendations and to go ahead full blast with its belligerent policies and militarization of tribal areas. How will these get 'ordered' out?

Postscript (2023)

As this book goes to press, in mid-2023, the situation in Bastar is not very different from what it was in 2011. Soon after the Supreme Court judgement on Salwa Judum in that year, the SPOs were disbanded, but then inducted almost immediately (except for some who were underage) into a new police force created for this purpose, the Chhattisgarh Auxiliary Force. What was not disbanded in the judgement or in practice was the impunity granted to the paramilitary and police forces at the time of the Salwa Judum operation. Salwa Judum was followed by other counter-insurgency operations including Operation Green Hunt, Operation Haka, Operation Prahar, Operation Samadhan, and so on, and the impunity was extended without a hiccup to the new forces that were created for these operations be it the Koya Commandos, District Reserve Guards or Bastar Fighters (amongst others), in which local tribals—including surrendered Maoists—were recruited to be the eyes, ears, hands and at times even shields of the paramilitary (CRPF). A tribal battalion of the CRPF was also created, called the Bastar Battalion. Every time a new force is announced, local youth—men and women—queue up in thousands to join, as an employment opportunity. The large number of those who do not make it become vulnerable, for they have earned the suspicion and displeasure of the Maoists for wanting to join the police ranks.[23]

Over the long years of conflict, Adivasi communities at the village level have got badly divided. The cohesion and community life that Adivasis had achieved over centuries, a marker of the Adivasi way of life, are now much weakened in conflict-torn areas of Bastar. Adivasis have been forced to take sides and have been targeted for the side they chose to support. The uniforms on both sides hold bodies, a large number of whom are of local Adivasis—insurgents and counter-insurgents. The Maoist movement in Bastar is mostly an Adivasi movement, based on local recruits. In village after village, there are stories of people who have been killed or incarcerated as alleged Maoists or Maoist sympathizers. Likewise, in the towns, there are colonies of displaced Adivasis who were forced to vacate their homes and fields by the Maoists, or left of their own accord, for their safety.

The government proudly claims that it has a three-pronged strategy to counter the Maoists: *vishwas, vikas* and *suraksha* (trust, development and security). However, it has failed on each front because its definition of each of these is its own and ignores the views of the largely Adivasi population of this region. The political representatives of the Adivasis in the State Assembly and the Parliament, who are Adivasis themselves, toe the party line, be it the BJP or the Congress. The roots of the conflict remain unaddressed. Worse, the state continues to fan discontent amongst the Adivasis by trampling upon their basic rights over local resources—*jal, jungle, jameen* and now *khanij* (water, forest, land, minerals)—in favour of corporate interests. People's protests are quelled by brute force, or simply by ignoring their legitimate demands even when they are made through peaceful means.

When the Congress came to power in Chhattisgarh in 2018, after three terms of BJP governments, one of the promises it had made to the electorate (in its manifesto) was to initiate a political dialogue with the Maoists. This promise was not kept. Instead, the state has continued to militarize the area and rely on the use of force.

The Wheels of Justice

Periodic incidents of human rights violations have continued unabated after 2011, including fake encounters, sexual violence, fabricated cases and routine harassment. Some illustrations are included in the next three chapters. Even when the scale of state-committed crimes was colossal, the wheels of justice remained rusted and skewed. The effort of the state was to maintain the status quo.

Sarkeguda and Edesmetta Massacres

Two notorious examples are the massacres that occurred in Sarkeguda and Edesmetta (Bijapur district) in the intervening nights of 28–29 June 2012 and 17–18 May 2013 respectively.[24] In Sarkeguda, seventeen civilians including six minors were gunned down by CRPF personnel when security forces on a night operation mistook a peaceful assembly for Maoists. In Edesmetta, eight civilians including four minors were killed when CRPF personnel opened fire on a peaceful gathering celebrating the Beeja Pandum, a local seed festival prior to the beginning of the agricultural cycle.

In both cases, a judicial commission was formed to probe the incident. The Sarkeguda incident was probed by a one-man commission consisting of a retired judge of the Madhya Pradesh High Court, V.K. Agarwal. The report, submitted in late 2019, rejects the police claim that the victims were Maoists killed in an encounter ('the incident did not take place as is being described by [the] Security Forces').[25] It concludes, instead, that they were civilians killed at close range. The report also notes that one of the victims, Irpa Ramesh, was beaten and killed on the morning of 29 June, well after the alleged encounter. The night firing was attributed to a 'panic reaction' when the security forces chanced on the gathering in an area where Maoists were suspected of being active.

The Edesmetta incident was also probed by a one-man commission, consisting of the same retired judge. The commission's report was submitted to the Chhattisgarh government in September 2021 and tabled in the State Assembly in March 2022. The report concludes that those assembled in Edesmetta on 17 May 2013 were unarmed civilians and blames the security forces for the killings, possibly due to 'panic firing'.[26] The commission's conclusions are consistent with those of an earlier investigation of the Human Rights Forum (2013).[27]

These two massacres are noteworthy not only for their heavy toll but also for the fact that both were thoroughly probed by a judicial commission, unlike many other incidents of this sort. The commission reports clearly hold the security forces responsible. In spite of this, no action has been taken against anyone for these massacres.

Fabricated Cases, Jails and Courts

It is no secret that countless Adivasis in Bastar have been jailed under fabricated charges, often draconian, and that many of them languish in jail as their trials drag on for years. Even if most are eventually acquitted, the process is a harsh punishment. In March 2019, the Congress government in Chhattisgarh formed a committee chaired by a retired Supreme Court judge, Justice A.K. Patnaik, to examine the possibility of securing the release of *nirdosh adivasi* (innocent tribals), a telling admission that many Adivasi undertrials were victims of fabricated charges. The committee, however, restricted itself to those who were charged under sections that carried a punishment of up to seven years. Within the confines of this self-imposed restriction, it was able to provide relief only in excise cases and made no real difference to 'Naxali' cases since most of them invite a punishment of more than seven years.

Aside from Jagdalpur Central Jail, there are several jails and sub-jails in Bastar, with around 3500 inmates, most of them Adivasis. Most of these jails are overcrowded well beyond capacity. Only a small fraction of the inmates are convicts, the rest are undertrials. Working as a human rights lawyer in the District and Sessions Courts of Bastar in the last few years has given me a clearer view of the criminal justice system. I have been able to better understand how Naxalite cases work: the false nature of accusations in the FIRs, the continuance of falsehood in the chargesheets, and the often excruciatingly slow trial process.

After a Maoist attack or incident be it an ambush, IED blast or encounter, the FIR is usually made out against *agyat* (unknown) persons, allowing the police to arrest a large number of people on mere suspicion from the surrounding areas, and to charge them under various sections of the IPC along with the Arms Act, the Explosive Substances Act, and special security legislations such as the Chhattisgarh Special Public Security Act, 2005 (CSPSA) and Unlawful Activities (Prevention) Act, 1967 (UAPA). The UAPA and many CSPSA cases are tried in the National Investigation Agency (NIA) courts. In these cases, as well as in other Naxalite cases, the complainant, the investigating officer and most witnesses tend to be part of the police and security forces. The speed of the trial, therefore, depends on the availability and cooperation of the police, including officers who may have been transferred far away. Typically, summons have to be sent many times before witnesses appear in court, causing endless delay. The cases drag on for years.

A telling example of justice delayed is the Burkapal case, which caused 121 accused (all Adivasis except one) to spend five years in jail before they were all acquitted.[28] They had been arbitrarily rounded up and charged under the UAPA as well as other Acts and IPC in 2017, after a Maoist ambush in Burkapal (Sukma district) where twenty-five CRPF jawans lost their lives. During these five years, they were produced in court just twice—once at the initial stage and once for examination—when it is mandatory to produce the accused in person at every hearing. Despite Bastar being the most militarized zone in the country next to Jammu and Kashmir, the excuse given each time was that there were not enough police personnel to accompany the accused to court. The Burkapal case is a symbol of the grave injustices being done to the Adivasis of Bastar in the name of anti-Maoist operations.

As undertrials languish in jail, their families endure the worst hardships. They have to make frequent long trips to the courts and jails, often in vain, with no money for food or stay. Most are Gonds who may not know Hindi and have difficulties communicating with the non-Gondi speaking lawyers, and have no clue as to what is happening in the court since lawyers rarely take the time to explain even if they are able to communicate. Often, the families have to sell their meagre belongings to cover the court-related expenses. They are rarely informed about legal-aid facilities, such as they are.

When cases don't move, people's lives get held up. This feeling of being stuck in a stagnant pool, the murky workings of which are obscure to them, can also take a toll on the mental health of prisoners and their family members. For a human-rights lawyer, it becomes hard to explain the delays and keep hope alive. Bail, a possible relief, is rarely granted in these cases and almost never to those charged under the UAPA. This is so common that it has become unwritten law.

Often, helpless families of undertrials fall prey to false promises from unscrupulous lawyers and end up parting with large sums of money. Bail applications and the promise of a speedy trial are a sure bait. These lawyers, in turn, corrupt the system by paying bribes—to the clerk for an early hearing, to witnesses for singing to their tune, or even to some judges. Law practice becomes a business, dashing all hopes of justice being achieved through fair means.

Militarization, Mining and Protests

Camps and Mining

Unbeknown to the Indian public, the Bastar region has been the site of epic public protests during the last few years. The main issue is the proliferation of para-military camps across Bastar—there are 142 as of now according to Inspector General of Police,[29] and more are being built or planned. There have been peaceful mass protests against these camps at multiple sites (at least two dozen), sometimes lasting for months or even years.

One of these protests, in Silger village of Sukma district, has made history of sorts. A police camp had been set up there in the dead of night on 12 May 2021, without informing the villagers let alone seeking their consent through a gram sabha or otherwise. From 14 to 16 May, large numbers of women and men from Silger and neighbouring villages assembled in protest outside the camp. Every day the police tried to disperse them, sometimes with lathis, sometimes with *mirchi pataka* (pepper sprays) or tear gas. On 17 May, there was a lathi charge, some protesters started throwing stones, tensions rose, and then the police fired on the crowd.[30] Three protestors were killed on the spot (one of them just sixteen or seventeen years old), at least another three had bullet injuries and as many as forty were injured.[31] The families filed a police complaint immediately and there were huge protests, prompting the Chief Minister to promise that an SDM enquiry would be completed and made public within a month. However, nothing happened afterwards. Not only was that camp retained but another one was set up in the village, again by stealth. The powerful Silger protest, however, gave birth to a sea of struggles in the area and the formation of the Moolvasi Bachao Manch, which has now spread all over the Bastar division. Membership of the Manch is mainly of youth who were children at the time of Salwa Judum and important witnesses of those times. These youngsters are now seeking to bring about a change through peaceful means, but rather than listen to them the state has chosen to repress the movement and even label it as a front of the Maoists! A person or an organisation should be judged by what they do—actions speak louder than words. Why, then, does a democratic government continue to use force (e.g. burning of the *dharna manch*, forcible eviction, lathi charge, and threats or false charges against leaders) as a substitute for dialogue with its citizens?

The police camps in Bastar serve a dual purpose. On one hand, they help to crush the Maoist movement. On the other, they pave the way for mining operations. Only the first purpose is officially acknowledged, but the second may be more important. Indeed, with or without the Maoist movement, mining operations are bound to encounter massive resistance in this overwhelmingly Adivasi area where mining is an existential threat for local communities. The camps are making the area safe for mining interests.

The government sometimes claims that camps are needed for the purpose of building roads, viewed as necessary for local development. The real purpose of roads, however, is often to facilitate mining. That is why wide roads are being built, in an area where few people have a motorbike let alone a car. Adivasis in Bastar do not generally oppose small link roads—in fact, they often welcome them. But many do oppose wide roads that encroach on their land, destroy the environment and pave the way for mining companies. If mining interests were not involved, there would be no need for wide roads, and link roads could be built without opposition, obviating the alleged need for camps on this count.

Most of the camps are set up without due process, as are the mines. Quite often, they are set up in the middle of the night without consulting or even informing local communities, as happened in Silger. This is a gross violation of their right to prior informed consent under PESA and the Forest Rights Act. Further, the creation of a camp almost invariably exposes local communities to harassment, brutality, theft, sexual exploitation, arbitrary arrests and worse. This is the main reason why Adivasis oppose the camps as well as mining operations.

Intensified Militarization

Militarization in Bastar continues to intensify today with new tactics, operations and technologies. Among recent developments is the use of drones for extensive surveillance. On several occasions, it seems that drones have also been used to facilitate aerial bombing or firing. This happened in southern areas of Sukma and Bijapur districts on 11 January and 7 April 2023 respectively, and on two earlier occasions as well.[32] Security forces contest these reports, but people's testimonies leave little room for doubt that some sort of aerial bombing or firing occurred there.

The fallout of militarization can be felt by villagers in unexpected ways, not only in conflict areas. One morning in April 2022, one of my neighbours in a settlement on the outskirts of Dantewada town, who is an anganwadi helper, showed me a video clip of miniature rockets that small children had picked up that morning and brought to the anganwadi, thinking they were toys. She and the anganwadi teacher asked the children where they had found these objects and went to the spot, where other remnants were found. The anganwadi teacher informed her husband, who is a policeman. When thana personnel came to investigate, their first instruction was not to touch these objects. After insistent enquiries, we learnt that these objects were expired 'para-bombs' that had been taken to a pit near the Dankini river the previous night, along with other expired explosives, to be defused (intermittent sounds of explosion were heard that night in the neighbourhood). These para-bombs are used by security forces for signalling purposes. They are certainly not meant to fall into the hands of children, even after they have 'expired'. In the course of being defused, some of these para-bombs had flown as far as the village grove.

In this instance, the ammunitions had been defused, or so we were told. But this is not always the case. Later the same year, on a visit to Bhurji (Bijapur district) where people had been agitating against a camp, a farmer told me that he had found an object in his field a few days earlier and that he had not handed it over to the police for fear of being labelled as a Maoist. He showed it to me, and it was also a para-bomb. We informed the police and handed it over to the thana police personally. When the Bomb Disposal Squad (BDS) team eventually defused the para-bomb in front of us, we understood that it was still live.

War without Witness

The first casualty of war is truth. In Bastar, too, relentless efforts have been made to suppress dissenting voices ever since the war began. At the time of Salwa Judum and Operation Green Hunt, there was an atmosphere of intense fear and it was almost impossible for outsiders to move in interior villages of Bastar or even in smaller towns. In those days, local journalists who dared to speak out were targeted by the police and Salwa Judum, as happened to Kamlesh Paikra and Afzal Khan in Bijapur and Sanjay Reddy in Konta. Independent local organizations were few and even a Gandhian NGO like Vanvasi Chetna Ashram (VCA) that had been working in the region for many years, often in collaboration with the government, was targeted after it started aiding visiting investigative teams and later itself raising questions about the brutality of Salwa Judum in courts and otherwise. The Ashram was demolished in 2009. Javed Iqbal, then a freelance journalist, was beaten during the demolition of the Ashram. He continued to work in Bastar until 2011, when threats of a false case began to follow him. Kartam Joga, one of the petitioners in the composite petition against Salwa Judum in the Supreme Court, was jailed under a false murder charge and spent twenty-nine months in prison before being acquitted in January 2013.

This pattern of quelling dissent continued later on, and extended not only to journalists and social workers but also to lawyers and researchers. For several years, police repression was led by the then Inspector General of Police (IG), S.R.P. Kalluri, who used unarmed civilian vigilante forces like the Samajik Ekta Manch, Mahila Ekta Manch and later the Action Group for National Integrity (AGNI) to hound those who were raising uncomfortable questions and were seen as Maoist sympathizers.[33] In 2015, local journalists Santosh Yadav and Somaro Nag were incarcerated under false charges, as was Prabhat Singh in March 2016. Also in early 2016, threats and other tactics were used to build pressure on Jagdalpur-based journalist

Malini Subramaniam of Scroll and the Jagdalpur Legal Aid group (JagLAG), until they left Bastar. BBC's Chhattisgarh correspondent, Alok Putul, also received threats around this time and had to leave Bastar half-way through an assignment. Many other local journalists faced threats and harassment in those days including Anil Mishra, Kamal Shukla, Lingaram Kodopi and Mangal Kunjam. During this period, Adivasi activist Soni Sori too was being harassed through diverse means including an attack on her using a corrosive substance in early 2016. Also in 2016, four members of an independent fact-finding team (Archana Prasad, Nandini Sundar, Vineet Tiwari and Sanjay Parate) were harassed in the form of an absurd murder charge that was later dropped by the Chhattisgarh government, after the National Human Rights Commission intervened.[34]

I had a taste of this repression myself beginning in October 2015, when my landlord in Jagdalpur told me that I would have to move out without giving a good reason (he was a tailor who made police and CRPF uniforms). I moved to a rented house in Parpa village, close to Jagdalpur. In March 2016, a hostile rally was taken outside that house and pressure was built on my Adivasi landlady to evict me. A leaflet calling me a *Naxali dalal* (Naxal agent) was also distributed in the area. In the following months, harassment continued through other means, the most dramatic being the simultaneous effigy burning of civilian actors (including myself) by the police in several locations in Bastar. Other means included anonymous threatening letters sent to me through the local sarpanch and snatching of my mobile in September 2016 when I was covering the massive anti-Maoist Lalkaar rally in Jagdalpur, organized by AGNI with police patronage. Finally, in January 2017, a police-sponsored vigilante group attacked my house in Parpa and tried to drive me away from Bastar. This happened within hours of my return from Bijapur, where I had assisted a visiting NHRC team that was investigating the Peddagelur and Bellamlendra rape and sexual assault cases by the security forces (see Chapter 18, Rape by the Way).[35] In September

2019, I discovered that I was among those who had come under intense surveillance (almost certainly from the Indian government) after their phones had been hacked using the infamous Pegasus software.

I had a bitter experience of the ordeals involved in seeking justice when I sought action against those who had attacked my house. I filed an FIR and provided ample evidence (photo, vehicle number, etc.) to the police and the court of the facts of the incident and the identity of some of the miscreants. The police also had direct evidence since they had started video recording as soon as they reached the site (a clip of this video was circulated by an AGNI member), but they chose to ignore it and applied for *khatma* (closure) of the file on grounds of lack of evidence in late October 2017. The case was heard in the CJM's court, but the court also chose to look the other way. The absurdity of the legal process came to the fore one day on a hearing date of the khatma, when the mob leader was also produced. It was his hearing date too, in another case. I pointed at him in front of the CJM and said: 'Sir, he is the person who was leading the mob!' I was astounded when he replied: 'I can't do anything about that; my task is to decide whether the case should be closed or not.' I was not surprised when the CJM upheld the closure in April 2019, as did the Court of Appeal in Jagdalpur in September 2021.

This is just a small sample of the numerous attempts that were made to suppress dissent in Bastar over the years. The Indian government—with full cooperation of the state government—has done its best to turn counter-insurgency operations in Bastar into a 'war without witness'.[36]

The Brunt of Maoist Violence

The problematic aspects of 'revolutionary violence', discussed in the previous chapter, apply to the Maoist struggle in Bastar. Besides violent incidents like IED blasts, ambushes aimed at the security forces, and the occasional loss of lives of many civilians killed as 'collateral damage' in a Maoist action, there are more everyday types of deliberate killing.[37] In this last category are the chilling deaths, reported only too frequently in local newspapers, of the alleged *police mukhbir* (police informers). But police informers are not the only targets of Maoist violence.

Just to mention a few personal memories here. In 2008, when I was trying to understand Salwa Judum, I once spoke to some children in Bhopalpatnam, Bijapur district. One of them described how her father was captured, tied, dragged at some distance from the house and then beaten to death. While hearing this, I kept thinking that she was referring to the Salwa Judum. But later it dawned on me that the child was actually speaking about the Maoists.

In Kutru, one of the areas (also in Bijapur district) where dissent against the Maoists had started, I came across a young woman who had become an anganwadi teacher. She described how her father and brother, who were sleeping in the verandah of the house, were killed by Maoists. She and the other women of the house were sleeping in the inner room. They clung to the rods of the sole window of the room, from where they could see what was happening, pleading with the Maoists that they should spare their lives. '*Mat maro, mat maro* [stop hitting],' they kept shouting. But their pleas fell on deaf ears. She said that her last memory of her father was of him cowering against the wall, bare-chested, with his arms raised to protect himself from the blows before he was overpowered and killed. Her seventeen-year old brother, who was sleeping on the cot besides their father, was also killed. 'The Maoists had an issue with my father, why did they kill my brother too?' she lamented.

In Narayanpur, in 2009, the Maoists were after a PDS dealer as they said he was corrupt. They came to his house at night. When they could not find him, they took his wife who was an anganwadi teacher. Her body was found on the road four days later.

In 2013, a sarpanch in Bijapur told me that he was a former sangam member and that he used to help the Maoists by hiding guns at his house. Despite that, the Maoists killed his father as they suspected him of being against them. 'Why did they kill my father?' he asked. For this reason, he said, he left the Maoists and joined the Salwa Judum.

In 2016, I learnt that a pastor had been killed in a village near the Telangana border. I had met an Adivasi pastor there a few years earlier, and I was worried that it might be him, but it turned out to be his younger brother. The slain pastor's wife and son told me that the Maoists had come to their house that night and were asking for the whereabouts of his elder brother. When he refused to cooperate, he was taken a short distance away and killed. 'It is because the Maoists couldn't find his brother that they killed my husband,' said the victim's wife. I recalled the senior pastor and the story he had told me. He used to be a *vadde* (an Adivasi purohit) in a Sukma village but converted of his own free will and became, as he said jokingly, Jesus's Commander (in contrast with the Maoist commanders). But because of the constant pressure from the Maoists, who stopped him from preaching, burnt his Bible, and demolished the church, he had run away to this border village, and his family had also followed. His nephew said that even here he was under constant threat, so he had shifted base again recently.

Local journalists have also come under pressure from the Maoists from time to time. Two have even been killed—Sai Reddy and Nemichand Jain. Sai Reddy had been forced to move out of his village Basaguda (Bijapur district) after his house was demolished by the Maoists, who accused him of having plans to rent it to the police. On 6 December 2013, on a visit to Basaguda with his wife, he was chased, overpowered from behind, and his throat was slit. Incidentally, Reddy had, in 2008, spent time in jail under the CSPSA on suspicion of being a Maoist supporter. Thus, he was targeted from both sides. The same happened to Nemichand Jain, a local journalist from Tongpal in Sukma district. He was accused by both sides of supporting the other side. On 13 December 2013, he was killed by the Maoists on suspicion of being a police informer.

It is when we meet and hear the victims of such incidents or their families that we are able to believe them, otherwise these stories may seem like anti-Maoist propaganda.

The War Must End

We have all been so caught up in understanding the contours of the war in Bastar—the shape of the beast so to say—that we have forgotten to fight against the war itself. The protracted war between the Indian government and the CPI (Maoist) in the heart of India has taken a huge toll on the lives of its Adivasi residents, not to speak of the combatants on both sides—Adivasi and non-Adivasi. In so many villages, hidden amidst hills, trees and rocks are graves of those who died untimely deaths. As a new grave is dug and a body lowered, sometimes near older ones, more tears soak into the earth, but few others care.

Every time there is fresh violence, counting of the dead begins. Generally, the public outcry is loudest when members of the paramilitary die. When the Maoists die, it is nobody's business but that of the Maoists. And when civilians die, it is a private matter. The combatants on both sides are hailed as 'martyrs' and their families are compensated by each side in its own ways. But when a civilian is killed by a state bullet, responsibility is rarely taken, though the state sometimes compensates those who are killed by the Maoists if a police complaint is lodged to that effect. Whatever the details of the aftermath of each death, the plain truth is that too many people have died. There has been too much suffering.

Human beings are odd—we get used to anything. We don't mind that an entire people, officially amongst the poorest in the country, who were promised special protection by the Constitution—the

Adivasis—are the ones who are suffering the most. A large majority of those who get killed, especially amongst the civilians, Maoists and state police, are Adivasis. Most of those who are arbitrarily picked up by the security forces, detained by the police, jailed as undertrials for many years or convicted by the courts are Adivasis. So are those who are kidnapped by the Maoists, killed on suspicion of being police informers, maimed or killed in IED blasts, or forced to leave their villages to save their lives or for other reasons.

And yet there is silence from the ordinary citizens who live in the towns of Chhattisgarh—people who know what is going on but do not speak out because their own lives are not affected. This also applies to people in Bastar, where speaking out entails a real danger of undesirable consequences. Among those who do speak out, some irresponsibly exhort the government to intensify the militarization and 'finish off' the Maoists, despite knowing that the brunt of the onslaught would be borne by the Adivasi residents of the war zone.

From the Maoist side, there is a similar call for a fight to the finish. Depending on which side you are on, you count or ignore the dead. There are numbers and statistics on both sides. Both prefer to forget the third side—the civilian Adivasis residing in the war zone, who may be caught in between or sideways or whichever way. As far as the state is concerned, all those who reside in the war zone are Maoists, or at least suspected Maoists. As far as the Maoists and their supporters are concerned, any suggestion that civilians are caught in the crossfire is seen as contempt for the agency of Adivasis and inability to take sides—mainly the Maoist side.

Both sides claim that that they are waging the war 'on behalf of the people' and 'to save them'. The war, like a conveyor belt, keeps rolling year after year even as evidence on the ground indicates that it has been counterproductive. We are familiar with the political economies of wars and know that there are many who gain, who become fat and rich and cynical on the blood money that they make. Their interest is to see that the war continues. Any suggestion that the state should explore and exhaust non-violent means of negotiation before the use of force is generally ridiculed. Non-violence is seen as a weakness in these quarters (not only in the Maoist camp). The government also shows its disrespect for non-violence when open and democratic people's movements are suppressed with a heavy hand. Today, Maoism has become a convenient excuse to silence all dissent in Bastar and beyond.

The war in Bastar must end. There have been enough killings and counter-killings. Actions of both sides have contributed to taking the society backward instead of forward. A public call for ceasefire should be given. In the interest of the people of Bastar, both sides should respect it and work towards a political solution. The ordinary citizen should no longer remain a mute witness to a war that has lost all meaning and in which there will be no winners.

18

Rape by the Way[*]

The tarred blackness of the road stood out in the headlights. Its smoothness reminded me of times not so smooth. Some may think that times have changed, but the twelve women inside the vehicle know better. They are returning to their homes in Bellamlendra after five days in Bijapur where eight testified to gang rape and all to looting and threats by the police and security forces. Some are with small children, three of whom were diagnosed with malaria while in Bijapur. It is a cold night but all the children and most of the women are barefoot. Clothed in thin cotton, with bright prints in warm colours.

Rape is not uncommon, but one knows something is very wrong when it becomes common. In the last three months, three instances of large-scale sexual violence on Adivasi women by police and security

---

[*] First published in *Outlook* as 'The Pegdapalli Files' (February 2016). This essay is based on conversations I had with the affected women (individually and collectively) as well as documentary evidence, including the FIR and testimonies that were recorded in my presence by the local SDM. Names of affected women have been changed to respect privacy. Some of the inquiries reported in this essay were made with other members of the Women Against Sexual Violence and State Repression (WSS) collective. The WSS later documented these incidents in their report *Bearing Witness: Sexual Violence in South Chhattisgarh* (2017).

forces, while on combing operations, have surfaced in Bastar (south Chhattisgarh): in Peddagelur-Chinnagelur and Bellamlendra villages of Bijapur district and Kunna village of Sukma district.

Peddagelur

The first incident occurred in October 2015, when three women— Parvati, Somi and Lakke—were gang-raped and at least fifteen other women were sexually assaulted in the twin villages of Peddagelur and Chinnagelur.

We learnt about this incident by chance, in the weekly bazaar at Basaguda on Friday, 30 October 2015. Parvati, Somi and Lakke were not present then, but we met many other women who recounted what happened between 19 and 24 October, when hundreds of security forces left a trail of excesses and atrocities as they passed through Pegdapalli, Chinnagelur, Peddagelur, Gundem and Burgicheru villages on combing operations.

One of our team members had a video recorder. The women's testimonies were recorded and shown to the District Collector, Yashwant Kumar, the same evening. The collector promised to take immediate action if we helped these women to reach the district headquarters. The villages were 60–75 km from Bijapur. The next morning, we returned to the area and with the help of local sarpanchs and teachers who had motorcycles, we headed towards the villages.

Parvati is a fourteen-year-old Dorla girl who lives in the Patelpara of Peddagelur, home to seventy families of Dorla and Madia Gond Adivasis. The villages of this area are close to the Telangana border and this was reflected in the way Parvati was dressed—in a long skirt, Telangana-style. Her aunt, Nagamma, who brought her up after her mother died when she was a child, told us that on 21 October, they had gone to the jungle to graze cattle with a few others when they met the security forces who chased them. 'I was also caught and beaten severely. They were able to isolate Parvati. She was taken to the bushes on one side, blindfolded and raped many times until she lost consciousness.' Nagamma found her in a badly bruised state. She said that she had to nurse her with traditional medicine for days afterwards. Parvati does not seem to have recovered yet and wears a withdrawn look.

Somi and Lakke live in Mettapara, another hamlet of Peddagelur with about sixty Madia Gond households. Somi is Lakke's daughter-in-law. In her early twenties, she married Unga two years ago and was four months pregnant with their first child when the forces came on the day before Dusshera (21 October). It was afternoon. Somi was out grazing the cows and Lakke was at home. Somi said that she was near the stream when they surrounded her. They stripped her and pushed her into the water many times. Some of them also removed their clothes. Then, they raped her and left her by the stream.

Lakke listens to Somi in silence. She had talked to us about what had happened to Somi but remained quiet about herself. We learnt about her story only later, when something she said made us realize that she was talking about herself. On closer questioning, Lakke opened up and said that the forces also came to her house that afternoon. 'They began chasing my hens, so I objected. "Why are you catching my hens? Do your own work," I said. At this, they hit me with a *danda* [baton], blindfolded and dragged me to the jungle where they raped me. I heard them say in Gondi that they would kill me there itself.'

Besides gangrape, at least fifteen women from Peddagelur and Chinnagelur mentioned being molested, beaten and threatened by the security forces. Some women were chased out of their homes, which were then occupied by the forces and used for their stay. We heard statements such as these: '*sone ko bol rahe the* [they were asking us to sleep [with them)]', '*bacchon ki maon ke stan se dudh nichoda* [they squeezed the breasts of lactating mothers for milk]', '*kapada utha kar jango aur chithodo par mara* [lifting our skirts, they hit us on our thighs and buttocks]', '*kapada uthao, andar mirchi dalenge* [lift your skirt, we will put chillis up your vagina]'.

Beatings were reported from villages where sexual assault happened as well as where it did not. Batons were used, at times even guns. Some women were holding their infants when they were hit from behind. Some had their hair pulled and their heads banged against the ground. We saw their bruises.

Looting was common. We heard so many stories and statements of this kind that one lost count: '*ghar-ghar se murgi liya* [they took hens from every house]', '*paanch paili chaval, teen murgi, barbatti, mirchi ek bora, tel ek tina* [the equivalent of ten kilos of rice, three hens, beans, one sack of dried chillis, one tin of oil]', '*sabun-tel tak nahi chode hai* [they did not leave even soap and hair oil]', '*kapada jalaye* [they burnt our clothes]', '*paisa churaye* [stole money]', '*chor company hai* [they are a band of thieves]'.

By late evening, we were able to return to Bijapur with some of the women. Later, in the district collectorate, in the presence of the Collector, the Superintendent of Police and the Assistant Superintendent of Police (Naxal Operations), they related what had happened. Based on these testimonies, a police complaint was filed and an FIR was registered on 1 November. The following day, their testimonies were recorded by the SDM, and again by the DSP, and their medical examinations were conducted.

Bellamlendra

Basaguda police station had acquired an unenviable notoriety. In ninety days, no chargesheet in the Peddagelur case was in sight, but another incident, more widespread, had occurred in Bellamlendra village (also known as Nendra). As in the Peddagelur case, this was also during a combing operation of a few days, from 11 to 14 January 2016, when the security forces camped in the village. Bellamlendra had ninety-eight houses of Madia Gond Adivasis

distributed in four paras. According to the WSS investigating team
of which I was a part, at least thirteen instances of gang rape had
occurred. Eight women testified in front of the SDM and police.
Six of the eight were from one para—Gotumpara—that had a total
of twenty-two houses.

When I first met Bali, she was sitting in the corridor of the
collectorate in front of the SDM office waiting for her turn. Her boy,
Hadma, no longer an infant, stayed close to his mother all the time.
Bali had a quiet dignity about her. I have often been struck by the
restraint that Adivasis exercise in the face of sorrow. Their sufferings
seem to settle in them.

Bali, a mother of three, said that the forces came to their village
on Monday, 11 January. That day, they raped Kosi.

I was at a little distance and saw one policeman holding Kosi's
legs and another raping her. I had gone there upon hearing her
shout. She was in her backyard plucking vegetables when they
came. They had thrown a black-coloured cloth on her face. Their
own faces were also covered with black cloth. Hearing her shouts,
Hidme dokri (an old woman) also rushed there. She threatened
them with her danda. Seeing her, they ran away. After that,
Hidme gathered nine to ten women of the para and we went with
Kosi to the place where the forces were cooking their meal, near
the handpump.

We asked: *Aisa galat kaam kyon kar rahe ho? Apne sahab se baat
karao* (Why are you doing such condemnable deeds? We want to
speak with your officer).

They said: *Sahab nahi hai* (Officer is not here).

We asked: *Kaun aisa kiya? Usko dikhao* (Who has done this? Bring
him).

They said: *Yahan nahi hai. Tum log halla nahi karo. Ghar jao* (He is not here. Don't make a scene. Go home).

This was Monday. On Tuesday, I was raped.

The forces came from the side of the Gotum hill. It was late evening. Hearing them come, my husband Deva fled. Two came inside my house. They overturned the cot I was sleeping on with Hadma. They cornered me, removed my lungi and tore my petticoat. One held my feet while the other raped me. They covered my mouth to stop me from screaming. But an elder relative had heard the noise and came with a danda and torch. Seeing the light, they ran away. It was dark and I could not see their faces, but I heard them speaking in Gondi.

The forces included Gondi as well as Hindi speakers. Those who forced themselves on Hidme, Tulsi and Paike, also in Gotumpara, were speaking in Hindi. Tulsi said: 'I was alone at home with my three children. At around five in the evening on Monday, three men in police dress came to my house. They were speaking in Hindi. *Do jan mujhe pakde the aur ek ne galat kiya* (Two were holding me while one raped me). Hearing my cries for help, my sister Avlam Devi came to my rescue. Seeing her, they ran away. The next day, I went to my mother's house. My neighbours told me that five of them had come again.'

A fiercely independent-looking Paike paid the price for asking payment for her hens from the two intruders who came to her house on Tuesday. So did Raimati in Masodpara, also on Tuesday, in the afternoon. 'They were three,' she said. 'They took four kilos of rice, promising money. When they started helping themselves to the hens, I stopped them saying I had planned to sell them and buy clothes. They got angry and covered my face with a fishing net and then pushed me inside the house. They were speaking in Gondi and Hindi. My mother-in-law, Uike Deve, hearing me yell, came and hit the back of the policeman who was on me. He stopped, then dressed and escaped with the two others, picking up four hens as they left.'

Three women recognized ex-Naxalites among those who had assaulted them. Four have been named in their testimonies, one is from their own hamlet (Gotumpara). Their presence suggests that District Reserve Guards (DRG) were part of the combined security forces involved in this combing operation. The DRG was formed three years ago. Surrendered Maoists comprised half its strength. The other half were recruited through a formal process of advertisements; these would be the Hindi speakers.

Women were threatened with a worse vengeance. Ungi, a forty-five-year-old woman who was also raped, was told, '*Tum log naksalion ke sath rahte ho, tumhare gharon ko aag laga denge* [You people are with the Naxalites, we will burn your houses].' Jogi, in her early twenties, was told, '*Yeh baat kisi ko bhi bataogi to agli baar goli mar denge* [If you divulge this matter to anyone, we will kill you next time].' She was raped by three, including two ex-Naxalites whom she recognizes. Kosi recalled them saying, '*Tendu patta jaise udta hai, vaise udaenge* [We will make you (and your men) fall like the leaves of the tendu tree].'

Kunna

Strangely, or perhaps not so strangely, between 11 and 14 January 2016—the same dates as in Bellamlendra—another combing operation was taking place in Peddapara of Kunna village in Sukma district. This combing operation also boasts of features that are now familiar. Twenty-nine persons, including some women, were rounded up and dragged to the school, one kilometre away from the para. En route, they were beaten up, women's clothes were torn and verbal and physical sexual abuse followed. Six women suffered severe sexual assault. Three men of the village were arrested.

The police and security forces often complain that the men run away when the forces go to the villages and argue that this is a sign of guilt. In Kunna, the men did not run away, but they were treated with brute force. One youth died due to the brutal beatings of the forces. Laloo Sodi's mother told us that her twenty-one-year-old son was in the field when the forces caught him and beat him black and blue. He was unable to eat or drink anything that night, not even pej (rice gruel). He died the next day, on 14 January. The family cremated him without a post-mortem.

Fighting for justice is not easy, more so in an area where the ordinary villager is regarded with suspicion and hostility by the administration, especially the police. Even registering an FIR becomes a challenge. It is a myth that any citizen can go to a police station and get an FIR registered. Not in Bastar. At the thana level, there is blatant refusal. At the SP level, one is told that there will be a *janch* (investigation) first. Both refusal and delay are clear violations of the law (Section 154, CrPC).

Under these circumstances, the filing of the FIR in the Peddagelur case seemed like a victory of sorts. This became the first case in the country after the amended rape law (2013) allowed for the indictment of central and state security forces (Section 376 2c, IPC). With much difficulty, FIRs have also been registered in the Bellamlendra and Kunna incidents.

What is happening now is beginning to look like the early years of Salwa Judum, in 2005–06, when villagers reported more than ninety-nine incidents of rape. There was no FIR then. Women are speaking out now. They have come forward and testified despite the fear they must feel. Relating and reliving such incidents is always traumatic for the victims; many times, one saw women staring into space, tears welling up in their eyes. But the impunity of the police and security forces remains unshaken—so far.

The Quest for Justice

As often happens, justice has eluded the victims of these incidents of rape and sexual violence in Bastar. The National Human Rights

Commission initiated suo moto proceedings in 2016 in response to media reports and conducted a spot investigation. On 7 January 2017, the Commission directed the state government to ensure that detailed statements of all the victims were carefully recorded (NHRC, 2017). Taking the view that there was prima facie evidence of rape and sexual assault by the security forces, the NHRC also directed the state government to pay compensation to the victims, adding to Rs 37 lakh. When the compensation was finally ready to be disbursed from the Bijapur Collectorate in 2019, the women refused on the grounds that they wanted justice, not compensation.

Separately, the National Commission for Scheduled Tribes took suo moto cognizance of the matter. In a rare initiative, Chairperson Rameshwar Oraon personally visited the area in April 2016 with an NCST team to hear the victims. The NCST prepared a useful report and recommended a Criminal Investigation Department (CID) inquiry.[1] The state government accepted this recommendation.

In 2017, a writ petition was filed in the High Court of Chhattisgarh by twenty-eight petitioners from Peddagelur and Chinnagelur, most of them women. The petition languished until 9 May 2023, when a two-judge bench (including the chief justice of Chhattisgarh) ordered the CID to submit its report within three weeks. The court ignored other prayers of the petitioners, such as compensation of Rs 10 lakh per victim and the constitution of a Special Investigation Team from outside Chhattisgarh, and disposed of the petition.

Aside from the NHRC and NCST, many other delegations visited Bijapur and Sukma in 2016 and conducted their own investigations into the gang rapes and mass sexual assault, including the State Commission for Women, the National Commission for Women, the Adivasi Mahasabha and delegations of many political parties. All this attention created some local tension in the area. Anti-Maoist groups that included families of victims of Maoist violence wanted state and national authorities, activists and media persons to also pay attention to their own situation, which they felt remained unaddressed by most. Local police and government functionaries were fanning their discontent. Soon after the Nendra FIR was lodged, for instance, one such group accosted human rights activists outside the police station; slogans were also shouted outside the Bijapur circuit house when the National Commission for Women held a meeting there with some of the victims and activists. It was also around that time that the wave of repression against dissenting voices in Bastar, mentioned in Chapter 17 (Salwa Judum and After), intensified.

In spite of so many efforts and so much public attention, no one has been arrested let alone convicted for these acts of sexual violence.

The Lohandiguda Assaults

Before 2015–16 as well as afterwards, there have been many other instances of rape and sexual assault in the conflict areas of Bastar. In these parts, assaults on women's bodies have become routine during searching and combing operations. Some seem planned, some not— both ways they have become an integral feature of counter-insurgency operations. Their incidence is much higher than reported. Even the Peddagelur cases came to light only by chance, after an unexpected encounter in a bazaar.

However, at least one of the incidents I have investigated tells us that sexual violence on Adivasi women by security forces is not restricted to areas of Maoist influence, and is also a way of suppressing Adivasi dissent in other contexts. In early 2007, a major incident involving one rape and what seemed to be organized molestation of ten women occurred in two villages of Lohandiguda block in Bastar district. The villages were known to be strongholds of the Communist Party of India (CPI). There was, at the time, an ongoing conflict between the tribal residents of ten gram panchayats of Lohandiguda block and the government. Roughly 6,000 hectares of land of these gram panchayats were slated to be acquired by the

Tata Steel Company. The government was all set to push the project at all costs even though the people were unwilling. Resistance was getting more intense as was repression.

The main grievance of the affected people was that even basic information regarding the project had not been provided to them. They had not seen the MoU signed between the state government and the Tatas nor the compensation package. Even the MLA of the area, a member of the ruling BJP, admitted in public that he was not privy to these documents.

The affected Adivasis of these ten gram panchayats were well aware that Bastar district came under the Fifth Schedule of the Indian Constitution that offered them special protection. They also knew that the Panchayat Extension to Scheduled Areas (PESA) Act empowered the gram sabha to have a say in land acquisition for any project, public or private.

Gram sabhas were held on 20 July 2006 in eight gram panchayats and on 2 August 2006 in the last two. However, these gram sabhas were held under duress in the coercive presence of a large number of police personnel as well as administrative staff including the District Collector, Sub-Divisional Magistrate and Superintendent of Police. In spite of the coercion, the people in these gram panchayats put forward thirteen demands on which they wanted further discussion with the government before taking a final decision. Months passed, but the government did not meet them. This led the sarpanchs of six gram panchayats to declare that they would reconvene the gram sabhas on 24 February 2007.

Police action in these villages was escalating. Even before the gram sabhas were held in 2006, sixty or so of the most vocal leaders of these gram panchayats were arrested under false charges. Some of them stayed up to sixty days in prison. The property of the main leaders was also destroyed. A police camp was set up in Sirisguda, regarded as a 'rebel' village. Following that, men of these villages used to keep away from their homes in order to evade wrongful arrest or harassment. With their men mostly absent, women had to manage their homes, children, cattle and fields on their own. The 2006 winter harvest in Sirisguda was done single-handedly by women.

The assault on women on 26 and 27 February 2007 needs to be understood in this light. In the early morning of 26 February, a contingent of police force came to Kandkipara of Sirisguda and went in two or threes inside homes while their colleagues kept guard outside. Sexual violence that morning included molestation of ten women—six of these women were less than sixteen years old, and the youngest was only twelve. In the evening of the following day, in Marigudapara of Takraguda, a twenty-year-old mother who was alone at home with her infant was raped by one policeman who came to her door on the pretext of asking for water to drink.

In this incident of mass sexual assault, it became clear that the women had been targeted by the police in a planned manner to punish them and their communities for daring to exercise their right to say 'No'—a right that was theirs by law.

Following our investigation, affidavits of the eleven women were prepared and a complaint was sent to the NHRC on 28 March 2007.[2] However, nothing came of it. After considerable foot-dragging, the NHRC finally responded, only to say that the case had been sent to the DGP Chhattisgarh for investigation. Meanwhile, people's resistance against displacement continued and ultimately succeeded: Tata Steel withdrew from the project in 2016, and soon after Congress came to power in Chhattisgarh in 2018, in a rare step, acquired lands were returned.

Justice Delayed, then Denied

These incidents join a long list of other incidents of rape or sexual violence by security forces that have remained unpunished. Among other prominent cases that come to mind are the 1991 incident in Kunan-Poshpora (Kashmir), where twenty-three women filed complaints of rape by members of the CRPF and BSF; several cases that were reported in Doda (Jammu) between 1994–2001 of rape by members of 19 Sikh Regiment, ADA-322 battalion, 15 Bihar Regiment and 8 Rashtriya Rifles; the alleged rape and killing of Thangjam Manorama Devi by members of the Assam Rifles in Manipur in 2004; and the gang rapes of Kondh Adivasi women by members of the Greyhound force in Vakapalli in 2007 and Baluguda in 2010, both in Visakhapatnam district, Andhra Pradesh.[3] The Justice Verma Committee has aptly analysed the pattern behind these multiple incidents: '. . . rape and other forms of sexual assault have been found to be consistently deployed as an expression of power . . . by State and private persons in conflict areas'.[4]

So far, there is only one instance of mass sexual violence by the security forces being punished. This is the Vachathi case of gang rapes of eighteen Adivasi women in Dharmapuri district (Tamil Nadu) in 1992. Judgement was delivered in 2011, indicting 215 surviving accused including forest department officials, police officials as well as tehsildars.[5] This exception shows that impunity need not be the rule.

19

Fake Encounter in Nulkatong*

At the best of times, it is difficult to ascertain the truth. Sometimes, it is more so. A long row of body bags in black polythene, strung up with green and yellow plastic rope, caught the eye of newspaper readers in Bastar on 7 August 2018. The security forces, we were told, had had resounding success in a major encounter in Nulkatong village of Sukma district in which fifteen Maoists had been killed. The encounter, part of Operation Monsoon, was being heralded by officials as 'the biggest success of anti-Naxal operation in Chhattisgarh'.

Whether an encounter is real or fake cannot be ascertained unless one goes and talks to the people. Even then, a sceptic may ask, how can you be sure that the people are telling the truth? That, in my view, is a matter of judgement. Like everyone else, people too may prevaricate, hide or tell half-truths. Between the crevices of such silences and speech lies the 'truth' about a particular incident.

It was raining hard in Bastar those days and Nulkatong, nestled deep in the forests of Konta block, was difficult to reach—a trek of 20–25 km by any route. There is a straightforward route from

---

* An edited version of this essay was published in *Caravan*, December 2018. Some names have been changed to protect anonymity.

413

the Konta block headquarters that has a paved road until Banda. If you manage to win the confidence of CRPF personnel when they stop you in front of their camp, you may be allowed to pass after becoming a register entry with all the requisite details. But sometimes the CRPF may say that you have to get a written permission from the police, and then at the police station they may say that permission is not required but refuse to put that in writing—tried ways of stopping citizens from reaching the site.

Having experienced this before, I decided to ward off trouble and take the Andhra route through Koya villages in the East Godavari district that borders Konta block. This route also had its challenges that local people have to contend with every monsoon when the rivers expand their bosoms and swell and swirl in merriment. Difficulties come with lighter moments, as happened when I was waiting with other Koya families to cross the first river—Gunabirji by name, because she usually flowed under a bridge, although she was happily flowing over it that evening. At times like that, when one with nature, you wonder whether the river can hear you, so we shouted above the rain: '*Areem*, Gunabirji (Allow us to pass, Gunabirji)!' And she did hear, after an hour or so, when the water level receded. It took two days of travelling mostly on foot, wading through six more excited rivers and staying overnight in two villages en route, before I reached my destination on 14 August, but I learnt much about the incident from those I met on the way.

On the Road

People on the Andhra–Chhattisgarh border said that two trucks full of local police from Konta had reached Mallempeta (a village on the border) by late afternoon on Saturday, 4 August. After dropping them, the trucks returned to Konta. According to early reports, this was a joint operation of the District Reserve Guards (DRG) and Special Task Force (STF) from Konta and Bhejji police stations.

In the next two days, they spread themselves in the area in three directions. This was towards the end of the Maoists' 'Martyrs Week' that starts each year on 28 July. Celebrations may be held in one place or in several places depending on the security situation in the area. From the police point of view, there is a chance of finding an assembly of Maoists at that time.

I met him by chance—the youth on a bicycle who had stopped by at the grocer's shop. 'He is from Nulkatong,' said the shopkeeper, by then aware of my purpose. The youth, in neat shirt and trousers, was carrying one of those plastic bags with multi-coloured stripes that villagers often use for their shopping; an umbrella was tucked in the frame of his bicycle. In response to my questions, this is what he said along with interjections by another person (henceforth 'villager') from a village close to Nulkatong, who was also there.

Youth: The incident occurred on Monday morning (6 August) at 6.30 a.m. The previous night, we were at home when we learnt that the police was close by, so all the youth went to the *laadi* (a thatched structure that villagers build close to their fields in the monsoon, where anyone can take refuge if it rains). Women, the middle-aged and old people stayed back. A few militia persons were there that night. Some people had gone there when they heard that the panchayat mukhiya was also there. Except for the militia, all others were ordinary members of the public. There was no meeting there that day.

Villager: *Andarvalon ka system alag hai* (The system of the Maoists is different). They have their own panchayats. Gompad, Nulkatong, Velpocha and Kindrepal fall under one panchayat. Militia are people of the village. They are in *sada* (ordinary) dress and live and work in the village like everybody else. They play a supportive role. They may be unarmed, or have bows and arrows, or a knife, or sometimes a *bharmar* (a muzzle-loading gun, an archaic nineteenth century weapon).

Youth: Some of the militia had a bharmar but there was no exchange of fire that morning. The police attacked the laadi and started firing. Six persons were killed (from Nulkatong). One of them was a militia member; five were public (*sic*). One militia managed to escape.

Villager: Police always do that. They do not differentiate between a *naxali* (Naxalite), militia or *aam-janata* (civilians)—all are treated in the same way. This is what the police do when they come. *Jinda kaatte hain* (They kill people in cold blood). That day also they must have just seen the bharmars and started firing.

Youth: Madkam Lakma, the militia who was killed, was around thirty years old. He had no formal education. He was unmarried and lived in the village and cultivated his fields like everyone else. He had been a militia member since 2010.

Villager: We also saw his body. His left leg was completely destroyed; there was almost no flesh, only bones. His head had been bludgeoned as though with a *sambal* (an iron rod with a pointed end, used in agricultural work). Those who were wounded but still alive after the shootout must have been hit with the sambal or the end of rifles to finish them off.

Youth: The villagers who were killed included three cousin brothers (Muchaki Deva, Muchaki Hidma and Muchaki Muka) and Sodi Parbhu. Muka and Parbhu were younger than me (he said he was fifteen or sixteen years old). Hidma and Deva were about two years older. Out of the six, only Unga (sometimes pronounced Hunga) was married. He was in his twenties. The force also took away two sangam (village committee) members that day.

The youth and the villager said that six had been killed from Gompad, including three militia members; two militia members managed to get away. About the persons from three other villages, the youth said, '*Aur ek militia Velpocha ka tha, ek Kindrepal ka tha, ek Etegatta ka tha—veh bhi khatam* [And there was one militia from Velpocha, one from Kindrepal, one from Etegatta—all of them were killed].' The villager added that 'guruji' from Etegatta may have come as a *mehman* (a guest), visiting relatives. Somebody from a neighbouring village who was translating for us in Nulkatong the next day mentioned later to me that the person from Etegatta was in the *dalam*—Local Guerrilla Squad (LGS) and that he had come to meet the jan-militia that day.

Villager: After the incident, all men from Gompad and Nulkatong ran to Durma (a neighbouring village) out of fear. They stayed there from ten in the morning till late afternoon. They were not at the site of the incident, but were scared that if the police (as security forces are referred to) found them, they would also be killed. Whenever police go to any village, they harass and trouble people—steal money, drink *daru* (liquor), slay hens, beat people and sometimes take them away. I went to Durma to meet them. *Veh vikat ro rahe the* (They were crying a lot). Those who had run to the laadi in the fields that day had gone with the hope of saving themselves. *Jeene ke liye kahan jaen? Kahin chup kar rahe kone mein, veh soche* (Where do we go so that we can stay alive? Let's hide in some corner, they thought.) Youth are often fiddling with their mobiles. Perhaps the police got to know where they were from that or from the light of the fire they may have lit that night in the laadi.

I showed them the photos of confiscated items and dead bodies, taken at Konta police station, that had been circulating on WhatsApp. Looking at the former, they said: 'Jholas belonged to the militia, not the *boris* [sacks].' They recognized the blue backpack as belonging to somebody who had managed to escape. '*Rassi* [rope] was not there that day.' Most of the guns on display [the police had claimed there were sixteen] were rifles, only a few were bharmars. 'They have been planted,' they said. 'From where did the two tiffins come?' they wondered. [Tiffins are often used as containers for an improvised explosive device (IED).]

I could not easily read the expressions on their faces as they saw the photographs of the dead. They knew and I knew that it could easily have been them. Their first comment was: '*Police ne baad mein dress dala* [the police dressed the victims into uniforms after the event].'

'I know him', one said, pointing at the photo of a young man, his eyes in still surprise, clad in a green checked shirt. 'He was from Gompad. He was not a militia.' He could not recognize two others but pointed to Parbhu, with a string of blue beads around his neck, Unga, with a sharp nose and neat moustache who seemed to be sleeping peacefully, and Hidma, in a red and black striped shirt—all three from Nulkatong.

Talking about death is hard. We had been sitting on the muddy portico of the shop. It was time for the youth to leave. The villager had other things to do before going home, but he arranged for me to go with two women who were heading in the same direction. I gathered the clothes I had set out to dry and soon we were on our way. It is always good to find walking companions amongst Adivasis. Their slim, erect bodies and steady pace help to measure your own in likeness, enabling you to walk longer distances with greater ease. I stayed that night at the house of a relative of the villager, who returned later that evening, and accompanied me to Gompad the next day.

What the People of Gompad Said

I first heard about Gompad in 2009, when Operation Greenhunt was in full swing, and nine persons were killed there. Investigations revealed that seven were from Gompad itself and two were from neighbouring villages (one each from Velpocha and Nulkatong). In 2016, a young woman called Madkam Hidme was raped and killed, dressed in a Maoist uniform and said to be a member of the Kistaram area platoon number 8. In December 2017, security forces opened fire on four women who were fishing, injuring one called Soyam Rame (she later left the village out of fear).[1] I had investigated the 2009 and 2016 incidents—projected as encounters by the police—and found the allegations of deliberate killing to be credible.

This is not to say that the Maoist movement is absent in Gompad. A large water tank built many years ago by the villagers of Gompad and surrounding areas is testimony to their presence. The martyr-memorial columns in the village also tell a story of a kind, besides other facts like the absence of voter ID cards. Darker evidence also emerged at the time of Hidme's death, when it emerged that those responsible for torturing and killing her included surrendered Maoists who had joined the DRG—persons who had been coming to the village for years.

Gompad's sorrow is therefore of a different nature—sorrow inflicted by 'intimate' enemies as well as a ruthless state.

This time, Gompad lost six more of its residents: four from Muria para and two from Dorla para. One survivor who witnessed it all is Kadti Mangal of Muria para. He said: 'Police has been coming to our village very often. Every time they come, they beat and harass people. They especially target young persons and pick them up if they can find them. On 5 August, when we heard that a large number of police were close to our village, around twenty to twenty-five people ran towards Nulkatong. My son, Aayata, was amongst them. Worried for my son, I ran after him.'

Mangal continued: 'There were around forty persons that night in the laadi. In the morning, the forces attacked suddenly. Everybody was running, I too ran. A bullet hit my leg. Somehow, I managed to run and save myself. In the confusion, I could not see Aayata. My son was killed.'

Aayata's older sister brought a photo that had been taken a year earlier. Mangal said that Aayata was studying in an ashram school in Konta but came home because he did not get admission in sixth class. He was fourteen years old.

We learnt from Mangal that three other persons from their para were killed that morning: Madavi Nanda (son of Hidma), Kadti Hadma (son of Deva) and Madavi Deva (son of Hadma; he was married and had two children).

Amongst those assembled at Mangal's house while we were talking was Madkam Lakshmi, Hidme's mother. She had fought bravely in the campaign for justice for Madkam Hidme, travelling many times to the High Court in Bilaspur and other places. She stood silently, listening to Mangal. Like Mangal, who had run after Aayata but could not save him, she had not been able to stop those who had pulled Hidme out of her bed (she was ill) and taken her away in front of her. We left them, mother and father, in shared grief, with a hurt that would never heal.

In Dorla para, a few minutes' walk from Muria para, we met the family members of Soyam Sita and Soyam Chandra who had also been killed that fateful morning. Santosh, Sita's brother, said that his brother was in his mid-twenties while Chandra was a few years younger. Chandra's young wife, holding her one-year-old daughter, confirmed that Chandra and Sita had run with others towards Nulkatong when they heard that *charon or police bichi hui hai* (police is spread on all sides). Chandra was the sarpanch of the village, like his father before him. Chandra's younger brother Mallesh, who is a student in Konta, took us to the *margath* (the burial ground) and showed us their graves, next to those of the four victims from Muria para. In the drizzle, we saw the six overturned cots on the graves with other personal belongings of the deceased. Aayata's school bag was on one of the cots and a backpack and shoes hung from the branch of a nearby tree. 'Those belonged to Sita,' said Mallesh.

The Grieving Women of Nulkatong

Gompad and Nulkatong are a few kilometres apart. On reaching Nulkatong, our guide first took us to *neeche para* (the lower hamlet). The hustle-bustle in a nearby house attracted our attention and I was surprised, gladly so, to hear that a *chetti* (naming ceremony) was going on. The little one deserved to be treated well, as per custom, and the family was celebrating. Pork had been cooked and it was nice to see this sign of life.

In the same para is Muchaki Sukadi's house. She is sitting in the mud-plastered verandah of her house near a low fire. A bicycle is leaning on the side frame of the verandah, not used since 6 August. 'That was his cycle,' she says. She is Muchaki Muka's mother. She shows us his photograph. 'When we heard that the police had come,' she says, 'all youth ran to the laadi out of fear. Muka also went with them.'

We asked her to tell us more about Muka. 'Muka did not attend school. He was younger than Boda.' We had just met Boda, brother of Tati Unga who had also been killed on 6 August. Boda's age is fifteen according to his Aadhaar card. Muka must have been around thirteen or fourteen years old.

This was the second time that a member of Sukadi's family was killed at the hands of the police. We learnt that in 2009, her husband Botti was killed by the security forces and Salwa Judum. 'He was not part of the Maoist organization at any level. He was feeding wood in the fire while making daru when he was nabbed and killed,' she said. Muchaki Sukadi's youngest son is studying in Class VII in Konta. But now she doubts that he will be able to continue.

Boda, too, had mentioned that he might have to drop out of school. He is a Class IX student. But now that his brother Tati Unga has died, he may be needed at home. Unga was in his early twenties. He is survived by his wife Lakke and a daughter who is about seven years old. Boda said that when Unga heard that the police was coming, he went to sleep in the laadi. *'Par yahan rehne se bhi marte* [But he might have died even if he had stayed at home].' Lakke's mother Bhime cannot contain her tears. She keeps breaking down and crying. She said that she was so burdened by her thoughts that she felt ill.

While we were talking with the relatives of the deceased, one person quietly handed to us folded sheets of paper and went away. This was the two-page press release of the CPI (Maoist) on the incident. Another, older person came a little later and took out six used cartridges from the pocket of his frayed khaki shirt. He showed them to us, cradling them in the palm of his hand, without saying a word.

Arrests and Beatings

The police had, in a self-congratulatory note, claimed that they had arrested two wanted Maoists in Nulkatong, a man (Madkam Ravi) and a woman (Payko). Ravi, they said, was a 'wanted Naxali' who had a reward of Rs 5 lakh on his head. Disputing the police claim, Ravi's wife Idme said: 'He was with them [the Naxalites] for a year or so. I don't know what work he did for them. But he had some health problems and returned. Since then, he has been staying home. That night, he had also taken refuge in the laadi out of fear.' It turned out, as explained below, that the police had confused two persons called Ravi—Ravi from Nulkatong and another Ravi from Gompad.

Kandri, Payko's mother, was too worried to say much when we met her. It had already been eight days since Payko was taken away. Kandri said: 'Hearing that the *paike* [police] are coming, Payko went to the *khet* [field] to sleep. A few other girls also went with her. The police took her, and now I do not know where she is or how she is.'

According to her Aadhaar enrolment slip, certified by the sarpanch and sachiv, Payko is only nineteen years old.

Besides Ravi and Payko, the police party had also caught two youth, Madavi Bhima (son of Marka) and Sodi Kanna (son of Ravi), from the laadi. Both were from Nulkatong, and according to the youth and villager I had met on the way, they used to be sangam members. On 14 August, when I was returning to Konta with some journalists I had met in Gompad, we saw Madavi Bhima and Sodi Kanna walking back to Nulkatong with their family members.

They said that they had also gone to the laadi for safety that day. When the firing started, they tried to run away but they were caught. The police took them to Konta police station where they were kept for eight days, just before we met them. However, when I talked to the Superintendent of Police of Sukma district later, he claimed that Bhima was not present in the laadi that night (see below).

In Nulkatong, women who had gone to the site in a group soon after the firing ended were beaten up by the police. Local journalists circulated their photographs on social media. The dark marks on their legs, buttocks and backs suggest severe beatings. Even a woman who was obviously pregnant was not spared. The SP, however, just called these beatings 'dhakka-mukki' (see below).

Family members went to Konta the same day (6 August) to claim the bodies. The bodies had been taken to Sukma for post-mortem. It was not until Wednesday, 8 August, that they could finally take the bodies home. The police had left the bodies in Banda from where they had to be carried for at least 15 km. That evening itself, they were cremated or buried.

Varying Versions

On 9 August, the South Bastar Division Committee of the CPI (Maoist) issued a two-page statement condemning the fake encounter in Nulkatong and calling for a Bastar Bandh on 13 August. The statement included a list of those killed and a description of the incident. The list has a slight discrepancy in names and a larger age discrepancy (only one victim has been shown as a minor). The party's account of the incident is at odds with what I learnt from the villagers. The CPI(Maoist) statement describes the incident as follows:

> As part of a special operation, more than 200 police from Konta, Bhejji and Golapalli camps surrounded the villages of Nulkatong, Velpocha, Gompad, Kindempad (*sic*) and Kannaipad on 5 August, held more than fifty persons captive and took them away. Next day on 6 August, at six in the morning, they took them near the Nulkatong hill, tied the hands and feet of fifteen *nishastra grameen* (unarmed villagers) and fired indiscriminately—killing them mercilessly. A few of them are still in captivity of the police. Many are missing and injured.

Turning to the police version, this is what the SP of Sukma district told me in a telephonic interview on 18 August 2018:

> The jan militia of three villages joined to form a militia platoon. A militia platoon has twenty to thirty members. That day, the militia of many villages were together. They had formed a platoon because our (police) parties were dominating in the region for some time. A meeting of the militia platoon was held in Gompad on 31 July. The police reached there at seven the following morning but missed them. Evidence of the meeting was there; they had slaughtered a cow. After that, our parties returned to Bhejji and Konta camps. After taking rest, this operation was launched on 4 August.
> There are four eyewitnesses of the 6 August incident: Ravi, Kanna, Payko and Bhima. Kanna and Ravi were sleeping in the laadi. At 9 p.m. or 10 p.m., they heard a sound. They started running from there. Commander Sita said, '*Hum log hain* [It is

us].' The militia party was there, around twenty-five of them. *'Hum bhi yahin ruk jaate hain* [We will also stay here].'

In the morning, they rose before 5 a.m. Sunrise is at 5.30 a.m. these days. After freshening up, except for the sentry, the rest were attending the roll call—their duties are assigned at that time. The police party had stayed on the other side of the hill while they were on this side. There was only a distance of one-and-a-half kilometres of forests between them. The police did not know about their presence. We noticed them from the hill and started moving in their direction. The Naxal sentry was standing towards the south. He was the first to see our approach and fired. The police parties spread themselves. None of them entered the village.

After that, there was an encounter. They were armed and opened fire. We had advanced weapons. Even a PLGA (People's Liberation Guerrilla Army) company may have less than five automatic weapons. But when firing is taking place from the other side, you cannot know what weapon is being used. There was also a PLGA cadre that day; Baman from Etegatta was a member of the military platoon 4. He had a .303 rifle.

Kanna was working in the sangam for two years. He was a low-key member. Bhima was also a low-key member of the sangam for one year. He used to support the Maoists by providing food. Bhima was not in the laadi that night. He was going from the village to his fields at dawn. When the firing started, he sat down where he was and was caught on the spot.

On Ravi's arrest, the SP accepted that it was a case of mistaken identity. 'We mistook him for Ravi of Gompad, who is the adhyaksh of the Revolutionary People's Council (RPC). He is wanted in twenty cases, including the incident that occurred on 11 March 2017 in which twelve jawans were killed. The militia members killed in this incident were recruited by him. He was also present that morning but managed to escape. Ravi of Nulkatong was no big shot. He was in the militia for a few years and a member of the Local Organizing Squad (LOS) with Commander Mangru. He developed pain in his knees and left the LOS. He has warrants against him in two cases. He was produced before the magistrate on 7 August and is in jail in Sukma.'

About Payko, he said: 'When our party captured (*sic*) Payko, she said that she was hit by a bullet. When somebody is hit by a bullet, sometimes there is no oozing of blood. Therefore, she was put on a cot. She was taken that evening to the hospital in Sukma, where a lady doctor examined her and said that her hip was dislocated. She was produced before the magistrate on 7 August, and on his orders, is being treated first before being arrested.

Payko has told us that she had joined the militia three-and-a-half years back and had left the organization six months ago. But after a couple of months, Soyam Sita came to her home and forcibly took her. He threatened to kill her if she did not come. She was roaming again with the militia party during the last three months.'

On minors, he said that there were two borderline cases which were being medically examined. Results were awaited. On the presence of women other than Payko, he said that there were none. He said village women confronted the police on the Konta-Gollapalli road when they were returning to the camp (not at the site of the encounter), following which there was some dhakka-mukki (scuffle) between them.

'Had it not been an actual encounter, why would there be eyewitnesses?' he asked. 'We are not stopping people from going to the villages. They should also know the truth,' he maintained.

Interestingly, this account of the events is somewhat different from the initial press note issued by the Sukma police. That note gives the impression of an ambush-like incident, where armed Maoists had attempted to ambush the police and the police retaliated. There were forty to fifty Maoists, who—according to that statement—ran away after realizing that the police had the upper hand.

A third version from the police was reported on 7 August in *Nai Duniya* newspaper and attributed to D.M. Awasthi (Special DG, Naxal Operations). In that version, the Maoists were sleeping in their camp when the police reached the spot based on an intelligence tip-off. The police attacked the camp and the Maoists 'tried to retaliate' (*Achanak hui* firing *ke baad Naxaliyon ne jawabi hamla karne ki koshish ki*).

In short, the police versions of the event are not only inconsistent with those of the villagers, but also inconsistent with each other.

On 7 September, I went to meet Payko in the central jail at Jagdalpur. She said that she had been taken to court only once, after two weeks in the hospital. 'In the court, I was told to say that fifteen persons died and that I am a Naxali. I was made to put my thumb impression on a blank sheet of paper.' This was perhaps the 'confessional statement' that the SP was referring to when I spoke with him.

At present, both Payko and Ravi are in the Jagdalpur jail. They have been charged under the IPC Sections 147, 148, 149, 307, 120B (rioting, attempt to murder and criminal conspiracy); Arms Act Sections 25, 27 (using prohibited arms); and UAPA Sections 38, 39 (membership and support of a terrorist organization). These are all serious offences carrying prison sentences of several years—up to ten years in the case of UAPA offences.

Encounter or Massacre?

Our main concern is to determine whether the fifteen who were killed in the morning of 6 August were killed in a real encounter, as the police claims. A real encounter would mean that there was an exchange of fire and proportionate use of force by the police.

Even though the police officials maintain that there was an exchange of fire, the people I spoke to—including those who said that a few militia members were present—denied that there was an exchange of fire. They all maintained that the police surrounded the laadi and opened fire.

The laadi was a bamboo and thatched enclosure which allowed easy visibility of the occupants; there were trees only on one side. The SP had mentioned that their parties had seen the laadi from the hill. The 200 police who surrounded the laadi must have been able to see immediately that those present were in plain clothes. This fact alone would tell them about the 'combatants' they were facing. Even if they were a militia platoon, as SP Meena claims, the police would be well aware of the kind of weapons in their possession. The SP's observation in this regard is quite clear—'We have advanced weapons. Even a PLGA Company may have less than five automatic weapons.' The police parties knew that a militia member may be unarmed, or armed with local weapons like bows and arrows, or at the most with an archaic bharmar, which is no match for automatic weapons. The SP said that one person was a PLGA cadre with a .303 rifle and that when the firing is going on you do not know what weapons are being used. But this is difficult to believe—those trained in warfare would have a fairly accurate idea. Also, except for the SP, nobody else mentioned that there was a better weapon than a bharmar in the laadi that day.

According to those who were present in the laadi, there were approximately thirty to forty persons there on the night of 5 August. This would mean that the police-people ratio was as high as 6:1 or even 8:1. Clearly, the police parties had an overwhelming advantage of numbers as well as weaponry. What, then, stopped them from overpowering and arresting the suspects?

Just as a real encounter has some discernible features, so does a fake one. A fake encounter has to be staged as a real one and efforts are made to obfuscate the truth. Tampering of facts related to uniforms of the deceased, ammunition and material seized, post-mortem, media reports and the judicial process is common. A fake encounter is successful when the police are given a clean chit. In this case, too, we have early evidence of the moves made by the police in this direction.

Some of the bodies—four according to one account—were found wearing the upper half of a camouflaged uniform. Curiously, these uniforms had no blood stains and one of them had a Bharatiya Sena (Indian Army) logo. The villagers stated that the police deliberately dressed the victims in these uniforms; their relatives were all in everyday clothes that day.

At this point, a word should be said about the involvement of the DRG. As mentioned by the SP to the media, two of the police parties were of DRG and one of STF. The DRG is made up of local persons, many of whom are Adivasis or surrendered Maoists. In earlier investigations of fake encounters (including the killing of Hidme in Gompad), relatives of victims have often recognized ex-Maoists, now DRG, who played a leading role in identifying and sometimes killing the victims. Since they are local, often from the same area or villages, they know persons by name as well as the extent of their involvement with the Maoists. There have been occasions when relatives of the victims have accused the DRG of targeting young men and women they had themselves recruited earlier into the Maoist movement.

In this incident, my contention is that the force opened fire on an unsuspecting group, of which around nine were members of the jan-militia of their villages. The identity of the jan militia was no doubt known to some DRGs. The jan-militia members were targeted—killing six of them. Two of them (Madkam Lakma of Nulkatong and possibly Soyam Sita of Gompad) were not only shot at, but their heads were bludgeoned and Lakma's leg was mutilated with knives or other sharp instruments. The seventh organizational person who was killed was the lone LGS member from Etegetta (according to one source), who was also in plain clothes. The other eight victims were all civilians and at least four of them were minors. All this indicates that this was not a real encounter where casualties occur in an exchange of fire.

The fact that more than half of those killed were civilians suggests that the firing happened indiscriminately on the group as a whole. There was no meeting that day. The jan-militia members are local persons of the same villages, as are LOS or LGS members, and they have relatives in each other's villages. It is quite normal for people to get together socially. Even if there was a meeting, it does not imply that there was an exchange of fire and nor would it justify indiscriminate firing.

Opening fire indiscriminately cannot be justified on any grounds, least of all the argument that the police *thought* that the other side might have sophisticated weapons. In warfare, there are ways for soldiers to protect themselves—wearing protection gear, for instance. They can, if they wish, use only as much force as necessary to subdue their targets. But all this means nothing when the firing is part of a deliberate strategy to kill as many 'Naxalis' as possible, without being mindful of the nature or degree of their involvement, if any, in the Maoist movement.

The conclusion that the Nulkatong incident was a massacre and not an encounter is consistent with several other facts. First, none of the police were injured despite the firing going on for an hour and a half in their own account. Second, the victims' bodies were quickly put into body bags, whereas after an encounter, the dead bodies are usually brought to the police station and displayed as they are. The reason, quite likely, is that the police did not want anyone to see that many of the victims were minors, and in any case, not uniformed Maoists as they had claimed. Third, according to a reliable source, post-mortem was conducted on just thirteen bodies instead of fifteen. Could it be that the two remaining bodies were those of Madkam Lakma and the other person, possibly Soyam Sita, whose head had been bludgeoned? It is unlikely that the police would have liked this act of brutality to come to light, since it would contradict their encounter story—this would be another reason for putting the bodies in body bags in a hurry. Finally, as mentioned earlier, the uniforms allegedly worn by some of the victims were uniforms of the Indian Army. This, again, suggests a cover-up.

Afterwards

Even though SP Meena said that the police encouraged people to find out the truth, the situation on the ground was quite different. Independent investigations were not welcome. Even as this inquiry was in progress, on 13 August 2018, a rally took place in Konta where a crowd mobilized by former Salwa Judum leaders shouted hostile slogans against me and Soni Sori (who had already gone to Nulkatong with a fact-finding team of the Aam Aadmi Party). A group of journalists who were accompanying Soni Sori on 18–19 August was obstructed and reached Nulkatong with much difficulty. On reaching, they found an empty village. They learnt later that the police had instructed the people of Nulkatong to leave for Durma (on the pretext of possible firing due to Maoist presence in the area), and also to stay clear of outsiders.

Abuses and threats were also aired on social media. For example, on 19 August, on the WhatsApp group 'Yuva Sangh Chhattisgarh' (administered by members of the Action Group for National Integration [AGNI] among others), some persons made wild allegations against Soni Sori and journalists Lingaram Kodopi and Prabhat Singh, claiming that they had taken money from the Maoists in return for speaking in their favour. On the same group, someone called me '*suar ki beti, murdabad*'. Prabhat, who was countering these abuses in a civil manner, even received a death threat ('*main hi tere ko dauda-dauda kar marunga*'). On 21 August, another prominent anti-Maoist leader of Sukma circulated a press note mentioning that a police complaint had been lodged against Soni Sori and myself by some villagers of Nulkatong, claiming that we were putting pressure on people to give false testimonies. Soni Sori later received a notice from Konta police station on 27 August.

In spite of these acts of intimidation, many local and national journalists as well as fact-finding teams investigated the Nulkatong 'encounter' and found it to be a fake one. The difference, if at all, is in their understanding of whether all those killed were plain villagers or some were also jan militia.

No police complaint was made at the Konta police station under which Nulkatong falls. This is because at the time, as happens in these cases, relatives are more concerned about getting the dead bodies from the police so that they can perform the last rites (there have been instances where the handing over of a dead body has been refused and the police has disposed of it). In any case, they knew that the police force of their own thana was involved in the encounter and that this could not have happened without the knowledge of the district SP; this also discouraged them from seeking 'justice' through available institutional channels. Authorities could have taken suo moto notice based on the many media reports of the encounter, but did not do so. Later, a petition was filed in the Supreme Court by the Civil Liberties Committee, Telangana, arguing that the encounter was fake and that civilians had been killed, but nothing came of it so far.

The Nulkatong villagers were very worried about the four who had been taken away by the police on the day of the massacre. Two were released after eight days and later made prosecution witnesses. The other two, Ravi and Payko, were jailed and charged as mentioned earlier. Their families appointed me as their lawyer, enabling me to follow the case closely. Incarcerated in the Jagdalpur central jail, they were rarely brought to court during their long years behind bars. Ravi's wife could visit her husband only two or three times because of the distance (about 200 km) and expenses involved. Payko's father Rama was able to come a few more times, breaking journey on the way. Despite the strain, he still had a gentle smile every time I met him, but the anxiety took its toll. A few months before the case was disposed, I heard that he had lost his mind and disappeared.

The prosecution took four years to examine fourteen witnesses. Except for the two who were from Nulkatong, all were police and security force personnel of the DRG and STF parties that had gone to Nulkatong that day. The judgement was delivered on 3 February 2023, acquitting Ravi and Payko who could finally go home.

A Similar Encounter in Gadchiroli

There are telling similarities between the Nulkatong encounter and another encounter I had investigated earlier with a team of students from the Tata Institute of Social Sciences in a village called Mendhari, just across the Chhattisgarh border in Gadchiroli district, Maharashtra.[2] This was another case of unwarranted killing in broad daylight, on 7 July 2013.

Six Maoists, all Adivasi women (said to be from Rajnandgaon district in Chhattisgarh), were killed that day by security forces on a combing operation. Local villagers said that the forces were around 300 in number. According to the district SP, they included C-60 commandoes of the Maharashtra state as well as CoBRA commandoes of the CRPF.

We visited Mendhari a few days after the incident and heard consistent accounts of it from multiple local witnesses. We learnt that the Maoist women had taken shelter in the jungle close to the village and were having their morning tea when the forces closed in on them. The women had guns, of the most primitive sort. A short encounter ensued, with no casualties. Feeling overpowered, all six women started running towards the village with the force on their heels. The villagers saw them as they ran through the main lane towards the paddy fields on the western side of the village.

Four of them were in one field and two at a little distance when another section of the force appeared from the other side. The four were surrounded. They dropped their guns and raised their hands in surrender, yet they were shot at and killed from close range. One of the other two who was near a giant mahua tree was shot in the head from behind, damaging her face beyond recognition. Her mate, the sixth woman, had climbed the tree in a futile attempt to save herself. The branches of that tree still bore the marks of the bullets that had rained at her from below.

The villagers said that they had been harassed by the police: 'They took us forcibly to identify the bodies. When we said that we did not know them, they beat us brutally, saying, "You give them food and say you cannot recognize them?"' One young man was abused, beaten, and then caught by the neck and made to stare at the face of one of the mutilated women. 'Seeing the dead bodies, and the face of the dead woman from so close, I lost my head and ran towards the jungle,' he said. The police fired at his retreating back. Fortunately, they missed him and he survived to tell the tale.

As in the Nulkatong case, the Gadchiroli SP too admitted that '[the six women Maoists] had only twelve bore guns. We have automatic weapons.' Perhaps this cold-blooded killing of six Adivasi Maoist women who had surrendered was celebrated by the security forces as a victory in their 'hunt' for Maoists. Executions of this sort, however, negate the rule of law.

NHRC Guidelines

The NHRC, in a letter sent to chief ministers on 12 May 2010, lays down guidelines and procedures to be followed in cases of 'death during the course of police action'.[3] In this letter, the NHRC clearly states that 'the police do not have a right to take away the life of a person'. It mentions three specific circumstances where causing death can be justified. These are: (a) in exercise of the right of self-defence during an encounter; (b) in the course of dispersal of unlawful assembly; and (c) in the course of effecting arrest, when 'Section 46 of the Criminal Procedure Code . . . authorizes the police to use reasonable force, even extending up to the causing of death, *if found necessary* [emphasis added] to arrest the person accused of an offence punishable with death or imprisonment for life.'

The letter affirms: 'Thus, it is evident that death caused in an encounter if not justified would amount to an offence of culpable homicide'.

Even in a war situation, if soldiers surrender and are not involved in any form of active combat at that time, killing them would be a breach of human rights and a violation of Article 21 of the Indian Constitution (*'No person shall be deprived of his life except according to procedure established by law'*). In their response to a complaint filed by Andhra Pradesh Civil Liberties Committee (APCLC), dated 5 November 1996, NHRC invokes Article 6 of the International Covenant on Civil and Political Rights that states: *'Every human being has the inherent right to life. This right shall be protected by law. No one shall be arbitrarily deprived of his life.'*

In the Nulkatong and Mendhari 'encounters' we can see that none of the three circumstances mentioned above are applicable. These are therefore clear cases of fake encounter and should be treated as 'culpable homicide'. The police, an arm of the state, has infringed the Constitution of India.

Concluding Thoughts

The Nulkatong massacre is symbolic of the ruthless nature of anti-Maoist operations in Bastar. There is huge pressure to 'finish off' the Maoist movement without delay, and to show results, mainly in the form of Maoist casualties. Many of the so-called Maoists being killed, however, are innocent villagers, or members of local militias who are also ordinary villagers armed with the most rudimentary weapons if any. Security forces are unleashed on them with overwhelming force and full impunity.

It is well known that the number of the jan militia and others who constitute 'the base force' of the Maoist movement is much larger than that of the PLGA cadre. According to a press report of 2010, PLGA has a strength of 3000, compared with 30,000 for the jan militia. When the Salwa Judum operation was launched in 2005, the state had candidly asserted its intention of 'draining the water so that the fish cannot survive'.[4] At that time, as we know, hundreds of villages were burnt and many hundreds died in targeted killings of those thought to be involved with the Maoists in any way. The situation today is much the same: jan militia are deemed 'Naxali' since they are at the lowest rung of the Maoist structure. As mentioned earlier, they are very poorly armed. It is comparatively easy for the state to use its powerful forces to launch operations targeting them and others in the base force. The emphasis is on '*kitne shav la paye kiya*' (how many dead bodies could you get). That those who were killed were only the gatekeepers of the Maoist organization does not count. As the villager I met on my way to Nulkatong the first day put it, 'Police . . . do not differentiate between a *naxali* [Naxalite], militia or *aam-janata* [civilians]—all are treated in the same way.'

The Nulkatong massacre also raises a troubling question about the responsibility of the CPI (Maoist) towards those who make up its base force as well as towards the people in the villages where the party has a strong presence. The militia members, let alone ordinary people, are in no position to defend themselves in this sort of situation, unlike higher-level PLGA cadre who have a better chance since they have military training and modern weapons. The militia members and the LOS are soft targets for security personnel who have to show results. In Gompad, a village of fifty houses, at least fourteen people (including children) have been killed since 2009 in successive 'encounter killings'.

Murders have become an inevitable part of the counter-insurgency strategy in Bastar, as we have witnessed since 2005. Several such cases have been challenged in the courts, but there is no progress. A government indulging in criminality as a matter of policy does not give us hope for either justice or peace in this tormented land.

20

Nowhere to Hide*

The three incidents below occurred between 2 February and 8 March 2019—within just over a month. They will, I hope, give an inkling of what is happening in Bastar on a regular basis since 2005.

Three Bullets for Three Women of Godelguda

There are things we do every day without knowing that it may be the last time. This applies everywhere but more so in a conflict area where 'war' intrudes in your life without a warning in unforeseen ways.

It was something like that for Podiyam Sukki that early morning on 2 February 2019, when she left her four sleeping children, picked up her axe, and joined two other women from her hamlet, Kalmu Deve and Podiyam Hungi. They started for the forests at some distance from their village Godelguda in Sukma's Konta tehsil, to collect firewood.

They crossed the village pond and were walking on an open stretch interspersed with a few trees and tendu bushes—within half a kilometre of the village—when they noticed security forces coming

---

* This chapter is based on three articles published in Wire in 2019. Some names have been changed, to protect anonymity.

from the opposite side. They turned back in fear and then heard a gunshot. Alarmed, they lifted their arms and axes, shouting that they were out to collect firewood. But before they knew it, Sukki and Deve had been hit, a bullet missing Hungi only because she is short-statured.

Night had fallen by the time we reached Godelguda a few days later. In the headlights of the motorcycles, we could make out the outlines of the houses and courtyards we passed. We stopped in an open space close to a house where a few women were sitting on the mud-caked floor. A beautiful and healthy infant lay asleep on a colourful cotton cloth. The child, all of three months, was the youngest of Sukki's four children.

Some of us sat on the small string cot that was brought out for us. I was trying the stump of a tree as a seat when Deve and Hungi arrived followed by Deva, Sukki's husband, with their other three children in tow. The oldest is six-year-old Joga.

Deve and Hungi are young women in their twenties. Deve's attractive face is full of consternation as she recounts what happened that morning. 'Sukki was hit in the stomach,' she says. Pointing at her upper left thigh she adds, 'I was hit here and became unconscious; only Hungi was left who could help us.'

Hungi, still distraught, said, 'I managed to somehow drag Deve to the village. Sukki was calling out to her mother and asking for water when we left her.'

Soni Sori, who had gone to the village soon after the incident with a team including Aam Aadmi Party members and other Adivasi activists, said, 'Upon learning what had happened, a few village women went to the spot with water for Sukki and saw security forces slipping a Maoist uniform over her. When they protested, the forces wrapped her in a polythene sheet instead, even though she was still alive and asking for water.'

Deva said that his family members informed him about the incident over the phone. He was in a Telangana village where he had gone to work in the fields as a casual labourer. He said that the security forces took his wife, who was around twenty-seven years old, to the CRPF camp in Puswada, saying that there was a field hospital there. By the time his mother and others of the village reached the camp, Sukki had died. Her dead body was returned late at night that day, after his relatives were kept waiting for many hours. The forces had put pressure on the family to cremate the body quickly, without completing the customary rites.

Encounter, Crossfire or Plain Killing?

Local newspaper reports of the incident quoted then Superintendent of Police (SP) of Sukma district, Jitendra Shukla. The SP first claimed that CRPF forces from the Puswada camp and district police personnel were returning from an area domination exercise in Rangaiguda forests when there was an encounter with Maoists close to Godelguda in which a Naxali woman was killed and another was injured and apprehended. In response to allegations of a fake encounter, the SP modified his statement slightly, accepting that the women were civilians ('they were not in Maoist uniforms') and claiming that they were killed in crossfire during an encounter with the Maoists.

However, the SP's encounter and crossfire stories are at odds with what Deve, Hungi and other villagers have maintained—that there were no Maoists around that day and no exchange of fire. The secretary of the Konta Area Committee of the CPI (Maoist) also stated in a press release (dated 5 February 2019) that there was no Maoist movement in the area that day.

Local journalists who went to the spot found fallen axes but a curious absence of blood-stained earth or grass, suggesting an attempt by the forces to tamper with evidence. They also found that the site of the alleged 'encounter' was not a forest, as is usually the case, but open land with sparse tree cover.

From available facts, it is clear that three bullets were fired—deliberately—at the only three persons who were out in that stretch of open field that morning. Three young women were shot at, and one killed, on a fleeting suspicion of being Maoists, or even knowing that they were civilians.

Compensation as Justice?

Kawasi Lakhma, Congress MLA of Konta constituency in which Godelguda falls and a minister in the state cabinet, also maintained that the encounter was fake, that the victims were unarmed village women. In a letter to the Chief Minister on 8 February 2019, he said that such incidents 'erode people's confidence in the government'. Indeed, angered by the killings, Adivasi organisations like the Sarva Adivasi Samaj called for a bandh in Sukma.

The families of the deceased and injured later received monetary compensation from Kawasi Lakhma (Rs 5 lakh and 1 lakh respectively) as well as from the district administration (Rs 25,000 and Rs 20,000).

SP Jitendra Shukla informed the press three days after the incident that an FIR had been lodged in the Polampalli thana against 'unknown persons for murder' and that a judicial inquiry had been initiated.[1] However, faith in inquiries has understandably shrunk in Bastar.

Lingaram Kodopi, an Adivasi journalist who investigated this incident wryly commented: 'When the forces go to the jungle on a Maoist operation, perhaps they think they are going on *shikar* (hunting). After the shikar, dead bodies of Adivasis are wrapped in polythene sheets, tied with rope, and paraded in front of the media and public as Maoists.'

If the rule of law prevailed in Bastar, CRPF jawans who fired the three shots would have been booked under IPC Sections 302 (murder) and 307 (attempt to murder), arrested, and tried like anyone else who is so charged. But the rule of law does not prevail in Bastar.

Nightmare in Abujmarh

At dawn on 5 March 2019, thousands of Adivasis of Abujmarh—a densely forested region of Bastar considered as 'a liberated area' by the CPI (Maoist)—were walking towards the Indravati River. There were women and men, and children hanging on to their parents, some of whom were also carrying bags of rice and vegetables to cook on the way. Wading through the river, they reached the opposite bank to join throngs from the other side heading in the same direction. Even from the riverbank, it is a long walk—about ten kilometres—to the public ground in Bhairamgarh town. Many had walked more than 20 kilometres from their villages.

On 7 February, only five days after the Godelguda incident in Sukma district, the lives of ten Adivasi youth were lost in an alleged encounter in Tadballa, a tiny village on the northern side of the Indravati in Abujmarh. The youth were from six villages—Utla, Jhilli, Kolnar, Chotepalli, Tadopot and Tadballa—of Bhairamgarh tehsil, on both sides of the river.

People of these villages had come out to protest for the first time since the Salwa Judum, to demand accountability. After assembling in Bhairamgarh, they held a public meeting where many locals spoke up. Women were particularly vocal in their indictment of the security forces and the government. The speakers also included Vikram Mandavi, an ex-Salwa Judum leader of the area who is now an active Congress party leader and the MLA of Bijapur constituency.

The Incident

There were around a dozen mostly middle-aged Adivasis in that small room, sitting or resting. It had been a long day and they looked tired.

They may or may not have known each other before, but their shared grief brought with it a certain intimacy unlikely to fade with time.

It was evening. Parents and other family members of all those who were killed had stayed back to discuss a possible case with lawyers from the high court of Chhattisgarh who were keen to represent them. They began talking about the day of the alleged encounter.

'A few party [Maoist] persons had come to our village two days before the encounter. They said that they were organising two days of sports for the youth and needed help with preparations,' said Oyami Budhuram of Utla village. He said that it takes around two hours to reach Tadballa from Utla by foot. Four other villages where the Maoists went to ask for volunteers are also at a walking distance of one or two hours from Tadballa.

Budhuram's son, Raju, and four other youth from Utla (Parsa Sukku, Barsa Sukko, Kadiyami Shankar and Madvi Vijjo) were among those who were killed on 7 February.

The incident occurred at around 10 a.m. in the Patelpara of Tadballa village. The location is a ground with a few mango trees. At a short distance, there is a stream. There are more trees and hills at a distance.

The party members had asked the volunteers to come a day in advance of the event with cooking pots and other utensils as well as rice. There were tasks to be done like clearing the ground of leaves and twigs and making it suitable for a sports event. A group of young persons at the site had just finished cooking rice and were cutting vegetables. Relatives said that as the day advanced, many more would have come to watch the event.

Hundreds of security personnel (they were District Reserve Guards and Special Task Force from Bijapur and Bhairamgarh camps) then attacked the assembly of around seventy youth at the venue. The attack went on for around two hours.

According to one testimony, there were three Maoists in uniform at the site, who managed to escape. It is not clear whether they were armed or not, but in any case, there was no exchange of fire. A few *bharmars* (archaic muzzle-loading guns) were allegedly found at the site by the police.

Palo's father Sodi Hidma and mother Aayte who live in Tadballa said, 'We were quite close to the ground and could hear the shots and then the screams of our daughter. We tried to go to her, but the forces prevented us. They had cordoned off the site.'

They said that when they received the body from the district hospital at Bijapur, naked and wrapped in polythene—all the bodies were handed over to relatives in the same condition—they saw that she had been sexually assaulted. Some of her fingers had been cut and one eye had been taken out. There were marks on her forehead of heavy blows as though with a stone. She had also been stabbed in the chest and had two bullet entry and exit wounds. Palo, they said, was around fifteen years old.

Five women and five men were killed in this incident. All of them were very young—in their early twenties and even younger in some cases. Aside from Palo, Shanti (daughter of Aarki Paklu) of Kolnar village and Shankar (son of Kadiyami Lakku) of Utla village were also minors, according to their parents. Except for Barsa Parmesh of Utla, they were all unmarried. Most of them were illiterate.

The testimonies of other parents also suggest unspeakable brutality. Bullets, knives and stones were used to kill and mutilate. Many bodies—such as those of Raju, Sukku, Palo, Shanti and Somdi—showed that two and sometimes even three bullets had been fired at them. Knives were also used: Raju's and Shankar's throats had been slit, and stab wounds were found on the bodies of Somdi, Parmesh, Palo and Sudri. Like Palo, fifteen-year-old Shanti was sexually assaulted and her genitalia were mutilated. Somdi's body also showed signs of sexual assault.

Parents and relatives said that their children were dressed in casual clothes. Women, for example, were wearing the customary lungi and blouse. But a group photograph of the bodies circulated by the police shows them in shirts, and in a couple of cases, what looks like a Maoist uniform.

Clothes and other personal belongings that the police found at the site were burnt on the spot. Vessels show hole marks and other damage. 'Villagers of Tadballa told us that after the incident, the police butchered chicken and a pig for their meal that they cooked and ate there,' said Madvi Jabbo, Vijjo's mother.

Many parents said that while claiming the bodies, they were asked for the Aadhaar cards of the victims. The Aadhaar cards, which include age among other information, were not returned by the police in the case of Shanti and Shankar—both minors, according to their parents and relatives.

Somdi's mother, Parsa Nendo, of Chotepalli village said, 'Such an incident has not occurred before in our parts. We do not want compensation. We want justice.'

Seeking Justice

A very good indicator that an encounter is fake is when people protest—they do not protest after every encounter.

From testimonies and other facts, we can conclude that there was no encounter that day. The victims were not Maoists, but youth who were living in a 'liberated area'. Perhaps they were under the influence of Maoists and did participate in events organized by Maoists such as this sports event. If people join open activities organized by Maoists in an area where there are no other organisations and a few sources of entertainment, can they be blamed?

Without ascertaining the details of the 'encounter', the government was quick to hail it as a great victory of the security forces over the Maoists. According to the police's version of the incident, quoted in media reports, the site was a training camp and there was an exchange of fire. All this, however, was emphatically denied by the parents and relatives of the victims.

This is not the first time that security forces have opened fire on an unarmed assembly in areas that are known to be under Maoist influence. On 17 May 2013, in Edesmetta village of Bijapur district, the security forces fired on an unarmed assembly of villagers who were celebrating *beeja pandum* (seed festival), killing eight Adivasis. A similar incident occurred in Sarkeguda, also in Bijapur district, on 28 June 2012, killing seventeen Adivasis. In these regions, security forces get suspicious whenever they see villagers assembled in large groups. In both cases, judicial inquiries concluded that there had been unprovoked firing on unarmed civilians (see Chapter 17—Salwa Judum and After).

At the end of the Bhairamgarh meeting, a petition was submitted to the local MLA. The petition demanded that a counter-FIR should be lodged in accordance with the people's version of the facts (an FIR had already been filed by the police). It also called for a judicial inquiry commission, an opportunity for people to testify before it, and strict action against those responsible for the atrocities perpetrated on 7 February. Copies of the petition were sent to the highest officials (President, Chief Justice of India, Chief Minister of Chhattisgarh, Chief Justice of the High Court), without any result.

In the last week of April 2019, according to local news reports, three Adivasis of three villages near Tadballa were killed by the Maoists after a 'jan adalat' where they were accused of being police informers. There have been no protests against these killings, suggesting that people either support the Maoist execution or lack the freedom to protest in such matters.

Who Killed Sodi Deva?

With a trembling hand, Podiyam Ganga reached for the stamp-pad to put the impression of his left thumb on the police complaint. Ganga was amongst ten or so Adivasis who had come from Bodhrajpadar village of Konta tehsil to Sukma, the district headquarters, on Saturday

16 March 2019. They were there to register police complaints on two related incidents.

A Fatal Leaflet

On Friday, 8 March, around thirty-five to forty villagers of Bodhrajpadar were travelling on a tractor (often the only means of public transport in these parts) to Bheji thana, seven kilometres from their village. Amongst them was Sodi Deva, a twenty-year-old youngster. Ganga, the patel of the village in his early fifties, was not far behind on a cycle. The previous day, when some of the villagers were returning from the Konta weekly market, they had gone once more to Bheji thana to demand the release of four persons from their village, amongst them Deva's father Dula, who had been in police custody for a month. They had made the same request many times during the previous month, but had always been turned away. This time, however, they were told that if all the villagers came to the thana the next day, the four would be set free.

Around 1.5 kilometres before the thana and half a kilometre from Bheji village, Deva and a few others in the tractor noticed sheets of paper held on the ground with stones, on the edge of the road. They knew these were Maoist parchas. Ganga, on his cycle, had also seen them. When Deva noticed two policemen at a grocery store further up the road, he jumped off the tractor and also stopped Ganga when he caught up with him. 'We told them about the parchas,' said Ganga. 'We do not know their names but both have the surname Markam [a common Adivasi surname]. They asked us to go back and get the parchas. We refused. They started abusing us in foul language. "*Bhosadike,* do as you are told if you want to meet your relatives," they shouted.'

Deva borrowed a cycle and, reluctantly, headed to the spot with Ganga. At a short distance from the spot, Ganga had an urge to pee and pedalled towards a thicket of trees on the side of the road. 'From where I was, I could see Deva as he stopped near the parchas. There were a few of them and he started picking them up. He was bent over the last one when there was a terrifying blast, a roaring fire and smoke. I saw Deva fly far above the ground, higher than a giant tree nearby. Then I saw him fall.'

Scared of going closer, Ganga turned back towards the thana. According to him and other villagers, after being alerted the police made the villagers lead the way to the site. 'Why did they not go in the front?,' they asked, 'they have machines . . . there could have been another bomb.' Deva's lifeless body with a missing right arm lay face down on the gravel, only there was no face.

Illegal Confinement

As Ganga related what had happened, others listened. Amongst them were Dula, Deva's father, as well as the other three who had been in police custody.

The first person to be taken in, on 20 January, was Kawasi Lakhma. Tall and lanky, Lakhma is in his mid-twenties. He said that he was sleeping at home when a posse of mostly Gondi-speaking force picked him up, at around 4 a.m. He was first taken to the nearby CRPF-DRG camp at Elarmadgu, where he was kept for three days, and then to Bheji thana. 'I was beaten up at the camp and the thana by police after they had consumed daru. Amongst them was one called Kashyap. They kept forcing me to surrender. I told them that I used to work for them [the Maoists] but left two years ago, why should I surrender?'

Kawasi Lakhma was joined in Bheji thana by three others from the village, who were all picked up at dawn on 7 February. Two of them, Sodi Dula and Dirdo Deva, are older men in their mid-forties while the third, Podiyam Nandu, is in his twenties. Like Lakhma, they were all kept in the camp for several days (even weeks in one case) before being taken to the thana. All three said that they were beaten up when they were first taken in—Dula in the village, Deva in the thana and Nandu in the camp.

Nandu was under pressure to surrender, like Lakhma, but he resisted. He told them that he used to be part of the jan militia but had left it after a year. That was a few years ago; he has been living at home in the village ever since.

Deva said, 'I was not asked to surrender but a drunk Major Sham kept asking me to speak in Hindi ["*Hindi bol*"] and beating me for being unable to do so.'

Dula said that he was accused of having slept in his uncle's house the previous night 'because he was hiding out of fear.' What had actually happened was that after having a few drinks of tadi (palm toddy) he was too drowsy to go home.

While in police custody, they were kept in a room next to the office section of the thana. In the camp as well as the thana they were made to do odd jobs like sweeping, chopping wood, cutting vegetables, washing utensils and cleaning the yard. Family members went to the thana many times, but their pleas were ignored. Sometimes they were told that the four would be released whenever the sahib came. They were finally released on 8 March, after the blast.

The Code of Criminal Procedure does not allow a person arrested without a warrant to be detained in police custody for more than twenty-four hours (Section 57); the period may be extended, up to fifteen days, only by an order of a Judicial Magistrate (Section 167). A police official who did not want to be named said that permission from a Magistrate is hardly ever taken—it is very unlikely that it was taken in this case.

The illegal confinement of four persons for weeks is not unusual in the conflict-ridden districts of Bastar. It is not clear whether an entry about their 'arrest' was even made in the police station diary.

Futile Complaints

For the IED blast, an FIR has been registered. The FIR bears the signature of Podiyam Ganga as the person who filed it two hours after the incident. This is mystifying, since Ganga came to Sukma to file a police complaint after a week. Perhaps he was too shocked at the time to know what he was signing. The FIR, made out against unknown Maoists, states that the villagers were on their way to the bazar that day, that Deva picked up the parchas on his own volition, and that the IED planted there was an act of criminal conspiracy with the intention of causing death.

On 16 March, the Superintendent of Police, D.S. Meravi, gave a patient hearing to the aggrieved group from Bodhrajpadar. He ordered the immediate transfer of the two Assistant sub-inspectors at Bheji thana, Budharuram Markam and Chainuram Markam. Further punitive action would be taken, he assured. He said that Deva's father would receive the monetary compensation that is due when a civilian is killed in a Maoist action (Rs 5 lakh) and that a family member or relative would get a job in a government office.

So, who killed Sodi Deva? It can be argued that if the police had not so callously forced Ganga and Deva to get the parchas, Deva would be alive. It is also possible that, instead of him, a tractor-full of people would have died, or a villager on her way to the market, or just a wandering cow or goat. It is not the first time that the planting of IEDs by the Maoists, to target the police, has backfired.

The 8th of March is celebrated as international women's day. In Bodhrajpadar, however, it will be remembered as a day when a Maoist leaflet—celebrating women's day—killed Sodi Deva.

21

Adivasi Christians
Attacked in a Sukma Village[*]

Our first glimpse of Chingavaram, a village of Sukma district in Bastar, was in the dark. It was early evening, on 28 November 2020, and the village was quiet and seemingly peaceful. There was nothing to show that this had been the site of communal violence just a few nights earlier.

A youth sat on a bench in the verandah outside the local grocery shop, browsing on his mobile. 'Yes, there had been trouble three nights ago. The Christian houses are there,' he said pointing down the road. We found no one there, however, except for a few elderly women.

The Attack

The next morning, we spent two hours in the company of the *virodhi paksh* (opposing side). This included influential members of the

---

[*] Originally published in Scroll, December 2020. Similar incidents in other parts of Bastar, before and after the attack reported here, point to organised attempts to incite local communities against Adivasi Christians in this entire region during the last few years.

village: the sarpanch-pati, patel, pujari's son, a teacher, a leader of the Koya Samaj from a neighbouring village and a few others.

We asked them to describe what had happened. Budra Madavi, the sarpanch-pati (who was not among the attackers), said:

> The incident occurred on the intervening night of 24 and 25 November. It began at around 1 a.m. Some families in our village have been *Isu* (Jesus) believers for the last five-six years. We sat with them two or three times and tried to reason with them. *Humne unko kaha ki Isu mein mat mano. Hum pehle se devi-devta mein manne wale hain. Tum hum logon mein aao. Par vo log nahi mane* (We told them, don't believe in Jesus. We have always believed in *devi-devta*. Be with us. But they did not listen).
>
> That evening, around sixty persons from outside had come to Mukka's house. A DJ (sound system) was being used. Loud songs were being played and people were dancing. The Christians had not taken permission from the patel or pujari. We asked them, why are you doing this? That time we were fifteen-sixteen of us. Afterwards, men of the whole village went and beat them up.

Chingavaram, he said, was a village of around 130 households of Gond Adivasis. More than half of the households, including three of those we were talking with, participated in the 'attack'. They called it *maar-peet* (beating). When asked how they had beaten people up, they said that they had used their hands and *dande* (thick wooden or bamboo sticks). They said that some managed to run away and that they beat up whoever they could catch—men or women. When asked whether there was any retaliation, they said: '*Humi log, gaon wale . . . mare. Veh log vapas nahi kiye* [We, the village people . . . beat them. They did not hit back].'

In one version of the story, the reason for anger was that the Christians had convened their gathering without permission just one day after the rest of the village had celebrated the traditional harvest puja for two days.

It seemed that the attack had been led by the village patel, Somda Madavi, and the pujari, Deva Madavi, among others. A large number of those who participated in the attack were from Patel para where the sarpanch, patel and pujari reside, and Mirkum para. Somda, the patel, said much the same thing as Budra, the sarpanch-pati. He said that he had also talked to Mukka, in whose house the programme was being organized, hoping for a *samjhauta* (compromise). 'He did not listen, so we beat them up.' He said that they were celebrating something, but they did not say what. He did not think that it was a wedding or a chetti (naming ceremony).

Somda also mentioned casually that a cow had been slaughtered for the feast, but no one made an issue of it—all of them eat cow meat from time to time. It turned out later that no cow had, in fact, been slaughtered.

The Victims

Later in the day, we managed to find the affected Christians in Sukma. They had taken refuge there in a makeshift camp, with the help of the church they were part of (New Bethesda Jesus Christ Tribal Ministries). We had a long discussion with twenty to twenty-five men, women and children. Their account of the incident was consistent with what we had heard in the village, but far more alarming. Many of them had wounds—broken limbs, fractured ribs, beating marks and so on. We learnt that four persons had to be hospitalized for serious injuries while fifteen to twenty others sustained minor injuries.

Their version of the event is as follows. On 24 November evening, a programme was organized at Mukka Madavi's house in Naka para, at one end of the village. A hut had been built in Mukka's courtyard three years ago that serves as a church.

The programme started at around 7 p.m. The guests, around forty in number, who attended the event were from nearby villages and districts. A prayer meeting was followed by chetti celebration of Prakash, Mukka's nephew. After that everyone had a meal of chicken, lentils and rice. Then most went to sleep or were talking amongst themselves, while seven to ten children and youngsters were dancing to the tune of songs being played with an amplifier, but not very loud, they said.

They were suddenly attacked by a large group of persons from their own village who were armed with dandas, rods, bows and arrows, and sickles. Many of them were drunk. Shouting abuses and threats, they started beating whoever they could catch. The attack went on for a long time. Madka Madavi, around forty years old, said: 'I managed to hide during the night, but I was caught early in the morning by Somda patel, Deva pujari and four others. They dragged me in front of our church and thrashed me mercilessly, fracturing my arm and a rib.'

Laxman Madavi, a college student, related how his fifty-year-old father Mukka, the host of the gathering, was hit by an arrow in the lower back and was hospitalized, as was Sodi Ganga, who had been beaten with a danda and rods. Bending on the mud-plastered floor, Jaisingh lifted his shirt and showed us the dark marks on his back. Sanni Madkam, a young woman, raised her bandaged hand to show us where she had been hit by a rod. Three other women took me behind the house to show me severe bruises on their buttocks, as did Gangi Madavi, who had bruises all over her body. She had been attacked by Mura Madavi who, like Gangi, also lived in Naka para.

They mentioned that the assailants heaped all possible belongings of the guests in a pile and burnt them. In the pile was also a Bible and Rs 15,000.

Kikir Lakka, a Christian from Sukma and one of the invited guests, said that he managed to run away that night while the attack was going on. He ran to the nearby CRPF camp, less than half a kilometre down the road. He begged the CRPF to intervene. But they flatly refused, saying: '*Bhago yahan se! Hum log raat me nahi aayenge* [Go away. We will not come in the night]!' He and six others refused to leave and stayed outside the camp until the police arrived from the Gadiras thana 12 km away.

The sub-inspector of the thana told us that he had learnt about the incident at 6 a.m., from a thana staff who was at the CRPF camp at the time. He went there soon afterwards with an ambulance. The district collector and the Superintendent of Police also visited the village later that day.

An FIR was filed by Bhima Madavi on the same day (25 November). It names sixteen persons, who were charged under Sections 147, 149, 294, 506B and 323 of the IPC. Eleven of them were apprehended that day itself, but released after three hours on a personal bond of Rs 30,000. Likewise, five others were arrested and released the next day.

The Christian families sheltering in Sukma are terrified of going back to their homes in Chingavaram. They were told in no uncertain terms that if they came back, there would be 'murder'. Mukka, his wife Pojje, son Laxman and Madka are said to be 'targets'—at greater risk.

The Issue

Discussions with both sides shed some light on the reasons behind this conflict. Christian families said that there have been tensions even in the past, but they did not lodge a complaint. For example, in 2019, Mukka's house was surrounded by the same miscreants, but he got wind of it and escaped. In March–April 2020, a village meeting was held in which Joga Madavi, a teacher we met, tried to reason with the Christian families, but when they refused to give up their faith, other villagers at the meeting gave them a thrashing. It was in the preceding two years especially that incidents of this sort had multiplied.

The attackers had several misgivings about the Christian families. Their main grudge is that the Christians stay aloof and are giving up on the collective traditions and practices of the village such as chanda and puja. '*Unko alag hi samjho* [Consider them separate]', one of them said. However, it was not clear whether the Christians were staying aloof or being kept aloof.

Some also mentioned other grudges. For instance, one person expressed a fear that Christian organizations would gradually convert the whole village: '*Pehle ek jan tha Isu ka, phir dhire-dhire badha, dhire-dhire pure gaon ko kabja karte hain*' (Initially, there was only one Christian, then slowly their numbers grew and gradually, they will take over the entire village). Another said that people are being converted by giving them unscientific information—e.g., if you become a Christian, you will have children or you will be cured of an illness—or material inducements. One Koya Samaj leader from a neighbouring village argued that Adivasis who became Christians should not be entitled to reservation. He also argued that in a 5th Schedule area, where people have their own way of life and institutions, outsiders should not be allowed to come and disturb the local culture by taking advantage of innocent locals. Some of these grudges suggested that the speakers themselves were under some outside influence (the Bajrang Dal, for one, has a presence in the area).

The Christians saw it differently. Madka, who had been beaten badly, said, 'I became a Christian because of the *dukh* (pain) in my life.' Others mentioned that the regular meetings, collective prayers and *dua* (blessings) made them feel better. They said that they had changed their lives, for instance by giving up liquor, and were now better off, causing others some annoyance.

Government in Denial

In the Bastar division, this was the second mob attack on Christian Adivasis by other Adivasis from the same village in two months. In late September, an attack on Christians of four villages of Kondagaon district made headlines. A National Alliance of People's Movements (NAPM)–PUCL team led by Medha Patkar had investigated the incident a month later. Subsequently we met the Chief Minister, Bhupesh Bhagel, and warned him of the imminent dangers.

The ruling Congress party seemed reluctant to antagonize the Adivasis in these villages by taking strict action. The Christian vote bank, as they see it, is with them in any case. While in Kondagaon, the district administration chose to attribute the incident to routine intra-village tensions, the Sukma case is also being viewed superficially. There again, the assailants are trying to downplay the issue as ordinary maar-peet and the police is going along with it: none of the IPC sections in the FIR relate to communal violence. The police, we were told (from reliable sources in the government) had been instructed to hush up the communal nature of the incident and avoid taking sides.

However, the question here is not of the Congress or the BJP, or for that matter the CPI that has a strong presence in Sukma district. It is a deeper question of Adivasi identity and culture. While Adivasis of Bastar would be right in asserting their singular histories and traditions, the fact is that for long they have been exploited by dominant forces. Hinduization of Adivasis in India is an old phenomenon and has been carried out by successive governments irrespective of political affiliations. Some Adivasis have turned to Christianity as one way out of their dukh, as Madka explained. For others, it may be a response to the administration's gross indifference towards their struggle for survival, school education, health care and other basic needs. While forced conversion would of course be wrong, voluntary conversion is a fundamental right under Article 25 of the Constitution of India.

Having said this, perhaps the Christian missionaries need to ask themselves a question (often asked locally) whether good cannot be done for Adivasi communities without conversion. The 'call of Jesus' of Christian congregations, such as New Bethesda Jesus Christ, is an expansionist project that aims to spread in Adivasi areas under their 'Tribal Ministries'. The fact that Adivasis also have a way of life that needs to be protected and nurtured may not be appreciated or understood by even well-meaning missionaries. Also, some of these congregations have a lot of money (often from foreign sources) and it becomes difficult for local non-Christian organizations to compete with them. Christian missionaries may feel that they are 'saving' people when they convert them, but if conversions end up dividing Adivasi society and bringing strife, then they are hardly serving people's interests. Conversion activism also gives a foothold to right-wing organizations, such as the Bajrang Dal, that have their own expansionist and communal agenda.

The questions are many and deep. Further communal violence in the area can be avoided only if all sides abide by the constitutional principles of secularism, freedom of religion and respect for Adivasi culture.

22

A Stone in My Hand

Four Months Kashmir Will Never Forget*

An average Indian vaguely knows that there is a problem in Kashmir—if only from periodic news in national dailies about skirmishes at the Line of Control, 'encounters' with militants, ambushes, killings, disappearances, curfews and protests. Yet, by and large, our awareness has remained peripheral. We have continued with our lives without concerning ourselves overly with what the Indian army and government are doing in Kashmir.

Like many others, I had gone to Kashmir on a family holiday as a child. Kashmir's beauty is indeed overwhelming. As the bus chugs on the winding mountain road, roadside boards keep reminding us that Kashmir is 'the pride of India' or 'the paradise of India'. Indeed, the majestic mountains, dense forests of deodar or chinar trees, the green valleys, and glimpses of the fast-flowing Chenab in the gorges below hold one spellbound.

---

* This essay is adapted from material written in 2011 (see text), based on investigations in Kashmir in October 2010, including a join fact-finding visit with Ravi Hemadri, Sukumar Muralidharan and Vrinda Grover.

But this is only how Kashmir looks. It tells us little of how the Kashmiris live or what they feel or think. I was rudely jolted into awareness of their situation in 2001, when I returned there as a member of a joint fact-finding team of five human rights organisations. By way of preparation, some of us visited the offices of Kashmiri dailies in Delhi and browsed through newspapers of the preceding months. We made notes of alleged incidents and their locations. And thus, we arrived at an itinerary. The visit took us to the side alleys of Srinagar and other towns as well as to villages in far-flung areas. It gave us a chance to listen to the Kashmiri people in their own homes in the valley, in the hill villages of Doda and also in the camps of Kashmiri pandits in Jammu. This experience was an eye-opener, as was a similar visit in 2007.

We realised that the beauty of Kashmir hides a deep suffering, so vast has been the loss of human lives, so extreme the methods of torture, so long the lists of the disappeared, so constant the fear and humiliation. Almost every house has a painful story to tell. Even a short visit of this sort is enough to make anyone otherwise proud to be an Indian want to hang their head in shame.

Even before one reaches Srinagar, some of the story begins to unfold. Bus halts prove revealing. A halt at a wayside dhaba makes one wonder whether it might be a military canteen, full as it is of men in uniform: the Border Security Force (BSF), CRPF and the Commandos with their black headscarves. All of them are armed with AK47s or other lethal weapons. On the road, countless trucks and buses transporting military personnel and equipment; body search and sniffer dogs at Banihal Pass; repeated inspection of the identity cards that Kashmiris are supposed to carry at all times; all this and more gives the feeling that one has entered a war zone.

In mid-2010, Kashmir witnessed over a hundred violent deaths, during a summer of turmoil seen by some as an *intifada* (uprising) for freedom. Aside from the fatalities, more than 500 persons suffered bullet injuries. In most cases, lethal force was applied against unarmed civilians—protestors, mourners, mere bystanders and those who inadvertently got drawn into the cycle of protests. The pattern was similar in many parts of the valley, whether rural or urban. Instances were rife of the armed forces firing on unarmed assemblies or protests.

This uprising was the latest expression of the Kashmir struggle for self-determination—a struggle that goes back to the early days of India's independence but intensified from 1989 onwards, when militancy broke out in Kashmir. This happened primarily because, in the four preceding decades, India went back on its promise of allowing the Kashmiris a choice about their future. Instead, the Indian government kept restricting Jammu and Kashmir's autonomy, undermining democracy, rigging elections and installing puppet regimes. The state's geographical position as a border region also made it a pawn in the continuing hostility between India and Pakistan. The real issue—the right of self-determination—has been trampled upon by all sides.

Militancy continued to varying degrees from 1989 onwards. But the 2010 intifada was very different: it was an open mass uprising rather than an armed underground insurgency. It was largely based on non-violent methods such as marches, vigils, strikes and sit-ins. Stone-pelting, however, was also routine wherever the security forces turned up, and became the most visible part of the movement for the media and the Indian public. Many of the victims of the uprising died in these clashes.

In October 2010, I visited Kashmir again as part of a four-member team of independent citizens. The other team members were Ravi Hemadri, Sukumar Muralidharan and Vrinda Grover. This essay is based on the joint fact-finding that we conducted as well as a fortnight I spent in the valley afterwards, to continue the investigation of incidents documented in our report.[1] Most of the accounts are based on testimonies from victims, their families, or witnesses. My main purpose in this essay is to convey their version of the events.

Background

Militancy in the valley, some believed, was on the decline since 2004. However, after the controversy over the Amarnath land allotment in 2008, the suspected rape and murder of two women in Shopian in 2009 and the cold-blooded killing of three civilians in Machhil (portrayed as an armed encounter) in April 2010, popular discontent was simmering. The dam burst with the killing of Tufail Mattoo in June 2010. In the weeks that followed, the people of Kashmir, especially the youth, took to the streets in protest. They were unarmed, but many picked up stones when the security forces provoked them, often with lethal firepower. The stone-pelter or sangbaaz became the face of political protest through the summer.

Sections of the Indian media and some security and intelligence officials have suggested that a hand from across the border lurks behind the protests. Those whom we met were positive that they were in the movement of their own volition and that the beginning of the cycle of protests lay in the spontaneous rage provoked by the army and police excesses. Syed Ali Shah Geelani—the seniormost leader of the Hurriyat Conference—was late in comprehending the nature of the uprising, though he soon adapted to it by issuing periodic 'calendars' laying out the schedule of protests and demonstrations. Once this element of order was introduced into the demonstrations, days of bandh or *hartal* (strike) alternated with 'working' days, when people caught up with necessary activities that were otherwise on hold. The days when 'normalcy' was declared were busy for the people, with milling bazaars and crowded roads. Such was life in the Kashmir valley between June and early September, when the long cycle of protests began to wind down—with no clarity as to what would happen next.

Most of those who were killed were youngsters, the youngest a mere eight-year-old. What follows is a modest attempt at assembling some narratives of these disturbing events.

Death of Tufail Mattoo[2]

Tufail Mattoo died on 11 June 2010, just eighteen days short of his eighteenth birthday. The cause of death was identified, after much early confusion, as a grievous head injury. Tufail was an only child, who had spent several years in Dubai and Mumbai where his father had a handicraft business. He was keen to pursue his studies and a career, without getting involved in the tensions that were enveloping Kashmir. At the time he was killed, he was on his way to his grandmother's residence in the Nowhatta area of Srinagar, after a session of private tuition. He alighted from a bus to begin the short walk to his grandmother's home.

The record of the events that followed tends to get a little confused. A demonstration was happening in the vicinity of the Ghani Stadium, but Tufail was reportedly some distance away. Eyewitness accounts have mentioned a J&K police contingent at the venue, under the command of Deputy Superintendent Abdul Hamid Saka. Tufail's family believes that he was far from the demonstrators but perilously close to the police contingent that was then gearing up for crowd control.

Certain media reports have said that Tufail was probably walking through the open field of the Ghani Stadium when he got caught in the exchange of projectiles between the demonstrators and the police. As reported in the *Indian Express* of 13 June: 'Tufail . . . was caught in a skirmish between a group of protestors and the police.' An eyewitness account from one of the protestors has it that Tufail 'was inside the playground when they (the police) fired (a tear-gas shell) at him. It hit his head and he fell down.' Three policemen then reportedly 'got down from their vehicle' and one of them 'kicked

[Tufail's] body and told the other two that he was dead'. Then the police personnel reportedly 'fled'.[3]

Local newspapers did not manage to uncover any further forensic details. Once the body of the young boy was received in Srinagar's SMHS Hospital, the local authorities, it seems, sought to strike a compromise with the family, but the family refused. As Tufail's body was being taken away from the medical facility for a burial that the family intended as a private affair, it was intercepted in the Rainawari area. Angry demonstrators snatched the body from the Mattoo family, insisting on laying him to rest in the burial ground that has come to be known as the 'martyr's graveyard' in Srinagar.

The *Kashmir Times* reported then: 'Thousands of people defied the curfew restrictions and held massive protest demonstrations. Police had to fire in air, burst smoke shells and resort (*sic*) to lathi charge to disperse the protestors. Even excessive force (*sic*) was used on the people in the funeral procession of Tufail at several places. At some places including Zinda Shah Masjid the protestors were forced by cops to keep the coffin, carrying the body of Tufail, on road amid heavy shelling and firing in air.'[4]

Details of the autopsy conducted after Tufail's death soon emerged. The autopsy concluded that death had been caused by a tear-gas shell striking at high velocity and close range.[5] The police, for its part, sought to first put out one version and then another. One held that Tufail had been fatally hurt in stone throwing by the demonstrators. Another attributed the fatal injury to a brawl that the boy got into while playing cricket.

Despite the autopsy report, the police showed little urgency about registering a case. On 18 June, Tufail's uncle Manzoor Ahmad Mattoo moved an application before the Chief Judicial Magistrate, Srinagar, asking the police to register a case and begin investigations. The FIR that was subsequently filed reflected none of the findings of the autopsy and clung to the story that death was a consequence of a cricket-field brawl.

The Senior Superintendent of Police (SSP) of Srinagar, Riyaz Bedar, had, to an extent, cooperated with the effort to establish the circumstances behind Tufail's death, by providing a specimen tear-gas shell to the medical staff at the time of the autopsy. He was transferred on 22 June. The investigation has made little progress since.

In early December 2010, an eleven-member delegation from an independent research foundation based in Delhi—the Centre for Policy Analysis—and diverse regional and left-wing political parties visited Kashmir. Since Tufail's death had proved a pivotal event in the year's disturbances, the delegation's first visit was to his father, Mohammad Ashraf Mattoo.[6] The suspicions of the local police and security agencies were reportedly aroused by this visit. Since then, the elder Mattoo has reported several visits by security personnel, who have urged him to accept the cash compensation of Rs 5 lakh on offer and withdraw his petition seeking an investigation into his son's death.[7]

July 6: Violence Erupts in Srinagar[8]

On 7 July 2010, the Indian Army came out on the streets of Srinagar for the first time in several years. Earlier, it had pulled out of Kashmir's main urban areas as part of a failed return to so called 'normalcy'. This reversal was prompted by the events of 5-6 July, when four innocent persons were killed: Muzaffar Ahmad Bhat, Fayez Ahmad Wani, Abrar Ahmad and Fancy Jaan. This reversal, prompted by the events of 6 July, was an admission that the pretence of normalcy was running thin.

This spate of violence was set in motion in the afternoon of 5 July, when a minister of state in the J&K government, Nasir Aslam Wani, visited the Tengpora area of Srinagar, adjoining the Gangbugh bypass on the highway to Baramulla. He came with the intent of examining the damage inflicted on civic life as a consequence of the tactics that security forces had been adopting to quell the growing tide of protests—including breaking windows and shattering household items.

The minister's visit was seen in the locality as a publicity gimmick. Reflecting the public sentiment, a group of young boys bathing in a canal that runs along the pathway into the neighbourhood jeered at him. There is no evidence that any stones were hurled, though some media narratives seemed to accept without serious inquiry that the protest against the minister's visit did involve some stone pelting.

Subsequent events, as reported in the media, are somewhat confusing. *Greater Kashmir* says that Muzaffar Ahmad Bhat was one among a group of boys that was surrounded by the CRPF after protests erupted during the minister's visit. Muzaffar, for reasons yet unknown, was taken in, while his companions were let off.

Other media reports say that all the boys were chased down the road by an angry contingent of policemen. The boys, indeed, may not have been quite so innocent and may have pelted stones at the minister's entourage. With uniformed personnel after him, Muzaffar may have leapt into the Gangbugh canal in panic.

Muzaffar's Death: A Different Account

Muzaffar was the third child of Bashir Ahmad Bhat, a small farmer in the area. As his father narrates the events, Muzaffar, aged seventeen at the time, was working in the fields with him till about 2 p.m. on 5 July 2010. They both came back home for lunch, following which Muzaffar went out to bathe in the canal.

The minister arrived on his inspection visit around 3.30 p.m. that afternoon and was met by irate protesters. Shortly after he left, a group of policemen came back into the village on what seemed like a mission of settling scores. Muzaffar and his friends, still bathing in the canal, were the first target they spotted. Muzaffar was picked up from among the group and taken away, for no reason other than the need for the police to make an example of somebody.

As word spread of another disappearance, the entire neighbourhood came out and gathered on the highway to Baramulla, shouting slogans and demanding Muzaffar's release. By late evening, the highway was choked and traffic movement paralysed. The top police officials—from the Superintendent to the Inspector-General—turned up to negotiate an end to the blockade. Tengpora was unwilling to relent and tear-gas shells and lathi charges proved to be of little use in dispersing the demonstrators.

Muzaffar's father, Bashir, had meanwhile visited the two police stations in the vicinity, at Batamaloo and Shergarh, where he had been told that there was nobody matching his son's description in their custody. Suggestions were made by the police that his son may have fallen into the reservoir adjoining the highway while fleeing the security crackdown. As Bashir recounts that day's incidents, the reservoir was then searched by a group of local residents, but the boy remained untraced.

By 5 a.m. the next morning, the siege of the highway was lifted, in part because the protesters were in a state of fatigue. Bashir suspects that Muzaffar's lifeless body was surreptitiously brought to the site after the crowd dispersed. The body was found at the point on the highway where the road turns in towards Tengpora. A crowd soon assembled, again shouting azadi slogans and demanding justice for the slain youth.

Fayaz: Collateral Damage

This was the context in which Fayaz Ahmad Wani, an employee of the state government's department of parks and gardens, set out for work on 6 July. The highway was blocked and there was a company of the CRPF advancing towards the demonstrators, but Fayaz was moving in another direction, with no intent other than reporting for duty on time.

Saqib Nazir Wani, Fayaz's younger brother, was—by his own admission—part of the demonstration. But as he tells it, Fayaz was not, and there is no evident reason at all why he should have been the target of CRPF gunfire. There were a number of others among the demonstrators who were injured in this firing, but Fayaz, hit in the neck, was the only one to die.

Abrar: Death after Death

Fayaz's body was laid out and wrapped in a shroud alongside Muzaffar's. The highway to Baramulla became the scene of one of the largest gatherings of mourners and protesters that Kashmir had seen in several years. Faced with this explosion of rage, the police force used brutal methods to control it. Even Abdul Ghani Bhat, Muzaffar's uncle, in an image widely publicized and seen through the valley, was harassed by the police as he kept a vigil over the body of the slain youth.

As news of the deaths in Tengpora spread, crowds came out in other parts of the valley. The most vigorous protests occurred in the Maisuma Bagh area of Srinagar, where Fayaz had been a resident with his family, until they relocated to Tengpora. Abrar Ahmad, an eighteen-year-old, was killed there in a police firing.

All through that morning of 6 July and well into the afternoon, most of Srinagar was in turmoil. In the Lakshmanpora neighbourhood under Batamaloo police station, protests began after announcements were made from the mosques about the killing of Muzaffar and Fayaz. Sometime in the afternoon, J&K police forces charged down the main street of the neighbourhood, dispersing the crowd with several bursts of tear-gas.

Fancy Jaan: Accident or Crime?

Some of the tear-gas shells were fired down a side street on which Abdur Rahim, a casual worker, lives. As the fumes started entering the home, his daughter Fancy Jaan noticed that they were causing some distress to her asthmatic mother. Fancy went up to the first floor to draw the curtain on the windowframe. The home had no windows then since a minor renovation was underway and curtains were the only protection. Fancy may have looked out of her window for a fraction of a second. At that precise moment, she was hit by a bullet fired by a policeman patrolling the main street.

Considering the distance and the angle at which the shot was fired, perhaps the bullet was thought unlikely to hit any live object, let alone prove fatal. Yet Fancy was hit in the chest and died almost immediately. Even if it was a shot fired on impulse—with intent to intimidate rather than kill—it was certainly done without care for consequences.

It was mid-afternoon. Fancy's family brought her out in order to take her to the hospital, even though they had little hope of her life being revived. They were forced to retreat indoors by massive tear-gassing. Fancy's body was left on the main road and the security forces reportedly left in a hurry, rather than take responsibility for the killing or its aftermath.

Unlike others caught in similar situations, Fancy's family chose to lodge an FIR at the local police station, but they encountered great difficulties in the process. Despite their dire circumstances, they refused compensation. Fancy herself did *kravel* embroidery work to supplement the family income. Though her neighbourhood had frequently been swept up in the fervour of the protests engulfing Kashmir, she had never been an active participant. Her death, in the words of her parents, shows that no place is safe in Kashmir—not even the supposed haven of a family home.

The Death Trail

Shooting the Sangbaaz

Logripora is a village of around 200 houses in Sopore tehsil of Baramulla district, known to have been at the forefront of the militancy since its early days. People in Sopore regard the estimated two thousand martyrs they have contributed to the struggle as a matter of some pride.

On Friday, 13 August 2010, Samir Ahmed Lone and Farhat Ahmed Meer of Logripora were killed. In his early twenties, Samir was a carpenter by profession and had his own shop in Silu, three kilometres away. At around 2.30 p.m., Samir and five other youth (including Farhat, a Class X student) started for the nearby town of Bomai. As a neighbour recalls: 'During those days, there was a protest almost every day in Bomai. There has been a CRPF camp in Bomai since 2009. Before that, there was an RR (Rashtriya Rifles) camp for ten years. We waged a long struggle to get the RR camp removed from our village. RR forces had committed many atrocities. In one instance, in an RR shooting Firdauz of Bomai was killed and one other youth was in coma for a long time. Both were innocent. Due to such atrocities of the RR, we had protested and fought for the camp's removal. After that the CRPF came.'

Soon after Samir and his friends reached Bomai, they fell victim to a shootout by the CRPF. Samir and Farhat were killed on the spot. Many others from the group sustained bullet injuries. Those we spoke to said that there was no stone pelting in the protest that day, but the security forces opened fire nonetheless, without the slightest effort to use the non-lethal options prescribed as first recourse, such as water cannon and tear-gas. Farhat's father Mohammad Maqsood Meer, a landless agricultural labourer, is unable to accept his loss and asks how bullets could be regarded, even in the event of a stone being flung by protesters, as the appropriate response. Farhat, he says, was hit by up to four bullets in his stomach, fired from the front.

From Bomai, the bodies of the two youths were brought in a *janaza* (funeral) procession of several thousand to Logripora, when personnel believed to be of the Special Operations Group (SOG) of the J&K Police—who were accompanying the CRPF—opened fire.[9] Up to twenty were injured in this shootout, including several women. One of the injured, Kausar, a Class XII student, had to be taken to Srinagar. Family members of the deceased informed us that an FIR could be registered only six days later at the Bomai police station.

Not all families think it necessary to file an FIR. This sentiment was clearly expressed in the case of eighteen-year-old Tajamul Bashir Bhat. Tajamul lived in a small mohalla of around twenty-five households called Ashanmodan, around five kilometres from the main Logripora village. His mother, Zarifa Begum, said that the family depended mainly on agriculture and wage labour for a livelihood. Tajamul was the oldest of her five sons, studying in Class X in the nearby village of Silu.

Zarifa still suffers a profound sense of loss but is factual and dispassionate when she relates her son's death to his participation in the struggle for freedom. People from the mohalla, she said, were part of the protest march that started towards Sopore around mid-morning that day. In her recollection, around fifteen thousand people were there; most were men, women and children of the Jhanger area, which comprises around sixteen villages. Two hours later, at around 1.30 p.m., when the protest reached the Sopore Khapra neighbourhood, the security forces started tear-gas shelling and firing. People scattered. Tajamul was hit on the left side of the chest and died on the spot. Five or six others—from Silu, Nethipora and Model Town in Zafira's recollection—were seriously injured.

Tajamul was first taken to the sub-district hospital in Sopore and then brought home. His body was taken for burial to Vodra village where he was born and where the family had lived till not long ago. In response to an inquiry regarding the filing of an FIR, a local youth said bluntly that the struggle for freedom does not allow any manner of accommodation with the security forces—'*Azadi ki ladai mein FIR kis baat ka? Hum to police aur fauj ke khilaf jate hai.*'

(In the struggle for freedom, where is the question of an FIR? We are opposing the police and army.)

By the same principle, any compensation offer made by the state government would be turned down.

Harassment of youth who are accused of being stone pelters, often arbitrarily, is common. Two days prior to our visit to Logripora, a young boy called Bitta (a Class IX student) had gone to the fields to get his cow when a person in civilian attire, believed to be from the SOG, caught him and accused him of being a stone pelter. He was then pushed into a jeep and taken to Bomai. The entire village turned up in protest at the police station and Bitta had to be released. In another instance, some nine students of Bomai were accused of being *sangbaaz* and threatened with arrest under the state's Public Safety Act (PSA). The parents were asked to pay a certain amount if they wanted their children back. Even on that occasion, the entire village turned up in solidarity and secured the release of the boys.

'In response to the stones, the government is using the PSA or firing bullets,' said one villager. Added another: 'The security forces have in some instances photographed our youth while they were in town and later gone to their homes in the night and accused them of being sangbaaz.'

Shooting to Kill

It cannot be said that the killings we came across were all targeted in the sense that the identity of the victim was known to the security forces when they fired their lethal bullets. There is a broad consensus among the people of Kashmir that lethal force is often applied without regard to possible human consequences. There was, in other words, an intent to kill, though without any specific person being the target. The purpose could be to intimidate the protesters and quell the uprising by spreading fear, with scant regard for the attendant loss of young lives.

Yasir Rafiq (called Raju at home), a resident of the Maisuma Bagh area of Srinagar, suffered pellet injuries on 30 Aug 2010 and died a fortnight later. The day he was shot at was a day of curfew, but there had been no reported incident of stone throwing or any other form of demonstration. Two of Raju's friends, eighteen-year-old Ishfaq and seventeen-year-old Sajid, were playing a game of carrom in the narrow lane outside his house. Such activities, though strictly speaking disallowed, are normally tolerated, except during the worst days of shutdown imposed by either side. Raju had come down the stairs and was standing in the doorway watching the game, when he was hit at close range. The pellets were fired by a J&K police person who suddenly came around the corner and just as quickly vanished from the scene. After a few days in the hospital, Raju was flown to Delhi for urgent medical attention, but his life could not be saved.

Raju is Yasin Malik's nephew. The day he was hit was the fourth since Yasin's release from over two months in preventive detention. The family feels that the policeman who shot Raju was familiar with the identity of his target, since anybody deployed in the area would have known that the inhabitant of that modest dwelling was Kashmir's most widely known face of political dissent.

From all the evidence that we have been able to access, it seems undeniable that the policeman who fired at Yasir had the clear intent of harming a family member of one of Kashmir's leading dissenters. Whether there was an intent to kill or not is a matter for criminal investigation. In any case, his immediate superiors—and indeed, the Director General of J&K Police, where the buck finally stops— should be held accountable under the general principle of command responsibility.

The Three Pampore Deaths

On 12 September 2010, the day following Eid, young Maqbul and Nura set off from their village Tengen (Chadoora tehsil, Budgam district) for Pampore town, 2 km away. Maqbul's married sister lives there. He stayed there overnight and was heading back home the following day after lunch when, at Kadalbal Chowk, he was shot in the head and killed on the spot. Maqbul's family takes this to be a case of shoot-at-sight by the security forces. Curfew had been imposed that day in Srinagar, though not in Kadalbal. But because a hartal had been called by Kashmir's dissident political formations, all shops were shut and the roads empty.

Maqbul was first taken to Ahmed Private Hospital in Naugam, fifteen kilometres from Pampore, where his brother Nazir Ahmed works. Until then they were under the impression that he was only injured.

'*Yahan jakhmi ko uthana bhi jurum hai* [To help the injured is also a crime here],' said Firdouz, brother of Maqbul's friend Riyaz, who was with him that day. After Maqbul fell, Riyaz and a few others were trying to carry him into a nearby vehicle to take him to a hospital, when Riyaz was hit on the head with a brick by a CRPF man. He started bleeding profusely and until as late as October, when we met him, he had to visit the hospital regularly. As his brother recounted, Riyaz was a school dropout who used to earn a living as a casual labourer. Since this incident, he has been unable to do any work.

The second victim of the day's events was Eizaz Ahmed Gojari, who lived in the Meer mohalla in Kadalbal, Pampore. According to his elder brother Hilal, Eizaz was aged around thirty and worked in a family-owned shop selling electrical goods. He was married in 2007 and had a two-year-old son. On 13 September, around 3 p.m., he had gone to the market—only five minutes' walk from their house—to buy some fruit. There was no declared curfew in place, though a hartal had been declared. Certain vital services are allowed to function even during hartal days, such as the *nanvai* (bakery), the chemist and a few others. Vegetable and fruit sellers are also allowed to work in certain circumstances, since people need to eat and also recognize their need for a livelihood. According to Hilal,

Eizaz was shot and killed by the CRPF or other security personnel stationed near the shops. Either they confused the hartal with a curfew, or they were deliberately trying to disrupt the hartal. 'The lane on which Eizaz was killed is not a major thoroughfare. Even during hartal, these interior areas remain open and children continue to play there,' said his brother.

Javed Iqbal Rathar, aged a little over thirty years, was the third victim that day. Javed's joint family also lives in the Meer mohalla of Kadalbal, Pampore. His brother, Bilal, informed us that Javed had gone to the local shop that afternoon to get some bread when he was shot and killed. There was no curfew or protest that day, and in any case, even when imposed, curfew is only believed to be in force along major thoroughfares and the national highway running through the state. Free movement is generally allowed within the mohallas, even during curfew time. That day, however, people were inside their homes and the streets were empty, because it was a festive day when families get together.

Javed's family runs its own business and is reasonably affluent. Nobody in the family has been involved in political activity. Javed got married just last year. He was a graduate as is his wife.

Bilal related at some length the problems they faced while taking the three victims (Maqbul, Eizaz and Javed) to the Sri Maharaja Hari Singh (SMHS) Hospital in Srinagar. Their experience speaks volumes about the treatment received by injured persons at the hands of the security forces.

After the firings, the three of them were taken to Srinagar in two vehicles that belonged to Eizaz's family. Eizaz and Maqbul were in one vehicle and Javed in another. They started from Tolli mohalla where one of the incidents had occured. From Tolli mohalla their vehicle had reached Kadalbal Chowk when, according to Bilal, CRPF and J&K police broke the windows of their vehicles and beat up the people inside. A boy was injured but they pressed on. From Kadalbal Chowk, they took the usual route towards the highway. On the way, near the Punjab National Bank, their vehicles were attacked again—stones were thrown and batons rained down at the window panes of the vehicles. At Darangbal Chowk and Irestabal Chowk, they had the same experience. Another boy in the vehicle was injured and had to be admitted for two days. In Bypass Chowk, barbed wire had been laid across the road, due to which a tyre of one vehicle was punctured. Somehow, they reached SMHS Hospital. Eizaz died there. Javed was put on a ventilator and shifted to the Sher-e-Kashmir Institute of Medical Sciences (SKIMS) at Soura. He died at 7.45 p.m. Maqbul had died on the spot.

The following day, curfew was imposed in Pampore. On the night of 15 September, the security forces raided Kadalbal (which includes Kadalbal, Meer, Tolli and other small mohallas). Around fifteen to twenty boys were arrested. The security forces visited around two dozen houses. At every house, they first fired in the air and then took the youth of the house with them to the police station at Pampore and then to Srinagar Central Jail. Later, these youth were granted bail, but with fabricated charges against them.

With the Chinar Tree as Witness

Mubina Akhter, a twenty-one-year-old graduate, lived in Nethipora village of Sopore tehsil (Baramulla district). Her elderly uncle, Ghulam Mohammed Wani, said that on Sunday, 19 September 2010, there was a public protest that started at 9 a.m., in which around ten youth of their village had joined. The protest continued till mid-day and dispersed without any untoward incident. At 6.30 p.m. that evening, Mubina had joined three other women—Mahmuda and Shakila, her close relatives, and a friend Parveena—on the road a short distance away from his home, for a casual chat. According to the three women who witnessed the incident, a shot was fired at them from a CRPF vehicle parked under a chinar tree a few hundred metres away. Mubina was hit in her lower abdomen. She was rushed to the sub-district hospital at Sopore and referred to Srinagar. According to the SMHS Hospital records in Srinagar, she was 'brought dead'.

Sopore's First Pellet Gun Victim

The state government has justified the use of pellet guns in crowd control on the grounds that it is a weapon that deters but does not kill. This, however, is not the experience of those who have been hit by these guns. If fired from close range, as often happens, the pellet gun is certain to create multiple organ injuries, with a definite possibility of death. The first victim of a pellet gun in Sopore tehsil was Mudassir Nazir.

Mudassir, from Aarampora in the Hazam mohalla of Sopore, was in his early twenties and worked with the Aircel telecom company. On 19 August, he had gone to Vatlab Zurimanz village, some 15 kilometres from Sopore. It was the month of Ramzan and that evening, he came out of a masjid at *iftar* time, around 6.45 p.m. According to his family, Mudassir was hit at close range from inside a CRPF vehicle as he was passing by its side on a narrow road. Mudassir was hit a little above his right thigh, but close to the stomach. Initially, nobody could understand what kind of weapon had been used. Local residents were aware that small shrapnel wounds can occur even in grenade blasts. Only later did they understand that Mudassir had been shot at with a pellet gun.

'*Pellet gun janwaro par istamal kiya jata hai, inhone insaano par kiya. Agar doori se kiya jaye to insaan jakhmi hota hai, par inhone paas se kiya. Doctor keh rahe the ki pet ka koi hissa bacha nahi hai jisko si saken* [Pellet guns are used on animals, but they used them on human beings. If fired from a distance, it only causes injury, but they fired it from close range. The doctor was saying that nothing of the stomach remained that could be stitched],' said Mudassir's cousin. Apparently, around forty to fifty pellets had shredded with his abdomen.

'*Koi jhagde ke bina CRPF ne* firing *ki* [The CRPF fired despite there being no tension],' said his mother, Nasima. Mudassir's family has received compensation money. An elder of the community remarked—'*Sarkar ne hamara* rate *lagaya hai* [The government has fixed our rate].'

This is a rare instance where the local police subsequently registered a murder case against CRPF personnel.[10] According to the same report, two other persons were injured in this incident of 'unprovoked firing of pellets', as the police described it.

Snuffing Out Dreams

Mudassar Bashir Kachru, all of twenty years, was a software engineering student and star footballer who captained the J&K state junior team. He was born in a humble family in Khushal Matoo mohalla in Sopore town. He was killed on 15 September 2010, shot twice through the chest while coming out of a masjid after the evening namaz. There was neither a curfew nor hartal in force at the time, nor was there any demonstration going on. Bashir Ahmed Kachru, his father, says that they have registered an FIR but refused compensation. 'The government first kills our youth and then gives us money,' he said. 'Our youth have faced a lot of brutal repression. I am not a rich man. A son is a support for his father. They are killing us poor people.'

Firing on Janazas

Many lives have been lost during these four months in attacks on funeral processions. Typically, when a death occurs, people gather in thousands. A person killed by the security forces is seen as a life sacrificed for freedom and becomes a martyr. The mourning of a martyr is not just a social occasion but also turns into a cry for freedom. Tearful cries of personal loss become chants for azadi.

We came across many cases of firing on such processions, often leading to more deaths than were being mourned. After Faizan

Rafiq Buhroo, a Class VII student, drowned as he tried to flee in terror from the CRPF—or perhaps after being thrown vindictively into the fast-flowing river—on 17 July 2010 in Baramulla, the security forces (CRPF and SOG) opened fire on the funeral procession of several thousand, injuring around thirty to forty persons, including women, as well as killing a civilian on his way home, Faiyaz Ahmad.[11]

Civilian Deaths Following Deaths of Militants

In the Karaltaing mohalla of Sopore, we came across one case which showed us how civilian deaths may occur following so-called 'encounters' with militants. On 26 June 2010, on the bridge in the south side of Sopore town, an encounter had taken place in which two militants (allegedly belonging to the Lashkar-Taiba [LeT]) were killed. One of them, Firdoz, was from Sopore. After that, the security forces opened fire on protesters, killing two civilians (Bingli of Sopore and Lalad of Amargadh, close to Sopore). As tension mounted, the local authorities imposed a curfew.

The following day, after the *teesri namaz* at 5 p.m., Bilal Ahmed Wani, a youth in his early twenties, was returning home when he became conscious of a commotion in a nearby lane. As he peeped into the lane to see what the problem was, a CRPF contingent fired in his direction. He was hit in the throat, according to a friend, by a rubber bullet. Still on his feet but realizing that he needed urgent medical attention, Bilal started walking towards a doctor's clinic in the mohalla. He collapsed on the way, but was carried by others to the clinic where he was administered first aid and referred to a hospital. He died on the way.[12]

Bilal was the sole wage earner in his family and his loss is going to be heavily felt. His father is old and had to leave his job as a driver in a sawmill after an injury at work. Bilal left school after completing his higher secondary due to his family's poverty. He was the fourth child after three daughters. He has left behind his aged parents, one divorced and two unmarried sisters. The family has received the *ex-gratia* amount, but as Bilal's teacher said: 'Government ex-gratia *de rahi hai, par* justice *nahi.*'

Bilal's teacher said that during curfew times, there is often stone pelting. It is quite possible that somebody had thrown a stone and that the forces, in reaction, opened fire. Bilal's teacher also reported that a Sikh officer—of DSP rank—in the task force had admitted to him that the situation did not justify the use of firing with bullets.

Killing of Bystanders and Injured

On 2 August 2010, Bashir Ahmad of Wachi village was killed. He was a mechanic and had his own shop on the highway. He was from a poor family and had stopped studying after secondary school. He was only sixteen at the time of his death. He was not part of the protests that happened that day. When the crowd of demonstrators reached his shop, he stepped out to have a look, and he was hit by two bullets—one in his chest and the other in his neck. According to his family, this happened as security personnel stationed at a nearby bridge were firing at the demonstration.

An FIR has been registered by the police in the Sangam police station. The family has not received a copy, though they went to the police station. They did not insist or protest, out of fear. They know about the compensation provided for victims, but they have not received any formal communication on this from the government, either in writing or in person. There is nobody in this family who can follow up since the grandparents are old and both Bashir's father and brother are labourers who are busy earning a living during the day. A neighbour said: 'From the police behaviour it seemed like the police wanted a bribe before they gave a copy of the FIR.'

Killing by Unidentified Gunmen

During this investigation, we came across only one instance where a civilian was killed by unidentified gunmen. Ghulam Nabi Wani was a resident of Chakura village (Pulwama district). This village, around fifteen kilometres from Pulwama, has around 450 houses. There is a high school there, though the nearest hospital is in Bijbehera or Anantnag. The village has three mohallas: Khanpora, Mirpora and Sherpora.

Ghulam Nabi Wani, thirty-seven years of age, lived in Sherpora mohalla. At around 10 p.m. on 23 August 2010, he was killed by unidentified gunmen on his way back from the local masjid. Ghulam has been an active member of the National Conference, especially since Omar Abdullah came to power. He did not participate in pro-azadi protests. He was also the panchayat secretary. That evening, he got out of the masjid earlier than others. Those who were pro-azadi shouted slogans after coming out, as was customary at the time. Ghulam's thinking was different and he did not hide it. The previous year, some persons had attacked his house at midnight and broken the windowpanes. At the time, he had also received a warning from the Hizbul Mujahideen (HM), but after his death in August, HM denied having any hand in his killing. The group's usual practice is to own up to any political assassination. Nobody can be sure of who was responsible for Ghulam's killing. It could be the militants, or a political party that opposed the National Conference, or surrendered militants now acting as agents of the police and armed forces, or anybody at all with a personal grievance. Some of the locals think that the killing could also have been by the security forces, since the Rashtriya Rifles camp was just about four kilometres from the mohalla. RR personnel, present in the village for many years, had frequently engaged in crackdowns, harassment and destruction of property.

An Eight-Year-Old Killed

Samir Ahmad Rah was anything but a security threat when he set out from his home in the Batamaloo area of Srinagar on 2 August 2010. He was only eight years old, and though the area was under curfew, few in his family saw any danger in his playing in the back alleys close to his home.

That day, Samir had not strayed very far from his home when he encountered a CRPF picket. His family is convinced that he was attacked without provocation.

Rising Kashmir (a local newspaper) reported the next day, ostensibly based on eyewitness accounts, that Samir may have shouted an azadi slogan on seeing the uniformed men. If that indeed is the case, then it was obviously a child's innocent emulation of a pattern of behaviour seen among elders all around. But the CRPF contingent, apparently, made no distinction between an informed slogan shouter and an eight-year-old imitator.

Eyewitnesses speak of Samir being hit violently on the head with a rifle butt and a lathi being thrust down his throat. The boy was then abandoned where he fell. Personnel of the J&K police happened to reach the site soon afterwards. Samir was taken to the nearest police control room and then, at 3.45 p.m., to the SMHS Hospital. He died there a few hours later.

Samir's neighbourhood, meanwhile, had erupted in protest. Later that evening, water and electricity supply to the neighbourhood was cut off and cable television went off the screens.

Samir's father, Fayaz Ahmad Rah, told us that the head of the local police station had visited him the next day. Privately, he admitted that a great wrong had been committed. Yet the FIR he registered afterwards recorded the cause of Samir's death as injuries caused in a stampede. Fayaz, who ekes out a modest living selling fruits off his pushcart at a nearby street corner, has refused to accept this finding. Indeed, the post-mortem report mentions no injury aside from a 'bruise on the occipital region, not actively bleeding'. There was no other mark of injury on Samir's body, nor any evidence of bleeding. This seems to rule out the possibility that the boy was killed in a stampede.

Youth at Risk

Many of the victims of state violence in Kashmir in 2010 were youngsters. Most of them did not do anything that would justify the use of lethal force, even if some hurled the odd stone at the security forces. Security personnel in Kashmir tend to look at youngsters as a threat; at the slightest provocation, they respond with overwhelming force. Some of the people we spoke with felt that the induction of former militants into the police force had contributed to this lack of restraint. These surrendered militants once worked as low-profile foot soldiers of the counterinsurgency operations with the support of security agencies. Some of them now occupy official positions—even key positions—in the chain of command.

Among other events that drew our attention to these issues is the killing of twelve-year old Faizan Buhroo in Baramulla on 17 July 2010.[13] We met Faizan's family, including his father Rafiq and his older sister Rizwan. Rafiq works as a blacksmith in Uri, and normally goes there every day, but the recent turmoil has made it difficult for him to continue going back and forth. Like much of Kashmir's population at this time, Rafiq's family lives in precarious circumstances.

Faizan was studying in Class VII. According to his sister Rizwan, curfew had been relaxed in Baramulla on 17 July in view of the school exams. Faizan returned home early after it emerged that the day's exam would not be held. A little later, he went with some friends to the Azadganj bridge, about half a kilometre away. This new bridge across the Jhelum had become a popular recreation spot for the people of Baramulla. There was no reason for the family to feel anxious about Faizan going there.

What happened after that they can only guess from what they heard. A confrontation of some sort evidently happened between the children and security personnel. It seems that a truck of security forces, known as a 'civil truck', was coming across the bridge as the children were reaching it. Seeing armed personnel jump from the truck, the children made a U-turn and ran away. An older boy jumped into the river, but Faizan did not because he did not know how to swim.

According to eye-witnesses, Faizan and two of his friends had stayed on the bridge and were soon overpowered by the forces. Another boy, even younger than Faizan, suffered a serious ear injury and was later taken to the hospital in Srinagar. Faizan was also beaten. As his sister saw it: 'Faizan had an old injury on his forehead. They must have thought that he was a stone pelter. He was beaten mercilessly with tear gas guns and dandas.' After this beating, we were told, Faizan was thrown into the river.

Faizan's mother reached the scene a little later, after hearing that a child was drowning. The child, she was told, had been struggling to swim and shouting for help, but no-one had been able to help him because of intimidation by the security forces. Meanwhile, Faizan's older brother Faisal heard that the child in question was none other than his own brother.

Faizan had disappeared. The word spread through the town and many joined the search. By the evening, the local administration and army command also offered their assistance. An army boat with a team of experienced divers joined the search. But it is only on 20 July that Faizan's body was handed over to his family after being purportedly found the same day. Faizan's family suspects that his body was actually found earlier and that the local administration kept it for some time to tamper with the evidence.

The family carefully examined Faizan's body after it was handed over to them. He had been bleeding from a nose injury, and three other injuries were also visible on his head. One of them was

particularly severe and they thought it might have been caused by a
rifle butt.

As often happens in Kashmir, this event led to a show of
solidarity. During the three days when Faizan was missing, thousands
of local residents were watching or searching on both sides of the
Jhelum day and night. After the body was found and handed over,
a large crowd assembled and took a procession through the town.
Thousands joined the procession as it made its way to the district
headquarters.

As mentioned earlier, security forces opened fire on this
procession in Baramulla. About thirty to forty were injured and one
was killed: Faiyaz Ahmad, who died on the spot after he was shot in
the chest as he was returning home at the end of the day.

According to some residents of Baramulla, the person who
was leading Faizan's beating and possibly bore responsibility for
his death was a former militant who had turned into a counter-
insurgency element under police supervision. They believe that he
is now an officer in the Special Operations Group (SOG) of the
J&K Police.

Alienated Youth

At least 112 persons were reportedly killed in the civil uprising that
took place in Kashmir in 2010. The information we have suggests
that perhaps twenty-seven of them were under eighteen years of age.
In the short time available, we were unable to collect testimonies for
more than a few of these adolescent and child deaths. But we did
survey quite a few of them in specific areas, including Sopore and
Anantnag. In these areas of frequent unrest, some of the victims'
families acknowledged that their children had actively participated
in the demonstrations. As they joined the protests, they must have
known that they were risking their lives. This is a telling sign of their
despair.

Attack on Pattan Hospital

Pattan is a small town located in Baramulla district, on the highway to Srinagar. There is a government hospital there. Not far from Pattan, a few kilometres away, is a village called Palhallan. This village had experienced severe repression for many weeks when we visited the area. It was more or less under siege for more than two months, without attracting much attention until shortly before our visit. During this troubled period, the government hospital in Pattan was the first point of medical help whenever someone was injured in Palhallan.

On 30 July 2010, a disturbing incident happened there.[14] As the doctors and other staff remember it, armed CRPF personnel barged into the health centre early in the evening, shortly after injured civilians had been admitted for urgent attention. The security forces vandalized the hospital, breaking doors, shattering windows and smashing essential medical equipment. The hospital staff and patients were terrified. Surgeons conducting life-saving procedures in the hospital's small operation theatre were alerted to this violent irruption of CRPF personnel and advised to stay put.

The senior surgeon soon heard loud thumping on the door of the casualty ward. There were a dozen patients in the ward at that time, including some with grievous injuries. The casualty ward was also packed with volunteers who had brought the patients in one way or another, in the absence of ambulance services. Opening the door carried a risk of mass panic in the casualty ward, which could have proved fatal for some of the patients. But the surgeon felt that it might be even riskier to ignore the violent thumping on the door, so he opened it.

No sooner had he opened the door than three rifles were aimed at his chest from close range. Taken aback, the surgeon tried his best not to panic and to explain calmly that the injured patients needed his urgent attention. The CRPF allowed him to return to his surgery, but they roughed up many other staff and volunteers in the ward and beyond. They also smashed a brand-new ambulance and the chief medical officer's car. There was mayhem all over the hospital premises.

Still according to hospital staff, the CRPF did not even spare the women's ward. They broke the door open and barged in before the bewildered staff had a chance to retreat into the adjacent room. Fortunately, there was just enough time for a local visitor to interpose and lock the staff in, attracting the intruders' fury to himself. Had it not been for this quick diversion, the female staff fear that they would have been maltreated too. Three doctors also managed to escape the rampage by locking themselves inside a bathroom.

We heard many other disturbing details of this incident. Reconstructing the full sequence of events would take a more in-depth enquiry, but at least one other story is worth recounting for the light it throws on the extremes that security forces are capable of in Kashmir.

We heard this story from Mohammad Ramzan Sheikh, a resident of Palhallan. Like many of his neighbours, he had been taking part from time to time in protests against the security forces in the last few months. Sometimes he was accompanied by his twelve-year old son Adil Ramzan Sheikh, as he was around mid-day on 30 July when both of them were heading towards the venue of the day's protest. Mohammad always made sure that his son remained at a safe distance from the frontline of the demonstrations, but that day, he lost sight of Adil.

Mohammad searched for him in vain, until he received a phone call around 3 p.m. informing him that his son was lying dead at the Pattan hospital. He had been rushed there after a bullet had grazed his shoulder, causing a lot of bleeding. His wound was dressed after he was admitted, and he was put on intravenous (IV) drip. Soon after that, Mohammad was told, the CRPF personnel raided the premises.

In the rampage that followed, they tore the IV cord from Adil's arm, pulled him out of the bed, and shot him dead.

Mohammad requested the body to be sent back to Palhallan for burial. Meanwhile, however, the roads had been sealed by the security forces. It was late in the evening by the time some people managed to reach Palhallan with Adil's body on their shoulders. On examining the body, Mohammad noticed one wound near Adil's shoulder and another one in the lower chest that looked like it had been caused by a bullet fired at close range.

Adil was buried later that night. The family does not have any documents related to this incident. No FIR has been registered, nor is the family aware of any post-mortem report. In short, there is no trace of this gruesome incident.

The doctors at Pattan hospital also remembered Adil. They said that he was already grievously injured when he was admitted, and that his chances of survival seemed low. His wound must have been dressed by way of first-aid. How and why he was fatally shot inside the hospital is not entirely clear to the doctors. They are guessing that perhaps he fled for shelter in the chaos and turmoil that followed the CRPF incursion, when some people were even jumping out of windows. According to some eyewitnesses they had heard, Adil was trying to run towards the boundary wall of the hospital, adjoining a school, when he was fatally shot at close range.

Whatever the details of how Adil lost his life, the fact is that he was fatally shot within hospital premises. It is also clear that the hospital was the target of a brutal CRPF attack that day. An armed attack on a hospital is a serious crime and a violation of international humanitarian law. This should have called for an urgent independent investigation, but nothing of the sort happened. According to the Director General of the J&K Police, Kuldeep Khoda, the police did file charges against a few of its own men as well as against some army and CRPF personnel. This is an unusual admission of excessive use of force, of a sort that routinely happened all over Kashmir during this long summer of civil unrest.

The attack on Pattan hospital belongs to a long list of similar incidents that never became the object of serious investigations. Security forces have repeatedly crossed all limits with brazen impunity. They have not even spared health centres, medical personnel or ambulances—facilities and persons that are meant to be exempt from the use of force at all times, in all circumstances.

Doctors and other staff at Pattan hospital were naturally appalled by the 30 July attack. However, they were reluctant to seek redressal because of this climate of impunity. They have not even sought any intervention from the doctors' association, believing this to be futile. As for demanding criminal prosecution, they laugh at this naive idea. 'Who should we file an FIR against?' —asked someone who had witnessed the attack—'Against all of India?'

The Injured

The story of injuries suffered through Kashmir's long months of unrest in 2010 is as shocking as the story of deaths. According to official figures, as many as 515 persons suffered bullet injuries between June and mid-October; the actual numbers are likely to be much higher. The injured are more fortunate than the dead, but not much.

Commenting on the patient overload, the Deputy Superintendent at SMHS Hospital, the largest government hospital in Srinagar, remarked: 'The patient load after June increased manifold. Patients were from all districts of Kashmir. Most were young, many were just teenagers. While injury patients increased in number, routine patients decreased significantly due to curfews and hartals.'

Doctors at the SMHS hospital shared a special concern about the use of pellet guns. A top surgeon explained their dire consequences: 'If a pellet gun is fired from a distance, it will not penetrate the body, but if it is fired at close range then it can cause devastating injury and even death. Multiple pellets can injure different organs. Earlier, pellet guns of a different type were used and perforation was single. Single pellet is manageable, but multiple pellets are devastating and sometimes fatal.' The routine use of pellet guns against civilian crowds is a matter of enormous popular resentment in Kashmir. And this is just one of the brutal means of crowd control being used there with abandon.

Doctors also complained about the hurdles and harassment that ambulance drivers and medical staff face when they attempt to extend timely help to the injured or to take them to hospitals at times of curfew or hartal. The Deputy Superintendent recalled four instances where SMHS ambulance drivers had been beaten by the police or security forces. Another senior doctor recalled a few instances when ambulances were smashed and medical staff were beaten.

The plight of the injured struck me forcefully when I visited Khushal Matoo, a working-class neighbourhood in Sopore. In one of the narrow lanes, hearing that an *insani huqooq* (human rights) person had come, family members of the injured came out of so many houses that the lane was full. They were so many that it was difficult to record each story before darkness fell.

Just to mention one story, consider Posha, mother of Aizaz and Mudassar, twenty and twenty-two years old respectively. Her husband is disabled and unable to work. Her sons used to work as domestic labourers and the family was somehow limping along on their meagre earnings and a small fruit shop. In July, Aizaz was hit in the arm by a CRPF bullet. His arm is more or less paralysed. One month later, Mudassar was shot in the thigh by a CRPF constable as he was standing in the doorway of his house. Posha said that they had to sell half of the fruit shop to pay for the treatment of her sons. Both are unemployed today, and mostly sitting at home with their disabled father.

Concluding Thought

Such are the stories that one hears after just a few days in Kashmir. The most startling aspect of it all is that so little of this is known to the Indian public. The events of mid-2010, dramatic as they were, went virtually unreported in the Indian media. When they were reported, it was usually based on a lopsided narrative where Kashmiris were blamed for the violence. Even the international audience remained more or less in the dark: international human rights organizations are rarely allowed in Kashmir. This silence is part of the climate of impunity that has made these atrocities possible.

23

Student Protests in the Garo Hills[*]

Certain days get marked in the history of a region forever. For the people of the Garo Hills in Meghalaya, 30 September 2005 will always bring up agonizing memories. On that day, the state police and armed forces opened fire on unarmed peaceful assemblies of students being held at Tura and Williamnagar, headquarters of the West Garo Hills and East Garo Hills districts, respectively. Nine persons lost their lives, including five school students and two university students. Besides, dozens were injured—some received multiple bullet injuries. One twenty-six-year-old post-graduate student who was hit on his spine has been crippled and is now condemned to spend most of his life on a bed, or in a wheelchair at best. Guns— AK47s and SLRs—were aimed directly at these youngsters, in most cases at their receding backs. The playgrounds at Chandmari (Tura) and Rongrenggire Government High School (Williamnagar), where the very same students had spent many happy hours playing football

* This essay is based on my contribution to the report *Police Firing on Demonstrations in Garo Hills, Meghalaya*, published in 2006 by the Other Media, New Delhi. The other members of the fact-finding team were Kamal Mitra Chenoy, Rajashree Dasgupta and Sukumar Muralidharan. We visited the Garo Hills together in early September 2006.

and other games, will no longer be associated with days of carefree abandon. Instead, history books have come alive in a strange and sad way: students are recalling the Jallianwalla Bagh tragedy and wondering why this should recur in independent India.

The Protests

The peaceful protests that had been planned on 30 September 2005 in Tura and Williamnagar relate to an issue that may seem relatively unimportant from a distance but matters a lot to the people of Meghalaya: the location and functioning of the Meghalaya Board of Secondary Education (MBOSE). Ever since the formation of Meghalaya in 1972, MBOSE had been located at Tura. The Khasi Students Union demanded that it should be moved to Shillong. Among other reasons, they mentioned the difficulties that students from the Khasi Hills faced to go to Tura: in the absence of a good direct road between Tura and Shillong, they had to make a long and expensive detour via Guwahati in Assam. The Garo people, of course, face the same problem every time they have to go to Shillong, the state capital.

The students and people of the Garo Hills insisted that the headquarters of MBOSE should remain in Tura. They argued that MBOSE was the only major state government institution located at Tura, while all others were at Shillong. This imbalance reinforced a deep-seated feeling of neglect that the Garos have felt in Meghalaya regarding their development, infrastructural facilities and generally not being on par with the Khasis. To a large extent, this is due to the historical advantage that the Khasis have had over the Garos, as Shillong was always the hub ever since the days when it was the capital of undivided Assam. However, even after the formation of Meghalaya, and despite adequate representation of the Garos in the Assembly (indeed, except one, all the Chief Ministers of Meghalaya so far have been Garos), many differences persist. For example, there is a world of difference between Shillong and Tura: even though it is the main town of the three districts of Garo Hills, Tura still wears a small-town look, and crucial public institutions like the civil hospital are bereft of basic facilities. This acute feeling of neglect amongst the Garos is not new. It was at the root of the demand for a separate Garoland being voiced by the Achik National Volunteer Council (ANVC)—an armed underground movement until it entered into a ceasefire agreement with the Indian government in 2004. All this helps to understand how a simple matter like the location of the MBOSE gradually became a controversial political issue.

Student organizations had been agitating non-violently for some time. No incident of violence had occurred before 30 September 2005. In fact, just two days earlier, on 28 September, a dharna had taken place in front of the Deputy Commissioner's (DC) office in Williamnagar. One of the participants, Gamchi Timre R. Marak (Secretary, Achik Social Vigilance and Protection Team), clearly recalls the peaceful atmosphere of the dharna: 'They told us not to sit inside the DC's compound, so we said okay and we sat outside the compound. There were lots of CRPF men, they were happy seeing our peaceful dharnas because we didn't create any problem.'

Based on this experience, the organizers of the 30 September protests in Tura and Williamnagar expected to receive permission for the event. And indeed, an impression was given to them on 29 September that permission would be given. Little did they know that their attempt at a peaceful protest would end in a major firing incident, the first of its kind in the living memory of the people of the Garo Hills. I shall restrict my observations here to the incident in Tura since I did not visit Williamnagar.

The Firing in Tura

A few days earlier, the Joint Action Committee (JAC) had asked the District Magistrates of West and East Garo Hills for permission to hold a public meeting and a rally in Tura and Williamnagar on 30 September 2005. The permission was initially granted. However, at 6 p.m. on 29 September, the Tura DC called the leaders of the Joint Action Committee and informed them that the permission had been revoked because of apprehensions of a violent incident, based on intelligence reports. The JAC leaders refused to sign the agreement on the grounds that it was too late to inform all the people. The district administration later claimed that the PR division went that evening to some crucial locations in the town and announced that the permission had been revoked; a television announcement was also made. But physical announcement through a megaphone has its limitations, and the TV announcement was done at a time when families have other things to do than watch TV, if they have a TV in the first place.

What was not done is also noteworthy. For instance, no attempt was made to block the main entry points to Tura on 30 September, or to prevent people from entering the Chandmari grounds, a school playground in Tura, where the meeting was to be held. According to survivors and witnesses, after thousands of people had assembled, an official announcement was made that the assembly had been banned and that people should disperse. A banner with a similar message was also unfurled.

John Leslee K. Sangma, Member of the District Council (MDC), intervened to say that at least fifteen minutes should be allowed for people to disperse. At that point, Sengrak D. Marak (Chairman of the Joint Action Committee, Tura, and a popular leader) went in front of the crowd with a megaphone and appealed to people to disperse peacefully. He had barely begun when armed guards held him from both sides and started taking him away. Seeing Sengrak being taken away, the students in the front started protesting and tried to pull him back. This was the beginning of the disturbance. Eyewitnesses say that within minutes tear-gas shells were released in the air and almost immediately the firing began.

The Chandmari ground is not very big, but as mentioned earlier, there were thousands of people who in all probability had not been able to understand what was going on in the front, or what was being said, given that only a megaphone was used by the administration (the same megaphone was also being used by Sengrak). According to a video taken by a local reporter as well as first-hand accounts of witnesses and survivors, students and the rest of the public were trying to disperse and get out of the field as soon as they possibly could. This was difficult since the Chandmari ground is closed on three sides: there is a boundary on the right, a stream (flowing around 20 feet below) on the left and a seating arena at the far end facing the only entrance to the playground from the main road.

Meanwhile, a large number of CRPF personnel, Special Operations Teams, and state police forces had taken position at the entrance as well as other potential exit routes. Eyewitnesses said that before the firing began, the crowd was still trying to disperse in an orderly manner. But as soon as the tear-gas shells were fired and gunfire started, there was confusion and panic. In the absence of any escape route people picked stones and started throwing them at the police, though there were few stones to be found on the playground. In desperation, some jumped into the stream twenty feet below. The firing continued unabated for a considerable length of time. Shocking video footage is available of careless firing by a CRPF jawan: with his hands and AK47 raised above his head, hopping from one foot to another, he can be clearly seen showering bullets on the crowd not just for a few seconds but minutes. He was finally restrained by one of his own colleagues while the DSP stood by just a few feet away.

We heard moving accounts of how, in the midst of the firing, some people did not run away but stayed to help others escape and to attend to the injured. For example, seeing one person fall down in front of him, one youngster took off his shirt and tied it around the victim's wound to stop the flow of blood. Similarly, Becking Marak, who was hit on his spine and is now crippled for life, had stopped to help an injured person and assist a girl to safely climb the boundary wall. Another witness said that he was running to save himself but stopped when a mother admonished him not to run but to help others. He stayed back and later sustained several bullet injuries.

The injured were taken to a Christian hospital close by for first aid, and then moved to bigger hospitals. At the government civil hospital, they could not be treated immediately since the doctors were in the operation theatre. One injured person died in the meantime. Others were treated to the extent that was possible and then referred to Guwahati. The civil hospital in Tura is an impressive building but the doctors are frustrated by the lack of basic facilities. They showed surgical gloves that had holes and an X-ray machine they could not use since there was no operator. Medicines were also short, they said. They felt helpless since their complaints went unheeded.

Meanwhile, within an hour of the firing, people—a large majority of them students—took to the streets in a silent protest that passed the Collectorate and other government offices. The DC and other government officials had barricaded themselves in their offices, as had policemen and members of the armed forces. A young woman at the front of the procession held the Indian flag high and resolutely. Under the Indian flag, in its care so to say and with it as witness, they could be seen to be demanding justice from Indian democracy. 'Tell us, is this the behaviour of violent people?' asked a Garo activist who was sitting quietly by my side when we were watching a video of the procession.

Three Testimonies

Testimony 1: Raksan M. Sangma

In his early thirties, Raksan M. Sangma now works as a laboratory assistant at the Government College in Tura, a job he got as compensation for being injured in the firing. Here is how he remembers the event:

> I was one of the victims that day in the rally. Soon after I reached the venue, the Magistrate unfurled a banner on which was written that the [meeting] had been declared illegal. I was afraid that something was going to happen. A public leader, Sengrak Marak, asked permission from the Magistrate to speak for fifteen minutes. The Magistrate gave Sengrak permission to speak. He had spoken for only a few minutes when he was stopped and the megaphone was taken away from him. Students got agitated and tried to pull Sengrak from the grip of the police. All this time the public was orderly, but the tear gas started. The students started running. I told the students not to run so that everybody could disperse slowly. I never expected that we would be fired at since no incident like this had ever occurred in Tura. I was leaving the field when I was shot at by a policeman who was behind a jeep a short distance away. I was hit on my left elbow and on the side of my chest. A boy took his shirt off and tried to stop the gushing blood before I fell unconscious. I was first taken to the Christian hospital and then to the civil hospital. The next day I was shifted to Guwahati. After surgery, my arm has become short and I can lift that arm only a little. I can move the fingers of that hand but cannot hold anything. I returned from Guwahati after nearly three months but had to make many trips there for continuing treatment. The district administration delayed payment to the hospital and the hospital would not allow me to leave without payment. I was given a job in the laboratory only because of the efforts of a local NGO.

Testimony 2: Grikseng D. Marak

> I am from Jenggitchakgre village which is 12 km from Tura. Soon after I reached the ground that day, three to four tear-gas

shells were fired. This was my first experience with tear-gas and tears were rolling down my face while I tried to exit from a small opening in the wall. But a mother called me back to the field saying that I should not feel scared and should have the courage to die for the country. I went back to her. She was then in the middle of the field. The police, who were watching us from the front of the field, suddenly started rushing towards us and firing. I was running towards the end of the field when I was hit. Later, I learnt that they had pumped five bullets into me: two near my right shoulder, two near the waist and one near the hip. I was bleeding profusely. I was taken to the Christian hospital where they stitched up the wounds without taking out the bullets in order to stop the bleeding. At the civil hospital, they took out two bullets. A bullet near the liver could not be taken out. Bullets in the back of the right elbow are near some nerves and require an operation. Besides, there were four bullet fragments embedded in my back. I have already had three surgeries.

I know that whatever happened on 30 September is illegal according to the Indian Constitution and universal human rights. We are accused of throwing stones, but some who threw stones did so only because there was no exit and they could be killed any moment by the rain of bullets all around.

Grikseng, a BA student, could not appear for his final examinations due to this incident. His family is dependent on agriculture. We asked him whether he would go again if there was another rally in Tura. He replied without any hesitation that he would.

Testimony 3: Becking Marak

Becking Marak, a post-graduate student of Garo literature at the North-Eastern Hill University (NEHU, Garo Hills) at Tura, lives in a village called Dalu, bordering Bangladesh. When we went to see him in Dalu, Becking lay on his bed, his outstretched legs already in a wasted state. This is what Becking had to say:

> There was no need to shoot where I stood because there was nobody throwing stones at them from that side. I was hoping to help an injured man I had seen falling, close to where I was. Four others who were with him were calling for help. Most people had managed to run away from the shooting that was still going on. I was moving towards this injured person when I saw the DSP, Dalton P. Marak, gesturing to his Personal Security Officer (PSO) who was shooting in another direction to shoot at us. Realizing what was about to happen and seeing a girl who was in a shocked state, I turned and tried to take the girl with me. The PSO was now shooting in our direction with his AK-47. Only twenty metres separated us. When I saw him aiming at us, I attempted to jump into the stream with the girl. She was saved, but I was hit and I fell down. After a few minutes I tried to turn around, but I could not move my legs. I could only turn my upper body and saw the DSP and some CRPF jawans standing close to us. One of them pointed to a bruise on his forehead and said, 'Look what you have done to me.' I could not move. Two men tried to lift me. One bullet had hit me in my spine and the other on my side.
>
> I have been going to Guwahati for treatment, but there is still no sensation below my waist. The government is bearing the medical expenses, but the doctors have given up. I can't move at all. I am unable to do anything now. I feel very depressed. Instead of protecting us, how could the government send soldiers to shoot us?

Unanswered Questions

I have referred earlier to video footage of the incident. This video footage was taken by a reporter who was risking his own life. It shows the whole sequence of events, until the peaceful procession that was taken after the incident. The faces of some of the key officials, police and, CRPF personnel are visible in the video.

When we met the Secretary to the Home Minister as part of our investigation, we pointed out that not one officer—not even the CRPF jawan who was mindlessly firing at the crowd—had been suspended even as a temporary measure. We felt that the authenticity of the video could not be doubted for at least two reasons: first, it was consistent with the sequence of events as narrated by all the eyewitnesses we met, and second, the video clearly showed known public figures like the DSP and magistrates aside from the jawans. Yet, the Secretary maintained that the video was 'doctored'.

Many troubling questions remain. Can bullets be showered on a defenceless crowd that includes a large number of school children and youth, just to disperse them or even in response to stone throwing? After tear-gassing, why were other stipulated methods like water cannon or lathi charge not used for crowd dispersal instead of resorting to gunfire immediately? Most of the victims had bullet entry wounds in their backs, why were they fired upon when they were running away? Why were bullets fired above the belt? Who ordered the firing? Why did the security forces include the Special Operations Teams that are supposed to be used only to tackle 'militants'? If the stone-throwing was really so intense that the police was constrained to respond with force, why have only a few policemen been injured and that too with minor injuries? Why did the district administration not take active steps to stop the entry of people from outside Tura after the permission was withdrawn the previous evening?

These are some of the questions that remained unanswered as we completed our inquiry into the Tura incident. We were disturbed to learn that the incident in Williamnagar on the same day was of a similar nature. The disconcerting similarities almost suggest that the two incidents had played out in coordination or were even pre-planned.

An Inquiry Commission was set up to investigate the Tura firing. It consisted of a single member, Justice D.N. Chowdhury, who submitted his report in April 2007. The report includes a succinct account of the numerous testimonies that were presented to it from both sides. It comes to the firm conclusion that there was excessive use of force by the police: 'The materials on record unerringly lead to the conclusion that the quantum of force resorted to by the police was unjustified and excessive in the facts and circumstances of the case . . . The security forces . . . went berserk and conducted themselves in a recklessly irresponsible manner' (pp. 103, 110). Further, the report held specific officers responsible for the incident, including L.R. Sangma (District Magistrate at the time of the incident), S.N. Marak (Additional District Magistrate) and O. Pasi (Superintendent of Police). Unfortunately, this report later gathered dust and to this day no action has been taken against any of these officers or anyone else.

A similar report was submitted for Williamnagar by a two-member Enquiry Commission headed by Justice D.N. Baruah. That report, however, concludes that there was no excessive use of force in the circumstances.

The Deeper Questions

Meghalaya is a different world. If you have not been to the Garo Hills, there is much that will enchant you there, from the winding roads around green hills to the proliferation of a variety of trees. The colourful flowered or striped *mekhlas* (traditional dress) of Garo women are likely to catch your attention as are the women themselves, whether behind the counter of a shop or walking on the streets, their confidence perhaps a legacy of the traditional matrilineal system. Most of the Garos are Christians and some western influence can be observed in their everyday life. For instance, one may come across guitar-carrying youth on roads and buses. I was told that guitars are popular in church services and for serenading a sweetheart!

Meghalaya was carved out of Assam in 1972. Garos and Khasis, the two main tribal communities, had fought together for a separate state. However, three decades after its formation, the two have reached a point where the Garos are now aspiring for a separate Garoland. The principal reason for this aspiration is the feeling that they have been neglected and are still deprived in comparison to the Khasis. As it is, the Khasis were ahead educationally and economically due to the fact that Shillong—located in West Khasi Hills—had been the capital for a long time, first of undivided Assam and now of Meghalaya.

Garos are still fighting the historical disadvantage that they feel vis-à-vis the Khasis. Those who are better off in a society often do not realize that if they are what they are, it is not due to their own merit but because they have benefited from historical advantages. Sadly, empathy gets little space in political discourse or practical decision-making. The Garos themselves do not always have much sympathy for Bangladeshi immigrants.

What happened in Tura and Williamnagar should also be seen in the wider context of the history and politics of the north-eastern states in the post-colonial period. Widespread militarization and serious transgressions of human rights have marked this region. What happened on 30 September 2005 is by no means exceptional. In fact, it is symptomatic of the manner in which the Indian government has handled unrest in the north-eastern states. As we saw, little effort was made to address the real issue, and instead, overwhelming force was used against civilians. Militarization has been a short-cut and a long-cut to curb and control dissent through special laws like the Armed Forces Special Powers Act (AFSPA) that was imposed in 1958 in Nagaland (then part of Assam) and later extended to most of the north-east under the pretext of countering insurgencies. Needless to say, excessive use of force perpetuated or intensified both popular discontent and insurgency movements.

It is astounding that the burning issues of the north-eastern region remain largely unnoticed and unquestioned in other parts of the country. Taking a cue from the government, mainstream media focus mostly on militancy and violent incidents, eclipsing the real issues and perpetuating our ignorance and lack of meaningful engagement with the societies and politics of this region. Meanwhile, the Indian state, like a ruthless shark, continues to swallow so many colourful fishes and confine them to its dark underbelly.

24

The Struggle for Self-Rule in
Manipur's Hill Districts[*]

Around 30 km from Kohima is Mao Gate, the border between Nagaland and Manipur. Mao Gate takes its name from Mao village that falls on both sides of the border and the Mao community of the Nagas that inhabits this region. This border area is part of Senapati district, which along with adjoining Ukhrul, Tamenglong and Chandel districts (four of the five hill districts of Manipur), form a continuum of present-day 'Nagaland' in every sense—topographically, socially and culturally. This southern stretch is now in Manipur only due to the arbitrary boundaries that were created by the Indian state. These boundaries took off from the British occupation of the historical political entity 'Nagalim' (the homeland of the Naga people) and its division between India and Burma (Myanmar). After Independence, the Indian state further divided the Naga areas under its control, despite it being a contiguous area, into (parts of) four states: Nagaland, Assam, Manipur and Arunachal Pradesh. Likewise, the Nagas under Burmese occupation were divided between Sagaing sub-division and Kachin state.

---

* Originally published in *Economic and Political Weekly*, 31 July 2010.

It is in the context of this historical injustice done to the Naga people that we need to understand the tensions of May 2010 between Manipur and Nagaland. The crisis that started on 1 May when the Manipur government banned Thuingaleng Muivah, general secretary of the National Socialist Council of Nagalim-Isak-Muivah (NSCN-IM) from visiting Somdal, his village in Ukhrul district (after more than four decades of being away), is not about a person or a village but about the illegitimate power of a government over a people. It is about the quest of a people for their homeland that was unjustly wrested from them, the quest of a people for sovereignty that was not respected, when a legitimate demand was quelled by brute force, when every trick was used to sap their fine spirits and make them bend under the weight of an unjust rule. And now after a history of pain, even when a formal peace process has been in place for the last thirteen years, no consideration is shown towards the leader of a people by the state government, even though the central government is supposedly negotiating with NSCN at the highest level as an equal. How are self-respecting people supposed to understand this?

This is yet another instance where the government resorts to militarization, allegedly to avoid tension and maintain 'law and order', but instead plunging the entire region into a full-scale crisis—social, economic and political. Its belligerent stand led to protests that have by and large remained peaceful. The protests have, however, failed so far to make the government rethink its decision. Instead, the government has stubbornly stuck to its original line thereby continuing to cause hardship to the citizens on both sides, fuelling the tension that was already created and sowing seeds for a possible larger conflagration.

In Mao Land

The story began on 1 May 2010 when all the local dailies announced that the Manipur government had denied permission to Muivah on

the ground that it might cause 'communal disharmony endangering
the peaceful coexistence of different ethnic communities'. This
decision came as a jolt since the centre had already given its consent
to the visit.

The tone was set the following morning, when a heavy
deployment of hundreds of Manipur armed forces including police
commandos, Manipur Rifles and Indian Reserve Battalion (IRB)
personnel moved into the border areas and villages at Mao Gate (on
NH 39) to prevent Muivah's visit, scheduled for 3 May. One of the
first actions of the forces was to pull down the traditional welcome
arch and banners put up by the Naga community to welcome Muivah
at Mao Gate. Soon after, Section 144 CrPC was imposed in Senapati
and Ukhrul districts and curfew was clamped in the area.[1] By then,
a tense atmosphere prevailed at Mao Gate, with police flag marches
and armoured vehicles on display. People in the hill districts had
started protesting against the imposition of Section 144 and the ban
on Muivah's entry. In Ukhrul town, there was a public meeting of
over 10,000 persons followed by a candlelight vigil. Women of nine
villages around Mao started an indefinite protest in Mao village, as
did women of thirteen surrounding villages in Tadubi. Even as news
came of peaceful protests from all Naga-inhabited areas of Manipur,
one also began to hear of more direct action like the attack by a group
of women on a police station in Ukhrul and the torching of five
stranded trucks with Manipur number plates by unidentified persons
late at night on 3 May.

I visited Mao Gate on 4 May, as part of a women's team that
included two leading Naga activists.[2] Just outside Kohima, our
vehicle started climbing a winding road through villages and forests,
leaving the terraced fields at a distance below. We could see that
the past loomed above and everywhere in many ways. The 'security'
forces occupied entire hill ranges. As we went past the Assam Rifles
camp, we saw a board outside which boldly declared: 'Friends of
the Hill People'. We went past Kigwema village and sure enough

the Kigwema 'army' camp was right above. Be it the Indian army, paramilitary or the police, there have been so many different armed forces and for so long—more than five decades—that for the Nagas, this 'friendship' under the shadow of the gun has become part of their daily life and landscape.

A little beyond Viswema, 8 km before Mao Gate, we saw a truck burnt to cinders and soon another four vehicles in a similar state. At Khuzama village, we met some members of the Naga Students' Federation (NSF). We learnt that NSF is the oldest civil society organization there, older even than the Naga Mothers' Association (NMA) and the Naga Peoples' Movement for Human Rights (NPMHR). Each tribe has its own students' union and all are under the NSF. The organization also covers all the Naga youth in Nagaland as well as the Naga-inhabited areas. Later, together with these NSF representatives, NMA women of the Mao area and some local media persons, we proceeded to the border.

We were stopped at the border by the Manipur police, who said they had orders not to allow any 'media' to enter. Eventually they allowed us entry for a short while. We were able to visit the women's protests in Mao and Tadubi villages, where we found impressive assemblies of thousands of Mao Naga women in traditional black and red shawls, of all ages, many with children, settled on both sides of the National Highway 39. These were 'silent' protests, but not if one read the scores of placards women were carrying: 'Muivah has a right to visit his birthplace', 'Respect Indo-Naga ceasefire', 'Down with the Ibobi government', 'We want peaceful settlement', 'Nagas are one', 'No more militarization', 'We want peaceful coexistence', 'Expedite peace process', amongst others.

'Why were curfew and Section 144 imposed? There was no turmoil here, no reaction, even after they directly provoked us by pulling down our welcome gate,' said one member of the Mao Naga Women's Welfare Association. Another woman in her thirties said: 'I have never seen so many forces in the last three decades. Why have they been deployed? We are not having a war.' Other women and men said: 'This is unconstitutional and undemocratic', 'Our future is threatened' and 'Such actions are inviting ethnic clashes'.

Despite these democratic protests, the Manipur cabinet reaffirmed its earlier decision to deny permission to Muivah. Meanwhile, feelings of indignation and anger were building up. The students were irked by the government's stand and use of armed forces to deny entry to the public as well as to turn away Naga Hoho, NSF, NMA and NPMHR leaders from the border.[3] The NSF maintained that by denying them access to the Nagas on the other side and 'an entry in our own land', the government had insulted all the Nagas. On 3 May, the NSF had issued an ultimatum demanding that the Manipur government revoke Section 144 in Naga-inhabited areas and issue an apology within twenty-four hours, else there would be a bandh on all Manipur vehicles in these areas. Since these conditions were not met, the indefinite bandh started from the evening of 4 May. This bandh obstructed vehicular movement on the main road connecting Manipur and Nagaland.

On the evening of 5 May, a villager from Songsong was assaulted by IRB personnel. The next day, when women of Songsong and other villages protested against this assault and demanded that the forces should leave, they were tear-gassed by police commandos and then fired upon by IRB personnel. Two college students, Daikho Loshuo (twenty-three) and Neli Chakho (twenty-one) from Kalinamai village, were killed on the spot and Lokho, a postgraduate student from Songsong, was critically injured. As the public ran for cover, the security personnel fired tear gas, injuring at least seventy people, mostly women since they were at the front, though the exact number of injured is not known as many fled to the jungles.[4] The inspector-general of police however denied the firing in a media interview, saying that 'We did not have any firing order so there was no open firing'.[5]

A black flag march was held at Mao Gate the following day and 6 May was proclaimed as 'Black Thursday'. Six independent Naga members of the Manipur legislative assembly resigned. Meanwhile, fearing further armed action, hundreds of villagers fled from their homes and crossed the border to Nagaland. With just enough time to gather their children and no available transport, most of them took the jungle route. Initially the villagers of Khuzama, the first village across the border, sheltered them in the local church. Later they were shifted to Kisama. A headcount that week showed that there were 444 'internally displaced persons' in the Kisama camp besides another 2,000 who were reported to be in Kohima and Dimapur, sheltered by relatives. The bordering villages of Mao Gate wore a deserted look after the 6 May incident.

Despite direct provocation, the reaction of the Naga organizations by and large remained non-violent. Diverse forms of non-violent resistance were used, such as press statements, public meetings, dharnas, rallies, bandhs, blockades and solidarity actions in other parts of the north-east and the rest of India. However, the mainstream media failed to appreciate this entire spectrum of non-violent resistance, its cause, or the absence of an adequate response from the state government. Instead, most of the attention was on the blockade, with the Nagas being shown as the culprits, calling for a closer examination of its origin.

The Case of the Two Blockades

First of all, it is important to register that two blockades, not one, started at different times and for different reasons. The first blockade was imposed on 11 April by the All Naga Students' Association of Manipur and All Tribal Students' Union of Manipur to protest against the elections scheduled for 26 May for the Autonomous District Councils (ADCs) under the controversial Manipur (Hill Areas) District Councils Act (Third Amendment), 2008. The second blockade was imposed by the NSF on the evening of 4 May and was reaffirmed after the 6 May firing. Following this, a counter-blockade was imposed by the All Manipur United Clubs Organization and United Committee Manipur on 6 May. Since the chronology of events clarifies the reasons behind the second blockade, let us examine the causes behind the first.

Administration in the Hill Areas

The five hill districts of Manipur cover around 90 per cent of the area of the state and are home to twenty-nine government-recognized tribal communities (besides smaller communities that are not yet recognized).[6] According to the 2001 Census, the tribals are 34 per cent of the state population but 92 per cent of the population of the hill districts. The tribal population can be clubbed under two broad ethnic groups: the Nagas (eighteen tribes) and the Kuki-Chin-Zomi (seventeen tribes).[7] The Nagas are a little more than half of the tribal population, followed by the Kukis, Mizos and other smaller tribes. While the presence of Nagas is highest in Ukhrul (93 per cent) and Tamenglong (78 per cent), they are a little over half in Senapati (55 per cent) and almost half in Chandel (47 per cent).[8] The Kuki-Chin-Zomi tribes are the majority in Churachandpur district. The Meiteis (often referred to as Manipuri), Pangals (Manipur Muslims) and other communities such as Bhamons make up the third, 'non-tribal' group and live primarily in the state's valley region; their population is 66 per cent of Manipur's total population of 23 lakh (according to 2001 Census).

After Independence, the government of India attempted to safeguard the interests and well-being of its tribal population by including special provisions in the Fifth and the Sixth Schedules of the Constitution. While the Fifth Schedule outlined the structure of governance of scheduled areas in tribal interests, the Sixth Schedule was conceived as an instrument of tribal self-rule. Tribal areas in nine states of mainland India are included under the Fifth Schedule and the Sixth Schedule covers such areas in four north-eastern states:

Assam, Meghalaya, Tripura and Mizoram (with special constitutional provisions as Article 371B in Assam and Article 371G in Mizoram). Arunachal Pradesh was in the Sixth Schedule but has subsequently adopted the panchayati raj (with some additional safeguards as in Article 371H). Nagaland, though theoretically under the Sixth Schedule, was never governed by its provisions in practice, and since 1962, when it became a state, has been governed as per Article 371A. The hill districts of Manipur, however, were not included in either the Fifth or Sixth Schedules. Manipur is the only state of the seven north-eastern states where the provisions of the Sixth Schedule have never applied.

Instead, the dual system of administration for the hills and the valley—that came into existence after the British annexed the independent kingdom of Manipur in 1891—continued after independence and also after 1949, when this kingdom along with the hills merged into the Indian union. During the period of Manipur's transition from being a union territory to statehood in 1972, a succession of Acts attempted to administer the hill areas: The Manipur Hill People's (Administration) Regulation Act, 1947; the Manipur Village Authorities (Hill Areas) Act, 1956; the Manipur (Hill Areas) Acquisition of Chief's Rights Act, 1967; and the Manipur (Hill Areas) District Councils Act, 1971. Besides, a Hill Areas Committee (HAC) comprising elected members of the legislative assembly from the hill areas was in place since Manipur was a union territory. It would have ceased to be operative after Manipur became a state but was kept in place by the introduction of a special provision (Article 371C) through a constitutional amendment in 1971. Article 371C also empowered the governor to report directly to the president regarding the administration in the hill areas and stipulated that '. . . the executive power of the union shall extend to the giving of directions to the State as to the administration of the said areas.'

Though the stated objectives of the said Acts and provisions were 'to safeguard the interests' of the Scheduled Tribes, the tribal communities did not believe this. They saw these Acts as an attempt by the state to extend its control in the hill areas. For instance, the 1956 Village Authorities Act was seen as an attempt to weaken the customary basis of the village polity by introducing the concept of a village authority whose members would be elected and whose size would depend on the number of taxpaying households in the village—this was a change from the 1947 Act which upheld the customary system in this respect. This was in contrast with the traditional system based on clan representation—as in the case of Tangkhul Nagas where the representative is nominated or elected by his clan members and can be removed only by them and not even by the chief, or nomination—as in the case of the Kukis where the chief of the village used to nominate members. The Act also tried to weaken the powers of the chiefs, for example, the role they played in village courts. A government report asserts: 'This Act may be regarded as one of the first steps towards the democratization of hill administration in Manipur. By placing certain restrictions on the powers of the chief and by introducing adult franchise at the lowest level of administration . . . the common villagers became aware of democratic values and practices.'[9] But the tribals took a different view. The Act was opposed quite strongly by most of them, especially the Kukis, who believed that the Act was an attempt to 'do away with the rights of the chiefs over land'. It was this insecurity that led the Kuki National Assembly to demand a Kuki state (within the Indian Union) in 1960.[10] The Act was however implemented in 1957 and 725 village authorities were constituted in seven subdivisions of the hill districts.

The 1967 Acquisition of Chief's Rights Act could not be implemented. As the name suggests, the Act aimed at abolishing the traditional system of chieftainship, compensating the chiefs and extending the Manipur Land Revenue and Land Reform Act, 1960, to the hill areas, thereby authorizing 'the state government to acquire the rights, title and land in the hill areas'.[11] The Act was seen as a way of weakening the authority of the chief and thereby the autonomy of the tribe and clan especially in respect to land.[12]

Resistance to the Manipur (Hill Areas) District Councils Act

Such being the experience of the tribal communities with legislations, they could not greet the Manipur (Hill Areas) District Councils Act, 1971 with anything resembling enthusiasm. The Act met with severe opposition from its inception on the grounds that it posed a danger to the autonomy the tribal communities enjoyed under their traditional systems of self-governance in all spheres of life. The unified demand of all tribal communities—despite protracted tensions between some of them such as the Nagas and Kukis, Paites and Kukis, or Kukis and Zomis—was that the Act be modified to include the provisions of the Sixth Schedule of the Constitution.

Opposition notwithstanding, the Act came into force and six district councils were put into place in the hill areas in 1973, though they could function only until the late 1980s, after which they had to be suspended due to continuous resistance. Things came to a head during the 1984 assembly elections, when the district councils started demanding greater autonomy. Until then and even later, the seventeen subjects that were supposedly under the 'control and administration' of the district councils (as per Section 29 of the Act) were not so in reality because the required devolution never happened—the Act mentions that these functions were 'subject to such exceptions and conditions as the administrator may make and impose'.[13] In the next two decades, council elections were successfully boycotted.

The government responded by taking one step forward and two steps backwards. The First Amendment Bill, passed in 1975, was followed by a more substantial move towards making the district councils 'autonomous' with the Manipur Hill Areas Autonomous District Council Bill, passed in July 2000. However, no further progress was made on this and a Second Amendment Bill was passed in March 2006 effectively revoking it. After another two years of silence, the Third Amendment Bill was presented in the legislative assembly on 19 March 2008. However, there were allegations of irregularities in the processes that followed and the bill was eventually withdrawn. Two irregularities were pointed out:

(i)   The state assembly constituted an extra constitutional body called the Select Committee to work on [the Principal Bill 2008] introduced by the HAC. Three of the five members . . . are not elected from the Hill Areas of the state.

(ii) Many clauses in the report of the Select Committee . . . were found in bad taste. [It] wanted to delete the word 'Autonomous' from the title . . . [replace] 'Self-Government' [with] 'Local Self-Governance', 'Tribals' [with] 'People of the Hill Areas' . . .[14]

The Manipur government then attempted to get an ordinance promulgated by the governor. People wondered as to why this was being done because the life of an ordinance cannot exceed seven and a half months and it would have to be presented in the next assembly session (within the first six weeks) as a bill or it would cease to operate (Constitution of India, Article 213: 2a). Moreover, this legislative power of the governor was an emergency power for taking immediate action at a time when the legislature was not in session—so what was the emergency? However, the governor having been 'satisfied that circumstances exist[ed] which render[ed] it necessary for him to take immediate action' (Article 213: 1) gave his acceptance to the ordinance, after the initial draft was amended, on 12 May 2008.[15] It should be noted that 'An ordinance promulgated under this article [has] the same force and effect as an Act of the legislature of the state assented to by the governor' (Article 213, Clause 2) and 'Notwithstanding anything in the Constitution, the satisfaction of governor mentioned in clause (1) shall be final and conclusive and shall not be questioned in any court on any ground' (Clause 4).

There was some talk of the fact that the cabinet had not consulted the HAC at this stage and also that the proposed ordinance had used the special provisions of 371C to include the Bill under Article 243M of the panchayat (73rd Amendment) Act, 1992—to which the corresponding provisions in the 11th Schedule would apply—so that the district councils would be under the control of the state legislature. Accordingly, the State Election Commission had been vested with powers of preparation of the electoral rolls while earlier it was the office of the administrator who undertook this through the Hill ministry of the state.[16]

On 10 October 2008, the Manipur (Hill Areas) District Councils (Third Amendment) Bill, 2008 was presented in the legislative assembly. As the excerpt below from the proceedings shows, there was little discussion on the bill before it was passed in the Legislative Assembly. A few members did express dissatisfaction that the bill had been presented in the house and referred to a select committee after promulgating the ordinance, thus not allowing them a chance to have a discussion on the Principal Bill. One member even cautioned that 'passing of the Bill without any discussion of the Principal Bill would have serious consequences'. There were suggestions that public opinion should be solicited, procedural lapses rectified, suitable amendments made and only then should it be passed. A question was also raised about a new insertion regarding a 'hill department'. But these objections and suggestions (of six MLAs) were brushed aside by the chief minister who argued that the bill was not very different from the 1971 Act and hence could be passed without much discussion:

> Shri O. Ibobi Singh, Hon'ble Chief Minister, clarifying to the discussion pointed out the need for passing the bill in order to conduct the long pending election of the district councils due

to which development of the hill area had been hampered and
added that the government had no intension (*sic*) to pass the
bill arbitrarily. He further said that the present bill was the same
Act of 1971 and the house had discussed it many times in the
past and hence, another discussion was not very necessary and
therefore, appealed to the members to pass the bill unanimously
in the interest of the hill people . . . (Manipur Legislative Assembly
Secretariat 2008).

Interestingly, D.D. Thaisii (Tribal Development Minister) reiterated
that the bill needed to be passed 'in the interest of the hill people . . .
and the necessary amendment can be done later on'. The opinion
of the chief minister and the tribal development minister (both of
the Indian National Congress) along with one independent MLA
prevailed over the opinion of the six MLAs—four of whom were from
the Manipur People's Party, one from the National People's Party
and one from the Indian National Congress—who had demanded
further discussion, rectification or amendment. After deleting the
words 'the hill department of', the Manipur (Hill Areas) District
Councils (Third Amendment) Bill, 2008, was passed that day.

How should we understand this? What was the need to hurry on
an issue that had waited for nearly forty years for a fair resolution?
Especially considering that the original Act was not only rejected by
the people, but in a sense by the government too, since it introduced
a new version in the form of the 2000 Bill, even though the changed
version was also subsequently revoked. A review of the Act is called
for in order to comprehend why it has been termed 'dangerous'.[17]

Why Is the District Councils Act Deemed 'Dangerous'?

Even from a quick look one can see that there is much in this Act
that would justifiably make any freedom-loving tribal nervous.
First, the district councils as envisaged in the Act are certainly not

autonomous. In fact, they are under the control of the deputy commissioner of the 'autonomous district', who would be appointed by the 'administrator' (one understands this position to be that of the governor). For instance, the deputy commissioner would have the power (Section 46: 3) to suspend the execution of any resolution or order of the district council and prohibit the doing of any act if he may see it to be 'in excess of the powers conferred by law' or 'likely to lead to a breach of the peace, or to cause annoyance or injury to the public or to any class or body of persons'.

Second, while there is scope (under Section 29 (1) of Chapter 3) for the district councils to have various executive functions such as maintenance of schools, dispensaries, roads and also some aspects of the management of land and forests, this is only insofar as these matters are entrusted to them by the administrator in consultation with the HAC. The Act does not confer any legislative powers on the councils although Section 29 (2) authorizes them to make recommendations to the government on specific issues such as appointment or succession of chiefs, inheritance of property and social customs. All judicial powers remain with the state government. Similarly, all cases in the district would have to go to the district court for adjudication. To sum up, the powers of the district council are rather limited:

> The district administration exercises supreme control over the district council in executive, legislative and judicial matters. The proposals for framing rules, regulations and by-laws, developmental works and executive and judicial matters are submitted to the district administration after these are passed in the district council. The district administration has to approve the proposals. Generally, the important executive, legislative and judicial activities are carried out by the district administration . . . The district council does not possess the financial, administrative and functional powers of an effective local self-government . . .

Thus, the autonomy granted to the district councils under the Act remains elusive (Institute for Human Development 2006: 242).[18]

In these and other ways, the Act vindicated the fears of tribal organizations that it could seriously jeopardize the rights of the tribal people and put them at the mercy of the deputy commissioner, who had overwhelming power over the district council despite it being a body of elected representatives. The district council, for its part, had the power to curtail the decisions of the village authority. As one commentator put it, 'The Manipur government turned the district councils into its agents instead of truly autonomous bodies.'[19]

Sixth Schedule Denied

As mentioned above, the tribal communities of Manipur have been waging a protracted struggle for the hill areas to be included in the Sixth Schedule of the Constitution. It is quite striking that there is almost no specific mention of the hill areas of Manipur in the significant debates and documents on the subject.[20]

The hill people of the areas that were included in the Sixth Schedule had expressed reservation at the time of inclusion, as admitted by J.J.M. Nichols Roy during the Constituent Assembly debates: '. . . these hill people feel that even this Sixth Schedule has controlled them too much and that they have not got enough [of] what they would like to have', and the last decades have borne this out to some extent. Nevertheless, the Sixth Schedule is clearly superior to the 1971 Act in its vision, philosophy and content.[21]

The Sixth Schedule allows for greater autonomy in the structure as well as the functions of the councils.[22] It has divided tribal areas in the states of Assam, Meghalaya, Tripura and Mizoram into autonomous districts and has empowered the governor to further divide the districts into autonomous regions, if there are different scheduled tribes in the district, as well as to change the size and number of existing districts. Each autonomous district would have a district council of not more than thirty members, four of whom would be nominated by the governor and the rest elected, and each autonomous region would have a regional council.

The schedule gives legislative powers to the district and regional councils, where the district council would have the power 'in respect of all areas within the district except those which are under the authority of regional councils, if any . . .' (paragraph 3). The regional council therefore would be free to make laws related to the use of land (except land lawfully acquired by the government for public purpose), management of any forest (except reserved forest), use of water, regulation of shifting cultivation, policing, appointment or succession of chiefs, inheritance of property, marriage and divorce as well as social customs. However, these laws would come into effect only after the assent of the governor. Likewise, executive powers for the administration of basic services and judicial powers have been accorded to the regional and district councils within a framework of rules that are to be worked out jointly with the governor. Besides, amongst other powers, the district councils would be able to make regulations for the control of money-lending and trading by non-tribals, and for the collection and sharing of land revenue, taxes and royalties (including mining of minerals).

For our purposes a crucial difference between the 1971 Act and the Sixth Schedule is that even though the latter does not grant complete autonomy (regional and district councils are subject to approval, consultation, correction, suspension and dissolution by the governor), nevertheless, it offers a 'charter of autonomy' and a real potential for democracy. For instance, under the Sixth Schedule there is no single officer like a deputy commissioner with power over the district councils, and the councils have not only executive but also legislative, judicial, developmental and financial powers and functions that are mandatory. Additionally, while in the present administrative structure in Manipur, the HAC offers some protection to the tribals under Article 371C, much depends on the initiative and energy of the MLAs from the hill areas who are its members. In fact, tribal communities recognize that the complacency of the HAC members has contributed to their adverse situation.[23]

The case for the Sixth Schedule has also been made by many high-level government committees, but it has been disregarded. For instance, the National Commission to Review the Working of the Constitution (chaired by Justice M.N. Venkatachaliah, former Chief Justice of India), in its report submitted in March 2002, recommended that the Sixth Schedule be extended to the hill districts of Manipur.[24] Nearly a decade earlier (1994), another government report of MPs and experts had bemoaned the fact that these areas had been excluded from the Fifth and Sixth Schedules (Report of MPs and experts 1994). State cabinet meetings have endorsed this demand not once but thrice (13 May 1991, 17 August 1992 and 28 March 2001), though with an inserted clause—'. . . with certain local adjustments and amendments'—about which the central government has sought clarification many times.[25] Besides, the HAC has also passed resolutions recommending the Sixth Schedule, as early as in 1974.[26]

Despite the legitimate claim for the Sixth Schedule and the rejection of the Act, it became clear to the tribals in March-April 2010 that the state government was planning to hold the ADC elections soon. This led to a revival of the earlier agitation on the issue. The chief minister's announcement of the election schedule (on 26 April) caused an uproar. The Manipur Tribal Joint Action Committee and All Manipur Tribal Union declared the day as 'Black Day' in the history of the tribal people of Manipur, accusing the chief minister of attempting to get the ADCs in place 'manipulatively'.[27] Other tribal organizations like the Kuki Inpi Manipur (the apex body of the Kukis) reiterated the objection and demanded that the elections be held under the provisions of the Sixth Schedule 'to fulfil the aspiration of the tribal people of Manipur and to protect the integrity of the State'.[28]

The tribal organizations then approached the governor, prime minister and home minister and sought their urgent intervention. The governor told them to cooperate with the election process and said that all necessary amendments would be made after the elections! This was unacceptable to these organizations, which maintained that nothing short of the Sixth Schedule would be acceptable. They believed that once the elections were held under the Act, 'the tribal people would be victims of economic and political exploitation and stagnation for another generation to come'.[29]

Hence, the blockade continued and later merged with the other blockade, started after Muivah's visit was stopped by the armed forces. The two blockades are two ends of the same story. A step-by-step escalation in response to the decisions and actions of the state government, these blockades raise the crucial question of how a people should express disagreement and dissent in our democracy. In this case, the government completely disregarded the sustained non-violent democratic movement of tribals. Nothing came of the decades of resistance or self-imposed deprivation (under suspended district councils, little planned development happened after 1988). Instead, the government chose to revert to the 1971 Act, the root of the problem. If this is not undemocratic governance, what is? What must a people do to register their protest and be heard?

Humanitarian Crisis vs Humanitarian Crisis

Aside from these two blockades, there is a third blockade—which has existed for so long that it has become part of everyday life and therefore invisible—of the state against the tribal people where the democratic rights of the citizens of hill areas have been trampled upon with impunity for decades. Any mention of 'humanitarian crisis' caused by the road blockades should not overlook the other 'humanitarian crisis' due to years of neglect, discrimination, political marginalization and subjugation that has been inflicted on the tribal population in general and Nagas in particular in Manipur.

This is not to downplay the negative effects of the recent road blockades. As a consequence of the blockades, the prices of essential commodities (including food, fuel and medicines) have shot up in Manipur, causing much inconvenience to the people, especially in the Imphal valley. However, it is unfortunate that the media projected this as a conflict between Nagas and Meiteis. The blockades were against the seat of government and if the seat had been elsewhere, no doubt the site of the blockades would have changed too. While the ill-effects of the blockades necessitate rethinking of this mode of agitation (or at least of how long it can be stretched), one should not lose sight of the political question and injustice that led to the agitation in the first place. One should also not overlook the fact that neither the blockades nor their adverse effect had any impact on the state government's stance.

It would have been useful if the people of the valley had also taken up the cause of the tribal people as their own, and restrained the government from taking recourse to militarization and district council elections, as it did with almost no opposition from the valley districts. But this is perhaps too much to ask: there is a conflict of interest here, and in the face of one's own interests, few can stand firm on principles, values and duty. The fear and insecurities displayed by the chief minister and his colleagues are largely shared by the people in the valley districts. This is the fear of a dominant community which is restricted to around 10 per cent of the total land area of the state—not because they were pushed to this state of confinement by the hill people but because this is the way it always was. The valley districts have a functional panchayat system since 1960 (later enhanced with the 73rd and 74th amendments) and there has been sustained development there, even if its pace and quality have been unsatisfactory. But for their future expansion, the hill territories would be important.

The tribal people feel that one significant reason why they have been denied the Sixth Schedule so far is that the state can gain control over their land through other means. They want to protect themselves from laws that could exploit them and alienate them from their land and other resources. This is not just a matter of livelihood but also an attempt to safeguard their way of life since their economic, social and political systems are interlinked. No survey has been done of land ownership in the hill areas since the land is mostly collectively held. In the absence of land records and titles, people are not only deprived of some credit facilities but also vulnerable to 'outsiders', i.e., non-tribals, if the constitutional protection that they have so far is lifted or circumscribed. Already, the government has made several attempts to extend the Manipur Land Revenue and Land Reforms Act 1960 to the hill areas. When it was first enacted, the hill areas were clearly exempt. But later (in 1967) the government made an abortive attempt to cover the hill areas through the Chief's Act.

Subsequently, the sixth amendment to the Land Reforms Act (in 1989) attempted to open a passage to the hills by inserting an exception to the exempt clause that allowed the state government to extend whole or part of any section of the Act to any of the hill areas by a notification in the official gazette. This filled the tribals with dread.[30] This amendment, however, was opposed and could not be implemented. Nevertheless, the 1960 Act was able to make a move into the hill territories. The Act meant only for plains was extended also to the plain areas of the hill districts. Since the Act involved conducting a survey, conferring ownership rights and collection of revenue, its implementation led to privatization of land in some plain areas of three hill districts.[31] During the last few years, there has also been a campaign for a uniform land law for the entire state. Tribals have been opposing it and demanding a separate land law for the hill areas, but nothing has come of it.

This fear of land alienation into non-tribal hands is quite real since this has been the experience in most scheduled areas of the country. Also, there are international examples of how the demography of 'occupied territories' (e.g., West Bank) can be changed over time by state-sponsored settlements and laws, ultimately leaving the original residents with a fait accompli.

The tribals are also wary of land being taken away in the name of 'public purpose' as is happening in many other parts of the country, often without any compensation. Already, large 'development' projects are located or planned to be located in the hills and inroads have been made by contractors into their forests. At the root of all these problems, in their view, is a structure of governance that does not allow them to be in control of their present and future. The struggle for the Sixth Schedule is therefore a fundamental struggle for their very existence and way of life.

Nobody can deny that the demand for the Sixth Schedule in the hill districts is a valid one and is pertinent for all the tribes and not only the Nagas. Fear of the Sixth Schedule is an old one—even the Constituent Assembly debates on the subject reveal the feudal mindset of some legislators and leaders who believed that by allowing the tribals to be autonomous, one would lose them to China or Burma, or they would go the Tibet way; one member even warned that '[t]he Communists will come and they will have a free hand . . . [and] we will have no government there'![32]

In Manipur, granting of Sixth Schedule for the hill districts is often seen as tantamount to acceding to the demand of Nagalim and a separate Kuki state; conversely, Naga and Kuki insurgents have started viewing 'the Sixth Schedule as a means of suppressing their demands . . .'[33] But the state cannot have it both ways—refuse to grant the Sixth Schedule and also talk about 'territorial integrity' at the same time. The government has lost all moral integrity on which to rest its case. It could have done so if it had treated its tribal citizens (including Nagas) justly. By not conceding the Sixth Schedule and forcing the district council elections, the government has only alienated the tribals further. The hill areas have been deprived of what is due to them for decades—this hardly helps to persuade them to stay within the fold. The disenchantment with the Manipur state is not of Nagas alone. Through its decisions and actions, the state government has only exposed its own fear psychosis—the fear of the wrongdoer.

Some may view further developments, in May–June 2010, as an indication that the conflict is over. The elections to the district councils were held as per schedule, the blockades were lifted and police and paramilitary were withdrawn from the border villages. But in crucial respects, the situation has deteriorated. The Naga civil society organizations have declared the elections in the Naga inhabited areas as 'null and void'. Further, they have affirmed that they were severing all ties with the Manipur government and would like the central government to make alternative arrangements.

This kind of breaking point was expected.

In the absence of a suitable self-governance structure or of any response from the state government to their democratic resistance, and with the AFSPA 1958 still in force in the hill districts (the ceasefire agreement notwithstanding), the Naga organizations had started a civil disobedience movement against the Manipur government in 2005: the United Naga Council submitted hill house tax of 93,227 households for 2006 to the prime minister in June that year; prescribed textbooks for secondary schools were surrendered and 156 private schools adopted the Nagaland Board of Secondary Education syllabus; and schools and colleges in the Naga inhabited areas sought affiliation with the Nagaland Board and Nagaland University.[34] The struggle with the state government, however, had not disrupted relations with the people in the valley, especially the Meiteis. However, in May this year when the crisis around Mao Gate and the blockades was escalating, especially after the firing incident, and there was little solidarity from the Meiteis (who are the dominant community not only in society but also in the state government and legislature), the Naga Hoho announced that the Nagas could no longer continue to relate with the Meiteis. This unfortunate development is the result of the recent deadlock, created by the Manipur government in the first instance, but also by the central government, which continued to watch while the situation worsened without making any timely or meaningful intervention.

Peace Without Justice?

One would like to think that control by denying basic democratic rights cannot last forever, but in this case, it has already lasted for more than six decades. The conflict(s) in Manipur can be resolved if there is political will, if the government respects the rule of law and if it is willing to treat all its citizens equally. And above all, if it does not resort to militarization. There has been militarization here for long years as in few places in the country, and it has not solved anything—on the contrary. Yet, no lesson has been learnt.

A large part of the present crisis has been due to the heavy deployment of armed forces at the border. Several additional companies of the paramilitary were sent by the centre to lift the blockade—though this decision came at the same time as that of the blockades being lifted—with the intention of stationing two companies permanently. At the most this would mean that blockade as a form of protest will be curtailed, but will the cause of the conflict be addressed through this? The mere presence of armed forces in large numbers is likely to cause problems. We have to only recall how the armed forces thoughtlessly opened fire on villagers in Tamenglong in May, when the truck carrying essential commodities that they were escorting slipped off the road on its own accord. These hill districts have been a site of many serious human rights violations in the past. One has to only pick up a NPMHR report to see the scores of instances of killing, rape and torture that are part of the memory and that have shaped the psychology of the people of this region. The ceasefire agreement between the Government of India and the NSCN does not apply to Manipur. The AFSPA is still in force. During the present crisis, people have protested peacefully and with restraint, but by deploying such large contingents of armed forces, is the government not being provocative? And if there is slippage, would that by default be attributed to 'rebel forces' and all toll on human life dismissed as 'collateral damage'?

In the present conflict, the state has missed an opportunity to strengthen peace. It does not require an exceptionally discerning eye to see that this was a completely avoidable turn of events. The stance and actions of the governments made a mockery of the ongoing peace process. Practising peace requires another kind of sincerity and commitment than talking peace. The simple desire of the Naga leader to visit his village could have been met in a dignified manner. Despite the fact that central questions like the NSCN demand for Nagalim is on the negotiating table, the Manipur government had stated earlier that it would not allow Muivah to enter Manipur until the demand for Nagalim was withdrawn, and also that Muivah could enter if he was simply going to visit his home but not if he had a political agenda. Can one really expect a political person to go anywhere without his politics? The fear, of course, was that he would speak about integration of the Naga inhabited areas of Manipur with Nagaland. And this could not be allowed, especially at the time when the district council elections were due. But is there no freedom of expression? Muivah's visit was going to be only for four days. Even if he did speak about integration during the four days, which he surely would have, what was stopping the Manipur government from campaigning on 'territorial integrity' for the remaining 361 days?

No peace can be achieved without the ability to respect the other and in the present context, this would necessarily mean being respectful of the rights of the other. The Naga people have a right to live together—a desire that has been expressed since 1920, which would mean redrawing state borders. Borders are seen to be sacrosanct in a world view where a people may well get divided, but the border must stay intact. As the Naga leaders have emphasized, the land they are asking for is theirs and not an inch of anybody else's land. Why then should this just claim be denied? The Naga quest for justice should of course not obviate consideration of other tribes residing in the same regions or neighbouring ones. However, the recent trajectory of events has reaffirmed the struggle of the Nagas to redraw the borders so that no authority can turn a Naga away from her home or land. Peaceful coexistence is possible only with the fulfilment of rights.

25

Awaiting *Nachiso*

Naga Elders Remember 1957[*]

Time is known to be a great healer, but the injustice of some wounds cannot be forgotten. The Naga people had a land of their own until 1826, when the British colonialists, through the Treaty of Yandabo, drew the Indo-Burmese boundary, thus arbitrarily dividing the Naga tribes and their lands between the two countries. The Naga resistance to British subjugation began in 1832, when the British army entered their 'homeland' for the first time. The Naga Hills, then part of Assam, were classified by the Indian Home Rule Act (1919) as 'Backward Areas' that were to remain outside the purview of the Assam Provincial Assembly. In 1929, the Naga leaders sent a memorandum to the Simon Commission asserting that after the British left, the Naga people wanted to be left as they were before the advent of colonialism—independent and free. There was some hope when the Government of India Act (1935) declared the Naga Hills as 'Excluded Areas' from both British India and British Burma.

In June 1946, the first agreement was signed between the Naga National Council (NNC)—the first all-Naga political organization

* This was originally published in Himal Southasian in August 2011.

formed earlier that year—and the interim government of India. The agreement stated that a protected state would be formed in 'Nagalim' under the NNC, with India as 'the guardian power' for ten years, at the end of which the agreement would be reviewed. However, on 14 August 1947, the declaration of Naga independence by the NNC led to a dramatic volte-face and the interim government deemed the previous agreement to be invalid. Thereafter, in May 1951, a Naga-organized plebiscite in all Naga-inhabited areas resulted in an overwhelming vote in favour of Naga independence. The Indian government responded by sending the Assam Rifles to the Naga Hills.

These circumstances led the Nagas to take up arms, presenting the Indian state with a rationale to silence the insurgency with brute force. Security forces were sent in large numbers and severe repression of both the underground cadres and ordinary Nagas ensued. In 1962, the state of Nagaland was officially created, following a sixteen-point agreement between the Indian government and Naga leaders. These leaders were actually intermediaries between the government and the underground leaders, but the latter were excluded during the crucial negotiations.

That, briefly, is how the Naga people were 'integrated' into the Indian Union. Today, the Naga tribes and lands are divided between India and Burma, and in India they have been further sub-divided across four states: Nagaland, Manipur, Assam and Arunachal Pradesh.

During 1956–57, the Indian state used 'strategic hamletting'—a counterinsurgency strategy first employed by the British in Malaysia and the US in Vietnam—to isolate the Naga insurgents from the people. These forced amalgamations of villages, called 'groupings', proved to be one of the most trying experiences that civilians were subjected to. In mid-2010, I spent some time in Mokokchung district of Nagaland, listening to recollections of those times from people who were old enough to remember them. Here are some extracts from our conversations.

The Groupings

Tekayangshi (eighty-four) and his wife Tepdakyangla (seventy-nine) live in Mangmetong village in Mokokchung district. Three years after their marriage, in 1953, Tekayangshi joined the underground, commonly called UG, as did many other 'volunteers' from their village. He remained underground for the next two decades. The Naga Hills were then part of undivided Assam, and the Assam police arrived in the area in 1953. They were based in Longkhum village of which Mangmetong is an offshoot. Although harassment of villagers and burning of granaries started soon, large-scale and systematic aggression began only after the arrival of the Indian military in 1956.

The 'grouping' of villages began in earnest later that year and continued into 1957. This involved moving the entire population of adjacent villages to one village, typically close to a road or an army camp. In February 1957, the whole population of Mangmetong was taken to Longkhum. The thousand-odd families of Longkhum and Mangmetong were moved into an area enclosed by two bamboo fences; in some places, spikes were installed between these fence lines. Families of individuals who had gone underground were further segregated from the general population (referred to as 'General') with a third fence around them. Tepdakyangla said that they received a one-week advance warning before being forced to move.

> They had burnt our house and destroyed our granary stores before the grouping. We took whatever rice remained and slaughtered our biggest pig. Those days there were no shops, but I managed to buy a tin of rice later in Longkhum. We also collected leaves of the sura tree to make our shelter in the grouping.
>
> Our daily lives were full of difficulties. We did not have enough food to cook. We did not even have clean drinking water. We were not allowed to collect firewood and there was no space to store wood. We cooked in milk cans and everybody got only a

small portion to eat. Toilet facilities were a major problem. In the absence of any open space, we had to defecate on leaves, which we then tied up and threw on the roof of our huts. Most of us slept on the floor, except some who were able to find enough material to make mats. The army gave us a few blankets, which we shared, and sometimes they surprised us by giving food and clothes.

My eldest daughter was born there on 30 July. My older son was with me, but I had kept him with my brother, who was in the General. My mother-in-law, who was very old, also stayed with my brother's family. When my daughter was born, the child had to be washed with drainage water. I sent word to my husband through some people who were allowed to work on their paddy fields. But it was impossible for him to come and see the child—he saw her only in March 1958, when we were allowed to return to our village. That year, three other babies were born in the grouping.

Every morning there would be a roll call. If we did not go, we were fined one rupee. The armed forces were there in large numbers. They would be there all the time, checking, questioning and so on. But the greatest difficulty of all was that those of us who were segregated were not allowed to go to the paddy fields. And even those who were allowed had fixed timings.

We were not beaten in the camp. Before the groupings, a lot of rapes were committed. The Assam police would come home and commit rapes. Even mentally unbalanced women were not spared in Longkhum. But during the grouping, no rape or sex work took place. After the grouping, however, the army came, and whenever they got a chance, they continued to molest and rape women, up to 1974. The peace accord was signed in 1975, halting the atrocities. In those days, women would smear soot over their faces and act as though they were mad, so that they would not be raped. Here most will not admit it, but it was very common in those days.

During the grouping period, three people were shot dead by underground cadres on suspicion of being army informers. Before the grouping, two other members of the village had been shot by the Assam police. After the grouping, civilians were also shot, including one from this village, leading to the suspension of two army personnel. From this village, twenty of those who were in the underground were killed. Tepdakyangla continued:

> All of us called this 'grouping' without knowing the meaning [of the term], because that is what the government called it. The younger generations now call these groupings 'concentration camps'. When we asked the security forces why they were troubling us like this, they would reply, 'Since you are demanding independence . . . So that you have no link with the underground . . . So you can't supply food to the underground.' The groupings were therefore done both to terrorize us and to cut off the supplies to the underground.
>
> One morning around 3 a.m., they came and started banging on the sides of our houses and told us that we could now go back. After returning, we rebuilt our houses. Even before the grouping, our house had been burnt more than three times. After the first time we would make only temporary houses, but they would come and set fire even to those.

Tepdakyangla said she was happy that Tekayangshi was in the underground during the grouping period, as he was serving their community. Today, however, Tekayangshi expressed unhappiness at the state of the underground groups, saying that there were too many factions with no united aim. He also complained that some of the rebel leaders had been corrupted by money, others by power. He also said that he has hopes from the peace process and that India was a good friend.

How could he call India a 'friend' after all that had happened? Tekayangshi said that even though the Nagas have suffered so much,

'Because we are neighbours, we will have to live together. Therefore, we must live as good neighbours and friends.' However, this did not mean that he had forgotten the dream of an independent Nagaland. He continued to use the word Nagalim—the term for the historical, and hoped for, Naga homeland.

Internal Autonomy

In Ungma, on 12 May 2010, I spoke with Bengangangshi, a Naga elder, leader and intellectual who used to be active in the underground. He told me:

> 1957 was the year of groupings in most parts of what is now Nagaland. The government's objective was to apprehend all those underground, and this was difficult without the groupings. By grouping, the area of operation is reduced, therefore, the army can function effectively. People were allowed to go out only for farming. A single grouping covered a large distance [5 or 6 km]. Because of this, the economic situation of the people was reduced to nothing. They could not cultivate like before. Medicines were also not available and it was difficult for sick people to go to hospitals, since there were no vehicles.
>
> Even when the people went for cultivation, the army was in the jungle. If they saw anybody in the jungle, they could simply shoot—even kill a man for no reason. A hawaldar could shoot a man or two and no one could question his authority. Women could be raped while in the fields or jungle, but again, no one could question the army—even married women were not spared. They could just carry them away in their vehicles and keep them for days, weeks or months, and then release them. Nobody could question their authority. All these areas have witnessed all this.
>
> Whenever we would go for cultivation, the army would detain women and also men whom they suspected had links with

the UG. They were constantly looking for UG freedom fighters they could round up and kill. Whenever any incident took place, their argument always was, 'You people have given them shelter and food'—as though this was a good reason to round them up and rape them.

The groupings did not have the desired effect, however, because the people were indeed supporting the UG. Wherever the cadres went, people would freely give them food. In those days, Bengangangshi was also in the UG. He and others would come to the grouping from the back, remove the fencing and put it back; in this way they would carry away the rations. He said:

> The groupings did not weaken the UG. But it did cause immense suffering to the common people, just because they were supporting the UG. People would supply [arrowroot-like] puglashi, and they would themselves consume local vegetation and grasses in the absence of rice, meat or vegetables. Extreme poverty prevented people from supporting the UG as they had done earlier, before the grouping period.
>
> When the army personnel would come, they would stay in the churches and carry away the women there. It was all very open. There was no shame at all. All this went on for one year—1957—from the beginning to the end.
>
> In those days, the big leaders were trying to bring about a solution. Periodic meetings were held in Mokokchung, Kohima and Wokha. Through that initiative, the Naga People's Convention (NPC) was born. The aim of the NPC was to bring the underground and Indian leaders together. But during the final stages of negotiation, even though the Indian government had given assurances to the UG leaders that they would be involved, they cheated and called only the overground NPC leaders to Delhi and signed the sixteen-point agreement with them.

In 1956, thousands of houses were burnt, including churches.
People were shot and killed. Granaries were burnt to ashes.
During this period, not only the freedom fighters but much of the
general public also went underground, since they were all in any
case without food or shelter. Schools had been closed down. At
that time there were only two high schools and the army occupied
their hostels. Therefore, many of the students went underground.

Bengangangshi joined the UG just after his matriculation exam,
in 1956. He was there until 1958, when he was so badly wounded
that he had to be admitted to the mission hospital in Jorhat. Before
joining the UG, he had been an active supporter. He continued:

It is difficult to say what the strength of the UG was during
1956–57. Every tribe had its own collection of names, its own
organization and registration. But these papers could not be kept
intact, because if they were written one day, they would need to be
burnt the next day. At that time all the tribes worked together, and
there must have been a few thousand underground cadres.

UG action started in the Mokokchung area in 1956. It started
in Tuensang in 1954 and there was heavy fighting there in 1955.
Fighting continued until the ceasefire on 6 September 1964, even
though an agreement was reached in 1960. The second ceasefire
was in 1975. The third ceasefire started in 1997. It has now been
fourteen years and nothing substantive has been achieved—it has
continued without bearing any fruit.

The demand from the Naga side is very simple—we want
freedom from India; it has been put in writing and has been placed
before India. But it is no longer rigid.

Before, the demand was only sovereignty. But 'sovereignty'
was never defined. Sovereignty in the present context is defined
in other ways. We want an 'honourable settlement'. In the present
context, it is like a give-and-take policy. We would like two

constitutions, one for India and one for Nagas. We would like it to be as in a federal system, where there are certain rights that would be with the Nagas and there would be certain portfolios that would be given to the central government, such as external affairs. In short, we want internal autonomy.

A large number of Nagas are also in Burma, where we have ancestral lands. In 1953, Nehru allowed the Burmese government to occupy our land, even though the Burmese people never claimed that it was theirs. That land is also a part of the Naga Hills. The Indian government does not want to consider our demand for greater autonomy, because it would involve disintegration of some states as they are organized today. But our demand will be continued by the coming generations, because Nagas cannot forget their demand. The Naga people will never swallow the bitter pill that India wants us to swallow.

Then and Now

Chuchuyimpang is a village of 861 houses, six kilometres from Mokokchung. On the way up, my companion points to the college and the church, which he says during the late 1990s was pockmarked with bullets due to intense fights between the two factions of the National Socialist Council of Nagalim—the Isak-Muivah (IM) and Khaplang (K) factions, which were created when the NSCN split in 1985, five years after its formation. The army did not intervene in this intense fighting.

The Chuchuyimpang forest was not burnt before or after the grouping. However, sexual assaults on women were fairly common and men of the village were frequently asked to do labour for the army. The grouping in Chuchuyimpang brought four villages together, around 1150 houses in total. It started in March 1956 and continued for the following year. This grouping was fenced, with one gate at each end, but the UG families were not segregated. No food (cooked or uncooked) was allowed to be taken when the farmers went to their fields since the officials believed that this would be passed on to UG cadres. Thus, farmers were forced to go without food for the entire day. Elsewhere, people suffered every day to meet their basic needs of water, firewood and food—for everything, permission was mandatory. In one incident, a woman from Longmisa had gone home to get rice from the stores that her family had hidden without the army's permission and was shot dead while returning. During that period, many people chose to live in the jungle, even though they were not with the UG; many died there due to malnutrition and illness.

In Chuchuyimpang, we met with three elders who were also good friends, Soupongyanger (eighty-three, a retired schoolteacher), Nungsangtemjen (eighty-six, also a retired school teacher) and C. Aliba (eighty-five, a retired government employee). None of the three were ever in the UG. The story that follows was told collectively by these three:

> The severity of the army action on a village depended on its relationship with the UG. Some villages were burnt many times. They could get all the necessary information about hide-outs, etc, from the CIDs [police informers]. When even this did not meet their objectives, they started the groupings. During that period, selected persons were also taken to the army camps, where many were tortured and killed. Before the grouping in a village, the army personnel would come and check the village. They would first group all the men in the open ground. Then, they went for checking in the homes when only the women were there. Many women were raped during such checks and household valuables were stolen.

In 1956, before the grouping, there was a major ambush in Chuchuyimpang in which seven army men and one UG were killed. After that, the army returned and took all the men aside and selected four suspects. C. Aliba was one of them. Severe beatings followed, he said, on the soles of their feet, behind the ears, on the head and knees. With rifle butts they would prod and pound their bodies. Aliba said that he still felt dizzy sometimes due to the beatings he received on his head. He is the only one of the four who is still alive.

Soupongyanger recalled the story of Toshinungsang, the first man from their district to be shot by the Assam police, though he escaped death. The incident occurred on 27 February 1956. He was not in the UG and he was in the village when he was shot. Soupongyanger, who witnessed the shooting, was also taken into custody, along with one other witness. He said they were taken to the army camp, where they had needles inserted under their nails and were beaten repeatedly. They were kept in a prison in Mokokchung for three months; he had to pay 500 rupees for his release. Even after his release, he had to report to the army every day for a month—punishment for refusing to divulge information on the location of the UG camp, details on the rebels' weapons, etc. Information about them had evidently been given to the army by informers, of which there were four in the village at the time. Indeed, 'The CID system continues till today,' said Soupongyanger. 'Since we have not gotten independence yet, they also need CIDs.'

These three elders believe that they will get independence one day. They said:

> Our ideology was simple. Phizo told us that we will take the full rupee coin. Not more, nor less.
>
> Even today we believe in this. For that one-rupee coin we have struggled. If we do not get our sovereignty, then what use was our sacrifice? Even if we die, we will get our independence. Our relationship with mainland India is only for political reasons—for all other reasons we are different.

As I took leave and turned to go, one of them called out: 'When you write, do not forget our sovereignty!'

As I walked down the hill, I thought of Tareptsuba. It was late evening, like the other day when we were preparing to leave Longkhum and I was told there that one other person wanted to meet me. Eighty-eight-year-old Tareptsuba had come after he learnt that an Indian had come to their village. An old shawl draped around his shoulders, leaning on his cane, he insisted on standing while speaking, as though making a formal deposition before a court of law. I felt humbled and disturbed.

'We are still waiting for nachiso (independence),' he began. 'In 1951, I put my thumb along with the rest of the Nagas for independence. Why is it that Nagas have still not got their independence? Right after that we were tortured—my teeth were smashed. Today, you are asking all these questions. Will you send the Indian Army? We might not be able to wield weapons against mighty India, but our willpower will win.'

Epilogue

The Last Leaf

'Don't tell me the moon is shining; show me the glint of light on broken glass,' wrote Chekhov, reminding us that ultimately, it is practical change on the ground that matters. When we look at how India is changing, our yardstick must be the lives of the people. Throughout this book, my effort has been to examine issues from the perspective of ordinary Indians who are virtually invisible beyond their own confines—people who don't count for much in India's exclusive democracy.

In the late-afternoon stillness today, as I mull over the story as I have told it—in fits and starts, bits and pieces—clichéd phrases come to mind like 'a bitter harvest' or 'a quagmire'. For those of us who think from their hearts, feelings say it all. And the feeling in this case is one that draws you down with each swirl, its shadowy shades exemplifying the sultry disquiet at the situation around us, many aspects of which are not only unsatisfactory but have also gone terribly wrong.

One is of course not speaking for everyone. One is not speaking, for example, about the privileged classes. Some of them may also be hurt if the promises made in the preamble of the Constitution of India are not kept. But they will find their feet and perhaps even fly to greener pastures. Not so the multitudes whose 'tryst with destiny' is still very much on Indian soil, often within a few kilometres from where they were born.

Still Forgotten

As I look back at these writings, I am struck by the fact that little has changed. The confidence one had about the fundamentals of our democratic framework has itself been shaken, portending calamitous changes that may undermine the very idea of India.

Most of the issues discussed in this book have not yet been resolved. In many cases, the situation is worse today than it was at the time of writing. For instance, the poisonous communal climate that prevailed in Gujarat in 2002 (discussed in the first chapter), has now spread to many other states like Uttar Pradesh, Rajasthan and Karnataka. Worse, now that the Bharatiya Janata Party (BJP) has come to power at the centre with an absolute majority, Hindu nationalism is as good as official. The ruling party's agenda seems to begin with harassing Muslims in every possible way, whether it is the Citizenship Amendment Act, the National Register of Citizens, population policies, the Uniform Civil Code, the release of Bilkis Bano's rapists, the bogey of 'love jihad', restrictions on the sale of meat, or more direct acts of state-sponsored lynching and bulldozing.

What is less well understood is that Christians, also unwanted guests in India as per Hindutva ideology, have also been a target of sustained persecution in recent years. In Chhattisgarh, incidents of harassment of Christians (illustrated in Chapter 19) have become more and more common. In countless villages, right-wing Hindu-nationalist groups are inciting local Adivasis against the Adivasi Christian minority, often leading to active harassment, for instance, in the form of depriving Christian families of land to bury their dead.

In Kashmir, repression continues. What we witnessed in 2010 happened again in different ways, year after year, until 2019. In

August 2019, soon after the BJP returned to power at the centre, Article 370 of the Indian Constitution was abrogated and the state of Jammu and Kashmir was divided into three Union Territories— Jammu, Kashmir and Ladakh. The abrogation of Article 370 was an old commitment of the Rashtriya Swayamsevak Sangh (RSS) and took the country one step closer to their dream of a Hindu Rashtra. Of course, it was done in the name of the Kashmiri people's interests, but it was actually an attempt to snuff out their hopes and defuse their protests. Needless to say, protests continue and Kashmiris are still living in an atmosphere of anger, fear and violence.

In the North-East, too, earlier conflicts have remained unresolved even as new sites of intense violence have emerged. Manipur, for instance, has been engulfed in unprecedented violence for months as this book goes to press. Had the long-standing demand of the hill districts for autonomy under Schedule 6 of the Constitution been met, it is possible that Manipur would not be where it is today. In other parts of the country, too, the autonomy of India's indigenous people is under threat. Their resources are being plundered for corporate profit while their way of life is being sacrificed in the name of development. Nowhere is this clearer than in Bastar, where all the atrocities discussed earlier continue—forcible displacement, false cases, fake encounters, police brutality, sexual violence and so on. A whole class of 'internal enemies' seen to be at war with the 'nation' has been created.

Beyond specific conflicts, there is a wider pattern of growing authoritarianism and concentration of power. On one side, corporate power and Hindu nationalism are colluding to undermine democracy. In many pockets, like Bastar, this is aided and aggravated by growing militarization. On the other side, safeguards for the protection of vulnerable groups are being weakened or dismantled, from the Right to Information Act to PESA and the Forest Rights Act. The Brahmanical Hindutva project to redefine India uses traditional Indian culture and values to hoodwink the Indian public.

As a result, the constitutional values of liberty, equality and fraternity feel more than ever like a distant dream.

This is not to deny that there have been some signs of hope and improvement. For instance, the lives of the Sahariyas in Baran are significantly better today than they were twenty years ago. Bonded labour, for one thing, is much rarer today than it was at that time. Incidentally, their liberation from bondage has been facilitated by a range of social security measures introduced over this period under public pressure, such as food subsidies, school meals, social security pensions and jobs under the National Rural Employment Guarantee Act. The fact remains that they could have better control over their lives if they also had access to land, quality education and decent jobs.

Similarly, there have been sporadic successes of popular resistance against state repression and corporate plunder. In Jharkhand, for instance, the Koel-Karo project was scrapped in 2003, soon after the firing incident reported in Chapter 10. Not far from there, the Netarhat field firing range was denotified in 2022, after decades of peaceful protests against it by local Adivasis. There have been other impressive movements of this sort in the recent past, such as the farmer's movement against the Modi government's corporate-driven 'farm laws' in 2020–21 and country-wide protests against the Citizenship Amendment Act (CAA) and National Register of Citizens (NRC) in 2019–20. These achievements, however, are a small dent in the juggernaut of authoritarianism that is rolling across India today.

Conflict and Anger

As the stories in this book make clear, India is a conflict-ridden society. The Dalits of Rajasthan, the mazdooras of Bihar, the Adivasis of Bastar, the widows of Gujarat, the oustees of the Narmada Valley, the students of Meghalaya, the squatters of Sanjay Basti, and the people of Kashmir and Nagaland have all been struggling against forces that curtail their freedom. In one form or another, conflict dominates their lives.

Living with conflict for long years makes you sick. That sickness does not go away easily. Each day becomes an agony. The pain may be physical at times but is almost always mental. In some cases, this can become a lifetime of sorrow. Individuals caught in conflict are constrained to live lives with constant worry, frustration, uncertainty, fear, hopelessness and despair—sometimes even anger, repressed or expressed. Living thus is a slow death.

In our divided society, conflicts may be inevitable. But it is our collective responsibility to ensure that they are resolved quickly. Only a life devoid of conflict is truly free. It is only in that free air that you can breathe easily and fully. It is only then that the flowers can bloom and plausible futures be explored.

Attempts to settle some of these conflicts through violent means have not been successful. Nor are these means easy to justify in any case. Quite often, violence has created new conflicts even as they left old ones unresolved. It is hard for the end to justify the means when there is no end in sight.

Democratic institutions have also failed to resolve most of these conflicts. Instead of fostering a just resolution, they have become another battleground—an uneven one that is slanted against the victims of injustice. This applies, for instance, to the judicial system. Even as hundreds of thousands of ordinary people languish in jail as undertrials, complaints against powerful criminals are not even registered.

These institutions are unlikely to succeed without a stronger and wider commitment to democratic values. There is a long way to go in this respect and no shortcuts. Today, even the basic courtesy of listening to people's grievances is missing. How then can there be genuine progress? For only if you listen, will you be able to empathize. Only if you empathize, will you be able to understand. Only if you understand, will you be able to act.

Unfortunately, both democratic institutions and democratic culture are under severe attack today. Freedom of expression has been throttled and rational thinking has been devalued. As media and communications are increasingly driven by artificial intelligence, we are told and shown what we want to hear and see. Prejudices are reinforced on all sides and informed debate is rare. Even in social movements committed to democracy, a truly democratic culture is often lacking. The question remains: How best to motivate ethics and morality in personal and political life?

As I contemplate this impasse, an image that has stayed with me over the years resurfaces. This image is of Lahanya Bhiku, the main character in the 1980 film *Aakrosh*.

'Aakrosh' can be translated as anger but it is closer to rage—a burning rage that trembles with its own force, tumultuous and all-consuming. The film conveyed the dashed hopes of the swathes of the landless for redistributed land, the undiminished power of the local 'government' of upper-caste landlords, police and politicians, and the feudal and patriarchal society they commanded with violence and impunity while labourers toiled like oxen in their fields yet remained in their debt, subjected to unspeakable indignities as a matter of routine.

Aakrosh is the story of Adivasi Lahanya Bhiku, and how his family is destroyed by the power, lust and violence of the local politician and his henchmen. Nagi, Lahanya's wife, commits suicide after being raped. Lahanya is framed and imprisoned. A young lawyer, the only exception in an otherwise unresponsive district judiciary, impresses upon him the need to speak out: 'If you don't speak, how will I help you?' But Lahanya maintains a stunned, stony silence.

Later, it is at the cremation of his father that Lahanya breaks from his past. On grounds that mark death and endings, the rising flames of his father's pyre behind him, Lahanya in a sudden move grabs an axe and heaves a blow at his young sister who is already being eyed lusciously. Unable to protect his loved ones, Lahanya chooses to become an offender of a system that has turned predatory and let him down, though the violence of this final act also hurts his own. Lahanya's wounded self then cries out, repeatedly, full-throated piercing screams that rent the air.

Long after the last scene, it is the torment of the soul that takes the form of anger, depicted so well by Om Puri as Lahanya, that stubbornly lingers, dragging us into the abyss of Lahanya's stunned, stony silence.

As we can see, the anger of the oppressed is a natural outcome of severe injustice. The first person to be affected by the anger is the one who feels it, who lives with it, who may express it through legitimate means, and in the absence of a satisfactory response, let it kill him or take a volatile form—violence to end violence.

Hope

In 'The Last Leaf', a short story by the American writer O. Henry, a poor art student who is ill with pneumonia believes that she will live as long as a leaf remains on the ivy on the wall outside her window. 'When the last leaf withers and dies, I shall die too', she tells her friend. One night when there is wind and rain, the last leaf is seemingly bound to fall, but it is still there in the morning, renewing her will to live and helping her to recover. It soon emerges that that cold night had claimed the life of her elderly neighbour and artist friend who had caught pneumonia, but not before he had successfully painted a leaf on the wall after the last leaf fell.

Morality is an old-fashioned word. While some cringe at the word, some refuse to listen if the argument is a moral one. Yet, those of us who love stories may remember the many stories we heard in our childhood when a question was put at the end, asking us what we thought was the 'moral of the story'. The moral of the story was meant as a takeaway, a lingering aftertaste, a do-not-forget reminder, a lesson learnt or conclusion drawn, an observation or question so stark that one could ignore it only at one's own peril. To my mind, no harm comes one's way if we reflect on the moral of a story. One's thinking does not get straightjacketed nor is any freedom taken. Instead, perhaps, this occasional pause may help us over time to underline the basics of what defines us as humans and how not to stumble on the path of life.

The moral of 'The Last Leaf' seems to be that hope keeps us alive at the worst times. Indeed, in hope, there is hope. The story also highlights how selfless friendship—where one has the capacity to love the other as one would one's own self—can be a life-giving force.

In these dark times, we all need a last leaf to keep us hopeful. I have thought hard about what is my last leaf. For me, hope lies in all the goodness I have seen over the years. I have learnt that while human beings are capable of the worst, they are also capable of the best. Most chapters in this book are tales of injustice and violence, but if you have noticed, they also include inspiring stories of courage and selflessness. The Darbars who sheltered Muslim victims of communal violence in Sabarkantha, Babulal Bairwa when he defied upper-caste norms to bathe in the Chakwada pond, Rampuneet Devi who stood up for her rights, the community leaders in the Narmada Valley who refused to be bought, Marwari Mallah who opened his house to terrorized Dalit neighbours in Bathani Tola, Grikseng Marak who braved police firing in Tura to help others and Bilal who risked his life to take his injured friends to a hospital in Srinagar— all showed humanity at its best. Without much need to think, they knew what they had to do. As Robert M. Pirsig wrote in the classic *Zen and the Art of Motorcycle Maintenance: An Inquiry into Values* (1974):

'And what is good, Phaedrus,
And what is not good —
Need we ask anyone to tell us these things?'

As and when the numbers of such good people swell, and they have more power, instead of being ruled and ignored, India is likely to become a better place.

But this is only my view. The infirmity of reason to establish a definitive truth is well accepted. Each person would need to exercise their own freedom of thought in this respect. I leave it to you, the reader, to decide for yourself what is your last leaf.

List of Original Articles and Sources*

1. 'A Step Back in Sabarkantha', *Seminar*, 513, May 2002.
2. 'Massacre on the Banks of the Sone', *Economic and Political Weekly*, 20 December 1997.
3. 'Of Human Bondage in Baran', *Economic and Political Weekly*, 30 June 2012.
4. 'Dalit Rebellion against Untouchability in Chakwada', *Contributions to Indian Sociology*, 40:1, 2006.
5. 'Social Action with Rural Widows in Gujarat', in Chen, M. (ed.) *Widows in India: Social Neglect and Public Action* (Delhi: Sage. 1998).
6. Unpublished material.
7. 'Lush Fields and Parched Throats: The Political Economy of Groundwater in Gujarat', *Economic and Political Weekly*, Special Article, 28 (51–52), 19–26 December 1992.
8. 'Fighting the Invisible Enemy in Jadugoda', *Survey of the Environment, The Hindu*, 2001.
9. 'Resistance and Repression', *Frontline*, 3 March 2001.
10. 'Forced Evictions in the Narmada Valley', in Drèze, J.P., Samson, M., and Singh, S. (eds.), *The Dam and the Nation: Displacement and Resettlement in the Narmada Valley* (Delhi: Oxford University Press. 1997).
11. 'Competing Concerns', *Economic and Political Weekly*, 19 November 2005.
12. 'The *Mazduras*', chapter from PhD thesis submitted to the University of Cambridge, 2000.

---

* The serial numbers refer to the corresponding chapters. In some cases, the original titles (listed here) are different from the chapter titles used in this book.

13. 'The Naxalite Movement in Central Bihar', *Economic and Political Weekly*, Special Article, 9 April 2005.
14. Unpublished material.
15. 'Justice, Not Vengeance: The Bathani Tola Massacre and the Ranbeer Sena in Bihar', *Economic and Political Weekly*, 21 September 2013.
16. 'On Armed Resistance', *Economic and Political Weekly*, 22 July 2006.
17. Unpublished material.
18. 'The Pegdapalli Files', *Outlook*, 22 February 2016.
19. 'Monsoon Massacre: What Really Happened in the Nulkatong Encounter?', *Caravan*, 31 December 2018.
20. 'Who Killed Sodi Deva?', Wire, 26 March 2019; 'Three Bullets and Three Women: A "Fake Encounter in Bastar"', Wire, 26 April 2019; 'The Anatomy of a "Fake Encounter": How 10 Adivasis were Killed in Abujmarh', Wire, 14 May 2019.
21. 'Why are Christians being Attacked in Adivasi Villages in Chhattisgarh?', Scroll, 14 December 2020.
22. Contribution to *Four Months the Kashmir Valley Will Never Forget: An Enquiry Into the Mass Uprising of 2010* (New Delhi: The Other Media), available at https://kafilabackup.files.wordpress.com/2011/03/kashmir-fft-report.pdf.
23. Contribution to *Police Firing on Demonstrations in Garo Hills, Meghalaya. A Report by an Independent Fact-finding Team* (Guwahati: North East Peoples' Initiatives, 2006).
24. 'Justice Denied to Tribals in the Hill Districts of Manipur', *Economic and Political Weekly*, 31 July 2010.
25. 'Awaiting Nachiso', Himal Southasian, 1 August 2011.

Acknowledgements

Researching and writing this book, in tempest and solitude, has been a dialogue with mirth and melancholy. Like all quests, this one too was made possible only by the companionship of many individuals I was fortunate to meet—exceptional people whose thoughts and actions informed and inspired me, and made this an important experience of my life. And then there were those who helped me in myriad ways while I was on the road, out of the goodness of their hearts, and expected nothing in return. I take this chance to thank and think of these friends, some of whom I name here and significant others whom I thank in silence.

First and foremost, I remember with much fondness and nostalgia my early years of working life in Gujarat. My colleagues at Shramjivi Samaj and Shramjivi Mahila Sangathan in the then Sabarkantha district, especially Karsanbhai, Heerabhai, Chandrakant, Mohan, Ramila, Naina, Shildaben and Hansa as well as the many remarkable persons from so many villages where we worked—Nanjibhai and Savitaben of Kalidungri, Khemiben and Kankuben of Mau, Kamliben, Santuben and Bhikhiben of Janali Tanda, Kamlaben of Dodisara—were all dear friends who taught me so much. Setu: Centre for Social Knowledge and Action at Ahmedabad, of which

I was then also a part, was a nurturing soil. I remember warmly the times spent with Medha Patkar, Achyut Yagnik, Bharti Patel, Ashok Shrimali and Rohit Jain, and thank them for their intellectual and personal support. I remember the many discussions that were almost always imbued with humour with Girishbhai Patel, an institution in himself.

My work in Bihar in the mid-1990s would not have been possible without the generosity and friendship I encountered on an everyday level. Chaiwalas, rickshawalas, fellow travellers in buses and trains, activists, journalists, teachers and scholars—all were exceptionally generous with their time and support. Sitting on broken benches in tea stalls, crowded trains or elsewhere, with much patience and goodwill, they shared their insights on Bihar. Especially so, the members and supporters of the Naxalite movement who cooperated with my research in spite of some danger to themselves. I would like to thank Lok Sangram Morcha in Patna and the local offices of CPI (ML) Liberation in Sahar, Ara and Jehanabad for taking a researcher into their fold with almost the same degree of warmth as they would a fellow activist. I am also grateful to Bihar Dalit Vikas Samiti for logistical support during my stays in Jehanabad, and to the A.N. Sinha Institute of Social Studies in Patna for hosting me from time to time.

I would like to thank Bhuwaneshwarji, Damayanti, Karuji, Mahendra, Pushpendra and Sarita for a supportive and stimulating starting point in Bihar. Tilak Dasgupta was an intellectual anchor during the first year of fieldwork. I have benefited from extensive discussions with him and also with Prasanna Chaudhury, Bani Dasgupta, Hetukar Jha, M.N. Karna, Nandkishore, Daisy Narayan, Pradhan Prasad, Uttam Sengupta, Arvind Sinha, Indu Sinha, M.P. Sinha, Prabhakar Sinha, Sudha Varghese, amongst others in Bihar. Since Jharkhand was part of Bihar in those days, I would also like to thank Ghanshyam Birulee, Xavier Dias, Malancha and Tridip Ghosh, Meghnath, Sunil Minj, Shashibhushan Pathak, Stan Swamy and Biju Toppo among those who helped and guided me there.

My work in Bastar and surrounding areas was made possible by the generous help and companionship I found on the way. Whether it was in the villages on the banks of the Sabari, Indravati, and Godavari across the state borders or in interior villages, I have found much kindness from numerous people who were themselves often quite impoverished. Over the years, I have also learnt from various organizations who were working on people's issues in these parts. In the first phase of fieldwork in Telangana with the Bastar Adivasis who had sought work and refuge there after being displaced, Sitara, ASDS, and Action Aid (Hyderabad) were most helpful; in south Bastar, members of the Communist Party of India (CPI), the Jagdalpur Legal Aid Group, Human Rights Law Network, Moolvasi Bachao Manch, Chhattisgarh Bachao Andolan and the People's Union for Civil Liberties have been valued associates. Special thanks for the initial help and hospitality to Himanshu Kumar, Veena Bhalla and their team members at Vanvasi Chetna Ashram, especially Bhuwaneshwari, Kopa Kunjam, Lingoo Markam, Uday Nag and Sukhdev. I am grateful to J. Rajeshwara Rao in Konta, Badde and Podiyam Panda in Chintagufa, Manish Kunjam in Sukma, NRK Pillai in Dantewada, Mangal Kunjam in Kirandul, S. R. Ramteke in Bijapur, Fr. Toby in Gangaloor, Afzal Khan in Bhopalpatnam, Ramnath Sarfe and Arvind Netam in Jagdalpur, as well as to many local journalists. For steadfast support in 2016–17, I am most grateful to Ramnath and Raimati Maurya of Parpa village who continued to rent accommodation to me despite facing harassment and threats. During the same period, the friendship of Mangal Kashyap and Saraswati, also of Parpa village, and Kandari Kashyap, Arjun Nag and Anita Netam in Jagdalpur was invaluable. Dharampal Saini was a wonderful friend all along.

Over the years, I have had the occasion to share my work and thoughts with many scholars, activists and friends who were generous with their comments and insights. I would like to thank Javeed Alam, Janine Almeida, K. Anuradha, K. Balagopal, Sanjoy

Barbora, Prashant Bhushan, Shiraz Bulsara, Anand Chakravarti, Uma Chakravarti, Marty Chen, Stuart Corbridge, Nikhil Dey, Arundhati Dhuru, Abhay Dubey, Peter D'Souza, Walter Fernandes, Vidyadhar Gadgil, Nuria Garro, Haris Gazdar, Ramachandra Guha, G. Haragopal, David Hardiman, John Harriss, Geoffrey Hawthorn, Ajit Jha, Avinash Jha, Rajalaxmi Kamath, Dolly Kikon, Sanober Keshwar, N. Kodandaram, Sanjay Kumar, Moti Lal, Brian Lobo, Manoranjan Mohanty, Neelabh Mishra, Vimala Morthala, D.L. Nagaraj, Gautam Navlakha, Aditya Nigam, Nandini Oza, Eleanor O'Gorman, Rosalind O'Hanlon, Vishram Patil, Pradip Prabhu, B. Pradeep, J. Prakash, Ashok Prasad, Vijay Pratap, B. Ramulu, V.V. Rao, Rajendra Ravi, Reehana Raza, C. Rammanohar Reddy, Aruna Roy, Meera Samson, S.R. Sankaran, E.A.S. Sarma, Vira Sathidar, K.B. Saxena, Harsh Sethi, Anomita Sen, Binayak Sen, Ajay Skaria, Ghanshyam Shah, B.D. Sharma, D.L. Sheth, Rakesh Shukla, Siddhartha, Ashley Tellis, Bojja Tharakam, Joe Thomas, V. Vasantha Lakshmi, N. Venugopal, Shiney Varghese, Rahul Verman, Shiv Visvanathan, Yogendra Yadav and B.N.Yugandhar.

In the course of human rights investigations in various states, I have been part of a number of fact-finding teams, including teams convened by the Human Rights Forum (HRF), People's Union for Civil Liberties (PUCL), People's Union for Democratic Rights (PUDR), Coordination of Democratic Rights Organisations (CDRO), Committee on Violence on Women (CAVOW) and Women Against Sexual Violence and State Repression (WSS). I have learnt much from many team members including N. Babaiah, Shahana Bhattacharya, Sudha Bharadwaj, Praful Bidwai, Rajshree Dasgupta, Harish Dhawan, Paul Diwakar, Rosemary Dzüvichü, B. Ganesh, Vrinda Grover, Ravi Hemadri, V.S. Krishna, K. Sudha, Ruth Manorama, Vincent Manoharan, Lyla Mehta, Asha Mishra, Sukumar Muralidharan, Bittu Kaveri Rajaraman, Debaranjan Sarangi, G. Sampath, Shoma Sen, Ilina Sen, Neikesanuo Sorhie, Kavita Srivastava and Vani Subramaniam. In Jammu and Kashmir, amongst those who helped us, I would especially like to thank Parveena Ahangar, Anuradha Bhasin, Ved Bhasin, Shujaat Bukhari, Parvez Imroz, Masooda Parveen, Khurram Parvez and Balraj Puri. Likewise, in Nagaland, activists of the Nagaland Peoples' Movement for Human Rights (NPMHR) were most helpful.

Some chapters of this book were written when I was associated with academic institutions: the Centre for the Study of Developing Societies (CSDS, Delhi), the National Institute of Rural Development (NIRD, Hyderabad) and the Tata Institute of Social Sciences (TISS, Bombay). I am most grateful to colleagues and students there as well as for the campuses and libraries that were kind to the eye and to the mind. I would especially like to remember Prof. S. Parasuraman, then director of TISS, for his kind support, which actually goes back to the early 1980s when he was my teacher at the same institution. At TISS, I have also benefited from Gauri Galande's able assistance.

The entire team at Penguin deserves much credit for facilitating the production of the book and cooperating with multiple rounds of revision. I am most grateful to each one of them, especially Karthik Venkatesh, Aparna Abhijit and Richa Burman. Thanks also to Divya Choudhary, Jasmin Naur Hafiz and Kalyani Raghunathan for help with copy-editing and proofreading.

A special nod of appreciation to Jean, a kindred spirit, who has been a companion of this volume. He was almost always the first person with whom these stories were shared.

Being with Somari, my dog-daughter and Sellotape companion of the last ten years, and, from 2017, her children—Imli, Tora, Bija and Jagli—was the perfect balm in troubled times. My woes got licked and worries flicked, gently and generously! I could not ask for better friends.

A warm thank you to Ritu, Rajiv and Bindu for being a part of me.

There are many others whom I shall not attempt to mention here in black and white. What I owe them needs a different canvas and different colours. But what needs to be said will be.

Notes

Chapter 1: A Step Back in Sabarkantha

1 Some of the background information in this section draws on the Sabarkantha District Gazetteer, 1974.

2 In Gujarat, only Dangs district has a higher rural/urban population ratio.

3 The incidents narrated in this section are based on multiple interviews with and testimonies from victims of the violence as well as from other witnesses. Names have been changed to ensure anonymity. The role of right-wing Hindu-nationalist organizations such as the Bajrang Dal and Vishwa Hindu Parishad (VHP) in the wave of communal violence that swept through Sabarkantha and other parts of Gujarat in March 2002 is clear from *Tehelka*'s investigative report 'The Truth: Gujarat 2002', published in a special issue of *Tehelka* in November 2007. See also Human Rights Watch (2002) and Varadarajan (2002), among others.

4 Information received from the District Collectorate, Himmatnagar.

5 This section is based on testimonies of victims, visits to police stations and an interview with the Deputy Superintendent of Police, Sabarkantha district. Police complicity with communal violence in Sabarkantha and other parts of Gujarat in March 2002 is well established from multiple reports, including those cited earlier (Note 3).

6 On the BKS and its influence in rural Gujarat at that time, see e.g., Bose (1987).

Chapter 2: Massacre on the Banks of the Sone

1   Arwal became a separate district in 2001.

2   This section is based on first-hand testimonies from residents of Bathe. Their accounts are consistent with the findings of multiple investigations (e.g., Human Rights Watch 1999 and other sources cited there) as well as with testimonies presented at a 'public hearing with the survivors of Bathani Tola and Bathe massacres' held in New Delhi on 18 December 2013. The involvement of the Ranbeer Sena in the massacre is a recurrent theme of all these investigations and testimonies. On this, see also Chapters 13 and 15 (The Naxalite Movement in Central Bihar and Justice, Not Vengeance).

3   Besides the main village of Laxmanpur-Bathe are its four tolas: Batanbigha, Siyahibigha, Dankabigha and Mahavirganj. The main village and Batanbigha tola were multi-caste. The two main landowning upper castes, Bhumihars and Rajputs, roughly in equal strength (thirty and twenty houses respectively) lived in the main village. Besides, in the main village and Batanbigha there was a high proportion (about 85 per cent) of Dalits and lower backward castes, a large proportion of whom were landless. The other three tolas had a large proportion of upper backward castes like Koeris and Yadavs.

4   These figures were collected by me in the village itself, just a few days after the massacre. They are consistent with subsequent reports, e.g., Human Rights Watch (1999).

5   See Chapter 15 (Justice, Not Vengeance).

6   A similar statement from witnesses ('the killers shouted pro-Sena slogans') is reported in an independent investigation by United News of India (UNI 1997); see also Human Rights Watch (1999).

7   The Bathe massacre is just one of the series of massacres that took place in Bihar in the years of protracted violent conflict between Naxalite organizations and various 'caste senas' including the Ranbeer Sena. The role of the Ranbeer Sena in the Bathe massacre is not in doubt and the Sena itself has never denied it. In fact, Sena members openly admitted this role in a sting operation by Cobrapost in 2015 (Bhatnagar 2015). For further discussion, see Amnesty International (1997), People's Union for Democratic Rights (1997), Human Rights Watch (1999), Sinha and Sinha (2001); see also Chapters 13 and 15.

8   The nexus between Ranbeer Sena and the BJP is clear from the Cobrapost exposé 'Operation Black Rain', released in 2015 (Ashish 2015; also available on YouTube: https://www.youtube.com/watch?v=jJRbpcIVGOU). The Sena, however, has also had supporters and sponsors from other political parties. These connections were due to be exposed in the Amir Das Commission

Report, but the commission was dissolved in 2005 by the Bihar government and the report was never released.

9   For details of this incident, see People's Union for Democratic Rights (1997).

10   Ranbeer Sena Chief Brahmeshwar Singh, also known as 'Mukhiya', was not arrested until 2002; in an interview with *Times of India* in 1999, he openly justified the killing of people who 'provide shelter to the Naxalite *dastas* (squads)', adding that 'Hanuman in his fight against Ravan set on fire the whole of Lanka' (quoted in Sinha and Sinha 2001, p. 4095).

11   On this, see Human Rights Watch (1999).

12   These three examples are based on detailed accounts of these incidents in People's Union for Democratic Rights (1997). For further discussion of police harassment in the area, see also the joint fact-finding report of multiple human rights organizations presented in Bhatia (1998a).

13   For further discussion of this widely reported statement, see Arslan et al. (1997).

Chapter 3: Of Human Bondage in Baran

1   See Srivastava (2005) for a comprehensive overview of the incidence of labour bondage in India.

2   See Godbole (2003), Rajalakshmi (2003), amongst others.

3   Ali (2011).

4   Verbal communication from the District Collector, 10 January 2012.

5   The list is available on the website of the Ministry of Tribal Development (https://tribal.nic.in/ST/StatewisePvTGsList.pdf).

6   The official land ceiling in this area is forty-eight bighas.

7   The reference here is to Sankalp, a voluntary organization working in Baran district since 1983. Motilal was the secretary of this organization until he died in 2016. Sankalp has helped form local organizations of women (Jagrut Mahila Sangathan in 2002) and youth (Yuva Shakti Sangathan in 2003–04).

8   'Rajasthan's Jat-Sikhs are OBC, clarifies social justice department', *Times of India*, 25 July 2012 (https://timesofindia.indiatimes.com/city/jaipur/rajasthans-jat-sikhs-are-obc-clarifies-social-justice-department/articleshow/15134270.cms).

9   This is an edited version of a chronology prepared by Jagrut Mahila Sangathan, Kishanganj, the local organization that had invited us (the inquiry committee) to the area.

Chapter 4: Dalit Rebellion against Untouchability in Chakwada

1   Phagi, the tehsil headquarters, is only 6 km from Chakwada.

2   These rules were laid down by the panchayat, which existed in pre-modern times. Even though this panchayat was known as the 'village panchayat', it was not representative of all social classes and its members were all from the upper castes.

3   According to Babulal Bairwa, the main protagonist of the Chakwada rebellion, this was out of fear. Muslims were feared due to the power of their badshah over the local rajas; and Meenas (an Adivasi community) were feared because the Meena tribe had a reputation for being deft at theft (interview to the author, 22 May 2004).

4   The Bairwas felt this to be unfair from a practical point of view as well. Equal contribution (in cash or as *shramdan*—donation of labour) was taken from them towards the maintenance of the pond, but equal access was denied.

5   I was struck by this analogy of a tongue between the teeth. It reminded me of another instance when exactly the same analogy had been used by a Rajput farmer in Nannor village (Sahar block, Bhojpur, Bihar) during the 1996 Lok Sabha elections, following a retaliatory massacre by the CPI (ML) Liberation of eight Bhumihars on the day prior to the election (see Chapter 15) as a result of which the upper castes had stayed indoors on election day—the fate of the Dalits in this region in most of the previous elections until then. While the analogy was understandable in that case, its usage in the Chakwada case seemed out of place. What it conveyed was the acute sense of persecution that the upper castes—comfortable in the traditional social order—felt at the slightest attempt by the Dalits to change the status quo.

6   Ambedkar, B.R., *Annihilation of Caste*. In Writings and Speeches, vol. 1, pp. 40–41.

7   Interview with Babulal Bairwa, 25 September 2002.

8   Interview with Laduram Solaniya (former MLA, Phagi), 25 September 2002.

9   At the time of my visit, there were six other, smaller temples including three of Baba Ramdev in the Dalit hamlets. Dalits were prohibited from entry in all the temples, except their own. Interestingly, Baba Ramdev was remembered as a Rajput from Jaisalmer who had fought for Dalit rights. Even though the Bairwas pointed out that they had no desire to enter these temples, temple entry remained an unfulfilled democratic right of Dalits in Rajasthan. A prominent case was that of the famous Shrinath temple in Nathdwara, one of the most celebrated pilgrimage shrines of India. In mid-January 2004, activists participating in a national Dalit Swadhikar rally organized by the NCDHR were denied entry, in spite of a strong court judgment affirming that the right of Dalits to enter the temple unhindered was protected under Article 17 of the Constitution. The judgment was given in 1988 when Swami Agnivesh sought the protection of the Court before entering the temple with a group of Dalits.

In spite of the Court order, their attempt had failed (Iqbal, Mohammed, 'Dalits Barred Entry Into Temple', *The Hindu*, 14 January 2004).

10   A sub-inspector in the Phagi thana later acknowledged that according to official directives, '*Soochna milte hi mokai par jana jaruri hai* [We are required to reach the site as soon as we receive information]'.

11   I am grateful to P.L. Mimroth for sharing a letter written by Chandalal Bairwa (Bairwa Samaj, Phagi) and R.S. Dev (National Campaign for Dalit Human Rights) to the CDHR in October 2002, which contained some of the details mentioned here.

12   The Bairwas are not usually expected to wash their glasses in local teashops, even though some other communities—such as the Bhangis and Vaghris—still are.

13   Besides the above-mentioned cases, a few instances of encroachment of Dalit owned land by the dominant castes also occurred but have not been reported here since accurate details could not be gathered.

14   Caste sentiment, it seems, had also influenced decision-making in previous elections. As Babulal pointed out with some pride: 'In all previous elections, except in two instances, we have always had a Bairwa MLA.'

15   Meeting of the PUCL fact-finding team with Ashok Tanwar, September 2002.

16   One frequently invoked reason for this relatively high status is that, before Independence, Meenas used to be in charge of the treasury of some of the Rajput rulers. As a result, they considered themselves at par with Rajputs and others also regarded them as such.

17   In Rajasthan, the Chamars are known by these different names in different regions. For example, in the eastern part of the state, they are known as Jatavs and Chamars, in the central region largely as Bairwas, in western and south-eastern regions as Meghval, Balai and Meghvanshi. Even the present day Bunkars in Rajasthan used to do leather work, though they have now taken to weaving.

18   Interview with Babulal Bairwa, 22 May 2004.

19   In Rajasthan, there are other examples of public announcements by Dalits of their intention to convert to Islam. A recent one was by Gopal Krishan Dhankiya (Nimora village, Bassi block, Jaipur district), who was prohibited by the upper castes of his village from worshipping Hanuman. Not allowed to enter the public temple, he constructed a private temple with an idol of Hanuman, larger than the idol in the main temple. The upper castes objected to this and imposed a series of restrictions and punishments on Gopal and his family, finally leading to their ouster from the village. The local police colluded with the upper castes and his complaint was deemed to be 'false'. Gopal approached higher officials and the SHRC, but when all his efforts came

to nothing, he announced his intention to embrace Islam. (See Mimroth, P.L., 'Dalit Warrior', Countercurrents.org, 20 May 2004.)

20 It is possibly under the influence of the dominant castes that Harishanker Bairwa wrote to NCDHR in late 2003 and asked the organization to drop Chakwada from the itinerary of a proposed rally for Dalit human rights, which they did. His argument was that all was well in Chakwada, that the Bairwas had won their bathing rights and that the rally might have unwanted repercussions.

21 See Rajasthan Election Watch (2004).

22 In states such as Bihar and Andhra Pradesh, Dalits joined movements such as the Naxalite movement in large numbers in order to redress their grievances against the local landlords who continued to flout the law and exploit them economically and oppress them socially, in full view of state authorities; see Chapter 13 and Bhatia (2000, 2002).

23 Gupta (1991), p. 12.

24 Gupta (2004), p. x. For further discussions on this theme, see Gupta (2000) and various contributions in Gupta (1991, 2004). For related interpretations of the caste system, see also Srinivas (1996), Fuller (1997), Deshpande (2003), among others.

25 The slogan 'Jiyo aur jine do' can be understood as an expression of this sentiment.

26 As Chandra Bhan Prasad states in his critique of Dipankar Gupta's thesis: 'Are varna/caste groups free to abandon occupations . . . which are not "regarded as prestigious"? If that were the case, no Dalit would have remained a sweeper, or a cobbler, or a washerman. While not all Dalits are sweepers or cobblers or washermen—all sweepers, all cobblers, and all washermen are Dalits! Are they so by choice? Or is there no opportunity to "abandon these occupations"?' (Prasad 2000, p. 19).

Chapter 5: Ekaki: The Pain of Lonesome Marginality

1 The broad socio-economic characteristics of Sabarkantha district were introduced in Chapter 1 (A Step Back in Sabarkantha).

2 Karsanbhai Parmar, the principal leader of the Mau-Bhambi struggle, played a critical role in the latter struggle as well, when he joined hands with Bhanubhai Adhvaryu, a veteran socialist leader who was its chief protagonist. They were supported by Achyut Yagnik, Ashok Shrimali and others at Setu: Centre for Social Knoweldge and Action in Ahmedabad.

3 The process of formalization started in 1981, with the registration of the eight agricultural cooperative societies. This was followed by the formation of a sangh (union) of these cooperatives. However, a need for a broader forum was

felt—a forum through which other agrarian questions and issues related to oppression and infringement of democratic rights of the underprivileged could be addressed. This took the form of Shramjivi Samaj, which was registered as a trade union in 1983. There are no women in the working committee of any of the cooperatives of the sangh, but the working committee of the Shramjivi Samaj includes five women out of a total of twenty-one members; two of these five women are widows.

4   Many other peasant organizations with a 'mixed' membership, i.e., both men and women, have had a similar experience (Shramik Sangathana in Dhule, Maharashtra is one such example). This urge of peasant women to assert their autonomy has often been seen as divisive, but in reality, it facilitates their emancipation as well as their active participation in the larger struggle. Organizations that have failed to address this need often find women members withdrawing from the struggle in large numbers.

5   See Drèze (1990b).

6   In Bhiloda taluka, women in most caste groups are used to meetings of their respective caste panchayats, but not as active participants. In a Vanjara village council, I have witnessed Vanjara women, keen to follow the deliberations, eavesdropping from the inner rooms of the houses, while male members or the council sit on charpais (rope-stringed wooden cots) in the open space outside. In the Bhambi caste panchayats also, women are not active participants. Not unlike the Vanjara women, Bhambi women can be seen sitting here and there, always on the ground and in the background, while the all-male panchayat members and other men of the village sit on elevated positions. Women may occasionally contribute a word or a passing comment, but even that is a privilege of the older women only. While tribal women tend to enjoy less unequal treatment than other Indian women, their participation in village panchayats and inter-village councils is again unusual.

7   Most of these women observe *laj* (semi-purdah), not only when older males are present but also, in some castes, in the presence of their mother-in-law or other female elders in their husband's family.

8   This, of course, was not the cost of the form but the bribe paid to process the form.

9   Interestingly, while the sammelan was of single women, after the sammelan it was always referred to as the *vidhva sammelan* (widows' gathering). Most of the participants were widows, rather than separated or divorced women.

10   The list of 'below poverty line' (BPL) households is widely used as a target group for government schemes such as rural housing, schemes to provide land to the landless, credit-based schemes, and so on. The list is supposed to be

prepared by the *gram sevak* (village-level government officer) in the *gram sabha* (village assembly).

11   In each panchayat, there are fixed days when the sarpanch and talati are supposed to be available, but these arrangements are not always observed. Even if the concerned officials are available, their attitude is often far from helpful. Few of them consider it their duty to deal with these requests; if they do it at all, it is more as a personal favour, or (in the case of the sarpanch) as a means of winning votes.

12   The work of Shramjivi Mahila Sangathan with single women was initially restricted to Bhiloda taluka, but later spread to Idar and Vijaynagar talukas of Sabarkantha district. Efforts were also made to campaign on this issue with other women's organizations in the state. For instance, a state-level *mahila milap* (women's convention or rally) was organized in Khedbrahma, Sabarkantha district in 1990.

13   Most women do not even consider the possibility of claiming their inheritance rights to a share of their father's land because they can hardly think of 'fighting' with their own brothers. They tend to think of their brothers as persons who may protect them in various adverse circumstances (especially after the death of their father). A conflict with one's brother means a psychological rupture of that protective bond as well as a practical loss of potential help. Also, even talking about one's 'own' share of family property is seen as divisive behaviour, going against the emphasis on the togetherness of the family.

14   The belief in dakans (witches) is deep-rooted in the Adivasi mind. When I was talking about dakans with Kesarben Parmar, the district Social Security Director, who knew little of this belief, she called her Adivasi peon and asked him, '*Dakan hoi? Dakan boli nai shu karai* [Do witches exist? What do people do about them]?' The peon replied, '*Dakano hoi ben, mari nakhvi pade* [Yes, sister, witches exist no doubt, and they have to be killed]!'

15   The non-Adivasi male leaders of the Shramjivi Samaj also argued that since this was an Adivasi issue, the leadership should come from the Adivasi community. This view was hotly contested by some of the female activists, who felt that in the absence of such initiative from the Adivasi community, the Samaj (which had members from various castes and communities) should take up this issue, which was not only a women's issue but also a basic human rights issue.

16   Widows often have a special concern for the education of their daughters, because they consider education as a form of security against the kind of destitution they have experienced themselves. Nevertheless, girls are often withdrawn from school more readily than boys when poverty forces these women to compromise on their children's education. Another common reason

is the need for someone to take care of young children when a widow is forced to go out for casual labour.

17 Kesarben Parmar, Social Security Director, mentioned that when a complaint is received prior to the holding of a child marriage, they try to stop it from taking place; if the complaint is received after the event, then they file a case against the parties. In 1983–84, when 1231 complaints were received, only 152 child marriages were stopped and legal sentences were passed in ninety-five cases.

18 The bandharan mentioned here actually applies to the twenty-eight villages in the barasi pargana; Bhambis of different parganas (groups of villages) have different constitutions.

19 Census of India 2011, Table C-02. Separated and divorced women accounted for another 2.4 and 0.9 million single women respectively. In addition, there were more than 9 million unmarried women above the age of twenty-four years in 2011.

Chapter 7: Lush Fields and Parched Throats: Groundwater Politics in Gujarat

1 See e.g., *Gujarat Relief Manual*, 1979, section on 'The Historical Survey of Calamities in Gujarat'.

2 Loveday (1914), pp. 25–27.

3 The local names of these droughts, in many cases, reflect the date of their occurrence in the Hindu calendar (known as 'Vikram Samvat'), which is ahead of the British calendar by fifty-six years. Thus, the year 1956 in the Hindu calendar witnessed a famine remembered as 'Chappaniyo' (*chappan* means fifty-six in Gujarati).

4 Baird Smith (1861), quoted in Srivastava (1968), p. 53.

5 Government of India (1880), Appendix I, p. 205.

6 Even in the pre-Independence period, this strategy was pursued on a number of occasions, with mixed results. For a detailed discussion of famine prevention in India before and after Independence, see Drèze (1990a).

7 Water scarcity is clearly mentioned for the first time by the Famine Commission of 1901, which states that on account of the failure of water supply in the Princely States, people were often left with no alternative but to emigrate to British territories during famines. The description of the drought of 1911 in Bharuch district also refers to the distress of the people on this count. But it is only from the drought of 1960-61 onwards that consistent mention is made of the problem of water scarcity—see Government of Gujarat (1976), pp. 13, 19–24.

8   Bhailalbhai Patel (1970), *Bhaikakana Sasmarno* ('The Memoirs of Bhaikaka').
9   Bhailalbhai does mention the existence of a surface-water drought and of increased dependence on groundwater for water needs. See J. Gupta (1988) for further discussion.
10   A 'no source' village is a village with no public well within a distance of 1.6 km, or where the public well dries up in the summer, or where the water level is more than 15 m deep.
11   Government of Gujarat (1987).
12   In Gujarat, the person hired to lift water from a well through the traditional *kos* (i.e., the leather bag pulled by bullocks) is known as *koshia*.
13   This section omits a number of tables and maps presented in the original version of the article along with detailed evidence of various symptoms of groundwater depletion in Gujarat.
14   Two other manifestations are 'salinity ingress' and rising fluoride content of groundwater (for further discussion, see Bhatia, 1992). Note that rising levels of salinity and fluoride content also result in a lower *quality* of groundwater. Hence, the scarcity of groundwater increases not only in quantitative but also in qualitative terms.
15   According to Phadtare (1988) and Bradley and Phadtare (1989), overexploitation and well interference have caused dramatic declines in water tables in large parts of Mehsana. Official information even suggests that most of the phreatic aquifer system in Mehsana has dried up (personal communication from the Gujarat Water Resources Development Corporation).
16   These ecological and economic processes, of course, themselves have deeper causes, relating for instance to the structure of property rights. For further discussion, see Bhatia (1992).
17   Agarwal and Narain (1985). In addition, some experts believe that trees help in bringing rain, by cooling the warm air masses and thus supporting the process of condensation. On this, see also Meher-Homji (1988).
18   Government of Gujarat (1984). The figures were originally obtained from the Forest Department, Government of Gujarat. These misleading figures are due to the simplistic reporting system in the Forest Department, which describes the forest wealth in terms not of tree cover but of the extent of the areas which stand notified under one section or another of the Indian Forest Act 1927, regardless of whether these areas possess any tree cover or not. As Vohra (1989) rightly points out, 'There is a tendency on the part of the Forestry establishment to take shelter behind these misleading figures.'
19   Centre for Science and Environment (1985).
20   Vohra (1987).

21 District-level data shows a particularly high incidence of well irrigation in Sabarkantha around this time. According to the Sabarkantha Gazetteer (1974), in 1968–69, wells accounted for as much as 95 per cent of the district's irrigated area.

22 It should be stressed that this grouping is based on the *economic* prosperity of different castes and not on their ritual status in the traditional caste hierarchy. Economic and ritual statuses are, of course, often closely related. But insofar as they diverge, our interest is in the former rather than the latter.

23 In many cases they have also had to work without pay for the money-lenders over long periods to repay the balance of the loans that remained after they had lost all their land.

24 For a similar observation in the context of the 1970–73 drought in Maharashtra, see Brahme (1983) and Oughton (1982). In *unirrigated* areas, one does sometimes observe a larger proportionate decline in income for large farmers during drought years, reflecting their dependence on agriculture (see e.g., Desai et al., 1979).

25 Dhawan (1987), p. 1554.

26 Jacob (1989).

27 Ratanlal and Dhirajlal (1987), p. 321. Individual rights to groundwater resources, however, always remain 'subject to the state's sovereign right . . . to regulate [these resources] in the public interest' (Jacob, 1989, p. 2).

28 Chandrakanth (1989), pp. 3–4.

Chapter 8: Fighting the Invisible Enemy in Jadugoda

1 K.K. Beri, the technical director of the UCIL, argued in an interview that this was necessary from the cost-benefit point of view.

2 This information is based on the findings of a health survey conducted in the area by scientists Surendra Gadekar and Sanghamitra Gadekar; for further details of this survey, see Centre for Science and Environment (1999). On health hazards in Jadugoda, see also Sagar (2018) among others.

Chapter 9: Resistance and Repression in Koel-Karo

1 The account presented in this essay is based on first-hand testimonies from witnesses. I visited Tapkara in the first week of February 2001, immediately after the incident. For other reports on this incident, see e.g., Balagopalan et al. (2001) and The Indian People's Tribunal on Environment and Human Rights (2002).

2 These allegations are consistent with similar complaints against R.N. Singh recorded in the reports cited in the preceding note.

3 This scene is described in similar terms by other witnesses in Balagopalan et al. (2001).

4   Anuj Kumar Sinha's partial list of police firings in Jharkhand (before and after it became an independent state in 2000) has twenty-eight entries (Sinha, 2017). In 2003, when a journalist pointed out to then Chief Minister Babulal Marandi that fourteen instances of police firing had occurred in Jharkhand within three years of its creation, the CM reportedly replied: 'There is nothing new about such firings. They will keep happening.' See Down to Earth (2003).

5   See e.g., Manthan (1999).

Chapter 10: Forced Evictions in the Narmada Valley

1   These benchmarks were accepted by the Executive Board of Directors of the World Bank and the Government of India.

2   For details of the Gujarat government's official resettlement package, see Bhatia (1997a).

3   These eleven resettlement sites are not the only sites where displaced persons from the study villages have been relocated. The residents of these five villages have been dispersed in dozens of different sites.

4   See Bhushan et al. (1993).

5   Sometimes it was difficult to identify these households, because they had not been clearly informed about their status.

6   Survey data collected by the Centre for Social Studies, Surat.

7   'An "oustee" shall mean any person who since, at least one year prior to the date of publication of the notification under Section 4 of the Act, has been ordinarily residing or cultivating land or carrying on any trade, occupation, calling, or working for gain in the area likely to be submerged permanently or temporarily.' (NWDT Award, Clause XI, Sub-clause 1)

8   This sentiment was almost always expressed by members of the same hamlet, especially those who belonged to the same tribe. Resettling a hamlet as a unit is administratively easier than resettling a whole village (as envisaged by the Tribunal Award). During the course of my survey, however, I did not come across any instance where this had been achieved.

9   According to government workers, the wood would be auctioned, 30 per cent of the sale price would be deducted for expenses (cutting, carting, etc.) and with the rest would be given to the owner. I did not come across a single instance where the owner had been paid.

10   In places where the more-than successful resettlement of village leaders is apparent, one often notices a loss of unity in the community. Some leaders, however, have chosen to stay with their people and share their hardships.

11   For further details see Bhatia and Mehta (1993). Accounts of this well-known incident are also available in Rathod and Kumar (2002) and Mehta (2009).

Chapter 11: Forest Rights: Competing Concerns

1   See Haimendorf (1990), p 74.
2   See Elwin (1937), p 13.
3   Memory of a conversation with Ajay Skaria; see also Skaria (1999).
4   For a moving account of the life and times of Paraja Adivasis in Odisha, see Mohanty (1987).
5   For the background of this order, and wide-ranging testimonies on eviction drives, see Campaign for Survival and Dignity (2004).
6   For instance, according to Valmik Thapar (a leading critic of the bill), 'this bill is an open-ended land distribution programme (2.5 ha per tribal nuclear family to be given out)' (Thapar 2005a), and the bill 'de facto makes the entire 64 million hectares of forest land available for distribution to individuals as private property' (Thapar 2005b).
7   Government of India (2005b).
8   Government of India (2005a), p. 6.
9   Government of India (2005a), Chapter 3.
10 Government of India (2005a), pp. 14–20.
11 *Kora Rajee*, directed by Biju Toppo, is a telling documentary on this.
12 Note also that the land ceilings usually apply to land for cultivation; the ceiling of 2.5 hectares in the bill, on the other hand, includes both cultivation land and homestead land.
13 Government of India (2005b).

Chapter 12: The Mazdooras of Bihar

1   The 1981 figure is from Sharma (1994), Table 1, based on census data; the corresponding 1991 figure was calculated from Census of India 1991, Table B-4 (available at censusindia.gov.in).
2   Sharma (1994), Table 4. This figure pertains to 1982, but the concentration of land ownership steadily *increased* in rural Bihar from then on (until 2013, the latest year for which data is available); see Sharma and Malik (2021).
3   The zamindars were local landlords who also collected land revenue on behalf of the colonial administration.
4   On zamindari abolition and land reforms in Bihar see Das (1983), Government of Bihar (undated), Jannuzi (1974), Yugandhar and Iyer (1993), among others, and also the report of the Bihar Land Reforms Commission chaired by D. Bandyopadhyay.
5   Joshi (1970), pp. 37–38. The statement refers to India as a whole, but it is clear from the same study (e.g., p. 43) that it applies with particular force to Bihar.

The large-scale eviction of tenants at the time of zamindari abolition in Bihar is also mentioned in Jannuzi (1974) and Jha (1994), among others.

6   Under the Bihar Land Reforms (Fixation of Ceiling Area and Acquisition of Surplus Land) Act, 1961, the ceiling ranges between fifteen and forty-five acres depending on the quality of the land.

7   According to the Land Reforms Act, 1950, gairmajurwa land was to remain in the possession of the erstwhile landlord, though the Act restricted the uses that could be made of it (e.g., gairmajurwa aam land could neither be leased out nor cultivated by the landlord himself). Later legislation, however, stipulates that gairmajurwa land belongs to the state.

8   See Blair (1981). After 1931, information on caste (other than broad categories) was dropped from the decennial census questionnaires.

9   The shares of the last three groups in the 1961 population were 12.5 per cent, 14.1 per cent and 9.1 per cent respectively; see Blair (1981), Table III, where data from the 1931 census is also presented.

10 On the mindset of the Bhumihars, including their 'tendency of asserting their caste superiority through violence and domination', see Nandan and Santhosh (2019, 2021).

11 For further discussion of the Bhumihar self-perception, see Tully (1995). Francis Buchanan, in his report on Shahabad in 1812–13, aptly called them 'military Brahmins' (see Jha et al., 1985, p. 17).

12 For an interesting case study of this mutual hostility, see Singh (2005).

13 Risley (1915), p. 310.

14 For details on specific scheduled castes, see Singh (1993).

15 Later, labour migration became another major source of livelihood for Dalit households in rural Bihar and for casual labourers generally.

16 This is reflected in the very name Musahar (*musa* + *har*) meaning rat-eater. Even today, it is not uncommon for Musahars to catch and eat rats.

17 As mentioned earlier, the focus of this essay is on living conditions in rural Bihar in the mid-1990s. Living conditions there have improved later in absolute terms, but they remain abysmal compared to most other states (except Jharkhand, carved out of Bihar in 2000). For updated facts and figures, see e.g., Drèze and Sen (2013), International Institute for Population Sciences (2017, 2022), Chakravarti (2018), NITI Aayog (2021).

18 Government of India (2014), Table A7; the reference year is 1993–94. These estimates are based on the Lakdawala Methodology, where the poverty line is supposed to correspond to the level of per capita expenditure required to satisfy minimum calorie norms, taking into account the consumption patterns actually observed in the population. Interestingly, the same point applies as recently as 2015–16 based on the more recent 'multidimensional poverty'

method: Bihar is still the only state where a majority of the population lives in poverty (NITI Aayog 2021, p. 34).

19 Nanda (1991b), p. 194, based on 1991 census data. By 2011, the share of agricultural labourers in the workforce ('main workers') had risen further to 45 per cent in Bihar as a whole and 49 per cent in rural Bihar (Census of India 2011, Table B-4, available at censusindia.gov.in).

20 Das (1992), p. 1, based on earlier research by historian D.D. Kosambi.

21 On trends in real wages until the 1970s, see Jha (1994).

22 One such legend is that of Mahtin Dai, in whose memory a temple stands at Behea, Bhojpur. According to one story, when Ran Pal Singh, the local raja who was known to be a tyrant, compelled her for *dola*, there was severe resistance resulting in a clash, in which Mahtin Dai's supporters and husband were killed, following which she performed *sati* (Mukherjee and Yadav, 1980). For further discussion of sexual exploitation in rural Bihar, see e.g., Lata (2019).

23 Mukherjee and Yadav (1980), p. 53.

24 Das (1992), p. 122.

25 Mukherjee and Yadav (1980).

26 See Jha et al., (1985), p. 26.

27 The size of a bigha varies between different areas; in the area where the study villages are situated, there are 1.6 bighas to an acre.

28 This is also the case with respect to the bulk of gairmajurwa land in this region. In most of the study villages, this land too was under the illegal occupation of individual upper caste maliks who used it for their own benefit.

29 The term *saamanti* is used to refer to practices such as high-handedness, arbitrary beatings, public humiliation, sexual harassment and other forms of insulting and exploitative behaviour. This local term closely approximates the term 'feudal'.

30 The term mazdoora is a diminutive form of mazdoor, often used by the maliks with a pejorative connotation. The mazdoor in different parts of Bihar may also be known by different names; for example, in Bhojpur, the word *banihar* is often used.

31 The plight of the bonded labourer has found a place in the literature of the dispossessed in Bihar. In particular, see Pathak (1991), and Mahasweta Devi's writings in Ghatak (1997).

32 The sexual exploitation of female labourers can also be seen as part of this mindset, whereby the members of the lower castes are just bodies that can be mobilized at any time without consent, remuneration or apology.

33 Middle peasants of upper castes who cannot afford to employ a halwaha for a whole year but need to employ one because upper-caste social norms do not

permit them to plough, may keep a halwaha for six months (the whole of *kharif* and the beginning of *rabi*).

34 Grierson (1885), p. 315.

35 Ibid., p. 229.

36 Traditionally, it is the *malikini* who hands the due grain wages to the labourers. This seems to follow from the fact that she is responsible for overseeing the grain once it has been stored in the house. According to the labourers, the malikini (who had no earnings of her own) often appropriates a small portion of the labourer's wages and keeps it for herself. The malikini, therefore, further exacerbated the exploitation of the labourers while trying to redress her own.

37 Similar improvements apply to halwahas. In addition, the land given to them for self-cultivation has increased from five katthas to ten, fifteen or even twenty katthas (according to the status of the malik).

38 Bharti (1990).

39 See Grierson (1885), pp. 196–98.

40 Ibid., p. 198. In addition, Grierson describes other systems where the landlord got *less* than half the total produce. However, he mentions that these systems are also exceptional 'as in time of drought, or when a jungle or waste land has to be brought under cultivation, or when land requires much labour on the part of the tenant'.

41 Men usually wear a lungi with a ganji (vest) and gamcha. As their economic status improves, they start wearing kurtas and pyjamas or dhotis, or shirts and pants (more popular among educated youth).

42 India accounted for 60 per cent of global polio cases in 1994, just before its Pulse Polio Immunization Programme began; it was officially declared polio-free in 2014 (World Health Organization, 2021).

43 On the state of schooling in central Bihar and how the Naxalite movement has affected it, see Bhatia (1998b).

Chapter 13: The Naxalite Movement in Central Bihar

1 Insightful studies of the Naxalite movement in Bihar include Mukherjee and Yadav (1980), Urmilesh (1991), Nimbran (1992), Gupta (1993), Singh (1995), Sinha (1996), among others; see also Banerjee (1984). In addition to these major studies, articles have been published on specific aspects of the Naxalite movement in Bihar, such as women's participation, electoral participation or the evolution of the movement in specific areas. Party literature and media reports provide a rich source of primary material (see particularly Sen et al., 1978, CPI (ML) Liberation, 1986, and Ghosh, 1992).

2 Ranajit Guha (1982) also argues for a politics of the people in the context of the history of Indian nationalism. He contrasts this approach with the elitist historiography of Indian nationalism which 'fails to acknowledge, far less interpret, the contribution made by the people *on their own*, that is, *independently of the elite* to the making and development of this nationalism' (Guha, 1982, p. 3).

3 The year 1977 is an appropriate demarcating line because it marks the end of one phase of the Naxalite movement not only in Bihar, but also in India as a whole (see Bhatia, 2000).

4 The AICCCR was an interim organization formed in Calcutta in November 1967 (shortly after the Naxalbari uprising) in an attempt to unite all revolutionary communist groups. Some groups that supported the Naxalbari struggle did not join AICCCR, notably the 'Dakshin Desh group', which included the original leaders of the present Maoist Communist Centre. On 1 May 1969, AICCCR was disbanded and CPI (ML) was formed.

5 This section draws on interviews with Vinod Mishra (15 January 1996), then general secretary of the CPI (ML) Liberation, Pawan Sharma (21 April 1994), then secretary of the Bihar state committee, and Ramjatan Sharma (17 October 1996), then secretary of the Bihar state committee.

6 The Liberation group started contesting elections in 1985. Until the 1995 assembly elections, it was contesting under the banner of IPF, from 1995 onwards, it started contesting as CPI (ML).

7 This section is based on primary literature of the party as well as interviews with prominent members of the party and its front organizations.

8 These were: Centre for Unity, a small West Bengal based organization; a faction of CPI (ML) CT which called itself the Coordination Centre and was functioning in Punjab; and the Bihar faction of the CCRI (ML), which was active in the Khagadia district of north Bihar. For further details, see Bhatia (2000).

9 The two other trends consisted of (1) individuals and groups who ceased to appreciate anything positive in the Naxalbari movement and the CPI (ML), and either left it or 'turned towards a right deviationist, liquidationist or revisionist line'; and (2) others, who were not ready to admit that mistakes had been made, continued to propagate the original line and 'drifted towards extreme forms of left sectarianism' (CPI [ML] Party Unity, 1997, p. 1).

10 At the local level, the organization continues to be called 'Sangram Samiti' or 'MKSS'; hence, I have continued to refer to the organization as MKSS in this essay. This is also to avoid confusion with other names (e.g., Mazdoor Kisan Mukti Manch) by which the organization was known in different regions in 1986–94, in order to circumvent the ban.

11   I have used the word 'party' for MCC, as I have for Liberation and Party Unity; however, in MCC's case the term is not strictly accurate since MCC considers itself a 'coordination committee'. In practice, MCC is often referred to as a party and the term also helps to distinguish the underground organization from its mass fronts.

12   See *Liberation*, July 1971–January 1972, Vol. 5, No. 1; reprinted in Sen et al., 1978, pp. 313–20.

13   This includes not only the Scheduled Castes, but also lower backward castes. It is important to note that while most Scheduled Caste families are landless, the converse is not true: a large proportion among the landless belong to lower backward castes.

14   Observations from MCC's area of influence have not been possible since I was unable to conduct fieldwork in those areas.

15   This and the following quotes are from Party Unity cadres and squad members.

16   In some cases, individuals were reported to have joined the movement for seemingly trivial reasons, which no doubt mattered a great deal to the person concerned. For example, an activist of MKSP reported that Ajit had joined the open front in Gaya because he had lost his bullock and wanted help to find it. Another person approached MKSP for help in a dispute involving a neighbour's newly constructed window that allegedly infringed on the privacy of his own courtyard.

17   By this, he did not mean that Bhumihars were self-cultivating. Due to social restrictions, Bhumihar men do not touch the plough and Bhumihar women do not even go to the fields. Bhumihars are therefore highly dependent on hired labourers for cultivation.

18   Mukherjee and Yadav (1980), pp. 43–44.

19   Ibid., pp. 53–54.

20   Sankh Singh himself was killed by the Naxalites, about two years after I interviewed him.

21   They also claimed that they used to have good relations with the mazdoors, based on mutual dependence. As Sankh Singh maintained, '*Mazdoor hamara hath ba, goud ba* (Labourers are our hands and feet).'

22   This account of struggle on the ground is not exhaustive. Some important aspects of the Naxalite movement, such as the response of the state as well as of upper castes and classes, internecine conflicts within the movement and engagement with electoral politics, are dealt with in Bhatia (2000).

23   However, one disadvantage of wage struggles is that they are often partly directed against small farmers who employ wage labour; this narrows down the support base of the movement (personal communication from Abhay, a PU leader).

24 Interview with Arvind, Secretary, Mazdoor Kisan Sangram Parishad (MKSP), July 1996.

25 In some instances, the police were protecting these gang leaders. For example, even though the government had announced a cash prize of Rs 50,000 for Ramanand, a dacoit, when the Naxalites targeted him, the police gave him wholehearted protection (in spite of which he was eventually killed).

26 MCC, for its part, has a policy of poll boycott and often threatens sanctions against people who vote. However, MCC's poll-boycott campaigns have been relatively unsuccessful (Bhatia, 2000).

27 Interview with PU leader, July 1996.

28 Interestingly, many agricultural labourers refer to the mass fronts as *hamara party* (our party). The word party therefore has different meanings and has to be interpreted in context.

29 As one person put it, '*Jiske paas paisa hai uska yeh sarkar hai; jiske paas paisa naheen hai uska duniya mein koi sahara naheen hai* [Whoever has money, the government is his; those who have no money are without protection in the world].'

30 The issue of factionalism within the Naxalite movement is dealt with in Bhatia (2000), Chapter 7.

31 Further, the spiral of violence contributes to a negative perception of the Naxalite movement in the minds of many observers, even those who are otherwise sympathetic to the ideals of the movement.

32 This concluding section builds not only on the material presented earlier, but also on other aspects of my study of the Naxalite movement in central Bihar (Bhatia, 2000).

Chapter 14: Might Is Right in Champaran

1 The Musahars are known as one of the poorest Dalit communities in Bihar. Most of them are landless labourers. For further discussion of their living conditions, see Chapter 12 (The Mazdooras of Bihar). On the history and culture of the Musahars, see e.g., Nishaant (2019).

2 For further details of these events, widely reported in the local media, see Ahmed (2002), Sahay (2002), and especially Pandey (2002).

Chapter 15: Justice, Not Vengeance: Bathani Tola and the Ranbeer Sena

1 The role of the Ranbeer Sena in this massacre is clear from multiple reports, aside from the testimonies presented in this essay; see e.g., Sinha and Sinha (1996), Human Rights Watch (1999), Banerjee (2010, 2012), Bhattacharya

(2012), Teltumbde (2012), Chakravarti (2016). See also the proceedings of 'Jan Sunwai with the survivors of the Bathani Tola and Bathe Massacres', a public hearing held in New Delhi on 18 December 2013 (some of the testimonies are available at https://www.youtube.com/watch?v=BM1z1HdX810), and the Cobrapost exposé 'Operation Black Rain' (Ashish, 2015). It is another matter that the High Court found it difficult to endorse the lower court's conviction of specific individuals, whether due to lack of evidence or lack of will.

2   The case was lodged as the Sahar PS Case No. 0098 of 1996, dated 12 July 1996, instituted under Sections 147/148/149/302/307/324/ 326/436 of IPC, Section 27 of the Arms Act and Section 3 (v) of the SC and ST (POA) Act. Out of the initial sixty-eight accused, fifty-three were tried; proceedings against the remaining fifteen were dropped because a few died, some absconded, or for other reasons.

3   The High Court judgment is available at https://www.academia.edu/6942790/Patna_High_Court_Judgement_in_Bathani_Tola_Massacre_case.

4   As reported in Ajay Singh (1996).

5   Ibid.

6   The reference here was to Manoj Singh, 20 years old, and Santosh Singh, 25 years old (both sons of Deepan Singh), Bela Singh, 25 years old, and Subedar Singh, a retired *jawan* with a criminal record. The ages are as per information available at the time of the massacre; later, in 2010, as they were being sentenced by the sessions court, the first three claimed to have been juveniles at the time of the massacre.

7   Both Saddam and Baby, who were said to be out of danger in late July, succumbed to their injuries the next month.

8   The circumstances of these killings are not entirely clear. According to Liberation sources, some attempt was made by upper-caste hoodlums to disrupt the march violently; the killings occurred in the tussle that followed.

9   On 19 April 1986, just three days after C.R. Kaswan took charge as the first SP of Jehanabad sub-division, he ordered the police to open fire on a peaceful assembly of agricultural labourers against the illegal eviction of nine landless Dalit families from a small piece of land (26 decimals). This massacre, known as the Arwal massacre after the place where the meeting was being held, claimed twenty-one lives and was denounced as the 'Jallianwalla Bagh of Bihar'. The state government's claim that the police fired in self-defence when an armed mob attacked the police station was proved baseless by many investigations, reports and the proceedings of the Indian People's Human Rights Tribunal.

10 One exception is the Kisan Sangh, a caste sena which includes members of several landed castes. Rajput senas in Bhojpur have included Ganga Sena and Kunwar Sena; the Brahmarishi Sena was a Bhumihar Sena.

11 Bhumihars and Rajputs, with roughly the same social and economic status, are said to have always had an antagonistic relationship in Bhojpur as well as in the rest of Bihar, a consequence no doubt of inter-caste rivalry in the pursuit of power and control; both castes rarely inhabit the same village.

12 This account of the incident is based on interviews with local Liberation activists, a conversation with Deepa Musahar and further inquiries in the area.

13 A mukhiya is the elected head of a gram panchayat in Bihar. Mukhiyas and other panchayat members have played a prominent role in the Ranbeer Sena. Brahmeshwar Singh, its main leader, is a mukhiya.

14 This section owes much to senior counsel Girish Patel. I am immensely grateful to him for patiently explaining the knots in criminal jurisprudence as well as discussing the Bathani Tola verdict despite his ill-health.

15 The statement of another important witness, Naimuddin, was deemed inadmissible by the HC-J (not the LC-J) due to alleged discrepancies in successive versions. Immediately after the carnage, Naimuddin, who had lost five family members, was in no condition to give a statement. Later, he gave two oral statements and a written one. Some additions were made to the first oral statement and this made his testimony suspect in the eyes of the HC judges.

16 In another recent case similar to that of Bathani Tola, on 1 March 2013, the Patna High Court acquitted eleven Ranbeer Sena members who had been found guilty by the Ara sessions court of a massacre of ten CPI(ML)Liberation supporters on the night of 11 November 1998 in Nagari Bazaar (Charpokhari block, Bhojpur district).

17 This is a long bamboo at the end of which an iron spade is attached. It is used to maintain the *aari* (the boundary of the field).

18 Badu, a Bhumihar, was considered a 'bad element' and was not short of enemies. One week prior to the cigarette incident, he had allegedly misbehaved with a woman passenger and this had led to a squabble. He was the main accused in a 1993 murder case where the victim was an old man of the Chamar caste. He had also earned the ire of the Yadav community for the alleged murder of a man belonging to the Bijendra Yadav group (Bijendra Yadav is a Janata Dal leader who enjoys considerable clout in the area).

Chapter 16: On 'Revolutionary Violence'

1 The lives of guerrilla fighters have inspired many writings; see, for example, Anderson (1992).

2 Revolutionary groups in other countries have also used extortion and other illegal means of getting funds with similar dilemmas. This also emerged in a talk I had with a former party leader of Peru's *Sendero Luminoso* (Shining

Path), who related how in his teens, when he first joined the party, the work during the day mainly involved petty theft, e.g., pickpocketing, stealing watches, looting banks, etc., in order to garner funds for the party. (Interview, Leiden, 11 February 2006.)

3   'Maoists Beat Woman to Death', NDTV report, 15 August 2005.

4   Mahesh (1999).

5   This is not to overlook the fact that when these very disadvantaged communities (for example, the Musahars in Bihar), who had so far always been at the receiving end of repressive violence, were first given guns, it did make them feel empowered in a certain way. However, this initial empowerment was followed by the highs and lows of violent struggle and the Dalit critique has to be viewed in the light of this overall experience.

6   In Andhra Pradesh, for example, after the breakdown of the peace process in January 2005, nearly forty sarpanchs had been killed by the second week of March (Kannabiran, 2005). In Bihar, internecine killings have plagued the movement since the mid-1980s.

7   The same attitude of intolerance contributes to discouraging dissent and debate within the party.

8   Estimate provided by the Human Rights Forum, Hyderabad.

9   See Ngugi (1964).

10   In this context, the concept of *shantimaita* is an important one. In contrast with *ahimsa,* which does not envisage or allow any violence, shantimaita commits itself to peacefulness and non-violence, but does not rule out the possibility of violence erupting in situations of severe social and political upheaval. This concept was introduced by Jayaprakash Narayan and was practised by the Chhatra Yuva Sangharsh Vahini in Bodhgaya from 1978 onwards.

11   Chomsky (1970), p. 40.

12   Bhagat Singh (1930), p. 15.

Chapter 17: Salwa Judum and After: Internal War as Counter-Insurgency

1   The district names used in this chapter correspond to the boundaries applicable at the time of my fieldwork in 2006–09. Some districts were bifurcated later on, e.g., undivided Dantewada was split into Bijapur (carved out in 2007), Sukma (created in 2012) and Dantewada districts. The Bastar division of Chhattisgarh now has seven districts.

2   *The Hindu Business Line,* 20 August 2006.

3   Singh (1994), p. 294.

4 That the word 'camp' was a misnomer was proven right when the Chief Minister of Chhattisgarh explicitly admitted that the intention was to create durable settlements.

5 Many testimonies are also available in petitions submitted to the Supreme Court in the Salwa Judum case, discussed further in this chapter. However, they were not in the public domain at the time of my fieldwork.

6 See e.g., Asian Centre for Human Rights (2006), Committee Against Violence on Women (2006), Human Rights Forum (2006, 2013), Independent Citizens' Initiative (2006), People's Union for Civil Liberties and others (2006), International Association of People's Lawyers (2007), Human Rights Watch (2008a), Sundar (2016), Bhardwaj (2020).

7 This claim was later found credible by the National Human Rights Commission (NHRC); see Sharma (2010a).

8 High Court at Bilaspur, Writ Petition (Cr.) No. 2111/2008. Madkami Aayete and five others vs. State of Chhattisgarh and seven others. 8 April 2008.

9 Statement of Kudami Somdu, as dictated to Sanchita Bakshi and Omprakash and submitted at the NHRC hearing in Dantewada, 10 June 2008.

10 On this incident, see also Indo-Asian News Service (2008), One India (2008), Sharma (2010b), among others. This is a rare case where the authorities owned up to the killing of innocent people (a woman and child), compensated the victims' families and registered criminal cases against CRPF personnel.

11 For early reports on both massacres, see Sethi (2010a, 2010b, 2010c, 2010d). Further atrocities happened in Gompad later on (see Chapter 19, Fake Encounter in Nulkatong).

12 For details, see Purkayastha (2014).

13 See nhrc.nic.in/press-release/nhrc-concludes-its-two-day-camp-sitting-raipur-recommends-20-lakhs-monetary-relief. To my knowledge, there has been no independent investigation of this massacre and its details are still shrouded in mystery.

14 See Sharma (2011).

15 I was accompanied by B. Ganesh, a journalist from the *Sakshi* newspaper in Telangana.

16 See Sethi (2010d).

17 In late 2009, twelve villagers from Gachanpalli and Gompad along with Himanshu Kumar of Vanvasi Chetna Ashram filed a writ petition in the Supreme Court demanding a CBI investigation of these massacres and compensation for the victims. In a startling judgement delivered on 14 July 2022, the Supreme Court embraced the police version of the events, imposed a fine on Himanshu Kumar, and allowed the Chhattisgarh government to initiate further action against him for making false allegations against the

security forces (for further details, see Himanshu Kumar's interview by Astha Savyasachi in Wire, 21 July 2022; also Sundar 2022). The judgement breaks all norms of judicial impartiality and blindly sides with the police against the petitioners. It sets an ominous precedent of courts turning against social workers who seek legal remedies for human rights violations.

18   See Chandra Bhaskar Rao (2009).

19   This section is based on Bhatia (2011).

20   A PIL was filed in the Supreme Court by Nandini Sundar, Ramachandra Guha and E.A.S. Sarma in 2007 (Writ Petition–civil–no. 250) followed by another PIL filed by Manish Kunjam, Kartam Joga and Dudhi Joga (Writ Petition–criminal–no. 119 of 2007), and an impleadment by K.G. Kannabiran. The first PIL drew on independent fact-finding and the second on an important set of 100-odd testimonies collected by the Adivasi Mahasabha and CPI at a meeting in Cherla in early 2007. All these were treated as one composite case by the Supreme Court. At the time, other petitions against specific atrocities related to Salwa Judum had also been filed in the High Court of Chhattisgarh at Bilaspur and the Supreme Court.

21   The judgment does say that all security forces should function within the limits of the constitution: 'The primordial [constitutional] value is the responsibility of every organ of the state to function within the four corners of constitutional responsibility. This is the ultimate rule of law.' (Para 69) However, the implications are drawn only with specific reference to SPOs, who are deemed unconstitutional. Likewise, the order for '. . . investigation of all previously inappropriately or incompletely investigated instances of alleged criminal activities' is restricted to Salwa Judum.

22   Planning Commission (2008).

23   On this issue, see also Goswami (2023).

24   For detailed accounts of these incidents, see Agarwal (2019) and Human Rights Forum (2013) respectively.

25   See Agarwal (2019).

26   See Shantha (2022).

27   I was part of this fact-finding team and filed a complaint in the Gangalur Police Station immediately after the investigation on behalf of the team, on 26 May 2013.

28   See Bhatia (2022).

29   Personal communication, June 2023.

30   For a short report on this incident, see Bhatia and Drèze (2021).

31   One of the injured, a pregnant woman, died within a few days.

32   See Saikia (2023). The basic facts had already emerged from an earlier investigation by the Coordination of Democratic Rights Organisations

(CDRO). The police tried every means to scuttle the first attempt of the investigating team (of which I was also a part) to reach the villages; facing harassment at every step, the enquiry had to be aborted. However, the CDRO successfully completed its investigation later on.

33 AGNI was formed in 2016 after the dissolution of Samajik Ekta Manch. AGNI itself was dissolved soon after S.R.P. Kalluri was transferred from Bastar in early 2017.

34 For further details of these incidents, see e.g. Agarwal (2016), Bhardwaj (2016), Bhatia (2016b), Mishra (2016), Sharma (2016a, 2016b), Wire Staff (2019), among many other reports.

35 For further details, see Kumar (2017) and Mahaprashasta (2017). I had made complaints to the District Collector after every incident of threat and had filed FIRs after the mobile snatching and house attack. Following the public uproar after the house attack and my refusal to leave Bastar, the Collector had to allot a two-room government house to me in a colony of government employees on subsidized rent for my safety. However, surveillance continued in the form of unarmed 'guards' (despite repeated written requests for their withdrawal) until late 2018.

36 See Bhatia (2016b).

37 Sometimes the Naxalites have also burnt or looted the houses of those who had gone with the Salwa Judum.

Chapter 18: Rape by the Way

1 See National Commission for Scheduled Tribes (2016); the report is in Hindi, but extracts in English are available in Women Against Sexual Violence and State Repression (2017), Appendix 11. See also Choudhury (2016).

2 'Police atrocities on Madia (Gondi) adivasi women in Lohandiguda, Bastar', complaint to NHRC by Ramuram Maurya (President, Prastavit Tata Steel Jan Adhikar Samiti) and the author, 28 March 2007.

3 On these incidents, see Amnesty International (1999), Andhra Pradesh Civil Liberties Committee and others (2001), Human Rights Watch (2008b), Human Rights Forum (2013), Batool et al. (2016), Venkatesan (2023). In the Vakapalli incident, involving rapes of 11 women, the judgement was finally delivered on 6 April 2023 by the Special Sessions Judge for the trial of cases under SC&ST (Prevention of Atrocities) Act and all the accused were acquitted. The judges blamed the shoddy investigation by the Investigating Officers for their inability to indict anyone. However, they maintained that the victims were entitled for compensation (two women died in the intervening period) and ordered that suitable compensation be worked out and paid to them.

4   Government of India (2013), p. 220.

5   I am grateful to Uma Chakravarti for drawing my attention to this. On the Vachathi judgement, see e.g. Arivanantham (2011) and Palaniappan (2011). The convicts filed an appeal in the Madras High Court (Soundaraya Athimuthu, 2023), but the High Court upheld the convictions (Pandey and Krishnan, 2023).

Chapter 19: Fake Encounter in Nulkatong

1   For detailed accounts of these incidents, see Sethi (2010), Subramaniam and Shukla (2016), Kritika A (2018), among others. These two cases were taken to court (Supreme Court and High Court respectively). Unfortunately, they are two of the recent cases where the court not only dismissed the petition but also, in one case, turned against the petitioner.

2   The other team members were Varun Kumar, Pramod Mandade and NS. We also made a submission to the SDM, Etapalli tehsil (Gadchiroli), for the Mendhari village Magisterial Enquiry on 23 July 2013.

3   This letter is a modified version of an earlier letter sent by the NHRC to chief ministers on 29 March 1997, revised on 2 December 2003.

4   See e.g. Bharadwaj (2009).

Chapter 20: Nowhere to Hide

1   *Patrika*, 6 February 2019.

Chapter 22: A Stone in My Hand: Four Months Kashmir Will Never Forget

1   See *Four Months the Kashmir Valley will never Forget* (Fact-Finding Team to Kashmir, 2011). Other useful accounts of the events of that summer include Centre for Dialogue and Reconciliation (n.d.), Subramanian (2010), Ali et al. (2011), Kak (2011). For earlier reports on human rights violations in Jammu and Kashmir, see e.g. Andhra Pradesh Civil Liberties Committee and others (2001), Human Rights Forum and others (2007), Jammu Kashmir Coalition of Civil Society (2012, 2015).

2   The killing of Tufail Mattoo, which sparked the 2010 unrest in Kashmir, was widely reported in the national and international media; see e.g., Polgreen (2010) and NDTV (2011). Tufail's family has been waiting for justice ever since, year after year; see Amnesty International (2013), Ashiq (2017), Javeed (2018), Bazaz (2020), The KashmirWalla (2021).

3   See 'Valley Schoolboy was Killed by Teargas Shell', *Indian Express*, 13 June 2010.
4   Accessible at http://www.kashmirtimes.com/ on clicking through the 'archives' link to 12 June 2010.
5   Subramanian (2010).
6   *Hindustan Times*, Delhi edition, 4 December 2010.
7   *Greater Kashmir* in Srinagar reported the story on 28 December 2010 under the headline 'Tufail's father looking for asylum'. *Hindustan Times* followed the next day in its Delhi edition, with a story titled 'Scared, Tufail's father mulls asylum'.
8   On the events reported in this section and the situation in Kashmir at that time, see also Anjum and Varma (2010), Bhasin Jamwal (2010), Bukhari and Varadarajan (2010), *Economic Times* (2010), *Mumbai Mirror* (2010), among other articles in the Indian media.
9   Exactly when and why the security forces opened fire is not very clear. According to a police officer speaking to Associated Press, this happened 'after thousands of protesters gathered and threw stones at the troops' (Associated Press, 2010). The same report, however, also states that '[l]ocal residents maintained the protest was peaceful and clashes only erupted after the shooting'. That is also what we heard from eyewitnesses.
10   See Bashir (2010).
11   On this incident, see also Bashaarat Masood (2010). On other incidents of attacks on funeral processions, see Irfan (2010a).
12   NDTV (2010) covered this incident and some of the tensions that followed.
13   On this incident, see also Irfan (2010b).
14   This incident was covered the next day (on 31 July 2010) in *Greater Kashmir* and *Kashmir Times*; see Fact-Finding Team to Kashmir (2011) for further discussion.

Chapter 24: The Struggle for Self-Rule in Manipur's Hill Districts

1   Section 144 of the Criminal Procedure Code, a relic of the colonial period, empowers some magistrates to issue preventive orders in 'urgent cases of nuisance or apprehended danger'.
2   The other team members were Vani Subramaniam, Rosemary Dzüvichü and Neikesanuo Sorhie.
3   Naga Hoho is the apex body of all the Naga tribes, be they in Nagaland, Manipur, Assam, Arunachal Pradesh or Myanmar.
4   This figure is from the community hospital at Kalinamai.
5   See Sagar (2010).

6   Scheduled Castes and Scheduled Tribes Lists (Modification) Orders 1956, Part X Manipur.
7   There are altogether sixty-eight Naga tribes (including those in Myanmar). 'Kuki' is the term for the Zo or Chin who migrated from the Chin Hills of Myanmar, though the generic name Kuki has become controversial and many ethnic groups are now struggling for recognition or their own identities (Shimray 2009: 91).
8   These estimates are according to the 1991 Census.
9   Institute for Human Development (2006).
10   Gangte (nd), cited in Takhellambam (2009), p. 148.
11   Shimray (2009), p. 92. The Act met with disfavour also because it had been pushed 'despite a difference of opinion between the Hill Areas Committee and the Legislative Assembly . . . the former did not agree with several provisions of the Bill'. Institute for Human Development (2006: 240).
12   See Kamei (2009) for the resistance of the Kuki-Chins to the Act because of which it could not be implemented in their areas.
13   This also had other worrying consequences, e.g., that development projects could be sanctioned in the hill areas without the district councils having any say. See Chamroy (2008).
14   Chamroy (2008).
15   Zolengthe (2008).
16   Chamroy (2008).
17   See Mashangva (2010) and Chiphang (2010), among others.
18   Institute for Human Development 2006: 242.
19   Chakma (2010).
20   See e.g., the compilation by Justice B.L. Hansaria (2005).
21   See in particular the 'Bardoloi Sub-Committee Report on the North-East Frontier (Assam) Tribal and Excluded Areas' on which the Sixth Schedule is based and the 'Constituent Assembly Debate Relating to the Sixth Schedule' in Hansaria (2005).
22   The version of the Sixth Schedule referred to in this section is as it existed on 29 April 2005, included in Hansaria (2005).
23   This is not unlike the experience with the Tribal Advisory Councils in the Fifth Schedule areas.
24   See Chapter 9 (Part D) of the report in Hansaria (2005).
25   Shimray (2009), p. 112.
26   Haokip (2009), p. 321.
27   Newmai News Network (2010).
28   Correspondent (2010b).
29   Correspondent (2010a).

30 So great was the resultant apprehension that it led to the formation of the Kuki National Front in 1988–89 'with the view to . . . perpetuate the political demand of the Kuki National Assembly . . . [for] the creation of a Kuki Homeland (Kuki State), within the framework of Indian Constitution . . .' (Gangte as quoted in Takhellambam, p. 149).

31 The extension of the Act was made in eighty-four villages in Churachandpur (in 1962), fourteen villages of Senapati (in 1965) and fourteen villages in Tamenglong (Dena 2010).

32 Constituent Assembly Debate in Hansaria (2005), p. 285.

33 Haokip (2009), pp. 321–22.

34 Memorandum submitted to the Prime Minister of India in June 2006.

References

Agarwal, A., and Narain, S. (1985), *The State of India's Environment 1984-85* (New Delhi: Centre for Science and Environment).

Agarwal, Shikohi (2016), 'Is the Attack on Soni Sori Part of a Larger Plan for Bastar?', Wire, 21 February.

Agarwal, V.K. (2019), *Report of the Judicial Enquiry Commission in the Matter of Incident of Encounter at Villages Sarkeguda of Police Station Basaguda, District Bijapur and Villages Silger and Chimlipenta of Police Station Jagargunda of District Sukma, on the Night Intervening between 28th & 29th June 2012* (available at http://bhumkalsamachar.com/wp-content/uploads/2019/12/Sarkeguda-Judicial-Inquiry-Report.pdf).

Ahmed, Farzand (2002), 'Mass Protests after Bihar Minister Purnamasi Ram Assaults CPI (ML) Leader of Bagaha', *India Today*, 22 April.

Ali, Syed Intishab (2011), 'Malnutrition claims 3 kids in Baran in 1 month', *Times of India* (Jaipur), 22 November.

Ali, T., Bhatt, H., Chatterji, A.P., Khatun, H., Mishra, P., and Roy, A. (2011), *Kashmir: The Case for Freedom* (London: Verso).

Ambedkar, B.R. (1944), *Annihilation of Caste*. Reprinted in Government of Maharashtra (1989), *Dr. Babasaheb Ambedkar: Writings and Speeches*, Vol. 1 (Mumbai: Education Department).

Amnesty International (1997), 'India: Stop Killings in "Lawless State"', press release, 3 December.

Amnesty International (1999), Press release concerning the safety of Gulsham Bano, Raja Begum and Muhammed Shafi Wani, 8 June (available at https://www.amnesty.org/ar/wp-content/uploads/2021/06/asa200231999en.pdf).

Amnesty International (2013), 'India: Authorities Must Reopen Investigation into 2010 Killing of Tufail Mattoo', 17 June (available at https://www.amnesty.org/fr/wp-content/uploads/2021/06/asa200282013en.pdf).

Anderson, J.L. (1992), *Guerrillas: The Inside Stories of the World's Revolutionaries* (London: HarperCollins).

Andhra Pradesh Civil Liberties Committee and others (2001), *Grim Realities of Life, Death and Survival in Jammu & Kashmir* (available at https://pudr.org/grim-realities-life-death-and-survival-jammu-kashmir).

Anjum, A., and Varma, S. (2010), 'Curfewed in Kashmir: Voices', *Economic and Political Weekly*, 28 August.

Arivanantham, R. (2011), 'Rape Convicts Sent to Jail', *The Hindu*, 30 September.

Arslan, M., Kothari, S., Lewis, P., Ray, A., and Vanaik, A. (1997), 'Gunshots and Silence: The Killings in Siwan, Bihar', report of an independent fact-finding mission (available at http://www.unipune.ac.in/snc/cssh/humanrights/02%20STATE%20AND%20ARMY%20-%20POLICE%20REPRESSION/C%20Bihar/12.pdf).

Ashiq, Peerzada (2017), 'Justice eludes man whose son's death sparked protests', *The Hindu*, 1 March (available at https://www.thehindu.com/news/national/other-states/justice-eludes-man-whose-sons-death-sparked-protests/article17384908.ece).

Ashish, K. (2015), 'Operation Black Rain: Revisiting the Killings of Dalits of Bihar and Confessions of their Killers', Cobrapost blog (available at cobrapost.com); the Cobrapost exposé is also available on YouTube.

Asian Centre for Human Rights (2006), *The Adivasis of Chhattisgarh: Victims of the Naxalite Movement and Salwa Judum Campaign* (New Delhi: ACHR).

Associated Press (2010), 'Kashmir protests erupt into violence after government troops kill four', *The Guardian*, 13 August (available at https://www.theguardian.com/world/2010/aug/13/kashmir-protests-killed-ramadan).

Balagopalan, S., Ghosh, K., and Meghnath (2001), 'Massacres of Adivasis: A Preliminary Report', *Economic and Political Weekly*, 3 March.

Bandyopadhyay, J. (1987), *Ecology of Drought and Water Scarcity: Need for an Ecological Water Resources Policy* (Dehradun: Research Foundation for Science and Ecology).

Banerjee, Shoumojit (2010), 'Death for three in Bathani Tola massacre case', *The Hindu*, 14 May.

Banerjee, Shoumojit (2012), 'For residents of Bathani, it is a horror they cannot forget', *The Hindu*, 19 April.

Banerjee, Sumanta (1984), *India's Simmering Revolution: The Naxalite Uprising* (New Delhi: Selectbook Service Syndicate).

Bashaarat Masood (2010), 'Labourer killed in police firing, Valley back on boil', *Indian Express*, 20 July.

Bashir, Sheikh Imran (2010), 'Protests Spread In Kashmir, Death Toll Rises To 62', posted at countercurrents.org (available at https://www.countercurrents.org/bashir200810.htm).

Batool, E., Butt, I., Rashid, M., Rather, N., and Mushtaq, S. (2016), *Do You Remember Kunan Poshpora?* (New Delhi: Zubaan).

Bazaz, Junain Nabi (2020), '10 Years of Tufail Mattoo's Death and His Father's Fight for Justice', *Kashmir Reader*, 12 June (available at https://kashmirreader.com/2020/06/12/10-years-of-tufail-mattoos-death-and-his-fathers-fight-for-justice/).

Bharadwaj, Sudha (2009), 'The situation in Dantewada, Chhattisgarh today', posted at sanhati.com, 21 September (available at http://sanhati.com/excerpted/1787/).

Bhardwaj, Amit (2016), 'After Three Days, Missing Bastar Journalist Prabhat Singh Posts On Facebook', Newslaundry, 19 September (available at www.newslaundry.com/2016/09/19/where-is-bastar-journalist-prabhat-singh).

Bhardwaj, Ashutosh (2020), *The Death Script: Dreams and Delusions in Naxal Country* (New Delhi: Fourth Estate).

Bharti, Indu (1990), 'Mobilisation of Agricultural Labour: Jehanabad Experience', *Economic and Political Weekly*, 2 June.

Bhasin Jamwal, Anuradha (2010), 'Fuelling the Rage in Kashmir', *Economic and Political Weekly*, 10 July.

Bhatia, Bela (1992), 'Lush Fields and Parched Throats', *Economic and Political Weekly*, 19–26 December.

Bhatia, Bela (1993), 'Forced Evictions of Tribal Oustees due to the Sardar Sarovar Project in Five Submerging Villages of Gujarat', report submitted to the Gujarat High Court, 15 July.

Bhatia, Bela (1994), 'Narmada Widows Get Raw Deal', *The Tribune*, 23 January.

Bhatia, Bela (1997a), 'Forced Evictions in the Narmada Valley', in Drèze, J.P., Samson, M., and Singh, S. (eds.) (1997), *The Dam and the Nation: Displacement and Resettlement in the Narmada Valley* (New Delhi: Oxford University Press).

Bhatia, Bela (1997b), 'Anatomy of a Massacre', *Seminar*, February.

Bhatia, Bela (1998a), 'After the Massacre', *Economic and Political Weekly*, 4 April.

Bhatia, Bela (1998b), 'Rethinking Revolution in Bihar', *Seminar*, April.

Bhatia, Bela (1998c), 'Social Action with Rural Widows in Gujarat', in Chen, M. (ed.)(1998), *Widows in India: Social Neglect and Public Action* (Delhi: Sage).

Bhatia, Bela (1998d), 'Widows, Land Rights and Resettlement in the Narmada Valley', in Chen, M. (ed.)(1998), *Widows in India: Social Neglect and Public Action* (Delhi: Sage).

Bhatia, Bela (2000), 'The Naxalite Movement in Central Bihar', PhD thesis, University of Cambridge.

Bhatia, Bela (2002), '*Naxalvaadi bante dalit: andolan ke bhitar andolan*', in Dubey, A. (ed.) (2002), *Adhunikta Ke Aine Mein Dalit* (Delhi: Vani Prakashan and CSDS).

Bhatia, Bela (2005), 'The Naxalite Movement in Central Bihar', *Economic and Political Weekly*, 9 April.

Bhatia, Bela (2011), 'Judging the Judgment', *Economic and Political Weekly*, 23 July.

Bhatia, Bela (2016a), 'The Pegdapalli Files', *Outlook*, 29 February.

Bhatia, Bela (2016b), 'The War without Witness', *Outlook*, 18 June.

Bhatia, Bela (2019a), 'Who Killed Sodi Deva?', Wire, 26 March.

Bhatia, Bela (2019b), 'Three Bullets and Three Women: A "Fake Encounter in Bastar"', Wire, 26 April.

Bhatia, Bela (2019c), 'The Anatomy of a "Fake Encounter": How 10 Adivasis were Killed in Abujmarh', Wire, 14 May.

Bhatia, Bela (2022), 'Adivasi Life in Bastar: Burkapal Is a Tip of the Repression', *Outlook*, 6 August.

Bhatia, B., and Drèze, J.P. (2021), 'Facts and Fiction of Firing in Silger (Bastar)', press note (available at https://countercurrents.org/2021/05/facts-and-fiction-of-firing-in-silger-bastar/).

Bhatia, B., and Mehta, L. (1993), 'Police Terror in Antras: The Rape of a Tribal Woman', report submitted to the Gujarat High Court, April.

Bhatnagar, Vivek (2015), 'Confessions from Bihar's Killing Fields Set to Singe BJP, and Nitish Too', Wire, 17 August (available at https://thewire.in/rights/confessions-from-bihars-killing-fields-set-to-singe-bjp-and-nitish-too).

Bhattacharya, Dipankar (2012), 'Bathani Tola II: Miscarriage of Justice', *Economic and Political Weekly*, 2 June.

Bhushan, P., Jaiswal, K., and Tewatia, D.S. (1993), 'Report of the Team of Observers on the Human Rights Violations in the Sardar Sarovar Project', mimeo, 6 June.

Blair, Harry W. (1981), 'Caste and the British Census in Bihar', in Barrier, N.G. (ed.) (1981), *The Census in British India: New Perspectives* (New Delhi: Manohar).

Bose, P.K. (1987), 'Kulaks on the Rise', *Economic and Political Weekly*, 20 June.

Bradley, E., and Phadtare, P.N. (1989), 'Paleohydrology Affecting Recharge to Overexploited Semiconfined Aquifers in the Mehsana Area, Gujarat State, India', *Journal of Hydrology*, 108.

Brahme, S. (1983), *Drought in Maharashtra 1972* (Pune: Gokhale Institute).

Bukhari, S., and Varadarajan, S. (2010), 'Army May be Deployed as Violence Escalates in Kashmir', *The Hindu*, 6 July.

Campaign for Survival and Dignity (2004), *Endangered Symbiosis: Evictions and India's Forest Communities* (New Delhi: CSD).

Centre for Dialogue and Reconciliation (n.d.), *Behind the Numbers: Profiling Those Killed in the 2010 Unrest* (available at https://kipdf.com/behind-the-numbers-profiling-those-killed-in-kashmir-s-2010-unrest_5ab565a71723dd329c641e1e.html).

Centre for Science and Environment (1985), *The State of India's Environment 1984-85* (New Delhi: CSE).

Centre for Science and Environment (1999), 'A deformed existence', *Down to Earth*, 15 July.

Chakma, Suhas (2010), 'Why the Road Blocks Really Started', *Hindustan Times*, 23 May.

Chakravarti, Anand (2016), 'Who Killed at Bathani Tola?', *Indian Express*, 18 January.

Chakravarti, Anand (2018), *Is This 'Azaadi'? Everyday Lives of Dalit Agricultural Labourers in a Bihar Village* (New Delhi: Tulika).

Chakravarti, Uma (2020), 'From the Home to the Borders: Violence Against Women, Impunity and Resistance', *Social Change*, 50(2).

Chamroy, N. (2008), 'On Autonomous District Councils in Manipur', 6 May.

Chandra Bhaskar Rao, D. (2009), 'Maoists Suffer Major Blow in Chhattisgarh', *The Hindu*, 19 September.

Chandrakanth, M.G. (1989), 'Issues in the Management of Ground Water in India: An Institutional Perspective', paper presented at a workshop on Efficiency and Equity in Groundwater Use and Management held at the Institute of Rural Management (Anand), 1 February.

Choudhury, Chitraganda (2016), 'The NCST's Report on Gangrapes and Assaults in Bastar Says There is a Breakdown of Discipline Among Security Forces', *Caravan*, 12 May (available at https://caravanmagazine.in/vantage/bastar-ncst-report-gangrapes-assaults-result-breakdown-discipline).

Chiphang, Addie (2010), 'Ukhrul Denounces ADC 2008 Act', *Sangai Express*, 6 April.

Chomsky, Noam (1970, 2005), *Government in the Future* (Delhi: Leftword).

Committee Against Violence on Women (2006), *Salwa Judum and Violence on Women in Dantewara, Chhattisgarh* (Nagpur: CAVOW).

Correspondent (2010a), 'Manipur ADC Poll Hits Wall of Protest', *The Telegraph*, 12 April.

Correspondent (2010b), 'KIM for ADC Polls under Sixth Schedule', *Lanka Times*, 28 April.

CPI (ML) Liberation (1986), *Report from the Flaming Fields of Bihar* (Calcutta: Prabodh Bhattacharya).

CPI (ML) Liberation (1997), 'Crossing the Barriers', *Liberation*, April.

CPI (ML) Liberation (n.d.), 'CPI (ML) Liberation: Firm Defender of the Revolutionary Legacy of the Indian Communists', unpublished party document.

CPI (ML) Party Unity (1987), 'Documents Adopted at the 2nd Central Conference Held on 17–23 April 1987', unpublished party document.

CPI (ML) Party Unity (1997), 'Political and Organisational Review', unpublished party document.

Das, Arvind (1983), *Agrarian Unrest and Socio-economic Change in Bihar, 1900-80* (Delhi: Manohar).

Das, Arvind (1992), *The Republic of Bihar* (New Delhi: Penguin).

Dena, Lal (2010), 'Manipur Hill Tribes Still Waiting for Justice', *Mizoram Express*, 20 May.

Desai, G.M., Singh, G., and Sah, D.C. (1979), 'Impact of Scarcity on Farm Economy and Significance of Relief Operations', CMA Monograph No. 84 (Ahmedabad: Indian Institute of Management).

Deshpande, Satish (2003), *Contemporary India: A Sociological View* (New Delhi: Penguin).

Dhawan, B.D. (1987), 'Management of Groundwater Resource: Direct versus Indirect Regulatory Mechanisms', *Economic and Political Weekly*, 5–12 September.

Down to Earth (2003), 'Police firing will keep happening', interview with Babulal Marandi (available at http://www.indiaenvironmentportal.org.in/content/24836/police-firing-will-keep-happening/).

Drèze, J.P. (1990a), 'Famine Prevention in India', in Drèze, J.P., and Sen, A.K. (eds) (1990), *The Political Economy of Hunger*, Volume 2 (Oxford: Oxford University Press).

Drèze, J.P. (1990b), 'Widows in Rural India', Discussion Paper No. 26, Development Economics Research Programme, London School of Economics.

Drèze, J.P., and Sen, A.K. (2013), *An Uncertain Glory: India and Its Contradictions* (New Delhi: Penguin).

Economic Times (2010), 'Teenager Killed in Srinagar Violence, Day's Toll Hits 3', 6 July (available at https://economictimes.indiatimes.com/news/politics-and-nation/teenager-killed-in-srinagar-violence-days-toll-hits-3/articleshow/6135600.cms?from=mdr).

Elwin, Verrier (1937), 'Myths and Dreams of the Baigas of Central India' (summary of a communication by Verrier Elwin, December 1, 1936), *Man*, Vol 37.

Elwin, Verrier (1947, 1991), *The Muria and their Ghotul* (Oxford: Oxford University Press); special reprint.

Fact-Finding Team to Kashmir (2011), *Four Months the Kashmir Valley Will Never Forget: An Enquiry into the Mass Uprising of 2010* (New Delhi: The Other Media).

Fernandes, W., and Barbora, S. (eds.) (2009), *Land, People and Politics: Contest Over Tribal Land in North-east India* (Guwahati: North-Eastern Social Research Centre).

Fuller, C.J. (ed.) (1997), *Caste Today* (New Delhi: Oxford University Press).

Gangte, Thangkhotinmang S. (n.d.), *Land Problem and Ethnic Tension in North-east India with Special Reference to Manipur*, unpublished monograph.

Ghatak, Maitreya (ed.) (1997), *Dust on the Road: The Activist Writings of Mahasweta Devi* (Calcutta: Seagull Books).

Ghosh, Suniti (ed.) (1992), *The Historic Turning-Point: A Liberation Anthology*, 2 volumes (Calcutta: S.K. Ghosh).

Godbole, Girija (2003), 'Free Meals Make them Dependent, so Should They go Back to Eating Grass?', *Infochange*, January.

Goswami, Prasoon (2023), 'Embrace Guns or Death by Maoists: People in Bastar Face Bizarre Choice', *Outlook*, 22 June.

Government of Bihar (n.d.), *Memorandum on Land Tenure System in Bihar and Measures Taken in the State for Abolition of Zamindaris* (Patna: Revenue Department).

Government of Gujarat (1974), *Gazetteer of India, Gujarat State: Sabarkantha District* (Baroda: Government Press).

Government of Gujarat (1976), *Gujarat Relief Manual*, Volume 1 (Gandhinagar: Government Central Press).

Government of Gujarat (1984), *Gujarat Agriculture Compendium* (Ahmedabad: Directorate of Agriculture).

Government of Gujarat (1987), *Memorandum to Government of India on Scarcity 1987-88* (Government of Gujarat: Revenue Department).

Government of Gujarat (1992), *Gujaratma Samaj Surakshani Pravarti* (Ahmedabad: Government of Gujarat).

Government of Gujarat (n.d.), *Samajik Salamati Yojnao* (Ahmedabad: Social Security Department).

Government of India (1880), *Report of the Indian Famine Commission 1880* (London: HMSO).

Government of India (1986), *Groundwater Development in India* (New Delhi: Ministry of Water Resources).

Government of India (2005a), *Joining the Dots: Report of the Tiger Task Force* (New Delhi: Ministry of Environment and Forests).

Government of India (2005b), 'The Scheduled Tribes (Recognition of Forest Rights) Bill, 2005', powerpoint presentation by the Ministry of Tribal Affairs at the Prime Minister's Office, 30 September.

Government of India (2013), *Report of the Committee on Amendments to Criminal Law* (available at adrindia.org/sites/default/files/Justice_Verma_Amendmenttocriminallaw_Jan2013.pdf).

Government of India (2014), *Report of the Expert Group to Review the Methodology for Measurement of Poverty* (New Delhi: Planning Commission).

Grierson, G.A. (1885), *Bihar Peasant Life*, 2nd advanced revised edition, 1926 (Calcutta).

Grigson, W.V. (1938), *The Maria Gonds of Bastar* (London: Oxford University Press).

Guha, Ranajit (1982), 'On Some Aspects of the Historiography of Colonial India', in Guha, R. (ed.) (1982), *Subaltern Studies I: Writings on South Asian History and Society* (Delhi: Oxford University Press).

Gupta, Dipankar (2000), *Interrogating Caste* (New Delhi: Penguin).

Gupta, Dipankar (2004), *Caste in Question: Identity or Hierarchy?* (New Delhi: Sage).

Gupta, Dipankar (ed.)(1991), *Social Stratification* (Delhi: Oxford University Press).

Gupta, J. (1988), 'Development Plans Caused Chaos: Water Problem in Gujarat', *The Statesman*, New Delhi, 6 May.

Gupta, Tilak Das (1993), 'Recent Developments in the Naxalite Movement', *Monthly Review*, 45.

Haimendorf, Christoph von Fürer (1990), *Life among Indian Tribes: The Autobiography of an Anthropologist* (Delhi: Oxford University Press).

Hansaria, B. L. (revised by Vijay Hansaria) (2005), *Sixth Schedule to the Constitution*, second edition (Delhi: Universal Law Publishing).

Haokip, T. T. (2009), 'Critically Assessing Kuki Land System in Manipur', in Priyoranjan Singh, 2009.

Horam, M., and Rizvi, S.H.M. (eds.) (1998), *People of India: Manipur* (Calcutta: Anthropological Survey of India and Seagull Books).

Human Rights Campaign on Narmada (1993), 'Respect Human Rights: Violations of Human Rights in the Narmada Valley', memorandum submitted to the Sardar Sarovar Project Review Group, 10 October; available from The Other Media, New Delhi.

Human Rights Forum (2006), *Death, Displacement and Deprivation: The War in Dantewara* (Hyderabad: Navya Printers).

Human Rights Forum and others (2007), *Kashmir: Will the Pain Never End?* (available at http://humanrightsforum.org).

Human Rights Forum (2013), *The Terrible Cost of an Inhuman Counter-Insurgency* (Hyderabad: Navya Printers).

Human Rights Watch (1999), *Broken People: Caste Violence Against India's 'Untouchables'* (New York: Human Rights Watch).

Human Rights Watch (2002), *'We Have no Orders to Save You': State Participation and Complicity in Communal Violence in Gujarat* (New York: HRW).

Human Rights Watch (2008a), *'Being Neutral is Our Biggest Crime': Government, Vigilante, and Naxalite Abuses in India's Chhattisgarh State* (New York: HRW).

Human Rights Watch (2008b), *'These Fellows Must be Eliminated': Relentless Violence and Impunity in Manipur* (New Yord: HRW).

Independent Citizens' Initiative (2006), *War in the Heart of India: An Enquiry into the Ground Situation in Dantewada District, Chhattisgarh* (available at https://cpjc.files.wordpress.com/2007/07/ici-warintheheartofindia.pdf).

India Today (2010), 'Fresh violence in valley, 4 killed, Srinagar under curfew', 6 July (available at https://www.indiatoday.in/india/north/story/fresh-violence-in-valley-4-killed-srinagar-under-curfew-78099-2010-07-06).

Indian Express (2010), 'Three killed, 70 injured as violence erupts in Srinagar', 6 July (available at https://indianexpress.com/article/india/latest-news/three-killed-70-injured-as-violence-erupts-in-srinagar/).

Indo-Asian News Service (2008), 'Tribals, rights activists seek recall of CRPF troopers', press release (available at https://twocircles.net/2008may24/tribals_rights_activists_seek_recall_crpf_troopers.html).

Institute for Human Development (2006), 'Manipur State Development Report', draft report sponsored by the Planning Commission, Government of India, Delhi.

International Association of People's Lawyers (2007), 'Preliminary Observations and Findings of the IAPL Team on the Human Rights Situation in Chhattisgarh, India' (available at https://cpjc.files.wordpress.com/2007/12/iapl_report.pdf).

International Institute for Population Sciences (2017), *National Family Health Survey (NFHS-4), 2015-16* (Mumbai: IIPS).

International Institute for Population Sciences (2022), *National Family Health Survey (NFHS-5), 2019-21* (Mumbai: IIPS).

Irfan, Shams (2010a), 'Desecrating the Dead', *Kashmir Life*, 18 July (available at https://kashmirlife.net/desecrating-the-dead-650/).

Irfan, Shams (2010b), 'Chased to Death', *Kashmir Life*, 26 July (available at https://kashmirlife.net/chased-to-death-757/).

Jacob, A. (1989), 'The Existing Legal Regime of Ground Water', paper presented at a workshop on Efficiency and Equity in Groundwater Use and Management held at the Institute of Rural Management (Anand), 1 February 1989.

Jammu Kashmir Coalition of Civil Society (2012), *Alleged Perpetrators: Stories of Impunity in Jammu and Kashmir* (Srinagar: JKCCS).

Jammu Kashmir Coalition of Civil Society (2015), *Structures of Violence: The Indian State in Jammu and Kashmir* (Srinagar: JKCCS).

Jannuzi, F.T. (1974), *Agrarian Crisis in India: The Case of Bihar* (Austin: University of Texas Press).

Javeed, Auqib (2018), 'The Never Ending Wait for Justice to Tufail Mattoo', TwoCircles.net, 12 June (available at https://twocircles.net/2018jun12/423704.html).

Jha, H., Sinha, J.B.P., Gopal, S., and Tiwari, K.M. (1985), *Social Structures and Alignments: A Study of Rural Bihar* (New Delhi: Usha).

Jha, Praveen (1994), 'Stagnation of Agricultural Wages in Rural India', PhD thesis (New Delhi: Jawaharlal Nehru University).

Joshi, P.C. (1970), *Land Reforms and Agrarian Change in India and Pakistan since 1947* (Delhi: Institute of Economic Growth).

Kak, Sanjay (ed.) (2011), *Until My Freedom Has Come: The New Intifada in Kashmir* (New Delhi: Penguin).

Kamei, Gangmumei (2009), 'Ethnicity, Identity and Land in Tribal Manipur', in Priyoranjan Singh, 2009.

Kannabiran, K.G. (2005), 'Vempenta Killings and Maoists', *Deccan Herald*, 11 March.

Khetan, Ashish (2007), 'Sabarkantha: Nowhere to Run', *Tehelka*, 3 November.

Kritika A. (2018), 'In the Gompad trail: An account of 15 'encounter' deaths and bloodied facts in a haystack of security fiction from Chhattisgarh', Leaflet, 27 August (available at https://theleaflet.in/in-the-gompad-trail-an-account-of-15-encounter-deaths-and-bloodied-facts-in-a-haystack-of-security-fiction-from-chhattisgarh/).

Kumar, Raksha (2017), 'As Bastar Mob Hounds Researcher Bela Bhatia Out of her Home, Little has Changed for Activists Here', Scroll, 24 January.

Lata, Kusum (2019), 'The Women's Question in the Naxalite Movement in Bihar', Working Paper 2019/1, Department of Sociology, South Asian University, New Delhi.

Loveday, A. (1914), *The History and Economics of Indian Famines* (London: A.G. Bells and Sons), reprinted by Usha Publications, New Delhi, 1985.

Mahaprashasta, Ajoy Ashirwad (2017), 'Academic Bela Bhatia Attacked, Threatened in Bastar', Wire, 23 January.

Mahesh (1999), 'Which Way is Your Journey', letter to the Committee of Concerned Citizens; reprinted in the Third Report of the Committee of Concerned Citizens (Hyderabad, 2002).

Manipur Legislative Assembly Secretariat (2008), *Bulletin Part I (No 48)*, Manipur Legislative Assembly Secretariat, 10 October.

Manthan, Sri (1999), 'Displacement related to the Subernarekha dam in Jharkhand', report prepared for the Society for Participatory Research in Asia (PRIA), New Delhi.

Mashangva, Somi (2010), 'Why Manipur District Council Act Is 'Dangerous' for Hill Tribes', *Mizoram Express*, 27 May.

Meher-Homji, V.M. (1988), 'Deforestation, Ecological Destabilisation and Drought', *Social Action*, 38(2).

Mehta, Lyla (ed.) (2009), *Displacement by Development: Confronting Marginalisation and Gender Injustice* (New Delhi: Sage).

Mimroth, P.L. (2004), 'Dalit Warrior', Countercurrents.org, 20 May.

Mishra, Ishita (2016), 'BBC Journalist Receives Threats in Bastar, Leaves Assignment', *Times of India*, 22 February.

Mohammed, Iqbal (2004), 'Dalits Barred Entry Into Temple', *The Hindu*, 14 January.

Mohanty, Gopinath (1987), *Paraja*, translated by Bikram K. Das (Delhi: Oxford University Press).

Morse, B., et al., (1992), *Sardar Sarovar: Report of the Independent Review* (Ottawa: Resource Futures International).

Mukherjee, K., and Yadav, R. (1980), *Bhojpur: Naxalism in the Plains of Bihar* (Delhi: Radhakrishna Prakashan).

Mumbai Mirror (2010), 'Army Out in Srinagar as Turmoil Worsens', 7 July (available at https://mumbaimirror.indiatimes.com/news/india/army-out-in-srinagar-as-turmoil-worsens/articleshow/16032350.cms).

Nanda, A.R. (1991a), *Provisional Population Totals: Rural Urban Distribution*, Census of India 1991, Series 1, Paper 2 of 1991 (New Delhi: Office of the Registrar General).

Nanda, A.R. (1991b), *Provisional Population Totals: Workers and Their Distribution*, Census of India 1991, Series 1, Paper 3 of 1991 (New Delhi: Office of the Registrar General).

Nandan, A., and Santhosh, R. (2019), 'Exploring the Changing Forms of Caste-violence: A Study of Bhumihars in Bihar, India', *European Journal of Cultural and Political Sociology*, 6(4).

Nandan, A., and Santhosh, R. (2021), 'Associational Structures and Beyond: Evolution and Contemporary Articulations of Bhumihar Caste Associations in Bihar, India', *Journal of Historical Sociology*, 33.

National Commission for Scheduled Tribes (2016), '*Chhattisgarh rajya ke Bijapur evam Sukma zilon mein suraksha balon dwara 40 adivasi mahilaon ke saath kathit roop se dushkarm kiye jane sambandhi angrezi "Outlook" patrika ke 22-02-2016 ke ank mein prakashit samachar ki janch ki report*', a report on sexual violence by security forces in Bijapur and Sukma (available at https://ncst.nic.in/sites/default/files/219scan0030.pdf).

National Human Rights Commission (2017), 'NHRC Finds 16 Women Prima Facie Victims of Rape, Sexual and Physical Assault by Police Personnel in Chhattisgarh', press release, 7 January.

NDTV (2010), 'Violence in Kashmir Valley', 28 June (available at https://www.ndtv.com/photos/news/violence-in-kashmir-valley-7651#photo-87180).

NDTV (2011), 'One Year On, Tufail Matto's Family Still Awaits Justice', 12 June (available at https://www.ndtv.com/india-news/one-year-on-tufail-mattoos-family-still-awaits-justice-458285).

Newmai News Network (2010), '26 April to be Observed as Black Day for Tribals', 28 April.

Newmai News Network (2010), 'Tribal Rights Body Says, Rules under ADC Act Full of Errors', 17 April.

Ngugi, Wa Thiong'o (1964), *Weep Not, Child* (London: Heinemann).

Nimbran, Amrik Singh (1992), *Poverty, Land and Violence* (Patna: Layman's Publications).

Nishaant, T. (2019), *Musahars: A Noble People, A Resilient Culture* (Delhi: Media House).

NITI Aayog (2021), *India: National Multidimensional Poverty India* (New Delhi: NITI Aayog).

Nongkynrih, A. K. (2009), 'Privatisation of Communal Land of the Tribes of North-East India: Socio-logical Viewpoint', in Fernandes and Barbora, 2009.

One India (2008), 'CRPF companies withdrawn in firing incident', news report, 24 May (available at https://www.oneindia.com/2008/05/24/crpf-companies-withdrawn-in-firing-incident-1211636131.html).

Oughton, Elizabeth (1982), 'The Maharashtra Droughts of 1970 to 1973: An Analysis of Scarcity', *Oxford Bulletin of Economics and Statistics*, 44(3).

Outlook Web Bureau (2017), 'Activists, Scholars Appeal To "Restore Rule Of Law" In Bastar', *Outlook*, 31 January.

Palaniappan, V.S. (2011), 'A Long, Agonising Wait for Justice Ends', *The Hindu*, 30 September.

Pandey, B.B. (2002), 'CPI(ML) Unearths a Major Scam by an RJD Minister', *Liberation*, April (available at https://www.archive.cpiml.org/liberation/year_2002/april/report%20bihar.htm).

Pandey, G., and Krishnan, P. (2023), 'Vachathi: India Court Upholds Convictions in 30-Year-Old Rapes', BBC News, 30 September (available at https://www.bbc.com/news/world-asia-india-65248208).

Patel, Bhailalbhai (1970), *Bhaikakana Sasmarno*, memoirs of Bhaikaka, a posthumous publication (Ahmedabad: Sastu Sahitya Vardhak Karyalaya); extracts ('Chhapaniyo Drought') published in *Setu Patrika*, No. 8, June 1988 (Ahmedabad: Centre for Social Knowledge and Action).

Pathak, M. (1991), *Gagan Ghata Gahrani* (Dhanbad: Kata Publications).

People's Union for Civil Liberties and others (2006), *Where the State Makes War on its Own People* (New Delhi: PUCL).

People's Union for Democratic Rights (1997), *Agrarian Conflict in Bihar and the Ranbir Sena* (Delhi: PUDR).

People's Union for Democratic Rights (2010), 'Findings of fact-finding team into 17th September and 1st October murders by security forces in Dantewada', report of a joint fact-finding team (available at https://www.pudr.org/findings-fact-finding-team-dantewada).

Phadtare, P.N. (1988), 'Geohydrology of Gujarat State', Central Ground Water Board, Ministry of Water Resources, Government of India, West Central Region, Ahmedabad.

Planning Commission (2008), *Development Challenges in Extremist Affected Areas* (New Delhi: Planning Commission).

Polgreen, Lydia (2010), 'A Youth's Death in Kashmir Renews a Familiar Pattern of Crisis', *New York Times*, 11 July (available at https://www.nytimes.com/2010/07/12/world/asia/12kashmir.html).

Prasad, Chandra Bhan (2000), 'Misunderstanding Caste', *Biblio*, Vol. V, Nos. 7–8, pp. 19–21.

Purkayastha, Sharmila (2014), 'Where is Sodi Shambo?', *Himal South Asian*, 16 October.

Rajalakshmi, T.K. (2003), 'Baran's Call', *Frontline*, 26 April.

Rajasthan Election Watch (2004), 'Lok Sabha Elections 2004: A Compilation of Background Information and Analysis taken from the Affidavits of all 185 Candidates from the 25 Constituencies in Rajasthan', Jaipur.

Ratanlal, R., and Dhirajlal, K.T. (1987), *The Law of Torts* (Nagpur: Wadhwa and Company).

Rathod, P.V., and Kumar, V. (2002), 'The Working of the Scheduled Castes and Scheduled Tribes (Prevention of Atrocities) Act, 1989 in Gujarat', in Shah, G. (ed.) (2002), *Dalits and the State* (New Delhi: Concept Publishing).

Risley, H. (1915), *The People of India*, 2nd edition, W. Crooke (ed.) (1969) (New Delhi: Oriental Books).

Sagar (2018), 'Endorsed by Courts and the Government, Uranium Mining Continues to Create Health Hazards in Jadugoda as the UCIL Expands Its Operations', *Caravan*, 3 January.

Sagar, Narain (2010), 'Mayhem in Mao, Two Students Killed', *Eastern Mirror*, Dimapur, 7 May.

Sahay, Anand Mohan (2002), 'Criminal Case against Bihar Minister in Rs 61 Billion PDS Scam', Rediff.com, 4 April (available at https://www.rediff.com/news/2002/apr/04bihar1.htm).

Saikia, Arunabh (2023), 'Bastar villagers Allege Aerial Bombing by Security Forces. What is the Truth?', Scroll, 4 May.

Savyasachi, Astha (2022), 'Interview: When a Quest for Justice Was Treated Like a Crime', Wire, 21 July.

Sen, S., Panda, D., and Lahiri, A. (1978), *Naxalbari and After: A Frontier Anthology*, 2 volumes (Calcutta: Kathashilpa).

Sethi, Aman (2010a), 'Gompad Case: Police Exhumed Seven Bodies Last Month', *The Hindu*, 6 February.

Sethi, Aman (2010b), '"Police Killed Them" Say the Villagers', Kafila, 22 February (available at https://kafila.online/2010/02/22/police-killed-them-say-the-villagers/).

Sethi, Aman (2010c), 'Witnesses Allege Biggest Anti-Naxal Operation of 2009 was Fake', *The Hindu*, 20 March.

Sethi, Aman (2010d), 'The Day of Long Knives', Kafila, 21 March (available at https://kafila.online/2010/03/21/chhattisgarhs-day-of-long-knives/).

Sethi, Aman (2010e), 'In Chhattisgarh, Jail is the Cost of Filing a Public Interest Litigation Plea', *The Hindu,* 17 January.

Shantha, Sukanya (2022), 'Edesmetta Encounter: Instead of Seeking Justice, Govt Is Now Targeting a Rights Activist', Wire, 25 November.

Sharma, H.R. (1994), 'Distribution of Landholdings in Rural India, 1953-54 to 1981-82', *Economic and Political Weekly*, 24 September.

Sharma, H.R., and Malik, S.H. (2021), 'Distribution of Landholdings in Rural India, 1982 to 2013', *Economic and Political Weekly*, 4 September.

Sharma, Supriya (2010a), 'NHRC questioned police version of Bijapur killings', *Times of India*, 21 June.

Sharma, Supriya (2010b), 'How a 15-yr-old vendor became a "dead Maoist"', *Times of India*, 25 July.

Sharma, Supriya (2011), 'Agnivesh, Journalist Assaulted on Way to Burnt Villages in Dantewada', *Times of India*, 26 March.

Sharma, Supriya (2016a), '"Don't Tarnish the Image of the Police": Home of Scroll. in Contributor Attacked in Chhattisgarh', Scroll, 8 February.

Sharma, Supriya (2106b), 'How the Chhattisgarh Police Succeeded in Hounding out Those who Questioned it', Scroll, 19 February.

Shimray, U. A. (2007), *Naga Population and Integration Movement* (New Delhi: Mittal Publications).

Shimray, U.A. (2009), 'Land Use System in Manipur Hills: A Case Study of the Tangkhul Naga', in Fernandes and Barbora, 2009.

Singh, Ajay (1996), '*Inka kasur kya tha?*', *Hindustan* (Patna edition), 20 July.

Singh, Bhagat (1930, 2003), *Why I Am An Atheist* (Patna: Samkaleen Prakashan).

Singh, K.S. (1993), *The Scheduled Castes* (Delhi: Oxford University Press).

Singh, K.S. (1994), *The Scheduled Tribes* (Delhi: Oxford University Press).

Singh, Mangi S. (2009), 'Land, Ethnic Relations and the 9th Assembly Elections in the Hills of Manipur', in Priyoranjan Singh, 2009.

Singh, Prakash (1995), *The Naxalite Movement in India* (New Delhi: Rupa).

Singh, Priyoranjan (ed.) (2009), *Tribalism and the Tragedy of the Commons: Land, Identity and Development: The Manipur Experience* (New Delhi: Akansha Publishing House).

Singh, Shashi Bhushan (2005), 'Limits to Power: Naxalism and Caste Relations in a South Bihar Village', *Economic and Political Weekly*, 16 July.

Sinha, A., and Sinha, I. (1996), 'State, Class and Sena Nexus: Bathani Tola Massacre', *Economic and Political Weekly*, 2 November.

Sinha, Anuj Kumar (2017), *Unsung Heroes of Jharkhand Movement* (New Delhi: Prabhat Prakashan).

Sinha, Arvind (1996), '*Naxalbari ke teen dashak*', *Philhal*, Vols. 18 and 19, 16 September and 1 October.

Sinha, A., and Sinha, I. (2001), 'Ranveer Sena and 'Massacre Widows'', *Economic and Political Weekly*, 27 October

Skaria, Ajay (1999), *Hybrid Histories: Forests, Frontiers and Wildness in Western India* (Delhi: Oxford University Press).

Smith, Baird (1861), *Report on the North Western Provinces Famine of 1860-61* (London: HMSO).

Soundaraya Athimuthu (2023), 'Vachathi's Women Accuse Foresters of Rape: Is Justice Near After 30 Years?', Quint, 6 March (available at https://www.thequint.com/south-india/vachathi-adivasi-women-tamil-nadu-police-rape-assault-justice-after-30-years#read-more).

Srinivas, M.N. (ed.) (1996), *Caste: Its Twentieth Century Avatar* (New Delhi: Penguin).

Srivastava, H.S. (1968), *History of Indian Famines and Development of Famine Policy 1858-1918* (Agra: Sri Ram Mehra & Co).

Srivastava, Ravi (2005), *Bonded Labour in India: Its Incidence and Pattern* (Geneva: International Labour Office).

Subramaniam, M., and Shukla, K. (2016), ''A stark nude body wrapped in plastic': What happened to a young woman in Chhattisgarh', *Scroll*, 27 June (available at https://scroll.in/article/810601/a-stark-nude-body-wrapped-in-plastic-what-happened-to-a-young-woman-in-chhattisgarh).

Subramanian, Nirupama (2010), 'Feel Our Pain, Say Kashmiris', *The Hindu*, 24 November (available at https://www.thehindu.com/opinion/op-ed//article61768069.ece).

Sundar, Nandini (2016), *The Burning Forest: India's War in Bastar* (New Delhi: Juggernaut).

Sundar, Nandini (2022), 'Chhattisgarh Judgment Upends Justice, Fraternity and Basic Common Sense', Wire, 4 August.

Takhellambam, Bhabananda (2009), 'Contesting Space, Competing Claims, Shaping Places: Violent Conflicts and Development in Manipur', in Priyoranjan Singh, 2009.

Tehelka (2007), 'The Truth: Gujarat 2002', special issue, 17 November.

Teltumbde, Anand (2012), 'Bathani Tola and the Cartoon Controversy', *Economic and Political Weekly*, 2 June.

The Indian People's Tribunal on Environment and Human Rights (2002), 'An Independent Enquiry into the Police Firing at Tapkara and Resistance to the

Koel-Karo Project, Jharkhand', IPT Secretariat, Mumbai (available at https://justicesachar.com/wp-content/uploads/2019/11/Koel-Karo-An-Independent-Enquiry-Into-The-Police-Firing-At-Tapkara-And-Resistance-To-The-Koel-Karo-Project-Jharkhand-1.pdf).

The KashmirWalla (2021), 'Eleven years on, Tufail Mattoo's family awaits justice', 11 June (available at https://thekashmirwalla.com/eleven-years-on-tufail-mattoos-family-awaits-justice/#:~:text=On%2011%20June%202010%2C%2017,summer%20civilian%20uprising%20of%202010).

The Wire Staff (2019), 'Chhattisgarh Police Drop Charges Against Nandini Sundar and Co-Accused', Wire, 12 February.

Thapar, Valmik (2005a), 'Inputs on the Tribal Bill', note prepared for a meeting convened by the Prime Minister on 30 September.

Thapar, Valmik (2005b), 'Comments on the Draft "Scheduled Tribes (Recognition of Forest Rights) Bill 2005"', letter to the Ministry of Tribal Affairs, 8 July.

Tully, Mark (1995), *The Heart of India* (New Delhi: Viking).

United News of India (1997), 'Bloodbath at Midnight', news report (available at https://www.rediff.com/news/dec/03kill2.htm).

Urmilesh (1991), *Bihar ka Sach: Krishi Sankat aur Khetihar Sangharsh* (New Delhi: Prakashan Sansthan).

Valmiki, Omprakash (2003), *Joothan: A Dalit's Life* (Kolkata: Samya).

Varadarajan, Siddharth (ed.) (2002), *Gujarat: The Making of a Tragedy* (New Delhi: Penguin).

Venkatesan, V. (2023), '"Shoddy Probe, Bias?': Questions Surround the Acquittal of All Accused in Vakapalli Gangrape Case", Wire, 10 April.

Vohra, B.B. (1987), 'Issues in Water Management', *Wasteland News*, August-October.

Vohra, B.B. (1989), 'Plantations not the Answer: Failure of Forest Policy', *Indian Express*, Ahmedabad, 21 April.

Women Against Sexual Violence and State Repression (2017), *Bearing Witness: Sexual Violence in South Chhattisgarh* (available at https://wssnet.org/2017/02/06/bearing-witness-a-wss-book-on-sexual-violence-in-south-chhattisgarh/).

World Health Organization (2021), 'A Push to Vaccinate Every Child, Everywhere, Ended Polio in India' (available at https://www.who.int/india/news/feature-stories/detail/a-push-to-vaccinate-every-child-everywhere-ended-polio-in-india).

Yugandhar, B.N., and Iyer, G. (eds.) (1993), *Land Reforms in India: Bihar—Institutional Constraints (Vol. I)* (New Delhi: Sage).

Zolengthe (2008), 'ADC Ordinance Promulgated after Governor's Assent', 14 May, zspdelhi.wordpress.com; source: *Imphal Free Press*.

Name Index*

Aam Aadmi Party 431, 438
Abdullah, Omar 480
Achik National Volunteer Council 493
Action Group for National Integrity
  (AGNI) 392-94, 431, 583
Adhvaryu, Bhanubhai 564
Adivasi Mahasabha 408, 582
Adivasi Samaj 103–4
Adivasi Samanvay Samiti 162
Agarwal, Anil 568, 582-83
Agarwal, V.K. (J) 385
Agnivesh, Swami 374, 562
Ahir, Rameshwar 269
Ahmed, Farzand 577
Akhter, Mubina 475-76
Ali, Syed Intishab 561
Ali, Tariq 584
Aliba, C. 538-39
All Manipur Tribal Union 520
All Manipur United Clubs
  Organization 510

All Naga Students' Association of
  Manipur 509
All Tribal Students' Union of Manipur
  509
All-India Bairwa Mahasabha 66
All-India Coordination Committee
  of Communist Revolutionaries
  (AICCCR) 252, 575
Ambedkar, B.R. xxii, xxiv-xxv, xxvii,
  57, 67, 562
Amir Das Commission 560
Amnesty International 560, 583-84
Anderson, J.L. 579
Andhra Pradesh Civil Liberties
  Committee (APCLC) 435
Anjum, Aaliya 585
ARCH-Vahini 214
Arivanantham, R. 584
Arslan, Mehdi 561
Arvind 577
Ashiq, Peerzada 584

---

* Individuals, institutions and organizations. Organizations of special relevance
  (e.g. communist parties and Hindu nationalist organisations) are listed in the
  Subject Index.

Subject Index

Abujmarh 349, 382, 441; fake encounter in 441-45

Adivasis* xvi, xviii, xxiv-xxv, xxvii, 1, 3, 4, 12-15, 31-51, 54, 56, 70, 72, 78, 87-88, 90-91, 100, 102-4, 155-225, 293, 295-96, 346-457, 542, 544, 546, 566; Hinduization of 14-15, 456; non-scheduled 222; seen as encroachers 219; recruited by police 381-83; sharp observers of nature 157-58; tend to stick together 372; way of life 204, 371-72, 383, 455, 457; witch-hunting among 87, 100, 104, 566; and communal violence 12-13, 450-57; and the war in Bastar 397-99; in Bastar 346-457, 542, 544; in Bihar 293, 295-96; in Gujarat 1, 3, 4, 12-15, 87-88, 90-91, 100, 102-4, 177-215, 566; in Jharkhand 155-76; in Rajasthan 31-51, 54, 56, 70, 72,

78; in Telangana 216-17, 362-67; see also Manipur, Meghalaya, Nagaland, Scheduled Tribes, tribal groups

agricultural labourers xvi, xviii-xx, 23, 25, 28, 84-85, 31-51, 90-91, 117, 138, 226, 228, 232-49, 267-79, 284, 287, 289, 293-98, 310, 313-14, 328, 343, 546, 573-74, 576-78; categories of 239-43; living conditions 245–48; see also bonded labourers, labourers

Amarnath, land allotment 461

ambushes 374, 377, 387, 394, 426, 458, 538

Andhra Pradesh 216, 222, 292, 334–35, 337–39, 341–42, 352, 357, 381, 412, 414, 435, 564, 580, 583–84; Naxalite movement in 292, 334-42

Annihilation of Caste, Ambedkar xxii, 57

---

* The word Adivasi has not generally been used in this book to refer to tribal groups in the north-east, where this term is not well accepted.

613

74–75, 82, 548; *see also* bathing
rights

poverty xiii-xv, xvi-xviii, xx, xxiii, xvii,
6, 22, 24-25, 31, 34, 54, 80, 96,
111, 115-17, 133, 144-45, 160-
61, 216, 225-27, 232-35, 239-49,
274-76, 281, 287-90, 293-94,
296, 307, 321, 335-36, 340, 342,
374, 397, 478, 535, 547, 577;
as '*dukh no dungar*' xx; *see also*
hunger, starvation

Prevention of Terrorism Act (POTA)
291

protests xiv, xxiv, 47, 52-53, 63, 71,
98, 145, 153, 162, 166-67, 170,
225, 384, 445, 544; against big
dams 166, 172-74, 176, 209-10;
against police repression or fake
encounters 298, 368, 438, 441,
444; against paramilitary camps
in Bastar 388-390; against the
Citizenship Amendment Act xxiv,
544; of farmers xxiv, 544; of Garo
students 491-503; in Kashmir
458, 460-63, 464-71, 474-
75, 478-81, 484, 486, 543; in
Manipur 505-9, 526-27; in Silger
389-90; of labourers 39, 298;
Naxalite-led 270, 277, 294, 314,
325, 329, 331; *see also* rebellion

public distribution system (PDS) xxv,
92, 98, 247, 300, 340, 371, 395

Public Interest Litigation (PIL) 162,
177, 179, 300, 377, 582

public ownership of bores 146, 153–54

Public Safety Act (PSA), in J&K 471

pumpsets 135–37, 139–40, 142; *see
also* borewells, groundwater

'Purification Hunt' to 'Green Hunt'
372–74

radiation 156-57, 159, 161–63

Rajasthan xix, xxiv, 2, 4, 11, 15-16,
31-32, 45, 54, 56, 62, 69, 71,
76, 78-79, 113, 221, 542, 544,
561–64; *see also* bonded labour,
Chakwada

Rajasthan, places in: Baran 31–51;
Ganeshpura 34–37, 45, 51; Iklera
34, 38, 44, 47–51; Kansel 64–65;
Kishanganj 31–32, 34, 46–47, 50-
51; Pushkar 4; Shahbad 31–33,
50-51; Sunda 40, 45, 50–51;
Sunda-Chenpur 33-34, 36, 38,
40–41; *see also* Chakwada

Rajputs xviii, 2-3, 12, 15, 26-28, 38,
40, 45, 56, 67, 93–95, 102-5,
140, 230-231, 234, 236, 266,
275, 308-12, 331-32, 560, 562-
63, 578–79; women 93–94, 104–5

Ram dhuni programme, by upper castes
63

Ranbeer Sena xxi, 19, 21-29, 268, 270,
277, 290, 301, 310, 312–15,
321–32, 560-61, 577, 579; *see
also* Bathe massacre, Bathani tola
massacre

rape xxvii, 11, 38, 266, 276, 327,
411-12, 546, 583; testimonies of
400-406; in Antras 209-10; in
Bathe 19, 22; of Adivasi women
in Bastar 346, 351, 364, 367-
68, 378, 400-12, 419; of Dalit
or labouring women in Bihar
234, 275, 283, 313; in Kashmir
411-12, 461; in Manipur 526; in
Nagaland 532-35, 538; *see also*
gang rapes

Rashtriya Swayamsevak Sangh (RSS)
12, 15, 72-73, 543

Scan QR code to access the
Penguin Random House India website